With love to
John Peter Fountas,
whose vision, spirit, and
passion for life and learning
inspires us each day
to make a difference.

Contents

Acknowledgments

Writing a second edition for our first book, with a gap of twenty years in between, has been both a humbling experience, and a learning experience. In the process, we have learned from so many of our colleagues. We are deeply grateful to them and want to acknowledge their contributions here.

A superb editorial team at Heinemann contributed hugely to this effort. We especially thank our extraordinary publisher, Mary Lou Mackin, and our calm, insightful editor Betsy Sawyer-Melodia for their brilliant leadership, their unending patience and hard work, and their highly competent contributions to the writing. An excellent and skilled team has contributed to the design and production of this edition; we appreciate and respect the meticulous and artistic work of Michael Cirone, Lynne Costa, Monica Crigler, Suzanne Heiser, and Angel Lepore. The production team worked endlessly with care and patience. Samantha Garon has contributed invaluable advice on the language, content and design of the publication. We thank Lisa Fowler for her brilliant artistic design and also thank Kimberly Capriola, Alana Jeralds, and Jill Backman who have always provided expert support with skill and enthusiasm. David Pence has contributed in numerous ways as he worked with us to conceptualize *The Literacy Continuum* that is foundational to this work. We thank Deanna Richardson whose magic gets our work to teachers in beautiful form. We also thank Vicki Boyd for her steadfast leadership at Heinemann and Cherie Bartlett, Mim Easton and Gina Cullen for organizing the professional development that will extend this work.

We would also like to thank the following schools for generously opening their classrooms to us and sharing the work of their teachers and students: Horace Mann Laboratory School, Mather Elementary, Mary C. Dondero Elementary, City Park Elementary, Park Creek Elementary, Hanson Elementary, Blue Ridge Elementary, and Marguerite E. Small Elementary.

We are constantly grateful to the energetic and talented teams who implement the Literacy Collaborative at The Ohio State University and Lesley University. We admire and appreciate their efforts to inform our efforts and to extend communication about this work. At Ohio State, we recognize Pat Scharer, who heads it all up, as well as Sherry Kinzel, Marsha Levering, Jenny McFerin, Lisa Patrick, Shelly Schaub, Wendy Sheets, Carla Steele, and Nikki Woodruff. At Lesley University, we recognize the gracious contributions of Elizabeth DeHaven, Cynthia Downend, Jill Eurich, Jessica Sherman, Wendy Vaulton, Helen Sisk, Heather Rodman, and Toni Czekanski, as well as the enthusiastic administrative team- Barbara Brammer, Melissa Fasten, Kelly Adams, Candice Campbell, Diane Tan, Kristen Mosher, Julie Travers, Vickie Aldin, and Amanda Bedford.

The preparation of this edition involved seeking feedback on many parts of this book. We thank Eva Konstantellou and Kathy Ha for meticulous and thoughtful feedback on our drafts and Diane Powell, Linda Garbus, Jill Eurich, and Cindy Downend for reading chapters and giving valuable constructive feedback all along the way. Their generosity and collegiality is highly valued. In addition, we are continuously appreciative of the feedback of teachers every day, as they have informed our work.

We could not have produced this volume without the expert assistance of Cheryl Wasserstrom, Sharon Freeman, and Andrea Lelievre. We particularly appreciate their willingness to be flexible and to put in extra effort when needed.

The second edition of *Guided Reading* represents an expansion in scope and a refinement of ideas. All of the changes we made are based not only on reading and rereading the work of Marie Clay and other current research, but on the work of gracious and generous teachers who are constantly refining their practice. We cannot name all of the individuals who have welcomed us into their classrooms and who have contributed to the films and artifacts that we study. The examples in this book are based on their work.

Finally, we would like to acknowledge three individuals with whom we no longer work closely but who have supported our work and inspired us for many years. We owe special thanks to Mike Gibbons who made the decision to publish the first edition of *Guided Reading*, and helped us extend our work through the years he was with Heinemann, and whose ideas are always forward-thinking. We will always be grateful to Lesa Scott for her brilliant leadership and vision and to Buzz Rhodes who could think through a splendid delivery system to get our work to educators. We would not have been able to accomplish our vision without their unwavering belief in our work.

As always, we thank our families, our friends, and our dogs for their loving support and encouragement throughout this very long project.

INTRODUCTION

Introduction

Our work in guided reading has been a journey of over two decades. Like most journeys (at least those that are worth taking) there is a lot of learning along the way. For over twenty years, we have spent time in classrooms, observed teachers and children, tried out techniques, and talked with a wide range of educators (including administrators, teachers of English language learners, policy makers, and literacy coaches). We have read the research literature and talked with scholars. We have written books on many other topics related to classroom life and literacy, and each time, immersed ourselves more deeply in some aspect of teaching.

We have been delighted—even grateful—to see the results of our work reflected in the faces of children, and to hear it in their talk. As with everyone who shares ideas and thinking, we sometimes worry about the unintended consequences and misinterpretations (or "over interpretations") of our work. In the busy rush of schoolwork, it's easy for educators to occasionally combine and merge ideas that really don't belong together and come from different sources.

A couple of years ago, we were invited to write an article for *The Reading Teacher,* and we were honored to have the chance to speak to such a wide audience on the topic of guided reading. It was published with the title, "Guided Reading: The Romance and the Reality." Thinking about and writing that article confirmed our belief that it was time for a new edition of *Guided Reading: Good First Teaching for All Children.*

Our Process

As we reread the first edition of *Guided Reading,* it became evident that the new edition could be no "cut-and-paste" operation. We had to start over. As a result, every chapter in the book is, in a sense, new. But we're also aware that there is much of value in the first edition, so while writing a completely new text, we have tried to maintain some of the practical features that many teachers felt were helpful, and we have added much new material that we hope readers will enjoy and find useful.

Perhaps the greatest difference in the second edition of *Guided Reading* is that we have taken a wider view of the population of children served by guided reading, and this is signaled by the change of subtitle to "Responsive Teaching Across the Grades." The subtitle also signals that, while we continue to include the "nuts and bolts" of how to use guided reading, we have placed more emphasis on responsive teaching—those moment-to-moment decisions that teachers make as they observe and analyze their students' behaviors. It is the observation and analysis of the students' reading behaviors that informs your next teaching moves. No matter how well you plan and structure learning tasks, it's the one-on-one interactions that inform the power and effectiveness in your teaching. This responsive action is the highest and most difficult task of teaching. It often takes years to develop, and excellent management and planning are needed to create a situation in which you can use your expertise with flexibility and ease.

Since 1996, when *Guided Reading* was first published, we have worked to create tools that support teachers in their development of decision-making skills. The most important of these is *The Continuum of Literacy Learning,* which is being published in an expanded edition (*The Fountas & Pinnell Literacy Continuum* 2017). Over the years, we have grown in our realization that teacher language is all-important in responsive teaching. We want our statements, prompts, and questions to be as clear and precise as possible. We agree with Marie Clay on the necessity of "spare" language that communicates with clarity. We have produced a number of tools that will help you hone your language until it becomes an automatic part of your teaching, ultimately making the tools unnecessary (or necessary only for planning). These tools include: *Prompting Guide Part 1 for Oral Reading and Early Writing; Prompting Guide Part 2 for Comprehension; Genre Prompting Guide for Fiction;* and *Genre Prompting Guide for Nonfiction, Poetry, and Test Taking.* Much of the thinking behind these tools, and many examples from them, are reflected in this book.

Over two decades, you can expect a great deal of social change, and that has certainly happened since 1996. Change isn't good or bad—it's simply inevitable. Our world has grown much smaller and there is an increasing need to prepare the children of today to become global citizens. Almost every community across the world is welcoming immigrants from other countries and cultures, and our classrooms often include many students who are learning to speak English. Some schools serve a population that includes specifics of as many as forty to fifty different native languages, with English being only one. In the coming years, diversity will be the norm, and we value that change. Diversity in the classroom stretches us as teachers and focuses extra attention on the all-important area of language. We make reference to teaching ELLs in many chapters of this book and Chapter 7 addresses the unique ways we need to adjust teaching to serve these students well.

If you are familiar with the first edition of *Guided Reading,* as well as some of our other books, you will encounter many ideas here that will be familiar to you. Over the years, a body of information has built up around the practice of small-group reading instruction. We have not changed how we approach basic concepts about guided reading or our belief in it as a sound classroom practice. But we have refined our descriptions and developed a deeper understanding of its complexity. You will see that we have made some changes, and we hope you find that we have articulated our ideas more clearly.

Section One: Using Guided Reading to Help Individual Readers Construct an Effective Literacy Processing System

Section One includes seven chapters that introduce readers to the topic of guided reading. Chapter 1, "What Is Guided Reading?" offers an introduction to the topic with a full example of a lesson. In this chapter, and elsewhere in the book, we emphasize that guided reading is only one component of a comprehensive literacy design. Although it is important, guided reading is not intended to be the only literacy instruction a student receives during the day. We emphasize that guided reading should be embedded within a coherent literacy program, and that message carries over to Chapter 2, "Guided Reading Within a Multitext Approach: Levels of Support for Literacy Learning." In this chapter we describe a range of contexts for literacy teaching—ranging from high teacher support to independent work.

Chapters 3 and 4 may be surprising to readers who are expecting an introduction to guided reading. Chapter 3 is titled "From Shared to Guided Reading in the Early Years," and Chapter 4, "Shared and Performance Reading Across the Grades." These two chapters focus on the re-emerging role of shared reading as a highly beneficial way to engage readers in complex texts. Across time, shared reading can "lead" guided reading forward by providing the level of support readers need so that they can process texts that are more challenging than they can take on in guided reading or independent reading. Shared reading contributes to all systems of strategic actions—not only those related to oral reading but also all apects of comprehending. Readers think continually about the meaning and make their voices reflect it.

The next two chapters in Section One are designed to help you get started. Chapter 5, "Planning for Effective Guided Reading Lessons: Building a Strong Early Reading Process," and Chapter 6, "Planning for Effective Guided Reading Lessons: Lifting the Competencies of Every Reader," describe the steps in implementing a guided reading lesson—from observing and assessing the readers, to analyzing the text, to teaching the lesson. You likely have students who are at a certain level as your primary concern, but we encourage you to read both of these chapters. In any classroom, you are likely to have a wide range of readers and need to be able to shift up and down the text gradient.

The final chapter in the first section, "Using Guided Reading for Effective Teaching of English Language Learners," underscores the importance of teaching in different ways to meet the needs of students who speak another language in the home and community. Apply the principles introduced in this chapter to the entire book.

Section Two: Using Systematic Observation and Assessment to Form Groups and Guide Teaching

The four chapters of Section Two address the area of observation and assessment, which is critically important if you are to engage in responsive teaching. Highly skilled teaching can never be accomplished if you are blindly following a preordained script and sequence of steps. Of course, we all need good tools, guides, and materials, but learners don't always fit neatly into a specific system. It's up to the teacher to know the readers and make the materials accessible to them. Chapter 8 is titled, "Understanding Reading as a Complex Process." This chapter lays out a theoretical explanation of the reading process on which the teaching in guided reading is based.

Chapter 9, "Observing and Assessing Readers to Inform Teaching Decisions," focuses on the procedures you use to gather student data, analyze it, and use it in guided reading. These procedures enable you to set up a successful context within which you can teach successfully. Chapter 10, "Using Assessment to Form Dynamic Groups and Document Reading Progress," supports you as you use grouping in a thoughtful and dynamic way. Chapter 11, "Using Running Records and *The Fountas & Pinnell Literacy Continuum* to Guide Teaching," describes the bridge between assessment and instruction as well as the use of *The Literacy Continuum* as a powerful tool to plan for, guide, and assess teaching.

Section Three: Using High-Quality Texts to Support Responsive Teaching

The three chapters in Section Three focus on texts. Every classroom needs a rich text base that can support and extend student learning. In Chapter 12, "Creating a Collection of Texts to Support Literacy Learning," we describe the classroom collection, which goes beyond leveled books. Chapter 13, "The F&P Text Gradient™: A Tool for Teaching," focuses on leveled books and the purpose and use of the gradient as a teacher's tool. Look here for a description of how the gradient is used (and how we do not recommend using it). Chapter 14, "Selecting and Introducing Texts for Guided Reading," moves back to instruction to discuss important aspects of selecting and orienting students to process texts successfully.

Section Four: Effective Decision Making Within the Guided Reading Lesson

Although this entire book is about teaching, we have informally called the six chapters in Section Four the "teaching chapters" because they go deep into teaching/learning interactions. Every example in this book is based on thousands of observations in classrooms and via video that capture teaching in guided reading. No lesson is perfect; what matters most is your ability to reflect on your teaching in an analytic way, so these chapters are full of examples of teacher language.

Chapter 15, "Teaching for Systems of Strategic Actions in Guided Reading," connects the theoretical base to the kinds of teaching moves that support strategic actions. The next four chapters extend this goal to specific areas of strategic activity: Chapter 16, "Teaching for Monitoring, Searching, and Self-Correction Behaviors"; Chapter 17, "Teaching for Visual Processing over Time: Solving Words"; Chapter 18, "Teaching for Phrased, Fluent Reading in Guided Reading Lessons"; Chapter 19, "The Role of Facilitative Talk in Supporting Change over Time in Processing Systems," and Chapter 20, "Teaching for Comprehending: Helping Students Think Within, Beyond, and About the Text." These chapters discuss how you can put into action your detailed knowledge of students and of texts.

The Fountas & Pinnell Literacy Continuum offers a detailed description of the behaviors and understandings that readers need to control at every level of the gradient, but in Chapter 19, we identify high-priority *shifts* in learning across time. Also, specific teacher language is suggested for each of these high-priority areas. You can consider these priorities as you observe your students in guided reading groups, making sure that these shifts occur.

Section Five: Thinking, Talking, Reading, and Writing in a Classroom Community

In Section Five we turn again to the classroom context as a whole. Guided reading cannot be successful unless we have excellent management systems. All students learn best within an inclusive, respectful, and supportive social community, where people collaborate with and help each other. In our experience in education, there is a tendency to concentrate on creating a warm, supportive community and good relationships but without enough attention to rigorous learning. Or, educators tighten down achievement in the attempt to create rigorous learning, and in the process they undermine the sense of community that exists within a school (and consequently within classrooms). We believe that you can't really have one without the other. The chapters in this section help you create a learning environment within which literacy and language can flourish.

Chapter 21, "Building a Community of Readers Across the Grades," focuses on the strong link between emotions and learning and the need for each student to feel a sense of belonging and self-efficacy. In Chapter 22, "Managed Independent Learning in the Early Grades," we discuss two approaches to managing the literacy activity in classrooms for younger children. Chapter 23, "Managing Literacy in the Intermediate/Middle Grades," focuses on the transitions you can make as students develop more self-regulation. Chapter 24, "A Design for Language and Literacy Instruction," places guided reading as an important element within a coherent approach—one that has many texts for different purposes and that develops students' competencies across a broad spectrum.

Summary

As you read, you will find both familiar and new ideas. We hope that this volume supports your teaching and helps you expand your expertise. You may find ideas that you agree with and others that you disagree with. You may feel a sense of dissonance. Remember, the first step in learning is this dissonance, so value it. The secret to having a rewarding and engaging career in education is to keep learning. The idea of community receives much more emphasis here than it did in the first edition of *Guided Reading*, and that is the result of recent research and our work with teachers. As writers, we can only present our ideas. What you do with them in your own classroom makes the difference for students. We invite you to continue the conversation about these ideas through some of our blogs and Twitter chats. And you can always find new information, continuously updated, on www.fountasandpinnell.com.

Online Resources Access Information

Resources for *Guided Reading,* Second Edition are available through the *Fountas & Pinnell Online Resources* site.

To access these resources, follow the steps below:

- Visit **http://resources.fountasandpinnell.com**
- Do one of the following:
  - If this is your first time at the site, please click on the **Register** button, enter the product code **FPGR2E7216** and set up your account. You will need to enter your email address and create a password.
  - If you previously registered a different product at this site, simply log in, click the "Add a New Product" plus sign just above your current products, enter the product code **FPGR2E7216** and click **SUBMIT**.

You will now be able to access resources for *Guided Reading,* Second Edition. For technical assistance, please email technologysupport@heinemann.com or call 877-331-7290.

SECTION **ONE**

Using Guided Reading to Help Individual Readers Construct an Effective Literacy Processing System

The chapters in Section One introduce the concept and structure of guided reading. It may be surprising that two chapters on shared reading are also included in this introductory section. In these chapters, we make the case that shared reading is a highly effective context (across the grades) for engaging students in processing more complex texts than they are able to process, at present, in guided or independent reading. Shared reading *leads* guided and independent reading forward by making it possible for students to read and understand more challenging texts, because the teacher and the group offer a high level of support.

Chapters 5 and 6 take you through the process of implementing guided reading, step by step. The process involves observing and assessing students, analyzing texts, planning an introduction, and teaching the lesson. These chapters are designed to help you get started!

Guided reading has always been an important way to provide for the diverse needs of learners in our classrooms, but in the last two decades, classrooms around the world have welcomed more students from other countries and cultures, many of whom speak languages other than English. Many schools are now serving a multilingual population, and these students have highly diverse needs. Chapter 7 in this section addresses specific ways that teaching English language learners must be different in order to meet the unique needs of this growing population.

CHAPTER 1

What Is Guided Reading?

> *Guided reading is a form of group instruction in
> which we introduce children to the techniques
> of reading new or unseen material for personal
> satisfaction and understanding.*
>
> –Don Holdaway

In our highly literate society, the ability to read is an important component in an individual's quality of life. Not only is a high level of literacy the key to education and careers, but it also enriches lives, brings personal pleasure, and expands the individual's understanding of the world and its people. Reading can be an escape from tension and worry, and it feeds the imagination. Teaching children to read is the challenge and the responsibility of *every* teacher who enters the profession. Those most concerned, usually, are teachers of young children, and the early grades tend to get the most attention from policy makers, researchers, and publishers. But in the long run, the work of *all* teachers is affected by and affects students' literacy at every level of education. The responsibility resides with every teacher of every subject in every year of schooling.

Guided reading takes place *in the classroom,* and that is where students live a literate life in schools. We believe that a literate life is the right of every child, and most children need expert teaching to have access to that life. Each year, students grow in reading ability, developing increasingly complex and effective systems of "in-the-head" strategic actions for processing and understanding written texts. These actions enable them not only to read the words on a page but also to understand the meaning—both directly and indirectly stated—of the language. With this deep understanding comes appreciation of the craft of writing, expansion of thinking, and increased enjoyment, which are goals for every year of school. Simultaneously, an effective processing system enables them to learn *from* reading and learn more *about* reading. It is amazing what students can achieve when high quality literacy instruction supports them year after year.

Guided reading provides a context for responsive teaching—teaching that is grounded in the teacher's detailed knowledge of and respect for each student, supporting the readers' active construction of a processing system. As Clay says, "just as a listener tunes in to a speaker, so a teacher must observe, listen to, and tune in to a learner," (1998). The responsive teacher provides differentiated instruction to meet the needs of each student. He observes readers and writers very carefully, weaving a valuable set of understandings about each. Then, in a continuously evolving process, he tailors his precise responses to the readers' strengths and needs. In guided reading, with a group of students, and a text that is selected specifically to provide just the right amount of challenge, it is possible to address individual student needs in a powerful way. Responsive teaching involves moment-to-moment teaching decisions that enable the learners to take different paths to common outcomes.

There is great diversity among the students in every classroom. Some come to school with a wealth of language and literacy experiences, while others may have had rich language experiences but little exposure to print. Some learn quickly, while others need more support. It is inevitable that some children will enjoy reading more than others, but all students need the reading ability that will allow them to open doors and access deeper thinking and learning. The key is good teaching.

Guided reading offers a context within which students engage with a rich variety of texts and are taught how to build an effective and efficient reading processing system. You bring students together in a small group—students who are similar in their reading development—for efficient teaching. Then, you select a text that is appropriate for all students in the group—one that is accessible to them *with the support of skilled teaching*. That means that the text also offers the kinds of challenges that enable all the students to learn more about the process of reading. Within each daily guided reading lesson, students learn how to think like readers and expand their in-the-head network of systems of strategic actions. With the opportunity to process one text, they learn how to think in new ways as readers and take their expanded competencies to every other text they read.

Guided Reading Within a Coherent Literacy Design

This book focuses on guided reading, which takes approximately 15 to 25 important minutes of a student's day. But as important as it is, small-group guided reading instruction is not the only context that contributes to a student's reading growth. Effective reading instruction involves a combination of powerful instructional settings. For example, within a school day (or span of several days), a student should also experience the following text opportunities to engage with high quality texts.

Reading and Talking About Reading

▶ *Interactive Read-Aloud* of age-appropriate, grade-appropriate texts (for students of all ages) promotes the joy of reading, expands vocabulary and the ability to think, talk, and write about texts that fully engage their interest, many of which are beyond students' current ability to decode.

▶ *Reading Minilessons* allow for specific, explicit instruction to help students become independent readers for life.

▶ *Reading Conferences* allow the teacher to differentiate instruction for individuals while also gathering important information about each reader.

▶ *Shared Reading* of texts (usually enlarged) helps students learn to construct meaning in a supported context so they can enjoy reading and learn critical concepts of how texts work. It also helps all students develop reading fluency and the ability to interpret texts with the voice.

▶ *Book Clubs* (literature discussion) bring students together for in-depth discussion of a self-selected book they have read (or listened to), extending thinking about and enjoying age-appropriate material. Students have the opportunity to think more deeply about a text and its illustrations as they talk with one another and co-construct new, richer understandings than any one reader could gain from reading it for himself.

▶ *Independent Reading* offers the opportunity for a student to develop tastes as a reader and to read a large number of self-selected books on his own, with the support of individual conferences with the teacher. Here, you can make specific teaching points in brief conferences that take the individual reader forward.

▶ *Group Share* is designed to bring the entire classroom community together to talk about the books they are reading independently. They may recommend books to others or talk with a partner or a small group to share their reading experiences.

Writing and Talking About Writing

▶ *Writing Minilessons* provide short and explicit instruction to help students understand the characteristics of good writing and write in a variety of genres with purpose and voice.

▶ *Writing Conferences* allow for differentiation of instruction for individuals while also providing the teacher with important information about each writer.

▶ *Shared or Interactive Writing* is a highly collaborative activity that involves the teacher and students composing and constructing a text together. It introduces students to the way written language works, while encouraging excitement, interest, and confidence.

▶ *Guided Writing* allows for differentiated learning in order to address the common needs of students in small groups. You can teach on the cutting edge of a student's learning since you are providing explicit teaching based on the writers' needs at a particular point in time.

> *Independent Writing* engages students daily in a structured routine that provides massive opportunities to write. They become excellent writers by applying principles related to the conventions, craft, and process of writing.

> *Group Share* brings the class together as a learning community. You can reinforce new understandings, provide a genuine audience for writers, and create a community of writers who share ideas and insights.

All of the above contexts, described further in Chapter 2, foster authentic language and literacy learning; that is, students engage in thinking, reading, writing, and talking in a way that reflects the world of literate people. An authentic literacy approach involves a combination of whole-class, small-group, and individual teaching.

Guided reading is *not* the entire reading program. But it is through guided reading that students learn how to engage in every facet of the reading process at a level that provides maximum opportunities to grow in reading competence. They take their reading competencies to all literacy contexts. The purpose of guided reading is to support the reader's building of an effective processing system, enabling them to expand their reading power over time.

Defining Guided Reading

Guided reading is a small-group instructional context in which a teacher supports each reader's development of systems of strategic actions for processing new texts at increasingly challenging levels of difficulty. Students in the group are similar (although not exactly the same) in their development of a reading process, so it is appropriate, efficient, and productive for them to read the same text. The text offers each reader the opportunity to learn how to read more effectively, creates a shared text experience, and allows you to teach with greater impact. The essential characteristics of guided reading are:

> A teacher works with a small group of students.

> Students are similar in their development of a reading process so that it is efficient to teach them in a group.

> The teacher selects a text that is appropriate for the group in that it offers a small, but significant, amount of challenge. Students read the same book so that they share the experience, and the teaching is meaningful for all members of the group.

> The teacher introduces the text in a way that provides just enough support to allow students to process this more challenging text with accuracy, fluency, and understanding.

> The teacher guides students in a discussion of the text in a way that encourages them to express their thinking and learn from the thinking of others.

> Based on observations of the reading and discussion, the teacher makes specific teaching decisions directed at systems of strategic actions and designed to help students learn something new that they can apply to all of their reading.

❱ The teacher engages students for a few minutes in quick, hands-on work with letters or words to develop the students' flexibility and word analysis skills.

❱ Students may write about reading to reflect on and share their understandings.

The ultimate goal of instruction is to enable readers to work their way through a text independently, so all teaching is directed toward helping the individuals within the group build systems of strategic actions that they initiate and control for themselves. Guided reading leads to the independent reading that builds the process; it is the heart of an effective literacy program.

We summarize the role of teacher and students across a guided reading lesson, below (Figure 1-1).

Before the Reading	*During* the Reading	*After* The Reading
Teacher		
● Selects an appropriate text, one that will be supportive but with a few problems to solve thus providing opportunities to learn ● Analyzes the text to determine challenges and learning opportunities ● Prepares an introduction to the text ● Briefly introduces the text, keeping in mind the challenges in the text, and the knowledge, experience, language competencies, and skills of the readers	● Observes the reading behaviors of individuals for evidence of strategic actions ● Sometimes "listens in" to individuals' oral reading ● Confirms children's problem-solving attempts and successes ● Interacts with individuals to assist with problem-solving after error or at difficulty (when appropriate) ● Makes notes about reading behaviors observed	● Talks about the text with the students ● Invites personal response ● Returns to the text for one or two teaching opportunities such as finding evidence or confirming a reader's problem-solving actions ● Assesses students' understanding of the text ● Engages the students for two to three minutes of letter/word work (as appropriate) ● Sometimes engages the students in writing about reading ● May invite students to do some "close reading" (rereading a portion of the text for a particular purpose)
Students		
● Engage in a conversation about the text (may make predictions, activate background knowledge, or raise questions) ● Build expectations ● Notice information in the text ● Notice the genre of the text ● Notice graphics and important text features such as headings	● Read the whole text or a unified part to themselves (softly or silently) ● Request help in problem-solving when needed ● Think actively while reading to understand the story or topic ● Recognize or take apart words while reading for meaning	● Talk about the whole text or a unified part ● Check predictions and react personally to the story or informational topic ● Revisit the text at points of problem-solving as guided by the teacher ● Engage in "close reading" (reread a portion of the text for a purpose, such as noticing aspects of the writer's craft) ● May reread the story to a partner or independently (early readers) ● Engage actively in two or three minutes of letter/word work (as appropriate) ● May write/draw about reading

FIGURE 1-1 | The Role of Teacher and Students Across a Guided Reading Lesson

The Teacher's Role

As a teacher, you play a highly intentional and powerful instructional role. The group is small, so that it is easier to tailor your teaching for individual members. So even though guided reading occupies only a short time for each student, it can have a big impact.

Before the Reading

Knowing the competencies of the individuals in the small group, select a new text that all will read. The text is one that includes some challenges, but is within readers' power to process with proficiency (given supportive teaching). The text offers an opportunity for readers to apply everything they know about reading to a new text. There are opportunities to expand the processing system through successful problem solving. Students are expected to achieve proficiency on the first reading. Your goal is the reader's successful problem solving on an extended piece of text.

Introductions are brief and vary according to the readers' strengths and needs as well as the characteristics of the text. Your goal is to interest the students in the information or story, relate it to their experiences, and provide a frame of meaning that will support independent problem solving. Discuss the title and author and provide an overall sense of what the book is about and how it "works" (the structure or organization). Based on your knowledge of the students, you may suggest personal connections to the story. The introduction is conversational rather than a prescribed story review or series of questions. You can use new or important vocabulary and syntactic structures that may be unfamiliar to the group. Proper names that may be difficult to pronounce can be emphasized. The introduction "debugs" the book for the students by directing their attention to features they will need to use in their problem solving.

Don't use the introduction to "pre-teach" words although you may call attention to a word in context, sometimes asking students to locate it, say it, and notice specific features such as the beginning letter, an ending or word part. Assure that students understand the meaning of some new and complex words. Guide the readers to look at some of the illustrations or graphic features, hear some of the language, and understand the structure of the text and critical aspects of meaning. When working with inexperienced readers, you may go all the way through the text talking about almost all of the pictures, but this is rare. Sometimes a briefer summary-like overview will provide enough support for students to read the text successfully.

During the Reading

The students read the whole text at their own pace. Children who are just beginning to learn to read are asked to read softly to themselves; soon, they begin to read portions of the text silently. At higher text levels, students process the entire text silently. The ultimate goal of guided reading is independent silent reading. You are there to support them if they need help or become confused; but, in general, they read without interruption. You may "listen in" or ask a specific student to read aloud softly. This sample enables you to look for evidence of problem solving and intervene as needed to support the reader's construction of effective strategic actions. Any interactions you have with readers should be very brief. Your observations help you plan quickly what to teach for after the first reading. This is a good time to take notes on a clipboard to document progress and use for planning.

After the Reading

First, invite students to share their thinking about the text. The discussion focuses on the meaning and any aspects of the story or nonfiction text that are critical to understanding. Don't ask students to "retell" the text as if to prove they read it! Don't ask literal questions like a test. This is an opportunity for teaching not testing. The conversations should be friendly and natural; you can ask some questions or share some of your own thinking. You can encourage extended discussion by prompts such as, "can you say why you think that?" or "who would like to add to that?" The discussion is not long because of the need for time management; but you will be surprised how much students can say about a text in a short time when they become accustomed to articulating their thinking. Notice and note evidence of their grasp of the key understandings of the text.

Following the discussion, you have the opportunity to interact with students to do some quick teaching for strategic actions. The teaching is very specific and focused on some aspect of reading. The teaching point can be directed toward any of the systems of strategic actions; selection of the point is based on your knowledge of the readers and what they need to learn how to do. You may preplan your teaching or have several possible emphases in mind; but you may also change it in response to your immediate observation of the students' reading behaviors. Sometimes, especially with younger readers, you might call attention to an example of successful problem solving. For more sophisticated texts, you might engage students in "close reading." In this case, students return to a segment of the text and reread it with a purpose in mind; for example, to detect evidence of character change, to think about what the dialogue tells you, or to notice a writer's use of problem and solution. You can also revisit the text to work for fluency.

At the end of the lesson, spend a few minutes in active, "hands-on" work with letters or words. This work helps students develop a flexible range of strategies for solving words and to use them rapidly and with ease. You are working not so much with the precise words in the text but with the features of words and the kind of problem solving they need to do at this text level. Children who are just learning how to look at print or how words work may sort letters in a variety of ways or make words with magnetic letters. Students may sort words according to features or work with base words and affixes. They may notice the parts and put words that are alike together. This word work does not take the place of the phonics/word work minilesson that students experience as part of the literacy program; it provides quick, rapid practice to develop flexibility and fluency.

Sometimes, you may want to engage the students in writing about reading. They may write a paragraph in a reader's notebook to express their thinking about the text, or they may engage in any of variety of ways to write about reading—charts, quick writes, drawing with writing, summarizing, character sketches, lists of interesting words, and so on. There is seldom time to do much writing during the guided reading lesson, but once you have shown students what to do, they can work independently. Beginning readers will benefit from shared or interactive writing.

Sometimes you might want to take a brief time—no more than one or two minutes—right after the group meeting to jot down important observations while they are fresh in your mind. Teachers have different routines for taking reading records for continuous assessment, but one productive time is immediately before the lesson using the previous day's new book. This reading record not only reflects the students' processing but helps you check on the effectiveness of your teaching. Keep careful records of your guided reading lessons, including books read, runnng records (or reading records), and any notes on specific reading behaviors of individual readers.

The Students' Role

Students are expected to play a very active role throughout the guided reading lesson. The lesson is fast-paced with several important learning activities packed into a short period of time.

Before the Reading

Students learn that their role during the introduction is to engage in conversation with you and with each other about the story or topic. They ask questions and build expectations. The introduction supports their thinking about the story or topic so that comprehension is at the forefront. Each reader needs to hold a copy of the book to view while you introduce it. It is important to bring the readers into the text and set them up to work through it successfully.

During the Reading

Each student has a copy of the book and reads the whole text (occasionally, in the intermediate or middle grades, you might have students read a longer text over several days). The reading is usually soft (beginning readers) or silent, but all members of the group are operating independently as readers at the same time. This is not "round robin" reading, in which students take turns reading aloud while others listen and follow along. In guided reading, each student has the opportunity to solve problems while reading extended text and attending to meaning. They construct meaning throughout the process, from their initial predictions about the story to examining the details of print in the text to their reflections after the story is read. Because they are similar in their development, the students in the group can read the carefully selected book at about the same rate and level of success, preferably with an accuracy rate above 90 percent (levels A-K) or above 95 percent (levels L-Z). This procedure ensures that students can process the print and language successfully without losing meaning. With an appropriate introduction to the text, they should need very little teacher help as they read it. Students sustain attention while problem solving an extended piece of text and, in doing so, build "in the head" systems of strategic actions that they can use for reading other texts.

After the Reading

After the reading, students are invited to talk about the book they have read (see Figure 1-2). Since each reader responds individually to every book, it's important to value and recognize individual responses and opinions. As part of the discussion, with teacher or student prompting, they may revisit parts of the text to show evidence, search for information, or notice aspects of the writer's craft.

You can then make one or two teaching points that help the readers process more effectively, such as self-monitoring, searching for and using a source of information, or noticing interesting language. You may ask students to engage in "close reading." They will quickly learn the routines for this activity, which can also be called "revisiting the text." The students reread a short portion of the text with a clear purpose in mind—usually one that is set by the teacher. It might be to notice aspects of the writer's craft (for example, the "lead," how a character is revealed, the turning point in a story, the arguments in a nonfiction text, the author's message). They learn to read quickly and then respond, articulating their own thinking, and listening and responding to that of others. Revisiting the text offers an opportunity to "think again," reaching a deeper level.

Students then engage in two to three minutes of letter or word work to develop flexibility in taking apart words (not optional for early readers). Over the year, students learn many ways to write about their reading. Occasionally, you may ask them to write something specific about the new text they just read.

Across the lesson, guided reading allows you to teach in a responsive way, taking into account your analysis of strengths and needs of individual readers. You are responsive in the way you select texts, introduce them, notice reading, discuss texts, and make teaching decisions after the reading, always making sure they that they provide the right learning opportunities, engage readers, and allow them to make personal connections with the texts.

FIGURE 1-2 A Guided Reading Lesson

Evaluating Guided Reading

As with any instructional approach, as a teacher you ask yourself, "How do I know when I am using guided reading successfully?" Ultimately, the test is whether the approach responds to the students' learning needs and helps them develop a self-extending system for processing texts, one that fuels its own learning and enables the reader to continue to learn through the act of reading. Effective readers have self-extending systems; they are self-initiating, self-regulating, and independent. You do not have to wait for the results of end-of-year testing to know that your guided reading instruction is successful. You know if students read each new harder text with high accuracy, fluency, and comprehension, and you also know that guided reading is effective if moment-to-moment observations and running records show that the readers are expanding their reading power across increasingly challenging texts. They self-initiate problem-solving actions and consistently search for and use multiple sources of information as they read for understanding.

Developing readers need to:

- Enjoy reading even when texts offer new challenges.
- Be successful when tackling more complex texts.
- Have opportunities to problem solve while reading.
- Read for meaning even when they must do some problem solving.
- Learn ways of taking actions that they can apply to their reading of other texts.
- Use their strengths.
- Self-confirm their active problem solving.
- Use what they know to get to what they do not yet know.
- Talk articulately about and respond to what they read.
- Expand their knowledge and understanding through reading.
- Make connections between texts they have read and between their own world knowledge and reading.
- Develop questions and become curious through reading.
- Learn and think deeply about the world they meet in books.
- Learn to read like a writer, noticing aspects of the writer's craft like structure and language.
- Develop knowledge of a wide range of genre and their characteristics.

We sometimes mistakenly assume that these needs can be met just by providing good books and encouraging students to explore them. In fact, what most readers need cannot be found in books alone. The process of reading must be dynamically supported by an interaction of text reading and good teaching. Guided reading serves this important goal.

A Rationale for Guided Reading

A great deal of tension surrounds decisions about whole-group, small-group, and individual instruction. Some instruction lends itself very well to whole-group instruction where students experience the same text (for example, interactive read aloud or shared reading); however, accelerative reading instruction requires that the individual reader be able to process a text with proficiency and, within a short time, take on the necessary understandings and behaviors to process texts of similar difficulty independently. Then, the instruction moves to more demanding texts with the same result.

Individual instruction can occur in a classroom (for example, you make time to have short individual conferences with students that focus on their own reading of the texts they have chosen). Conferences support independent reading, but these short conferences do not take the place of responsive, explicit small-group instruction that is designed to be generative using a carefully selected instructional level text. Conferences are brief and you cannot meet with every student every day. You simply do not have the time to teach every single student individually. It makes sense to bring students together in small groups so that you can tune in to the repertoires of the individuals, engage them in discourse about texts, and provide excellent instruction with efficiency. With good organization and time management, it is possible to give every student a guided reading lesson three to five days a week (balancing frequency with student need).

Teaching Tools for Guided Reading

As a skilled and responsive teacher, you have some powerful tools at your disposal. These include: your understanding of the reading process and your careful observations of your students; your ability to analyze the demands of texts; and, your repertoire of teaching actions that enable readers to develop self-initiating, self-regulating reading behaviors.

Know the Readers

The better you know the students in your class, the more effective and the more responsive you will be as a teacher of reading. You gain evidence by closely observing students as they read orally, by talking with them and by examining what they write about reading to get evidence of their understandings.

Systematic observation involves asking the student to read orally and noticing reading behaviors like multiple attempts at words, self-corrections, rereading, and phrased, fluent reading. Even when a student makes an error, the behavior tells you something about what the reader knows or almost knows how to do. For example, an individual reader reads this sentence: "They squawked and squabbled all day." But the reader reads, "They squawked and squidded all day." The substitution is an error, but the teacher notices that the substitution is partially correct. The substitution:

- is a verb, (even though a non-word, it has all the characteristics of a verb). which fits grammatically with the language structure (notice the past-tense ending);

- starts with the appropriate sounds, which indicates that the reader has noticed visual features of the word; and,

- ends with an *–ed,* which also indicates that the student is aware that past tense is appropriate.

Since there was no self-correction, it may be that the word *squabbled* is not in the students' oral vocabulary; however, the substitution shows a high level of word-solving competence. The teacher can go quickly back to the word *after* the reading to help the student examine the visual information more carefully and talk about the meaning.

After reading, engage the student in a brief conversation to process together the meaning of the text. You will gain evidence of whether the reader has followed and understood the ideas in the text and inferred what the writer implies as well as the main idea(s) of the text. It's also important to determine the degree to which the reader has noticed aspects of the writer's craft such as organizational structure, figurative language, plot construction, characterization, or underlying text structures such as problem and solution or compare and contrast in informational texts.

Systematic observation of each reader in the group provides rich and useful information related to your readers' current processing abilities—not just the level of text each can read with high accuracy. It reveals important reading behaviors signaling current processing abilities.

We recommend the use of a benchmark assessment system (see Chapter 9 for more about *Fountas & Pinnell Benchmark Assessment System*) at the beginning of the school year to know where to begin teaching. Administering the same standardized assessment to all students will give you a good profile of the class and serve as the basis for forming initial groups and planning for the emphases in teaching. The benchmark assessment can be used at year-end to document progress (and sometimes at midyear for particular students). In between benchmark assessments, the systematic use of running records (a coding of the students' oral reading) at selected intervals will be essential to guide your teaching in guided reading lessons across the year and to monitor progress (see Chapter 11).

Know the Texts

Your knowledge of texts is another tool for successful teaching of reading. The first step in preparing for a guided reading lesson is to read the text yourself and think about the characteristics. Ask yourself: What demands does this text make on readers? In other words, puzzle out what a reader has to do to read the text with comprehension, accuracy, and fluency. You can refer to the text descriptions for each level in the Guided Reading section of *The Fountas & Pinnell Literacy Continuum.*

What you notice about a text must be very specific. Consider the difficulty of the deeper meaning of the text, the words and their meaning, sentence complexity, literary features such as figurative language, how the text is organized, the genre, the length, and many other factors, all of which play a role in the demands that are made on the reader. In Chapter 13 you will find descriptions of ten key text characteristics as well as the gradient of text we have created as a teacher tool. The gradient describes text characteristics from A, the very easiest level, to Z, the most complex and sophisticated reading. Alongside the text characteristics we have described the demands of each level of text on readers in *The Literacy Continuum*. This document specifies a composite of behaviors and understandings showing what readers must be able to know and be able to do to meet the challenges of each level. The ordered categories show the difficulty of texts, A to Z, but the most important resources for you as a teacher are the detailed descriptions of reading competencies—the behaviors and understandings to notice, teach for, and support at each level of text. You can use these detailed descriptions to plan lessons, guide discussion after the text reading, make powerful teaching decisions after the reading, and evaluate the effects of your teaching.

Develop Expertise in Teaching

Each element in a guided reading lesson is directed at helping students build their independent processing power. The real key to helping the readers take control of the problem solving is the language that you use to support the reader's learning across the lessons. Through your specific language, you: (1) provide an introduction to the text that scaffolds reading; (2) intervene briefly to do some powerful prompting for strategic activity while students are reading; (3) guide the discussion so that students grasp the meaning and deepen thinking; and (4) do some specific teaching that reveals something important for students to notice or problems for them to solve. The students leave a guided reading lesson with understandings they can use to read other texts.

An Example of a Guided Reading Lesson

On the following pages you will see one example of a lesson from which you can glean the general principles of effective teaching in a guided reading context. Remember that this is only one example to introduce you to the shape of the lesson. In this book, you will find different teaching examples at a variety of instructional levels.

Information on the Readers

Mrs. M is working with a group of five students who read instructionally at level N (see Figure 1-3). That means that her benchmark assessment revealed that they can read books at level N on the text gradient with between 95% and 97% accuracy and with satisfactory comprehension. They can read books at level M and below in independent reading (though we do not recommend students choose independent reading books by level. See Chapter 12).

FIGURE 1-3 Mrs. M and Her Students

These students have a wide and flexible range of strategies for solving words that includes but goes beyond simple letter and sound correspondence. They use multiple sources of information to solve unfamiliar words but not consistently. They often make connections among words with similar features and can use some word parts to solve words of several syllables. They have learned a large number of high-frequency words that they recognize automatically without conscious attention.

They have experience in searching for and using information across some complex sentences and in simple graphics. They are able to identify and talk about the problem in a fiction story and follow it over multiple episodes. They have begun to understand the characteristics of several fiction and nonfiction text genres, although this ability is still developing. The students are able to use their background knowledge and information from the text to make predictions and to synthesize new knowledge.

Mrs. M wants to support their ability to infer the larger message of a text as well as the attributes of characters, to understand the characteristics of different genres, and to notice strong verbs that add to the description of action. Below are some of the behaviors from *The Literacy Continuum* that she wants to support:

▶ Take apart new multisyllable words to solve them

▶ Read verbs with inflectional endings that add meaning

▶ Predict the ending of a story based on knowledge of how plots work and understanding of characters, setting, and the story problem

▶ Infer character traits, feelings, and motivations from what characters say, think, or do and what others say and think about them

▶ Understand and describe characteristics of fables

▶ Infer the writer's message

Selecting the Text

Mrs. M pulls out six copies of *The Rooster and the Crow* (*Fountas & Pinnell Classroom*, in press), which is a level N book (see Figure 1-4). She calls the group members together at a table and gives each of the five students a copy of the book. This book is a fable that is probably not as familiar to students as several others they have read in that genre. Mrs. M wants to increase their awareness of the genre characteristics.

The Rooster and the Crow features two characters that exhibit undesirable attributes (foolish, constantly fighting, proud, boasting). The story also has a clever character that survives by using his wits. This story features complex sentences with phrases and clauses as well as a variety of unusual verbs to mark dialogue and the actions of characters. The plot centers on two competitive characters, neither of which deserves to win. The moral or lesson of the story is explicitly stated at the end (as is typical of a fable).

"True," cackled Rooster. "If anyone needs their beauty sleep, it's you."

"Very funny," said Crow. "Why don't you fly up here and say that?"

That was how it went, all day long.

Poor Worm flipped back and forth in Crow's beak, dizzy and dazed.

Rooster clucked to himself. Crow was so easy to trick.

"Oh, Crow!" he said. "Your feathers are as beautiful and black as a moonless night."

Crow was surprised. Rooster had never, ever said such pleasant things to him. But it was just the plain truth. Crow fluffed his feathers so everyone could see them.

FIGURE 1-4 *The Rooster and the Crow,* pages 4-5 and 10-11.

Teaching the Lesson

Introducing the Text

Mrs. M introduces the text by inviting students to talk about their expectations of fables. Students know that their role is to engage in conversation with the teacher and each other, access their present knowledge, and share their observations. In the introduction, Mrs. M raises their awareness of the characteristics of the genre of traditional literature, and also alerts them to notice character attributes and the resolution of the problem in the introduction (see Figure 1-5).

Text Introduction to *The Rooster and the Crow*, Level N

Speaker	Teacher/Student Interactions	Analysis of Interactions
Mrs. M	Today you are going to read a fable, *The Rooster and the Crow* by Casie Hermansson. Think about other fables you know and what you might expect in this story.	Remind students of the genre and ask them to share prior knowledge
Lanah	This is an Aesop fable like the one about the lion and the mouse.	Share what they know about the genre
Jake	A fable teaches a lesson.	Make connections between texts
Mrs. M	That's right, so you will want to look for the lesson in this story. A fable is a kind of traditional tale. What kinds of characters do fables usually have?	Alert them to look for characteristics they know Ask for specific genre characteristics
David	Most of the time they are animals and the animals talk.	Remind each other of specific genre characteristics
Carl	Some of them are not very nice to other animals.	
David	And they learn a lesson.	List important attributes of characters in a traditional tale
Mrs. M	In this story, the main characters are the rooster and the crow. Read the first paragraph and then share your thinking about the characters.	Introduce the characters and ask for thinking
Lorali	They sound like they are the foolish characters.	Demonstrates an awareness of a characteristic of the genre
Mrs. M	What does *foolish* mean?	Notice and talk about character attributes
Lorali	They are going to get in trouble.	Makes a prediction
David	They don't seem to like each other.	Infers characters' attitudes
Mrs. M	The writer uses the words *squawked* and *squabbled* to tell you that they argued with each other a lot. Say *squawked.* Find the word *squawked* on page 3. Get a good look at it. Say *squabbled.* Find *squabbled* and get a good look at the word. What do you notice about both words?	Point out how the writer reveals the characters Draw attention to key words that might be unexpected
Jake	They both start with *squ-.*	Notices word features

FIGURE 1-5 Text Introduction to *The Rooster and the Crow,* Level N

Text Introduction to *The Rooster and the Crow,* Level N

Speaker	Teacher/Student Interactions	Analysis of Interactions
David	And they end with *-ed.*	Notices word features
Mrs. M	Rooster and Crow both want to catch a worm. Who do you predict will win?	Ask for prediction based on character traits
Carl	The rooster will get it because he's closer to the ground.	Make a prediction
Mrs. M	That might be. So you will read to see what happens. Remember that both of these characters think that they are the best. Read *The Rooster and the Crow* and then let's talk about the lesson in the story and whether Rooster and Crow will act differently next time.	Prompt readers to confirm or disconfirm predictions Remind students to look for the lesson of the story and to infer character change

FIGURE 1-5 *(continued)*

Reading the Text

Students read the entire text silently, but Mrs. M listens and intervenes briefly with a few students to support their problem solving. Students know that when Mrs. M taps a student's hand, the student raises her voice so that Mrs. M can listen. (Sometimes teachers lean in to listen or walk around behind students and have the student turn briefly to read a little orally in a very quiet way.) In Figure 1-6, you can see examples of two interactions.

Reading the Text, *The Rooster and the Crow*

Interaction #1

Speaker	Teacher/Student Interactions	Analysis of Interactions
Lorali	I don't understand what this means. *[Reads from p. 9]* "Rooster has spoken the truth for once."	Doesn't understand the literary language and asks for help
Mrs. M	Read the second paragraph and ask, "What's different about the way Rooster is talking to Crow?"	Prompts to follow the plot
Carl	Rooster thinks Crow is great here.	Describes a character
Mrs. M	I agree. Read on and see what happens.	Prompts to follow the plot

Interaction #2

Speaker	Teacher/Student Interactions	Analysis of Interactions
Lorali	*[Stops]*	Shows need for help
Mrs. M	*[After reading p. 12]* Why did you stop?	Probes to be aware of self-monitoring
Lorali	What's that word? *[Pointing to* flattered*]*	Asks for help
Mrs. M	Look for a part you know *[covers -tered with finger].*	Prompts to notice word parts

FIGURE 1-6 Reading the Text, *The Rooster and the Crow*

Reading the Text, *The Rooster and the Crow*

Interaction #2

Speaker	Teacher/Student Interactions	Analysis of Interactions
Lorali	It says *flat* in the first part but that doesn't make sense.	Notices word parts and check meaning
Mrs. M	Now look at the next part of the word [moves finger to cover -ed only].	Takes apart multisyllable words
Lorali	-ter. Flattered.	
Mrs. M	Now go back and put *flattered* in the sentence to see if it makes sense to you.	Prompts for self-monitoring and correcting
Lorali	[Rereading the sentence] Oh, I see. Crow gave him a compliment.	Shows understanding
Mrs. M	You worked that out. Continue reading.	Confirms problem solving

FIGURE 1-6 *(continued)*

Discussing the Text

After students finish reading the text, Mrs. M invites personal response by asking them to talk about their thinking. Students know to respond to Mrs. M's open invitation to the discussion; they expect to immediately share their first thoughts about the text. Then, she selects questions and prompts that help students further expand their thinking. In Figure 1-7, you see an excerpt from the discussion. Mrs. M listens for understanding of the main ideas of the text (the writer's message(s)).

Discussing the Text, *The Rooster and the Crow*

Speaker	Teacher/Student Interactions	Analysis of Interactions
Mrs. M	So what did you learn about the characters?	Invites student thinking with open question
Jake	They were really dumb because the minute they thought they were being praised, they forgot what they were doing.	Analyzes character attributes and motivation
David	Each of them tricked the other one, but they were both dumb.	
Mrs. M	And why do you think that?	Prompts to explain thinking
David	Because they forgot that they wanted to keep the worm. They just did what they were proud of doing so they could show off.	Infers character motivation
Mrs. M	What happened to the worm? What do think about what the worm learned?	Prompts for interpretation of plot
Lorali	The worm escaped because he was smart enough to know that he could get away from both of them.	Infers character attributes

FIGURE 1-7 Discussing the Text, *The Rooster and the Crow*

Discussing the Text, *The Rooster and the Crow*

Speaker	Teacher/Student Interactions	Analysis of Interactions
Jake	The Rooster and the Crow forgot what they were doing, so the worm could get away.	Infers reasons for character behavior
Mrs. M	**So what could you say about the worm?**	Prompts to find evidence of outcome
Lanah	It's on page 15. The worm learned to be ready to escape.	Identifies evidence of character change
Mrs. M	**In a fable, the lesson is usually stated. Read the lesson in this story and think about what it means in your own words.**	Reminds students of a genre characteristic
Jake	*(Reading)* Pride and boasting will get you nowhere. I think this means that bragging and talking about yourself isn't a good thing.	Finds statement of big idea in the text

FIGURE 1-7 *(continued)*

Teaching Point

After the discussion, Mrs. M makes a teaching point that helps the readers look more closely at the text. The teaching point is shown in Figure 1-8.

Teaching Point, *The Rooster and the Crow*

Speaker	Teacher/Student Interactions	Analysis of Interactions
Mrs. M	**Take a look at page 16 and read the first paragraph. As you read, notice the way the writer describes what Crow and Rooster do.**	Prompts to notice how a writer reveals characters
Jake	They are really mad and they blamed each other.	Interprets the writer's language
David	They were making noise. One screeched.	Notices the writer's language
Mrs. M	**What does that word "screech" tell you about Crow?**	Draws attention to the meaning of a word
Jake	It's like he's yelling.	Clarifies meaning of a word
Mrs. M	**In this book, the writer chooses to use strong words like "screeched" and "stomped" to help readers understand the characters. The writer is choosing those words to show how unpleasant Crow is. Look at page 3 and see if you can find more words like that.**	Draws attention to writer's word choice
David	*Squawked* and *squabbled.*	Identifies strong verbs
Mrs. M	**All of those words—they are verbs—are what you might call strong or interesting verbs. They help make a picture in your mind. You can really tell what these animals are like as characters because of the writer's choice of words.**	Demonstrates noticing the writer's craft

FIGURE 1-8 Teaching Point, *The Rooster and the Crow*

Word Work

Following the teaching point, Mrs. M engages the group in a quick look at words with the inflectional ending –*ly*. Using magnetic letters she makes *slowly, quickly, softly,* and *sadly,* on a whiteboard and asks them to identify the base word for each and to think about how the ending changes the word meaning (see Figure 1-9).

Following word work, students move to page three of the book and locate *badly* to gain one more example and notice the base word.

Word Work, *The Rooster and the Crow*

Speaker	Teacher/Student Interactions	Analysis of Interactions
Mrs. M	What do you notice about all these words? *Slowly, quickly, softly, sadly.*	Invites students to engage in inquiry
Lorali	They all end in –*ly*.	Notices characteristics that connect words
Mrs. M	*[Moving* -ly *off of the word* slowly*]* What is the base word here?	Draws attention to an important word part
Jake	*Slow.*	Identifies the base word
Mrs. M	The –*ly* changes the meaning of *slow.* How does it change the meaning?	Asks for interpretations of the function of a suffix
David	It tells how you walk or move.	Identifies the function of a suffix
Mrs. M	Yes, adding the suffix –*ly* changes how something is done. Let's underline the base word for each of these words. *[Mrs. M has students/partners write four words on a whiteboard, underlining the base word of each.]*	States a principle of word analysis

FIGURE 1-9 Word Work, *The Rooster and the Crow*

Structure of a Guided Reading Lesson

1. Introduce the Text
2. Read the Text
3. Discuss the Text
4. Teaching Point
5. Letter-Word Work
6. Write About Reading (optional)

FIGURE 1-10 Structure of a Guided Reading Lesson

Structure of a Guided Reading Lesson

The lesson structure for guided reading is summarized in Figure 1-10.

The same basic structure is used in guided reading lessons from kindergarten through the upper elementary or middle grades; however, the texts, content, interactions, and goals change greatly over time as students grow in their ability to take on more complex texts. We have described the behaviors and understandings to teach for across the levels in *The Literacy Continuum*. Using your knowledge of your students, you can select the goals to prioritize in each lesson.

This example illustrates some of the essential components of the process—observation, clear examples, and support for the reader's ability to initiate problem-solving actions. While there are adjustments and variations related to the students' age and grade level and the text level, in guided reading the structure is consistent.

Teaching as a Decision-Making Process

There is no script for you to follow in guided reading. The lesson is highly structured and organized to support learning; however, your teaching interactions with students depend on their responses and the goals you see as important for them. Students quickly learn the organizational pattern so that lesson management (and directions from the teacher) are minimal. This leaves instructional time for learning conversations. The nature of the lesson is flexible, accounting for real conversation and the exchange of ideas. The instruction is directed toward developing student independence and initiative in thinking, problem solving and talking about texts.

For over a century, there has been a struggle within the educational community between scripted and rigidly controlled approaches and highly flexible approaches to reading instruction. We are advocating for a systematic structure within which responsive teaching can take place—teaching that is grounded in the observations of precise reading behaviors and responding to the reader in a way that enables the reader to construct in-the-head strategies that become increasingly complex. In fact, no single approach "works" for every child; but with guided reading, you vary your interactions and decisions to respond to the individual needs of each student in the group. Sometimes you invite students to engage in inquiry. Sometimes you teach explicitly. Sometimes you confirm successful problem solving. Sometimes you prompt for problem-solving actions. And remember, that within an excellent classroom literacy design, there are many opportunities for whole-class, small-group, and individual teaching, all directed toward building the competencies of each reader.

At every point in the guided reading lesson, your teaching decisions emerge from your professional knowledge of:

- The reading process and how it changes over time
- Your readers (gained through careful observation and interpretation of students observable reading behaviors)
- Your analysis of texts (complexity, genre, word difficulty, literary language, ideas, and themes)
- Your observations of the effects of teaching decisions on student learning

As a teacher, you will do some preplanning, for example:

- Create groups based on sound rationales (using assessment data and observational notes).
- Select a few teaching priorities or emphases for your students (as individuals and as a group). You will find the "Selecting Goals" section of *The Literacy Continuum* helpful in being specific about teaching goals (see Chapter 9).
- Select a text that is highly engaging and appropriate for the students and offers a few opportunities to learn (see Chapter 14).
- Analyze the text carefully to note opportunities for learning and also areas that need your support in the introduction to the text. Make a few notes on a sticky note and page numbers to plan the introduction.
- Plan some big idea questions and/or prompts to start student discussion based on text analysis of the deeper messages of the text.

Elements of Guided Reading

Preparation

1 Form a *Small Group*	Students are similar enough in their reading competencies so that a text at a particular level will offer learning opportunities for each of them.
2 *Identify Emphases*	Select a few behaviors and understandings to notice, teach for, and support from *The Fountas & Pinnell Literacy Continuum*.
3 *Select* a Text	The text is appropriate for the group. The text offers challenge and opportunity to learn.
4 *Analyze* the Text	Identify the demands of the text and opportunities for learning. Match with student needs.

Lesson

5 *Introduce* the Text	Provide support to enable proficient reading. Leave some problem solving to do.
6 Support Students' *Reading* of the Text	Observe reading behaviors. Intervene very briefly if needed to support strategic actions, not to test for comprehension.
7 Guide *Discussion* of the Text	Encourage students' expression of thinking. Encourage students to ground talk in the text and to cite evidence for their thinking. Observe for evidence of comprehension.
8 Engage in Specific *Teaching*	Provide specific teaching that is appropriate for the group based on your observations. Direct students' attention to something they can apply to not only this text but to other texts they read.
9 Support Students' *Work* with Letters and Words	Increase rapid word analysis skills. Increase flexibility in word solving.
10 *Extend* Understanding Through Writing About Reading (Optional)	Prompt students to write about reading. Encourage expression of thinking within, beyond, and about the text. Observe for evidence of comprehension.

FIGURE 1-11 Elements of Guided Reading

The better you know your students and the more thoroughly you analyze the text, the easier it will be to plan your guided reading lessons. We summarize key elements to keep in mind as you develop your expertise in guided reading (see Figure 1-11).

The lesson structure is especially helpful in supporting your ability to make good decisions within the act of teaching. Students engage in the same structure every day; the routines become automatic, and both you and your students develop an internal sense of the steps and approximate time each will take. They learn that participation in talk is essential. They learn that engaging in conversation during the introduction to the text and discussion supports their understanding of the book. Because students understand the lesson routines so well, attention is freed for attention to powerful teaching.

Becoming an effective teacher of guided reading takes time and effort; but the outcomes are worth it. As you teach students, you will have the satisfaction of seeing them apply today what you taught yesterday; you will notice behavioral evidence that they are taking on new understandings; and you will see them expand their competencies and move to higher levels of texts.

In the next chapter, we look at how various instructional contexts, including guided reading, contribute to the making of a reader.

Suggestions for Professional Development

The first step in implementing guided reading is to take an inventory of the status of language and literacy in your classroom. Over a period of two weeks, analyze your daily schedule (look back at lesson plans). Meeting with a colleague will help in problem solving.

1. How much time do I spend on reading instruction?
   - How much time for reading instruction is there in the weekly schedule?
   - How much specific reading instruction does each student receive each week?
   - How much time do students spend reading continuous text?
   - How much time do I spend in individual conferences? In whole-class instruction?
   - Where in my schedule can I teach small groups of students in guided reading?

2. Look at the texts that are available in your classroom and in your school. Do you have:
   - Single copies of high-quality books to read aloud?
   - Single copies of large-print books for shared reading?
   - Multiple copies of texts for small-group instruction?
   - Texts organized by level?
   - Individual copies of appropriate texts in a classroom library for students to select for independent reading?

3. After assessing the texts you have available, you will have a better idea of how much reading students currently do and what they need to have. You will also know what needs to be done in terms of acquiring and organizing the texts that you need to use in guided reading as an important element in the literacy design.

4. Create a weekly plan that reserves time for teaching several small groups in guided reading lessons.

CHAPTER 2

Guided Reading Within a Multitext Approach

Levels of Support for Literacy Learning

> *The truly literate are not those who know how to read, but those who read: independently, responsively, critically, and because they want to.*
>
> –Glenna Sloan

If you are a newcomer to any task, for example, cooking a soufflé, probably the first thing you want to see is a "live" demonstration of how it is done. Then, you start to try it out for yourself, perhaps with the expert sharing the task. As you work, you realize that there are nuances to the task that were not evident in the demonstration. When you try it yourself, it really helps to have an experienced soufflé chef working alongside you to guide the process. And soon, you feel confident enough to try the soufflé completely alone. The path to success in this simple task moves from a compelling demonstration, to a shared task, to doing it with someone reminding you of the tricks necessary for success, to performing it completely solo. Even after you become "expert" yourself, you occasionally want to watch a master at work to refine your skills or to learn variations that might be interesting. It is no wonder that cooking shows, which often include a novice learning from the master, are so popular.

Literacy learning is, of course, thousands of times more complex than cooking; nevertheless, there are comparisons. This book focuses on guided reading, but from the beginning, we emphasize that small-group instruction is more powerful when nested within a variety of instructional contexts with varying levels of support. In this chapter, we explore the broader literacy-learning context in which guided reading resides. All play an essential role; they contribute in different ways to each student's development as readers, writers, and language users. Let's think together about how you can vary the level of support depending on the demands of the text and the level of control by readers at any point in time.

Four Levels of Support and Five Kinds of Reading

Within the instructional design, we describe four levels of support for reading within five instructional contexts. (see Figure 2-1).

You vary from high to low teacher support depending on the level of control students demonstrate in relation to a text. This design fits with the "gradual release of responsibility" model of teaching and learning (Pearson and Gallagher 1983). As a teacher, you move from demonstration to sharing the task to turning it over to the students. If the text is too difficult for most of the students to read for themselves, you read it *to* them (read aloud or have them listen to an audio recording). If it is too difficult but within reach with strong support, you read it *with* them and share the task (shared reading). If it is challenging, but within reach with some support or little or no support, they read it *themselves* (guided or independent reading). Independent reading has the support of a strong set of routines, book talks, minilessons, teacher conferences, a rich classroom library, and group share as well as a rich classroom library. You are always demonstrating something harder, but students gradually take it on and engage successfully.

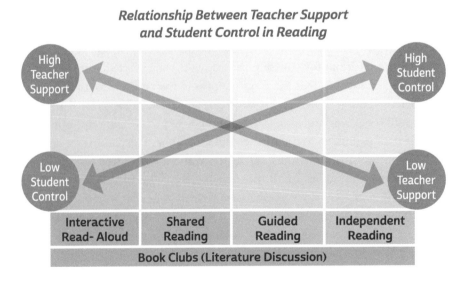

Relationship Between Teacher Support and Student Control in Reading

FIGURE 2-1 The Relationship Between Teacher Support and Student Control in Reading

Five Instructional Contexts for Reading

In the reading and writing classroom, we recommend five kinds of reading opportunities using a variety of texts across genres. Four contexts are shown in Figure 2-2. We discuss the fifth kind of reading, book clubs, later in this chapter. Book clubs include a variety of support levels for students to access the text.

Instructional Contexts for Reading

Read-Aloud	Shared Reading	Guided Reading	Independent Reading
Whole Class	Whole Class	Small Group	Individual
One individual print copy (though there are a few large-print picture books that children in the class can read)	Enlarged text/illustrations (big book, charts, computer enlarged, or small copies for each student)	Individual teacher-selected book for each child (the same for every child)	Individual self-selected book
Students are listening and can see illustrations	All eyes on the same text	Each reader in the group has a copy of the same text in hand	Reader has individual copy
Text level is beyond the level most or some could read independently	Text level beyond many students' instructional level	Text at reader's instructional level	Text at reader's independent level (though occasionally may not be)
Teacher reads aloud, occasionally pausing for conversation	Teacher reads aloud first time, with readers joining on rereading	Students read aloud softly or silently the complete text or unified part	Student reads silently the complete text
The text is usually new but occasionally some, or parts of some, are reread	The text is sometimes new and may be one that has been read before	The text is new. (Rereading of previously read texts may also happen before or after the lesson with early readers)	Text is new
Texts may be a variety of genres and formats	Texts may be a variety of genres and formats	Texts may be a variety of genres and formats	Texts are a variety of genres and formats
The focus is on constructing meaning using language	The focus is on constructing meaning using language and print	The focus is on constructing meaning using language and print	The focus is on constructing meaning using language and print

FIGURE 2-2 Instructional Contexts for Reading

FIGURE 2-3 Interactive Read-Aloud

FIGURE 2-4 Shared Reading

Interactive Read-Aloud. In interactive read-aloud, you select a text and read it to the students; interactive read-aloud is usually a whole-class activity (see Figure 2-3). The books have small print so students are listening to the story or nonfiction book. Most of your selections are picture books, so students can notice the illustrations or nonfiction text features. A high-quality picture book is a beautifully crafted short story or informational article with illustrations. There are many wonderful picture books with content suitable for every grade level and age group (some have serious and mature themes and content). As students listen, they engage systems of strategic actions for comprehending texts. The only difference is that they do not need to visually process the print (decode the words and attend to punctuation), but the thinking is the same.

This type of reading is called "interactive" because it is intended to spark discussion. The text is a basis for literature discussion among the whole group. As a teacher you identify places in the text to pause and invite students to turn and talk with a partner or respond to the whole group. Interactive read-aloud is a way to engage your students daily in comprehending and articulating their thinking about age-appropriate material (the level is generally beyond the instructional reading level of most of the students). Texts are carefully selected (and often organized into text sets) so that the students can make connections across the ideas and content and notice parallels in the craft of writing. Your read-aloud selections represent a variety of genres and formats. The lessons are carefully planned to expand student thinking. Students can also listen to texts read aloud at a listening center.

Shared Reading. Shared reading, too, is usually a whole-class context, although it can be used with small groups, particularly with early readers. You select an enlarged text (or enlarge a part of a regular-sized text). Your first step with a new book is to read it aloud to the students; but there is an important difference from interactive read-aloud: the print and other text features are visually available to the students (see Figure 2-4). Like interactive read-aloud, you use a variety of genres and formats and offer a high level of support. After you read the text aloud to students and talk about the story or informational content, invite students to read it (or a section of it) with you. For early readers, this usually means reading in unison or in parts. After the text has been read in unison several times, it is available for students to read independently or with a partner. For early readers, small versions can be available to reread for independent reading. We will discuss the lesson structure for shared reading later in this book.

Guided Reading. Guided reading is a small-group instructional context in which students move from high teacher support to full control of the reading process (see Figure 2-5). You select the text using a gradient of difficulty, and students have their own copies. Unlike interactive read-aloud and shared reading, you do not read the text to the students. Instead, you provide a carefully planned introduction to the text that enables each student to read (softly or silently) the whole text individually (see Chapter 14). The text is new to the students, so they have the opportunity to apply their processing systems across an unseen text, applying what they learned how to do as readers in the previous lesson. After reading, you guide a discussion of the meaning and then make a specific teaching point based on your observations of readers. Finally, you engage students in two or three minutes of active work with letters or words, if appropriate.

FIGURE 2-5 Guided Reading

FIGURE 2-6 Independent Reading

Independent Reading. Readers need to engage in massive amounts of choice, independent reading. The students have full control of the process in independent reading, although you support them by offering a rich, well-organized collection of books from which to choose (see Figure 2-6). You make sure that the collection offers engaging texts of varying genres and levels of difficulty so that all students will be able to find something that they can read and want to read. But students do not select books by level. A key factor in independent reading is *choice*. There are opportunities for students to share their thinking about books with other students in the class and through writing. Independent reading is placed within a strong instructional frame, through minilessons to help students apply understandings to their own reading and learn how to choose books they can enjoy, reading conferences to support thinking, and group share for further learning and assessment.

Book Clubs (Literature Discussion). You will notice in Figure 2-1 that book clubs (literature discussion) runs from high teacher support to low teacher support. We include book clubs as it involves a small group of students and can vary with the level of support needed for students to access the text. Students choose from a limited selection of titles and join a book club group to talk together about the text

Book Clubs (Literature Discussion)

Small group

Self-selected within limited options

Each reader has a copy of the text

Text level varies

Students read or listen to text

Text is new

Texts are a variety of genres and formats

The focus is on constructing meaning using language and print

FIGURE 2-7 Book Clubs (Literature Discussion)

FIGURE 2-8 Students and Teacher Participating in a Book Club

(see Figure 2-7). Because the text difficulty of the student's choice may not match the readers' competencies, she may listen to the text on an audio recording, or an adult may read the text to the student or even share the reading. The teacher gathers the students for a discussion, at first providing a higher level of support, but gradually with lessening support as students take over the discussion (see Figure 2-8).

If you think across these five contexts for reading, you can see that you are helping students build a rich text base. In all contexts, the focus is on constructing meaning using language. But, in shared, guided, and independent reading, the focus is on constructing meaning using language and print. When students engage as readers with a variety of texts, they are also learning about how to craft texts as writers. When you help your students read like writers and write like readers, they benefit greatly from the reading-writing connection.

Four Instructional Contexts for Writing

The four kinds of writing are roughly parallel to the contexts for reading in that they range from high teacher support to student control of the writing process (see Figures 2-9 and 2-10).

Shared Writing. In shared writing, you and the students create a text for a real purpose and audience. You serve as the scribe for sentences that the students work together to compose (see

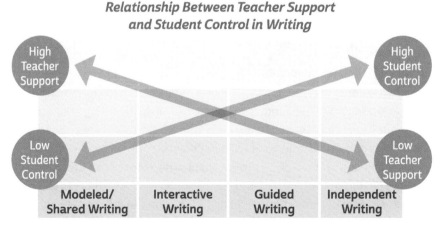

Relationship Between Teacher Support and Student Control in Writing

FIGURE 2-9 The Relationship Between Teacher Support and Student Control in Writing

Four Instructional Contexts for Writing

Shared Writing	Interactive Writing	Guided Writing	Independent Writing
Whole Class	Whole Class/Small Group	Small Group	Individual
Production of one enlarged text (chart or digital)	Production of one enlarged text (chart or digital)	Students work on their own pieces of writing with teacher support (usually focused on one aspect of writing)	Students work on their own pieces of writing
Students contribute ideas and language to one shared text Teacher shapes the piece and scribes	Students contribute ideas and language and sometimes write words and letters to produce one shared text	Students select their own topics and compose language with teacher support (usually focused on one aspect of writing)	Students select their own topics, compose language, and write the words, sentences, and paragraphs
Written language is beyond what the students can produce independently	Written language is beyond what the students can produce independently	Written language represents what students can do but is refined and extended through instruction	Written language represents what students can do independently (with occasional conferences with the teacher)
The text is reread using shared reading	The text is reread using shared reading	The text is reread by the student and may be read to the group	The text is reread by the student and may be refined through several drafts. Additional conferences with the teacher may be required
Written texts are in a variety of genres and formats	Written texts are in a variety of genres and formats	Written texts are in a variety of genres and formats	Written texts are in a variety of genres and formats
The focus is on composing the language of a text to communicate meaning for an authentic purpose	The focus is on composing the language of a text to communicate meaning for an authentic purpose, and on some of the actions needed to construct words, sentences, paragraphs	The focus is on composing a text to communicate meaning for an authentic purpose, and on constructing the words, sentences and paragraphs	The focus is on composing a text to communicate meaning for an authentic purpose, and on constructing the words, sentences and paragraphs

FIGURE 2-10 Four Instructional Contexts for Writing

FIGURE 2-11 Shared Writing

Figure 2-11). You write on a chart with a dark marker and the print is large enough for all students to see. (You could also use a keyboard and projected computer screen.) Students are freed from the acts of writing letters and spelling words, so they can concentrate on the meaning and language of the text (as well as the layout and text features). This context offers an opportunity to demonstrate the characteristics of just about any form of writing; often, the composition will be about a book that students have heard read aloud or about a topic they're learning about. Students concentrate on a common text, which is then available for rereading in a shared way. Charts have the advantage of being posted in the classroom as a reference or model. The composition can be any kind of text—summaries, lists, letters, short writes, and so on. The piece of writing is reread several times in a shared way during composition and once completed may be available for the group and individuals to reread. As students grow more sophisticated, shared writing still has benefits; for example, you can use it to:

- Demonstrate more complex sentence composition and punctuation.
- Get students' thinking down quickly and preserve it as a resource for other writing or talking about reading.
- Demonstrate writing in a new genre.
- Demonstrate aspects of the writer's craft.
- Show the organization of a text (for example, using a graphic organizer to show problem and solution).

FIGURE 2-12 Interactive Writing

Interactive Writing. Interactive writing is identical to and proceeds in exactly the same way as shared writing, with one exception: occasionally, as you make teaching points to help children attend to various features of letters and words, you invite a student to come up to the easel and contribute a letter, word, part of a word or punctuation (see Figure 2-12). You share the pen with students at selected points that have high instructional value. The parts of the text written by children foster close attention to sounds, letters, and word structure, give children more ownership of the piece, and capture their attention. Very often, kindergartners and first graders can tell you exactly which letters or words they wrote; but the technique should not be overused because it can slow down the production of text. When students are in full control of early writing behaviors and can spell many words, you may want to use shared writing most of the time for demonstration. The ultimate goal of interactive writing is to shift the control to the children as independent writers.

Interactive writing is a powerful tool for helping students build a strong early reading and writing process. Rereading to decide where to put the next word, saying a word slowly to decide what letter to write first (and next), attending to the spaces, help children develop awareness of early reading behaviors such as word-by-word matching, directional movement, and monitoring using sound and letter information. Both shared and interactive writing offer a way to engage students in composing and writing in different genres and forms ahead of the time they are expected to produce them independently. Usually, you use interactive writing with the whole class, but you may occasionally decide to use it in a small-group of early writers or intermediate writers who need a higher level of support. It may be used for writing about reading in small group guided reading instruction. It also provides a highly supportive language opportunity for English language learners. Since texts created in shared or interactive writing are created for authentic purposes for real audiences they become meaningful texts for shared or independent reading.

Guided Writing. You can bring together a small group of students with similar needs to engage them in guided writing (see Figure 2-13). You may have introduced a type of writing to the whole group but have noticed that these students need more support to take on the new learning. For example, students might need help in writing in a particular genre, using strong verbs, varying sentence structure, paragraphing, or text organization. You can provide an explicit minilesson based on the common needs of the small group. In the small group, you can also provide further support through shared or interactive writing. You can also bring in books you have read aloud to the class as examples, so that students learn how to use mentor texts to improve their own writing. Students can work on their own pieces while you observe them closely and provide specific guidance. Students can share their work with the group. The work in the small group is not daily, but it can give students a boost so that they can work more effectively on their own.

FIGURE 2-13 Guided Writing

Independent Writing. Students are involved daily in writing their own pieces (see Figure 2-14). Through writing, they explore a wide range of genres and topics for a variety of audiences. They also write about their reading about once a week (see Chapter 20). They also write from personal experience and from study in the academic disciplines. Over the course of elementary school (about ages 5 through 11), they should produce a large amount of

FIGURE 2-14 Independent Writing

written work independently. It's a wonderful idea to save samples from each year electronically so that there is a portfolio of progress. But students should produce so much that it would be hard to save everything! Many teachers ask students to select their best pieces each month for the portfolio.

Students engage in various aspects of the writing process that are appropriate to the age group, which is recursive, to include:

▶ Recording notes, sketches, and ideas in a writer's notebook ("planting seeds")

▶ Deciding on a topic and getting ideas down on paper in a blank, stapled book or on the computer ("drafting")

▶ Rereading and producing subsequent drafts of the piece ("revising")

▶ Doing final proofreading ("editing")

▶ Having the teacher edit and then moving to publication (optional)

With their pieces of writing, students are always somewhere along this process, and you may use a number of tools to monitor how they are progressing. You build a strong instructional frame around independent writing by providing a minilesson at the beginning of every writing period, conferring with writers, and having a group share at the end. The minilessons can focus on any aspect of writing (conventions, craft, or process), and students apply the principle of the lesson to their own writing. They learn how to analyze examples of good writing and use other writers as mentors. They learn how to use a rich variety of mentor texts in each genre so they can learn how to write from effective pieces.

With the combination of demonstration and guidance in these different writing contexts, students get the input they need to continually grow as writers. The focus in all four contexts is on the composition of meaningful texts in a variety of genres and text types for a real purpose and audience.

The Role of Talk in Reading and Writing

Across these levels of support, the vehicle for learning is talk. Talk is thinking. Students talk about mentor texts as readers and writers and become articulate about their thinking as they converse with you and their peers. Book clubs (literature discussion) take place in whole class, small groups, triads and dyads. (We define literature discussion as including the numerous high-quality nonfiction books students read as well as all genres of fiction.) Across contexts, students have maximum opportunities to process texts and use language that is grounded in texts.

Goals for Talking About Texts

Language grounded in texts is significantly different from conversations in other contexts. It is purposeful rather than casual. As a teacher, you can lift students' comprehension of texts as well as their ability to articulate their thinking by guiding the conversation and helping students to keep it grounded in texts. We are all familiar with young children's tendencies to engage in monologues about their own experiences, and there is a time for that. But engaging in book discussion means getting beyond casual sharing to make strong and explicit links between their own experiences and understanding and the larger ideas in a text. It's not just "a lot of talk." When students talk seriously and in-depth about books, the benefits are enormous (see Figure 2-15).

Building a literate community. When students bring their own thinking and experiences to bear on a text, they get to know one another in new ways and develop trusting relationships. A meaningful discussion grounded in a fiction text or nonfiction topic becomes a window on people and their world.

Voicing understandings and perspectives. As readers, we all understand more than we are able to successfully articulate. Even adults sometimes struggle for the right words to express their thinking, but the more opportunities an individual has, the easier it becomes. The group discussion is far different from a set of teacher-asked questions that, often, are designed to test rather than extend students' comprehension. Responding to the statements and questions of other students offers the challenge of communicating meanings to peers, which results in authentic discourse. Over and over again, students have the opportunity to express their understandings, a situation far different from writing responses alone.

Testing ideas. When students discuss literature with others, they are not in a testing or "grading" situation. The only requirement is courteous, collaborative participation. They can feel free to "float" ideas, listen to responses, and change their minds. They can state half-formed opinions and then decide if evidence supports them. Their thinking can evolve across the discussion because the group acts as a sounding board, and the group can extend and stretch the thinking of individual members.

Connecting big ideas to life. Every fiction or nonfiction text should have an overarching message or "big idea"—usually more than one—that has meaning or relevance for students' own lives, and can be connected to the world and other texts. Only then will reading come to be a highly valued lifelong activity. The group discussion should propel students' search for these bigger messages.

Learning conversational routines. An important life skill is the ability to enter into authentic conversation with others. Literature discussion is an ideal opportunity to practice conversational skills while talking about topics of significance. Many of these skills will require explicit teaching, but over

The Benefits of Talking About Texts

Students:

Build relationships with peers by learning more about them and their thinking.

Articulate their own understandings of, and perspectives on, a text.

Test ideas within a safe group context.

Develop and share understandings about the larger meanings of a text and how they connect to their lives, to other texts, and to the world.

Engage in turn taking and learn how to keep a meaningful strand of discussion going.

Become independent of the teacher in discussing texts with others.

Learn to value and respond to the thinking of other students.

Learn that there are different interpretations of texts and different perspectives on characters, plots, problem resolutions, and topics.

Learn academic language to use in discussing texts.

Build deeper, richer understandings of a text.

FIGURE 2-15 The Benefits of Talking About Texts

time they should become habitual and unconscious. Students can learn, for example, how to:

⯈ Listen carefully to others before responding.

⯈ Look at the person who is talking.

⯈ Speak to other students in the group (not just to the teacher).

⯈ Speak clearly so others can hear.

⯈ Talk in turn.

⯈ Disagree respectfully.

⯈ Build on ideas others have made.

⯈ Keep a strand of discussion going before changing the subject.

⯈ Include others in the group by asking for their thinking.

Early readers (and many intermediate/middle readers) will not automatically enter your class knowing these skills, and it won't happen just with telling. But teachers have become very effective at demonstrating, reminding, engaging students daily in their practice, and asking students to self-evaluate so that they develop the social conventions of book clubs over time.

Become independent. Many "school" discussions depend almost totally on the teacher's presence. Your goal in literature discussion is to develop in students the ability to have an exciting, meaningful conversation largely without your intervention. Your presence *is* essential to teach, demonstrate, support, and sometimes help them get back to the text; but the ultimate goal is independence. You can measure the growth of independence by noticing how many comments are directed toward other students and how many times students respond to others without your own talk in between.

Value the thinking of others. The discussion of literature is a place where the norm is respectful attention to others' comments. Students can disagree but should use language like, "I disagree with you because . . ." or, "tell me more about that so I can understand it." A hallmark of a community is respectful discourse. You will teach students to make sure that everyone in the group has a turn and that ideas are considered carefully. Thoughtful listening and responding from the teacher and peers is a better way to communicate value than words like "good."

Understand differences. The wonderful thing about fiction and nonfiction texts is that they require *interpretation*. It is important for students to understand that there will be different interpretations of the messages of texts and each person's perspective should be carefully considered. Over time, they should reach conclusions that are most strongly supported with evidence. Rubbing up against conflicting ideas sharpens thinking and makes discussion more lively and interesting.

Use academic language for talking about texts. As students discuss books they also acquire ways of talking about them. Even young children soon learn to use words like *author*, *title*, and *illustrations*. They enjoy having the technical vocabulary to talk about texts. As they grow over time, students acquire a whole range of technical terms, for example, *plot*, *character development*, *problem/solution*, *sidebar*, or *preface*. In *The Literacy Continuum*, you will find a suggested list of academic terms that might be appropriate at each grade level and at each level of text on the gradient. Academic language is acquired over a long period of time, and it is acquired through use. Learning to use such terms through conversation is far more effective than memorizing a list of definitions. Over time, the terms become part of students' repertoire and they use them automatically in discussion.

Build a deep, rich understanding of a text. With the benefit of the discussion, each student builds a richer, deeper understanding of a text than any one student could gain from reading it alone.

How Will You Know You Are Achieving the Goals?

You will want to develop some sharp observational skills so that you can detect when a discussion is going well and students are improving in their ability to enter into conversation and articulate their thinking. Often this means closely monitoring your own teaching moves. For illustration, let's look at two samples of interaction based on hundreds of observations in classrooms as well as our own experience as teachers (see Figures 2-16 and 2-17).

You may think that Sample A is exaggerated, but it is not. Any of us can find ourselves struggling with the discussion, repeating students' comments to fill time, and telling too much. At any point in time, our discussions might tend toward the tedious, forced discussion in Sample A to the dynamic discussion in Sample B, but our goal should be clear. And it will not happen without demonstrating and teaching students every day. One great first step is to avoid repeating students' comments and speaking after every student speaks. If you think a student has not spoken so others can hear, ask him to repeat it. Give wait time. You can spark a lot of discussion with comments like: "Can you say more about that?" "Would anyone

Sample A. Discussion of *A Long Walk to Water*

Ms. T	What do you think about the end of the book?
Ella	I think Salva did a good thing for the village.
Ms. T	Salva did a good thing for the village. What does somebody else think?
Brian	Nya will not have to carry water now.
Ms. T	Nya won't have to carry water. Anyone else?
Mayana	They get to meet at the end.
Ms. T	They get to meet. What about the tribes? How does that come into it?
Brian	She is from one tribe . . . the . . . uh.
Ms. T	Nya's from the Nuer tribe, and what about Salva?
Ella	He's from the other tribe . . . *[reads]* Dinka.
Ms. T	Yes the Dinka tribe. And those two tribes didn't get along did they? So that's important. How many thought this was a good ending?
Students	*[Raise hands]*

FIGURE 2-16 Sample A: Discussion of *A Long Walk to Water*

Sample B. Discussion of *A Long Walk to Water*

Ms. T	**Talk about your thinking about the end of the book.**
Mayana	They finally got to meet when Salva built the well in Nya's village. It's funny how they weren't in the same place until the very end.
Brian	Well, that's partly because it was two different time periods. Salva was grown up when Nya was just a little girl and so he couldn't meet her when he was a kid.
Ella	I agree, but it was also because they were in different tribes.
Ms. T	**That's true. The Dinka and the Nuer tribes were at war. What's different for these two people now?**
Ella	Salva has done something good for Nya.
Ms. T	**Say more about that.**
Ella	She won't have to carry water any more. So they can be friends.
Bryce	They probably think that the tribes and war aren't so important and people should work together. Does this mean the wars will end now?
Ms. T	**I'm not sure, but what do some of you think could happen?**
Mayana	If they keep on helping each other and getting to know each other, it could mean peace.
Brian	What I think about is how they each had to do so much walking, and really they had a lot in common. Water is so important.
Ella	I thought about that too, but also how he just had to keep putting one foot in front of another. Right up until he got the wells built and got people to give money.
Ms. T	**And does that remind you of anything?**
Mayana	It's like for us we have to keep on going to get our work done and to finish school.
Ella	I like how he didn't tell her his name until the very end.
	[The discussion continues]

FIGURE 2-17 Sample B: Discussion of *A Long Walk to Water*

like to respond to _____'s comment?" "Is there another way to think about that?" "Who can add to that?" "Do you all agree? Why? Or, why not?"

We have also observed that highly skilled teachers can do a lot with nonverbal gestures. We have observed a teacher gesturing with an open palm and looking sincerely at a student to encourage response, or gesturing with both hands to encourage everyone to think and offer an opinion. Looking at the students instead of talking can invite their participation. This kind of expert teacher behavior is hard to describe, but if you observe teachers and students in a rich discussion, no matter what age the students are, you will notice it.

Moving from Talk to Writing

Writing is thinking. Developing the ability to write about reading is an important outcome of literacy instruction. We want students to be able to express their thinking in writing not only to achieve on tests but also to gain general skills for expressing their thinking in written words. As most writers know, talking is a catalyst for writing. When you have had opportunities (sometimes over many days) to express your thinking by talking aloud to your friends, it makes writing easier. It is a kind of "rehearsal." Talking about reading will fuel excellent suggestions from participants in shared and interactive writing and will also give students the language they need to write in their reader's notebooks. A talk-filled classroom that is grounded in reading and writing will give students powerful learning opportunities. Often we need to increase student talk and lessen our teacher talk. The person talking is the one doing the thinking.

A Multitext Approach with Dynamic Talk

In this chapter we have explored a multitext approach to developing literacy learning. Guided reading is an integral part of such an approach. Across interactive read-aloud, shared reading, guided reading, independent reading, and book clubs, students experience varying levels of support and, ultimately, work toward independence in processing. At the same time, opportunities in interactive writing, guided writing, shared writing, and independent writing help them work toward independence as writers. The key concept is comprehending in each context and using talk to articulate understandings. What's important to remember here is that reading and writing are language processes and that the meaning is carried by language. Building on John Dewey's statement, "All learning floats on a sea of talk," James Britton had this to say: "People who know everything are silent; people who know nothing are silent. In between, there is talk. Literacy floats on a sea of talk," (Britton 1970). By participating actively in conversation surrounding texts, students engage in a meaning-driven use of language that supports comprehension and their ability to write about their reading. Reading is thinking, prompted by written words. Talk is thinking expressed, and so is writing. Your students will be thinkers when you value their thinking and connect them with the thinking of other writers throughout the day.

Suggestions for Professional Development

Work with a group of grade-level colleagues to share the work you have been doing on your schedule. This time, analyze the levels of support (from high to low) that you can provide within your current schedule.

1. First, work with the schedule toward a multitext approach with various levels of supports.

   ▶ Analyze the schedule using a grid something like the one in the facsimile shown in Figure 2-18 (a blank version is also available in Online Resources). For each level of support, write the reading and writing activities you currently use.

   ▶ Have a discussion of what you are missing and/or any imbalance you see.

   ▶ Look again at your schedule and make adjustments so that you are providing five levels of support for reading and four for writing. (If the task is too hard, you can work just on reading and address writing another time.)

2. Work with *The Fountas & Pinnell Literacy Continuum.*

   ▶ Select two or three important goals for guided reading at a level appropriate for your grade (or, a level where you know you will have a group reading).

   ▶ Find the same or a similar principle in the Interactive Read-Aloud continuum. Notice the first time it appears.

   ▶ Talk about why interactive read-aloud can take the lead on introducing understandings or principles.

3. Have an open discussion about how important goals can be accomplished across levels of support, with using high support to introduce a goal and then addressing it again with gradual release.

	Levels of Support	Reading	Writing	Other
High Support ↑	4			
	3			
	2			
↓ **Low Support**	1			

FIGURE 2-18 Analyzing Levels of Support

CHAPTER 3

From Shared to Guided Reading in the Early Years

Personal satisfaction from and the enjoyment of the story, as well as the conviction that reading is worthwhile and that it is for them personally, should be the long term effect of any shared book experience.

–Margaret Mooney

Three-year-old Jackson sits on his father's lap to share the reading of a favorite storybook, *Where's Spot?* by Eric Hill. In this popular book, a mother dog looks for her puppy, Spot. She asks a question on every page: "Is he behind the door? Is he inside the clock? Is he in the piano? "And so on. Each time, a whimsical animal saying, "no," is revealed by lifting a flap. This is a book in which a young child can truly participate.

Of course, Jackson is not really reading the print; his father, John, is doing that. Nevertheless, Jackson is a full participant, and his behavior indicates that some early literacy understandings are already emerging. This reading is about the fifth time for this book. We observe that Jackson:

▶ Expresses pleasure by saying, "Where's Spot?" when looking at his pile of books; in fact, he chose the book for this reading.

▶ Anticipates turning the pages and insists on grasping and turning the page himself and then looking automatically at the left page.

▶ Points to the pictures.

▶ Avoids covering the print with his hands.

▶ Chants along with John's reading (remembering the language).

▶ Shouts the word "no" after lifting each flap.

▶ Knows that when there are three birds in the piano, the reader says, "no," "no," "no."

▶ Knows when the problem is resolved and Spot is found (triggering different language, for example, "There's Spot").

▶ Joins in on the last page, "Good boy, Spot!

We can infer from the observations that Jackson is beginning to understand that:

▶ Reading is related to stories that are fun.

▶ When you read, you always say the same words and sentences in the same order.

▶ When you read a question, you often can expect to read an answer next.

▶ You have to see the print to read.

▶ The print is different from the pictures.

▶ You look at the left page first and then the right page.

▶ When there is one character, it says "no" once; and you can point to the character while saying "no."

▶ When there are three characters, each of them can say something ("no").

▶ You turn pages by taking the right page and turning it over the left page.

▶ You move through the book front to back.

▶ A book has a "name" (title) that has something to do with the story.

▶ There is power in the act of reading.

▶ Reading is full of pleasure.

Chances are, Jackson will not be able to remember a time when he did not consider himself to be a reader. He cannot yet recognize words and he doesn't know the letter names (although he can find his "J" on the refrigerator that shows a variety of colorful magnet letters); but he is able to fully participate as a literacy learner.

The conditions for developing early literacy behaviors are: "immersion, demonstration, expectation, responsibility, approximation, use and response," (Cambourne 1988). When the seven conditions of learning are present, the student can learn best.

1. Immersion—Readers need to be immersed in meaningful, relevant experiences with texts.

2. Demonstration—Readers need demonstrations of the reading process. The adult reads the texts inviting responses from the learners.

3. Expectation—Readers need to engage with texts with a high expectation that they can engage successfully in the process.

4. Responsibility—Readers need to be in control of the process.

5. Approximation—Readers need to feel they can take risks. Partially correct responses are valued.

6. Use—Readers need the time and opportunity to engage in the authentic literary task every day.

7. Response—Readers need continuous feedback in the form of gaining meaning from text.

Jackson is experiencing all of these conditions just about every time he participates in a "lap story." His father is not a teacher. John's objective is to have a pleasurable shared experience with his son (and perhaps to get him to go to sleep), but Jackson is soaking up all kinds of information about literacy. The opportunities of the lap book experience can be replicated in the early childhood classroom. Through shared reading, children can immediately assume the stance of a reader with the same conditions.

Holdaway (1979), the father of the "shared book experience," defined it simply as an approach where the teacher and a group of children read a text together, similar to the parent/child lap book or storybook experience. This seemingly simple act has enormous possibilities because it offers the same intimate job of the read-aloud but makes the text available to all students. It rests on the principle that what a child can do in cooperation today he can do alone tomorrow (Vygotsky 1978). For the young child, shared reading provides an easy entry into enjoying books and behaving like a reader. All the children can see and appreciate the print and illustrations. They are actively engaged with the language and the meaning of the text. As they read and then reread the text, the print features become more available. After several readings, they can read the enlarged print just like the adult model—smoothly and fluently.

Shared reading is especially powerful as a tool for including English language learners in the literacy community of the classroom. They can join in, producing the English they know, and they are supported by the teacher and the group. They can approximate English reading in a safe environment. Repeated readings are especially effective in helping them practice and internalize English syntax.

As children gain control of early reading behaviors, they can process several lines of print with your support. Your scaffolding makes available more challenging texts than students are able to read for themselves. The shared reading context enables you to engage the readers in using all systems of strategic actions so they can experience and build a processing system. Is this "real" reading? Not in the sense that children are independently solving all the words. But in every other sense they are behaving as readers.

Building a Strong Early Reading Process

In the early years of school, it is critical for children to establish a strong foundation on which they can build ongoing literacy learning. Reading and writing needs to make sense for them, and you want them to see themselves as readers and writers from the beginning. Young children need to:

▶ Actively engage in the reading process to develop a sense of agency.

▶ Learn to read by reading continuous text so that they understand that written language makes sense and sounds like language.

▶ Learn how to construct the meaning of the text through attending to the language and print.

▶ Use their own knowledge of language to process the text, which is a self-extending system (expands as it is used).

▶ Learn how to look at print and its features.

▶ Learn the relationship between reading and writing.

▶ Experience massive amounts of text to build knowledge of the syntax and vocabulary of written language.

Shared reading is especially powerful in this process because your level of support leads their learning forward.

Early Understandings

It is common to assume that early learning consists almost entirely of phonics understandings; in fact, young children develop knowledge along many important dimensions that *include* developing knowledge of the alphabetic system but encompass much more. In *The Fountas & Pinnell Literacy Continuum,* early behaviors and understandings to notice, teach for, and support appear in every section. Reading and writing are highly complex processes, even for beginning readers. Young children learn about how stories and information books work, how written language works, and how print works. You can find an extensive list of understandings in *The Literacy Continuum;* here we select some areas that are especially important.

Print Awareness: Letters, Sounds, Words, and How Print Works

Young children are developing an awareness of the alphabetic system, how symbols or signs represent sound, and how the symbols or signs are ordered to communicate language.

Letters

Emergent readers become aware that print is something special; it represents language. At first, children may scribble or make letter-like forms, and this shows that an awareness of print is beginning to emerge. Over time, as they notice the distinctive features of letters, their attempts become more letter-like.

The example in Figure 3-1 shows Brianna's early writing. Notice how she creates strings of letters, mostly from her name. She also knows that these marks on a page are a way to communicate and a way to represent her thinking. Young children often combine drawing and writing.

FIGURE 3-1 Brianna's Early Attempts at Writing

Before a child can learn the name of a letter and the associated sound, she must be able to notice the *distinctive features*—what makes this letter different from every other letter in the alphabet. This means the child needs to learn how to look at print. These differences are easy for us as adults to see; but they are actually quite small. Consider the differences between the four lowercase letters in Figure 3-2.

Lowercase *h* has a taller stick than *n* and *m*. Lowercase *u* is like *n* except that it is upside down. Direction or orientation makes a difference! Lowercase *m* has one more hump than *n*. At first glance, to the young child, these letters may not be appreciably different. After all, through his young life a child has learned to categorize his world. Dogs come in all sizes and colors. Some have short tails, some have long tails, some have no tails; and, if they roll over, they are still dogs. But in print, very small differences make a difference, and that's a good thing because it makes writing fast and efficient—with minimum effort. Through many experiences, children learn to manipulate and distinguish letters. For example, they can play with and sort magnetic letters; they can make their names and other words. They write their own names and names of family members; powerful words like "love" are learned as part of communication. But the real test of letter learning is whether children can use recognition of letters to monitor and solve problems while reading continuous text.

Sounds

From birth, children build implicit awareness of the phonological system of the language. It is fascinating that the process is the same for any language. They learn what talking sounds like and they approximate talking as they make noises like babbling. Researchers and parents have noted that young children are often observed to make series of sounds in their cribs right before sleep as if they are "trying out" sounds in combination (Weir 1962). Soon, a few words like *Mom* and *Dad* emerge, and the vocabulary grows from there. Words are put together in rule-governed ways even though the utterances are only two or three words. Gradually, the speaking vocabulary grows, and they learn to put together words in a grammar that makes sense to those around them. They learn that language has power.

Children delight in the sounds of language, and that is evident as they respond to and join in with nursery rhymes and nonsense. The acquisition of phonology is for the most part unconscious, with the child's focus on the meaning of the language. But at some point, the learner must become consciously aware of the individual sounds of language. This important ability is called *phonological awareness* or *phoneme awareness* when it refers to individual sounds. A large body of research points to phonological awareness as an important element in predicting success in reading (NICHD 2000). When children say words slowly, they can start to

FIGURE 3-2 Letter Differentiation in Four Lowercase Letters

FIGURE 3-3 Colin's Picture Name Writing

identify individual sounds within words, beginning at first with the dominant sounds they hear. This happens easily in writing; they learn to say the words and identify the first sound, the ending sound, and the sounds in sequence.

Early writing reveals children's developing understandings of letter-sound relationships. Colin was engaged in a very simple assessment task—writing picture names—at the beginning and midyear of kindergarten. Notice how he represented sounds with one or two letters at the beginning of the year, in the picture on top, but had much fuller word frames just a few months later (see Figure 3-3).

Words

Children do have an underlying concept of "wordness" because they put individual words together in different ways when they talk. But they do not necessarily know that oral language is composed of separate word units, and we cannot assume that they do. (Clay 1991). For example, a child may understand "gimme/the" as a unit. But as they encounter words in print, they need to learn that in reading, a word is defined by space on either side of a cluster of letters, ranging from one to many letters. A space indicates the end of a word and the start of a new word in print. We could see how Colin began to frame a word by putting together the sounds in writing. In reading, children need to be able to recognize words within continuous print, and shared reading is a key activity in helping them begin to build a reservoir of known words. Of course, children have several ways to solve words. They can recognize them from knowledge of their visual features; known words are a great resource for the beginning reader because "once the child has *read the new word aloud two or three times, it's phonological identity is available to him for closer analysis,*" (Clay 1991). They can also solve words by using the letters and sounds. Both of these ways of knowing allow the new reader to monitor the accuracy of his one-to-one correspondence in his reading (one spoken word matches one printed word) and to self-correct.

Ultimately, the reader must learn to use word-solving strategies in a smooth, automatic way while reading continuous text. Some approaches to teaching reading assume that children must learn all of the letters and sounds, how to "sound out" words, and have some sight words before they can actually read story books. Shared reading (and early guided reading lessons) offer a way for children to use everything they know immediately as they process continuous texts. They are learning how it feels to be a reader.

How Print Works

A strong early reading process includes a clear understanding of how written language "works," for example, a reader:

- Reads the print not the pictures (although the pictures offer extra information).
- Starts with the cover of the book and turn pages by taking the right page and turn it to the left.
- Reads the left page before the right page.
- Reads from top to bottom of the page.
- Begins on the left margin to read a line and returns to the left margin to read the next line.
- Looks at black marks and spaces to help notice the words.
- Reads from the top of the page to the bottom of the page.
- Reads left to right across print and sweeps back to left margin to read next line.
- Reads one word aloud for each cluster of letters.
- Knows that words are separated by spaces.
- Knows the difference between a letter and a word.
- Recognizes punctuation (as different from letters) and its functions.
- Knows that the letters in a word are always the same and in the same order, from left to right.

All of the above concepts are developed by processing continuous text. They represent the important idea that there are motor and directional elements in reading that are completely arbitrary. In English, you begin reading on the left, move left to right across the line, and return to the left again. That's just the way people invented writing in English and many other languages. In some languages, you read right to left and bottom to top. A first grader who is confused by any of the concepts listed above may be at risk of reading difficulty.

Language Awareness: Talking Like a Book

If you are a parent, you may have been startled to see your three-year-old pick up a familiar and beloved book like *Brown Bear, Brown Bear, What Do You See?* (Carle 1996) and appear to be reading it. The tone of voice, the cadence, and the vocabulary sound like someone reading aloud. The sentences are precise. Chances are, your three-year-old is "talking like a book," indicating his awareness of the syntax of written language, the vocabulary, and how it sounds when read aloud (Clay 1991). Written language is different in subtle ways from spoken language. For example, dialogue is signaled by words like, "he said." Young children who have great familiarity with hearing books read aloud will often exhibit this behavior. In fact, they are mostly inventing or reenacting the text, relying on memory and cued by the pictures. But it is amazing how they often get closer and closer to the actual text as they continue to work with it, and, pretty soon, they develop awareness of visual signposts.

Some children believe they *are* reading, but many understand that there are a few differences in their "reading" and their parents' reading, so they listen very closely and often join in during the bedtime story. Clay (1991) believes that talking like a book is an important step in learning to read because it signals that the child is aware that print can be read as speech and that it has a message. The picture is a guide to the message, and the same language occurs every time you read a book. The more a child reenacts reading, the more he learns about the act of reading and the closer he comes to recognizing some words.

Shared reading offers an opportunity for children to acquire the ability to talk like a book. They read engaging texts over and over, and after a time, they have almost memorized some of the sentences, so that they can reenact the book with high accuracy. It is important that these shared reading books have engaging language that children love to repeat. Because they are pointing to each word and moving left to right, they have maximum opportunity to use book language and attend to visual features of print.

Story Awareness: Language Structure, Meaning, and Organization

As they engage in shared reading, children have the opportunity to become more aware of the structure of a story, as well as nonfiction text characteristics. A story has a beginning, a problem, a series of events, and an ending. When children become familiar with storybooks through read-aloud, and when they participate again and again through shared reading, they become familiar with, and come to expect story elements. They know that characters and the problem in the story will be introduced in the beginning and that action will follow. They know that as they come closer to the end of the book, something will happen to bring the problem to a resolution. In nonfiction texts, they know they will learn some true information and in any one book, the information will be about the same (or explicitly related) topics. This early awareness supports their construction of meaning and their ability to predict language.

Successful Early Experiences

From the beginning, every child is successful in shared reading—that's the way it is designed. They are doing it together, helping each other, creating the demonstration of proficiency as a team, and having fun. This may sound a little "soft," rather than the rigorous approach to instruction that we advocate, but we assure you that success in reading has everything to do with emotion, confidence, and self-efficacy. These children are engaged in what they see as reading, and that is powerful.

We know that shared reading will not take them all the way. Eventually, each must be able to process a text individually and independently. But just imagine a preschooler's daily participation in shared reading, and the same in kindergarten. By the time these students enter a guided reading group, they will have experienced just about every aspect of beginning reading at the early levels. Our goal is to use shared reading to lead guided reading.

Finally, shared reading is a way to include English language learners in successful reading. They can find themselves reading English sentences with appropriate syntax, just like their native-English-speaking peers, and because it is so familiar, they know what it means.

Shared Reading

Shared reading provides the opportunity for your students to build an early reading process and have a strong foundation of letters, sounds, and words, as well as enjoyment in the meaning and language of books.

There are many values of shared reading for early readers that engage them in the reading process beyond their independent control (see Figure 3-4).

Shared reading is characterized by the following:

- All students have a clear view of the print and pictures.
- It is a warm, accepting, enjoyable social experience.
- You and your students share in the reading of a text.
- Students take on the behaviors of readers and learn new concepts about how texts work.
- Students have the opportunity to experience more sophisticated language and content than they can read on their own.
- You model and demonstrate effective reading behaviors.
- The text is usually read many times.
- You take the opportunity to discuss the meaning of the text with the readers.
- You can work in a highly intentional way to teach specific aspects of the reading process.
- You can revisit the text to help students notice letters, sounds, words, language structures, or other aspects of the writer's or illustrator's craft.

Value of Shared Reading for Early Readers

- Builds enjoyment in reading.
- Provides clear demonstration of the reading process.
- Engages readers in the reading process before they can read independently.
- Builds phonemic awareness (individual sounds, syllables, onsets and rimes, words and parts).
- Builds letter knowledge.
- Develops understanding of letter/sound relationships.

- Develops understanding of concepts of print.
- Builds word-recognition and word-analysis skills by providing the opportunity to teach a range of word-solving strategies.
- Provides social support within a heterogeneous group of readers.
- Builds language skills and enhances vocabulary.
- Builds knowledge of high-frequency words.
- Raises awareness of how reading should sound.

- Helps students understand that reading should be expressive and meaningful.
- Builds students' understanding of different types of texts, formats, and language structures.
- Encourages personal and critical response to texts.
- Develops systems of strategic actions for thinking beyond and about a text.
- Gives every child the experience of success.

FIGURE 3-4 Value of Shared Reading for Early Readers

Selecting Texts for Shared Reading

The first consideration is that the text for shared reading should be worth reading and rereading. That means the content, the story (if fiction), and the language must engage and delight the readers. In selecting texts, consider the readers' ages, previous experience, and level of expertise in processing texts. Choose many books with interesting words, refrains, and language play. What may seem too difficult for beginning readers becomes available because of teacher support, and because the texts are so engaging. Consider stories, poems, chants, and songs as well as fascinating informational books.

1. *Texts that provide early experiences with print.* Children in preschool and kindergarten generally need a simple text with bold, colorful illustrations and engaging content. To get started, use a text like *In My Bag* (*Fountas & Pinnell Classroom* in press), with only one line of print with clear spaces between words (see Figure 3-5). Print and illustrations should be clearly separated (see the Shared Reading section of *The Literacy Continuum*). A more sophisticated example of an early text, *Baxter's Red Ball* (*Fountas & Pinnell Classroom* in press), is shown in Figure 3-6. In this book, the story is slightly more complex. The verbs are more vivid. We see print against a white background, but the illustrations cross the page

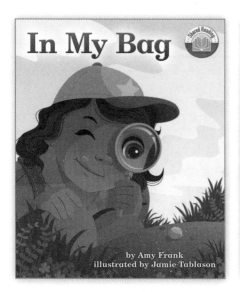 

FIGURE 3-5 *In My Bag,* Cover and Pages 4–5

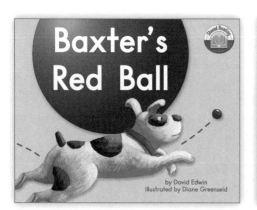 

FIGURE 3-6 *Baxter's Red Ball,* Cover and Pages 8–9

spreads and there are sound words from animals in speech bubbles. The story is carried by the pictures: Baxter runs after his red ball, continually avoiding obstacles. Figure 3-7, *Morning on the Farm* (*Fountas & Pinnell Classroom*, in press), is, again, a little more complex.

In fiction, select simple stories and nonfiction topics that are close to students' own experiences. The language should have some repetition with simple structures. You can also use simple four- or five-line poems for shared reading with young children. After a couple of readings, the rhyme and rhythm carry the readers along as in *Run, Jump, Swim*, (*Fountas & Pinnell Classroom*, in press), shown in Figure 3-8. It is easy to read when supported by the group and the teacher's pointer.

2. *Texts that lead the development of an early reading process.* Select enlarged texts that are just beyond those that most children can process in guided reading.

FIGURE 3-7 *Morning on the Farm*, Pages 12–15

FIGURE 3-8 *Run, Jump, Swim*, Pages 20–21

Students can read more lines of print and more complex stories or informational books with more text. These books should still have some repetition or longer repeating patterns, and language that engages students, as in *Chicken Licken* (*Fountas & Pinnell Classroom* in press) in Figure 3-9.

These students will also enjoy shared reading of poetry and songs to fully engage with the pleasurable sounds of language. Texts may have six or more lines of print and more complex patterns (see the Shared Reading section of *The Literacy Continuum*).

Students will enjoy reading poems in parts, and you can also involve them in reading an enlarged text as in readers' theater so that they read the specific dialogue in parts.

FIGURE 3-9 *Chicken Licken*, Pages 6–7

FIGURE 3-10 *Orange Butterfly*, Pages 8–9

3. *Texts that promote the construction of meaning and the development of language.* All high-quality texts support students' attention to the construction of meaning and the talk that surrounds it. Shared reading promotes opportunities for meaningful talk and the development of language structures.

Wordless picture books have enormous potential for productive work in shared reading. Using wordless big books like *Orange Butterfly* (*Fountas & Pinnell Classroom* in press) shown in Figure 3-10, children can engage in meaning making even without print. They can follow a story, search for information in the pictures, make and check predictions, make inferences—all of the searching processes that they will ultimately use on print. They can "read" and "reread" these wordless texts using rich language that is stimulated by the illustrations The illustrated text supports rich language use and development.

A wordless book can be a storybook or an informational text. There are many opportunities to apply strategic actions in advance of using them on texts with print. Lysaker and Hopper (2015) have identified (1) searching across images and readers' own experiences and knowledge; (2) cross-checking information with the narrative that is being constructed in oral language; (3) self-correcting to make the images and narrative fit; and (4) rereading or repeating to confirm or test hypotheses. The researchers suggest that "early print strategies identified by Clay—including monitoring, searching and cross-checking, rereading, and self-correcting—are emerging in the early nonprint experiences of wordless book reading" (Lysaker and Hopper 2015, 656).

Wordless books may be used with the whole class and in small-group settings. Students can take turns telling the story to each other. Sometimes, you may want to use shared writing to record their narratives on one or two pages. This small-group work is also excellent for English language learners.

Tools and Materials for Shared Reading

Have a meeting place in your classroom that accommodates all of the students in a way that enables them to see, hear, and participate. You will also need to consider how to make the books and charts available to students. Many teachers hang big books and charts on hangers with clips and put them on a stand. Alternatively, you can use a large shelf. Also, you will need to store materials so that you can reach for them quickly without delaying the lesson. We list basic materials for shared reading in Figure 3-11.

The easel should be very sturdy and large enough to hold big books or charts. It is helpful if it is wide enough to accommodate the page spread so that the big books do not flop

Basic Materials for Shared Reading

Texts:

- Large print/illustrated books—stories, songs, poems, chants, informational texts
- Large print poems, songs on charts—may be published or handmade with student illustrations
- Large wordless books
- Projected texts
- Shared/interactive writing texts
- Individual small copies of large text (if available)

Tools:

- Easel
- Plain pointer
- Wikki Stix
- Word cards
- Highlighter tape
- Magnetic letters
- Whiteboard
- Pocket chart
- Sliding masks or masks of various sizes
- Markers
- Correction tape and sticky notes
- Computer and screen to project an image

FIGURE 3-11 Basic Materials for Shared Reading

around. Ideally, to be most versatile, it should have a surface that magnetic letters will stick to. Another desirable feature is a whiteboard that is built into the easel so that you can write directly on it with erasable markers.

Be sure to use a plain pointer (a dowel rod with the tip painted red is ideal). Avoid thick pointers that have large objects on the end (like a ball, star, or hand). You need a pointer because if you extend your arm across the print and point with your finger or a short marker, the print will be obscured for some of the children. The major goal is to draw children's eyes to the print or feature you are looking at.

Wikki Stix® are sticky plastic straws that you can form into letters and/or use to underline or circle words or letters. They adhere to the paper and draw attention to the letter, word, or feature underlined or circled. They are easily removed and can be reused.

Highlighter tape comes in many different colors and widths. You can use it to help readers identify elements of the text. You can highlight a sentence, phrase, word, word part, or punctuation. Highlighter pens may occasionally be used, especially on pieces of shared writing that you do not plan to use with other groups. But highlighter tape performs the same function and peels off easily without damaging the document so that you can use it for different purposes and with different groups.

Word cards should be large enough for the group to see and read. An innovation is a magnetic word card, which you make by writing on magnetic tape that will stick to the easel (like refrigerator magnets).

Have a whiteboard that you can write on so that students can see. In addition, you will want a smaller hand-held whiteboard to write individual letters and words. The whiteboard can be used to do quick problem solving, show how words are divided into syllables, or give students a model so that it is easier for them to look for print features.

A pocket chart is very helpful for inserting word cards and sentence strips that then appear in a vertical space for readers. After a demonstration, students can work independently or with a partner to put together sentences in order or construct poems from the lines printed on sentence strips.

Sliding masks or masks of various sizes are useful for bringing sharp attention to words within continuous text (see Figure 3-12). The mask places a frame around a word so that you can quickly isolate it and then have students read it again within continuous text.

The mask or Wikki Stix®, like highlighter tape, has many uses and some of these are listed in Figure 3-13. You need masks in a variety of sizes to focus attention on a letter, a letter cluster, a word part, or a word.

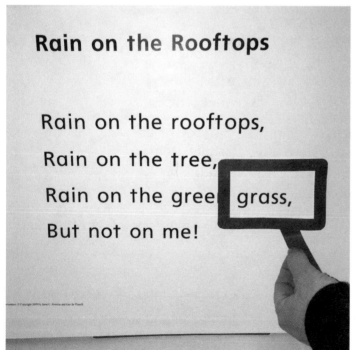

Rain on the Rooftops

Rain on the rooftops,
Rain on the tree,
Rain on the gree[n] grass,
But not on me!

FIGURE 3-12 Using a Mask

The Components of a Shared Reading
Lesson for Early Readers

The basic components of a shared reading lesson are shown in Figure 3-14. "The style of teaching in shared reading might be called invitational . . . an enthusiastic invitation to participate, contribute, take over the operation," (Holdaway 1979). From the first presentation of the text, shared reading should be joyful. *Nothing is hard. Everyone can do it. We can do it together.* You begin by a brief discussion that introduces the text and engages the children's interest. Then, you read the text to them. You might tell the children to listen carefully because next, "we'll read it together." This situation is very similar to a read-aloud. You may pause very briefly as you turn the page or at appropriate places to invite children's quick comment or to point out something in the illustrations. The goal is for students to understand the meaning of the whole text.

After reading the text, invite the students to read it with you. You will find that they mimic your intonation and phrasing. Keep up the momentum rather than slowing down to a drone. After reading, invite students to discuss the text, expressing their thinking and responding to the meaning. They may identify language they find funny or entertaining. Then, do some specific teaching that may address any aspect of reading: using information from pictures, locating words, noticing letters and letter clusters, identifying word patterns, noticing phrases, noticing punctuation, noticing repetition of words or language (see *The Literacy Continuum* for potential teaching). Don't try to teach too many things within one reading; be selective. Remember that you can revisit and reread the text many more times as long as children respond to and enjoy it.

Like the lap stories and bedtime stories, these texts are read over and over. In repeated rereadings, children play an increasingly active role. Repeated rereadings may focus on:

- Attention to concepts of print.
- Extending understanding of the meaning of the text.
- Building vocabulary and language understanding.
- Expanding understandings of concepts.
- Building quick recognition of words (locating words fast; finding words they know).
- Modeling word-solving actions.
- Noticing patterns or parts in words.

Use the Mask or Highlighter Tape to Draw Attention to:

- The letter____.
- A letter you know.
- The word _____.
- A word you know.
- A letter in your name.
- The letter your first (last) name starts with.
- The lowercase/uppercase letter _____.
- A word that rhymes with _____.
- A word that begins with the two letters (cluster) _____.
- A word that ends with the two letters (clusters)_____.
- A word that means the same as _____.
- A word the means the opposite of _____.
- A compound word.
- A word ending with _____ (ed, ly, ing).

FIGURE 3-13 Uses of Masks or Highlighter Tape

Basic Components of a Shared Reading Lesson for Early Readers

Teaching Action	Description	Teaching Possibilities
Introduce the Text	Say a few words about the text and invite conversation that is directed toward reading it.	◆ Point out author and illustrator. ◆ Discuss the cover, title, and illustrations. ◆ Build interest and curiosity. ◆ Invite thinking about the topic or story. ◆ Identify the genre. ◆ Allow active participation in predicting and responding.
Model Reading of the Text (First Reading)	Read the text **to** the students and have a brief discussion.	◆ Engage the readers in enjoying and thinking through the meaning of the text as you read it aloud. ◆ Pose questions or make brief comments as you turn a page to stimulate thinking. ◆ If appropriate, pause and invite predictions one or two times. ◆ Encourage brief attention to craft elements (e.g., punctuation, word choice, illustrations). ◆ Guide conversation about the meaning of the text and invite students to share their thinking after the reading.
Read the Text Together (Second Reading)	Have students read the whole text or selected parts **with** you.	◆ Encourage children to join in, especially on refrains, and to interpret the text with their voices. ◆ Give brief attention to craft elements (e.g., punctuation, word choice, illustrations).
Discuss the Text	Guide conversation about the meaning of the text and invite students to share their thinking.	◆ Engage readers in discussion of the whole text. ◆ Encourage children to share their thinking.
Teach for Specific Strategic Actions	Select a specific part of the text to revisit to make a teaching point. This can be accomplished over a number of subsequent readings.	◆ Select aspects of the text to draw students' attention to (letters, words, language structure, meaning). ◆ Have students locate words by predicting the first letter or another word feature. ◆ Make connections between words. ◆ Teach students how to use language structure by uncovering the next word or phrase in a sentence. ◆ Teach students how to check on their reading using meaning, structure, or visual/phonological information. ◆ Have students recognize and locate known words.
Repeated Readings	Revisit the text **with** students to read it again on subsequent days, making teaching points and supporting students in gaining independence.	◆ Continue to revisit the text, working on selected teaching points: known words, high-frequency words, word endings, punctuation, capitalization, rhyming words, repetitive language, letters and letter clusters, interesting words or language, dialogue, graphic features. ◆ When students can read the text without support, make it available for independent reading (either small copies or the enlarged text).

FIGURE 3-14 Basic Components of a Shared Reading Lesson for Early Readers

Basic Components of a Shared Reading Lesson for Early Readers

Teaching Action	Description	Teaching Possibilities
Independent Reading	Give students the opportunity to read the text independently or with a partner using the big book or small book version.	◆ Students can do the following: ◆ Listen to the text at the listening center, following along in the small book version. ◆ Reread the big book with a partner using a chopstick pointer. ◆ Use the small book version and read it in unison with a group. ◆ Read the book to a partner, taking turns reading pages or the whole book. ◆ Borrow the book to take home and/or keep one copy in the classroom browsing box.
Extended Language and Literacy Opportunities	Engage students in further exploration of the text if there is interest and need.	◆ Invite students to create a construction of or innovation on a text through shared or interactive writing. ◆ Invite students to create their own individual books like the shared reading book. ◆ Create a wall mural with pictures or cutouts made by children and sentences from the book as labels. ◆ Have a cut-up version of the poem or sentences from the book for students to put together in the pocket chart.

FIGURE 3-14 *(continued)*

❱ Locating and discussing punctuation.

❱ Noticing letters.

❱ Linking sounds to words.

❱ Finding expressions or language patterns.

❱ Noticing the writer's or illustrator's craft.

When the text has been read enough times that students are able to act independently with it, you can move it into independent work. Often small versions of big books are available. In this case, children can reread these texts independently. You can duplicate copies of poems children have experienced many times in shared reading and they can put them in their poetry notebooks. Children can explore the text independently or with a partner. They can listen to a recording by the teacher and use a chopstick to point along on a large or small version of the text. You can use shared or interactive writing to create an innovated version of the text. For example:

> I love chocolate,
> Yummy, yummy, yummy.
> I love chocolate,
> In my tummy.

This is an example of a text that is very easy to use for innovation. You don't have to rewrite the text; you can simply cover the word *chocolate* with a sticky note and write whatever food children suggest. You can substitute a child's name for "I" (and add "s" to "love"). Innovated texts provide many opportunities for more reading.

The shared reading text can also be used as a base for shared or interactive writing. Children can compose new texts for reading and rereading such as a book review or character summary. They can compose another version using the same pattern or text structure. They can use art to respond to the text, creating a labeled mural or a representation of the characters or puppets. They can enact the text with puppets or a play. They can engage in drama, pretending to be the characters. A well-constructed and well-selected, and now well-known, text has endless possibilities.

From Shared to Guided Reading

Whether you are working with early or intermediate readers, the behaviors and understandings attended to in shared reading can be revisited in guided reading so that students can apply them to independent processing of novel texts. If kindergarten children are accustomed to reading two, three, or four lines of text in unison with others and have also taken on the little books that have the same text, then, with a supportive introduction, they are very likely to be able to read one-line texts (level A) for themselves in a guided reading lesson.

Involve the whole class in the shared reading of large print books, songs, or poems that are more challenging than the texts that students can read in guided reading. Don't make the mistake of thinking that just because students can "read" the text in unison with others that they can independently process the print with accuracy. They still need to attend individually to the print. However, by participating in shared reading, they are building the language and conceptual knowledge they need, along with specific, supported attention to print. They have a reservoir of experience to bring to their own independent reading. In this way, shared reading can lead guided and independent reading forward.

A Shared Reading Lesson

In this section, we illustrate the basic components of a shared reading lesson with an example. Notice how the activity and goals change as the students revisit a text.

Selecting the Text

The fiction text, *The Wheels on the Bike* (*Fountas & Pinnell Classroom*, in press), is adapted from a song, "The Wheels on the Bus." This animal fantasy features a wonderful assortment of animals that ride the same bike "all through the town" as a cow and sheep pedal along.

While the text generally follows the pattern of the familiar song, a story frame is implied by the addition of a few new passengers and by the changing scenery. At the end of the story, these talented animals reach their destination and perform in a circus (see Figure 3-15).

Rhythm and repetition carry this story so that children can read quite a few lines of text. In addition, notice that a small picture is in an inset right under the

FIGURE 3-15 *The Wheels on the Bike,* Pages 2–3, 14–15, Last Page

text. The picture gives a clue as to the meaning of the text, and students soon learn key words that change as the text continues. This book lends itself to lively expression; students will find it easy to use phrasing to emphasize the repetition of phrases like "round and round." The next to last page ends with ellipses so that readers are prompted to suspend the voice in preparation for the surprise ending.

Introducing the Text

The shared reading text does not need a lengthy introduction. After all, you are going to read the entire book to the students! The goal is to engage the students with the text. But you do want to make brief opening moves that:

- Engage interest and curiosity.
- Get readers thinking about the author's and illustrator's meaning.
- Get readers thinking about the genre.
- Help students access relevant background knowledge.
- Foreshadow the "big ideas" that are in the text.

On the following page is an excerpt from the introduction to *The Wheels on the Bike* (Figure 3-16).

Introduction to *The Wheels on the Bike*

Speaker	Teacher/Student Interactions	Analysis of Interactions
Mr. S	We are going to read a big book together today. The title is *The Wheels on the Bike.* Since this story couldn't really happen, what do you call it?	States the title and invites student response about genre Calls attention to the illustrations
Rob	Fiction—It's a fiction book.	Identify the genre
Dion	There's a cow and a goose, and a sheep.	Notice the characters and actions
Sela	The cow is doing the pedaling . . . and the sheep too.	
Mr. S	Looks like a bicycle built for two. There are two sets of pedals so that the cow can pedal and so can the sheep. But there are more than two animals on the bike. What else do you notice?	Mentions a key word and calls attention the meaning Asks for observation of details
Ruth	It looks like there are some chickens. And they all have on helmets.	Notice information in illustrations
Dion	Is it like "The Wheels on the Bus"? The wheels on the bus go round and round.	Links to another text
Mr. S	You noticed that. It is like the song, "The Wheels on the Bus," but you will notice some differences. On the back it says, "Here's a new take on a favorite song." A "new take" means that a writer, like Anne Stribling, who wrote this book, starts with something you probably know but changes it a little. Think about that as you listen to me read it the first time. Then, we'll read it together.	Confirms connection to another text Tells students what will happen next

FIGURE 3-16 Introduction to *The Wheels on the Bike*

First Reading

The first time through the text, you will read it to the students. It's a good idea to remind them that you will be reading the whole book; often, but not always, they will be looking for something you mentioned in the introduction. Students who are experienced in shared reading may try to join in once they get the gist or repeated language of the story, and this is fine, but you should not expect them to be able to do so in the first reading. Mumbling along can interfere with understanding. If they are so eager to join in that it seems to interfere with listening and understanding, say, "Just listen the first time because I want to know what you think of the story. Then we'll read it together."

The goals are to ensure that students enjoy the story and think about the meaning, that they discover supports such as rhyme, rhythm, and repetition, and that they understand how the story "works." (See the Shared Reading section of *The Literacy Continuum.* Keep in mind that the goals for shared reading will be different each time you read the book). For example, every page of *The Wheels on the Bike* starts with attention to an animal or an object. They next three lines convey what the animal says or the object does. (The cow says, "Move on back." The pedals go "up and down.") The next two lines repeat the first two lines, and the last line ends with "all through the town." That's a fairly complex pattern for a five-year-old to remember and use. The pattern changes when they approach the circus, which is signaled by a red-and-white striped tent and shown on the last page. The voices and noises are repeated in speech balloons on some pages, providing an additional opportunity to notice a feature that appears in graphic texts.

You will generally read the text without interruption, focusing on enjoyment of language and construction of meaning, including illustrations. But you may occasionally pause very briefly to invite predictions or call attention to something important. You might make comments or pose a question as you turn a page. It is important to keep the momentum of the reading and also help students construct an understanding without bogging down. Figure 3-17 shows an excerpt from the first reading of *The Wheels on the Bike*.

Discussing the Text

You won't need a long discussion of the text because you'll want to go quickly to the second reading so that children can participate. But you will want students to share their first thoughts. The goal is to assure that students understand the meaning of the whole story. Plus, you want them to start to think about any messages the text might have. For example, *The Wheels on the Bike* is a fun story with a surprise ending. All through the book we see animals that are talented enough to ride a bike. They have on safety helmets, but the cow even has a pink tutu, foreshadowing a party or other festive occasion. Of course, they show their talents "all through

First Reading of *The Wheels on the Bike*

Speaker	Teacher/Student Interactions	Analysis of Interactions
Mr. S	*[Reads page 14 and 15, pausing at the ellipses.]*	Invites predictions
	Where do you think they're going? They've been all through the town.	Reminds readers of important language in the text
Tara	To the country.	Makes a prediction
Parvleen	It's not a town anymore.	
Dion	There are chipmunks and a barn. They're going to a farm.	Notices illustrations
Sela	But there's a striped house. Is it a party? And he's going in it.	
Dion	It's a tent.	
Mr. S	**Does it look like they really want to get there? I wonder why.**	Asks for inference
Eileen	Yes, because they are all together on one bike and they are really going fast.	Cites evidence
Dion	They want to have fun in the striped tent.	Makes a prediction
Mr. S	You are noticing a lot of things in the pictures. They give you clues. They are not in the town anymore. It looks like the country and they are going somewhere special.	Affirms student observations Takes students back into the text

FIGURE 3-17 First Reading of *The Wheels on the Bike*

Discussion of *The Wheels on the Bike*

Speaker	Teacher/Student Interactions	Analysis of Interactions
Mr. S	**What are you thinking about this story?**	Asks for articulation of the meaning
Parvleen	I didn't know it would be a circus. They are doing tricks on the bike now.	Notice details
Sela	They are good in the circus.	
Mr. S	**The first time I read this book, the circus was a surprise to me. I knew they were going somewhere . . .**	Acknowledges thinking
Dion	They're funny in the circus.	Use picture information
Geoffrey	The cow has a skirt. She's going to dance.	
Caleb	And they were going fast to get there.	Make predictions
Mr. S	**Yes, they really wanted to get there and be in the circus together. Now let's read it again and you can join in.**	Summarizes the story

FIGURE 3-18 Discussion of *The Wheels on the Bike*

the town" and there are hints that this is no routine ride. When they reach the circus, the purpose of their ride is made known (see Figure 3-18).

Second Reading

As you move into the second reading, it is useful to remember that this will be the first reading for children. They will be working to read the words and use their memory of the language of the text and of the story to move through it. *The Wheels on the Bike* is constructed in such a predictable way that most children are able to join in on the second reading. Of course, if you listened to each child individually, you probably would detect some error behavior, some dropping out and some listening and false starts before joining up again; however, shared reading is a group effort, just like a group sing!

During the second reading, you will read the entire text aloud with the students. Keep moving at a moderate pace with good expression. (Avoid the temptation to slow down too much so that all students can "get the words.") Too great a slowdown can lead to droning through the text in an expressionless way. For this text, you may want to explicitly point out that the picture under the print helps you read the page. Say, "You see the little picture of the pedals. Think about what the pedals do."

After the second reading you have the opportunity to encourage a deeper focus on meaning. Some possible areas for discussion might be:

▶ Attributes or motivations of characters.

▶ The exciting point in the story.

▶ Interesting details in the illustrations.

▶ The story problem and when it is resolved.

▶ Important "big ideas" or messages from the story.

Of course, you would not need to discuss every aspect of every text. Just think about what is important to understand for every text you use for shared reading. And, remember that you will be revisiting the text several times. During the second reading of *The Wheels on the Bike* this might be an example (Figure 3-19).

After a few shared readings, the entire text is now readily available to the students. They can revisit any part of it to engage in deeper thinking or notice more about the print or language. We sometimes forget that readers often do their best thinking about a text *after the end*. So, it doesn't really matter that students have experienced the text and know the ending, even if it is a surprise. We often have greater insights into the reasons for characters' actions, for example, when the outcomes of a story become visible.

Subsequent Readings

The shared reading book is now an available text that can be used as a tool for further learning. For example, you might use a cloze procedure, which involves concealing predictable words in a text and inviting children to use problem solving to predict and confirm the word. They predict the word using language structure and meaning and also may predict the first letter or letter cluster; then, they can check and confirm their choices. Sticky notes are very useful for this purpose.

Predicting the word *bike* and the first letter helps students focus in on the letter *b* (see Figure 3-20). Letters are chosen carefully for the cloze procedure. Parts of words may be masked as well (for example, the *ike* in *bike).* Sometimes they represent action words, content words, or high-frequency words or rhyming words.

Highlighter tape is also very useful in subsequent readings (see Figure 3-21).

Second Reading of *The Wheels on the Bike*

Speaker	Teacher/Student Interactions	Analysis of Interactions
Mr. S	*[After reading page 8 together.]* How can you tell that those animals have somewhere important to go?	Asks for inference and evidence from the text
Tara	They are going fast and beeping the horn. They won't stop for the rabbit.	Shares evidence
Parveen	They act like they want to get there fast.	Infers from behavior
Dion	It's because they want to be in the circus. Maybe they have to get there on time.	Makes prediction
Mr. S	Look at the faces. They are all looking like they are determined to get there in time. Maybe they want to hear the people cheering for them. And look at the next page. The rabbit just gets out of the way in time!	Draws attention to details in the illustrations Suggests character motivation
Tara	The geese are saying, "Honk, honk, honk."	Notices text

FIGURE 3-19 Second Reading of *The Wheels on the Bike*

FIGURE 3-20 Using Sticky Notes

FIGURE 3-21 Using Highlighter Tape

Below, students focus on the /*ow*/ sound, which is represented by two different letter clusters.

Your selection of teaching points depends on the needs of your students and the opportunities in the particular text to support new learning. We have provided an extensive list of examples you might select as teaching points in subsequent readings in Figure 3-22. The figure represents areas of discussion and action across interactive read-aloud, shared reading, guided reading, and independent reading. The difference with shared reading is that all children are viewing and discussing the same text and there is strong instructional support. Shared reading enables them to do the same kind of thinking and talking with a *more complex* text than they can read independently or in a guided situation. As opposed to interactive read-aloud, the text is visibly available to all students so that examples can be shared explicitly. The figure indicates an opportunity for powerful interactions with the enlarged text. The text is available to students in every way and motor actions identified with reading can be explicitly demonstrated.

Using Shared Reading in Small Groups

You may find it effective to use shared reading in small-group instruction. Working with a small group and an enlarged text is especially helpful to children who have difficulty attending in the large group. Using a shared text, children can attend closely to features and, if needed, touch the text to locate and identify features of letters, words, and sentences. You can pull together a small group of students for a more intimate shared reading experience using big books or poetry charts.

You can also use shared reading in a small group with multiple copies of the text. Here, each student has his own copy of a small version of the text and they have read it once previously. The text is thus available to students in a way similar to an enlarged shared reading text that all have read together. Students can read in unison with your lead to:

- Match voice to print.
- Use appropriate phrasing, word emphasis, intonation, or use of punctuation.
- Work out tricky syntactic patterns so that they can read them smoothly.
- Grow more familiar with a complex word and its pronunciation.

Shared Reading of Shared or Interactive Writing

When you construct group stories and nonfiction texts through shared or interactive writing, you create a text that can then be used for shared reading. As you compose and construct it many times, you will engage children in shared reading to:

- Remember what they previously wrote so that they can think of the next word or sentence.
- Check to see if it "sounds right."
- Check to see if the print reflects what they wanted to say.

After a piece is finished, it can be used as a shared reading text in all the ways that any big book or chart can be used. One difference is that children are intimately familiar with the text because they have been involved in making it. Children love to revisit the texts they have written together (and sometimes illustrated). Interestingly, when interactive writing has been used, children remember even months afterward the letters or words that they contributed!

Shared Reading to Independent Reading and Other Work

Shared reading provides an excellent base for a great deal of independent work on the part of students. Once a text has been made available through shared reading, students enjoy reading small versions of the text (if available) independently. This, of course, provides an ideal activity for them to do on their own while you are working with small groups in guided reading. All of the actions you have demonstrated for students in the group to do are now available for independent activity, for example, reconstructing a poetry chart by placing the lines of a poem in a pocket chart and then reading it with the pointer.

Related Goals

In this chapter we have shared the many values of shared reading; the texts, the tools and resources, and the shape of the instruction. There are strong links between interactive read-aloud, shared reading, guided reading book clubs, and independent reading. All of the goals in these instructional contexts are related to the development of strategic actions for comprehending texts. In all contexts, students are getting the message that books are all about making meaning using language and print. In order to do so, they need to attend to visual information and language as well as think about the meaning at the same time. Most of all, students are learning that reading is a joyful, satisfying experience.

Reading Behaviors and Teaching Points

CONCEPT

Thinking *Within* the Text

Rhyme: Words can sound alike at the end.

Word-by-word match: You read one word for each group of letters.

Directionality: You read left to right across the line and top to bottom down the page. Return to the left to start each new line.

Known words: A word always has the same letters left to right. You can find a known word by noticing the letters.

Word parts: You can notice parts of words to make connections between them and to read them.

Syllables: You can notice the syllables in words. You can read a word by dividing it into syllables.

Cross-check: Self-monitor by checking one source of information against another.

Search for and use information: Search for information in the print (letter/sound/words), in language structure, and in the meaning of the text (and the pictures) and use it to monitor and self-correct reading.

Fluency: Read aloud with phrasing, pausing to recognize punctuation, use appropriate word stress and intonation, and at an appropriate rate.

Summarize: Notice the important information in a text and tell about the story or informational text in a concise way.

Thinking *Beyond* the Text

Infer: Think about what is implied but not stated in the text.

Synthesize: Change your thinking in response to new information or ideas.

Thinking *About* the Text

Analyze: Notice aspects of the writer's craft for fiction (i.e., plot, characters, character change, beginning, ending) and nonfiction (i.e., categories of information, cause and effect, problem and solution).

Critique: Think about the quality of a texts and express opinions.

FIGURE 3-22 Reading Behaviors and Teaching Points

TEACHING

Highlight words on the page that rhyme.

Practice using a pointer to read word by word.

Practice using the pointer to read left to right with return sweep.

Find a known word by thinking about the sounds and letters. Highlight known words.

Highlight word parts. Find words that have the same part (letters, letter clusters, phonograms, endings like *-ing*).

Clap a word to notice the syllables. Highlight syllables in words.

Point to the match between picture and words. Reread to be sure it sounds right (or looks right). Check sound/letter against the meaning. Use cloze procedure to block off words and predict letters before revealing them.

Reread to see what would sound right and look right. Check the picture. Reread to think what would make sense (or be sure what you read make sense). Identify and use nonfiction text features such as headings and graphics. Use cloze procedure to block off words and predict letters before revealing them.

Reread to show the meaning through appropriate pausing, phrasing, word stress, and intonation. Highlight punctuation and talk about the meaning. Highlight words to stress.

Identify and highlight important facts and ideas. Identify important parts of a story. Tell important information from a text.

Discuss character motivation and feelings, causes for problems, importance of the topic, and other thinking that requires inference. Locate evidence in the text and illustrations to support inference.

Identify new information in a nonfiction text. Identify something exciting or surprising in a fiction text.

Identify characters, story problem, problem resolution, description of the setting, and descriptive language for fiction. Identify facts, categories of information, sequence, cause/effect, problem/solution, and other underlying text structures. Identify signal words such as *then*, *after*, and *finally*. Identify how the writer has used nonfiction text features and graphics.

Express opinions and support with evidence from the text.

FIGURE 3-22 (continued)

Suggestions for Professional Development

1. Gather a sample of enlarged texts (big books or poems) that you might use in grades PreK through 3. These texts will range from extremely simple to fairly complex. Try to have at least 9-12 examples and good variety of fiction and nonfiction.

2. Convene a group of colleagues who plan to use (or are using) shared reading in their classrooms (grades PreK to 3).

3. Work together to put the samples in order from easiest to hardest. To do this, use the Shared Reading section of *The Literacy Continuum,* Text Characteristics, Grades PreK to 3. Books for shared reading are not like books leveled precisely using the A-Z gradient; but you would, in general, select them keeping the children's current strengths and needs in mind. The creators of books for shared reading assume high teacher and group support. For example, preschoolers need simple texts but can chant along with a four-line poem. Second graders can attend to many lines of print, do not generally need the pointer under each word, can read in parts, and can attend closely to text features, like graphics.

4. Once the texts are in order, make four piles, from easiest to hardest.

5. For each pile, make a list of the learning and teaching opportunities. Try to specify a grade level and time of year when you might use the texts for shared reading. (You and your colleagues might suggest two appropriate grade levels or times of year. Or, you might identify specific groups of children for whom the texts might be appropriate.)

6. Have an open discussion about how shared reading can "lead" guided reading. Ground the discussion in specific ideas for teaching using the sample texts. For example, what teaching points would you use to:

   ▶ Help children who need to learn to self-monitor and cross-check?

   ▶ Help readers learn to use language structure?

   ▶ Help readers notice and use text features such as headings or graphics?

   ▶ Build readers' repertoire of known words?

   ▶ Help readers learn to take apart multisyllable words while reading continuous text?

7. End by having each teacher select a big book to take away and use with a group of children. Set up another meeting to share the results.

8. Hold a follow-up meeting to discuss:

   ▶ How did children respond on the first and selected gradient readings? What shifts did you see?

   ▶ What evidence do you have that children made shifts in literacy learning that they can apply to other settings (for example, guided reading)?

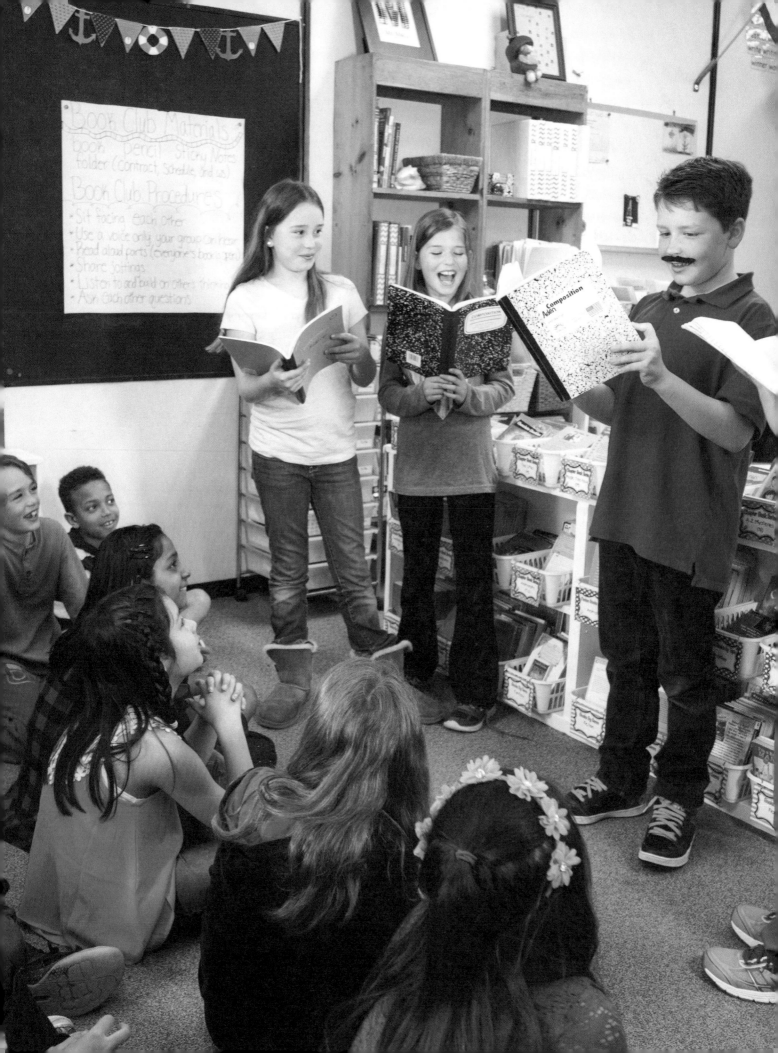

CHAPTER 4

Shared and Performance Reading Across the Grades

A great deal of teaching and learning happens every time active learners meet with a responsive teacher to read and reread shared books and to engage in discussion and analyses of texts.

–Brenda Parkes

When students have a well-established early reading process, they need to continue to expand their literacy processing systems. Shared reading can play an important role in expanding the systems of strategic actions using a variety of texts. In fact, a form of shared reading can be used at every grade level and is especially important for English language learners, who can benefit greatly from group support. You can use shared reading to establish early print awareness and a strong foundation, but also use the level of support and a greater variety of texts with intermediate or middle-level readers to develop their competencies in word analysis, vocabulary, fluency, and comprehension (see Figure 4-1).

Notice that the texts and goals change over time, but there are some constants:

- All eyes are on the same text and it is available to all students, making it an ideal setting for teaching to the group.
- Teaching points are selected on the basis of what students need to learn how to do *next* (in advance of what they are learning in guided reading).
- The text is carefully selected with learning goals in mind.
- A rich discussion directs attention to specific aspects of the reading process.
- The shared text is an ideal situation for engaging in analysis, supported by the group.

Shared Reading: Changes over Time

	Emergent Readers	Early Readers	Intermediate / Middle-Level Readers
TEXTS	◆ Big books ◆ Individual copies of small books ◆ Poems on chart paper ◆ Texts written through shared or interactive writing ◆ Posters and charts ◆ Electronic texts	◆ Big books ◆ Individual copies of small books ◆ Poems on chart paper and individual copies ◆ Scripts for readers' theater ◆ Enlarged pages of a regular sized texts (interactive read-aloud books, short stories, articles) ◆ Texts written through shared or interactive writing ◆ Posters and charts ◆ Electronic texts	◆ Scripts for readers' theater ◆ Individual copies of poems ◆ Enlarged pages of regular-sized texts (articles, novels, short stories, interactive read-aloud books) ◆ Plays ◆ Speeches and historical documents ◆ Charts, diagrams ◆ Advertisements ◆ Electronic texts
GOALS	◆ Learn how print "works" (left to right directionality, return sweep, etc.) ◆ Learn how to look at print ◆ Acquire a few known words ◆ Notice connections between words ◆ Develop the ability to monitor and search for information in print and pictures ◆ Understand simple stories and nonfiction texts ◆ Read 1–4 lines of print with support of the group ◆ Reread familiar texts independently ◆ Notice features of texts such as titles, authors, illustrators ◆ Become aware of the syntactic patterns of written language ◆ Make inferences from print and illustrations ◆ Develop a repertoire of known texts to return to for further learning ◆ Provide models for writing ◆ Build a sense of community	◆ Acquire known words ◆ Strengthen word analysis skills ◆ Expand vocabulary ◆ Increase knowledge of how texts "work" ◆ Expand knowledge of nonfiction text features and how they work ◆ Expand awareness of text structure (both overall and underlying) ◆ Read many lines of print in unison with others or in parts ◆ Read roles in a script with phrasing, pausing, word stress, and intonation ◆ Notice, recognize, and use punctuation ◆ Process complex syntax with proficiency and understanding ◆ Notice aspects of the writer's craft (beginnings, endings, story problem, narrator, problem resolution, descriptive language, character attributes and change) ◆ Provide models for writing ◆ Build a sense of community	◆ Strengthen word analysis skills ◆ Expand vocabulary to include literary language ◆ Use all dimensions of fluency (rate, pausing, word stress, intonation, and volume) to interpret a poem or script with the voice ◆ Expand knowledge of nonfiction text features ◆ Expand knowledge of nonfiction text structure (narrative, expository) ◆ Expand knowledge of underlying text structures (compare/contrast, sequence, problem/solution, and cause/effect) ◆ Notice aspects of the writer's craft (plot structure, character traits and development, narrator, description of setting, dialogue) ◆ Identify arguments and evidence that supports them ◆ Notice how the writer reveals purpose and the significance of a topic ◆ Compare and critique texts ◆ Provide models for writing ◆ Build a sense of community

FIGURE 4-1 Shared Reading: Changes over Time

▶ Shared texts provide a reference point for students that they can use in their own writing or in discussion in guided reading.

▶ The shared text makes it possible for students to successfully process a more complex text than they can read independently or in guided reading.

In the early years, shared reading plays a vital role in helping students understand how to find and use information from print—directional movement, one-to-one correspondence, words and letters, and the whole act of reading and understanding a story or nonfiction text. As readers become more proficient, shared reading continues to offer opportunities for more advanced reading work than students can do independently.

Value of Shared Reading for Intermediate/Middle-Level Readers

Shared reading has a number of benefits for readers at all levels of schooling using a variety of appropriate texts (see Figure 4-2).

The benefits of shared reading change greatly as students grow in the development of a reading process, but some principles are the same. Shared reading is a

Value of Shared Reading for Intermediate/Middle-Level Readers

- Creates a social situation in which students work together on a text.

- Develops a sense of community as students help each other notice aspects of the text.

- Provides a setting where you can demonstrate ways of working on problem-solving text.

- Provides a context for asking students to attend to aspects of the writer's craft (for example, text structure, the "lead" and "ending," sentence structure, transitions, word choice).

- Provides an opportunity for students to engage in processing increasingly challenging texts within a collaborative context.

- Builds confidence and knowledge.

- Makes difficult concepts and texts accessible.

- Helps students understand text features (for example, table of contents, headings and subheadings, photographs with labels, graphs, charts, maps, diagrams, insets, sidebars).

- Increases curiosity about words and builds reading vocabulary.

- Helps readers connect the information in print and graphics.

- Provides a forum for noticing and discussing conventions related to grammar and punctuation.

- Gives students an opportunity to notice the characteristics of genre.

- Increases collaboration and a sense of community among the group.

FIGURE 4-2 Value of Shared Reading for Intermediate/Middle-Level Readers

community experience, one that has enormous potential for including English language learners in a meaningful way. With high teacher support, you can lift students' understanding of critical concepts that they will eventually learn to apply in independent reading. It is important to note that learning to read is not a process that stops about the second or third year of school (the time which is usually seen as "learning to read"). In fact, readers keep expanding their abilities for the rest of their lives. Just compare a third-year reader and a fifth-year reader. The differences are tremendous. You might even have a third-year reader who can decode all or a high percentage of the words in a book like *A Long Walk to Water* (Park 2010) (see Figure 4-3). We would be tempted to say that this nine-year-old is "reading" at a sixth-or seventh-grade level; however, the comprehension demands of this book must be taken into account.

This book has dual narratives that take place in the same setting but at two points in time, twenty-three years apart. One narrative tells the story of Salva, one of the lost boys of the Sudan, from childhood to adulthood. The other tells the story of Nya, a young girl in Sudan who walks eight hours every day just to get water for her family. The setting is far from the experiences or background knowledge of almost all students. Background information about warring tribes in the Sudan, the challenges of living in desert climates, and the role of girls in tribal societies is needed. The messages are complex and mature. Readers must follow the perspectives of two very different characters and derive larger meanings across the

CHAPTER TWO

Southern Sudan, 2008

Nya put the container down and sat on the ground. She always tried not to step on the spiky plants that grew along the path, but their thorns littered the ground everywhere.

She looked at the bottom of her foot. There it was, a big thorn that had broken off right in the middle of her heel. Nya pushed at the skin around the thorn. Then she picked up another thorn and used it to poke and prod at the first one. She pressed her lips together against the pain.

Southern Sudan, 1985

BOOM!

Salva turned and looked. Behind him, a huge black cloud of smoke rose. Flames darted out of its base. Overhead, a jet plane veered away like a sleek evil bird.

In the smoke and dust, he couldn't see the school

building anymore. He tripped and almost fell. No more looking back; it slowed him down.

Salva lowered his head and ran.

He ran until he could not run anymore. Then he walked. For hours, until the sun was nearly gone from the sky.

Other people were walking, too. There were so many of them that they couldn't all be from the school village; they must have come from the whole area.

As Salva walked, the same thoughts kept going through his head in rhythm with his steps. *Where are we going? Where is my family? When will I see them again?*

The people stopped walking when it grew too dark to see the path. At first, everyone stood around uncertainly, speaking in tense whispers or silent with fear.

Then some of the men gathered and talked for a few moments. One of them called out, "Villages—group yourselves by villages. You will find someone you know."

Salva wandered around until he heard the words "Loun-Ariik! The village of Loun-Ariik, here!"

Relief flooded through him. That was his village! He hurried toward the sound of the voice.

A dozen or so people stood in a loose group at the side

| 8 |

| 9 |

FIGURE 4-3 Pages 8-9 from *A Long Walk to Water*

narratives, which come together at the end. The text involves tribal warfare, survival in a harsh climate, human rights, gender discrimination, and human loss. In fact, we could write for several pages about the comprehension demands of this book. Real reading of this complex text goes far beyond the reading of the words; the reader needs to deeply comprehend the text and be able to follow its nuances. Shared reading can be a vehicle for deeper understanding. In addition, every time you and your students share the meanings of a text, it contributes to a sense of community within the group.

A Sense of Community

The texts you read aloud to the class create a body of shared texts that students have in common. The same is true of texts used for shared reading; the difference is that when you use shared reading, the print, illustrations, and text features are visible to the students. Students can help each other notice aspects of a text that they might miss on a first reading. They can refer to specific examples that all students understand. They share a repertoire of texts that they can use in the discussion and interpretation of texts that they read in small groups and independently. Through both interactive read-aloud and shared reading, members of the community share:

▶ Literacy experiences in which all have participated.

▶ Access to complex ideas and information.

▶ Powerful models of fluent and sometimes expressive reading.

▶ The satisfaction of accomplishing something *in collaboration* with others (as opposed to individual competition).

Shared Reading Texts for Intermediate/ Middle-Level Readers

Any text that is age and grade appropriate can be selected for shared reading. You can use some enlarged print books created especially for this purpose, but you can also enlarge by scanning a page or short section of any book that has the particular features that you want to bring to students' attention. Or you can use chart paper to print a text yourself. Sometimes this may be a page of a book that you have previously read aloud to students, a part of an article, or a poem. An enlarged page gives you a chance to guide students to look closer at a particular use of language or text feature.

Intermediate/middle-level readers (as well as early readers) will also enjoy reading together to perform reading. For example, they enjoy readers' theater or choral reading of poetry. Here, they have to think deeply about the meaning of the text and discuss how they can use their voices to reflect emotions and messages.

For intermediate/middle-level readers, revisiting the text may involve a wide range of teaching. For example, you may cover part of the text to help students learn to anticipate language structure. You may draw attention to words, word parts, phrases, and sentences where the writer has communicated information about characters, the story problem, or the solution. You can demonstrate selective highlighting or marginal notes. You may bring parts of the text to students' attention to highlight, for example:

- The narrator of the text
- Characteristics of the genre
- How the writer and illustrator create a mood
- The writer's style (for example, short phrases for emphasis or a paragraph of description that creates visual imagery)
- The "lead" of the fiction or nonfiction text which is designed to engage interest
- The turning point of a story
- Character descriptions
- Markers of chronological sequence
- Connectives that show the relationship between ideas (*after, finally, meanwhile, nevertheless*)
- Figurative language and what it means
- Underlying structures such as compare and contrast or problem and solution

Big Books

Some enlarged texts are published for the purpose of shared reading by students who are beyond early reading. These students are well able to track print with their eyes and to perform the directional movements of reading. They have a repertoire of known words and can take words apart to solve them, using letters and sounds and word parts. They have developed the ability to study the structure or organization of the text or to look closely at text features. An example is *Saving Cranes* (*Fountas & Pinnell Classroom*, in press), shown in Figure 4-4.

This narrative nonfiction text tells the story of a unique effort to save whooping cranes, once threatened with extinction. The first few pages outline the problem and there is one page that shows fourteen flying cranes with a dramatic caption, "Once there were only about this many whopping cranes left in the wild." The book tells the story of how the scientists studied the cranes and then undertook to raise a flock and teach it to migrate. Some appropriate questions for discussion might be:

- The writer is telling this story in time, or chronological, order. Is this a good way to show how the scientists saved the whooping cranes?
- How does the writer use questions in this book?
- How does the writer show the passage of time?
- What do you learn from the graphic on page 8?
- What evidence does the writer present to show the amount of effort in researching the topic?
- Why did the scientists work so hard to save the species of whooping cranes?

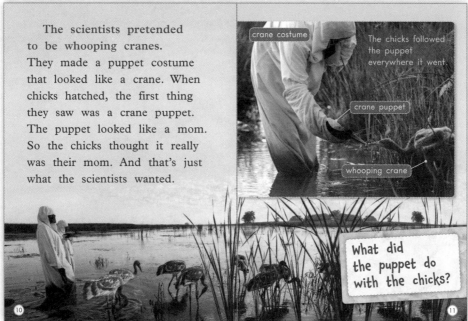

FIGURE 4-4 *Saving Cranes,* Pages 8–9, 10–11

> What is the problem and how does the writer show it in the text and the pictures?

> What is the solution, and how does the writer show that it works?

> What is the writer's message?

An advantage of the enlarged text is that students can identify evidence for the points they make and the print and pictures are available to all. (In a small group, students can also highlight words, phrases, titles, and other features of text using reusable highlighter tape.)

Another nonfiction example of an enlarged text for shared reading by proficient readers is *From Beans to Chocolate* (*Fountas & Pinnell Classroom*, in press), shown in Figure 4-5.

A major value of this text is the opportunity to attend to a graphic that appears on every page showing temporal sequence (from the cocoa tree to chocolate in the hand). Highlighted elements of nonfiction in the shared text are shown in Figure 4-6.

FIGURE 4-5 *From Beans to Chocolate, Pages 4–5, 14–15*

Poems

Students of every age enjoy poetry, songs, and chants. They can read them in chorus, using the voice as an instrument to interpret the meaning. Usually, students have their individual copies of the poem, but when introducing the poem, it helps to have an enlarged version on a chart. Read the poem to the students a couple of times and invite them to discuss the meaning. They can also talk about words that should be read in phrases, words that might be stressed, and so on. All dimensions of fluency apply to the reading of poetry, which packs a great deal of meaning into spare language. Sometimes a poem can be read in alternating parts or "solo" parts. For example, several poems are combined in *Rain, Sun, Wind, Snow* (*Fountas & Pinnell Classroom*, in press), shown in Figure 4-7 to use adjectives describing seasons.

A whole class can perform these poems with one-fourth of the group reading each one. Or, small groups can perform them as a sequence, talking about the characteristics of each season and varying the voice appropriately.

Sometimes poems can be found in prose or prose can be expressed in a poetic way for shared reading. In this short example of a poem

Highlighted Elements of Nonfiction in Shared Text

- Charts
- Diagrams
- Graphics
- Headings
- Index
- Key words
- Specialized language
- Table of contents
- Text structure
- Big ideas or messages
- Key information
- Underlying text structures

FIGURE 4-6 Highlighted Elements of Nonfiction in Shared Text

FIGURE 4-7 *Rain, Sun, Wind, Snow*, Pages 5, 8–9, 16, 18–19

adapted from the popular novel, *Hatchet,* Brian finds himself alone in the Canadian wilderness after a plane crash, with only a hatchet for survival. The poem expresses what it meant to Brian to be able to light a fire:

> I cannot leave the fire.
> So close and so precious,
> So sweet a thing.
> Yellow and red brighten the dark.
> Happy crackle of dry wood.
> I chop.
> I pile them up, burn them,
> Into the warm middle of the day.
> Smoke eddies and swirls.
> I will not let you go out—
> Not ever.
> My hungry friend.
> My good friend, fire. (Paulsen 1987)

Some popular novels, such as *Love That Dog* (Creech 1987) or *Out of the Dust* (Hesse 1997), are written in blank verse, so almost every page lends itself to poetic interpretation through shared reading.

Readers' Theater Scripts

Readers' theater is a dynamic process that is easy to implement in elementary classrooms. It is a fast and engaging way of making any literary text a type of play. The "script" is composed of dialogue and narrative from a fiction or nonfiction text, but liberties may be taken with the language to make it performable. Many readers' theater scripts are downloadable from the Internet, but you can easily create your own (or students can create them). Here is a script adapted from *A Long Walk to Water* (Park 2010), which shows the structure of this dual narrative based on a true story (Figure 4-8).

Notice how the action in Nya's story moves slowly, showing the monotony and drudgery of Nya's daily (all-day) walk for water. The action in Salva's story moves quickly, showing danger. This dramatic story has many possibilities for readers' theater.

Readers' theater requires only a script. It does not require costumes, props, or memorization. Performers are totally focused on how the voice represents the meaning. It can be performed for an audience, but most of the time, students engage it in for their own satisfaction. Readers' theater allows students to:

▶ Study characters in order to interpret their attributes and feelings.

▶ Develop ease and familiarity with new vocabulary words and language structure.

▶ Practice expressive reading for an authentic purpose.

▶ Self-assess their own reading performance.

▶ Build oral expression and speaking skills.

▶ Engage in oral reading for an authentic purpose.

Nya's Story Sudan 2009	Salva's Story Sudan 1985
Going was easy.	Nothing. Silence.
There was only heat, the sun, already baking the air.	Gunfire!
Heat. Time. And thorns.	Running into the bush.
	Away from home.
To the pond and back—	Men and women,
To the pond and back—	Boys and girls,
	Old and young,
Nearly a full day of walking,	Walking, walking . . .
Seven months of the year.	Walking to nowhere.
Daily. Every single day.	
Digging, scooping our handfuls of clay.	Walking into the morning sun.
Waiting for water.	Walking east.
Here, for hours at a time.	Ethiopia. Another country.
Every day for five long months.	Arm in arm with a friend.

FIGURE 4-8 A script adapted from *A Long Walk to Water*

To create a script for readers' theater:

1. Select an appropriate fiction or nonfiction text.
2. Decide which parts to turn into dialogue and narrative.
3. Have students work together to assign parts (characters and narrator).
4. Have students read the parts silently and think about how they will read them aloud.
5. Have students read the script a couple of times.
6. Have students read the script to others (optional).

Plays

As students grow more proficient, they will enjoy taking on the challenge of performing a play. It is useful for students to learn how to read plays. (There are substantial differences between reading a play and reading a straightforward narrative or descriptive text). The best way to learn how to read a play is to perform it. You can assign parts and let students read and study them, then read the play orally, just as you do readers' theater. Occasionally, students can memorize the words and perform a short play for an audience. This may or may not involve costumes and props, but we are not suggesting a long and time-consuming activity. Many plays that are especially appropriate for elementary students are available from the

Internet and other sources. But keep in mind that putting on a play can consume a great deal of time and effort, possibly detracting from your overall goal.

Speeches and Documents

Students can also benefit from performing speeches by practicing them (or segments of them) aloud. History is filled with famous speeches and documents that lend themselves to performance. You can find many famous speeches (or parts of them), that may be appropriate for students to perform. Famous documents can also be excellent resources for performance. When a student performs a speech or document for others, make sure that it:

- ▶ Is meaningfully related to ongoing inquiry in a content area.
- ▶ Has been read, discussed and understood by the student.
- ▶ Is a manageable piece of literature for both speaker and audience.

Students can also prepare and perform their own speeches, giving them opportunities to explore text types like argument and persuasion from the "inside" by creating them.

Enlarged Pages of Books

At any level, you can choose to select a page or pages from a fiction or nonfiction book and invite students to look closely at a segment of the text. You can enlarge the page so that each student can see the features you are asking them to discuss. (Students can have their own copies, if the cost isn't prohibitive.)

Writing in Response to Shared Reading

When students know a text very well, as is the case in shared reading, it can provide powerful fuel for writing. With an internalized text, writers have the text structure (organization) at their disposal along with vocabulary and ways of expressing meaning.

Innovations on Texts

Students across the grades can benefit from taking a known text and varying it to produce their own versions (Parkes 2000). As Holdaway has said, "The children respond with a delighted feeling of authorship, enjoying the opportunity for a genuinely personal and creative experience yet supported by the familiar structure" (1979). Innovating on a known text enables all writers to experience the success of producing longer and more complex texts than they typically can write independently. Of course, innovation does not take the place of students' independent writing for their own purposes, which would be going on at the same time in the classroom. But it does allow them to try out new text structures, language structures, vocabulary, and ideas.

The process starts during shared reading when you take an appropriate and well-known text and place sticky notes over some of the vocabulary. Students predict the correct word and can then check it. But after several readings, you may consider innovating by substituting a word. For example, this is part of the popular rhyme, "Peanut Butter and Jelly":

> Peanut butter, peanut butter,
> Jelly, jelly.
> First you take the dough and
> Knead it, knead it.
> Peanut butter, peanut butter,
> Jelly, jelly.

Students can substitute an infinite number of foods for the words *peanut butter* or *jelly* (for example, "pizza, pizza, cheese, cheese"). The teacher writes the substituted word on a sticky note. After students are very familiar with the poem, they can work with a partner to substitute words and read the text with the new words. Many poems and predictable texts lend themselves to this kind of substitution. Once they get the idea of innovation, they can make more substitutions, for example:

- Recreating a story within a new setting and characters.
- Telling an animal story with human characters or vice versa.
- Inserting new dialogue.
- Creating a sequel.
- Creating artifacts to go with the story (such as a letter or email from one character to another).

Shared and Independent Writing

Both fiction and nonfiction texts may be a resource for writing. In shared writing, you can demonstrate the process, acting as scribe and involving the students. (For early writers, it is useful to use interactive writing with students taking the pen at places that have high instructional value.) Students will soon begin to use shared reading texts as resources for their own independent writing.

In *On the Go* (*Fountas & Pinnell Classroom*, in press), a question-and-answer format is used along with descriptive words to show how animals move (see Figure 4-9).

The key words here are the animal names and the motion words. This text can easily be the basis of an innovation in which students substitute other animals and create words to describe the way they move.

Using the organizational structure of a well-known informational text, students can create

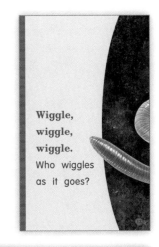

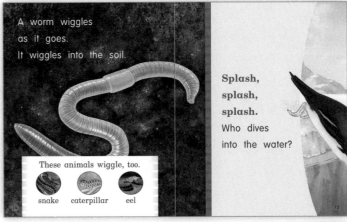

FIGURE 4-9 *On the Go*, Pages 13, 14–15, 16

their own book. Students may use chronological order to describe events that take place over time, or they may use the temporal order structure to describe a process. Graphics can be used for innovation, for example, life cycles or comparison charts. Students can extend a book by adding more categories of information about a topic and organizing them in the same way,

Teaching for Strategic Actions

Shared reading can be highly supportive to students in the development of strategic actions. Supported by the group, they can take on more complex texts; and, with your teaching, they can learn a great deal which they can then apply in guided and independent reading. Supporting the use of strategic actions through facilitative language is not fundamentally different from the way you interact with students in guided reading; however, you may be working with the whole class. Most of the time, though, you will want to use it within a guided reading context. In this way, shared reading can "lead" guided reading forward. Supported by the group and your teaching, they participate in skillful text processing ahead of what they can do individually. Shared reading is especially helpful to English language learners who are gaining control of English syntax.

As described in the previous chapter, for early readers, we explored the way shared reading can be highly supportive in teaching important early behaviors such as one-to-one matching. Through your prompting and questioning, they can learn to self-monitor their reading. You can make self-correction visible so that they realize their reading needs to "make sense, sound right, and look right." With group support, students can begin to use multiple sources of information in a coordinated way and then apply their understandings to the simpler texts they are reading independently. With the level of support in shared reading, students can usually read beyond their instructional or independent levels. The goal is for them, after much support, to be able to take on the reading for themselves, so it needs to be within reach.

At higher levels, there are opportunities to use shared reading to help students study a text closely. If you can enlarge a page or page layout from a text, then students can study it as a group and engage in collaborative discussion about the meaning. In addition, you can use underlining, highlighter tape, and other notation to point out aspects of text. The emphasis here is to uncover the techniques that the writer uses to communicate information and ideas to the readers.

You will want to be just as careful about the use of precise language in shared reading as in other settings. According to Brown (2004), "The teacher's use of rich, open-ended questioning is a powerful technique for engaging students in the exploration of texts in a shared reading lesson" (77). Open-ended questions probe students' thinking; they do not involve a specific answer that the teacher has in mind. Instead, they promote thinking and stimulate discussion. As you work with shared reading, you'll want to plan some specific language—both questions and prompts—that will help your students study the text in order to comprehend at a deeper level.

Alicia used these pages from *The Mysterious Fossa* (*Fountas & Pinnell Classroom*, in press) to help her students learn how to identify the problem and solution in a text (see Figure 4-10).

As these pages describe, the scientists helped people in many ways to become less dependent on farming. A deep discussion of these pages can help students uncover textual evidence to address questions such as:

▶ What contributes to the problem (the fossa facing extinction)?

▶ Why can't you just tell people not to cut down trees?

▶ What is a solution that protects an endangered species and at the same time helps people?

▶ What is important about the way the people in this book are working on their problems?

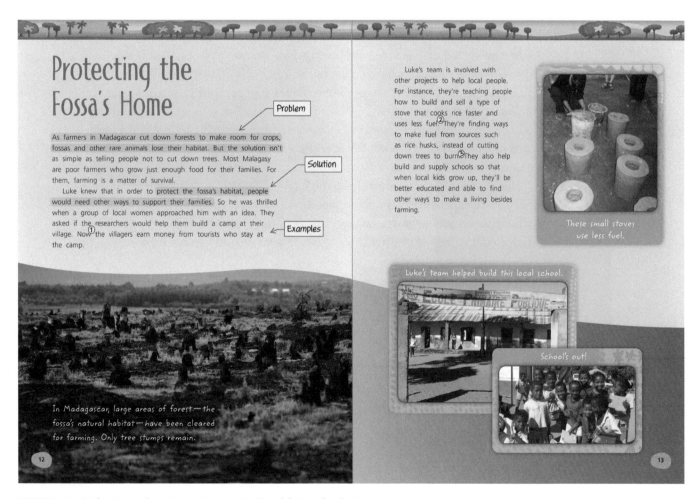

FIGURE 4-10 *The Mysterious Fossa,* Pages 12–13, with Teacher's Notes

At any age, students can profit from the opportunity to look together at a shared text. Shared reading can be used to support the full range of strategic actions.

From Shared to Guided Reading

In Chapters 3 and 4 we explored the potential of shared reading and its contribution to a powerful and coherent literacy instructional system. The topic of this book is guided reading, but the attention to shared reading underscores the importance of considering guided reading within a comprehensive literacy approach with varying levels of support that lead to the individual's competencies.

Interactive read-aloud, daily or even twice daily, engages students with highly complex texts, most well beyond students' own reading (or comprehending) levels, communicating and discussing ideas and concepts, using academic vocabulary, and internalizing complex language structures. In shared reading, students experience similar benefits, but they are working with a text that is *just beyond* their ability to read and comprehend in guided reading. Here, the print of the text is available so that they can match concepts, vocabulary, and structure to the print.

In guided reading, they are working at a level that they can process competently *with support and instruction*. After the introduction, they process the text mostly independently and their comprehension is supported by group discussion and your teaching points.

In independent reading, students competently process and comprehend a text *mostly* independently although they may share their thinking about the text with the teacher and with others.

These kinds of reading encompass the levels of support and challenge that students need to experience in a rich literacy approach every day. Your understanding of the rationales and instructional procedures of each instructional context will be critical to the success of a systematic, multitext approach to literacy success.

Suggestions for Professional Development

If you and your colleagues are inexperienced in implementing shared reading, the first step might be to try the most enjoyable context, readers' theater, for yourselves. If you are already using shared reading regularly, you might devote some meeting time to the collaborative creation of some good readers' theater scripts. Choose one of the two options below (or use them for two meetings consecutively).

Option 1: Book Club and Readers' Theater

1. Obtain several copies of *A Long Walk to Water* (Park 2010) and invite colleagues to join you in a book club. This book is a quick read and powerfully written (see Figure 4-3 in this chapter). Or substitute any book of your choosing with a readers' theater you have created.

2. Meet for a book club discussion. As the discussion winds down, introduce the readers' theater in Figure 4-8.

3. Have a discussion of the tempo and mood of each "story," and then assign half the group to read the part of Nya and half to read the part of Salva. Perform the piece as a choral reading, alternating each line—Nya, Salva, Nya, Salva, and so on. Then, try reading each as a separate piece.

4. Have an open discussion of the connections between comprehension and fluency and what students can gain from readers' theater.

Option 2: Readers' Theater/Poetry Workshop

1. Collect several texts appropriate as a foundation for readers' theater. Include several read-loud texts as well as some leveled books that you might use for guided reading. Most will be fiction, but try to identify some nonfiction. Argument, biography, and narrative nonfiction have good potential.

2. Have a discussion about the purpose of shared reading, and in particular, readers' theater. and the potential for increasing students' comprehension and fluency. Use this chapter as a resource. Read the poem drawn from *Hatchet* on page 86 and the script from *A Long Walk to Water* on page 87.

3. Have participants work with a partner to choose a book and then select it to create a script for readers' theater or a poem or script for choral reading. Consider language that:
   ▶ Expresses the emotions of characters.
   ▶ Shows the action and suspense of the plot.
   ▶ Reflects the writer's message.
   ▶ Makes the content interesting.
   ▶ Shows the qualities of the subject of a biographical text.
   ▶ Reflects the emotion in a memoir.

4. Have participants perform their scripts and share their thinking.

5. Copy and distribute to everyone for future use.

6. Each participant leaves with the goal of using readers' theater or a poem for shared reading.

CHAPTER

Planning for Effective Guided Reading Lessons

Building a Strong Early Reading Process

. . . Young children give overt signals about what they are attending to and what links they are making. Their behaviors provide signals that help teachers decide how best to lift their performance levels.

–Marie M. Clay

Shared reading and guided reading form a powerful instructional combination for helping early readers build a strong early reading process. Shared reading, in the early grades, supports building the processing system with a high level of support. It enables students to engage in reading continuous text in advance of the texts they can process independently. Students who have read (and reread) texts with one to four or five lines to a page and bold, clear illustrations, and rich language can transition seamlessly to reading very simple level A or B books in guided reading. And, they quickly build up a repertoire of books that they can read independently. Most independent reading at this point actually means *rereading* previously read books, but very quickly students will find that they can pick up easy books and read them, especially if they are supported by an introduction (see Figure 5-1). Shared reading provides a *transition to* guided, and ultimately, independent reading; and it continues to lead the expansion of the system. Throughout the first years of school, *in general*, students can read more complex texts in shared

Shared Reading
Provides the opportunity to process continuous text in unison with others. There is a high level of teacher and group support.

Guided Reading
Provides the opportunity to process continuous text individually with a moderate amount of support.

Independent Reading
Provides the opportunity to process continuous text individually with no or minimal support.

Level of Support

FIGURE 5-1 Independent, Guided, and Shared Reading: Levels of Support

reading than in guided reading and more complex texts in guided reading than independently.

In guided reading you focus on a small group of readers that you know in great detail. In reality, you are teaching *individuals* within the group to expand their reading competencies. You form groups of students who are similar to each other but they will never be exactly the same (see Chapter 9). As you involve them in lessons, you address their individual differences, which is possible in a small-group situation (as opposed to the whole class). During the first years of school, the goal of guided reading is to teach for the strategic actions needed to build a strong early reading process (see Figure 5-2).

It is obvious that in order to solve words, early readers must be able to take words apart and apply a range of phonics and word analysis skills; but it should also be obvious that much more is involved. In fact, early readers learn and use simultaneously the full range of strategic actions, even on very simple texts every time they read, although they may be limited in their ability to think in an analytic

A Strong Early Reading Process

- Early reading behaviors established and under control.

- Reading is characterized by monitoring and self-correcting behaviors (from overt to not noticeable).

- Using multiple sources of information (meaning, structure, and visual information) in an integrated way to read accurately with monitoring and self-correcting.

- Actively searching for information to solve words and understand reading.

- Applying a range of word-solving strategies "on the run" while reading for meaning.

- Demonstrating all dimensions of fluency.

- Making and articulating predictions and inferences.

- Distinguishing between known and new information and incorporating new ideas and concepts into their thinking.

- Using prior knowledge to understand texts.

- Understanding the difference between fiction and nonfiction and characteristics of some genres such as traditional tales.

- Noticing underlying structures in nonfiction like compare and contrast.

- Articulating opinions about texts and saying why.

- Supporting points with evidence from the text.

FIGURE 5-2 A Strong Early Reading Process

way about a text as a piece of writing (and texts at the early levels will not have as many features to think analytically about, even though many exhibit examples of excellent writing and art). Teaching students in a small group allows you to observe their reading behaviors closely enough to infer the in-the-head strategic actions that are taking place and provide just-in-time support to individuals to help them learn how to initiate problem solving as they work through a text.

In this chapter we outline the basic framework for guided reading, with emphasis on the early years of schooling. We outline the three primary considerations of the teacher in implementing guided reading: readers, texts, and teaching. As you read, keep in mind this summary of the steps for teaching groups in guided reading (Figure 5-3).

Steps for Teaching Groups in Guided Reading

Step	Action	Summary Description
1	Assess individual readers to form groups at the start of the school year. Select emphases from *The Fountas & Pinnell Literacy Continuum*. [During the year, use observational notes and regularly scheduled running records.]	Use systematic assessment to determine students' instructional and independent reading levels. Look at the reading record at the instructional level to note strengths and needs in processing. Use *The Literacy Continuum* to select a few emphases to guide reading.
2	Select and analyze the characteristics of the text.	Select a high-quality, engaging text that offers group members opportunities to learn. Analyze the text to determine opportunities and plan the introduction to the text.
3	Introduce the text.	Introduce readers to the setting, story problem, or topic of the nonfiction book, and other key aspects of the text.
4	Observe and interact as students read the text individually [softly or silently].	You can take the opportunity to observe students' oral reading [if they read softly], and you may sometimes interact very briefly with individuals to support their use of strategic actions.
5	Invite students to discuss the text.	Students share their thinking about the text. Guide the discussion toward articulation of the key ideas and larger messages of the text.
6	Make an immediate teaching point.	Based on your knowledge of students and your observation of their reading behaviors in the lesson, select a specific teaching point or two that will help readers expand their ability to read all texts.
7	Engage students in letter or word work.	Engage students in two to three minutes of "hands-on" work with letters or words that helps them apply an understanding of how words work or add words to their reading vocabularies.
8	Extend the lesson through writing or drawing about reading. [Optional]	When appropriate, you may wish to invite students to reflect on their understanding or interpretation of the text through writing or drawing.
9	Reflect on the lesson and plan tomorrow's lesson.	You will have a tentative plan of emphases for the week, but your observation of reading behaviors in this lesson may prompt you to make some adjustments for tomorrow. Consult *The Literacy Continuum*.

FIGURE 5-3 Steps for Teaching Groups in Guided Reading

Step One: Assess Readers to Form Groups

The first priority is to know the readers in your class. In one sense you are always observing and getting to know students. But you need a detailed analysis of precisely what they know and can do as readers. This takes systematic observation and assessment.

Systematic Assessment

Use an assessment system that gives you an inventory of each reader's current range of abilities. Engaging in assessment is well worth the time. With the information you get, you can:

> ▶ Identify the emphases for teaching.

> ▶ Select texts appropriately for maximum progress.

> ▶ Identify accelerative teaching goals.

> ▶ Use facilitative language to help students make leaps in learning.

> ▶ Teach with efficiency.

We created *The Fountas & Pinnell Benchmark Assessment System* (including Optional Assessments) as a systematic way to begin the year with good knowledge of the instructional needs and processing strengths of each student. Of course, you will need ongoing assessments on a regular basis, and for this we recommend taking running records of reading progress at selected intervals (see Chapter 11). Both the *Benchmark Assessment System* and continuous running records involve observing readers in great detail and forming hypotheses as to what they know and can do as readers to guide the direction of teaching within the lesson.

As an example, let's look at five children and what they could do at the beginning of the school year (see Figure 5-4).

Their accuracy profiles are similar in many ways, but they are very different in other ways.

> ▶ Tiara can monitor using visual information but needs to be more consistent.

> ▶ Alex consistently uses the first letter of words but needs to monitor his reading using language structure and meaning.

> ▶ Zach can read level D but only at 90% accuracy. His reading is slow and laborious with a great deal of overprocessing; and this was also characteristic of his reading at level C even though he had high accuracy (97%). He needs to read with more smoothness and ease.

> ▶ Bradley read level C at 93%, with three of his errors missing the same word (*asleep* for *sleeping*). He tends to neglect visual information cues, failing to monitor his reading; however, he can use visual information as shown by his correct reading of *sleeping* further on in the text.

> ▶ Donnie read level C at 91% and effective use of visual information. He needs to use language structure and meaning to monitor and search for information; and he needs to become more active in problem solving and to attend to meaning beyond the text.

This set of scores illustrates how identification of the "level" for instruction is valuable but does not tell the entire story of a reader. Your observations give much

Benchmark Assessment *System* Optional Assessments at the Beginning of the Year	Tiara	Alex	Zach	Bradley	Donnie
Letter Knowledge	44/54	42/48	48/48	42/48	46/48
Early Literacy Understandings	9/10	8/10	7/10	10/10	8/10
Text Reading					
Instructional Level Text (Beginning of the year *Benchmark Assessment*)	C	C	D	C	C
Accuracy	91%	90%	90%	93%	91%
Comprehension	Proficient	Proficient	Approaching Proficiency	Proficient	Approaching Proficiency
Fluency	1	1	0	2	0
Self-Correction Rate	1:2	1:5	1:3	nil	1:7
Observations	◆ Uses visual information at the first-letter level ◆ Not consistent in self-monitoring using visual information ◆ Uses structure and meaning to self-correct ◆ Comprehension excellent ◆ Work on phrasing	◆ Needs to use language structure more consistently ◆ Comprehension excellent within the text ◆ Needs to articulate inferences ◆ Work on phrasing	◆ Attends to visual features at first-letter level ◆ Needs to monitor and search for meaning and structure ◆ Comprehension satisfactory ◆ Work on phrasing	◆ Accurate reading ◆ Uses meaning to self-correct ◆ Smooth operation of early behaviors ◆ Comprehension excellent ◆ Work on phrasing	◆ Uses visual information at the first-letter level ◆ Needs to attend to language structure and meaning ◆ Needs to be more active in problem solving ◆ Comprehension satisfactory ◆ Work on phrasing

FIGURE 5-4 Reading Scores and Observations of Five Children

more information. All five readers have good letter knowledge and well-established knowledge of how print works. All need to work on fluency, but they are just beginning to phrase their reading and all are still pointing to the words as they read. All are just moving beyond the point of strongly establishing early behaviors such as directionality and word-by-word matching. They are just beginning to learn to read in phrases.

Each time you convene a group of students for guided reading, you will have some priorities in mind for the group. Mr. K identified a few emphases as teaching priorities using *The Literacy Continuum* to identify the important behaviors and understandings for the level (Figure 5-5).

With these priorities in mind, Mr. K looked for opportunities to do some pow-

Planning Sheet for Guided Reading Groups	
Priorities for the group:	

- Reinforce early reading behaviors: Continue to observe for evidence of word-by-word matching on several lines of print.
- Monitoring and correcting: Prompt for cross-checking meaning with visual information.
- Fluency: Prompt for phrasing and use of intonation, including reading the punctuation.
- Inferring: Demonstrate and prompt for thinking about how the illustrations reveal interpretation of a problem or of a character's feelings.

Tiara	Bradley
Prompt for self-monitoring using visual information.	Prompt for self-monitoring using visual information.
Alex	Donnie
Prompt for use of language structure and meaning.	Prompt for active searching and problem solving, cross-checking using language structure and meaning.
Zach	
Prompt for phrasing and smoother processing.	

FIGURE 5-5 Mr. K's Priorities for the Group

erful teaching, always realizing that *he could not teach everything to every student in every lesson.* After reflecting on students' strengths and needs, he selected a few behaviors and understandings to notice, teach for, and support in the lesson. He wrote them on a sticky note to refer to while teaching.

The second realization is that the priorities will continually change. But you will find that if you are fully informed about the readers and have your observational powers on alert, you are already halfway to making your teaching "count." That is, every teaching move you make can be powerful in shifting student learning. Consult the Guided Reading section of *The Literacy Continuum* as you plan for your teaching priorities.

Mr. K's Reflection on His Students' Strengths and Needs

The teacher, Mr. K, chose to teach his students in a group, selecting level C as a starting point. Once Mr. K had priorities in mind (see Figures 5-5 and 5-6), he consulted *Prompting Guide, Part 1 for Oral Reading,* a powerful tool for supporting his teaching (*Prompting Guide Part 1 App,* is searchable and very useful). This

I want to observe students' reading to be sure they are consistently matching word by word and using return sweep, but I probably won't need to prompt for these early reading behaviors. Also, all five have demonstrated that they can monitor their reading for accuracy, but as they take on more lines of print, I want to be sure that early behaviors remain under control. I will need to emphasize reading phrases.

FIGURE 5-6 Mr. K's Reflection on His Students' Strengths and Needs

guide suggests facilitative, precise language that can be used to direct the reader's attention. Using the *Prompting Guide,* Mr. K can use language to:

▶ Teach: Demonstrate the action and show the reader how to do it.

▶ Prompt: Remind the reader to take an action he has already learned to do.

▶ Reinforce: Affirm an action the reader has taken on his own.

Some examples of precise language to encourage self-monitoring, initiating problem-solving actions, and phrasing are shown in Figure 5-7. This specific language is effective because it tells the reader precisely what action is needed (or was used) and helps him build his processing system through effective problem-solving actions. Affirming the reader's specific actions gives him more information than vague language like, "good reading." Once Mr. K decides on his priorities for teaching, he jots down some language on a sticky note that he thinks might be effective if appropriate at any time in the lesson.

Examples of Precise Language

Strategic Action	Teach	Prompt	Reinforce
Self-Monitoring	That didn't make sense (sound or look right). You need to stop when it doesn't sound right (make sense or look right).	You knew something wasn't right. Think what would sound right (make sense or look right).	You stopped and made it sound right (make sense or look right).
Searching for and Using Information (Meaning)	You can try that again and think what would make sense. Let me show you.	Try that again and think what would make sense.	You tried that again and now it makes sense.
Phrasing	Listen to how I put these words (model phrase units) together to make it sound like talking.	Put your words together so it sounds like talking.	You put your words together and made it sound like talking.

FIGURE 5-7 Examples of Precise Language

Guidelines for Selecting Texts

Select texts that will engage readers' intellect, curiosity, and emotions.

Select texts that are accurate, and that reflect the diversity of our society and are culturally sensitive. (In particular, be sure that students see other children like themselves in many of the books they read and also that they see diversity.)

Select books that reflect high-quality writing even when geared toward early readers.

Select books that present high-quality and varied illustrations, both photographs and drawings.

Select a text that offers a reasonable challenge to the particular readers in the group. It should be one that they can read with proficiency and satisfactory comprehension given an introduction and supportive teaching. Use children's instructional level as a guide.

Select a text that can be read in one lesson most of the time.

Select texts that offer a variety of genres.

Select texts that focus on concepts and ideas that are age-appropriate for the group.

Select texts that are clear examples of the level (for example, consistent across pages).

Select texts that offer opportunities for students to build strategic actions that they can apply to reading other texts.

FIGURE 5-8 Guidelines for Selecting Texts

Step Two: Select and Analyze Texts

Mr. K's next step was to select and analyze a text that would give this group of readers opportunities to learn.

Selecting Texts

The text level is a guide, but that is certainly not all there is to text selection (see Chapter 12). The Guided Reading section of *The Literacy Continuum* offers detailed support for text selection. Level is not the only criterion, though it is important to have a text with appropriate amounts of support and challenge. The guidelines for selecting texts for a group in guided reading are summarized in Figure 5-8.

Remember that you are teaching the readers—not the text. Every action in text selection is directed toward helping the readers shift a little each day. The goal is not simply to learn how to read this book but to learn how to read. Your goal is the learning of strategic actions that they can apply in all of their reading.

Many teachers find it time efficient to select a few books to be used for the next several days with the group. Some teachers have their own collection of leveled books for guided reading, but a more economical approach is to house leveled books in a "book room" (see Chapter 12 and *Leveled Books K–8* © 2006). Multiple copies of leveled titles are housed by level on accessible shelves. Teachers can visit the book to "check out" the multiple titles, which they return after using them in lessons. For younger children, they may place one copy of a book that was previously used in guided reading in a browsing box for students to reread. Selecting books is part of planning for the week. You may select three to five titles, for example, and put them in sequence as you plan for lessons over a week's time. You can always change your mind if student behavior indicates: (1) the text is too easy (or the first three or four are consistently too easy) and you need to move to another level; or (2) the text is too hard and you need to analyze the readers' behaviors and your own teaching to decide what to do.

For the group of readers above, Mr. K selected four texts at level C: two nonfiction texts and two fiction texts. Both of the nonfiction books present a series of related ideas about several animals. The reader can see similarities between the animals. In *All Kinds of Eggs (Fountas &*

Pinnell Classroom, in press), all the animals (even though different species) hatch from eggs (see Figure 5-9). In *Animal Feet* (*Fountas & Pinnell Classroom*, in press), all of the animals (also different species) have feet that they use for different purposes (see Figure 5-10). Read in sequence, these two books offer the opportunity to talk about how animals survive.

 A Trip to the City (*Fountas & Pinnell Classroom*, in press) is a fictional story, presented in chronological order, of a young boy's day with his grandfather. The readers have the opportunity to notice aspects of the relationship between characters (see Figure 5-11). *Something for Dinner* (*Fountas & Pinnell Classroom*, in

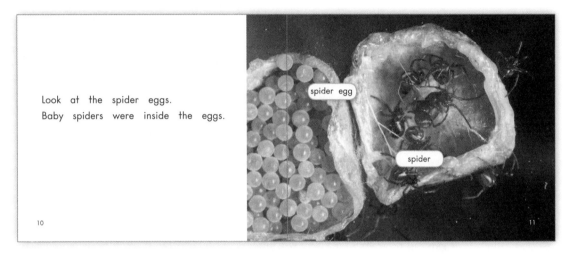

FIGURE 5-9 *All Kinds of Eggs*, Pages 10–11

FIGURE 5-10 *Animal Feet*, Pages 14–15

FIGURE 5-11 *A Trip to the City*, Pages 14–15

press) is the story of two children who reject each of the foods Dad offers them, but they end up loving the pizza that Dad has been making all along. This text offers the challenge of dialogue among three characters (see Figure 5-12).

Analyzing Texts

If you select texts carefully, you have already begun to think about the demands they make on readers. Give special attention to the needs of English language learners. Before you begin to teach the lesson, do some deeper thinking about each text. Some questions to ask are:

▶ What ideas and concepts will be challenging for students? How will this text stretch their thinking?

▶ What syntactic patterns (language structures) will be tricky and may need rehearsing? How will new language patterns help students expand their internalization of written syntax? What syntactic patterns will pose challenges to the English language learners in your classroom?

▶ What new words will students encounter? What can they add to their reading vocabularies?

▶ What words will require students to use word-solving (phonics) strategies? How will the word solving in this text help them learn *how to* solve words typical of this level?

▶ What new vocabulary will be challenging? How will this text help them expand their speaking and reading vocabularies? Does the text have any Tier 2 words that will need attention in the introduction? What words may need more explanation for English language learners?

▶ What opportunities are there for students to make connections to other texts?

▶ How can students connect this text to their own lives?

▶ How does this text help students make connections with essential questions?

So, for the teacher, text analysis is a complex intellectual activity even if the texts are from levels A to N. And, you need to perform this complex thinking "on the run" during your brief planning time. That's a challenge!

"Do you want some onions for dinner?" asked Dad.

Sam said, "No! I do not like onions!"

Pat said, "No! I do not like onions!"

FIGURE 5-12 *Something for Dinner, Pages 6–7*

We use ten text characteristics as a framework for thinking about a text (Figure 5-13). For a detailed description of each, see Chapter 13, Figure 13-3.

Using these ten characteristics a few times as an activity to analyze several texts will help you to develop a lens for quickly examining texts and noting salient features. From there, you can plan introductions that help your students.

With this kind of thinking, Mr. K was poised to provide a powerful introduction that would drive the readers into the text. He matched up his thinking about the text with his priorities for the readers.

Step Three: Introduce the Text

The introduction should be concise. There is no need to go over what students already know. Mr. K's goal was to unpack a few story components that would be essential to assure successful reading (for a description of what the introduction *is* and *is not*, see Chapter 14, Figure 14-4).

The book introduction is an orientation to the book. In a way, you are giving readers a kind of "road map" to the text. But it is not meant to take problem solving away from the reader. Your book introduction provides just enough support to enable readers to take on a more complex text. By engaging in the problem solving, they build their processing powers.

It is obvious that no one can write a "standard" introduction to a text that you use every single time. The introduction is always constructed with the particular readers in mind. As you work with a high-quality set of leveled books, however, you will find that it becomes easier to introduce well-known texts. You have a repertoire of texts that you have analyzed. Look through a book and make a few notes. For example, a thorough analysis of *Something for Dinner* would cover a page, but look at Mr. K's quick thinking and what he noticed about the text (Figure 5-14). You can look back at your notes and add new insights. Then, you adjust the introduction to fit the readers at your table.

Remembering the priorities for the group, let's look at an excerpt from Mr. K's introduction to *Something for Dinner* (see Figure 5-15). This introduction is rich in information yet does not "give away" the end of the story or even give attention

Ten Text Characteristics

1. Genre/Form
2. Text Structure
3. Content
4. Themes and Ideas
5. Language and Literary Features
6. Sentence Complexity
7. Vocabulary
8. Words
9. Illustrations
10. Book and Print Features

FIGURE 5-13 Ten Text Characteristics

Mr. K's Notes on *Something for Dinner*

Genre: Realistic fiction

- Three characters: Dad, Sam, and Pat
- Problem: Sam and Pat say they don't like anything Dad suggests for dinner. They can't see him cooking, so the perspective of the illustrations is important. Problem solved at the end as Dad serves pizza
- Dialogue among characters; extra space between speakers
- Punctuation: exclamation point, quotation marks, question marks
- Assigned dialogue: asked, said, speech bubble at end
- New high-frequency words: want, don't
- Content words: meatballs, onions, tomatoes, peppers, cheese (clear picture clues)
- Prepositional phrases
- Message: Don't say "no" without knowing the whole story
- Big idea: People in families love each other and take care of each other

FIGURE 5-14 Mr K's Notes on *Something for Dinner*

Introduction to *Something for Dinner,* **Level C**

Speaker	Teacher/Student Interactions	Analysis of Interactions
Mr. K	You are going to read a story today. The title is *Something for Dinner* and it's by Dagney Charles. This story is fiction. It didn't really happen, but as you read, think about whether it could happen. Look at the cover and you'll see two kids. Their names are Pat and Sam. "Dad is making one of his children's favorite foods." What do you think it is?	Introduces title, author, and genre Draws attention to illustrations and characters Asks for predictions
Alex	Tacos.	Make predictions
Donnie	Macaroni and cheese.	
Mr. K	You will have to keep wondering what it is. And whether Sam and Pat will like it. Turn to pages 2 and 3. What do you see in the picture?	Articulates story problem Draws closer attention to the picture
Tiara	They're playing a game and Dad is in the kitchen.	Notice information in picture
Alex	He's going to cook something.	
Mr. K	Looks like Dad has some peppers. Can you see them in the picture? He asks the children, "Do you want some peppers for dinner?" Can you say that? Say *want*. What letter do you expect to see first in *want*?	Uses high-frequency word Names a word and asks students to predict the first letter and locate it in print
Students	W.	Identify a letter
Mr. K	Put your finger under *want* and get a good look. On each page Dad asks *the* children if they want something for dinner. Turn to page 6 and 7. He will ask them if they want what? (Children locate the word *want*.)	Models language structure Makes prediction
Students	*Onions.*	
Bradley	I don't like onions.	
Mr. K	Say the word *asked.* Find it on page 6. Notice the first letter, a. Say the word *asked* slowly. Run your finger under it to check it like this. *[Mr. K demonstrates and students locate asked and say it.]* You see that word when someone asks a question. But what do you think Sam and Pat will say? `	Draws attention to a new high-frequency word and its meaning and visual features
Alex	He doesn't like onions.	Make prediction
Tiara	I don't like onions either.	
Mr. K	You are right. Sam said, "I do not like onions." On every page Dad asks Sam and Pat the same question.	Articulates how the book works
Donnie	They don't like the things Dad wants to cook.	Makes prediction

FIGURE 5-15 Introduction to *Something for Dinner,* Level C

Introduction to *Something for Dinner*, Level C

Speaker	Teacher/Student Interactions	Analysis of Interactions
Mr. K	Now look at page 12. Pat and Sam are talking and really can't really see what Dad is cooking for dinner, but they can smell something in the oven.	Draws further attention to the picture
Bradley	They smell something good.	
Alex	Maybe he's making chicken.	Make story predictions
Tiara	Or baked macaroni.	
Donnie	They won't like what he makes.	
Mr. K	**Will Dad find something Sam and Pat like?**	Articulates the story problem
Bradley	No, they don't like anything.	Predicts story ending
Mr. K	**Read to find out what Dad makes Pat and Sam for dinner. Then we'll talk about the story.**	Alerts students to be ready to talk about the meaning of the story

FIGURE 5-15 *(cont.)*

to every page. Students are reminded to use more than one way of solving words. They have the basic story structure (question and answer) and some repetitive language as a support for reading more complex sentences than they have encountered before. They also have background understanding and the illustrations to help them with the difficult food words (*tomatoes, onions, peppers*). The meaning and language structure will help them read words that they cannot yet fully decode, but they need to use the letter/sound information they have to be sure they are reading accurately. Mr. K asked them to look carefully at the word *asked* and to check it by looking through the word left to right. The content word *oven* is left for problem solving; students have a repertoire of known high-frequency words and the decoding skills to read the rest of the story. After the introduction, they are poised to read with high accuracy and understanding of the problem and outcome.

Step Four: Observe and Interact as Students Read the Text Individually

An exciting part of the lesson is observing your students as they read the text for the first time. Here, you can check on the effectiveness of your text analysis, planning, and introduction. Remember that 100% accuracy is not necessarily the "test" of effectiveness. You are looking for evidence of problem solving. Each student reads the text individually (rather than in unison with others). To support individual reading at the early levels:

▶ Encourage students to read softly (some teachers use the phrase "whisper read") and to think about the story.

▶ If needed, spread students apart so that they are not sitting very close together.

With an effective introduction, students should read the short text at a similar rate, but it is always the case that some will read faster than others. You can encourage students who finish quickly to pick up a previously read book from a basket in the middle of the table, to begin drawing or writing about the story in their reader's notebook, or to go back to reread. If rates are too disparate, go back to analysis. You may need to do some intensive teaching for fluency with students who are reading too slowly. Alternatively, notice students who are reading very quickly. Are they skipping words without attempting them? Are they leaving out lines of print? Are they leaving errors without working to self-correct them? The goal is for readers to move through the text at a good rate—not too fast and not too slow. Also, notice your own behavior. Are you interrupting your students too much? Interactions with individuals should be few, brief, and powerful.

One of your goals is to observe each student's reading behaviors, so be sure to listen and make notes. You will find a useful "shorthand" in the kinds of notation you use when taking a running record. Keep the students at the table as they read rather than sending them to their tables or desks. The early readers should be whisper reading, so you can lean in and interact as needed. When students are reading silently, you can listen to one student read at a time. You may need to ask an individual to raise his voice a little so that you can easily hear. You want students to stay focused so don't ask them to move around the table for you to listen. Instead, move around the table with a small portable stool or chair and ask a student to turn slightly toward you and read aloud.

After students get started with their reading and you can see that they are moving along well, interact with individual students as needed. These interactions offer an opportunity to tailor the teaching to individuals, but they should not interrupt the reading with a long series of teaching moves. They are brief and highly instructive. Use an economy of language. That means making a very specific point in a few words. Now is the time to use those examples of facilitative language you made note of as you were analyzing students' reading.

You will find *Prompting Guide Part 1 for Oral Reading* to be a helpful resource for the language of responsive teaching. Your interactions may arise when a student needs help. Remember that the text offers a challenge to the readers. (If it does not, then it has little instructive value.) It is at the point of difficulty or after an error that problem solving takes place and the learning opportunities are great. But often, you may want to intervene when the student does not notice mismatches or is not reading in phrases. These interactions call for decision making "on the run." Here are several examples from Mr. K's group as they read *Something for Dinner* (Figure 5-16, 5-17, and 5-18).

Something for Dinner—Student/Teacher Interaction: Zach

Zach   *[Reads]* "Do you want some t- *[pauses and looks at the teacher]*.

Mr. K   **Try that again and think what would make sense.**

Zach   *[Reads]* "'Do you want some tomatoes for dinner?' Dad asked."

Mr. K   **That makes sense. Does Dad have some tomatoes in the picture?**

FIGURE 5-16 *Something for Dinner*—Student/Teacher Interaction: Zach

Something for Dinner—Student/Teacher Interaction: Bradley

Bradley   *[Reads]* "'No, no! I don't look tomatoes', said Pat."

Mr. K   **It has to make sense. Try that again.**

Bradley   *[Reads]* "'No, no! I don't l- like tomatoes,' said Pat."

Mr. K   **Now that makes sense and looks right, too.**

FIGURE 5-17 *Something for Dinner*—Student/Teacher Interaction: Bradley

Something for Dinner—Student/Teacher Interaction: Tiara

Tiara   *[Reads]* "Dad put something in the" . . . what's that word?

Mr. K   **Would *oven* or *stove* make sense there?**

Tiara   *[Reads]* "Dad put something in the oven."

Mr. K   **Were you right?**

Tiara   Yes, it doesn't have an *s*, it has an *n* at the end.

Mr. K   **Yes, you made it make sense and it looks right, too.**

Tiara   *[Reads]* "Dad put something in the oven. It smelled very good." Yes, that makes sense.

FIGURE 5-18 *Something for Dinner*—Student/Teacher Interaction: Tiara

Step Five: Invite Students to Discuss the Text

After reading, the first move is to invite students to comment on the book. Make this an open question so that you can capture their first responses. Look for evidence that the students understood the story. You may have some prompts or questions in mind, but don't make the discussion an "interrogation." Rather than focusing on assessing, think about promoting text-based talk. As much as possible, the discussion should be a conversation. At the same time, try to not let the dialogue meander in a way that is not grounded in the text or results in nonproductive chatter. Also, be sure that all students have the opportunity to share their thinking rather than letting one or two dominate the conversation. Avoid constantly saying, "good" or "you're right." Instead, confirm students' responses by thoughtful listening and responding as you would in a conversation.

Guide the discussion in a way that encourages deeper thinking. Ultimately, you want students to articulate the deeper meanings of the text and any "big ideas" or messages that are implied in the writing. For example:

- For *All Kinds of Eggs,* a big idea might be: For many living things—even different species—reproduction involves eggs. Or, animals of different species can have many things in common.

- For *Animal Feet,* a big idea might be: Living things have bodies that perform essential functions to help them survive. Or, a body part can play a very important role in the survival of a living thing.

- For *A Trip to the City,* a big idea might be: Members of a family can have a special relationship even if they are different ages. Or, sometimes doing something is more fun if you share it with someone you love.

- For *Something for Dinner,* a big idea might be: It's a good idea to be open to trying new things. Or, don't reject something before you know what it is.

Of course, we would not expect seven-year-olds to express messages or big ideas in such academic language as that above. Instead, you would listen for a young child's version. You might hear: "It's a good thing lots of animals have feet because they need them to do stuff." Or, "They had a good day together and they love each other."

In Figure 5-19, you can see an excerpt from the discussion Mr. K's group had after reading *Something for Dinner.* These students are just beginning to be able to articulate messages from the simple texts they can read themselves. Remember, that they are talking about stories and nonfiction several times a day—in interactive read-aloud, shared reading, book clubs, guided reading, and reading conferences in independent reading. The ability to talk with each other about texts will grow over time.

Step Six: Make Teaching Points

Mr. K has been able to observe his students as they read orally and discuss the text. Now, he is ready to make one or two very specific instructional moves to help them expand their ability to read texts at this level. Teaching after the reading can be directed at any of the twelve systems of strategic actions. Mr. K has some teaching points in mind based on his recent observations, but he is open to decide on what will be most helpful to the readers' needs based on his lesson observations. Here are his teaching points after the discussion of *Something for Dinner* (see Figures 5-20 and 5-21).

Because the text is short and students read through it quickly, Mr. K is able to make two quick teaching points. You may have time for only one because you want your guided reading lesson to be about between fifteen and twenty minutes long at these early levels.

A Discussion of *Something for Dinner*

Speaker	Teacher/Student Interactions	Analysis of Interactions
Mr. K	**What are you thinking about this story?**	Asks for thinking
Donnie	It was funny. They didn't like any of it but then they liked pizza.	Share opinions
Tiara	I still don't like onions on a pizza.	Connect with characters
Zach	I don't like peppers.	
Alex	I love pizza, too.	
Mr. K	**What do you think about Pat and Sam on page 6? Look at their faces.**	Directs attention to pictures of the characters
		Asks for inference
Bradley	They just don't like anything. But look at their faces; they really don't like onions.	Notice and interpret illustrations
Zach	Look at Pat! She has her tongue out.	
Mr. K	**The picture can help you think about this part of the story.**	Directs attention to illustrations
Donnie	They aren't really thinking about it, about what it could be, and they don't even go and look.	Describes story events
Bradley	They probably know Dad will come up with something they like.	Makes an inference about the behaviors of characters
Mr. K	**Do you think that you could not like something and then like it when it is fixed a certain way—like on pizza?**	Invites students to connect with their own experience
Tiara	I used to not like mushrooms but I like them on pizza.	Relates own experience
Mr. K	**Do you think Dad is pretty smart? Why?**	Directs attention to another character
		Asks for inference and opinion
Donnie	He knows they like pizza so he's just kind of kidding them to ask about all those things, and the first thing they say is "no." They don't know they are getting pizza.	Makes inferences from character's actions
Mr. K	**So what do you learn from this story?**	Asks for articulation of message
Zach	You shouldn't just say "no." You should think maybe what you are going to get to eat might be good.	Articulates big idea or message of story
Tiara	But I would just pick the onions off and eat it. Everything else is good.	
Mr. K	**I agree. It's always a good idea to be open to trying new things.**	Confirms thinking

FIGURE 5-19 A Discussion of *Something for Dinner*

Teaching Point #1: Word Solving—Using Letter/Sound Analysis

Speaker	Teacher/Student Interactions	Analysis of Interactions
Mr. K	Go to page 8 and find the word *asked*. Take a good look at it and run you finger under it and say it.	Draws attention to a single word and its visual features
Students	*[Students locate the word]* Asked.	
Mr. K	*[Makes ask with magnet letters on the board and guides students to say the word, listening for the three sounds: /a//s//k/. Then he adds –ed to the end.]*	Makes the base word
		Points out letter/sound relationships in a word
		Helps students hear the sounds and connect them with letters in sequence
Students	Asked.	
Mr. K	You can see the word *ask* and notice the *–ed* ending, so the word is *asked* to show that it happened.	Points out *–ed* ending
Bradley	Why does it sound like a /t/ at the end?	
Mr. K	Sometimes the *–ed* at the end sounds like /t/ and sometimes it sounds like /d/. Read the sentence to a partner and check to be sure *asked* makes sense and looks right, too.	Points out two sounds that -ed ending is used to represent

FIGURE 5-20 Teaching Point #1: Word Solving—Using Letter/Sound Analysis

Teaching Point #2: Phrasing

Speaker	Teacher/Student Interactions	Analysis of Interactions
Mr. K	Turn to page 10 and think about how your reading sounds. Listen while I read this part. It's Sam's answer to Dad. *[Reads with phrasing and intonation]* "No, no! I don't like cheese," Sam said." What did you notice about my reading?	Models fluency and phrasing
		Asks for comments
Zach	It sounds like they are talking.	
Mr. K	They are talking in the story. Sam really means it when he says, "No, no! I don't like cheese." When you are reading and you see the talking marks, you need to make your voice sound just like Sam is saying it. Put your fingers on the talking marks that show when someone starts talking and stops talking. *[Students find quotation marks.]* Let's read it all together and put our words together and make it sound like Sam is talking.	Connects dialogue to phrasing
		Draws attention to quotation marks
		Models phrasing
Students	*[After reading, students take turns reading the page to a partner.]*	

FIGURE 5-21 Teaching Point #2: Phrasing

Responsive Teaching

In guided reading, your goal is to expand the reading competencies of the individual readers in the group. On the left side of the chart in Figure 5-22 are Mr. K's priorities for the group prior to reading. On the right side is the evidence of the actual teaching moves with the precise teaching language from the lesson.

Responsive Teaching

Teacher Priorities	Teaching Moves
Using Known Words to Monitor ◆ Begin to notice high-frequency words and use them to monitor	**During Introduction—page 4** ◆ Teacher: *What letter do you expect to see first in* want? ◆ Teacher confirms use of first letter: *Put your finger under the word* want *and look at the first letter.*
Searching for and Using Information ◆ Make meaningful attempts at unknown words	**During Reading—page 12** ◆ Tiara stops at difficulty: *"Dad put something in the . . ."* What's that word? ◆ Teacher: *Would* oven *or* stove *make sense there?* ◆ Tiara reads *oven.*
Fluency ◆ Use punctuation and intonation	**After Reading—page 10** ◆ Teacher models use of talking marks to make reading sound like the character: *I read, "No, no!" just like Sam would say it. Put your finger on the talking marks that show when someone starts talking and stops talking. Let's read it all together and put our words together to make it sound like Sam is talking.* ◆ Students read it like the character is talking.
Inferring ◆ Use of pictures to interpret characters' feelings	**After Reading—page 6** ◆ Teacher prompts readers to infer characters' feelings from the illustrations: *What do you think about Pat and Sam on page 6? Look at their faces.*

FIGURE 5-22 Responsive Teaching

Step Seven: Engage Students in Letter or Word Work

This quick two- or three-minute segment of the lesson does not take the place of the phonics/word work lesson that you provide in the comprehensive literacy design. But it gives students quick "hands-on" practice to apply what they know about how words work. Word work is pre-planned and designed to help students become quick and flexible at using principles that are important in solving words at this level. Here is an example from Mr. K's lesson using *Something for Dinner* (Figure 5-23).

Something for Dinner: Word Work

Mr. K	*[Gives each student an individual tray of magnetic letters (small cookie sheets or magnetic whiteboards). The letters are l, l, k, e, b, p, a, t, a, t, s, s, m (lined up at the top of the tray).]*
	Let's make some words. Here is the word *at*. Make *at*. Use both hands and pull the letters down quickly. Now use both hands and make the word *pat*.
Students	*[Students make* pat *with the letters.]*
Mr. K	Run your finger under the word *pat* as you say it.
Students	Pat.
Mr. K	Now make the word *mat* under the word *pat*. What do you notice about these two words?
Zach	They both have "at."
Bradley	They have different letters at the front.
Mr. K	Now make *sat*.
	You can make words that have the same part at the end.

FIGURE 5-23 *Something for Dinner:* Word Work

Some other choices for word work from *The Literacy Continuum* for this level include:

▶ Using magnetic letters to make words, take them apart, and make them again quickly.

▶ Using magnetic letters to make new words by changing the beginning (or the end, or the middle).

▶ Working with word cards to learn high-frequency words (saying, sorting, making connections).

▶ Saying words slowly and writing the sounds heard in boxes.

▶ Writing words quickly.

▶ Locating words quickly in the text.

Almost all students can profit from this quick application of some aspects of words. Even when students are expert decoders, they can still stretch their knowledge of words by taking words apart to notice meaningful units, which contributes to vocabulary growth.

Step Eight: Writing or Drawing About Reading (Optional)

Occasionally, you might want to ask students to reflect on their understanding of a text by drawing about it or writing about it. This option is particularly effective when a nonfiction topic or a story offers a great deal to think about. For example, a story might have an important lesson; a nonfiction topic might call for critical thinking or argument. The writing and/or drawing would not be completed in the guided reading lesson but can be accomplished independently as independent work. We caution against overuse of writing in response to guided reading lessons. It can be counterproductive; after all, readers don't necessarily write (as an assignment) every time they read!

This kind of writing is "writing about reading" and it supports comprehension. This written response to literature is one form of the writing in a multitext approach to literacy learning. There are many different options for writing about reading, such as:

Fiction

▶ Write about a character and what he/she is like.

▶ Write the lesson of a story.

▶ Write what you found interesting or were left wondering about.

▶ Write what you think will happen after the story ends.

Nonfiction

▶ Write about why you think the topic is important.

▶ Write what you learned about the topic.

▶ Write about what else you want to learn about the topic.

You can also use graphic organizers to bring structure to writing about reading. A graphic organizer is a kind of diagram that helps the reader think analytically about the structure of the text. The result is a visual display that shows relationships between facts, concepts, or ideas. For example, it might show sequence, cause and effect, or problem and solution. (Here, again, we use caution. Graphic organizers have been used as "fill out" worksheets, and we find no evidence of benefit from this, especially for early readers.)

You can find a great variety of graphic organizers, including many in our books, *Guiding Readers and Writers* and *Teaching for Comprehending and Fluency*. (Use your judgment about their appropriateness for early readers.) Students' first experience with graphic organizers are best supported by shared or interactive writing. Just take the basic diagram of a graphic organizer and draw it on chart paper. For example, you could draw two columns and label one "Problem" and the other "Solution." Or you could write a character's name in the center of a circle and draw lines out to attributes. All of this analysis is supported by rich talk between you and your students. And, you have to calculate the amount of time it will take. The first few times students are expected to use a graphic organizer you will want to use shared/interactive writing to teach students how to do it.

Step Nine: Reflect on the Lesson and Plan Tomorrow's Lesson

Step nine is not really a step. It's a signal that the cycle begins again. Make some notes as you finish the guided reading lesson. Even though you have some long-term goals for the students and a few pre-selected texts, you always want to adjust:

- The particular text or the level.
- The behaviors and understandings to notice, teach for, or support.
- The prompts you intend to use.
- The word work.

If you have implemented a good assessment plan and thought carefully about readers, not many adjustments will be needed.

Suggestions for Professional Development

1. Call a "planning workshop" with grade-level colleagues. Before the meeting, have colleagues visit the bookroom (or the collection of leveled texts) to select four books to be used with one guided reading group. (This would provide for about a week of instruction.) If you and your colleagues are new to guided reading and you are just beginning to collect the books, you may want to hold this session as you introduce a new collection of guided reading books. Have multiple copies of leveled books, as some pairs might select the same text.

2. Match up teachers who have a group reading at the same level and have them work as partners to create three guided reading lessons. Stress that these plans are concise and tentative because the teacher may make changes in response to students' reading behaviors.

3. You may want to create a form like the one in Figure 5-24 on the next page (also available as a blank form in Online Resources). Or, you can work with large sticky notes that can be placed on the front cover of each book. With three guided reading groups, lengthy plans are not possible.

4. At the end of the meeting, partners can share their plans.

Guided Reading Group			
Book Title	**1.**	**2.**	**3.**
Message			
Introduction ◆ Introductory Statement ◆ Points/Pages			
Reading ◆ Prompt for . . .			
Discussion ◆ Questions ◆ Prompts			
Specific Teaching ◆ Points ◆ Pages			
Word Work			

FIGURE 5-24 Planning for Guided Reading

CHAPTER 6

Planning for Effective Guided Reading Lessons

Lifting the Competencies of Every Reader

> *Over time, reading becomes a very fast and silent process and then we get little evidence of what the neural networks are doing.*
>
> —Marie M. Clay

Whether you are working with early or intermediate readers, the basic structure of the lesson remains the same; however, your teaching moves will show some important differences. In this chapter, we will again examine the steps in implementing guided reading and we'll provide some examples of those differences.

Implementing guided reading is a continuous process, so it is appropriate to show the steps as a cycle (see Figure 6-1). One of the practicalities of teaching is that it helps to have an overall plan for a week or two of teaching for each of your guided reading groups. That means having good assessment, a set of priorities for the group and for individuals within the group, and a selection of potential texts. You can make small, but significant, adjustments based on the systematic, ongoing observations.

There is an old saying: "In the first three years of school you learn how to read. After that, you read to learn." The problem with this common bit of wisdom is that it is simply not true. In the early years of school, students are indeed learning to read; and they are also learning ideas, content, and language and literary features *through* their reading. In the upper elementary and middle grades, students

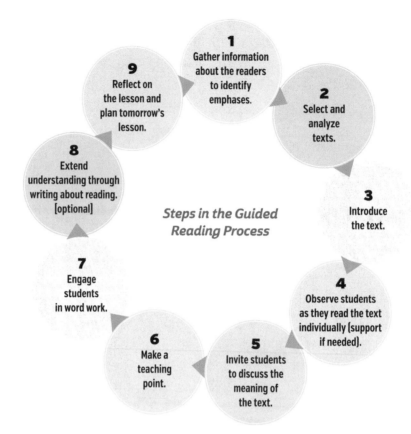

FIGURE 6-1 Steps in the Guided Reading Process

continue to expand their abilities to read even while they use reading as a tool for acquiring information. Reading is not something that is completely learned or "finished." People are always growing as readers; for example, even adults learn how to read texts in an unfamiliar academic discipline that offers challenging concepts, vocabulary, and ways of communicating knowledge. Expanding reading power and building mileage is especially critical in the years *after* students have established an early reading process, because entry level literacy is not enough, and because most students need continued teaching to develop a highly proficient reading process (see Figure 6-2).

The description above broadly represents the reading process of proficient readers as described in great detail in *The Fountas & Pinnell Literacy Continuum*. It is not enough to assign reading and then test knowledge of content. Across the grades, we need to teach students *how to* engage in the strategic actions they need to process increasingly complex fiction and nonfiction texts, for example:

⬧ Process increasingly complex texts and expand reading competency through problem solving.

⬧ Acquire vocabulary from reading, particularly the academic vocabulary necessary to comprehend in the disciplines.

⬧ Build background knowledge and also consistently apply it to reading new texts.

Throughout this book, we stress that reading is taught across many contexts; but it is in guided reading that you can provide highly specific, powerful teaching

The Reading Process of a Proficient Reader

Consistently using multiple sources of information in an integrated way.

Using a wide repertoire of flexible strategies for solving words rapidly and with little conscious effort.

Using a system for adding words to reading and writing vocabulary.

Consistently monitoring for understanding and active problem solving to clear up confusions.

Actively searching for meaning with automatic use of visual features of print (including letter/sound relationships).

Consistently demonstrating all dimensions of fluency.

Understanding and using characteristics of genre as a way of understanding and analyzing texts.

Adjusting purpose, expectations, and approaches to reading to fit with genre.

Making and articulating predictions along with active searching for information to confirm them.

Working actively to synthesize new knowledge during and after reading.

Noticing and using overall text structures (narrative, expository) to assist in comprehending texts.

Noticing and using underlying text structures in nonfiction texts (compare/contrast, description, cause/effect, problem/solution, temporal and chronological sequence) to comprehend texts.

Making and articulating inferences and support them with evidence from the text.

Thinking critically about the quality, accuracy, and authenticity of texts and articulating opinions.

Noticing and making comments on a wide range of aspects of the writer's craft.

Inferring and synthesizing the deeper messages of a text.

Applying the deeper messages in a text to their own lives.

FIGURE 6-2 The Reading Process of a Proficient Reader

that will lift individual students' reading abilities on a weekly and daily basis. Keep in mind that your teaching in guided reading will be much more effective if students are also participating in other reading contexts such as interactive read-aloud, shared reading, book clubs, and independent reading.

Step One: Know the Readers and Form Groups

The first priority is to know your students as readers. That's true across the grades, and it is just as important with intermediate/middle-level readers as with early readers. In Chapter 5, we briefly describe the *Fountas & Pinnell Benchmark Assessment System* as a systematic way to begin the year with good knowledge of each reader and the level at which to start teaching. You can begin to implement guided reading using any benchmark system or with your own selected set of leveled books. But it is important to find a place to begin with guided reading, and that means considering not only accuracy but also fluency, quality of processing, and comprehension. A systematic assessment system will help you know where to start. Once you have begun your system of regularly collected reading records, you will continue to inform the emphases of your teaching in the lesson.

As an example, let's look at six students in Mrs. A's fourth-grade classroom, several months into the school year. She has data from recent reading records, and notes on comprehension, as well as anecdotal notes from guided reading lessons (see Figures 6-3 and 6-4).

The data gathered from reading records, including the comprehension conversations, yields a great deal of information (see sample in Figures 6-5 and 6-6). As with early readers, the "level" students achieve is less important than your analysis and that includes the left side of the record where readers' specific actions are coded. The levels they read with high accuracy are similar, but analysis of the processing and comprehension notes indicate different needs. Most have excellent word-solving (sometimes called "decoding") strategies and can read with high accuracy. But Mrs. A notes some differences in processing, for example:

▶ Sam and Cardell are not consistently recognizing and using punctuation, but Craig, Julia, Cheyenne, and David are using punctuation to assist phrasing and intonation.

▶ Julia, Craig, Cheyenne, and David demonstrate most dimensions of fluency (pausing, phrasing, word stress, intonation, rate); but Sam and Cardell display some slow, laborious reading that does not reflect the meaning of the text. Most of these readers need to improve their oral reading fluency.

▶ Julia, Craig, and Sam read level S with 95–96% accuracy, and it looks like level S is the appropriate instructional level for them.

▶ Sam, David, and Julia are showing too much overt self-correction behavior.

▶ Julia has most aspects of the reading process under control. She reads with 95% accuracy. Her reading is smooth and efficient. Some overt processing can be observed as she self-corrects on six occasions on these pages. Two errors are the result of a syntactical miscue and the other error fit all three sources of information.

	Julia	Craig	Cheyenne	David	Cardell	Sam
Instructional Text Level	S	S	T	T	T	S
Accuracy	95%	96%	94%	97%	96%	95%
Comprehension	Approaching Proficiency	Approaching Proficiency	Approaching Proficiency	Approaching Proficiency	Proficient	Approaching Proficiency
Fluency	2	2	1	2	1	1
Self-Corrections	6	2	2	8	0	9

FIGURE 6-3 Reading Records from Six Fourth-Graders

▶ Craig reads with 96% accuracy and his reading is also smooth and phrased. He does some efficient problem solving on multisyllable words, rereads to self-correct one error based on structure, and on another he self-corrects immediately. All other uncorrected errors on this page fit meaning, structure, and visual information.

<table>
<tr><td colspan="2" align="center">*Guided Reading Observations*</td></tr>
<tr><td>

Julia, Level S

- Demonstrated many overt self-corrections
- Summarized in an organized way, including almost all of the important ideas and information stated in the text
- Articulated inferences but without citing evidence to support them
- Showed some evidence of ability to think analytically about the text
- Noticed text qualities that are interesting
- Provided evidence for opinions

</td><td>

Craig, Level S

- Summarized in an organized way with all the important information
- Stated some inferences with evidence
- Stated main idea in vague terms
- Used minimal academic language

</td></tr>
<tr><td>

Cheyenne, Level T

- Summarized events in an organized way
- Inferred mother/daughter relationship
- Noted character change but did not cite evidence for the change
- Had difficulty in analysis and critical thinking

</td><td>

David, Level T

- Summarized most of the important information
- Stated big ideas in vague ways
- Did not make predictions or connections between the problem and the solution
- Did some analysis but had difficulty with critical thinking
- Did not use academic language
- Demonstrated too much overt processing

</td></tr>
<tr><td>

Sam, Level S

- Summarized all of the important information in organized way
- Consistently read over punctuation
- Had slow processing of multisyllable words efficiently; too many self-corrections
- Inferred characters' motivations without citing evidence
- Was unable to clearly state the writer's message

</td><td>

Cardell, Level T

- Had laborious processing around text and didn't adjust reading of text features
- Tended to ignore syntax and read over punctuation
- Summarized some important information in organized way
- Stated big ideas

</td></tr>
</table>

FIGURE 6-4 Notes on Comprehension

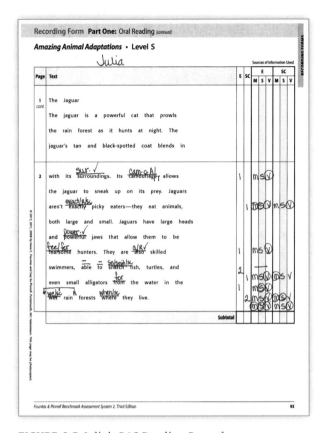

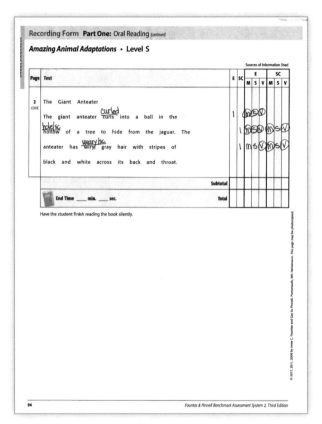

FIGURE 6-5 Julia's BAS Reading Record

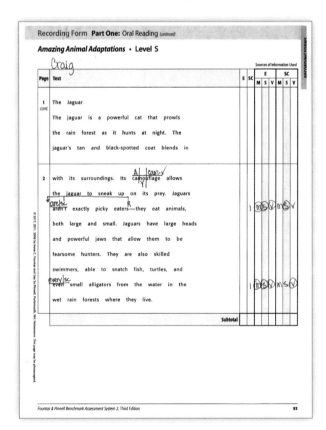

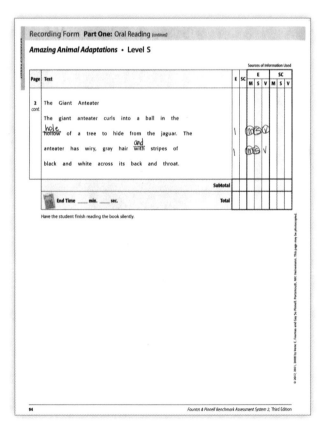

FIGURE 6-6 Craig's BAS Reading Record

Comprehension is best assessed on texts that students can read with high enough accuracy. Mrs. A notices some differences; for example:

▶ All of the students appear to be strong in literal comprehension (thinking within the text); but Julia, Cheyenne, Cardell, and David need to be able to make inferences with evidence, as well as connect ideas and content across texts, and generally bring more thinking to what is implied but not stated by the writer.

▶ Five of the six readers need strong teaching to be able to infer the writer's message.

▶ All of the students need strong teaching to be able to think analytically and critically about a text.

▶ All of the students need to expand their ability to use academic language and domain- (disciplinary-) specific vocabulary.

Reflecting on the data, Mrs. A places these students in a group and starts them on level S. You can read her priorities for the group in Figure 6-7. Each time Mrs. A convenes the group, she has these priorities in mind for the group and also for individuals. It helps to have notes on your priorities so you can refer to them. They will, of course, change over time.

Planning Sheet for Guided Reading Groups

Priorities for the group:

(1) Continue to demonstrate and prompt for all dimensions of fluency.

(2) Promote deeper thinking beyond and about the text and insist on citing evidence.

(3) Demonstrate and prompt for the use of academic language to talk about texts.

(4) Demonstrate and prompt for taking apart multisyllable words and noticing their meaningful parts (contributing both to word solving and vocabulary development).

Julia	David
Demonstrate and prompt for making inferences with evidence. Support ability to analyze texts and notice aspects of the writer's craft, including the big idea of the book.	Demonstrate and prompt for predictions and connections within texts. Support inferring the writer's message by citing evidence.
Craig	**Cardell**
Support deeper thinking in terms of analysis of the text. Help him notice aspects of the writer's craft and support inferences with evidence using academic language.	Prompt for aspects of fluency. Check on summarizing in a clear and logical way, as well as inferring problem and solution in nonfiction texts.
Cheyenne	**Sam**
Demonstrate and prompt for analytic and critical thinking about the text; help her to notice text features and underlying text structures. Prompt to support opinions with evidence from the text.	Demonstrate and prompt for phrasing, intonation, and use of punctuation. Support inferring and noticing aspects of the writer's craft

FIGURE 6-7 Priorities for the Group and Individual Readers

Your priorities may be written on sticky notes that you keep on a sheet inside the folder for this group or on one of the record keeping and planning sheets (see Chapter 10 and Online Resources). Having them handy will help you make some quick teaching decisions "on the run." After reflecting on students' strengths and needs (see Figure 6-8), Mrs. A selected a few behaviors and understandings to notice, teach for, and support in the lesson.

You draw out these priorities from the complex data available on students, but remember that you are always gathering more information. If you observe a behavior or evidence of understanding and find that a student is demonstrating it consistently, then there is no need to teach for it. As students approach different genres of texts, you discover new areas that need your teaching support. The goal is to make every teaching move powerful. As with early readers, you may want to use some language from *Prompting Guide, Part 1;* for example, prompts to encourage attention to fluency (see Figure 6-9).

It is apparent that Mrs. A needs to check on the fluency of some readers in the group and to prompt them to read with phrasing and use punctuation; however, at this level she wants a minimum of interruption while students are reading the text for the first time. Mrs. A can provide support in reading with phrasing and noticing punctuation in an introduction to the story and revisiting the text. Some of these readers are interrupting their own reading with too much overt processing. Thinking about the meaning and also learning more about taking words apart with efficiency will help to smooth out their reading. This kind of specific language is effective because it tells the reader precisely what action is needed or what the reader actually did (see Figure 6-10).

Mrs. A's Reflection

All students in this group are able to read level S with high accuracy. I'll need to make sure that all the readers have the support they need to comprehend at a proficient level. I may sample their oral reading several times as we begin to read this level text. I'll also sample oral reading from Cardell and Sam to help them strengthen their fluency at this level. Cardell can read at a higher level than S, but I am concerned about the amount and kind of processing he has to do. I'd like for him to read with smoothness and ease. Level S should provide a good instructional context for encouraging fluency. As he improves, he may move quickly to more challenging levels. Julia, Craig, and Cheyenne are well placed for reading with comprehension. Nonfiction texts at this level will offer opportunities to notice text features, underlying text structures, and disciplinary-specific vocabulary. I will want to get more information about their comprehension of fiction as they read and discuss texts. They will need some strong teaching to notice how writers structure plots and show character change. Everyone in the group needs to be supported in analyzing the text and thinking critically about it, for both fiction and nonfiction.

FIGURE 6-8 Mrs. A's Reflection

Prompts to Encourage Attention to Fluency

Strategic Action	Teach [Demonstrate the action and/or tell the reader what to do.]	Prompt [Remind the reader to take action in a certain way.]	Reinforce [Affirm an action the reader has taken independently.]
Intonation	• Listen to me read this and notice what I do at the punctuation. • Listen to me read this. Can you hear how I sound like the characters who are talking?	• Make your voice sound like the character is talking. • Make your voice show what you think the author means. • Make your voice show that you understand what the author means.	• You read the punctuation. • You made it sound like the character(s) were talking. • You made that story (part) sound interesting. • You showed the author's meaning in your voice.

FIGURE 6-9 Prompts to Encourage Attention to Fluency

Facilitative Language for Supporting Comprehension in the Discussion After Reading

Strategic Action	Examples of Language
Inferring	• Sometimes the writer says something and means more. What is the writer really trying to say? • What do you think this character really meant by saying that? [fiction] • How do you know [character] has changed? What does the writer want readers to know about _____ [character]?
Making Connections	• What do you know about these times [this place, character, situation]? • Were you reminded of anything in your own life? • How did the way this author told about the topic differ from the way _____ did?
Synthesizing	• How did this book change the way you think about _____? • How is what you learned different from what you understood before? • What can you learn about the genre from this piece? How does this fit with what you already know?
Predicting	• You know _____ [author, genre, content] of this book. What do you think it will be like? • Are your predictions confirmed or discarded? • How do you think the setting will influence the plot and characters? [fiction] • Now what are you thinking the big ideas of this story might be? • What details [words, phrases] does the author use that help you predict what might happen next? [fiction and narrative nonfiction]
Analyzing	• Why do you think the author chose this organization for the ideas he tells about? [nonfiction] • What is the problem and how is it solved? [fiction] • What does the writer do to make [character, topic, plot, setting] interesting? Can you take us to an example?
Critiquing	• How believable is the information? [nonfiction] • How do you feel about the story [topic] now compared to when you first started reading it? • Are the facts consistent throughout the book? How current is the information on the topic? • Did the illustrations [text features] help to support your understanding of the subject? How? [nonfiction]

FIGURE 6-10 Facilitative Language for Supporting Comprehension in the Discussion After Reading

You can also find some examples of facilitative language that draws attention to meaning making in *Prompting Guide, Part 2,* which focuses on comprehension. This kind of specific language is useful for boosting the level of the discussion after reading. When you provoke discussion using this specific language, you are asking students to share their thinking and simultaneously prompting them to "go deeper." There is no need to repeat their remarks, only to ask for elaboration or extension; and there is no need to label them as "right" or "wrong." Many students have learned to search for the answer the teacher expects; and, usually unconsciously, teachers ask until they get the answer they want and then say "right" or "good." It's very easy to fall into this pattern. The real goal of the discussion in guided reading is the expression of thinking and enjoyment in discussion; and you might even hope that students respectfully disagree with you or each other, because that is when thinking is sharpened the most.

Step Two: Select and Analyze Texts

The next step in the guided reading lesson is to select and analyze texts that give this group of students opportunities to learn, so Mrs. A's priorities will be a factor in her selection of texts.

Selecting Texts

For all students from the first years of school to upper elementary and middle school, text selection is very important. You can read about text selection in Chapter 14 and also see some guidelines in Chapter 5, Figure 5-8. The Guided Reading section of *The Literacy Continuum* also offers more support for text selection. Some additional things to think about when you are working with intermediate/middle-level readers are listed in Figure 6-11.

As with early readers, the goal with guided reading is to teach for strategic actions that readers can use in all of their reading. It is expected that all students are independently reading books of their own choice, every day. You provide minilessons to remind them of what they need to pay attention to as they read, and they share the observations of their reading.

We recommend short texts for guided reading even at intermediate and middle-grade levels. The things students learn reading short texts can be applied to longer texts in indepen-

Considerations for Selecting Texts for Intermediate/Middle-Level Readers

- Select nonfiction texts with compelling topics and stories that will engage readers.

- Select texts that have excellent examples of high-quality writing in the genre.

- Examine the illustrations to assure that nonfiction texts include complex graphics that help readers learn how to synthesize information from them and integrate it with the body of the text.

- Assure that fiction texts have high quality illustrations (where applicable) that enhance the meaning of the text and communicate the mood.

- Assure that the range of texts are accurate, culturally sensitive, and reflect the diversity of our world.

- Select texts that have deeper messages so that students can reach out for them.

FIGURE 6-11 Considerations for Selecting Texts for Intermediate/Middle-Level Readers

dent reading. Many good nonfiction texts are short; you could think of them as feature articles that offer challenges in reading but focus on a topic and communicate messages in 24 to 36 pages. When you use short texts, readers can apply their new learning on a novel text every day. Occasionally, you may want to use a novel for guided reading to build stamina, but we caution against reading the same book over weeks at a time. Move quickly with students reading several chapters each day to finish in one or two weeks.

Given that most of the texts you select for guided reading can be read in a day, you may want to select several books per group as you plan for a week of instruction. The practicalities of teaching demand that teachers make overall monthly/yearly plans and detailed weekly plans (and you always need to have them in case you need a substitute teacher).

Many schools where guided reading is implemented have a book room with multiple titles at each level (see Chapter 21). We suggest you visit the book room weekly to select and return multiple copies of the titles you need. Remember that you can always change your plans based on the reading behaviors of students from day to day. Then, you return the books to the book room. You do not need to keep copies of the book in the classroom unless a student specifically asks to read one again.

Most teachers select enough titles for a week (and sometimes two) of instruction, but remember that you are not locked in to your selections. You can use them in any order and also change your decision based on your observations of your students' reading behaviors. In general, students at the upper levels spend more time on a level because there are wider steps and greater variety between levels. The key is to make sure that they are comprehending what they read in a proficient way.

For the group of readers Mrs. A identifies, she concludes that these books are appropriate because each presents a variety of opportunities to expand the readers' systems of strategic actions:

▶ *Odoriferous Foods* (*Fountas & Pinnell Classroom*, in press) is an expository nonfiction text that focuses on potent-smelling foods from various cultures-foods that are considered delicacies, despite being very smelly foods (see Figure 6-12). Tier 2 words include *bacteria, fermented, durian, rinds,* and *herring.* Included in the text are tasting tips that tell the reader how to sample these foods for maximum enjoyment. Readers learn the history of each food's popularity, what makes it smelly, and where it can be found. Maps highlight the specific geographic areas where the foods originate.

▶ *Once Upon a Time Machine* (*Fountas & Pinnell Classroom*, in press) is a humorous science fiction story that gives readers opportunities to notice characteristics of the genre (see Figure 6-13).The story is told as a first-person narrative and features two main characters, Lydia and Jack. It's funny until the tale turns serious when Jack is stuck in the past and no longer exists in the present. Vocabulary includes Tier 3 words such as *stabilizers and teleportation.* The sepia-toned illustrations create an eerie mood at times.

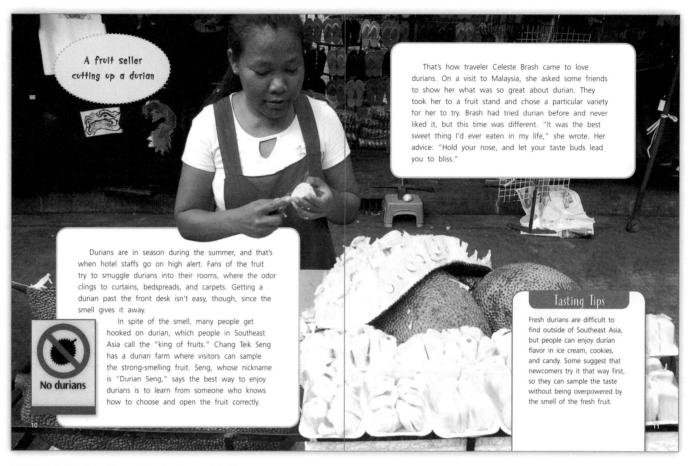

A fruit seller cutting up a durian

That's how traveler Celeste Brash came to love durians. On a visit to Malaysia, she asked some friends to show her what was so great about durian. They took her to a fruit stand and chose a particular variety for her to try. Brash had tried durian before and never liked it, but this time was different. "It was the best sweet thing I'd ever eaten in my life," she wrote. Her advice: "Hold your nose, and let your taste buds lead you to bliss."

Durians are in season during the summer, and that's when hotel staffs go on high alert. Fans of the fruit try to smuggle durians into their rooms, where the odor clings to curtains, bedspreads, and carpets. Getting a durian past the front desk isn't easy, though, since the smell gives it away.

In spite of the smell, many people get hooked on durian, which people in Southeast Asia call the "king of fruits." Chang Teik Seng has a durian farm where visitors can sample the strong-smelling fruit. Seng, whose nickname is "Durian Seng," says the best way to enjoy durians is to learn from someone who knows how to choose and open the fruit correctly.

Tasting Tips

Fresh durians are difficult to find outside of Southeast Asia, but people can enjoy durian flavor in ice cream, cookies, and candy. Some suggest that newcomers try it that way first, so they can sample the taste without being overpowered by the smell of the fresh fruit.

No durians

FIGURE 6-12 *Odoriferous Foods*, Pages 10–11

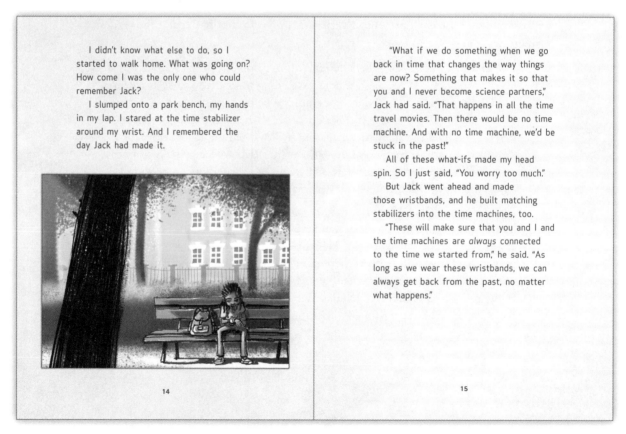

I didn't know what else to do, so I started to walk home. What was going on? How come I was the only one who could remember Jack?

I slumped onto a park bench, my hands in my lap. I stared at the time stabilizer around my wrist. And I remembered the day Jack had made it.

"What if we do something when we go back in time that changes the way things are now? Something that makes it so that you and I never become science partners," Jack had said. "That happens in all the time travel movies. Then there would be no time machine. And with no time machine, we'd be stuck in the past!"

All of these what-ifs made my head spin. So I just said, "You worry too much."

But Jack went ahead and made those wristbands, and he built matching stabilizers into the time machines, too.

"These will make sure that you and I and the time machines are *always* connected to the time we started from," he said. "As long as we wear these wristbands, we can always get back from the past, no matter what happens."

FIGURE 6-13 *Once Upon a Time Machine*, Pages 14–15

▶ *Bats in the City* (*Fountas & Pinnell Classroom*, in press) is a nonfiction expository text that features a massive colony of bats that live under a bridge in Austin, Texas (see Figure 6-14). The text includes Tier 3 words such as *nocturnal, pollinate,* and *conservationist.* Readers gain information about bats and how they live but also learn how public opinion is influenced by misinformation. The text structure is mainly chronological order. Graphics include a drawing that illustrates why the bridge is a good home for bats, as well as newspaper headlines and movie posters from the 1980s.

All three texts are short enough to read in one day and they present different opportunities. Science fiction, for example, offers some very specific challenges. Readers need to accept unworldly events as true within the story, and technology plays a role. Both nonfiction texts challenge the reader with complex ideas and a combination of underlying text structures. These three texts offered a good range of learning for Mrs. A's group of students over three guided reading lessons.

Analyzing Texts

You will find that text analysis will make a big difference in your teaching. As you select the texts for guided reading, you are already engaging in analysis. Almost always your analytic thinking about texts is accomplished informally, "on the run," as you are picking up and organizing materials for a week or two of teaching.

Analysis is an area of complex thinking because *no single factor makes a text easier or harder.* Instead you'll want to consider at least ten text features, each of which contains multiple characteristics. These factors are summarized in Chapter 5, Figure 5-13, and discussed more fully in Chapter 13.

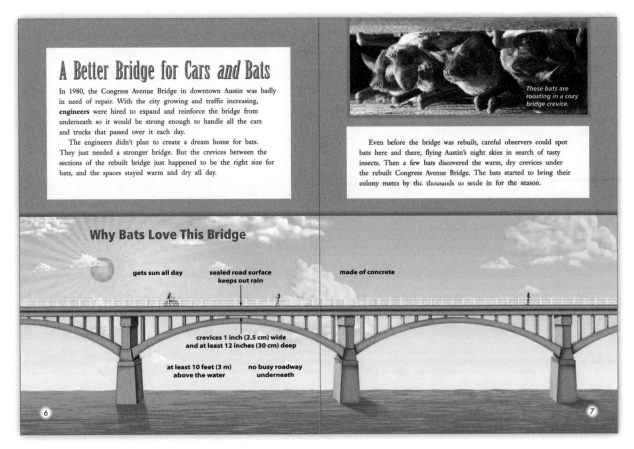

FIGURE 6-14 *Bats in the City, Pages 6–7*

The more you analyze texts with these ten factors in mind, the quicker and easier you will find it to select appropriate texts and plan your teaching moves. As discussed, you may occasionally want to use longer texts (for example, novels) in guided reading. That means you would need to break up the reading over several days. Many chapter books have been analyzed and leveled and appear on the Fountas & Pinnell Leveled Books website (*www.fountasandpinnell.com*). The process of introducing and reading the text is the same except that students read a section each day. In general, you can accomplish more and give students greater variety in reading experiences if most of the texts you use are short enough to be read in one day.

Some questions to ask when thinking about the texts for guided reading at levels L–Z are:

▶ What conceptual challenges will students find in this book? What ideas will they need to stretch their thinking to understand?

▶ What opportunities are there for students to learn something new about genre?

▶ What is the organizational structure of the text and how will it be challenging to students?

▶ What vocabulary will be challenging? (Notice Tier 2 and Tier 3 words.)

▶ What multisyllable words may be challenging for students to decode? (Notice words that offer opportunities for noticing meaningful parts of words.)

▶ What opportunities to acquire and understand new vocabulary (or to expand understanding of existing vocabulary) are present in this book?

▶ What academic language will be required for students to discuss the text?

▶ What are the "big ideas" (over and above the content of the book) that students will need to infer?

▶ What background knowledge will students need to access as they read the text?

▶ What challenges will text features such as graphics have for the readers?

▶ Can the content, ideas, or structure of this text be connected to any other texts they have read or heard read aloud?

▶ How does the content of the text (or the theme and plot of the story) connect to students' lives?

▶ How does this text help readers make connections with essential questions?

After this quick analysis (and with her extensive knowledge of readers), Mrs. A is ready to provide a powerful introduction. As you engage in this kind of reflection, you can anticipate the areas where this group of students might need more support. If they are familiar with graphics such as the ones on pages 6 and 7, for example, you might not need to focus on these pages in the introduction. But if you think they are unfamiliar with them, and they are important in comprehending the book, you may want to draw their attention to them. When you become accustomed to text analysis, your introductions will be more powerful and more concise.

Notes for *Bats in the City*

There will be no time for extensive written analyses of the texts you select and use in guided reading. Sometimes publishers provide some kind of analysis, and this may be helpful, but, ultimately, you will find it most useful to do your own thinking and make a few brief notes to help you in introducing the text. Here are Mrs. A's notes on her selection of *Bats in the City* (see Figure 6-15).

Bats in the City
- Expository nonfiction (with underlying structures of description and chronological sequence, problem and solution, compare and contrast
- Tier 2 words: adapt, co-exist, colony, crevice, massive, petition, proclaims, reinforced, thriving, roost
- Tier 3 words: nocturnal, pollinate, conservationist
- Dramatic lead
- Graphic: drawing showing conditions at the bridge
- Content: facts about bats, public attitude toward bats, power of education
- Tools: table of contents, headings, sidebars, glossary, captions, labels
- Complex sentences
- Connectives: while, at the very least, over time, once
- Big ideas: fear and misinformation are often at the root of prejudice. Education can influence public opinion. Different species of wildlife can live together and benefit from each other.

FIGURE 6-15 Mrs. A's Notes on *Bats in the City*, Level S

Step Three: Introduce the Text

The third step (but the first thing you do in the lesson) is to introduce the text. The introduction is concise, propels the readers into the text, and leaves important and productive reading work for them to do. Sometimes the introduction has been erroneously interpreted as "removing all the challenges of a text" or "telling the readers what to think." Nothing could be farther from the truth. (Refer to Chapter 14, Figure 14-4, to see our description of what the introduction is meant to do, and what it is not meant to do.)

If you use a text several times with different students, the process of introducing it will get easier because you will become very familiar with the demands of the text and your analysis will come readily to mind; however, each time, the introduction will vary because:

▶ The students and their current understandings vary.

▶ They will become involved in the conversation and turn it in new ways.

Over time, you will develop a repertoire of leveled texts that you have analyzed and used for teaching (always adding new high-quality texts we hope).

Remembering the priorities for the group described earlier, let's look at an excerpt from Mrs. A's introduction to *Bats in the City* (see Figure 6-16). You can see that intermediate readers vary a great deal in the background knowledge they bring to reading. It helps when students share some information.

The conversation during the introduction informs Mrs. A that her students have some background information (and some misconceptions) about bats. She

Introduction to *Bats in the City,* Level S

Speaker	Teacher/Student Interactions	Analysis of Interactions
Mrs. A	Today you are going to read *Bats in the City* by Martha Pickerill. This nonfiction book is about a large colony of bats that live under a bridge in Austin, Texas. You can see bats in flight over Austin on the front cover. What do you know about bats?	Introduces title, author, and topic Probes background knowledge
Cardell	They can fly at night and they don't have to see. They just feel their way.	Share background knowledge
Julia	I heard they can get in your hair and they are like vampires. They suck blood.	
David	Some people have a bat house because they are like birds and they eat insects like mosquitos.	
Sam	They're like vampire bats.	
Craig	I agree with Cardell. They have something kind of like radar.	
Cheyenne	I don't know much. They fly and they are kind of scary.	
Mrs. A	You know some things about bats but you are going to learn more in this book. The writer is telling the story of a particular group, or colony, of bats. A colony of Mexican free-tailed bats lives in the United States, Mexico, and South America. They migrate back and forth from Texas to Mexico. Do you know what that means?	Recognizes students' background knowledge and provides more Probes background knowledge
Sam	Maybe they migrate like birds. They go to warm weather when it's cold and then go back when summer comes.	Predicts word meaning
Mrs. A	That's what migration means. Look at pages 6 and 7. Get a good look at the drawing with labels and then let's talk about what you learned from it.	Affirms student knowledge Draws attention to graphic
Students	*[Work with a partner]*	
Mrs. A	**What did you learn?**	Asks for comments on reading
Craig	They like the bridge because it gets sun. Maybe the concrete gets warm like the road and it keeps them warm.	Share thinking with the group
Cheyenne	It's not in the water. I think it said it's 10 feet above it, so that's like a diving board. And they don't have to worry about the rain.	
David	What does *crevices* mean?	
Craig	I think it's the little grooves that maybe they hang on because they hang upside down when they sleep.	Contribute to each others' thinking

FIGURE 6-16 Introduction to *Bats in the City,* Level S

Introduction to *Bats in the City*, Level S

Speaker	Teacher/Student Interactions	Analysis of Interactions
Mrs. A	That might be true. Read the sidebar on page 7, and then let's talk about it.	Prompts to search for information
David	They liked the crevices and then they decided to all come there.	Shares information
Mrs. A	Look at pages 9 and 10 and read the headlines and the poster.	Prompts to search for information
Cheyenne	People are afraid of bats. Maybe they suck your blood?	Share information
Sam	People are afraid of the bats.	
Mrs. A	Many people in Austin were afraid and did not want those bats there. So, as you read, you will have to decide whether the people had the right information. Do you see the word in bold on page 9? *Conservationists*. Read the sentence. What do you think it means?	Prompts thinking
Julia	Conservation means taking care of the environment and animals.	Shares definition
Mrs. A	The suffix *-ist* means a person who does something. So look in the glossary to read the definition. Remember to use the glossary for a word in bold if you need to learn or think more about its meaning.	Clarifies a vocabulary word Reminds students of the glossary
Cheyenne	It's somebody who protects the animals and plants.	Shares glossary definition
Mrs. A	So conservationists want to protect the bats and help people understand them. You will find out why as you read. Think about how the people were so opposed to or afraid of the bats that there was a petition to get rid of them, and also think about why the bats were good for Austin.	Prompts for thinking while reading and tells students what they will be expected to talk about after reading

FIGURE 6-16 *(continued)*

does not try to give readers full information about bats, but prompts them to notice the information in the text. Not all of the technical words are discussed in the introduction; readers are reminded to use the glossary for terms they do not understand. But in the introduction, students are also prompted to read the word in a sentence and use context to think about the meaning. With this short introduction, this particular group of readers are now ready to read the text with understanding.

Step Four: Students Read the Text

At this level students are reading the text silently, so observation of the process is not possible unless you ask them to read aloud. The goal is for each student to have the time for serious concentrated processing of the entire text (or a substantial part of it). Sometimes the reading practice has been to introduce a page or two, have students read and then discuss it, and introduce another page or two. In our view, this practice makes reading a tedious process and breaks up the meaning so much that it may interfere with comprehension of the text as a whole. You might even feel that you are dragging the students through the book and it takes a very long time. Additionally, students need to develop the stamina to read page after page consecutively without stopping. Communicate the expectation that after the introduction, students will read individually and silently. You can be available for support if needed; but many teachers find that they can leave the students reading at the table and move around the classroom to have reading conferences with other individuals. (You want the students to begin reading with the introduction fresh in their minds, so it is not a good idea to send them to their own seats to read.)

If you want to check on an individual reader's processing, then you may sample some oral reading and teach for, prompt for, or reinforce strategic actions. One way to accomplish this is to lean in or move a chair or stool behind the student, have him turn slightly and read very softly—just loud enough for you to hear. You can take notes and perhaps have a brief interaction with the student that supports the problem solving through the text; but we caution against testing comprehension in the middle of the reading of a book. It will prevent the individual student from finishing the text and will, again, disrupt comprehension. Students will learn quickly that they can consult you at difficulty, but in general, they keep reading to the end.

If some students are reading too slowly (and the level is appropriate), you may want to interact briefly to support phrased, fluent reading. Some students may read too fast or skip words and lines, and you'll need to prompt for closer self-monitoring. In general, your students should finish reading the text about the same time so that you can move smoothly into the discussion but inevitably some will finish earlier and you don't want a long wait time. Set up some routines for students to use for a few minutes when they finish reading to allow for varied finish times. For example, they can:

- Go back in the text and use sticky notes to mark places they wish to discuss.

- Jot down any question they have about the story or nonfiction text.

- Use a reader's notebook to jot down first thoughts about what they read.

- Read their independent reading book.

Step Five: Discuss the Text

The discussion is a conversation, and each student should understand the expectation of contributing to it. The purpose is not to "test" students by asking question after question. You may want to open the discussion by getting students to respond to the ideas you left them thinking about in the introduction. You might begin the discussion with an open-ended invitation to students to share their thinking; for example:

- What are you thinking about this story (book, topic, biography)?

- Who would like to start the discussion by sharing your thinking?

- (Name of student), you had a question.

- Who wants to get us started on the discussion?

- Who has an idea to start us off?

Sometimes you may want to begin by asking students to "turn and talk" with a partner for a short time (about a minute). In this way, students can get their first thinking into words and then have something to share with the group.

Overall, you want to support students in the discussion so that they help each other reach for the deeper meaning of the text. Eventually, you want them to articulate (in their own words) the "big ideas" or messages that the writer intended. It is also true that as students bring their own thinking to the text, they construct meaning even beyond the writer's intent. There is no one "right" answer when you come to the point of discussing the messages of the text. There are important big ideas or messages you want to be sure all students understand, but they should also take their own meaning from the text and be able to offer textual evidence to support it.

You can use facilitative language to help students extend their thinking and to move the discussion along. Be sure to help students learn that they need to back up their thinking with evidence and much of that evidence comes from the text that they have just read. Also, you may want to redirect the discussion to keep students grounded in the text rather than taking it off to other (sometimes only marginally related) topics. You will find many examples in *Prompting Guide, Part 2* and *Genre Prompting Guides*, related to specific systems of strategic actions. Remember that the discussion time in guided reading lessons cannot be very long. Typically, students talk about the book for about five minutes and then you take the time to make a specific teaching point, which also may involve discussion. Examples such as these promote conversation as opposed to a chain of teacher questions and student answers.

- What is important about this story (or topic)?
- Is there another way to think about that?
- I hear you saying that _____.
- Say more about that.
- Let's return to what we were talking about before.
- Let's return to our discussion of _____.
- What makes you think that?
- Find an example that shows what you are talking about.
- Take us to the part of the story/book that makes you think that.
- This part makes me think _____.

In Figure 6-17, you can see an excerpt from Mrs. A's discussion of *Bats in the City.*

As the last example indicates, it's valid to share your own thinking and students will appreciate it. Also, you will occasionally want to demonstrate the use of academic language to talk about texts.

It probably will not be possible—nor would it be very interesting—to discuss every part of the book in an exhaustive way. You can encourage students to extend their understanding by doing research on the topic or reading other books. Also, any book that they enjoy in guided reading can be an example for sharing at the end of readers' workshop or a text to write about in a reader's notebook (see Chapter 23).

Discussion of *Bats in the City,* Level S

Speaker	Teacher/Student Interactions	Analysis of Interactions
Mrs. A	Talk with a partner to share your first thoughts about *Bats in the City.*	Prompts discussion
Students	*[Talk in pairs]*	
Mrs. A	Who has an idea to get us started?	Asks for comments
Julia	I didn't know that bats are really good.	Shares new thinking
Mrs. A	What evidence does the writer give us that bats are helpful to people?	Prompts to elaborate with evidence
Julia	On page 11 there's a whole list of things. *[Reads several facts aloud.]*	Provides evidence
Mrs. A	Julia is talking about an important point the writer made. Let's have some other comments on that.	Invites elaboration on a point
Craig	When they told people bats were good, then they changed their minds about them.	Share information and evidence
Cheyenne	They even named their hockey team the Bats.	
David	They found out the bats were good for plants and they won't really hurt people. I already knew about bats eating mosquitoes but I didn't know bats were good for plants.	
Sam	Some other places are building bridges now to have bats, and people like watching them.	
Mrs. A	You are giving some good evidence that bats and people can live in the same place and help each other. What was the problem in this book?	Prompts to talk about the problem
Craig	The people didn't want the bats. They started a petition to get them killed.	Identify the problem
David	They had all these movies and people were afraid they were like vampires.	
Mrs. A	Take us to the part you are talking about, David.	Asks for evidence
David	It's on page 8. There's a movie poster. Well, it says in the legend it's a fake, but it looks scary. And there are headlines and this is a real newspaper.	Provides evidence
Cardell	So people got scared and they wanted to get rid of them. But there was the bat conservationist group and they started giving people the facts. And then they got to be proud of the bats.	
Mrs. A	So you are saying that fear was really causing the problem.	Clarifies what students are saying
Cheyenne	It was because they didn't have the right information. They had the wrong information and it made them scared and want to kill the bats.	Provides evidence
Mrs. A	So now that we've determined the problem, let's see how the people solve the problem. Look at pages 10 and 11. Talk about how the people help the bats and how bats help people.	Prompts discussion of a specific idea

FIGURE 6-17 Discussion of *Bats in the City,* Level S

Discussion of *Bats in the City,* Level S

Speaker	Teacher/Student Interactions	Analysis of Interactions
Sam	The bats get a good place to live and now the people protect them, and bats do all the things that help people, like eating bugs.	Identifies solution
Mrs. A	**What do you think the writer's message is—the important, big idea the writer is trying to say to you?**	Asks directly for statement of the big ideas
Cardell	That people and animals can help each other and we should protect them.	Infer big ideas
Cheyenne	You have to get good information to help you overcome your fears.	
Julia	Sometimes if you want people to do the right thing you have to educate them.	
Mrs. A	**So we've identified the problem—fear, and we've identified the solution—education about bats. Sometimes authors organize a text using a problem and solution to help us understand a big topic. How do you think the author of this book feels about bats—or this topic?**	Moves to teaching for thinking beyond and about the text

FIGURE 6-17 *(continued)*

Step Six: Make One or Two Teaching Points

At the end of the discussion, move smoothly into some specific teaching that comes from your observations during the lesson. In the beginning, you may want to have in mind one or two ideas that you think will be helpful and change your mind based on your observation. Later on, when you know your students well, that may not be necessary. Here are two examples from Mrs. A's lesson on *Bats in the City* (see Figures 6-18 and 6-19).

This specific teaching is very quick and only takes a few minutes. It is sometimes hard to resist addressing three or even more, areas but too much teaching

Teaching Point #1: Analysis

Speaker	Teacher/Student Interactions	Analysis of Interactions
Mrs. A	**You have said the author, Martha Pickerill, feels very strongly about the protection of bats. Let's look a little deeper into what the author really means. Reread page 14 and then let's talk about what she does at the end of the book.**	Prompts for close reading
Students	*[Read silently]*	
Mrs. A	**What does the writer do here?**	Prompts for analysis
Craig	She kind of summarizes what they did and how people changed their minds.	Analyzes writer's craft

FIGURE 6-18 Teaching Point #1: Analysis

(continues)

Teaching Point #1: Analysis

Speaker	Teacher/Student Interactions	Analysis of Interactions
Julia	She also talks at the very end about what the whole thing means about people and animals. The habitats are going away and some animals have to live in cities. They can actually help people and they should try to create habitats for them in cities.	Analyzes writers craft
Mrs. A	**Did you notice the key word for the idea the writer is trying to persuade readers to believe?**	Draws attention to a central idea and vocabulary word
Sam	It's *co-existence*. It's not in the glossary but it means living in the same place. It's the co-existence of people and animals.	Identifies meaning of word
Mrs. A	**Here you can see clearly the difference between a summary of the problem and solution in the book and the larger idea—or the main idea—that we can take from it. The writer has done this in the last two paragraphs. The idea of co-existence is one that you may encounter in other reading.**	Restates larger idea

FIGURE 6-18 *(continued)*

Teaching Point #2: Reading with Fluency

Speaker	Teacher/Student Interactions	Analysis of Interactions
Mrs. A	**The author, Martha Pickerill, makes a strong argument in support of co-existence. Listen while I read the last paragraph and then you can tell me what you notice I do with my voice. I'll try to make my voice show the writer's meaning.** *[Reads the paragraph with good fluency and then pauses.]*	Draws attention to the quality of oral reading and its purpose
Sam	You paused at the comma and there. *[Points to the colon.]*	Shares observation
Mrs. A	**That is a colon, which introduces something. When you see a colon, you know that there will be an explanation or example of the idea in the first part of the sentence. In this sentence, the idea is that people have a choice; then there's a colon; and then, you read the two choices. You pause after the colon and then read the two choices. What else?**	Draws attention to punctuation and what it signals
Julia	You stressed the word *co-existence* like it is really important and you paused at the dash.	Shares observations
Sam	You sounded like you cared about co-existence.	
Mrs. A	**I'll read it again and then you read to a partner in the same way. Make the idea sound important.**	Prompts students to read with fluency

FIGURE 6-19 Teaching Point #2: Reading with Fluency

will overload the students' attention and make the lesson too long and tedious. It will also detract from enjoying the book and understanding its meaning. Decide to shape teaching to address one or two areas. Quick, well-chosen teaching moves are powerful.

Responsive Teaching

In guided reading, your goal is to expand the competencies of the individual readers in the group. On the left side of the chart in Figure 6-20 are the teacher's priorities for the students' needs before the reading. On the right side is evidence of teaching moves.

Responsive Teaching

Teacher Priorities	Teaching Moves
Solving Words: Derive meaning of words using flexible strategies (suffixes and content)	**Before the Reading:** ◆ Teacher directs readers to bold text to read the content ◆ Defines suffix *-ist* to readers ◆ Directs readers to the glossary
Solving Words—Vocabulary: Understand some academic language	**After the Reading:** ◆ Teacher and readers use academic language: author, summary, glossary, paragraphs, problem/solution, main idea
Analyze: Author's use of underlying text structure (problem/solution)	**After the Reading:** ◆ Teacher prompts students to identify problem ◆ Teacher helps clarify problem ◆ Teacher directs readers to the text to search for solutions to the problem
Fluency: Notice the use of punctuation: colon	**After the Reading:** ◆ Teacher draws attention to use of colon and what it means

FIGURE 6-20 Responsive Teaching

Step Seven: Working with Words

Even proficient readers often need more opportunities to learn efficient ways to take apart multisyllable words and also to relate the morphemes (smallest meaningful unit of words) to meaning. You can pre-plan word work based on the demands for word solving in texts at that level. It should take no more than two or three minutes using a whiteboard, chart paper, magnet words, or magnetic letters.

This short attention to words does not take the place of a lesson on words, their parts, and their meaning, but it can be very powerful. Mrs. A's word work from the *Bats in the City* lesson is shown in Figure 6-21.

Noticing meaningful parts is a helpful way for students to approach multisyllable words. In a scientific discipline, specific words very often may be broken down into meaningful parts. If students understand how to notice the parts of words, then they will not be intimidated by longer words and resort to sounding them out letter by letter, which is highly inefficient and doesn't help with meaning. You can use a whiteboard or students can write on their own whiteboards or in a reader's notebook. Some choices:

- Have students write some words that you've written on the whiteboard and then work with a partner to divide them into syllables.
- Give students word cards to sort. (For example, students could sort words by prefix, suffix, or base word.)
- Make word webs or chains (for example, *converse, conversation, convert, conversion).*

Bats in the City: **Word Work**

Speaker	Teacher/Student Interactions	Analysis of Interactions
Mrs. A	You are reading lots of multisyllable words in your reading. Let's look at *conversational*. [*Writes* conversational *on the whiteboard.*] What do you notice about the first part of the word?	Invites students to notice parts
Students	It says *converse*.	Notice word part
Mrs. A	And what does *converse* mean?	Elicits definition
Craig	It means to talk.	Gives meaning
Mrs. A	Yes, *converse*, comes from a Latin word that means "to talk." The first part of the word, *con*, just intensifies the meaning. What do you know about adding the suffix *-tion*?	Provides visual demonstration
Cheyenne	It makes it a thing.	Describes meaning of suffix
Mrs. A	*Converse* is a verb, but when you add the suffix *-tion*, you make it a noun—a process. So *conversation* is the process of talking with someone. Then, Cheyenne, you used the next suffix, *-al,* to add further meaning.	Explains function of a suffix Confirms student's work
Cheyenne	It means you're having a good conversation.	
Craig	*Conversational* means friendly talk.	Draw conclusions
Mrs. A	You can check the dictionary, but also, the parts of the word help you with the meaning and the pronunciation.	Summarizes the process

FIGURE 6-21 *Bats in the City*: Word Work

▶ Have students construct words with parts on cards.

▶ Have students use magnetic letters to build longer, multisyllable words.

Step Eight: Extend Understanding (Optional)

At this point in the lesson, your students may be ready to read another book. In guided reading, students should be exposed to as many books as possible to give them an opportunity to build the processing system. There is no need, nor is it desirable, to build a week of teaching around each book. You want students to progress through the books at a steady rate, reaching for more challenging levels. But occasionally, a book may lead students to engage in further inquiry. A fiction narrative may prompt deeper thinking and motivation to read other books with the same theme or in the same series. A nonfiction topic may inspire curiosity so that students do research on the Internet or seek books on the same topic.

Any guided reading book may prompt students to record their thinking in a reader's notebook. Some options are:

▶ Do a quick write.

▶ Make a character sketch.

▶ Write a summary of a story.

▶ Write one's thinking in response to the text.

▶ Describe the lesson of a story or the big idea of a nonfiction text and what it means to you.

▶ Use a graphic organizer to reflect text structure.

  ▶ Compare and contrast

  ▶ Problem and solution

  ▶ Part and whole

  ▶ Cause and effect

  ▶ Temporal sequence

  ▶ Chronological sequence (timeline)

▶ Write an argument (including counterarguments).

Use graphic organizers very carefully. Resist using them as "fill out" worksheets. Students can find them very tedious. A highly productive way to use graphic organizers is to have students work with a partner and discuss them as they work. Graphic organizers require analysis, and this kind of thinking is best supported by rich talk.

Step Nine: Reflection on the Lesson and Planning

After teaching, reflect on the lesson even if only for a short time. Usually, this reflective process is, again, performed "on the run." But reflection actually takes place throughout the lesson as you gather information from students' discussion and their responses to the teaching points. You will always have some long-term goals for the students, but your notes as you implement the lesson (and right at the end), will help in adjusting your teaching. You might change the book you use the next day, but it's more likely that you will slightly change the emphasis, the conversation, or the teaching in response to students. If today's text offers appropriate opportunity, you may want to follow up on your teaching with similar decisions on other books, or you can encourage students to make connections between texts.

You might be surprised at how the brief notes you make during a guided reading lesson mount up as a valuable source of information. They may suggest that you need to regroup, change emphases, or move to a new level with a group of students.

Using Guided Reading in a Flexible Way to Meet the Needs of Diverse Learners

We have described how guided reading contributes to the ongoing development of readers. While the basic lesson structure remains the same, you will be emphasizing different aspects of reading as the demands of texts increase. Readers may be proficient in upper elementary or middle school but even those with excellent skills have much to learn about comprehending texts. Deep, analytic thinking and academic language will be required of them. The work in guided reading changes in response to readers' current abilities. Within any classroom, you may have students who:

▶ Need to develop more fluency.

▶ Need work to take multisyllable words apart quickly and efficiently.

▶ Are reading with accuracy but not thinking deeply.

▶ Need to understand characteristics of genre.

▶ Need to derive the larger messages of a text.

▶ Need to develop academic vocabulary for talking about texts (e.g., *plot, setting, characters, organization,* or *structure*).

▶ Are expanding vocabulary (Tier 2 and Tier 3).

Guided reading is an excellent setting for helping students develop these advanced skills. Our goal is for all students to develop the competencies described at level Z. If they perform at that level, they will be highly critical and effective readers.

Suggestions for Professional Development

1. Convene a meeting of colleagues who work with the same grade level. Before the meeting, survey the group to see the range of levels for groups they teach (or are forming for teaching). Select a level common to the group of teachers and ask them to bring data on the students in that group. (If you and your colleagues are not far along to determine the instructional levels, choose one that is *likely* to have common interest.)

2. Select a good range of texts (about 5) at the level, which should provide for five to seven days of instruction (assuming that students are meeting about four days a week for guided reading). Be sure that texts have plenty to talk about; include a range of genres. Have the text characteristics handy for reference. Have multiple copies of each text (about eight).

3. Have each teacher read the texts and make some notes on a piece of paper. Keeping the text characteristics in mind, make notes on the challenges in this text for the group of students reading at this level.

   ▶ What will be interesting for them and engage them in the text?

   ▶ What will be challenging and what will they need support to understand?

   ▶ What are the learning opportunities in this book?

   ▶ How can this book help students with processing strategies?

   ▶ How can it help them expand comprehension?

4. Have each teacher read and work on one text. At a signal, have them pass the text to another teacher and add to the notes if they have more ideas. Have each book go all the way around the group if possible so that everyone has analyzed all texts.

5. Have teachers work with a partner to prepare two introductions. If possible, they should take notes that are clear enough that others can read them, but there is no need to write a "script."

   ▶ Work together to prepare an introduction to the book.

   ▶ Make some notes to guide the introduction and be sure that these can be read by someone else. You might organize them in bullet points.

   ▶ Write points to consider.

   ▶ Think about your own students, making adjustments as needed.

6. Have partners present their two introductions to the group, using their own language. Teachers can respond in terms of their own students. ("I wouldn't need to use that point because . . ." "I'd want to add a short discussion of . . .").

7. Type the bullet points for everyone and give each teacher a set of the books. Over the next two weeks, they can try out the introductions, using the notes but adjusting the introduction to fit the needs of their students.

8. Hold a follow-up meeting to share their experiences in using these four or five texts. Consider the following:

▶ How did you tailor the introduction to the text to meet the unique needs of your students?

▶ How did students respond to each book?

▶ What learning shifts did you observe during and after the reading?

▶ What happened in the discussions?

▶ What teaching points did you select?

CHAPTER 7

Using Guided Reading for Effective Teaching of English Language Learners

---

There will probably never be a formula for educating ELLs, just as there is no formula for educating students who already know English. What we can do is provide guidelines based on our strongest research about effective practices for teaching ELLs.

–Claude Goldenberg

One-fifth of people in the United States speak a language other than English as a first language, and populations are changing so fast that every figure we report is instantly out of date. One report, released by the Center for Immigration Studies in 2014 (Dinan, *The Washington Times,* October 6), found that nearly half of all California school-age children speak a language other than English at home, and six other states are similar. The percentage of ELL students in public schools is over 10 percent and that is changing rapidly. More than five million English language learners were enrolled in public schools in 2014, and that number has continued to expand. Spanish speakers dominate significantly, but the fastest growing groups speak Arabic, Chinese, and Vietnamese.

Other largely English-speaking countries (for example, Canada, Australia, and Great Britain) are also extremely diverse. In fact, the number of ELLs is increasing at a rate greater than the rate of increase for children of school age. The child's first language could be one of some 400! It is clear that we are moving toward a world in which it is common for children to grow up speaking several languages. This has long been common in many countries but is relatively new to the United States. We view this trend as highly positive. Bilingualism and bi-literacy (or multilingualism and multiliteracy) is a rich asset to the entire learning community as well as to the speakers; but it is still the case that having a large number of English language learners in your classroom presents a challenge to teachers, who are responsible for meeting their learning needs.

Most teachers in elementary schools today have experienced teaching learners whose first language is not English. ELLs are all ages and in all grades. Some have been learning English for several years; others are new to English. Many have classes with a variety of different home languages. If you do not teach English language learners now, it is highly likely that you will at some future time. In that case, adjustments must be made to instruction rather than continuing as usual and hoping that students will quickly learn English and fit in. Working with English language learners means taking action to make adjustments that will help the students acquire the language and learn successfully. The kind of language and literacy classroom you are developing can be highly supportive to English language learners.

We feel strongly that working effectively with ELLs does not mean just providing "good teaching." Of course, like all students ELLs need good teaching, but they have additional needs, which makes the situation more complex. They need teachers who understand their unique profile, and they need *additional* and *different* teaching. In this chapter we discuss how you can provide that extra, and different, level of support.

What Is an English Language Learner?

English language learner (ELL) is a broad term that refers to all students who need to learn to comprehend, speak, read, and write English. ELLs acquire language by hearing and understanding messages that are slightly above their current English language level, so entering and participating in conversation is *even more important* to these students. You will also find that inclusion of students who speak different languages and come from different cultures makes your classroom work richer and more interesting. The very term ELL signals a positive view of these students, their ability to learn, and their contributions as members of the classroom community.

It's also important to remember that even though we can apply this broad and general term of ELLs, the group is also highly diverse. ELLs vary in terms of:

▶ The first or home language they speak.

▶ The early literacy behaviors necessary to read the childrens' home language (e.g., some languages require reading right to left across a page).

▶ The geographical parts of the world they represent (even speakers of the same language come from many different places and there will be dialect differences).

▶ The cultures they represent.

▶ Any dialect (variation by region) of a language they speak (most languages include a variety of dialects just as English does).

▶ How long they have lived in the English-speaking country (ranging from second-or third-generation immigrants to just-arrived immigrants, to speakers of the ancient languages of native ethnic peoples).

▶ The level of English they can understand and speak.

▶ The amount of previous education they have experienced.

▶ The response of the individual to the move from their home country.

What they do have in common is that they are learning to speak English and their achievement of this goal is of critical importance. It's a simple matter of survival to be able to understand, speak, read, and write the dominant language in a country. In what are called the "English-speaking countries," English is the language of currency. Many English-speaking countries have moved farther in bilingual education, but in the United States, the following statement is still true:

> Language minority students who cannot read and write proficiently in English cannot participate fully in American schools, workplaces or society. They face limited job opportunities and earning power. Inadequate reading and writing proficiency in English relegates rapidly increasing language-minority populations to the sidelines, limiting the nation's potential for economic competitiveness, innovation, productivity growth, and quality of life. (August and Shanahan 2006, 1)

Although we agree that English is essential, at the same time, we recognize the need to create a multilingual society, and believe that at some time, that will happen. In our view, *every student* has the right to learn to speak, read, and write more than one language; in this chapter, we concentrate on the ELLs we teach today.

Another need ELLs have in common is that it is important for them to respect and sustain their native languages. Language is intimately tied to your identity as a person. Smith says: "Language is perceived to be the core of everyone's identity," (2005, 21) According to Clay, language is:

> An intimate possession, understood by loved ones . . . reflects membership of a particular speech group and identifies them with that group. It is personal and valuable and not just an incorrect version of a standard dialect. (*Literacy Lessons*)

We strongly encourage teachers in their work with families to emphasize the importance of their children maintaining and expanding their proficiency in their home or first language. Language is a means of communication with an important group of people and supports their transition to a second language. The children need to take pride in their home cultures and languages.

If it were possible, we would advocate for every student to have teachers who understand and speak his language; but that is out of reach at least for today. And, a large number of schools would have not just one additional language for teachers to learn but many. That means that we have to find ways to create classrooms that welcome and support ELLs even if we cannot supply many speakers of their language.

For all children, the language they bring from home is the greatest resource. All students who enter your classroom *have learned language,* which is in itself a self-extending system in that using it helps the speaker learn more language and learn more about language:

> Children who come to school speaking any language well have a preparation for literacy learning that is to be valued, whatever that prior language is. . . . we need to see them as competent children who speak and problem-solve well in their first culture and who are lucky to be learning a second language while they are young and active language learners. It is surprising how rapid their progress can be. (Clay, 2005, 6)

Language Proficiency in English

Levels, phases, or stages have been identified to describe the general progress of ELLs as they take on English (WIDA Classroom Consortium, (www.wida.us/); Cappellini 2005; Hill and Flynn 2006; Soltero 2011; Rodriguez-Eagle and Torres-Elias 2009). We summarize these in Figure 7-1. They apply to students of any age.

Whatever the terms you use, it is evident that achieving high levels of oral language and literacy takes about five to seven, and maybe even ten years. Even at the advanced level, language structures such as idioms or figurative language often confuse someone who is speaking, reading, and writing another language quite proficiently. In looking at this chart, you can see how it might help to guide your lessons in shared/interactive writing, shared reading, selection of texts for guided reading, and text introductions. Remember always that students' *receptive* understanding is probably greater than the language they can produce (productive language). Also, something to keep in mind is that it is not helpful (and is actually quite harmful) to correct students' grammar. Contrary to what seems logical to many people, we don't actually learn by being corrected; but we do learn by interacting, expanding, and in a natural way using grammatical structures over and over until it "sounds right" to us. Rather than correct, simply respond to the meaning and in the process you will demonstrate standard structure.

The challenge is not so simple as figuring out what to do to support all ELLs or even how to support all Spanish-speaking ELLS or all children from Ethiopia (where 77 tongues are spoken locally, most belonging to the Afroasiatic family). As you can see from Figure 7-1, it matters where the student is in the acquisition of a second language. Within one class, within one guided reading group, you are likely to have students at different levels. Even your assessment of their appropriate instructional and independent reading levels may not reveal this information precisely. If you have an ESL teacher in your school, use that resource to help you assess where a student is. You need to bring your teaching to where they are. Remember that you may need to respond differently to each member of the group, which is one of your goals anyway; but language differences add another layer of complexity. That said, some general guidelines will be helpful. We'll list those and

Progress in Acquisition of English

Step/Phase	Characteristics of the Learner	Approximate Time Frame	Teaching Decisions That Support English Language Learners
Beginning (Sometimes called "silent," "receptive," "preproduction" or "entering")	◆ Has a vocabulary of about 500 words (understanding but not necessarily speaking) ◆ May parrot or respond to pictures shared ◆ Uses pictorial representation of words ◆ Has minimal understanding ◆ Rarely verbalizes ("silent" much of the time) ◆ Uses gestures (nods "yes" or shakes head for "no") ◆ Learns a few common nouns ◆ Not comfortable speaking; uses actions and body gestures	0–6 months	◆ Give one-step commands or directions ◆ Make simple statements that allow for nonverbal answers ("show me ___"; "who has _____"; "get the _____.") ◆ Use simple sentences with "to be" ("I am _____." Name is _____") ◆ Make statements with nouns accompanied by pictures ◆ Use shared reading to provide high level of support ◆ Build vocabulary using visual support ◆ Don't force students to speak
Early (sometimes called "early production," "early intermediate")	◆ Has a vocabulary of about 1,000 words in speaking and writing ◆ Able to understand and use a limited vocabulary to meet basic needs ◆ Developing receptive and active vocabulary ◆ Speaks in one- to two-word phrases but understand more ◆ Makes negative statements ◆ Produces one- or two-word responses ◆ Uses key words to participate ◆ Uses pronouns and some phrases ("on the table") ◆ Uses subject statements ("there is," "here is") ◆ Utters a few simple sentences ◆ Uses some basic adjectives ◆ Uses some conjunctions ("and") ◆ Benefits from clear picture support	6 months–1 year	◆ Use questions that require only "yes" or "no" answers ◆ Use questions that involve a simple choice ("Is it big or little?" "Is it a big ball or a little ball?") ◆ Accept one- and two-word answers ◆ Have them read labels on pictures ◆ Provide listening activities ◆ Read simple books with predictable text ◆ Use shared reading to provide opportunities for repeating language structures ◆ Use shared and interactive writing ◆ Expand (without "correcting") contributions to shared and interactive writing when you understand the students' meaning
Intermediate (sometimes called "speech emergence," "developing")	◆ Has an active and receptive vocabulary of about 3,000 words ◆ Communicates with simple phrases and short sentences ◆ Uses verbs in present tense ("I go," "she goes") and past tense ("I played . . .") ◆ Uses possessive pronouns ("my," "his") ◆ Demonstrates subject/verb agreement ◆ Produces compound sentences ("We played ball and had lunch") ◆ Understands subordinating conjunctions ("because," "when," "before")	1–3 years	◆ Ask "why" and "how" questions that require more complex answers ◆ Accept phrases or short sentence answers ◆ Ask for explanation ("can you say how . . ."; "can you say more about that?") ◆ Explain jokes and idioms ◆ Continue reading aloud, shared reading (choral), shared and interactive writing ◆ Select simple stories close to experience

FIGURE 7–1 Progress in Acquisition of English

(continues)

Progress in Acquisition of English

Step/Phase	Characteristics of the Learner	Approximate Time Frame	Teaching Decisions That Support English Language Learners
	◆ Makes grammar and pronunciation errors in oral and written language but retains much of the meaning ◆ Misunderstands jokes and idioms ◆ Benefits from clear picture support		◆ Invite students to enjoy rhythm and rhyme in texts with repetition ◆ Provide access to books on audio (especially repeated reading of read-aloud and shared reading texts)
Early Advanced (sometimes called "intermediate fluency," "bridging")	◆ Uses reflexive pronouns ("myself," "yourself," "itself") ◆ Uses abstract nouns not concrete ("happy,' "sad," define a state) ◆ Uses more complex coordinating conjunctions ("however') ◆ Uses regular and irregular verbs, present, past tense ◆ Uses gerunds (verb that functions as a noun, "they like my going with them") ◆ Uses superlatives ("biggest," "highest") ◆ Uses some specific and technical language (academic language) ◆ Produces a variety of sentence lengths, both simple and complex ◆ Understands jokes and some idioms ◆ Produces multiple related paragraphs in writing ◆ Control more sophisticated syntactic structures ◆ Makes some grammatical errors (semantic) and errors in pronunciation that do not impede the comprehension of overall meaning in oral or written discourse	3–5 years	◆ Ask questions like "why do you think . . ." ◆ Ask questions requiring conditional tense, "what would have happened if . . ." ◆ Use abstract nouns but explain if needed ◆ Explain unfamiliar idioms ◆ Invite students to discuss and analyze figurative language ◆ Use plays, stories, and journals ◆ Provide visual and kinesthetic experiences ◆ Allow the use of native language to extend discussion of ideas and concepts ◆ Demonstrate academic language
Advanced (sometimes called "advanced fluency," "expanding")	◆ Uses verbs in all tenses including conditional ("if . . . I will," "if . . . I would," "if . . . I would have") and past perfect ("I had walked . . . by lunch") ◆ Uses auxiliary verbs ("could," "should") ◆ Uses relative pronouns ("who," "whom") ◆ Uses adverbial clauses ("Whomever runs in the race, I'll win it.") ◆ Uses contractions ("couldn't," "wouldn't") ◆ Uses embedded clauses ("She is the girl who won the race.") ◆ Uses subordinating conjunctions or "connectives" ("although," "whenever") ◆ Uses passive voice ("I was given the prize.") ◆ Uses and understands abstract language ◆ Understands and uses figurative language (metaphors and similes) ◆ Has developed some academic language related to the content areas	5–7 years	◆ Ask questions requiring conditional tense ("What would have happened if . . .") ◆ Invite students to share their thinking ◆ Ask questions to extend discourse ("What makes you think that?" 'What is your evidence for this argument?" "If that is the case, why do you think . . .") ◆ Support the use of more complex vocabulary and sentence structures ◆ Give extra support as needed ◆ Allow the use of native language to understand new concepts and vocabulary ◆ Use role play ◆ Use readers' theater ◆ Summarize talk with charts ◆ Expand academic language

FIGURE 7-1 *(continued)*

then discuss interactive read-aloud, shared reading, and interactive writing as valued contexts for supporting ELLs. Finally, we'll discuss some specifics for teaching in guided reading lessons.

Some Characteristics of Language

First, all languages and dialects of language are rule-governed. These "rules" by which people put words together in comprehensible sentences are called the "grammar" of a language (as opposed to what is sometimes called "correct" or "standard" grammar). The syntax, or grammar, of a language is gradually learned by the young child through interaction with others. If you observe very young children you will see communication with one word moving into two- and three-word phrases like "more book" or "more juice." Research has shown that in every phase of language acquisition, children speak in rule-governed ways. Gradually, they control more and more sentences that follow the rules of the language. So, they are learning much more than a collection of words. And this language is an invisible source of information in reading.

All children have some control over language. They know that you can't communicate with just a haphazard string of words. Speakers of a language other than English have learned much *about* language. They have internalized one set of rules and now they are charged with learning another, but they have one great advantage: *They have learned how to learn language.*

General Principles for Building Language

Below are some general principles, drawn from the literature on working with ELLs, from our experience, and from our conversations with teachers.

Create an inclusive environment. You can find many suggestions for creating a warm and welcoming classroom environment in Chapters 21, 22, and 23. Also think about the whole-school environment and how it welcomes and represents all students. This elusive factor is important for all students but is especially so when you are working with ELLs. Students need to see their own names in many places in the room and would be so pleased to see their names both in English and in their first language. They need to take pride in their home country and first language. If possible, use some of the languages students speak in the home to identify areas of the classroom. Label the calendar with several languages. All students enjoy encountering some words from other languages, so this would be educative for everyone.

Create a "context rich" environment. When possible, connect literacy experiences (read-aloud, shared reading, guided reading) with areas of study in the sciences and social studies so that students can build networks of understanding. In reading, select texts that have excellent picture support so that they support students in constructing meaning. Use many "modes" at the same time—visual, tactile, and kinesthetic to support learning. Take every opportunity to make it possible for students to use their knowledge of their own language as they read and write. They may not know English syntax, but they do know that language structure exists because they use it orally. They have an internal sense for nouns and verbs even if they do not have formal labels for parts of speech. You can encourage them to, "say it in _____." Then, have them say it in English. Encourage all students to use gestures and pictures as part of communication.

Respect students' progress toward English proficiency. ELL students are even more diverse among themselves than they differ from native English speakers. Part of that diversity comes in the length of time they have been learning English. Respect students in the "silent period," using mainly shared reading and writing, encouraging nonverbal participation, and using all the information you have to interpret a student's meaning. "Treat silence gently," (Saaverdra 2016, 67). Use appropriate wait time and avoid correcting students' grammar. Focus instead on what they mean. Immersion in a rich literate environment, with many opportunities for text-based talk, will help students to gradually take on English grammar and vocabulary.

Value partially correct responses. It helps our teaching if we realize that learning starts with what the child already knows. There is a tendency to notice language errors and faulty "grammar" instead of what the student is doing that is partially right. By being partially correct, the child progresses to more control over complexity in the use of language. Accuracy is the outcome not the process of learning," (Clay 1988, 251). As language teachers (and we are all language teachers), we need to assume that even ELLs who have very limited English are still competent language users. We need to tune into and expand their opportunities.

Talk with (not "at" or "for") students. It's not enough to simply flood children with talk. A huge amount of teacher talk may be meaningless and incomprehensible. Also, it is by using language that children learn it, so they must have the opportunity. Clay urges us to "be strong-minded" about holding meaningful conversations even when it is difficult. While you want to make children comfortable in the classroom, and you would not force them to speak, you want to make it clear that you value every kind of communication they do and are eager to hear or see more:

> If the child's language development seems to be lagging, it is misplaced sympathy to do his talking for him. Instead, put your ear closer, concentrate more sharply, smile more rewardingly and spend more time in genuine conversation, difficult though it is. (Clay *Becoming Literate*, 69)

Involving learners in conversation moves ELLs beyond the simple repetition of language samples, which is a very limited way to learn.

Create shared reading experiences. When you read texts aloud to younger students, they often join in on repetitive parts. This is an enjoyable activity and one that will greatly benefit English language learners. You can also involve them in shared reading (see Chapters 3 and 4). Shared reading at all levels provides ELLs with the opportunity to hear language while observing its phonological representation. Shared reading has three major benefits: (1) it provides very high support so that ELLs can join in on the parts they know but the group can carry the rest, thus giving them opportunity to fully participate as a member of the group; (2) it is natural in shared reading at all levels to read something several times, giving ELLs an opportunity to try on or repeat tricky language structures until they become familiar; and (3) support for meaning is high because the text is discussed and read several times. This third benefit is also true for interactive read-aloud; here, you not only have the opportunity to read the text to students in a meaningful way but you also clarify vocabulary, explain concepts, and involve them in a discussion of meaning.

Create a need to produce language. People seldom have good conversations about nothing. People converse because they have a need to communicate. Involve students in activities that spark their interest, including not only stories and simple nonfiction books but things they can touch, smell, and manipulate. Engage them in the co-construction of pieces of shared or interactive writing, in which students work together to record their explorations and thinking. ELLs can contribute a word or a letter to the words; interactive writing is an ideal setting in which students can construct language with high teacher and group support. The writing is reread many times, giving students the opportunity to internalize linguistic structures.

Provide opportunities to hear new sources of language. The texts you select for interactive read-aloud may be more complex than most ELLs (especially at the first three levels) can produce (or even repeat); but that is not a problem since you are offering high support and taking care to choose books that have large and helpful illustrations. You can begin with a richer introduction that will help ELLs understand what the whole story or that topic is about before they hear it read aloud. You may also consider rereading favorite or interesting parts so the students can hear and consider the language again.

Give them real texts. English language learners need to process texts that are easy enough for them to understand; but it is not be helpful to give them meaningless "exercises" reproduced on paper or books with highly contrived language (for example, "decodable" texts or highly repetitive sentences). They need comprehensible language, supported by interaction and discussion.

Know them as learners. Of course, you want to know all of your students as learners; but you may share more cultural understandings with those who are native English speakers. It will take more effort (but also be quite rewarding) to learn as much as you can about your ELL students. You may have assessment data on reading and writing; but it is also wise to gain linguistic and cultural information to put it into perspective and help you know more about how to respond to the child. Learn something about those patterns of syntax in the child's language; chances are, the learner is using some of the patterns even as he tries to use English words. Are there other English speakers in the student's home? For example, does he have siblings who speak more English? Learn the names of family members and ask how to pronounce them correct. Learn names for family members ("mom," "madre," "mami," "ema," "mamma," "ahm") and sometimes substitute them in shared reading or interactive writing. Learn about content that will be familiar to students (and which will not).

Select texts that reflect diversity in language and culture. Your selection of books for interactive read-aloud, shared reading, and guided reading, as well as the books in the classroom library, need to reflect the diversity of the world culture. Be on the lookout for books that reflect the various cultures in your students' particular homes and communities. All students need to see themselves in books and take pride in their native culture and language.

Ground talk in texts. When you read aloud to students or engage them in shared reading and also talk about those books, they have powerful linguistic resources on which they can draw. They may use some of the vocabulary or imitate the language patterns (especially if this is the second or third reading). Conversations should be genuine and include questions, sentence frames, and demonstrations of language about texts.

Accept variety in pronunciation and intonation. Many ELLs continue to employ the phonology and intonation patterns of their primary language, and instead of correcting them, respond using a standard structure. Remember that just about every speaker of English actually has an "accent" related to the region in which he lives. Children are good language learners and they can learn to use one dialect in one context, and a different one in another. The more opportunity ELLs have to speak, read, and write, the more they will take on the complex intonation patterns that reflect meanings expressed in English.

Teach routines, structure lessons in a predictable way, make expectations clear, and check for understanding. ELLs will benefit from a series of predictable classroom routines (see Chapters 21, 22, and 23), because they know what to do without having to understand complicated new directions every day. When directions are simple, make them short and clear. Try not to overload students with too many directions at once. Demonstrate routines explicitly. ELLs also benefit from predictably structured lessons. Use the same general framework for shared reading and guided reading so that students know what to expect. The book and conversation change and grow in complexity. Check to be sure they understand and use pictures and signals when possible.

Present vocabulary in context. It is meaningless for ELLs to study lists of words in isolation. While they may work with word cards and even be able to recognize and say the name of the word, they need to encounter words as meaningful language. The better scenario is to invite students to locate words in the context of a text they have read and understood and to talk about their meaning. Students can identify:

▸ How the picture helps

▸ How reading or listening to the sentence or paragraph helps

▸ The meaning they previously understood for the word and how that is different or the same as the meaning in this book

Use graphic organizers. Graphic organizers are a good visual tool for showing the information in a text. For example, a graphic organizer can show:

▸ The overall organization of the text

▸ Chronological sequence (for example, timeline)

▸ Compare and contrast (two or three column charts)

▸ Problem and solution (two column chart with arrows)

▸ Big ideas and details or examples

▸ The attributes of a character (a web with the character in the center and attributes around the edge)

▶ The problem in a story and how it is solved (two-column chart)

▶ The turning point in a story

▶ The structure of a story (beginning, problem, events, ending)

Graphic organizers are most valuable when you put them on a chart and create them with students through conversation. The graphic organizer helps them to see the essential features of a text and that supports comprehension.

Continue to teach challenging aspects of language even after students have reached intermediate and advanced levels. Achieving high proficiency in a language (and a high level of comprehension in reading) is more than just learning the meaning of words. Students may know well how to read accurately and even know the meaning of words, but they need to understand how words function in sentences to connect and convey additional meaning. Passive voice can be confusing and add to difficulty in comprehension. 'I was given this as a present" sometimes goes contrary to the naïve readers' expectations; it's harder and different in meaning from "I got a present."

Teach connectives or signal words. A particularly challenging area for many students is understanding and using subordinating conjunctions or "connectives" within a piece of written language. Connectives are signal words that range from very simple words like *and* and *with* to highly academic words such as *ultimately, presently,* and *in conclusion.* Connectives can signal:

▶ Addition of ideas (*and, also, moreover, another, equally important*)

▶ Time (*next, soon, in the meantime, meanwhile*)

▶ Order or sequence (*first, next, finally, before, then, hence, gradually*)

▶ Space and place (*behind, nearby, below, beyond, adjacent to*)

▶ An example (*for example, for instance, such as, furthermore, similarly*)

▶ Results (*as a result, hence, so, consequently*)

▶ Purpose (*because, for this reason, to this end*)

▶ Comparison (*like, as is, similarly*)

▶ Contrast (*but, yet, nevertheless, on the contrary, actually, in fact*)

▶ Summary or report (*in summary, in short, finally, in conclusion, as you can see*)

Connectives are important in any kind of formal communication but they are especially critical in articulating argument; yet, we often take it for granted that students understand and can use them.

Teach cognates. A cognate is a word that has similar meaning, spelling, and punctuation in two or more languages (e.g., in English and Spanish: *family, familia*). It is useful to teach ELLs to be aware of cognates and use them in their acquisition of English. It helps them make sense of the language. You can point out these words in the introduction to the text or in the teaching after reading.

Teach from whole to part. If you know the "big picture" of what something is about, it helps you understand what is happening, more than if you just look at the "bits." It helps to have larger meaningful categories. That's true for all of us, and it's the reason why many cooking shows on TV begin by telling you what dishes are going to be prepared and for what purpose, even showing finished products.

The intent is probably to entice viewers, but the effect is that each step of the recipe now has clearer meaning (and you have the larger context of what the whole process is all about). Imagine if someone on a cooking show just showed the equipment and the ingredients, naming the various labels, and then went through the steps without saying what the end product would be! Teaching from whole to part gives ELLs an idea of the whole topic or goal so that language is experience within a context. For example, helping them understand that the book, *Saving Cranes* (*Fountas & Pinnell Classroom,* in press) is about a species of bird that is about to disappear (as many other species have), helps them to understand that everything in this book will be about what scientists do to try to save the birds. They need to think about what birds need in order to survive—especially migratory birds. In *Coley's Journey* (*Fountas & Pinnell Classroom,* in press), they need to know that this book will be about the long journeys that many migratory birds make, and that the writer is going to show this journey day by day. Each part of the book will tell about Coley's experience in a different place along the way.

You may be thinking that all these suggestions just "sound like common sense," and that's a good thing. But you will want to constantly build these principles into your daily practice as you work with your ELL students. It's a lot like having a guest in your home—you find out their preferences and what they can and like to eat before they come. Except, in this case, you want students to feel not like guests but as owners of the classroom and valued members of the community.

Selecting Texts for English Language Learners

For students at the first level of learning, it would be great to give them access to books that reflect topics that are familiar to them; however, it is usually impossible to select texts that deal *only* with familiar ideas. Students will need your help in building the background information that will help them comprehend the texts. In addition, students will need to deal with new vocabulary and English syntax. ELLs do have vocabulary and internalized knowledge of syntactic patterns, but those understandings are in another language. Thus, the language knowledge they bring to reading in English is not as strong as native speakers, and they will need support. Each time you select a book, analyze it to determine the conceptual understandings, vocabulary, and language knowledge students will need to bring to it. That is especially true if you expect students to read the book for themselves instead of just listening.

Splash, Plop, Leap! (*Fountas & Pinnell Classroom,* in press) is a book with repetitive language that is designed for shared reading (see Figure 7-2). The book presents several animals that may be familiar to students (but they may not know the English labels). It also has number words; chances are students have the concept but may not have the English words. On page 5, the sentence has the adjective *four,* and subject and verb on the first line. The second line has a prepositional phrase. Then, you turn the page and you see a pronoun as subject, a verb, and a prepositional phrase. On the second line you see an article (*the*), a subject, a verb, and an adverb. This pattern is repeated throughout the book. This is not the very

FIGURE 7-2 *Splash, Plop, Leap!* Pages 5–8

simplest book to use in guided reading, but it does offer strong picture support and syntax that becomes predictable once the reader has heard the text and read it with the group several times. You'd offer very high support for this text by reading it to the students (more than once if necessary) and inviting them to join in. Some students may pick up the key words (*ducks, frogs, turtles*). They may also learn to use the number words quickly. It doesn't matter how much of the text they read—they are constantly supported by the group as they gain the ability to "read" much of the language of the text in an enjoyable way. These students are working on everything at once—the language patterns, the vocabulary, and the print and how it works. Shared reading is highly supportive for this kind of learning.

Students at the beginning level for language acquisition are very different from each other. Some have learned to read in their native language, and that means that they have early behaviors in place. They don't need to learn to look at print; they just need to acquire enough English language to read it. Some students may not be literate at all and will need an orientation to print. (Students who have learned to read in an alphabetic language are, again, different from students who have read other languages with different print features, and those students may also need to gain familiarity with English letter-sound system.)

Let's look at two examples of texts that you might choose for guided reading to examine the particular challenges for ELLs. The first, *The Yard Sale* (*Fountas & Pinnell Classroom,* in press), is a level A text (see Figure 7-3). *The Yard Sale* is a very easy book in terms of beginning readers. There is one line of print on each page. The same pattern is repeated on every page except for the last page. The story is told from the point of view of a boy in the story (first person). The only change for each page spread is the family member who "likes" something at the yard sale and the object that individual likes. As you analyze this text prior to introducing it to a group with English language learners, you would need to think about the following:

▶ Do students know what a yard sale is?

▶ What names for family members should I help students become familiar with?

▶ What labels for objects do students know and what do they need to repeat?

You'd want to be sure students understand the structure for the whole story (that everyone likes something and the boy ends up liking the kite). And, you'd

My grandma likes the dress.

My grandpa likes the book.

FIGURE 7-3 *The Yard Sale,* Pages 8–11

want to have them rehearse the language structure by choral reading or repeating the language of a page or two. This book is part of a series called "Family Series" that features the same characters over several books, so as they read more, students will have the advantage of familiarity.

Bird Feet (*Fountas & Pinnell Classroom*, in press) is a much more complex nonfiction text at Level K (see Figure 7-4). This text offers many challenges for ELLs, yet it provides many supports as well. Each section describes a different type of bird feet, including "Feet with Toes," "Feet Like a Blanket," "Feet for Icy Lands," "Fishing Feet," and "Feet Like Fingers." Each section has the name of one example of a bird, a description of the bird's feet and how they use them, sometimes a caption for the picture, and a "Did You Know?" sidebar. It's "reader friendly" because of the predictable text structure. The language is complex and natural sounding, but clear. It includes embedded clauses—both dependent and independent, adjectives (sometimes two for one known), and some figurative language such similes. Students would need to be clear on the big idea and focus, the organization or structure of the text, and hear you say some of the tricky language.

You might want to untangle any tricky syntax that might be difficult. For example, do they understand the phrase "that means" or how to read two modifying adjectives such as "wide, webbed feet." Do they understand how feet could be like a blanket? The introduction does not make everything in the book "easy." That

Feet Like a Blanket

The **booby** is a bird that spends most of its time on or near the ocean. A booby has **webbed** feet. That means it has skin between its toes. Most birds that swim have webbed feet. Boobies also use their wide, webbed feet to keep their eggs warm, like a blanket.

Boobies lay their eggs in the sand.

Why Boobies' Feet Are Blue
Boobies have colorful feet so they can show off to other boobies. When they are looking for a mate, they do a dance. They stick their heads up and their wings out. They lift one blue foot high in the air and then the other. Boobies use their dance to say, "Look at me!"

FIGURE 7-4 *Bird Feet*, Pages 6–7

would take away the tension of finding out new information by reading and make the lesson unnecessarily tedious. But if you scaffold the reading with some vital information that ELLs can use, there will still be plenty of problem solving to do.

If you teach ELLs, over time you will find that you read every book with a particular lens, one that keeps in mind the vast knowledge you have developed of your students and of ELLs in general. You will find that it becomes an integral part of the way you approach a text.

Using Interactive Read-Aloud to Support English Language Learners

In other chapters we have discussed many of the benefits of interactive read-aloud for all learners; this context is critical for students who are learning English. Through interactive read-aloud, you:

- Show students that reading is a meaningful and enjoyable activity.
- Provide demonstrations of language used for different purposes.
- Expose students to narrative.
- Get students listening to and understanding English syntax.
- Present new vocabulary within a meaningful context that includes illustrations.
- Have the opportunity to develop academic language to talk about texts and to discuss topics in content areas—a difficult task for all students but especially difficult for ELLs.
- Spark text-based talk, enabling ELLs to participate at whatever level they can.

Some new immigrants may have very little or highly interrupted education; others have received adequate schooling in their native country. Nevertheless, many ELLs, even those who have been in your own setting for several years, may have limited oral vocabularies (in English) and are reading below grade level. Select texts with language that is simple enough that students can understand it in context; books with repetitive language, rhyme, and rhythm are especially enjoyable and helpful. If students respond positively, you may want to reread some favorites; each time, students will understand more.

Using Shared Reading to Support English Language Learners

Shared reading is a context in which you and your students read together either from a single enlarged text or from individual copies of the same text. For younger students, this almost always means reading in unison with others. Perhaps you have had the experience of singing a song with others; for any word or phrase you don't know, you just drop out for a moment and then join in again. Often, the support of others brings a refrain or whole verse to mind. Shared reading offers that unison support.

Through shared reading you are implementing a pleasurable group activity that will help ELLs grow in every way related to reading English. It helps students expand vocabulary and internalize syntax because they find themselves repeating these patterns over and over. Yet, it does not feel like "drill" or "imitation." The experience helps students develop early reading behaviors like left-to-right directionality, return sweep, and word-by-word matching in a more advanced way than they will be expected to do in guided reading. After repeated readings, students will reach a point where they can read the text with a partner or on their own.

Shared reading has additional benefits because it is offers a meaningful context for learning about letters, sounds, and words. "Shared reading provides English language learners with an opportunity to hear language while observing its corresponding phonological representation" (Drucker 2003, 24). Once a text has been read several times, it will be more available to students. The familiarity of the text allows you to draw students' attention to individual words, for example:

> "What would you expect to see at the beginning of the word *book?*"
> "Find *my* on page 6. Now find *my* on page 8. Now find *my* on page 10."
> "Find a word on this page that starts like *Ken*. It's *kite*."

You can help children to do quick visual searching, using the distinctive features of letters and making connections between sounds and letters. Shared reading is particularly effective in helping ELLs learn English language syntax.

Select texts that are highly engaging and have large, clear, colorful illustrations. Holdaway encourages teachers to use "enchantingly interesting texts. For beginners, don't present pages full of print. Instead, find good stories and nonfiction texts with one, two, or three lines of print. Select texts with predictable language and repetitive language:

> . . . Children not thoroughly familiar with the syntactic patterns, idioms, and tunes of written English . . . require the joyful repetition of rich literature through the ear and across the tongue . . . [so that] the patterns of the book dialect are running through the automatic language system of the child. (Holdaway 1979, 194)

Using Shared and Interactive Writing to Support English Language Learners

Shared writing is also effective with intermediate students who are ELLs. You write the text with their input. By co-composing the text and acting as scribe, you can help students (and they can help each other) produce comprehensible text. Because they participate in the composition and construction (writing), it is available to them as a model that they can use as a resource. Closely related to shared writing is interactive writing.

Interactive writing involves a class or small group of students in creating a

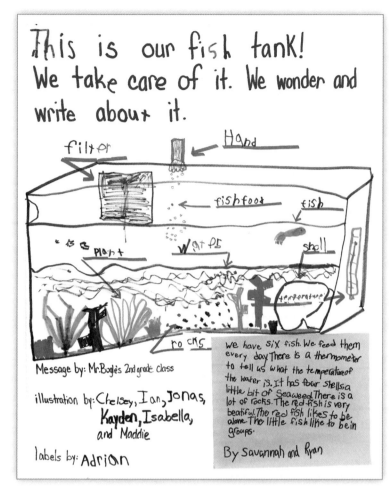

This is our fish tank!
We take care of it. We wonder and
write about it.

filter
Hand
fishfoot
tish
plant
water
shell
rocks
temperature

We have six fish. We feed them every day. There is a thermometer to tell us what the temperature of the water is. It has four stellsa little bit of Seaweed. There is a lot of rocks. The red fish is very beatiful. The red fish likes to be alone. The little fish like to be in groups.

By Savannah and Ryan

Message by: Mr. Boyles 2nd grade class

illustration by: Chelsey, Ian, Jonas, Kayden, Isabella, and Maddie

labels by: Adrian

FIGURE 7-5 Sample Interactive Writing by ELLs

common text (see Figure 7-5). ELLs can contribute a word or a letter to the words; interactive writing is an ideal setting because students write what they can and the teacher fills in the rest, but it is a true group product. (As interactive writing becomes more complex, the teacher writes words and phrases that students know very well so that the lesson moves quickly.)

Interactive writing is preceded and accompanied by a great deal of oral language. You can provide language frames that help ELLs turn a known word into a comprehensible sentence:

> "I learned _____."
> "I see _____."
> "I read _____ by _____."
> "_____ (Name) has ____ (number) sisters."

As these kinds of sentence frames are repeated in oral language, they can be recorded in written language by the teacher, sometimes "sharing the pen" with students. Then you and the children read the text again in a shared way.

Using Guided Reading to Support English Language Learners

Across the guided reading lesson, you will need to make adjustments to create maximum learning opportunities for ELLs.

An Example at Level C

Let's take a look at an example of an early lesson with English language learners.

Before the Reading

At the beginning level, the texts you select for guided reading have strong picture support and are based on concepts that are familiar or easy to explain to students. It is helpful to have repetitive sentence structures so that once students understand the syntax they can use the same patterns on several pages. *The Yard Sale* is a very simple example. *Making a Sandwich* (*Fountas & Pinnell Classroom,* in press), level C, shows another example of repetitive language, this time at a slightly more complex level (see Figure 7-6).

You can see that this book offers repetition of syntax, but the reader is working with larger pieces of language. These language patterns are what you might call

We got some lettuce
for the sandwich.

We put it
on the bread.

4

5

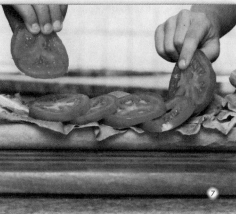

We got some tomatoes
for the sandwich.

We put them
on the lettuce.

6

7

Yum!

16

FIGURE 7-6 *Making a Sandwich,* Pages 4–7, 16

"high utility," in that they occur frequently in oral and written language and students can use them as frames. If they know the patterns of syntax, they can use them, substituting other words of the same part of speech.

Preview the book to judge how suitable it will be with the goal of having the students read the book fluently the first time. While rereading may have value for different teaching purposes, we are not talking about choosing a book that we have to "drag" students through, mostly reading it for them and rereading it many times before a proficient-sounding rendition is achieved. Choose texts that stretch students' language knowledge to a degree but not so complex that the language structures are beyond their ability to control after your introduction.

The purpose of the introduction is to prepare the reader for a mostly correct and fluent reading the *first* time. Let your students know that you are going to talk about the book before they read it. "Plan for the child to have in his head the ideas and language he needs to complete the reading," (Clay 2005, 91). Figure 7-7 is a sample from an introduction to *Making a Sandwich*.

An Introduction to *Making a Sandwich,* Level C

Speaker	Teacher/Student Interactions	Analysis of Interactions
Ms. T	You are going to read a book today. It's called *Making a Sandwich.* What do you like to get for your sandwich?	Reads the title Asks for background knowledge
Benyam	Bread.	Share personal preferences
Selina	Turkey.	
Abela	Cheese.	
Ms. T	You can see two boys making a sandwich on the cover. In this book, on every page they are going to tell what they get to put on their sandwich. I'm going to name some things they got for their sandwich and you point to them on the cover.	Orients them to how the book works Puts labels in their heads and connects them to pictures
	Bread, lettuce, tomatoes, peppers, meat, and cheese. Do you think it looks good to eat?	Asks for opinion
Hani	Yes. Peanut butter.	Indicates a preference
Ms. T	You can put peanut butter on a sandwich. They don't put it on this sandwich.	Clarifies the content
Abela	I like sandwich.	Relates to text topic
Ms. T	It looks like a good sandwich. Yum! Sometimes when you make a sandwich you get some bread first. Look at pages 2 and 3.	Uses a word from the end of the text Uses the same verb (different tense)
Selina	It is bread.	Notices picture information
Ms. T	You are right. The two boys are talking. This page says "We got some bread for the sandwich." Let's read that together and point under each word.	Gives students the precise language of the text Invites students to rehearse the language
Students	We got some bread for a sandwich.	Read in unison
Ms. T	Turn the page. Now what do they get?	Directs attention to the picture
Hani	Lettuce.	Notices picture information
Ms. T	Say the word *got*. It starts with a *g*. Run your finger under *got*.	Locate a new word
Ms. T	Say "We got some lettuce for the sandwich." Do you see where they put the lettuce? Point to it.	Directs attention to the picture
Abela	On the sandwich.	Uses book information

FIGURE 7-7 An Introduction to *Making a Sandwich,* Level C

An Introduction to *Making a Sandwich,* Level C

Speaker	Teacher/Student Interactions	Analysis of Interactions
Ms. T	They put it on the bread. Let's read the last two lines. "We put it on the bread."	Clarifies content
Students	"We put it on the bread."	Read in unison
Ms. T	Say *put.* What letter would you expect to see at the beginning of *put*?	Directs attention to the sound of the first letter to have children connect it to the letter
Students	P.	Identify a letter
Ms. T	Put your finger under the word *put* and get a good look. (Children locate *put.*) On every page, the boys will tell a new food that they *got* and *put* on the sandwich. Let's read this page together.	Directs attention to visual features of a word Tells how the book "works" Invites rehearsal of language
Students	We got some lettuce for the sandwich. We put it on the bread.	Read in unison
Ms. T	Let's go through the book and name some of the foods they got and put on the sandwich.	Directs attention to vocabulary
Students	*[Go through the book and name the foods. Whenever a food is named, everyone repeats it.]*	Rehearses labels for the food
Ms. T	(On page 10) That is *meat.* What would you expect to see at the beginning of *meat.* It starts like *me.*	Draws attention to sound/letter correspondence and invites connection to a known word
Students	M.	Identify a letter
Ms. T	Find the word *meat* and let's read this page together.	Draws attention to visual features of words Invites rehearsal of the language
Students	We got some meat for the sandwich. We put it on the peppers.	Read in unison
Ms. T	Look at page 13. What are they putting on the meat?	Draws attention to the pictures and asks students to use background information
Selina	Cheese.	Identify a word
Ms. T	They get one more thing to put on the cheese. What do you think it could be?	Asks for prediction
Abela	Lettuce?	Make predictions
Selina	More tomato?	
Hani	More bread. You put the bread on top.	
Ms. T	You will find out. And, you will find out if the boys like the sandwich. Let's go back to page 2. Read the book softly to yourself. Be sure to look at the pictures to help you and point under each word.	Asks for forward thinking to the end of the story Reminds students of word-by-word matching and the information in the pictures

FIGURE 7-7 *(continued)*

What you see in Figure 7-7 is a highly supportive introduction. Depending on your students' strengths, you might want to make it less or even more supportive. In summary, you can use the text introduction to:

▶ Help students understand how the book "works" (the organization, the events of the story, the way ideas are laid out on the page, the function of pictures, how the nonfiction text features function).

▶ Familiarize students with language structures that may be challenging.

▶ Get them thinking about the ideas and information in the book.

▶ Draw attention to the information in the pictures.

▶ Draw attention to new and important words (predicting the first letter, locating, saying, running a finger under it, talking about the meaning).

Vocabulary and word identification are important for ELLs. In the introduction above, a tricky part will be to say "put them on the tomatoes" instead of the (also likely) "put them on the sandwich." The teacher wants students to cross-check one source of information (syntax or meaning) with visual information (the first letter).

Language structure is also particularly important for ELLs because that is what they find most difficult. Searching for and using language structure is a very important factor in beginning reading. Language structure provides another source of information for cross-checking, monitoring, and searching that leads to self-regulation and independence. You don't want ELLs to acquire a large number of words that they cannot put together as language.

During the Reading

As you observe students reading orally, notice the sources of information they are using. Their accurate reading, substitutions, and self-corrections will provide important evidence of the reading behaviors they control.

▶ Are they using meaning (in the sentences and in the pictures)?

▶ Are they using language structure? Are some of their errors related to language issues, such as tricky syntax that they do not yet control?

▶ Are they using visual information (print) to monitor and cross-check?

▶ Are they checking meaning with visual information? Using structure to check is very difficult early on. The students need to first learn what it means for a phrase to sound right in English.

You can interact briefly with the student to teach, prompt, or reinforce effective behaviors, for example,

Early
"This is the way we say it in English." "Listen to how I say this."
"That makes sense. Say it this way _____ in English."
"It could be _____, but look at _____. (first letter)."

Later
"Try that again and think what would make sense and look right."
"That makes sense but it needs to look right, too."

Don't interrupt too much, try to correct everything, or teach too much at one time. It will be very easy for students to lose momentum in the language and/or the meaning of the story.

After the Reading

Discussing the text gives students an opportunity to express their ideas, and they are in a very good position to do so because some of the language of the text is immediately available to them. You want to hear comments like those in the discussion shown in Figure 7-8.

Students can also "borrow" some of the language structure from the book as they discuss it. You can ask questions or demonstrate by sharing your own thinking. Avoid responses like "right" or "good," because you want the situation to encourage talking, not shut it down by looking for a "correct" response until you get it.

After the discussion, teach for processing strategies that help readers make shifts in their learning. You might point out an example of cross-checking that you observed or work with the students on fluency. You might ask them to reread a page or short paragraph to think more about the meaning. Working with words in a "hands-on" way will help ELLs expand a repertoire of known sight words, which is very helpful to them; it will also help them connect words and learn the way words work. Working with words will help them grow in their ability to pronounce words as well because they are able to slow down the process and look closely.

ELLs may benefit from the use of interactive writing after reading, although this is an option rather than a regular part of guided reading lessons. Interactive writing provides the opportunity to again use some of the language of the text.

Discussion of *Making a Sandwich*

Ms. T	They put the bread and the lettuce and the tomatoes and the cheese.
Rohan	They got some lettuce and they got some peppers. They make big sandwich and they say 'yum'.
Leeta	I don't want tomato. I like cheese.
Regie	It's the biggest sandwich. I didn't know it was so big.
Abela	I like this sandwich.
Ms. T	It sounds like you are thinking it's a really, really big sandwich with all of those things on it. No wonder they say 'yum' at the end. Let's look at page 16 and read 'yum' just the way the boys say it. The last thing they put on the sandwich is?
Students	Bread.
Ms. T	Selina, you said it might be bread. They put another piece of bread on the sandwich.

FIGURE 7-8 Discussion of *Making a Sandwich*

An Example at Level P

After several years of school, many ELLs will be reading books like *Coley's Journey* (*Fountas & Pinnell Classroom*, in press), shown in Figure 7-9.

It's important to realize that even though these students can read many words in English, they will still need support in processing complex language and in comprehending deeply. It will help them if they understand what a text is all about and how it is organized before they actually begin to read it; that will give them more understanding of the context so that they can anticipate the meaning of the words. The text structure is critical to all readers' understanding, but that is especially true for ELLs.

Before the Reading

When you select a book for ELLs, examine it carefully and plan a supportive introduction, giving particular attention to language that is key to understanding concepts. There may be idioms, for example, that are confusing; you may need to help students understand a metaphor. ELLs not only have to cope with the technical words that are increasingly included in a text, but they also have to understand

FIGURE 7-9 *Coley's Journey,* Pages 6–7

many Tier 2 English words, so they face challenges that are greater than most native English speakers. Add to that, possible challenges in using English pronunciation, and complex English syntax! So, with this overlay of complexity, it's no wonder that ELLs can sometimes sound accurate but be unable to perform well when asked to articulate the larger ideas in a text or to explain complex plots.

Coley's Journey is the true story of Coley, an osprey, who is tracked with special technology on his long migratory journey from Columbia, South America, to New York in the United States. Ospreys migrate each year, enduring a long and dangerous journey of 2,600 miles (4,184 kilometers) in order to reach a summer habitat to raise their young. A small GPS was placed on Coley's back and a team of scientists tracked Coley's trip to South America (over 17 days). This text provides a record of Coley's return journey to New York. Entries are dated to show the passage of time. The text has literary quality that gives readers visual images; illustrations are actual photographs of ospreys. On the margin of each right-hand page, a map shows Coley's journey as he progresses.

The clear layout of this text, the signals of passing time, the maps, and the illustrations provide the support that will help ELLs understand the "big picture" of what is happening with the bird. Ms. B, the teacher, begins by giving students some background information (see Figure 7-10).

When working with ELLs reading at higher levels, you can use the text introduction to:

▶ Draw attention to helpful text features that reveal the overall organization of the text.

▶ Help students understand the "whole"—the topic, the categories of information, and the big ideas in the text.

▶ Clarify new vocabulary and concepts.

▶ Have students say complex and difficult language syntax or read it chorally.

▶ Draw their attention to pictures that will support understanding.

▶ Discuss complex ideas.

During the Reading

At this level, you do not want to interrupt students' reading, but you may want to sample some oral reading to observe the processing. You can also be ready to assist readers at a point of difficulty—to tell a word or direct them toward helpful information. You wouldn't want to stop frequently during reading and interrupt their attention to the meaning of the text, but you can make observations that will guide you as students revisit the text. As you observe, ask yourself:

▶ Are students reading accurately?

▶ What do intonation patterns and attempts at word pronunciation tell you?

▶ What kinds of confusions are evident?

▶ What elements of syntax seem challenging or confusing?

▶ What vocabulary do I need to clarify?

Introduction to *Coley's Journey*

Speaker	Teacher/Student Interactions	Analysis of Interactions
Ms. B	The title of this book is *Coley's Journey* by Jean Knox. Look at the bird on the front. That's an osprey. An osprey is a bird that migrates. Do you know what that means?	Provides background information and probes student understanding
Shara	They go south in winter because it's too cold.	Share understandings
Lin	Some birds don't do it, but lots of them do it.	
Ms. B	To *migrate* does mean to move back and forth from place to place. For birds, it usually means living somewhere warm in our winter and then going north in our summer. Some birds, like the osprey, have a very long trip, or journey, when they migrate. This whole book is about this osprey, Coley, and his journey or his trip. Read the back of the book and then share your thinking.	Defines a critical term and concept Provides background information Prompts articulation of thinking
Lin	They put a backpack on him that was like a phone or something so they could know where he goes.	Notice picture information
Dai	It was a GPS like in a car or on a phone.	
Maka	They didn't know where he went or anything about it.	
Ms. B	Look at the map on page 13. The red line shows you where Coley started in Columbia, South America, and how far he went. What are you thinking or wondering?	Draws attention to a graphic that will guide comprehension of the text Prompts articulation of thinking
Anh	It is a really long way.	Share responses
Shara	He goes to Cuba.	Pose wonderings
Anh	How long does it take?	
Dai	Is he by himself?	
Ms. B	It takes a long time and it's very dangerous. The scientists were able to see where Coley went because of the GPS and they could tell how long it took. Remember, he goes back and forth every year. They tracked him when he went from New York to Columbia, and that took 17 days. So we'll see how long it took him to come back. Look at pages 2 and 3 and share your thinking.	Provides background information Prompts articulation of thinking
Lin	He's a big bird like an eagle. He kind of looks like one.	Share observations
Shara	He goes a long way on the globe.	
Dai	He's in South America there. He looks kind of dangerous.	
Ms. B	You are probably looking at his talons—his feet. Say *talons*.	Draws attention to the illustration and label
Students	Talons.	Repeat word
Ms. B	Do you see the label in the picture? The talons are very important to Coley. He can hold on to branches and also catch fish.	Draws attention to the illustration and label
Dai	I saw a bird catch fish like that on TV.	Shares personal experience
Ms. B	You can see on the globe how far Coley has to go. He lives in a wildlife refuge in New York City, and he has to fly 2,600 miles to get there. Look at page 5 and read the sidebar.	Summarizes information in the text Directs attention to information
Maka	That's the little backpack. How do they keep it on?	Poses a question

FIGURE 7-10 Introduction to *Coley's Journey*

Introduction to *Coley's Journey*

Speaker	Teacher/Student Interactions	Analysis of Interactions
Kalu	It is little.	Shares observation
Ms. B	Look at page 6 and read the heading. What's happening?	Directs attention to information
Shara	He's starting off.	Shares observations
Dai	That's what they look like catching fish.	
Ms. B	Coley is starting on his journey. Do you see the dates, March 5 and March 7, on page 6? They look like they're on a tablet. That's the record that the scientist keeps. Until Coley gets to New York, you will see records, like a diary or your reader's notebook, with the dates from the calendar. Then, you will read what he does each day. Read the sidebar under the picture of Coley catching a fish.	Directs attention to information and explains chronological order Directs attention to the illustrations
Dai	He just hits the water and grabs it.	Relate information from text
Maka	It's slippery but he stabs it with his talons.	
Ms. B	This is an example of how he uses his talons. Do you see the word in bold, *hovers*? That's a word you may not know. Read the sidebar and then talk about what *hover* means.	Directs attention to vocabulary
Kalu	He just hangs there above the water for a minute and then he dives.	Provides definition
Ms. B	You know that you can look at the glossary if you don't understand the words in bold. Look at the next few pages and you can see the dates change. What do you notice about the map?	Prompts to use glossary Helps students use dates (timeline) and graphic Draws attention to details in the pictures
Dai	The red line shows how far he has gone. It keeps getting longer.	Relate information from graphic
Shara	He's going a lot of days.	
Ms. B	Look at pages 14 and 15. These two pages are really interesting. You find out more about ospreys. What do you notice in the pictures?	Directs attention to pictures
Kalu	They have a big nest and it says they use it every year. It's like their house.	Notice text information
Maka	He's got the backpack on there. What's that sticking up?	
Dai	It's like a thing for a radio.	
Ms. B	It does look like an antenna. That's how they track Coley. This bird, Coley, is described as the "star" of an important science project. Do you know why the writer would say that?	Checks on understanding
Shara	He's like a star in a movie?	Makes hypothesis
Ms. B	The star in a movie is often the main character. This whole scientific project is focusing on Coley and they are learning a lot from him, so the writer uses the word "star" to show how important Coley is. Always look at the dates and the red line. You'll notice that some days are skipped. So the writer does not include every day but you will read all the entries from March 5 to March 20, and you will see what Coley and his mate do when they reach Jamaica Bay in New York. Then, let's talk about your thinking.	Clarifies a metaphor Talks about how the whole text is organized Sets expectations

FIGURE 7-10 *(continued)*

After the Reading

ELL students benefit greatly from the discussion after reading. They have an authentic reason to put their thinking into words and to communicate with others. Students can become highly engaged in interaction. Use language that facilitates discussion and encourage students to use the same in responding to each other, for example:

> "What makes you think that?"
> "I agree because. . . ."
> "Say more about that so I can understand what you are thinking."

Discussing a text right after they have read it makes the language of the text more accessible to students and they can take on some of it themselves. Watch for comments like:

> "Coley's journey is so amazing because he could be killed in lots of places."
> "I wonder how he knows to start flying again."
> "They don't just study him. They do a lot of ospreys. It's not just him. It's what he teaches us about birds. Then you can protect the birds."
> "You can learn a lot because we have the GPS now."
> "They all migrate separately but why? But I don't know how the babies know how to do that."

One of the goals is to get students to talk to and respond to each other, but you also want to participate in a way that lifts students' thinking. It is not enough for ELLs to read accurately and have a superficial understanding of a text. They need to be able to manipulate ideas, make inferences, and detect the nuances of texts using a range of academic vocabulary. You want them to raise questions and search for answers. You can decide to revisit places in the text to support deeper understanding. You can also use graphic organizers to help students understand the way information is presented. For example, students could work together to make a timeline of Coley's journey or represent the route on a map. Or, you can use shared writing to list the benefits of the research project. Extending the text in this way will help students better understand the text, and they can use the language and vocabulary in the process.

Reflecting on Your Teaching

We began this chapter with a number of principles for working with English language learners. If you are new to this work, it may seem daunting. But don't reduce it to a seemingly endless set of "tasks" for you to add to your busy day. You can be successful if you try to see your classroom and the learning going on within it from the student's perspective. Saavedra says that empathy is the key. When you empathize, you put yourself in the learner's place, imagining what it would be like. Communication with empathy "lowers each student's guard and creates the conditions for rigorous learning," (2016, 69).

It will help to engage in ongoing self-reflection using the lens of an ELL. Put yourself in the students' shoes. Consider: What did the student do today that he could not do last week? How did I help and support this student? What adjustments did I make in my teaching to make it easier for the ELLs to learn? What do I need to do tomorrow? A hundred such acts will, over time, make a big difference for the students in your class; and, you will find that working with ELLs can be even more rewarding than working with native English speakers because their changes are so rapid and observable as they take on a new language.

Suggestions for Professional Development

1. Call a meeting in your school to talk about English language learners. (If this is not possible, engage in this activity as a self-reflection or invite a colleague from another school to join you.)

2. First, go through class lists or your own to identify all the home languages represented in your school. If you have time, make a circle graph showing the percentage of each language. You might be surprised at how many of the students do not speak English at home (or speak a language in addition to English).

3. Have each person at the meeting list the ELLs in his classroom and make an hypothesis as to the level of English acquisition for each student. (Confirming this list might take further assessment. The ESL teacher can be of great help if you have one in the school.)

4. Have each person find out something about the language and/or culture of at least one of the students. Learning about how the home language works will support students in understanding students' early reading behaviors in English.

5. If possible, find out about the student's prior school experience and presence of English speakers in the home. Understanding this can provide support in knowing what the student will need in understanding the logistics of how schools work in the new country.

6. Using the suggestions in this book (and any other good sources you have), make a list of how you can make the school more inviting. For example, what should students see as they enter the door and move down the corridors? You can have posters and signs in many languages.

7. Have grade-level colleagues work together to make a list of changes in the classroom environment to make it more inclusive. If one teacher is very experienced in this area, visit the classroom.

8. Make plans for a guided reading lesson and go over the introduction with the group. Consider the level of English acquisition with which you are working. Ask for suggestions about:
   ▶ What language patterns might need rehearsal?
   ▶ What vocabulary or background information do students need?

9. Call another meeting to discuss how the lesson went and what changes you have made in the classroom.

Working with ELLs will require ongoing professional work with colleagues. The number of languages students speak can make the work more complex, enormously challenging, and every bit as rewarding. As with all your students, these special learners rely on your expertise.

SECTION **TWO**

Using Systematic Observation and Assessment to Form Groups and Guide Teaching

The chapters in this section explore in detail the process of observing and assessing readers. Differences across years of growth are noted, and these chapters will help you understand how to group students for efficient teaching and learning. They offer a description of running records and the documentation of progress over time. Finally, we discuss the connections between assessment and instruction, using *The Fountas & Pinnell Literacy Continuum* as a tool.

We consider detailed assessment and careful grouping as essential for effective guided reading. You want to pull together students based on solid behavioral evidence, and use it to set the forward direction for your teaching. *The Literacy Continuum* is designed to help you teach for shifts in learning, which is the purpose of guided reading. It does little, if any, good for students to read a book that is too easy or too hard, and follow it with empty chatter. You can use *The Literacy Continuum* as a tool that can center your teaching and help you teach on the edge of the students' understandings, thus moving them forward.

CHAPTER 8

Understanding Reading as a Complex Process

The reader's successful strategic activity builds a neural network for working on written language and that network learns to extend itself.

–Marie Clay

Guided reading is only one component of an instructional system for literacy (see Chapter 2), but it is a critical component. It is in guided reading that you have the opportunity to lift students' ability to independently process texts or expand their processing system. With your support, they take on a more challenging text and read it with proficiency, learning more as they do so. When you teach a guided reading lesson, your richest resource is your knowledge of what proficient reading "looks like" and "sounds like." As teachers, we come to understand the reading process by observing what proficient readers actually do as they shift and change over time.

Even beginning reading is highly complex. Reading means constructing meaning from printed symbols arranged in regular patterns on a surface. It is tempting for people to assume that reading is the simple task of looking at letters (arranged as words), connecting the letters to the sounds of language—like cracking a secret code of abstract symbols. Connecting letters and sounds is indeed important and reading is processing language, but a large body of research indicates that reading is much more complex than decoding alone. We are constantly learning more about the complex range of in-the-head strategic actions that readers employ simultaneously as they process texts. In other words, as your eyes follow print, your brain is making an uncountable number of rapid and simultaneous connections and decisions.

"Reading is at once a 'perceptual' and a 'cognitive' process," (Rumelhart 1985, 722). Add to that, a motor element. In English and many other languages, readers need to track print left to right along the line and return to the left margin after finishing a line. They need to move from the left page to the right page, the top line to the bottom line, turn pages (or swipe pages) to move through a volume, front to back. Those motions are so completely routine for the proficient reader that they are unconscious, and we forget that they are arbitrary. Some languages don't work that way. All speech comes out in time, but when represented by written forms in space, languages differ, and they must be learned by beginners. From there, the description of reading becomes highly complex. Readers simultaneously:

▶ recognize letters and connect them to spoken words, a process that is rapid and unconscious;

▶ understand words arranged in recognizable syntax (language structure or grammar) that sounds like language;

▶ access the meaning of the words arranged in print;

▶ keep in mind the overall meaning of the text;

▶ keep adding to understanding and thinking about the ideas and information in the text.

Readers begin the process of comprehending from the moment they enter the text reading (and often, before they begin). Depending on the text, they can also feel a range of emotions as they read (and after they read).

The amazing thing is that almost all children accomplish the complex task of learning to read in just a few years, although they continue to expand reading ability for many years thereafter; and some aspects of reading are taken on even later in life (for example, when you begin to read a genre you have neglected or enter a new field of study).

The reading process and how it is learned has been a focus of research for the last one hundred years, and there are great disagreements as to its nature; but there is general agreement that it is highly complex (Clay 1979, 2001, 2015; Downing and Leong 1982; Juel 1991; McNaughton 1987; Meek 1988; Ruddell and Singer 1994; Rumelhart 1994). The most enlightening research has revealed what real children do as they read. For example, we can compare three readings of the same page of *Sticks and Stones for Little Monster* (*Fountas & Pinnell Classroom*, in press) shown in Figure 8-1.

Little Monster got
some weeds.
He put them
on the table, too.

8

9

FIGURE 8-1 *Sticks and Stones for Little Monster* Pages 8–9

All three children know some letters and their related sounds and recognize some words. They bring to the act of reading their knowledge of the language they have been learning since their first year of life. Their understanding of syntactic patterns is intuitive; they know when something doesn't "sound right." They also know to follow print left to right and to return to the left margin. And they understand that the language they see in print has to make sense and mean something (see Figure 8-2). All three are well on the way to reading.

1. On line one, Caleb read *gets* for *got*. On line two, he read *puts* for *put*. On line three, he substituted *the* for *them*. After he read *on*, he realized that *the* did not make sense or sound right. It may additionally be the case that he noticed the *m* at the end of *them*.

2. Riva read *gets* for *got* in line one and *puts* for *put* in line three. On line two, she inserted the word *and*. She did not pause; we can hypothesize that the substitutions made sense and sounded right to her. (As an additional confirmation, her substitutions were visually very similar to the correct words, so the discrepancies were not divergent enough to trigger a pause for self-correction at this point in her development of a reading process.) It is interesting that she used present tense on line one and preserved the present tense on line three, something that even adult oral readers are likely to do from time to time.

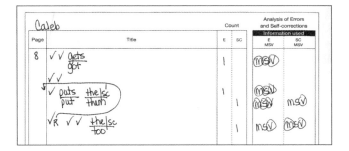

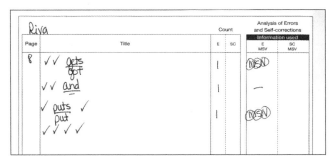

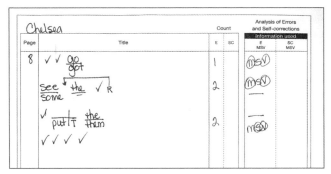

FIGURE 8-2 Caleb, Riva, and Chelsea Reading *Sticks and Stones for Little Monster*

3. Chelsea seemed to focus on using her knowledge of the sound system and graphic symbols. Using the first letter, she substituted *go* for *got* and *see* for *some*. She paused, however, and repeated *the weeds*, perhaps realizing that something was wrong. At the word *put*, she paused and was eventually told the word. On line three, she substituted *the* for *them*. There is evidence here that Chelsea was monitoring her reading and searching for information even if she was not ultimately successful.

All of these children are using several different sources of information and are learning how to check one against the other to be sure they make sense, sound right, and look right. The goal is the integration of all sources of information. Their errors and self-corrections offer a "window" on the reading process. Each of these children is making hypotheses and attempts based on them. The errors are not random guesses; each has logic behind it. Often, errors are the same part of speech as the correct word; very often they preserve meaning. Sometimes errors are based on the use of visual information. If something doesn't make sense, and readers notice it and act on it—they *self-monitor*. Then readers *search for* further information that they can *use* to *correct* the errors. A reader—even a very young one—who is making attempts, noticing errors, searching, and self-correcting is *active,* as Askew and Fountas point out in an article titled, "Active from the Start," (1998).

The foremost researcher and theorist of literacy processing and literacy learning is New Zealander Marie M. Clay. Her work has influenced researchers across the world, with tremendous impact on the work of teachers in classrooms. Clay was a developmental psychologist with a focus on cognitive growth. She studied children in great detail, documenting changes over time in their reading and writing behaviors. From her observations of how children's reading behaviors changed, she theorized changes in the way readers think. This was new territory in reading research at the time, and she referred to it as *an unusual lens.* Unlike other investigations, Clay

▶ made a very large number of detailed observations of children across time as they encountered their first year of reading instruction;

▶ observed children's behaviors as they read *continuous text* (rather than single letters or words only);

▶ looked at proficient learners (rather than children having difficulty only);

▶ identified multiple pathways to a fully integrated reading process.

She found that children can take many "different paths to common outcomes," depending on what they attend to at any given time and the rich resources and adult support available. Clay's theoretical perspectives reveal powerful messages for teachers in the classroom and have created a profound legacy. Below we examine some of the "big ideas" in Clay's theoretical frame.

Clay's theory of reading suggests that early readers must learn to look for four different types or sources of information in print and to check one against another as they learn how to build an early reading process (see Figure 8-3). Readers learn to look for and check one source of information against another to confirm a response.

They access what they know about the sounds of language, the visual features of letters and words (and their relationships to the sound system), and the structure of language. Overall, written language must make sense or have meaning. The sources of information are constantly cross-checked, one against another, so that the response "fits." Very early in the acquisition of the reading process, we can see behavioral evidence of these cognitive processes, but they rapidly become unconscious as readers learn more.

Clay's Theory of Reading

Sense, Meaning
Does it make sense?

Visual Cues
Does that look right?

Sounds
Say it. What can you hear?
What would you expect to see?

Structure/Grammar
Can we say it that way?

FIGURE 8-3 Clay's Theory of Reading (Clay, *Literacy Lessons: Designed for Individuals,* 2005.)

Language as a Self-Extending System

Clay was highly in tune with the research on language acquisition and development that was making breakthroughs at the time while writing *Becoming Literate*. She considered language to be the first example of a "self-extending system," one that grows, changes, and becomes more effective as it is used. When children engage in interactions with others, the process is much more than "practicing." They are building knowledge by trying out the language according to their working hypotheses. For example, parents are sometimes taken aback when a child who has been saying "I ran" suddenly says "I runned." That's not a step backward. It signals that the child has learned through interaction that very often the past tense is signaled by *–ed* and is overgeneralizing and applying the rule to all verbs.

It is sometimes said that no one has to "teach" children to talk; yet they master the huge and complex body of knowledge needed to use language by about age five. The young child's accomplishments are amazing. Every language has an infinite number of sentences, each with its own meaning, that are put together according to grammatical rules. By encountering and using language in the environment, children learn the rules that they can then use to generate an infinite number of sentences. Even typical early statements by children (*more juice, more cookie, more TV*) are not random utterances nor are they imitations of adult language. They are highly organized and meaningful statements that get responses from the adults with whom the children interact. By using a "rule" and applying it to more and more examples, they refine the use of language. In this way, language allows the learner to keep on learning by using it. Caregivers seldom correct their children. Instead, they encourage children to produce whatever they can—one-, two-, and three-word utterances. They listen and respond as if the child has produced a fully constructed meaningful sentence.

> Child: More juice.
> Mother: Oh, you would like some more juice? Here it is.

As children produce more, caregivers produce less of the conversation. Through learning language, children learn

- how the sounds of language are connected to meaning;
- how to negotiate meaning with others;
- how to notice details in the sounds;
- how to form hypotheses and test them through interaction;
- how to search for more information, revise concepts, and connect sets of understanding.

Our first language is always that of the home and community in which we lived as young children, but the learning opportunities—words, rules for generating meaningful statements and sentences, ways of pronouncing words and clusters of sounds—are there in every dialect of every language. Once children have learned to use any language, they have acquired a powerful self-extending system. Of the child entering school, Clay says,

> He has learned how to learn language. It is important for teachers to remind themselves of this when they seem to hear differences in a particular

child's speech. The child may not know as much about language as some of his peers, or he may find that the rules for talking in school are different from those in his culture or ethnic group, or he may see little similarity between talking in his family and the more formal teacher-pupil talk of the classroom, or he may even speak a different language from the teacher's. Yet in all these cases the child has already learned how to learn language. (1991, 26–27)

Language as a Resource for Taking on Print

Looking at a page of *We're Going on a Bear Hunt* (Rosen 1989), two-year-old Kristen says, "We're going on a bear hunt. We're gonna catch a bear, a big one. Can't go under it. Can't go around it. Swish, swish, swish." She is not looking at the print but at the pictures, but she makes hand gestures and tells the story using much of the vocabulary. She is learning about the language of books, which is different in many important ways from spoken language.

One of the things that makes reading difficult is that written language is not exactly "talk written down." Even in the easy texts that children read during the first year of school, the syntax of written language is different. For example,

"Wait," shouted John. "I want to go, too."

If you heard this sentence, even if you did not see the print, you would assume that the individual is reading because it sounds like "book talk." In fact, "talking like a book" is common in young children who have heard many stories read. Memorable language like "So he huffed, and he puffed, and he huffed, and he puffed" makes an impression on young learners and they take it on as oral language.

Because they live in a world that is full of meaningful print, they begin early to notice the signs of their favorite restaurants, the icons and names of electronic games, labels of favorite foods, and their own names when they appear in writing. These first understandings of print are very personal and highly idiosyncratic. Jackson recognizes his *J* before he truly understands the nature of the alphabet or even that there are a limited number of other letters. But for another child it could be *A* or *W* for the sign on the gate at the ranch. Children start to collect meaningful symbols.

Writing and Reading as Reciprocal Processes

When children have access to many books, they will learn a considerable amount about print before school entry. But even if their knowledge is limited, a print-rich environment can take advantage of children's natural tendencies to search for meaningful objects and signs. They learn about print rapidly, as shown in Figure 8-4. As they engage in these activities, literacy power is built through a com-

Learning About Written Language in Different Instructional Contexts

Context	Definition	Opportunity to Learn
Interactive Read-Aloud	Teacher reads to students.	◆ Internalize the structure and vocabulary of written language. ◆ Acquire knowledge of increasingly complex concepts and ideas they will meet in reading. ◆ Notice the writer's and illustrator's craft.
Shared Reading	Teacher and students read an enlarged text in unison.	◆ Follow print with the eyes. ◆ Notice distinctive features of letters and words. ◆ Say written language to learn the structure. ◆ Notice text features that signal organization and ideas (labels, headings). ◆ Attend to the writer's and illustrator's craft.
Guided Reading	Teacher works with a small group of students who are reading the same text.	◆ Engage in the act of reading a challenging text. ◆ Process print, bringing together language structure, visual information, knowledge of sounds, and meaning.
Independent Reading	Students independently read a text that is easy enough to read without support (or one that has been previously read).	◆ Engage in the act of reading a text, often one the reader has chosen. ◆ Process print, bringing together language structure, visual information, knowledge of sounds, and meaning.
Shared and Interactive Writing	The teacher and students compose a message while the teacher scribes and sometimes students contribute some of the print.	◆ Become aware of the layout of print (lines and spaces). ◆ Observe the formation of letters and words in the construction of a meaningful message. ◆ Sometimes make the motor movements necessary to form letters and words. ◆ Link the sounds of language to the symbols that represent them. ◆ Learn how to compose and lay out a variety of texts.
Guided Writing	The teacher pulls together students with a common writing need.	◆ Examine writing closely to confirm application of what was learned. ◆ Use mentor texts as examples to use in own writing. ◆ Learn planning, revising, and editing skills.
Independent Writing	Students write independently messages they have composed.	◆ Compose messages and stories. ◆ Slow down speech to link to letters. ◆ Draw and write to represent the stories and messages. ◆ Make writing decisions for a particular purpose and audience.

FIGURE 8-4 Learning About Written Language in Different Instructional Contexts

bination of reading and writing, between which there is a strong reciprocity. Processes are built up and broken down in both, but writing "slows down" the process and makes it more visible. In early writing experiences, children naturally and purposefully attend to the details of print, which provides strong support for early reading behaviors.

Very early writers may scribble, produce letter-like forms, strings of letters, or their names. They often combine drawing and writing, and sometimes attach a message or "story" only after writing. But with experience they recognize that print is different from pictures; it represents language that someone can read. And, when written language is read aloud, it says the same thing every time. They begin to develop a sense of "wordness," as it exists abstractly in spoken language and as words are defined by space on the page (Ray and Glover 2008). We love telling the story of the kindergarten student who asked, "Why can't I hear the spaces when I talk?"

Writing involves a complex series of actions. Children have to think of a message and hold it in the mind, think of the first word and how to start it, remember each letter form and its features, and manually reproduce the word letter by letter, left to right on a page. This immersion in the process begins to make literacy processing more visible.

In a well-designed instructional program, it is important to take advantage of the reciprocity between reading and writing. Children go smoothly from writing to reading, and reading to writing, always focusing on the uses of literacy for meaningful purposes.

Building Working Systems

At first, children may approach reading using primitive strategies such as "remembering" language and using it in response to the pictures, but as they learn more about print, they begin to do the following:

▶ Self-monitor. They know when something doesn't fit with the visual aspects of print or when something doesn't make sense. They pause.

▶ Cross-check one source of information with another to determine whether a word they have read "looks right," "sounds right," and "makes sense."

▶ Search for and use meaning, visual information (letter and sound relationships), and language structure to find a good fit.

▶ Self-correct to read accurately.

They do all of this with the goal of and for the pleasure of determining the meaning of language in print. In this process, they actually learn from making errors and correcting them. They become more independent in searching for and checking print. They automatically confirm and correct their reading. This "fast brainwork" builds a system for working on print and extends itself through successful problem solving on continuous text.

Expanding Strategic Activity

From the beginning, students need to understand (at increasingly sophisticated levels) what readers actually do. Early instructional influences may steer children toward incorrect or too narrow expectations. Some may believe that reading is simply saying words; they may process a text in a way that is not too different from a list. Others may believe that reading is just memorizing. Memory is certainly involved and so is using letter-sound relationships to say words, but reading is much more. Some readers do not understand how deeply they should expect themselves to comprehend a text.

If such confusions persist, students can move higher in the educational system with very low-level reading skills. Teachers sometimes say of struggling students that, "they can read it, but don't understand what they are reading." What they usually mean is that the students are reading the words without adequately understanding the meaning of the text. For us, meaning must be there. Reading without understanding simply isn't acceptable reading, and we have to do something about it to help students achieve their potential meaning must be the goal from the beginning.

Building a Strategic Base Across the Years

The goal in the early years of schooling is to help beginning readers build the strategic base they will need to engage in the highly complex and challenging reading they will do for the rest of their school years and in life. The meaning must always be there. Over time, readers learn to engage systems of strategic actions.

Searching for and Using Information

Readers search for and use information—a whole range of information: the visible information in print and the invisible information in language and meaning. In the earliest encounters, the child is learning how to look at the printed symbols, noticing their distinctive features. The process of problem solving in reading involves rapid, largely unconscious searching for the information needed. The rewards are accuracy and understanding. Using the eyes to quickly distinguish each letter form, particularly when they are arranged together, involves a large amount of visual learning. As they search, readers ask questions such as what would "look right," "sound right," and "make sense," (Clay 1993). As they grow more sophisticated, readers have more knowledge and information to bring to the reading process. From the process of reading, they acquire highly sophisticated knowledge of language structure, of words, of concepts and ideas, and of the way texts work in different genres.

Monitoring and Self-Correcting

Readers monitor and self-correct their reading. Reading is a problem-solving process and readers need to develop awareness of when they are inaccurate or don't understand what they are reading. They need to notice the mismatches and stop and problem-solve if their reading doesn't "look right," "sound right," or "make sense," (Clay 1993). As readers grow in proficiency, they develop highly sophisticated ways of using content knowledge, understanding of complex language, knowledge of literary features of genre, and insights into literary elements such as plot, character, and setting.

Solving Words

Readers solve words. They use a range of flexible word-solving strategies, which means not only decoding (or pronouncing) them but understanding their meaning. So word solving itself involves complex interactions. Clay (1993) theorized that readers use several sources of information, to problem-solve their way through a text. They use meaning that is built from the experiences in their lives. In other words, reading has to make sense. They use language syntax or structure; that is, they use predictable and acceptable grammatical structure to predict possible words. The word has to "sound right" in the sentence. Keep in mind that for English language learners, syntax is still being acquired and so access to English, which is so powerful for native speakers, may be weaker. (They do have deep knowledge of syntax in their own first language). They use the visual information that comes from knowing the relationship between oral language and its graphic symbols (graphophonic information)—the letters that are formed into words divided by spaces and arranged on the page. The word has to "look right." As they become more sophisticated, readers build their spoken and reading vocabularies. They develop a large number of known words that they recognize quickly and automatically, and they are able to take words apart in parts, thus solving long and complex words with efficiency.

Maintaining Fluency

Readers sustain fluent processing, which we assume is going on even when individuals are reading silently. Fluent processing means all strategic activity is taking place rapidly and smoothly. Fluency is not the same as reading "fast." In the beginning, young readers may slow down to point so that they control word-by-word matching and left-to-right directionality, but quickly they learn to move along with good momentum so that their reading sounds like language. Even in silent reading proficient readers move along at a good momentum, which is essential for understanding. Students who have to engage in processing, or "sound out" each word, and who read very slowly (word-by-word) typically have trouble comprehending what they read. And, individuals who try to "speed read" suffer large gaps in comprehension.

Adjusting

Readers adjust their reading in response to texts. They are flexible slowing down to problem-solve and speeding up again. They take action in flexible ways. (If one source of information is inadequate, they try another.) They read differently according to what they know about genre and features of text (for example, graphics, sidebars, or different kinds of text organization).

Summarizing

Readers summarize as they read. They remember important information and use it later in a text as information for problem solving and understanding. That means they do not remember every word or detail but distinguish and retain the important ideas and information from the trivial.

Predicting

Readers make predictions. They use what they know to anticipate what will happen next—the word, the sentence, or the events of the plot. They notice what characters are like and predict their actions. Prediction is a key part of thinking; we do it all the time and it is critical in reading. "You read with anticipation if you are to read with comprehension" (Clay 1979, 6).

Making Connections

Readers make connections as they read. They bring background knowledge to the understanding of both fiction and nonfiction texts. They empathize or identify with characters in stories. They connect books with their own lives, with other books, and with the larger world. As they acquire familiarity with more and more texts, they are able to make powerful connections between those they have experienced— for example, by genre, by author and style, by type of text structure, by attributes of characters, by plot, by theme, or by content.

Synthesizing

Readers synthesize new information and ideas from texts. Readers are always encountering new information and they incorporate it into their own sets of knowledge. As a result, they change cognitively. Their fund of information grows; they take on new perspectives, for example, from diverse cultures that they cannot directly experience or from gaining an understanding of history. Learning from texts is all about information and it goes beyond the "facts" to incorporating everything students learn about their world.

Inferring

Readers infer what writers imply but do not directly state. You might think a sophisticated strategic action like inferring is only for older readers; however, even the youngest readers can infer the feelings of characters or the "lesson" from a story. As readers encounter more sophisticated texts, the demands for inference are greater. The larger message of the text is very often unstated, but is very important for readers to infer.

Analyzing

Readers think analytically about a text. Not only do readers need to read a text with accuracy and comprehension; they also need to learn to be analytical. That means looking at the characteristics of the text—how the writer has organized and crafted it. Thinking analytically increases readers' deep understanding of a text and also contributes to enjoyment and awareness that can translate into writing skill. Analyzing is complex for early readers, but they can notice how a writer or illustrator created a funny character or helped readers understand a process. But as the demands of a text increase, so do the demands for analytic thinking. Deep comprehension usually involves noticing and understanding the nuances of the writer's craft.

Critiquing

Readers think critically about a text. Reading a text also involves forming opinions about it. We do not expect readers to accept what a writer says without evaluation. Early readers may simply think about whether a text is enjoyable, funny, or interesting and why; but as readers grow, they need to think about more complex criteria such as accuracy and authenticity. They need to learn to detect bias. Are characters believable? Is the argument soundly based on fact? Does the plot hang together logically? Is the writing of high quality? Sophisticated readers are also critics. They make judgments as to whether the characters seem real or the plot is believable. They evaluate the authenticity of a nonfiction text.

Systems of Strategic Actions

The strategic actions described briefly above are represented graphically in Figure 8-5 and on the inside front cover of this book. Readers use all of these actions simultaneously in a smoothly orchestrated way. They cannot be used or learned sep-

FIGURE 8-5 Systems of Strategic Actions

arately, but sometimes readers revisit or look back at a text after reading once to apply them in a more intense or focused way. Over time, we have called this revisiting "reading closely," "close analysis," or "close reading," to mean contemplating the meaning of a text or aspects of the writer's craft.

The strategic actions represent twelve categories within which we have clustered what are probably thousands of simultaneous actions that the brain engages in while reading. These categories represent the reading behaviors of proficient readers and provide a way to organize your thinking about teaching in guided reading, and they also give you a way to talk with colleagues about it. Strategic actions represent the teaching goals in guided reading. It may seem like a tall order, but by exposing students to texts that gradually increase in complexity, and providing skilled and supportive teaching, they can build these in-the-head actions over time. You are always "upping the ante" but assuring enough teaching that students can read with proficiency, and climb the ladder of success.

The Relationship Between Visible and Invisible Information

Clay's theory reveals an important concept—the relationship between visible and invisible information (see Figure 8-6 and also Figure 8-3). Some information is visible—you can see it in the text. Some is invisible—it exists in the reader's brain. Visible information includes what the reader sees as her eyes move across text or access information from graphics. It includes letters, words, word layout, punctuation, text tools, and text features such as captions, headings, sidebars, maps, graphics, and illustrations. Invisible information includes the reader's knowledge of language, content knowledge, personal experience, and understandings about texts. As readers process a text, they mix visible and invisible information to construct the author's intended meaning.

The reader notices the visible information in a text (print, punctuation, layout, text features, graphics, illustrations) and simultaneously brings to the process a wealth of knowledge that is invisible. Readers have opportunity to build experience with mixing visible and invisible information when processing continuous text. The reader searches for and uses both visible and invisible information in reading a text and the text itself, constructed by the author, provides both kinds of information.

The Relationship Between Visible and Invisible Information

Visible Information	Invisible Information
◆ Printed letters, clusters of letters, and words ◆ Punctuation and layout ◆ Graphics; illustrations	◆ Phonological information (associated with visible information in ways that vary by language) ◆ Syntactic or structural information (rules for stringing words together) ◆ Semantic (meaning) information (shown by the word and the placement in the sentence)

FIGURE 8-6 The Relationship Between Visible and Invisible Information

You will notice that visible information includes everything the eyes see, including print, graphics, illustrations, and other symbols. Invisible information exists in the readers head.

Self-Regulation

We wrote earlier about the early emergence of self-monitoring, cross-checking, and self-correction. These are sure signs of the self-regulation that will be important in the reading process throughout an individual's life. Successful reading of continuous text, with the ongoing construction of meaning, requires highly self-regulated behavior. A proficient reader keeps attention focused, uses all the information needed with efficiency, and is highly active—all this while sitting still and looking at print!

We know that "reading development is . . . strongly associated with the actual experience of successful reading," (Cormack 1992). Students need to get off to a good start and read with proficiency at every level, moving as fast as they can without the process breaking down. Self-regulation is an important element in the process; each time a student reads successfully, he should learn just a little bit more about the process of reading and grow in the ability to self-regulate. The development of a reading process is sometimes likened to the idea that "the rich get richer" based on a concept from the Gospel according to St. Matthew and has been called the "Matthew Effect" by Stanovich (1986). The better you read and the more you read the better reader you become. What this means is that we must assure successful reading, day after day, and year after year.

A Theory of Reading Continuous Text

Clay's research yielded a rich picture of the beginning development of a reading process because she studied readers as they processed continuous text. She could see evidence that children were using visible and invisible information as they self-monitored and self-corrected using multiple sources of information. We can see this same kind of evidence in the running records we code to capture and analyze reading behaviors (see Chapter 11). Other researchers have noticed how the features of texts assist and even "teach" the reader much about the structure of stories and informational texts (Meek 1988). Meek's convictions come from a five-year study of adolescents who had been determined to be "unteachable" but when they were given real books, they were able to learn.

All of this points to the idea that students should spend a large amount of time processing continuous text. As they do so, the process is *self-extending;* that is, like language, it expands with use. They develop independence and flexibility. In most cases, however, it doesn't happen without the careful and precise teaching that makes the difference in the acquisition of literacy.

Progress over Time

As you work with students, look for behavioral evidence of the strategic actions they control, partially control, or do not yet control. Some evidence comes from observation of oral reading; some comes from talking with students after reading or noting understanding from writing about reading. Each source of information is important as you make decisions about your teaching moves.

The Fountas & Pinnell Literacy Continuum: **A Practical Tool**

As a tool to use in this process, we have written a detailed description of progress over time. *The Fountas & Pinnell Literacy Continuum* is a compilation of the behaviors and understandings that proficient readers and writers develop over time in reading, writing and oral language. We have organized these specific descriptions along a continuum from the reading behaviors demanded by the easiest (level A) to the highly complex texts that adult proficient readers process (level Z). Also, the continua are organized according to instructional context to help you understand the possibilities for each kind of teaching as well as the evidence you can expect to see. The organization of *The Literacy Continuum* is shown in Figure 8-7.

    The Literacy Continuum is the backbone of a literacy curriculum. It allows you to do the following:

  ▶ Analyze the behaviors and understandings for individual readers and writers, noting strengths and needs.

  ▶ Select teaching goals and consider facilitative language.

  ▶ Notice specific evidence of progress over time.

  ▶ Plan for the emphases of teaching to help students expand systems of strategic actions.

  ▶ Evaluate the effects of your teaching on students' development of the behaviors.

    We will return to *The Literacy Continuum* in various chapters in this volume, but remember that the key to using it well is your own knowledge of readers, gained through close observation and interaction.

An Optimum Rate of Progress Through Skilled Teaching Support

We have provided a beginning description of a complex reading process along with information about how it changes from entry to a self-extending system. Individuals learn to read by reading; but most students need teaching in addition to time for reading and writing. And they need teaching even after an early reading process is established. Guided reading is an instructional context that allows you to help students move forward in reading development. Through specific teaching and careful text selection, you make it possible for students to learn more than they could learn on their own. The Russian psychologist Lev Vygotsky (1978; Rogoff, 1990) presented educators with a compelling and powerful idea. Vygotsky maintained that with the support of another, more experienced person, the learner is

Organization of *The Fountas & Pinnell Literacy Continuum*

	INSTRUCTIONAL CONTEXT	BRIEF DEFINITION	DESCRIPTION OF THE CONTINUUM
1	Interactive Read-Aloud and Literature Discussion	Students engage in discussion with one another about a text that they have heard read aloud or one they have read independently.	• Year by year, grades PreK–8 • Genres appropriate to grades PreK–8 • Specific behaviors and understandings that are evidence of thinking within, beyond, and about the text
2	Shared and Performance Reading	Students read together or take roles in reading a shared text. They reflect the meaning of the text with their voices.	• Year by year, grades PreK–8 • Genres appropriate to grades PreK–8 • Specific behaviors and understandings that are evidence of thinking within, beyond, and about the text
3	Writing About Reading	Students extend their understanding of a text through a variety of writing genres and illustrations.	• Year by year, grades PreK–8 • Genres/forms for writing about reading appropriate to grades PreK–8 • Specific evidence in the writing that reflects thinking within, beyond, and about the text
4	Writing	Students compose and write their own examples of a variety of genres, written for varying purposes and audiences.	• Year by year, grades PreK–8 • Genres/forms for writing appropriate to grades PreK–8 • Aspects of craft, conventions, and process that are evident in students' writing, grades PreK–8
5	Oral and Visual Communication	Students present their ideas through oral discussion and presentation.	• Year by year, grades PreK–8 • Specific behaviors and understandings related to listening, speaking, and presentation
6	Technological Communication	Students learn effective ways of communicating and searching for information through technology; they learn to think critically about information and sources.	• Year by year, grades PreK-8 • Specific behaviors and understandings related to effective and ethical uses of technology
7	Phonics, Spelling, and Word Study	Students learn about the relationships of letters to sounds as well as the structure and meaning of words to help them in reading and spelling.	• Year by year, grades PreK–8 • Specific behaviors and understandings related to nine areas of understanding related to letters, sounds, and words, and how they work in reading and spelling
8	Guided Reading	Students read a teacher-selected text in a small group; the teacher provides explicit teaching and support for reading increasingly challenging texts.	• Level by level, A to Z • Genres appropriate to grades PreK–8 • Specific behaviors and understandings that are evidence of thinking within, beyond, and about the text • Specific suggestions for word work (drawn from the phonics and word analysis continuum)

FIGURE 8-7 Organization of *The Fountas & Pinnell Literacy Continuum*

able to do more than he could on his own. Whatever the task, the learner is supported as he attempts it with assistance from the more capable partner. Gradually, the learner takes over the task and becomes expert, but meanwhile, the teacher, parent, or other learning partner works to extend the learner's knowledge and skills to a more advanced level.

Vygotsky used the term "zone of proximal development" to describe the experience of a learner who works successfully with the support of another and extends his knowledge in the process. Some educators refer to his heightened learning experience as "the learning zone" (see Figure 8-8).

The text you present in guided reading is not easy for the reader; in fact, it is challenging. However, your introduction and facilitative language make it possible for students to read it with proficiency. Day after day, they read with competence, working at the cutting edge of their understanding. As a teacher, you do not take problem solving away from the student. In fact, it is the problem solving that makes them grow.

With each guided reading lesson, you are using a "zoom lens" to provide very specific and focused instruction. You address your students' needs at one particular point on the developmental continuum in order to expand and refine their reading ability. They discover how to think about a text, and they use this ability across the literacy curriculum. Self-regulation is fostered. As Holdaway has said, "There is no better system to control the complexities and intricacies of each person's learning than that person's own system operating with genuine motivation and self-determination within reach of humane and informed help" (1979, 170).

Clay has described the process of taking on new learning and making it yours.

> This reading work clocks up more experience for the network with each of the features of print attended to. It allows the partially familiar to become familiar and the new to become familiar in an ever-changing sequence. Meaning is checked against letter sequence or vice versa, phonological recoding is checked against speech vocabulary, new meanings are checked against the grammatical and semantic contexts of the sentence and the story, and so on. Because one route to a response confirms an approach from another direction this may allow the network to become a more effective network. (Clay 1991, 328–329)

The Learning Zone

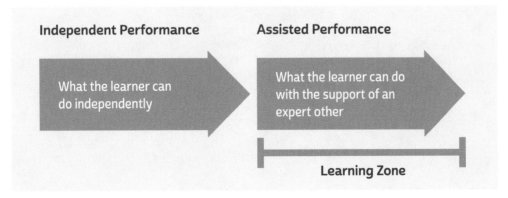

FIGURE 8-8 The Learning Zone

Clay has aptly described the day-to-day development of this complex learning. We see the gradient of text (and the constellations of behaviors and understandings texts demand at each level) as your tools for assisting your students in this learning process. Each day, in small-group instruction, readers learn a little bit more because they solve new problems and meet new challenges. Your teaching enables them not only to read one book with proficiency; they learn strategic actions that they can apply in all of their reading. We call this "learning generative." That's the goal of guided reading.

Suggestions for Professional Development

1. Work with a group of grade-level colleagues to take apart and understand the long quote by Clay about reading work on page 205.

   ▶ Work as partners or in small groups to make a diagram or drawing to represent the actions Clay is describing.

   ▶ Have partners or groups present their drawings.

   ▶ Discuss the role of successful experience in building the network.

2. Even if you and your colleagues are working with students at higher levels, it helps to examine lower-level examples because the reading behaviors are overt. Have partners or small groups work with the three running records in Figure 8-2. (You can download full-size blank versions from the Online Resources.) They can discuss:

   ▶ What evidence is there in each running record for the checking Clay has described?

   ▶ How are the three readers alike? How are they different?

3. Now go to the Guided Reading section of *The Fountas & Pinnell Literacy Continuum* if you have it (if you do not, you can use several leveled texts).

   ▶ Have group members examine one area of the text level of interest and talk about the goals.

   ▶ Then, have them go up two or three levels and, again, talk about the goals.

   Discuss:

   ▶ What teaching is needed today to assure success at their level?

   ▶ What will you expect to do in the next few weeks to enable students to lift their reading toward the next level?

CHAPTER 9

Observing and Assessing Readers to Inform Teaching Decisions

If children could work on literacy tasks most of the time at a level of success, we would have solved the biggest problem in learning to read and write.

–Don Holdaway

Powerful teaching in guided reading leads to an expansion of each student's reading abilities. Each lesson has the potential to result in "generative learning" that students can apply to other texts to extend the processing system. This is possible because you are working in the optimum zone of learning where, with support, students can read more than they could independently. The first step in effective guided reading instruction is to identify what students can presently do as readers, and that means using assessment that provides precise, reliable, and valid information. Two kinds of assessment are essential (see Figure 9-1).

Both kinds of assessment are essential and both are systematic rather than randomly applied. Assessment works best if it is used as an integral part of the rhythm of the school year and is built into the school day or week.

Two Essential Kinds of Assessment

Interval Assessment	Continuous Assessment
You use a standardized assessment to form a profile of each student.	You gather information or data on a continuous basis to give you a picture of individual progress over weeks of time throughout the year.
◆ This kind of assessment enables you to determine approximate beginning reading levels for individuals and to look across your classroom to form smaller groups for instruction.	◆ This kind of assessment helps you assess the impact of your teaching on a day-to-day basis.
◆ It is also useful in measuring the progress of the entire group.	◆ It is *formative* in that it helps you plan the emphases of teaching for individuals and groups on a daily and weekly basis.
◆ It can be *formative;* that is, it helps you make decisions about instruction at a distinct point or points in the school year.	
◆ It can also be *summative*, which means that it helps you assess the effectiveness of a half-year or a year of instruction on all of the students in your class.	
◆ It can function as part of the formal reporting system that is required in the school to document change in achievement.	

FIGURE 9-1 Two Essential Kinds of Assessment

Positive Outcomes for Assessment

- Finding out what each reader can do, both independently and with teacher support.
- Informing your teaching decisions on an ongoing basis.
- Documenting student progress over time.
- Summarizing achievement over a given period–six weeks, a year, or longer.
- Checking on the results (effectiveness) of your teaching.
- Providing information for reporting progress to families.
- Reporting to administrators, school boards, and various stakeholders in the community.

FIGURE 9-2 Positive Outcomes for Assessment

Rationale for Systematic Reading Assessment

Assessment has a number of positive outcomes (see Figure 9-2). Assessment begins with what students know: the evidence is in how they read, what they say, and what they write. Inevitably, then, assessment includes not only what students understand but also how well they can articulate their understandings. You should always keep in mind that English language learners almost always understand more than they can express. Your job in instruction is to provide safe daily opportunities to articulate understandings.

For the teacher of reading, observational assessment is an essential daily tool. A general view is that the role of assessment is to determine whether students have made progress; but that cannot be the sole purpose. If assessment does not result in improved teaching, then its value is greatly diminished. *Assessment allows us to see the results of our teaching* and to make valid judgments about: what students have learned how to do as readers; what they need to learn how to do next; and what teaching moves will support them.

Assessment is a form of scientific inquiry. A researcher gathers behavioral evidence in ways that are reliable and valid and then uses this evidence to build a pattern of knowledge about the phenomenon being observed. Evidence (which we will sometimes refer to as data or information) is organized and categorized by the researcher in a way that reveals important principles. Constructing these principles and testing them over time builds a theory or a set of understandings and beliefs that guide our work.

As teachers we have tentative theories (beliefs and understandings) about learning and teaching that we refine and revise every day as we work with students. Our theories are incomplete in that we are continually testing them against our observations of and interactions with individuals. Every student adds to our learning and enriches the theory, which is the foundation for our moment-to-moment decisions as we teach. The goal is to use assessment to grow in our understandings of our students and of the processes involved in learning to read.

All of us have internal systems or sets of understandings that allow us to make decisions "on the run." When you take on a new instructional approach, the tendency is to try to find good tools and guidelines to help you engage in teaching interactions and use facilitative language to support the learner's ability to construct understandings. Over time, we build a repertoire of ways of responding that are connected with our observations and interpretations of behavior.

We have to look closely at the strengths particular students bring to their literacy learning and build on those strengths instead of targeting deficits. There are many surprises in teaching; there is always some response that we did not predict. Students can make us revise our thinking. Being a teacher is to engage in continual inquiry; we are obligated not to hold our theory as static and unchangeable—a model into which all children must fit—when there is evidence to the contrary. One of the most important purposes of an assessment system, then, is to help us continually build a theoretical foundation or set of understandings out of which our teaching actions flow and against which we evaluate our decisions. Authentic assessment is the heart of student-centered teaching.

Characteristics of Authentic Assessment

Given that assessment plays a vital purpose in a design for literacy instruction, we need to select assessment systems that have several essential attributes.

Assessment uses accessible information, most of which can be collected as an integral part of teaching. The system must be practical and usable. It is not a separate and burdensome task but is woven into daily practice. Of course, you may do some initial assessment of students and may have regular, focused assessment periods, that involve children in productive activities such as reading stories and nonfiction books and writing and talking about them. However, the most powerful kind of documentation is the information collected as part of a daily routine. You will have to make practical decisions about how you use your time. It is better to gather and record useful information regularly than to have an elaborate and time-consuming test that requires study of completely different and unusual ways of responding and does not provide results that are helpful in teaching.

Assessment should involve students in tasks that are real acts of reading and writing. A student's time is not productive when filling in the blanks or bubbling answers. But time is not wasted when reading a good fiction or nonfiction book, talking about it, or writing about it. Just because the reading and talking individually with a teacher is called assessment does not mean that the student is not learning something by processing new texts. Writing about reading is another productive task.

When inquiring about validity, we need to ask, does this test really measure what we are trying to assess? Many writers have referred to this as *authenticity*. It is impossible for all assessment tasks to be completely authentic in the sense that the task is not one that the student has chosen for his own purposes and implements in an idiosyncratic way. Introducing a reliable and systematic approach inevitably leads to some contrived procedures, but assessment approaches must be as authentic as possible. Authenticity is an underlying principle of effective assessment.

Assessment approaches must be as close as possible to the task being assessed. This establishes strong validity of the assessment. Children learn to read by reading; we must assess their reading progress by observing their reading. The most powerful tool for assessment is the observation and recording of reading behaviors on continuous text.

Assessment includes systematic observations that will provide a continually updated profile of the student's current ways of responding. A highly organized system ensures the information is on hand for teachers to use. Clay (1991) admits that it asks too much of a teacher with a full class to carry in her head the particular learning history of each student for the past two or three weeks: "It is helpful for the teacher to have some systematic observations to refer to. . . . She needs to be on the same track as the child and systematic observations of how the child is working with texts from time to time provide the teacher with necessary information," (233). By systematic assessment, we do not mean the "unit tests" provided by core systems and/or standardized tests that are a regular part of the district's reporting procedures. These simply tell whether the student has "passed" or "failed." Observation that focuses on a student's reading behaviors can also be systematic and provide more valuable information. It captures the shifts in responding that indicate instruction is working.

Assessment provides reliable information about the progress of readers. The assessment system must be designed to yield consistent information. In other words, each time the assessment procedures are used, they build a database on an individual, one that allows you to ascertain the results of teaching. According to Smith and Elley, "Reliability means the consistency of the measures. If the same or a similar testing procedure is given after an extended period of time or by another person, we would expect the results to be similar if the procedure is reliable. The results should be accurate," (1995, 98). Of course, in the case of reading, if a great deal of time has passed, we should expect consistently higher scores (given effective instruction). A reliable procedure is applied in a standard way so that it yields consistent results across items and with different readers and different teachers.

Assessment is multidimensional. A multidimensional system provides the best chance to collect reliable and valid information on student progress. The system should include both formal and informal measures; for example, you might combine anecdotal records, lists of books read independently, running records taken on a regular basis (see Chapter 11), and writing about reading samples from a readers' notebook.

For early readers, we recommend some assessment of beginning knowledge of items related to literacy—the names of letters of the alphabet and awareness of print conventions. A multidimensional system also allows you to look across curriculum areas to find and use valuable information. For example, the assessment of a student's growth in writing can provide valuable information for helping him learn to read and vice versa.

Assessment provides feedback to improve the instructional program and the curriculum. A feedback loop sounds complicated but it simply means looking at the combined results of assessment and applying the results to instructional design and implementation. The first part of the loop, observational assessment, happens when you work with an individual student. Behavioral evidence, as Clay has said, "might cause a teacher to question her own assumptions and check them thoughtfully against what her children are actually doing, and to hold a watchful brief for when the child's processing behavior requires her to change her approach," (1995, 344). This questioning and reflective process can occur whatever the teacher's philosophy or instructional approach, because student response rather than a prescriptive model directs the teaching.

The second part of the loop takes place at the classroom level. In midyear, you might assess all students on one or two similar measures. Or, you might simply take a look at the last two weeks' collected observations in order to make some decisions about the instruction. If children are reading every day and there is little progress in the level of text they can read, something might be wrong with the way texts are selected for children in the group, or stronger teaching with more explicit demonstrations might be required.

A third and final part of the loop takes place at the school level. The leadership team or grade-level group could, for example, conduct a study of their results using the information across classes to make decisions about further professional development they might need or materials they want to purchase. They might set goals for the coming year.

Assessment identifies and directs steps to meet the needs of students who do not achieve despite excellent classroom instruction. Assessment is critical in identifying students who are not benefiting fully from the classroom program. Since intervention will be necessary for these students, assessment must occur early and be ongoing, so that no student moves on through the system without the level of support he needs to succeed. Intervention may take the form of a highly effective individual tutorial such as Reading Recovery (*What Works Clearinghouse*), which is applied at the end of the first year of school (beginning of grade one in the United States). Across the grades, you may consider high-quality, intensive small-group work that is systematically designed and has documented research results with diverse students. An example is our small-group reading intervention program, *Leveled Literacy Intervention* (Fountas and Pinnell 2009-2016), which is used in grades kindergarten through twelve.

Assessment involves students and families in the process. Assessment is most powerful when the learner is involved. Assessment systems for early, intermediate, and middle level students can provide the opportunity for them to reflect on their own strengths and goals for further learning. Involving families allows them to learn more about their children's strengths and provides you with additional reliable, valid information. It is not necessary for students or families to discuss, or even to know the specific text levels of the books students are reading. Those categories are complex and are used only as a teacher tool for instruction. You don't want to give the impression that a level is a "score" to achieve. But it is helpful for intermediate and middle-level students to describe what they have accomplished in reading and to set goals (for example, to read more in a particular genre). Families have the right to know whether their children are reading at, above, or below grade level, and to hear some simple descriptive statements about what the students can do as readers and what they need to learn next. The reader's notebook and samples of texts that students have read across time are wonderful tools to use in self-assessment and in family conferences.

Responsive Teaching: From Assessment to Teaching Decisions

If assessment is considered to be "separate" from instruction, it will always be superfluous, ineffective, even a dreaded and annoying interruption. Yet without effective assessment, instruction will be merely guesswork. We propose a seamless cycle from assessment to teaching that will enable you to engage in responsive teaching. Responsive teaching:

- Takes what the student already knows into account.
- Is coherent because it rests on a sound theory of how proficient readers build a reading process over time.
- Is generative in that students can apply new understandings to reading many texts.
- Utilizes precise teacher language that is meaningful to the student and does not interrupt processing.
- Works on the cutting edge of the student's ability to perform.
- Moves the reader forward in the use of independent strategic actions.

When students encounter responsive teaching in all literacy contexts, they get a powerful message: Reading is thinking. Readers are cued by the language they find in print, but understanding the ideas and information and thinking about it take place in the reader's head. Throughout the process, you want your students to be meaning seekers. The brain works and becomes efficient by recognizing and using patterns. They may take detours to study words and word parts or to see the patterns in word structure or sentence structure; but everything they read and do must make sense to them.

A design for responsive teaching is represented in Figure 9-3. The items in circles suggest that a cycle exists as you move from (1) observation of reading/writing/language behaviors to (2) making inferences about the students' control of strategic actions, to (3) prioritization of behaviors and understandings to notice, teach for, and support, to (4) teaching decisions, and back (5) for more observation.

At every point in the cycle, there are contexts and tools to gather the data and guide your teaching.

Step One: Observe Reading, Writing, and Language Behaviors

Teachers are always watching children; but observations can be random and diffuse. You always gather information about whether children are behaving appropriately, finishing their work, or performing tasks accurately. But you need to make your observations far more focused and productive when it comes to noticing the precise behaviors that relate to literacy learning. The secret to highly informative observation lies in your own brain, your ideas about learning, and in the way they inform your lens. Your efficient systems for capturing literacy behaviors within the act of teaching and in standardized contexts at selected intervals will make a significant difference in the effects of your teaching on student learning.

Contexts for Observing

You are always observing children's reading behaviors. Three contexts are highly productive for gathering data or information about literacy learning.

1. *Oral Reading: What you see and hear as a reader processes a text.* As you listen to students read aloud, notice significant behaviors such as pauses, repetitions, errors, and self-corrections. All of these behaviors offer a "window" on the activities that are going on in the brain. Very early readers read orally most of the time, so you will have natural opportunities to listen to reading while noticing accurate reading and other behaviors. Quickly, children begin to "drop" the voice and to read silently. When this happens, ask the reader to "raise" the voice to an audible level to read the text (or a meaningful part of it) while you observe briefly and sample the oral processing. Code the oral reading using a standardized notation method to record accurate reading and significant behaviors. You can use the process of running records to capture the processing for analysis and reflection (see Chapter 11). A system of coding allows you to save examples of reading behavior so that you can notice changes across time. Your analysis of the coded behaviors will reveal students' strengths and needs as readers. Using a standardized system enables you to share the data with other teachers and to pass along your analysis in the cumulative records.

2. *Talk: What you hear in what students say about their reading.* After reading, you engage students in a brief conversation about the fiction or nonfiction text they

FIGURE 9-3 Responsive Teaching: From Assessment to Literacy Instruction

have read. Your students' talk represents their thinking. During the conversation, you can use some precise prompts (either statements or questions) to elicit information about the students' understandings of the text, but the students do most of the talking. This conversation is not a "retelling"; it is not productive for the students to try to remember every detail, nor is "more," better. A reader who is trying to remember every detail, even very unimportant ones, may miss some of the bigger ideas of a story or nonfiction book. Look for the reader's ability to summarize, to infer what the writer is implying, to synthesize new information, to notice aspects of the craft of writing, and to think critically about a text. Gather evidence about the student's ability to comprehend a text and to articulate their understandings in oral language. Take observational notes, categorized as evidence of thinking within, beyond, and about the text. By taking careful notes within a framework of text understanding, you can keep a record of the evidence of comprehending. These notes will also help you notice change over time.

3. *Writing About Reading: Writing represents your students' thinking* Your students' weekly responses to texts in the reader's notebook provide rich data for assessing their understanding of a variety of texts. Students can also write in response to a carefully prepared prompt that asks them to share thinking about a fiction or nonfiction text they have read. These student artifacts provide evidence of comprehension as well as of the student's ability to articulate understandings in writing. Samples of students' writing about reading can be kept in the cumulative records and you can use them to notice growth over time.

Analyze the writing about reading. Each time a student responds to a text to share thinking, you have the opportunity to notice the same aspects of comprehension that you noted in the oral response. Writing about reading is not the old book report format, which yielded tedious reporting of detail after detail, nor is it a test of memory. Writing about reading may be: an open response; an open response with a segment that includes a prompt; or a response to a prompt that elicits certain understandings in a standardized way.

Step Two: Use Behavioral Evidence to Infer

It should be obvious that to gain a full picture of a student's reading ability you need to take a multistep approach. Use all of the behavioral evidence elicited through the contexts listed above to make inferences about what the student knows and can do. Your resource is your understanding of what the evidence "looks like" within the twelve categories of strategic actions discussed in Chapter 8 and below.

Systems of Strategic Actions

As students read orally, you gain evidence of the first five systems of strategic actions. Their talk and writing provide evidence of the last seven.

1. *Searching for and Using Information.* As you observe the student's reading behaviors, you can notice evidence of searching. The reader attempts to use all sources of information to provide a response. The student may take words apart, may make several attempts, may reread to use language structure as a resource.

The reader may reread to search for meaning or language or notice information in illustrations or graphics.

2. *Monitoring and Self-Correcting.* When coding reading, note when students pause after an error and make another attempt. Notice when the student stops at difficulty and does not self-initiate searching. Even if the student does not read the word accurately, his behavior can indicate an awareness of error. A self-correction is not counted as an error; however, it provides valuable evidence of self-monitoring. Look for evidence that the student is aware when comprehension is lost. If a student asks questions or is unsure of conclusions, he is on the way to understanding because he realizes he does not yet understand. Remember that accurate reading is, in itself, evidence that monitoring is going on.

3. *Solving Words.* As you notice a student's accurate reading, errors, substitutions, and self-corrections, you gain understanding of his ability to solve words. The student may recognize many words automatically and work at others by using word parts. In student talk and writing, you can form hypotheses about known vocabulary and also students' ability to derive the meaning of words from context.

4. *Maintaining Fluency.* Listening to oral reading is the only way to evaluate a student's reading fluency. The criterion is not just "reading fast." You listen for a voice that moves along at an appropriate pace for the piece being read and which reflects the meaning with intonation, pausing, phrasing, and word stress.

5. *Adjusting.* Readers are flexible. As you observe reading behaviors, you will notice the reader slowing down to problem-solve and then regaining momentum. They may search back to thoughtfully reconsider a difficult or challenging passage or examine a graphic. Readers read differently for different purposes and in different content disciplines and genres. Oral reading of nonfiction will actually sound different than oral reading of a suspenseful narrative.

6. *Summarizing.* In the talk after reading and in the writing, you can look for evidence that the student can concisely summarize the information and the big ideas in a text, leaving out irrelevant detail but including details that offer necessary evidence for thinking and understanding and reporting the larger messages.

7. *Predicting.* You can find evidence in students' talk and writing to show whether they can use the information they have to make predictions on such aspects as what characters will do, what might happen next in a story, or how problems might be resolved.

8. *Making Connections.* Again, in talk and writing, you can assess the extent to which a student can bring content knowledge, their own experience, or their understanding of other texts to the comprehension of texts they are reading.

9. *Synthesizing.* In talk and writing, you can find evidence that students are taking on new learning—ideas and information—from their reading. They self-report new thinking and changes in perspectives.

10. *Inferring.* As you listen to students talk and analyze their writing, you can look for evidence that students can think beyond the text to infer elements such as characters' feelings and motives, larger themes and ideas, causes of problems, and so on.

11. *Analyzing.* As you listen to students talk and read their writing, look for evidence that students are thinking analytically about texts—that they are noticing aspects of the writer's craft, such as the plot structure, the use of figurative language, or the use of persuasion or argument.

12. *Critiquing.* Talk and writing also reveal the extent to which students can think critically about their reading. Do they question the authenticity of the text or evaluate its quality? Do they think critically about the evidence offered to support an argument; do they consider alternative explanations?

It is obvious that no one source of information is sufficient to gather evidence along all of the complex dimensions of a reading process. In Figure 9-4, you see a summary of strategic actions and the contexts and evidence that serve as a resource for making your decisions.

Step Three: Prioritize Behaviors and Understandings to Notice, Teach for, and Support

The next step is to prioritize the behaviors and understandings that you want to emphasize in your instruction. A powerful tool to support this process is *The Fountas & Pinnell Literacy Continuum* (see Chapter 11). Texts we use for guided reading are categorized along a continuum of increasing difficulty. For each level, A to Z, we list goals, stated as behaviors and understandings to notice, teach for, and support. In Figure 9-5, you can see a page layout from *The Literacy Continuum*.

If you are working with a group of children whose assessment data indicate that level I will be an appropriate instructional level for the group, then you choose a book at that level (see Chapter 14). You then think about your observations of your students' reading behaviors and match them up with the behaviors and understandings listed in *The Literacy Continuum* for Thinking Within, Beyond, and

In Search of Evidence for Strategic Actions

STRATEGIC ACTIONS		EVIDENCE
Thinking Within the Text	◆ Searching for and Using Information ◆ Monitoring and Self-Correcting ◆ Solving Words ◆ Maintaining Fluency ◆ Adjusting ◆ Summarizing	◆ Code and analyze oral reading ◆ Notice evidence in talk and writing after reading
Thinking Beyond the Text	◆ Predicting ◆ Making Connections ◆ Synthesizing ◆ Inferring	◆ Notice evidence in talk after reading ◆ Notice evidence in writing about reading
Thinking About the Text	◆ Analyzing ◆ Critiquing	

FIGURE 9-4 In Search of Evidence for Strategic Actions

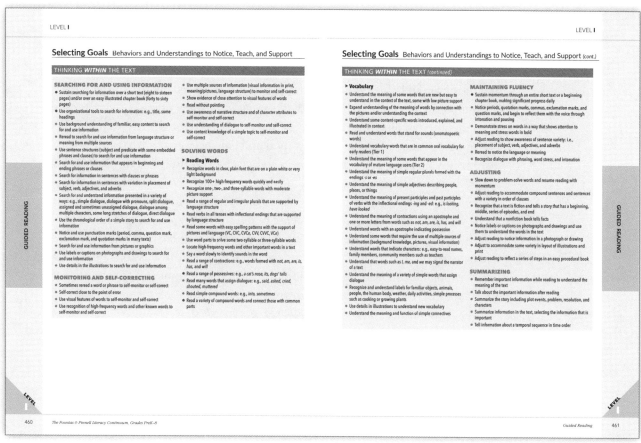

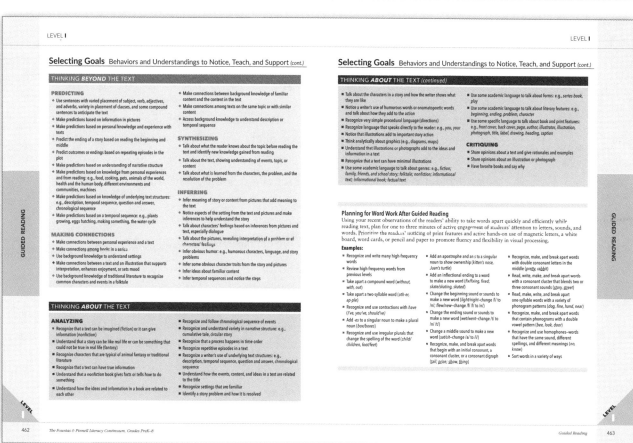

FIGURE 9-5 *The Fountas & Pinnell Literacy Continuum, Guided Reading, Selecting Goals, Level I*

About the Text. For example, you might notice that students are demonstrating knowledge of flexible ways to solve words (they notice words with easy spelling patterns). They can also understand the meaning of simple plurals and verbs with inflectional endings. And, they can use some organizational tools, such as the title and headings, and punctuation including periods, commas, question marks, exclamation points, and quotations marks. They can infer some obvious character traits from the story and pictures, and make connections between the text and illustrations in a way that supports interpretation and enhances enjoyment.

Identifying some priorities will help you teach powerfully at this level, deepening students' comprehension, before moving to a higher level with these students. Note that we are not saying you have one "focus" and continually hammer away at the same understanding at the expense of natural conversation and discussion. It does mean that you have some specific emphases that you have identified as needs and are part of your plan as you introduce texts, guide the discussion, and make teaching points. You also take into account what you see moment to moment to adjust your decisions as needed. With your plan in mind, look for opportunities or "teachable moments" that will lead the readers forward.

Step Four: Teach for Change in Strategic Actions

Once you have chosen your teaching emphases, demonstrate, prompt for, and reinforce the behaviors and understandings you have identified in various parts of the lesson as appropriate. Figure 9-6 shows sample pages from two tools that can serve as resources in this process.* *Prompting Guide Part 1 for Oral Reading and Early Writing*, and *Prompting Guide Part 2 for Comprehension* include precise language that teachers have found helpful in communicating clearly with students. Refer to the appropriate section and write two or three prompts that will be most helpful in your teaching. Alternatively, put a sticky note on one or two sections you might turn to as you teach. If you have the app you can open the page on your tablet or phone quickly.

For example, if you want to help students think in deeper ways about characters in the discussion after reading, you might use questions or prompts that call for readers to engage in thinking such as the following:

▶ This character doesn't usually act/talk this way. What might be behind his actions/words?

▶ That's what _____ (character) said. What did she really mean?

▶ How do you know _____ (character) has changed?

Once you have either demonstrated or prompted for strategic actions, observe for evidence that the student is engaging in these actions spontaneously and independently. Observations continue as students take on new behaviors and you keep prompting for more. The responsive teaching cycle is not a neat set of steps; observation is ongoing and your findings will be different for different students even

---

* There are four prompting guides: *Prompting Guide Part 1 for Oral Reading; Prompting Guide Part 2 for Comprehension; Genre Prompting Guide for Fiction;* and *Genre Prompting Guide for Nonfiction, Poetry, and Test Taking*. In this book, we refer to these simply as "prompting guides."

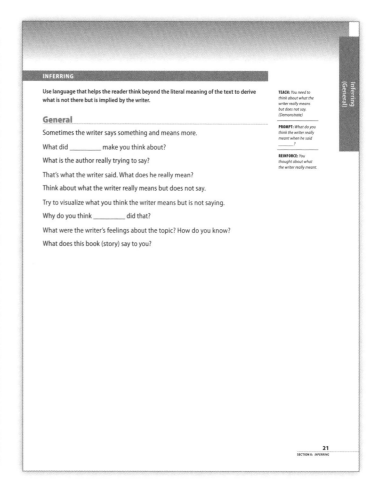

FIGURE 9-6 Pages from *Prompting Guide Part 1 for Oral Reading* and *Prompting Guide Part 2 for Comprehension*

within the same group. But having well-founded goals for your teaching will make it have a greater impact. You can gain the rich information you need from both interval and continuous assessment.

Using Standardized Assessment

Many school districts/boards require that all students are assessed using a standardized system so student progress can be documented and achievement patterns analyzed over time. We will discuss two types of standardized assessment that are essential for effective teaching in guided reading lessons: interval assessment and continuous assessment.

Interval Assessment

A benchmark assessment system is an ideal instrument for interval assessment for the following reasons:

- It involves students in reading continuous text while you measure factors such as accuracy, fluency, and comprehension.
- It can be administered by classroom teachers who keep data for their own purposes or who report it school-wide.

▶ It offers information that is useful for setting instructional goals at the classroom level, and, simultaneously, it offers useful information for administrators and boards.

▶ It provides a way for a teacher to determine whether he is meeting his goals and it simultaneously provides a way for a school or district to evaluate the effects of its literacy program.

A benchmark is a standard against which to measure something. A student reads a series of texts that represent the challenges at each level and then talks about each. The student's reading is matched against the benchmark level to find the highest level the student can read with satisfactory comprehension. The goal is to identify the level at which the student can work well in guided reading (a challenging or instructional text but within the student's grasp) as well as the level at which the student can read independently.

There are a number of benchmark systems available. Some teachers have established their own by selecting a set of trustworthy texts at each text level and creating protocols. The example we offer as a benchmark system for interval assessment is the *Fountas & Pinnell Benchmark Assessment System* (BAS). This comprehensive assessment system is linked directly to classroom instruction. Using the system, you determine three reading levels: (1) an independent level, which the student reads with very high accuracy and satisfactory or excellent comprehension; (2) an instructional level, which the student reads at satisfactory or excellent accuracy and comprehension; and, (3) a placement level, which reflects the teacher's final judgment after considering all information on the student.

At the beginning of a school year, the *Benchmark Assessment System* helps you determine levels that will be productive for instruction, and it can also be used to take an assessment of progress mid-year and/or at the end of the year. It is helpful in finding a good instructional reading level for a student who is new to the school. For every level, A to Z, a fiction and a nonfiction book is available. In the administration, you sample reading, alternating fiction and nonfiction as you move from level to level. Each book reflects the specific characteristics of its level as designated in the *Fountas and Pinnell Literacy Continuum*. The *Benchmark Assessment System* also includes a variety of optional assessments for diagnostic purposes.

A Protocol from the *Benchmark Assessment System*

In the next figures you see the text reading protocol for one student's reading assessment. Karl read a level I book from the *Benchmark Assessment System* at 99% accuracy with excellent comprehension, so the teacher asked him to read *More Than a Pet*, a level J book (see Figure 9-7).

Note his reading record (coded on a typed text) in Figure 9-8. Karl read the level J book with 94% accuracy and one self-correction. His fluency was satisfactory, and so was his comprehension. We can break down the comprehension conversation a bit more. He included all of the important ideas and information that are stated in the text. For example, he named the two kinds of dogs in the book and told what they do, with details such as "helping when people can't see well" and "making people feel better." He provided an excellent summary without

Do you know anyone
who has a pet dog?
Maybe you have a dog
in your family.
Dogs are good pets.

2

Two Kinds of Dogs

Some dogs are more than pets.
Two kinds of dogs do special jobs.
Dogs that make people feel better
are called **therapy dogs**. Dogs
that work are called **service dogs**.

3

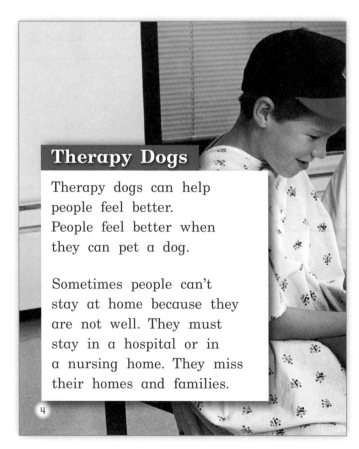

Therapy Dogs

Therapy dogs can help
people feel better.
People feel better when
they can pet a dog.

Sometimes people can't
stay at home because they
are not well. They must
stay in a hospital or in
a nursing home. They miss
their homes and families.

4

5

FIGURE 9-7 *More Than a Pet* from *Benchmark Assessment System* 1, Pages 2–3, 4–5

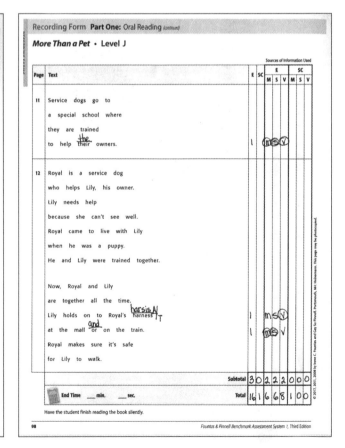

FIGURE 9-8 Karl's Reading Record for *More Than a Pet*

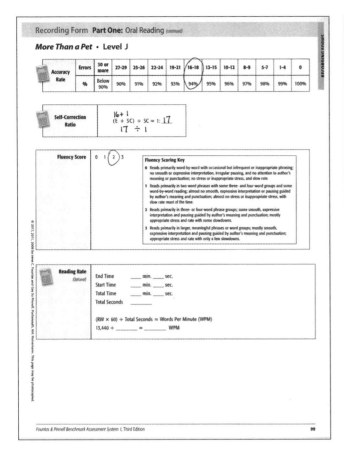

FIGURE 9-8 *(continued)*

irrelevant detail. He gave a logical reason that dogs can be helpful (because they can be trained) but did not fully describe attributes that would be important qualifications, which would require inference. He correctly identified the most important ideas that are implied in the text. Next, Karl read the level K book, *Edwin's Haircut,* but had significant processing issues. The teacher had him stop. This was his hard level. Level J was determined to be Karl's instructional level. Ideally, Karl would be reading books at level J in a guided reading group and receive strong teaching for comprehension.

Benchmark assessment is a very valuable tool that serves many purposes. You use it only two or three times a year to document progress at intervals. You would not want to administer the *BAS,* for example, to determine whether a student should move from one level to another in guided reading. For that purpose, you need continuous assessment in the form of running records (a record taken on a blank form) or reading records (a coded record on typed text).

Selected Additional Assessments

In addition to the text-reading assessment, you may want to administer some diagnostic assessments that pinpoint specific areas of interest. This is especially important when working with very early readers who may not be reading any text (or who may read only at very low levels). In these cases, this "item assessment" may be quite useful. For example, we cannot imagine a kindergarten classroom where knowledge of the letters of the alphabet is not assessed. Having a repertoire of letter, sound, and word understandings is basic to the early reader's ability to find "anchors" in print as they read continuous text. It is helpful for the teacher to use these assessments in a diagnostic way; an awareness of the precise letters, sounds, and words a student knows will help in prompting for strategic actions.

Optional Assessments

Below we describe some of these optional assessments that can be used to further analyze sub-skills across the grades. All are included in *BAS*.

Letter Recognition: Uppercase and Lowercase Naming

Readers say the names of the alphabet by recognizing the shapes of uppercase and lowercase letters. From this, you will be able to identify the letter forms that they can associate with the corresponding letter names. You can use this information to plan lessons on letters and also to decide what letters and letter features to bring to children's attention during interactive/shared writing and shared reading (see Chapter 3).

Early Literacy Behaviors

This assessment helps you learn about children's knowledge of the conventions of print. Read the book to the child. Then turn back to the front of the book and look at the second or third page.

- ▶ Point while I read. (One-to-one correspondence)
- ▶ Where do I start reading? Which way do I go? (Left-to-right directionality)
- ▶ Where do I go after that? (Return sweep)
- ▶ What's this? [Point to a period or exclamation mark.] What does it mean? (Meaning of punctuation)
- ▶ Show me one letter. Show me one word. (Difference between a letter and a word)
- ▶ Find a word you know and say it. (Locate a known word)
- ▶ Find a word that begins with *B*. (Locate an unknown word)

You can conduct this short assessment simply by selecting a level B or C book and asking the questions above. *BAS* also includes an abbreviated print awareness assessment. The idea of this assessment was Clay's (1993) original invention. You can use one of several published books to give the full Concepts About Print assessment (see Clay, *An Observation Survey of Early Literacy Achievement*). These early behaviors are critically important because a child who does not understand how print works may become very confused. Specific teaching will be needed.

Reading High-Frequency Words

BAS includes several lists of words for each grade level. It is useful for readers (from early to intermediate) to have a repertoire of known words. For early readers, you will want to have a record of all the words the child has added to her reading vocabulary. Early readers can use a small core of known words strategically while reading and problem solving. When working with groups at the earliest levels, the teacher may look through the assessments to find the words that many children hold in common (there will almost always be some known words after children have participated in interactive and shared writing and in shared reading for a week or two).

As students grow in sophistication, they add to the bank of words that they recognize instantly and effortlessly. Reading is a problem-solving process; and successful processing builds the system. But there should not be problem solving on every word. The reading work that students do should take place against a backdrop of accurate reading.

Students' attempts at words provide additional interesting information. By examining how they approach words in isolation, without the support of meaning or predictability in the text, you can learn more about the reader's ability to recognize features of words and also to take words apart. Often early readers will make an attempt that begins with the same letter as the word on the list or they will substitute a word that contains similar parts. When you use a high-frequency word assessment, begin to notice how a student reads the words while processing continuous text.

Phonological Awareness

The ability to hear and identify sounds in words is basic to word solving. To connect a sound with a letter, the reader must be able to "hear" it in a way that he can distinguish it from other sounds. That is not easy because sounds blend smoothly into each other when we say words. To isolate the sound, you must say it with a schwa, or "uh," sound after it—for example, /b/, "buh." It is helpful to know the extent to which children can hear sounds *in words*. Several oral tasks are included in *BAS* to determine whether children can do the following:

- ▶ Hear and match initial sounds in words using picture cards.
- ▶ Take individual sounds and blend them together to make words.
- ▶ Take a word and segment it into individual sounds.
- ▶ Hear rhyming words.
- ▶ Say words slowly and write them (word writing and picture names).

Word Writing

An assessment of word writing gives you a rich inventory of what a child controls, including what words she can spell accurately and what she is thinking about words and how they work. The child writes all the words she can. Encourage children to make attempts at words. Not only will you learn the words children can spell conventionally; you will also learn much about children ability to "frame" a word by representing sounds with letters and sometimes clusters of letters.

Writing Picture Names

A very simple and easy-to-administer assessment is the "picture names" test. You can administer this test in a group. Give children a sheet with pictures in each of six boxes (you can also use two sheets to make twelve). Use words like *kite, cat, box, pig*—all nouns that children will recognize. Say the words with the children. Then, each student writes the picture name; encourage attempts but do not say the words for children again. You will find this ready-to-use test in the *BAS* Optional Assessments.

Word Parts

Several assessments help you look closely at how students use the parts in words to read. These include

> ▶ Phonograms: A child reads words with simple to more complex phonograms to demonstrate the number of phonograms (spelling patterns like *-an, -at, -it,* and so on) he can recognize and read.

> ▶ Consonant Blends: A child reads words with consonant blends to identify the specific blends he controls in reading.

> ▶ Vowel Clusters: A child reads words with vowel clusters to identify the specific clusters he controls in reading.

> ▶ Suffixes: Students read base words and then read the word with the suffix. Or, you read a sentence and ask the student to circle the word you used (the base word or word with suffix).

> ▶ One-and Two-Syllable Words: (1) Students clap the correct number of syllables as you read a list of ten familiar one- and two-syllable words. (2) Give students picture cards and have them sort the pictures by the number of syllables.

> ▶ Syllables in Longer Words: Students read longer words, count the syllables, and place a line between syllable parts. This assessment tells you the particular words the student can read accurately and the accuracy and speed with which he takes words apart by syllable. In *BAS*, progressively more dif-ficult word lists are provided at each grade level.

There are a variety of other diagnostic assessments. The key is to use them only for a specific reason, not to gather information you already know.

> ▶ Six Dimensions of Fluency: Another optional assessment allows you to take a more complex look at fluency by breaking it down into six dimensions. You record a short piece of reading and then listen with the six dimensions in mind. You will find a rubric for fluency in Chapter 18.

> ▶ Suffixes and Prefixes: This quick assessment is designed to determine the extent to which students can read words that have affixes and base words. You give the student a list of base words in the first column, and the word with an affix in the second column. The student reads the base word and then the word with a prefix or suffix. Then, the student reads the word in a sentence and circles the base word within the word with an affix. You notice the number of words with suffixes or prefixes that the student can read.

> ▶ Synonyms and Antonyms: Students are given two lists of words and have them match synonyms and/or antonyms. This assessment will provide information on how well students can apply the concepts of synonyms and antonyms and also the ease with which they can connect words by meaning.

▶ Analogies: This assessment shows whether students understand the relationships between words. The words you use are slightly easier because you want students to concentrate on the relationships. Administer the assessment individually or give a written assignment to the entire class. Students need to select from the answer choices the pair of words that share the same relationship (see Figure 9-9).

Continuous Assessment

Running Record of Text Reading

A running record, or reading record, is a coding, analysis, and scoring of a student's actual reading of a text, providing both quantitative and qualitative information.* Running records are discussed in more detail in Chapter 11, because they are the most important tool in guided reading. Running records meet all of the goals of assessment and they can be used in two ways:

1. To conduct a benchmark-type assessment on unseen text at the beginning, middle, or end of the year to identify each student's instructional reading level and/or to identify students who need intervention to read at grade level. In this case, the students would be reading an unfamiliar text with only a brief (one- or two-sentence) introduction. This form of assessment is typical of the *BAS* and is the most accurate, efficient, and conservative way to assess a student's reading ability. That is, you learn what the student can do *without teaching*. We provided an example of how Karl's teacher conducted a *BAS* assessment earlier in this chapter.

2. A running record or reading record can also be used to measure continuous progress in response to teaching. In this case, you administer the running record at regular intervals (given the number of students in your class as well as student needs). You take the record on yesterday's new text, which has been

Word Analogies

How Are the Words Related?	Choose One Pair of Words That Are Related in the Same Way
1. courteous/polite	appropriate/suitable appropriate/eventual appropriate/incorrect appropriate/comfortable
2. expensive/cheap	exhilarating/cunning exhilarating/charming exhilarating/terrifying exhilarating/boring
3. pluck/string	disable/voice disable/disturb disable/engine disable/movement

FIGURE 9-9 Word Analogies

---

*What we describe here is a running record, as designed by Marie Clay. The teacher takes the record on a blank form, making checkmarks for each word and following the exact number of words in the line. For the *BAS* mentioned earlier, we provide forms with typed text, and so we call these "reading records." In all other ways, they are identical to running records. Typed text forms are provided for all books in *BAS*, *Leveled Literacy Intervention* and *Fountas & Pinnell Classroom*.

Pg.	*Boo!* Level D
2	Monkey saw Elephant. But Elephant did not see Monkey. "Boo!" Monkey shouted.
4	Elephant jumped. Her bananas fell to the ground.
6	Monkey laughed and laughed. "You are not funny!" said Elephant.
8	Monkey saw Zebra. But Zebra did not see Monkey.

Pg.	*Boo!* Level D
9	"Boo!" shouted Monkey. Zebra jumped. His ladder fell to the ground.
10	"You are not funny!" said Zebra. But Monkey laughed and laughed.
12	Monkey saw Hippo. But Hippo did not see Monkey. "Boo!" shouted Monkey. Hippo jumped. Her bucket fell over.
14	The water went all over Monkey.
16	"You look funny!" said Elephant and Hippo and Zebra. And they laughed and laughed and laughed.

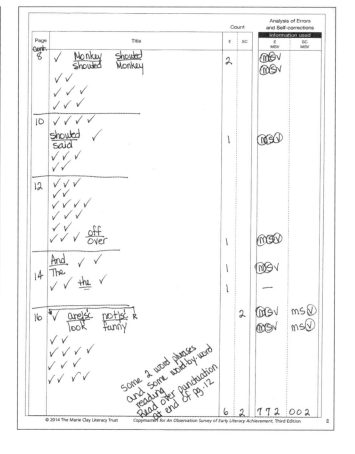

FIGURE 9-10 Brooklyn's Running Record for *Boo!*

read *once* with your teaching support. This gives you an ongoing check on the student's response to your teaching. The measure is a good indication of how the student is taking on new behaviors and applying what he is learning to reading texts. An example of a running record is shown in Figure 9-10. Notice that, like the *BAS* record, the teacher has coded, scored, and analyzed the reading. While the coding and scoring are important (that gives you the "bottom line" as to how accurately the student can read the book), the analysis is even more important (see Figure 9-11). Since this is the second reading, you would expect high accuracy and fluency.

Analysis of Brooklyn's Running Record

Brooklyn is early into her literacy journey and she's beginning to demonstrate those early literacy concepts. She was successful with her word-by-word matching and return sweep and didn't point while she was reading. She inserted one word, which didn't interfere with the meaning or structure. She read the text Boo!, level D, with 92% accuracy and a 1:5 self-correction ratio, meaning she self-corrected one in every five errors she made. She consistently used meaning (m) and structure (s) on her initial attempts as she read. About half the time she also used visual information (v). On many of her uncorrected errors, she used m, s, & v information initially: didn't/did not, on/to, shouted/said, and off/over. On page 8 she reversed two words: Monkey shouted/shouted Monkey and left them. She read And/The and inserted the on page 14. For these errors she used meaning and structural information. On page 16, she substituted are/look and not/funny as she continued the previously introduced pattern "You look funny", but realized something was wrong, reread, looked more carefully and self-corrected the two errors. Because she used m & s initially and self-corrected using v information, these would be examples of a reader cross-checking her reading— this time resulting in a self-correction.

Brooklyn read primarily in two-word phrases with occasional word-by-word reading. She used no stress or intonation during this reading, but usually used the punctuation appropriately (except not using!). On pages 12 & 14 she neglected to use the period at the end of page 12 and continued her thought as she read And/The on page 14.

FIGURE 9-11 Analysis of Brooklyn's Running Record

Analyzing Sources of Information Used

> **M** The error and/or the self-correction indicates that the student used MEANING as a source of information.
>
> **S** The error and/or the self-correction indicates that the student used STRUCTURE (language syntax) as a source of information.
>
> **V** The error and/or the self-correction indicates that the student used VISUAL INFORMATION (linked with phonological information) as a source of information.

FIGURE 9-12 Analyzing Sources of Information Used

You can learn more about coding, scoring, and analyzing running records in Chapter 11. But as you look at this analysis, you can notice that the teacher has analyzed each error and self-correction using a category system(see Figure 9-12).

Expanding Your Own Expertise

The more you code, score, and analyze running records (and reflect deeply on them), the more you will expand your knowledge of the reading process. As you think in a scientific way about each of your students, you will at the same time be adding to your own theoretical knowledge.

Guide for Observing and Noting Reading Behaviors

The Guide for Observing and Noting Reading Behaviors (available in Online Resources) is a tool for helping you learn how to notice the important behaviors readers may evidence in oral reading. Using the running record of a particular student, the Guide will direct your thinking to the evidence for each area of strategic actions observed in oral reading. In Figure 9-13, you see a completed form for Andy, an early reader. Notice that this form guides your thinking about whether the student controls early reading behaviors as well as some of the strategic actions related to early reading.

In Figure 9-14, you see a completed form for Elliot, an intermediate reader. Here, you make notes on the evidence you see for every category of the Systems of Strategic Actions.

Of course, you would not do such an in-depth analysis for every student or every time you take a running record. But as you are learning more about this kind of analysis, the use of this tool will orient you to think in these ways as you observe readers. You will learn more about each kind of behavioral evidence to look for as you observe your students processing text and as you quickly analyze the strategic actions on the left side of the running record.

Pg.	Food for Animals Level B
2	This is a bug. It is food for a frog.
4	This is a leaf. It is food for a giraffe.
6	This is an egg. It is food for a snake.
8	This is grass. It is food for a rabbit.

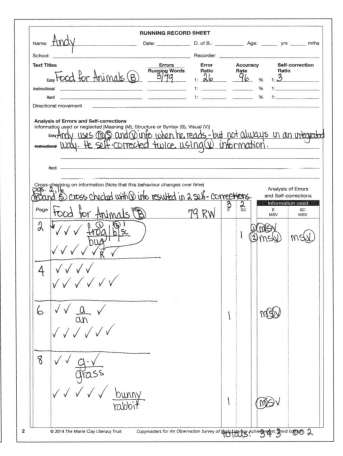

Pg.	Food for Animals Level B
10	This is a banana. It is food for a monkey.
12	This is a worm. It is food for a bird.
14	This is seaweed. It is food for a fish.
16	And this is a fish. It is food for a bear.

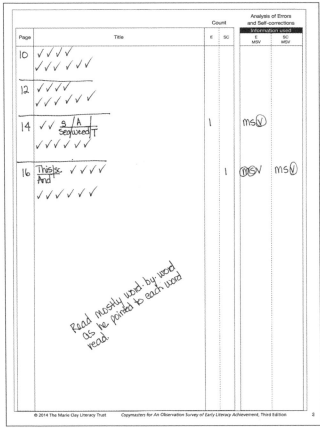

FIGURE 9-13 Andy's Reading of *Food for Animals* and Guide for Observing and Noting Reading Behaviors

(continues)

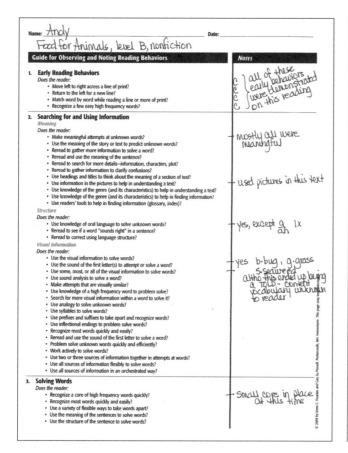

Name: Andy   Date: _____

Food for Animals, level B, nonfiction

Guide for Observing and Noting Reading Behaviors

	NOTES
1. Early Reading Behaviors *Does the reader:* • Move left to right across a line of print? • Return to the left for a new line? • Match word by word while reading a line or more of print? • Recognize a few easy high frequency words?	*all of these early behaviors were demonstrated on this reading*
2. Searching for and Using Information *Meaning* *Does the reader:* • Make meaningful attempts at unknown words? • Use the meaning of the story or text to predict unknown words? • Reread to gather more information to solve a word? • Reread and use the meaning of the sentence? • Reread to search for more details—information, characters, plot? • Reread to gather information to clarify confusions? • Use headings and titles to think about the meaning of a section of text? • Use information in the pictures to help in understanding a text? • Use knowledge of the genre (and its characteristics) to help in understanding a text? • Use knowledge of the genre (and its characteristics) to help in finding information? • Use readers' tools to help in finding information (glossary, index)?	*mostly all were meaningful* *used pictures in this text*
Structure *Does the reader:* • Use knowledge of oral language to solve unknown words? • Reread to see if a word "sounds right" in a sentence? • Reread to correct using language structure?	*yes, except g/ah 1x*
Visual Information *Does the reader:* • Use the visual information to solve words? • Use the sound of the first letter(s) to attempt or solve a word? • Use some, most, or all of the visual information to solve words? • Use sound analysis to solve a word? • Make attempts that are visually similar? • Use knowledge of a high frequency word to problem solve? • Search for more visual information within a word to solve it? • Use analogy to solve unknown words? • Use syllables to solve words? • Use prefixes and suffixes to take words apart and recognize words? • Use inflectional endings to problem solve words? • Recognize most words quickly and easily? • Reread and use the sound of the first letter to solve a word? • Problem solve unknown words quickly and efficiently? • Work actively to solve words? • Use two or three sources of information together in attempts at words? • Use all sources of information flexibly to solve words? • Use all sources of information in an orchestrated way?	*yes b-bug, g-grass s-seaweed* *altho this ended up being a TOLD - content vocabulary unknown to reader*
3. Solving Words *Does the reader:* • Recognize a core of high frequency words quickly? • Recognize most words quickly and easily? • Use a variety of flexible ways to take words apart? • Use the meaning of the sentences to solve words? • Use the structure of the sentence to solve words?	*small core in place at this time*

Guide for Observing and Noting Reading Behaviors *(cont.)*

	NOTES
• Use some of the visual information to solve words? • Use known word parts to solve words? • Use sound analysis (sounding out)? • Use analogy to solve words? • Make attempts that are visually similar? • Use the sound of the first letter to solve words? • Work actively to solve words? • Use known words or parts to solve unknown words? • Use syllables to problem solve? • Use prefixes and suffixes to take words apart? • Use inflectional endings to take words apart? • Use sentence context to derive the meaning of words? • Use base words and root words to derive the meaning of words? • Make connections among words to understand their meaning?	*g √ grass b/sc bug*
4. Self-Monitoring *Does the reader:* • Hesitate at an unknown word? • Stop at an unknown word? • Stop at an unknown word and appeal for help? • Stop after an error? • Notice mismatches? • Notice when an attempt does not look right? • Notice when an attempt does not sound right? • Notice when an attempt does not make sense? • Reread to confirm reading? • Use knowledge of some high frequency words to check on reading? • Check one source of information with another? • Check an attempt that makes sense with language? • Check an attempt that makes sense with the letters (visual information)? • Use language structure to check on reading? • Request help after making several attempts?	*only seaweed, otherwise attempted everything* *pg. 2 noticed mismatch after reading on - went back and s.t. error* *frog/b/sc (m-s) with pic bug bunny rabbit*
5. Self-Correcting *Does the reader:* • Reread and try again until accurate? • Stop after an error and make another attempt? • Stop after an error and make multiple attempts until accurate? • Reread to self-correct? • Work actively to solve mismatches? • Self-correct errors some of the time? • Self-correct errors most of the time?	*1:3 self-correction ratio* *pg. 2, pg. 16 This/sc And frog/b/sc bug* → *corrected some errors.*
6. Maintaining Fluency *Does the reader:* • Read without pointing? • Read word groups (phrases)? • Put words together? • Read smoothly? • Read the punctuation? • Make the voice go down at periods? • Make the voice go up at question marks? • Pause briefly at commas, dashes, and hyphens? • Read dialogue with intonation or expression? • Stress the appropriate words to convey accurate meaning? • Read at a good rate—not too fast and not too slow?	*pointing crisply at level B. Not yet focused on aspects of fluency*
7. Other	*96% accuracy*

FIGURE 9-13 (continued)

Pg.	**Odoriferous Foods** Level S
2	When a food gives off a mouth-watering aroma, you can't wait to take a bite. But what if a food smells like a garbage heap...or sweaty feet...or a dead animal? There are foods that smell like that—at least, that's how people describe them. Fans of these smelly foods, however, consider them delicacies. Each food is a prized part of its culture. Your taste in food often depends on where you grow up. If a food has a strong smell, people who

RUNNING RECORD SHEET

Name: Elliot   Date: _____   D. of B.: _____   Age: ____ yrs ____ mths

School: _____   Recorder: _____

Text Titles	Errors Running Words	Error Ratio	Accuracy Rate	Self-correction Ratio
Easy		1: ___	___ %	1: ___
Instructional Odoriferous Foods (S)	8/145	1: 16	95 %	1: 4
Hard		1: ___	___ %	1: ___

Directional movement _____

Analysis of Errors and Self-corrections
Information used or neglected (Meaning (M), Structure or Syntax (S), Visual (V))

Easy _____

Instructional *Elliot uses m and s consistently with visual information used often when reading initially. He uses visual and structural info to self-correct.*

Hard *Many uncorrected errors were m,s, & v information used initially. Some sampling of initial visual information.*

Cross-checking on information (Note that this behaviour changes over time)

FIGURE 9-14 Elliot's Reading of *Odoriferous Foods* and Guide for Observing and Noting Reading Behaviors

Pg.	Odoriferous Foods Level S
2 (cont.)	aren't used to it may find the smell disgusting. But to you and others who've grown up eating that food, the smell isn't bad or strange at all. You may even think of it as something yummy, because you connect it with good memories.

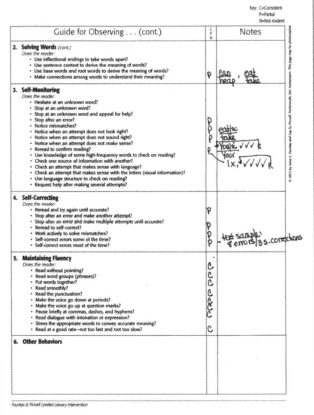

FIGURE 9-14 (continued)

The Impact of Literacy Assessment

Peter Johnston (2005) says:

> It is true that what is assessed is what is taught—perhaps truer than we have acknowledged. The ways we make assessments contribute to the development or demise of forms of literacy. Our assessment practices must help produce learners who are resilient and view literacy learning, rather than performance or ability, as their priority. They should produce literacy learners with the disposition to articulate their learning processes and perspectives, including their struggles, in ways that sustain strategic flexibility and mutual engagement. (686)

If what is assessed is what is taught, then we need to make sure that what we measure is real reading and real writing.

Suggestions for Professional Development

1. Prepare a set of materials for three students reading at various levels, to include:

   ▶ audio recording

   ▶ a running record (coded, scored and analyzed)

   ▶ copies of the books

   ▶ five copies of the Guide for Observing and Noting Reading Behaviors for each person (available in Online Resources).

2. Convene a meeting with colleagues to analyze the three readers. Taking each in turn, listen to the reading while following it in the text. Then have the teachers work with a partner or in a small group to analyze the reading. They can use the Guide for Observing and Noting Reading Behaviors for each reader to make notes in each area after listening and reviewing the running records.

   ▶ What evidence do you see of strengths?

   ▶ What does the reader nearly know?

   ▶ What does the reader need to learn next in each area?

3. Discuss how the Guide for Observing and Noting Reading Behaviors helped you understand and analyze the important reading behaviors observed in oral reading. Talk about how it will influence your observations and teaching discussions.

CHAPTER 10

Using Assessment to Form Dynamic Groups and Document Reading Progress

Grouping allows children to support each other in reading and feel part of a community of readers. It also allows for efficient use of a teacher's time.

–John Smith and Warwick Elley

When you use a systematic assessment system that is integral to school operations, you are in a position to engage in data-informed teaching. The data provide a solid foundation for making a whole range of decisions—grouping students for instruction and regrouping as indicated by documentation of progress, planning teaching moves using *The Fountas & Pinnell Literacy Continuum,* keeping records and charting progress, creating shared goals, and reporting. In this chapter we further explore the uses and outcomes of assessment.

Dynamic Grouping

Three assumptions are at work when a teacher is getting ready to group students for guided reading instruction: (1) there will be a wide range of experience, knowledge, and level of reading ability among any group of students; (2) every student will be different from every other student in some levels of knowledge and skill; and, (3) students will progress at varying rates. Daily, teachers face the problem of meeting individual students' needs while at the same time managing the learning of a large group. Look, for example at the record of *Fountas & Pinnell Benchmark Assessment System* data for a third-grade class (see Figure 10-1). The independent level shows the kind of texts that students can read independently; the instructional level shows what students can read with teacher support; and the placement level is the assessor's recommendation for an optimal level for instruction.

When the placement level differs from the instructional level (usually by one level), other factors are considered. For example, a student may read a text with

Benchmark Assessment Data
Ms. Reston—Grade 3

Name	Benchmark Independent Level	Benchmark Instructional Level	Placement Level	Notes
Talisha	G	H	H	Pretty fast. Ignores word endings.
Ernest	G	H	H	Slow, with many errors and SC's.
Reggie	H	I	I	Fluent, but limited comprehension.
David	I	I	I	Slow, accurate, but much inefficient word-solving.
John	H	I	I	High accuracy, limited comprehension.
Peter	H	I	I	Fluent and accurate. Needs to work on comprehension.
Larson	J	K	K	High accuracy. Needs work on multisyllable words.
Maha	J	K	K	Difficulty taking words apart. Lots of inefficient processing.
Remy	J	K	K	Reads fast. Lack of monitoring.
Courtney	K	K	K	Fluent reading. Satisfactory comprehension.
Sherrell	J	K	K	Fast, but little intonation.
Karin	K	M	M	High accuracy. Needs to monitor. Proficient comprehension.
Scott	L	M	M	Work on taking apart multisyllable words.
Curtis	M	N	N	Work on fluency. Proficient comprehension.
Sabrina	N	N	N	High accuracy. Limited comprehension.
Michael	M	N	N	Fast, robotic. Limited comprehension.
Amber	M	N	N	Satisfactory comprehension. Too much problem solving.
Roger	0	P	P	High accuracy. Limited comprehension.
Chris	0	P	P	Good phrasing and intonation.
Layla	P	Q	P	Too much processing–not smooth.
Sharon	0	P	P	Some difficulty with multisyllable words.
Keri	P	Q	Q	Fluent. Satisfactory comprehension.
Ray	P	Q	Q	Too fast. Proficient comprehension.
Nick	Q	R	R	Too fast. Comprehension barely meets criteria.

FIGURE 10-1 Benchmark Assessment Data

satisfactory accuracy and comprehension, yet read laboriously with a huge amount of inefficient, overt processing. The teacher might elect to work with the student at an easier level for a short time to teach for efficient processing. On the other hand, assessment results might indicate a particular instructional level; however, the error pattern and reading may provide evidence that the student can take on a slightly more difficult level. In general, you can trust the assessment process, but you should also trust your own observations and intuition. If you begin guided reading and find that, in spite of a supportive introduction and powerful teaching, a level is too hard for a student, you can adjust your groups the next day. If the books on the level are so easy that the student can't make shifts in learning, adjust accordingly.

Some core reading programs call for whole-class reading; that is, every student reads the same textbook (which might be any level since anthologies vary widely), and recently, there have been calls to present all students with more difficult material. In some places, this has been interpreted to mean that all students are required to read at a prescribed level at all times. That means that over half the class would spend most of their time trying to read material that is presently too hard. They would seldom experience proficiency. What this could mean for Talisha, Ernest, Reggie, David, John, and Peter is day after day of struggling through material they cannot read with a high degree of accuracy and of which they have limited, if any, understanding—that is, if they continue to try. Teachers may end up having to read the material to students. If these students do not process text for themselves day after day, they will not learn how to process texts for themselves and are in danger of becoming passive learners who will gain no satisfaction from the act of reading.

Figure 10-1 shows that typical Grade 3 material is probably too difficult (even with teacher help) for about 50% of the students. After all, the very definition of "average" is that 50% of the population is below average and 50% is above. Actually, if all of the students in this class are required to read at level O, then students reading at level P and above will not have many opportunities to learn. Students like Keri, Ray, and Nick will be reading well below their capabilities much of the time. They will not have the opportunity to increase their processing abilities; and, fluency and integrated problem solving may be undermined. At best, they will begin to see school as a tedious kind of place. It is not possible to raise reading achievement simply by assigning students to read harder books.

A student may explore, by choice, some harder texts on topics that interest him greatly; at the same time, a student may read an easy book because of interest. Requiring readers to read difficult texts day after day can have disastrous results. For example, early readers who are just beginning to understand important concepts about print need clear words with spaces between them and only one or two lines of text. When these readers are required to read text with many lines of text and hard words, their reading process breaks down to such a struggle that the reading makes no sense. They may perpetuate slow, word-by-word reading into the intermediate grades. If intermediate students struggle to read one word at a time, comprehension will suffer. Readers need material that they can process—with challenge, yes, but also within reach so they can climb the ladder of progress.

With the best of intentions, some teachers attempt to teach every student individually. But they are not able to give enough instructional time to each reader. For most teachers, individualized teaching just isn't practical given the number of students in the class. You can make time for quick individual conferences about a student's reading and writing; but supplying the full amount of instruction most students need is not feasible when you have twenty-five to thirty students.

You can differentiate instruction within the structure of small groups. Additionally, social interaction around texts enhances students' understanding and can make reading more enjoyable. Students learn how to support each other and respond to others' ideas. In a small group, you are able to make specific teaching points for individuals and to systematize instruction. It makes the teaching efficient and students benefit from the discourse.

Cautions About Grouping

Teachers often have valid concerns about grouping for reading instruction. Grouping can have negative consequences if not implemented with great care. In the past, grouping students often led to a "lock step" system in which students followed each other through a rigidly sequenced set of materials. This small-group approach was accompanied by a huge amount of busywork in the form of worksheets to keep students quiet. So changing groups meant they had to "catch up" on an enormous amount of paperwork. That seldom happened.

As a teacher of guided reading, you want to make sure that both the way you group and the context in which you do it work against such negative outcomes. In Figure 10-2, you can see a comparison of traditional and dynamic grouping. The guidelines in the right column indicate how to counteract negative consequences.

We describe guided reading as one component of a comprehensive design for literacy instruction. You want students to have many opportunities to work with other students as a class and in small groups. Guided reading is the only context in which students are grouped according to levels of progress. Students work in a range of heterogeneous grouping for other purposes, for example:

> Heterogeneous whole-group activities for reading aloud, shared reading, reading and writing minilessons, science and social studies inquiry, and other activities.

> Heterogeneous small-group activities for literature discussion (book clubs).

> Independent choice reading time (with individual conferences).

> Interest groups around literature and curriculum study.

The Process of Dynamic Grouping

As you look at the initial grouping of the third-grade class in Figure 10-3, consider how many reading groups you should form. Three groups can be problematic. Students are usually too widely distributed to serve them well with three groups, and you may fall into the trap of above-level, average, and below-level reading. Also, for most classrooms the groups would be too large.

Based on the wide range of scores of the students in this group, you could form as many as eight groups (with Nick being a group of one). However, that would create another dilemma: meeting every group daily would be impossible in terms of the time available, so, students would not receive instruction often enough. Or, you

Comparison of Traditional and Dynamic Grouping

	Traditional Reading Groups	Dynamic Grouping for Guided Reading
Assumptions	• General ability as determining factor • Progress through same phases at an established rate; change not usually expected • One kind of grouping prevails	• Ability to use systems of strategic actions at an instructional level is determining factor • May have accelerated progress as readers shift • Continuous change expected • Different groupings used for different purposes across the literacy program
Process of Grouping	• Grouped by general determination of ability • Static; usually remain stable in composition • Progress through a fixed sequence of books (same for all students) • May not skip materials	• Grouped by specific assessment for strengths in the reading process and appropriate level of text difficulty • Dynamic, flexible, and changeable on a regular basis • Books chosen for the group from a variety on the appropriate level–some overlap but generally not the same for every group • No required sequence for books other than level and teacher's text analysis; differences in books for different groups • No predetermined time on a level and may skip levels
Process of Teaching	• Words pre-taught • Skills practice follows reading • Limited number of selections buttressed by skills practice in workbooks or worksheets • Limited variety of selections • Controlled vocabulary • Selections usually read once or twice • Heavily focused on skills • Round robin reading; children take turns; each reading a page or line	• Introduction to the text foregrounds meaning and language with some attention to words in text • Unlimited number of selections; strategic actions demonstrated, supported, and reinforced, before, during, and after reading • Wide variety of selections • Many frequently used words but vocabulary not artificially controlled • Selections (or parts of them) reread for fluency and fast problem-solving • Focus on development of a network of strategic actions • All students read the whole text to themselves (with teacher support)
Process of Evaluation	• Evaluation based on progress through set group of materials and tests	• Evaluation based on daily observation and regular, systematic individual assessment

FIGURE 10-2 Comparison of Traditional and Dynamic Grouping

Initial Grouping of Third Graders

Level H/I	Level K	Level M/N	Level P	Level Q/R
Talisha (H)	Larson	Karin (M)	Roger	Keri (Q)
Ernest (H)	Maha	Scott (M)	Chris	Ray (Q)
Reggie (I)	Remy	Curtis (N)	Layla	Nick (R)
David (I)	Courtney	Sabrina (N)	Sharon	
John (I)	Sherrell	Michael (N)		
Peter (I)		Amber (N)		

FIGURE 10-3 Initial Grouping of Third Graders

would spend so much time teaching guided reading lessons that the other impor-tant areas of the curriculum would be neglected. Let's say that you have 75 minutes per day available for a reading period. You would take some time with opening moves such as a whole-class reading minilesson and some time at the end with a group share related to the independent reading or other activities students are en-gaged in. That would leave you about 60 minutes for guided reading.

Now, look at the class list again. When you teach students in small groups, some compromises must be made. You need to use practical reasoning to put to-gether a workable number of groups. Figure 10-4 shows how you might begin the year with guided reading groups for this third-grade class.

These groups work because nothing is written in stone. You wouldn't want to shuffle groups every day because that would make planning too difficult. But you do want to use continuous assessment (see Chapter 9), as well as your own notes

Third-Grade Guided Reading Groups at the Beginning of the Year

Plans for the Group	Groups	Expectations
This group will need to meet every day.	Talisha Ernest Reggie David John Peter	Begin at level H and expect to move quickly to level I giving extra support to Talisha and Ernest and extra challenge to others.
This group should meet at least four days a week.	Larson Maha Remy Courtney Sherrell	Begin at level K and expect to make steady progress toward grade level.
This group should meet at least three days a week.	Karin Scott Curtis Sabrina Michael Amber	Begin at level M with extra support to Karin and Scott and expect to move quickly to level N. Provide extra challenge to the others.
This group should meet at least three days a week.	Roger Chris Layla Sharon Keri Ray Nick	Begin at level P and expect steady prog-ress to level Q. Keri, Ray and Nick can read more challenging books during choice reading time. Be sure to confer with them regularly.

FIGURE 10-4 Third-Grade Guided Reading Groups at Beginning of Year

on reading behavior, to form and re-form the groups as needed. We illustrate this process in Figure 10-5.

The teacher of this class plans to meet with about three guided reading groups per 75-minute reading period. Time is flexible; she may meet with an extra group and/or confer with individuals. She may work with literature discussion groups. One or two days, she may be able to teach four groups, and on other days she may only have time for two. On average, she teaches three groups a day. The following schedule (Figure 10-6) shows a possible plan that offers differentiated instruction with more attention to students who need steady, intensive, daily instruction.

The number of groups you teach and your schedule should work together to accommodate the needs of your students. But if you make time for small-group reading on a regular basis and you build instruction day upon day, you will see progress in reading.

The last decision related to grouping is to watch closely for needed changes. *We expect changes,* so our initial decisions are tentative. Students respond as individuals to instruction. Some may move very quickly. One caution: *Do not assume a student should move to the next level simply because he is reading with high accuracy.* Engage in enough conversation with him to assure satisfactory

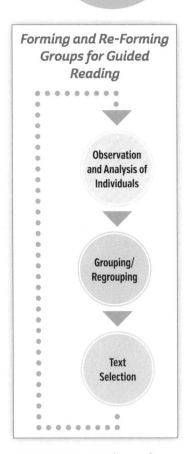

Forming and Re-Forming Groups for Guided Reading

Observation and Analysis of Individuals

Grouping/ Regrouping

Text Selection

FIGURE 10-5 Forming and Re-Forming Groups for Guided Reading

Guided Reading Group Schedule

Monday	Tuesday	Wednesday	Thursday	Friday
Talisha	Talisha	Talisha	Talisha	Roger
Ernest	Ernest	Ernest	Ernest	Chris
Reggie	Reggie	Reggie	Reggie	Layla
David	David	David	David	Sharon
John	John	John	John	Keri
Peter	Peter	Peter	Peter	Ray
				Nick
Karin	Larson	Larson	Larson	Larson
Scott	Maha	Maha	Maha	Maha
Curtis	Remy	Remy	Remy	Remy
Sabrina	Courtney	Courtney	Courtney	Courtney
Michael	Sherrell	Sherrell	Sherrell	Sherrell
Amber				
Roger	Karin	Roger	Karin	Talisha
Chris	Scott	Chris	Scott	Ernest
Layla	Curtis	Layla	Curtis	Reggie
Sharon	Sabrina	Sharon	Sabrina	David
Keri	Michael	Keri	Michael	John
Ray	Amber	Ray	Amber	Peter
Nick		Nick		

FIGURE 10-6 Guided Reading Group Schedule

comprehension. Review the behaviors and understandings to notice, teach for, and support at the level in *The Literacy Continuum* to identify the emphases for teaching at each level. The students should be able to infer the larger ideas in a text, grasp the nuances of character development, and notice the organization of the text. Figure 10-7 shows grouping changes in one class of students over a couple of months.

Moving students from one group to another does not have to be a big deal, nor does it have to be done all at once on a kind of "shuffle" day. Students should not be told that they are being "promoted." Readers should feel internal satisfaction and pride when they read with proficiency, every day. We suggest that you simply call particular students to join a group: "Would those of you who read *Coley's Journey* yesterday come to the table?" Or "Would those who read *Rules* join me now and Sabrina come too?" In an active learning classroom, students work in a variety of groups for different purposes. What matters is that every student, every day, reads a challenging text at a level of proficiency with enjoyment.

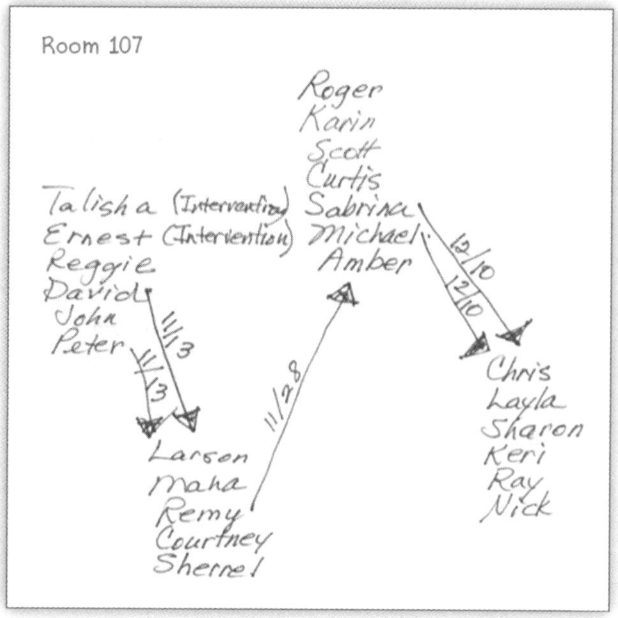

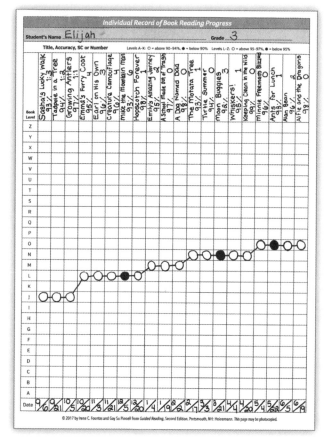

FIGURE 10-7 Dynamic Grouping of Third Graders

Monitoring and Documenting Individual Progress

The text gradient provides a reliable way to keep a record of individual progress during the time a student participates in guided reading instruction. In Figure 10-8, you can see a teacher's record of a third grader's reading (a blank form can be found in Online Resources). The teacher took a record of a student's reading about every ten days during the year. You can see that Elijah began the year at level J, which was well below grade level. Elijah participated in guided reading five days each week and in a great deal of choice reading. By mid-year, he was reading at beginning-third-grade level, and by the end of the year had reached grade level. Elijah is a student who needs excellent instruction on a steady basis, and he will continue to need that during the next few years. But he is building a system of independent proficiency.

Of course, today's technology can make it more efficient to record and report progress. In Figure 10-9, you can see a teacher's record of third-grader Larson's reading across a school year. His teacher took a record of his reading about every ten days throughout the year using the *Reading Record App* and the *Online Data Management System* (ODMS). You can see that Larson began

FIGURE 10-8 Individual Record of Book Reading Progress for Elijah

FIGURE 10-9 Individual Record of Progress for Larson—BAS Technology Version

the year at level I, which was well below grade level. He participated in guided reading five days a week and in a great deal of choice reading. By mid-year he was reading at beginning-third-grade level and by the end of the year had reached grade level. Larson is a student who needs excellent instruction on a steady basis, and will continue to need that during the next few years. But most importantly, he is building a system of independent proficiency.

This ODMS report, and others like it, can be very helpful when reporting data to administrators and school boards. (For more information on ODMS, see fountasandpinnell.com/odms.aspx.)

Figure 10-10 shows a school record that can be passed along with a student from grade to grade. These data were recorded using *The Benchmark Assessment System*, administered twice per year, and running records in between. You can see Heather's progress across six years during which time she progressed from level B in kindergarten to level U in grade five. This form, and a similar form for use with intermediate/middle-level readers, can be downloaded from Online Resources (resources.fountasandpinnell.com).

BAS, with the ODMS allows all of these data to be recorded and analyzed using technology with the ability to print reports as needed for individuals or

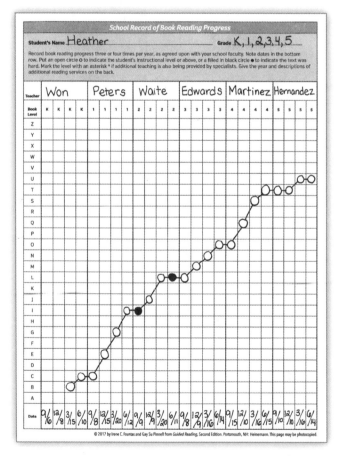

FIGURE 10-10 School Record of Book Reading Progress for Heather

classes. Reports like these are extremely helpful when reporting to administrators and school boards.

Continuous Monitoring Using Data Walls

A data wall, or a data board, is a visual tool used to keep up with the progress of all students in a class and, ultimately, in a school. It keeps student progress on display at all times. We emphasize that data walls are *a teacher's tool*. We have never recommended that students focus on their reading levels or that student reading levels be displayed in the classroom. It is not good practice to label students or label groups using text levels. During the course of a day or week, students should engage with a rich variety of texts. They should not choose books by level for their independent reading. In interactive read-aloud, shared reading, and book clubs, they should engage with texts of varying complexity.

But, for teachers, it is important to know the instructional levels students can currently process (and that includes the behaviors and understandings outlined by the level of text) and to have a vision for what teaching is needed.

When teachers work with a data wall in a private place in the school, it creates a sense of community and collective ownership of student outcomes. Teachers work toward the common vision that all students will make excellent progress over time. The whole-school data wall involves everyone.

A school in Dalton, Georgia, uses a type of data wall that is a foldable board. The grade-level teachers open it for their meetings and then store it away. There are different colors indicating the grade, as well as colored dots and arrows with additional information. (See Figures 10-11a, b, and c.) Data walls have many important uses, which are listed in Figure 10-12.

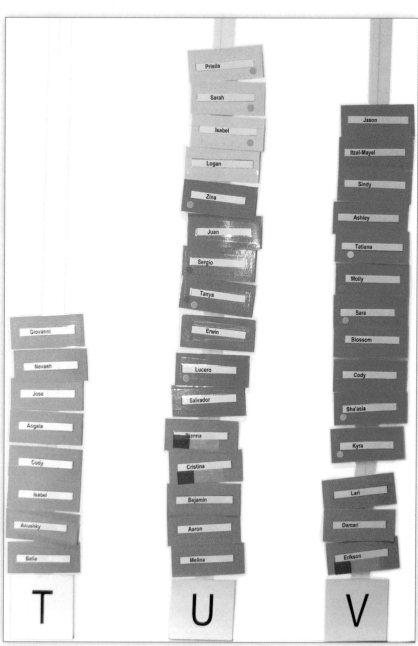

FIGURE 10-11a Three Levels on a Foldable Data Board

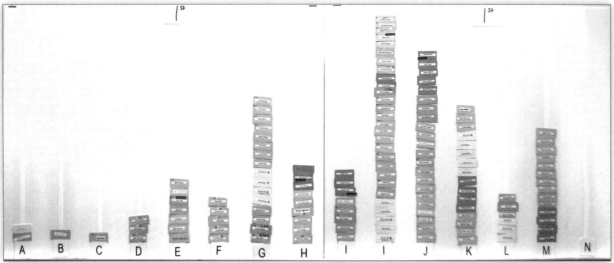

FIGURE 10-11b Foldable Data Board

Creating a Data Wall

Data walls can take various forms. We will describe one example. A data wall can consist of colored sticky notes (or cards with Velcro) that show students' first names and current reading level. The columns show text levels. There is a grade-level key for the colors of the sticky notes. (Each grade uses a different color, so that you and your colleagues can see at a glance where the cohort of first graders are reading, for example.) On the student's sticky note, you may want to place colored dots that provide more information. For example, a pink dot might be used to show a student is an English language learner, a green dot might indicate a student is receiving intervention services, and a yellow dot might identify a student with an IEP (see Figure 10-11c). If needed, you can indicate required test results by year. For getting started with a data wall, these suggestions may be useful:

▶ Convene teachers in a grade-level group (or some combined grade levels if needed).

▶ Have a large graph on the wall with text levels across the top and blank space to place sticky notes. Create a bracket or shading to indicate your district's grade-level expectations.

▶ Each teacher brings results of the first administration of text-based assessment, e.g., *BAS*, to the meeting.

▶ They record the student's first name and reading level on a sticky note with a uniform color for each grade level.

▶ Add colored dots if needed.

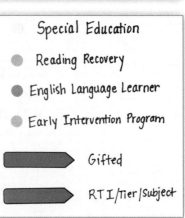

FIGURE 10-11c Grade-Level Key

Uses for the Data Wall

- Provide a visual reminder of the status of each student, of the class, of the grade-level cohort, and of the school population.

- Monitor change in readers over the course of a school year.

- Determine students who need intervention or extra support.

- Notice when students have stopped progressing at a satisfactory rate.

- Inform organization and instruction of guided reading groups.

- Offer an arena for collegial discussion and problem solving.

FIGURE 10-12 Uses for the Data Wall

▶ Place sticky notes under the appropriate column (text level) on the gradient.

▶ Create a key so that everyone recognizes the classroom or grade level and special designations.

▶ Have a discussion of what you notice as you look at the data wall and set some goals.

▶ Return to the data wall at regular intervals (often quarterly) for a continuing discussion. As time goes on and students progress up the ladder of text, teachers can move the sticky notes and place them at a higher level.

Now you have a visual profile of all the students in one place. The data wall becomes a living document that reveals the diversity among your students. The first thing teachers may notice is that each cohort spreads over more than a designated grade. Some second graders may be reading at a similar level as third graders, and so on. The data wall helps to blur grade-level lines and to remind you and your colleagues that you need to teach students where they are but give them impetus to go further.

As previously stated, the data wall should reside in the teacher's workroom. It is not a tool for students or families to see. Rather, it is an internal monitoring tool for those who are responsible for knowing the progress of the entire population of the school. According to Downend (2015), the data wall is a way to "embrace" data. The overall question on everyone's mind should be, have we made progress on the goals that are most important to us?

Downend offers these central questions to address in the discussion of the data wall:

▶ What do we want each student to learn?

▶ How will we know when each student has learned it?

▶ How will we respond when a student experiences difficulty?

▶ What do we do if a student already knows what we are teaching?

▶ What are our areas of strength and need?

▶ How many students do we have reading below grade level?

▶ What are the plans to provide extra support for students performing below grade level?

The conversation around the data wall goes far beyond text level. Use of *The Literacy Continuum* is integral to it. A student's name on the wall calls her to mind as an individual, and teachers soon find themselves talking about the behaviors and understandings that are essential to accurately read and fully comprehend a text at a particular level. It helps to create a culture of collaboration in which teachers can support each other in solving problems and have shared ownership of student outcomes. A culture of collaboration is: "A systematic process in which teachers work together to analyze and improve their classroom practice. Teachers work in teams, engaging in an ongoing cycle of questions that promote deep team learning" (DuFour 2004). This culture forms the fabric to support a high-quality instructional program for literacy.

Continuous Record Keeping

Your own observations, taken over time, are just as valuable as the levels and numbers you might record electronically. Take note of significant behaviors students demonstrate during guided reading. Even though you are teaching a group, you are noticing the behavior of individuals. This open-ended form is designed for ongoing record keeping. It can be downloaded from Online Resources (resources.fountasandpinnell.com). Place a sticky note on each square. On the sticky note, write the name of each student in the group, along with the date. This form is simple because of the flexibility it offers. Make quick observational notes on the sticky note for each student (see Figure 10-13). You may be able to record observations for several lessons on one note (each time writing the date); or, you may have so many notes that you use one note per lesson. When you are finished copy, the page to keep in your guided reading lesson folder for the group. Then take the sticky note off and stick it on a page that goes into the student's individual folder. These notes can be very useful for:

▶ Explaining student progress or lack of it.

▶ Planning guided reading lessons.

▶ Providing examples and information for family conferences.

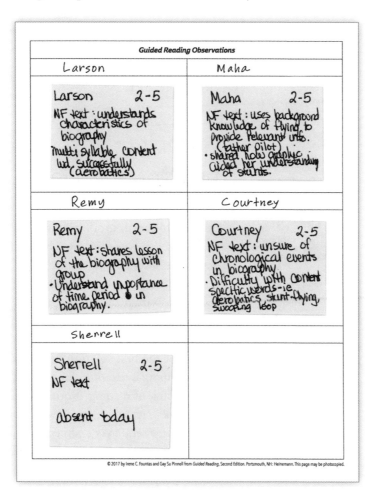

FIGURE 10-13 Guided Reading Observations

Another form (see Figure 10-14) is useful both for planning guided reading lessons and for taking observational notes. This form can also be downloaded from Online Resources.

Technology can certainly make observational notes more efficient to take and score. But even with handwritten notes, you will be amazed at the amount of good information you can accumulate about your students. Look back over your notes to determine evidence of your students' reading behaviors, such as:

- Initiation of problem-solving actions
- Behavioral patterns that show strengths and confusions
- Evidence of independent action
- Use of multiple sources of information to solve words
- Ability to take words apart while reading continuous text
- Inferences about the writer's message, about characters, and about plot
- Awareness of underlying structures such as compare/contrast, problem/solution, description, chronological and temporal sequence, cause/effect

Planning for Guided Reading and Taking Observational Notes

Group: Larson, Maha, Remy, Courtney, Sherrell

New Text and Level: Betty Skelton and Little Stinker (N) Biography

Introduce the Text	
• Engage student interest. • Establish the overall meaning of the text. • Talk about the meaning. • Introduce new language structures. • Call attention to a few new and important words if needed. • Point out aspects that are new or may cause confusion.	• Back flap – readers read. Author note – teacher reads parts. Why is plane named Little Stinker? • Pursuing one's dreams. • Time period (1926–now). Flew solo for 12 years. • Female paving way for other women. Never gives up on her dreams. • Photo of Betty, p. 2; aerobatics, p. 8
Students Read the Text	
• Notice the behaviors of individual readers. • Prompt for problem solving actions.	• See sticky notes. • Courtney — content-specific words.
Discuss and Revisit the Text	
• Begin in an open-ended way. • Have students talk about their thinking (**within, beyond,** and **about** the text). • Revisit to clarify, locate information, or provide evidence for statements.	• What did you think of Betty? Who is Little Stinker? Why that name? • Revisit diagram – p. 15 • Page 16 – stunt in 1949 – what are you thinking? • page 16 – timeline Anything you didn't understand about the stunt?
Teaching Points	
• Teach for one or two aspects of the reading process– **within, beyond, about** the text. • Ground teaching in text.	• Lessons learned (beyond the text) • Why did the author choose Betty as a subject? (about the text) • citing evidence from the text
Work with Letters/Words	
• Provide 2-3 minutes active, inquiry-based word work. • Focus on any aspect of word solving. • Help readers develop quick recognition and flexibility	• Multisyllable words – notice easy spelling patterns (CVC): how you can use known parts to figure out new multisyllable words. ham/hamster, cap/capture, win/window, dis/discovery, happen/happening, hop/grasshopper
Write About Reading	
• Talk/write about the text. • Use interactive, shared, independent, or dictated writing.	• Write a letter to Betty to share your thoughts about her accomplishments in your Reader's Notebook. Share with a partner.

FIGURE 10-14 Planning Guided Reading Lessons and Taking Observational Notes

The observational notes contribute greatly to your analysis of the students' strengths and needs. We reiterate that you should not rely on a "level" as a label or the sole source of information about a student. Elizabeth DeHaven shared her experiences in guided reading and notetaking comparing it to shopping for jeans! (See Figure 10-15)

Grouping: Essential but Not Sufficient

We have visited the difficult terrain of grouping students for small-group reading and documenting progress over time. These activities are key to the successful implementation of guided reading. The difficulty lies in the need to find your own system and make it work. We have tried to provide helpful examples, but we agree with Elizabeth that the simplest solution you can find is the best solution.

Grouping is essential for efficient and effective teaching of reading. Nothing has yet arrived to take its place, and we doubt that technology can adequately compensate, although certainly it can greatly enhance students' ability to work independently. Just as essential is the need to make grouping work in a flexible way

Finding a recording method for anecdotal notes is often a journey that takes on varying forms over time until you find one that suits you. It's a bit like shopping for jeans. You have to try on a few pairs, visit several stores, ask friends for recommendations and suggestions, and even buy a couple that don't fit quite right before discovering the pair you were born to wear. What works for someone else may not work for you. You may have to revise your system a few times before you find one that is both effective and efficient for you.

My own journey started with a sophisticated system of sticky notes and checklists, which was far more complicated and time consuming than it was effective. So I scaled down to a less-sophisticated system, replacing sticky notes with mailing labels and adding multicolored file folders and a binder. Scaling down looked an awful lot like scaling up.

I thought the more complicated and colorful the system the better I would be at recording information about my students. At the time I also thought fancy systems were the hallmark of a good teacher. What actually happened is that I maintained my system for roughly two days before becoming overwhelmed by the management required to keep it running that I neglected to take notes on the students.

I was more focused on creating a system with bells and whistles than finding a way to take and store meaningful notes about my students that would both be evidence of student learning and inform future work with these students.

Though this process of finding an effective system was long and expensive—I think I spent at least a week's salary at my office supply store on labels of various colors and sizes—I learned several things:

1. Less is more; simplicity is key. For me, what worked was using one sheet of paper for each guided reading group meeting with a box or space for each student.

2. It's easy to get caught up in the moment and energy of a lesson. Take time (before dipping in) while they read to jot down notes about what you observed during the text introduction. Do this again after conferring with a student and at the completion of the lesson. If you're anything like me, your memory will fail you if you wait too long.

3. Notes should reflect what students are doing as readers. A comment like "Ryan is a sweet boy" doesn't tell you much about how Ryan is processing text.

4. Ask the following questions to help focus your notes:
   - What can each student do as a reader? What are you learning about the way he or she processes text?
   - What processing strategies did you teach for and how did each student begin to take it on?
   - What are your initial thoughts about next steps?
   - Use The Fountas & Pinnell Literacy Continuum, PreK-8 to help you think through these questions.

FIGURE 10-15 Elizabeth DeHaven's Experiences with Guided Reading and Note Taking

without the negative effects that can arise. Good record keeping is an important key to the process of dynamic grouping but it must be accomplished within the space of your literacy period—that is, "on the run." Outside of that period you need time to read students' written responses and for other tasks, so record keeping shouldn't become another full-time job.

You will find that your observations become more valuable over time as you gain experience and expertise. They can fuel your teaching and your conversations with students' families (who are often delighted with some very specific "stories" of what their children have said or done). Working with colleagues will be very helpful in problem solving all of the activities related to managing guided reading lessons. We go to the next chapter knowing that grouping is essential and so are your observations and analytic thinking. They are essential because they make it possible for you to do your most powerful teaching.

Suggestions for Professional Development

1. Convene a group of grade-level colleagues to support each other in forming groups. Have each person bring a class list with assessment data (as in Figure 10-1).

2. Work together on the lists to form about four groups for each class (as in Figure 10-4).

3. Have each teacher reflect on the groups and write a brief statement of expectations with the group.

4. Create a data board with your colleagues to monitor progress with the cohort at your grade level. Schedule times to reconvene, and problem solve together.

5. Work toward completion of a whole-school data wall.

CHAPTER 11

Using Running Records and The Fountas & Pinnell Literacy Continuum *to Guide Teaching*

Assessing literacy demands that we have an intimate knowledge of literacy and its development so that we can make sense of the literate things students do.

–Peter Johnston

Developed by Marie Clay (Heinemann 2000) a running record is a standardized process for coding, scoring, and analyzing a student's precise reading behaviors In this chapter we will introduce you to the basic principles of this efficient, informative tool. Our *Fountas & Pinnell Continuum Teaching Video Library*, as well as our literacy systems for assessment and intervention, contain several running record video tutorials for your individual learning or professional development sessions. If you have one or more of these products, we encourage you to participate in one of the tutorials so you can get hands-on practice and realize how easy the process can be when you have had proper practice. Your goal should be to become so familiar with the process that it feels just like breathing. Clay's *Running Records for Classroom Teachers* (Heinemann 2000) contains a complete and thorough description of this technique and provides a blank running record form to be used for this purpose.

Taking running records of children's reading behaviors requires time and practice, but the results are well worth the effort. Once learned, the running record is a quick, practical, and highly informative tool. It becomes an integral part of

Purpose of Running Records

- Assess text difficulty
- Group and regroup for instruction
- Select appropriate texts
- Inform the introduction of texts
- Inform teaching decisions during the reading of a new book
- Inform your teaching decisions after reading
- Inform the letter-word work after reading
- Monitor individual progress over time
- Assess the effectiveness of yesterday's teaching

FIGURE 11-1 Purpose of Running Records

teaching, not only for documenting a student's reading behaviors for later analysis and reflection but also for sharpening your observational powers and your understanding of the reading process. A system for taking running records at selected intervals is essential to effective teaching in guided reading lessons. The record will inform not only the selection of an appropriate book but the specific emphases you need to prioritize on for your readers. You can use running records for many purposes (see Figure 11-1).

Taking a Running Record

Taking a running record involves sitting beside the student while he reads a text, usually one he has read once before (a seen text). At selected intervals, for example, at the beginning and end of the year, you may take a running record (or reading record) on a text the student has not seen before (unseen text) as a standardized benchmark assessment to begin teaching and document progress. In this case, the text may be typed on a recording form, and this is especially helpful when working with higher levels (beyond level J). When using paper and pencil, the only difference between a running record and a reading record is:

▶ A running record does not use pre-typed text. You make checkmarks on the blank page in the layout of the print. It's meant to be quick and used on any text the child is reading.

▶ A reading record uses pre-typed text. You have to acquire it or type it in the exact layout of the print.

At the early levels, you code the whole-text reading (about 150–200 words). At upper levels, you code about 150–200 words of oral reading to sample the processing, and students finish the text silently. Use a pencil on a form or use the *Fountas & Pinnell Reading Record App* for iPad to code the behaviors. The text should offer a bit of challenge but not be so difficult that the student's processing will break down.

Once you have begun the instructional program, use yesterday's new book (seen text) to take the record. You will be able to determine the appropriateness of the level, the current strengths and needs, and the effects of your teaching. Both you and the student are looking at the same text. The process is quite simple. Watch the student closely as he reads, coding behaviors on a separate form or tapping the screen of your tablet. Do not intervene; your role is that of a neutral observer. When the student needs help to move on, the most neutral thing to do is to say, "you try it" (if he verbally appeals) and then, if he balks, you tell him the word. Following the coding, note how the reading sounds, have a very brief conversation about the meaning, and make a teaching point. This process offers an opportunity to observe what the reader can do on his own without teaching.

In this chapter we will focus on assessment using paper and pencil. You need to learn this process. Once you are comfortable with the paper and pencil process, you may wish to increase your efficiency by using the electronic version (see page 275), which includes a video tutorial of the process. You will find that if you learn the paper and pencil process first, the app will be very easy to use.

Coding the Reading

Code all the accurate reading with a check (✓) for each word read accurately. Mismatches are recorded with a line, what the reader says above the line, and text information and all teacher actions below the line. This principle will become evident as the coding system is explained. The codes for significant behaviors you will observe are shown in Figure 11-2. This form can be downloaded from Online Resources (resources.fountasandpinnell.com). Look carefully at the first four columns in the chart. You will see the name for each observable oral reading behavior, what you see the reader do, how to code it, and an example of the behavior. You will notice that there is a second coding option for coding an insertion with a typed text. When you have coded all the behaviors, make a short note about how the reading sounds so you can reflect on the reader's fluency. Have a brief comprehension conversation. Then make an immediate teaching point based on your observation

Coding and Scoring Errors at-a-Glance

Behavior	What the Reader Does	How to Code	Example	How to Score	
Accurate Reading	Reads words correctly	Do not mark *or* place check (✓) above word	**No mark** *or* ✓ / environments		No error
Substitution	Gives an incorrect response	Write the substituted word above the word	worry / wonder	Substitution, not corrected	1 error
Multiple Substitutions	Makes several attempts at a word	Write each substitution in sequence above the word	speckles | spices | specials / species	Multiple substitutions, not corrected	1 error for each incorrect word in text
			adept | adopt | SC / adapted	Multiple substitutions, self-corrected (SC)	No error; 1 SC
			to | touch | teeth / tooth	Multiple misreadings of the same word, not corrected	1 error for each incorrect word in text
			Attic / Arctic	Multiple misreadings of names and proper nouns	1 error first time missed; no errors after that
			can not / can't; they're / they are	Misreading contractions (reads contraction as two words or two words as contraction)	1 error each time
Self-correction	Corrects a previous error	Write the error over the word, followed by SC	use | SC / usually		No error; 1 SC
Insertion	Adds a word that is not in the text	Write in the inserted word using a caret	very (over a caret ∧) *or* very (over a dash)		1 error per word inserted
Omission	Gives no response to a word	Place a dash (–) above the word	– / only	Skipping a word	1 error per word
				Skipping a line	1 error per word
Repetition	Reads same word again	Write R after the word	R		No error

Coding and Scoring Errors at-a-Glance (continued)

Behavior	What the Reader Does	How to Code	Example	How to Score	
Repeated Repetitions	Reads the same word more than once	Write R for the first repetition, then write a number for the additional repetitions	R_2 R_3		No error
Rereading	Returns to the beginning of sentence or phrase to read again	Write R with an arrow back to the place where rereading began	R		No error
	Rereads and self-corrects	Write R with an arrow back to the place where rereading began and a SC at point of self-correction	theirselves | sc R / They can wrap themselves		No error; 1 SC
Appeal	Verbally asks for help	Write A above the word	A / environments	Follow up with "You try it"	No error
"You Try It"	The child appeals, the teacher responds with "You try it"	Write Y after the word	A / environments | Y	"You try it" followed by correct word	No error
				"You try it" followed by omission, incorrect word, or Told	1 error
Told	Child doesn't attempt a word even after "You try it"	Write T after the word or the Y	A / environments | Y | T; A / environments | T		1 error
Spelling Aloud	Child spells word by saying the names of letters	Write the letters in all capital letters	E-V-E-R / ever	Spelling followed by correct word	No error
				Spelling followed by incorrect word	1 error
Sounding Out	The child makes the sounds associated with the letters in the word	Write the letters in lower case with hyphens between them	o-n-l-y | ✓ / only	"Sounding out" followed by correct word	No error; no SC
			t-em-per | temper / temperature	"Sounding out" followed by incorrect word or no word	1 error
			b- | SC / polar	Sounding the first letter incorrectly and then saying the word correctly	No error; 1 SC

FIGURE 11-2 Coding and Scoring Errors at-a-Glance

of the reader's use of strategic actions, including the information on fluency and comprehension.

Scoring The Reading: A Quantitative Analysis

Now you are ready to think about scoring the record.

Counting Errors

In scoring the running record quantitatively:

▶ A substitution counts as one error.

▶ If there are multiple attempts at a word, only one error is counted. You can't have more than one error for each word. You can't have more errors than words.

▶ Omissions, insertions, and "tolds" count as one error. Repetitions are not considered errors and are not counted in the scoring.

▶ Proper names count as an error only the first time.

▶ Self-corrections are not errors.

▶ Running words include all the words in the book or passage, not counting the title or other features outside the body of the text (e.g., sidebars, charts, diagrams).

Look at the last column in Figure 11-2 and you will see a summary of how to score each error.

Determining Accuracy Level

To determine the accuracy rate, subtract the number of errors from running words, divide by the number of running words, and multiply it by 100 (see Figure 11-3). As a shortcut, you can divide the number of running words by errors ($\frac{150}{15} = 10$), achieve a ratio (1:10), and refer to Clay's Calculation and Conversion Table (see Figure 11-4) to arrive at 90%. This chart can be photocopied and taped to the bottom of the clipboard you use to take running records.

Use the criteria for determining levels (Figure 11-5) to determine whether the text is independent, instructional, or hard. Reading at the instructional level provides good opportunities to observe reading work. As the reader works things out, you can notice the processing behaviors. The accuracy rate lets you know whether you are selecting books that offer the right amount of learning opportunity. The text should be neither too easy nor too hard. A good guideline is that the students should be reading with more than 90–94 percent accuracy (levels A–K) or 95–97 percent (levels L–Z) (see Figure 11-5). The point is not accuracy per se but whether you have selected a text in a range that provides opportunities for effective processing. Stretches of accurate reading mean there are appropriate sources of information that allow the child to problem-solve unfamiliar aspects of the text. Remember that you still need to assess the reader's comprehension. A student can read with high accuracy, but if he is not proficient in comprehension, the text is too hard.

When the text is too hard, readers cannot use what they know; the process becomes a struggle and may break down to using only one source of information.

Accuracy Rate

$$100 - \frac{E}{RW} \times \frac{100}{1}$$

$$100 - \frac{15}{150} \times \frac{100}{1}$$

$$= 90\%$$

FIGURE 11-3 Determining Accuracy Rate Table

From *An Observation Survey of Early Literacy Achievement,* Third Edition, by Marie M. Clay. © 2013 The Marie Clay Literacy Trust. Reprinted with permission.

Conversion Table

Error Ratio	Percent Accuracy	
1:200	99.5	
1:100	99	
1:50	98	
1:35	97	Good opportunities for teachers to observe children's processing of texts
1:25	96	
1:20	95	
1:17	94	
1:14	93	
1:12.5	92	
1:11.75	91	
1:10	90	
1:9	89	
1:8	87.5	
1:7	85.5	The reader tends to lose the support of the meaning of the text
1:6	83	
1:5	80	
1:4	75	
1:3	66	
1:2	50	

FIGURE 11-4 Clay's Calculation and Conversion Table

From *An Observation Survey of Early Literacy Achievement*, Third Edition, by Marie M. Clay. © 2013 The Marie Clay Literacy Trust. Reprinted with permission.

Levels A–K:	95–100% = independent 90–94% = instructional Below 90% = hard
Levels L–Z:	98–100% = independent 95–97% = instructional Below 95% = hard

FIGURE 11-5 Accuracy Criteria for Determination of Levels

The reader may stop attending to visual features of print and invent text, or the reader may rely on labored sounding that makes it difficult to read for meaning. You may have observed students produce nonsense words when struggling with a hard text. When the text is too hard, it is nonproductive in helping the student become an effective reader. To become an effective reader, the student must sustain effective processing over long stretches of meaningful text.

The accuracy rate, along with the comprehension information, helps you group readers effectively. For example, if a particular level of text is "right" for five to six readers, you can work effectively with them as a group even though they have differences in the ways they process text.

Finally, the accuracy rate lets you know whether the introduction to the text and other kinds of support during the first reading were effective. The introduction is especially important in helping readers process a text independently. High accuracy and evidence of effective processing indicate that the teaching was helpful to the student's developing independence in reading.

Determining Self-Correction Ratio

To determine the self-correction rate, add the number of errors and self-corrections, and divide by the number of self-corrections to calculate a ratio (see Figure 11-6). The self-correction ratio indicates the number of times the reader notices an error and corrects it. If the ratio is 1:3, the reader fixes one error for every three errors he makes. Over time, the overt self-correcting should become unseen and only a number of self-corrections indicated. Too much overt self-correction is inefficient in later processing.

Self-correction Ratio

$$\frac{SC}{E + SC}$$

$$\frac{5}{15 + 5}$$

1 : 4

One in four

FIGURE 11-6 Determining Self-Correction Ratio

From *An Observation Survey of Early Literacy Achievement*, Third Edition, by Marie M. Clay. © 2013 The Marie Clay Literacy Trust. Reprinted with permission.

Analyzing the Record: Qualitative Analysis

Qualitative analysis involves looking at the specific reading behaviors, thinking about how the reading sounds, and reviewing notes about how the reader understood the text based on the brief comprehension conversation.

Sources of Information Used

Look for evidence of the readers' use of sources of information and of the use of strategic actions such as searching for and using information, self-monitoring, checking one source of information against another (cross- checking), solving words or self-correcting. (It will be easier to see evidence of the reader's use of meaning, structure, or visual information (MSV) in younger readers because they make errors and self-corrections "out loud." With readers who are farther along, the processing "goes underground," and there is not so much observable behavior. Examine each incorrect attempt and self-correction and hypothesize about the information sources the reader might have been using up to the point of the error or self-correction (see Figure 11-7). In Clay's analysis, the sources of information form these major categories. Clay argues, "It is only when you go to the trouble of analyzing all the errors that you get quality information about the way the reader is working on print" (Clay 1993, 31).

Proficient readers use all of these information sources in an integrated way while reading for meaning. For example a reader might look at a word, make the sound of the first letter, search for a word that would make sense and sound right in the sentence, and check this prediction against other visual features of the word. In this case, the reader has initially used visual information, searched for and used meaning and structure, and then checked against visual information. Of course, all of this happens very quickly and most readers are not aware of the process. The result is accurate reading, but the operations reflect a complex integration of ways to use information. The reader's focus remains on the meaning or message involved.

Look at the running record of Alison's reading of *Sticks and Stones for Little Monster*, level E (Figure 11-8) to see an example of how to code errors and self-corrections as you think about the sources of information the reader was probably using up to the error. For each incorrect attempt and self-corrected error, the letters M S V are indicated in the Error column and the SC column, as appropriate. If meaning influenced the child's error, M is circled; if structure (syntax), S is circled; if visual information, V is circled (you actually write all three: M, S, and V, because you are analyzing sources of information *used*, and sources of information *neglected*). To circle M, S, or V in the self-correction column, you ask the question, "What information sent him back?" Or "What made him go back and search further?" A complete running record includes these analyses of each error and self-correction.

The value of this activity is to look for patterns in the reader's responses. You should not spend endless time trying to figure out each error, searching for the "right" analysis. The idea is to reflect carefully on the reader's attempt, make your best hypothesis, and then look at data through the whole reading and over time to

Analyzing Sources of Information Used

Sources of Information Used	Analysis	Ask Yourself
Meaning	Think about whether the reader's attempt makes sense up to the point of error. Think about the story or information from the illustrations or graphics, and the meaning in the sentence in deciding whether the reader was probably using meaning as a source. For a self-correction, think about what made the reader go back.	"Does the attempt make sense?"
Structure	Structure refers to the way language works. This information source is also sometimes referred to as syntax because unconscious knowledge of the rules of grammar in the language the reader speaks allows him to eliminate alternatives. In English you are asking if the attempt is an acceptable English structure or if the structure of the sentence influences the response. Using this implicit knowledge, the reader checks whether the sentence "sounds right." For a self-correction, think about what made the reader go back.	"Does the attempt sound right?"
Visual Information	Visual information includes the way the letters and words look. Readers use their knowledge of visual features of words and letters and connect these features to their knowledge of the way words and letters sound when spoken (phonological information). If the letters in the reader's attempt are visually similar to the letters in the word in the text (for example, if it begins with the same letter or has a similar cluster of letters), it is likely that the reader has used visual information. You are determining if the visual information from the print influences any part of the response. For a self-correction, think about what made the reader go back.	"Does the attempt look similar?"

FIGURE 11-7 Analyzing Sources of Information Used

identify patterns of responding. You will get a good sense of the reader's use of information, and an indication of the kinds of strategic actions the reader is using.

An important thing to remember about attempts is that they are not simply right or wrong but often partially correct. Partially correct responses involve the reader's use of some information on the way to using multiple sources of information. They indicate the reader's in-the-head strategic actions and provide a window through which you can observe for evidence of successful use of information while reading. You can observe whether the reader is actively relating one source of information to another, a behavior that Clay (1991a) calls "cross-checking" because the reader is checking one information source against another. At the top of the running record form, note sources of information used, sources neglected, and evidence of cross-checking behavior. Summarize how the reader used sources of information and patterns of behavior that are evident.

Pg.	Sticks and Stones for Little Monster — Level D
2	Little Monster got some stones. He put them on the table.
4	Little Monster looked for sticks. He put the sticks on top of the stones.
6	"I need worms," said Little Monster. He got some worms and he put them on the table.

Pg.	Sticks and Stones for Little Monster — Level D
8	Little Monster got some weeds. He put them on the table, too.
10	Little Monster looked for bugs in the grass. He put the bugs on the table. "I like bugs!" he said.
12	"I need mud," said Little Monster. He put mud on top of the stones and the sticks. He put mud on the worms, the weeds, and the bugs.
14	"Now I need one more thing," Little Monster said. He got a fork.
16	Yum!

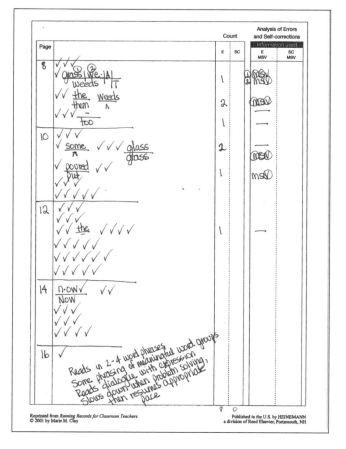

FIGURE 11-8 Alison's Reading of *Sticks and Stones for Little Monster*

Once sources of information are analyzed, think about questions like these that give you insight into the reader's construction of a processing system:

▶ Does the reader use sources of information in relation to each other?

▶ Does the reader check information sources against one another?

▶ Does the reader use several sources of information in an integrated way or rely on only one kind of information?

▶ Does the reader repeat what was read as if to confirm the reading thus far?

▶ Does the reader reread to search for and use more information from the sentence or text?

▶ Does the reader reread or use additional information to self-correct?

▶ Does the reader make meaningful attempts before appealing to you for help?

▶ Does the reader request help after making an attempt or several attempts?

▶ Does the reader notice when sources of information do not match?

▶ Does the reader stop at unknown words without actively searching for information?

▶ Does the reader appeal to you in a dependent way or appeal when appropriate (that is, when the reader has done what he can)?

▶ Does the reader read with phrasing and intonation? Does he use punctuation?

▶ Does the reader make comments or respond in ways that indicate comprehension of the story?

These kinds of reading behaviors provide a description of the reader's processing system (the list above is not exhaustive). It may be helpful for you to review and use an expanded list of observable behaviors to look for on a few running records. This will help you develop your lens for looking for precise reading behaviors in each of the categories of strategic actions. They reveal whether the reader is using in-the-head strategic activities, which include:

▶ *Early Literacy Behaviors* (at about levels A, B, C)

▶ *Searching for and Using Information.* Searching is an active process in which the reader looks for information that will support problem solving in some way. Readers search for and use all kinds of information sources, including meaning, visual information, and their knowledge of the syntax of language. The goal is for readers to use all sources of information simultaneously as they process a text (see Chapter 16).

▶ *Monitoring and Self-Correcting.* These strategic actions allow the reader to confirm whether he is reading the story accurately. Readers who are reading accurately are consistently using meaning, structure, and visual information to confirm their reading. This is not a conscious process, but the internal system tells them whether the reading makes sense, sounds right, and looks right. *Self-correcting* is the reader's ability to notice mismatches, search for further information, and make another attempt that accomplishes a precise fit with the information already known (see Chapter 16).

▶ *Solving Words.* Word solving involves recognizing words and taking them apart while reading. Readers often notice and use word parts, reread to think about the meaning and structure and read a word that fits all sources of information (see Chapter 17).

▶ *Maintaining Fluency.* Students are reading language, not words. This means they are processing units of meaning (phrases) and interpreting the writer's message. This processing involves not only phrasing but intonation, pausing, rate, stress and the orchestration of them all (see Chapter 18).

Assessing Fluency

When the student finishes reading orally, you make brief notes about how the reading sounds. You may want to use the holistic rubric (see Chapter 18) for a quick rating. This information will be very useful in selecting emphases for teaching. A reader who is not reading with phrasing and fluency is likely not using language structure and attending to meaning.

Assessing Comprehension

Once you complete the coding, you have a brief talk with the student, discussing the key understandings that were within, beyond, and about the text. You also have information from the discussion after the first reading of the text to consider as you evaluate the evidence of readers' ability to think within, beyond, and about the text.

A Look at the Processing Systems of Two Early Readers

Peter and Catherine are both reading at level G, working in the same group for guided reading lessons. Let's look at how their behaviors provide evidence of the way they are processing print (Figures 11-9 and 11-10). Although the quantitative analyses of their reading records were similar (92% accuracy and self-correction ratio of 1:5), you will see how each is building a reading process in a different way when you look qualitatively at the evidence of processing. Then you can think about how the emphases for teaching will differ within the same level.

Catherine's Reading

Catherine reads for meaning and uses language structure as is evidenced in her three substitutions, but she uses limited visual information on this selection. Two substitutions, however, that did not fit visually were attended to by Catherine, and she fixed them both immediately. The one substitution (*grass/ground*) is evidence of the use of all three sources of information (meaning, structure and visual information) but remained uncorrected by Catherine. She read word by word as if to demonstrate that reading was about reading each word accurately—she didn't use her oral language to attempt any unknown words. She waited six times for "tolds" by the teacher. Her accuracy rate was 92% and her self-correction ratio was 1:5, meaning that for every five errors she made, she self-corrected one. She falls into the instructional range for this reading, and her comprehension conversation scored her as proficient.

Pg.	**Animal Tracks** Level G
2	An animal made tracks in the soft mud. Turn the page to find out who made the tracks.
4	A bear made the tracks. The bear used its big paws to open a log and eat the bugs inside.
6	Who made the deep tracks?

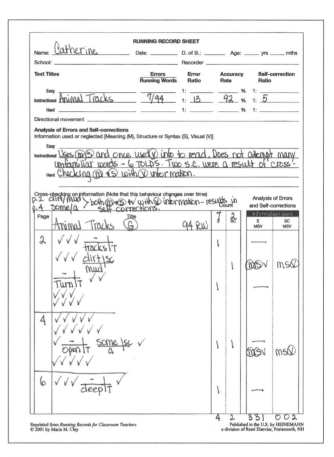

Pg.	**Animal Tracks** Level G
8	A deer made the deep tracks. The deer ran fast through the grass on its hard hooves.
10	Who made the thin tracks?
12	A bird made the thin tracks. The bird walked on the ground and pulled up a worm to eat.
14	Who made the bumpy tracks?
16	I made the bumpy tracks with my boots!

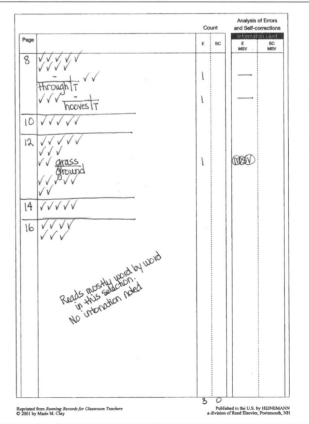

FIGURE 11-9 Catherine's Reading of *Animal Tracks*

Next Steps for Catherine

One of the most important things for Catherine to understand is that reading is about gathering meaning and/or information from a story. She shows evidence of self-monitoring her reading, but she's not doing anything after she comes to a difficulty. To do that, she needs to make attempts at unknown words so as to keep the storyline moving forward. When she waits for a "told," she interrupts the story and loses the essence of its meaning. She has shown evidence of her ability to use the visual information with her immediate self-corrections and her one uncorrected error. However, she's in a pattern of waiting at difficulty for someone to help her with the "hard" words. She needs to be in control of trying something herself. After the reading, then, her teacher could help her sort through her attempts so she could see how all three sources of information can work together to get to the "right" word.

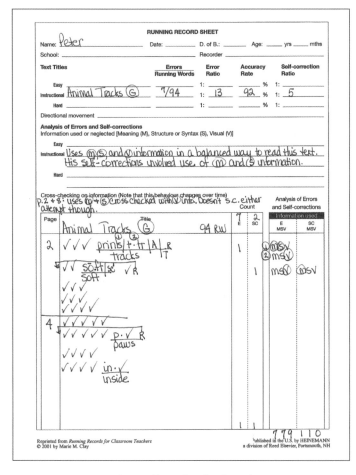
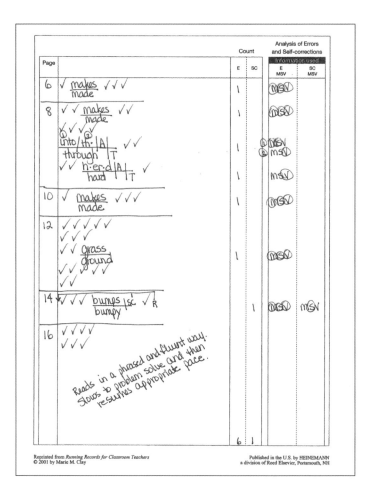

FIGURE 11-10 Peter's Reading of *Animal Tracks*

Peter's Reading

Peter is an active reader who understands that it's his responsibility to read the text as independently as possible. He reads using meaning, structure, and visual information in a balanced way—with a slight edge to the visual information. On two occasions, he made several attempts to problem-solve an unknown word (*tracks* and *through*) before appealing for help from the teacher. His first attempt involved meaning and structure, and the second attempt checked those information sources with visual information. Even though he was not able to correct those errors, he had a sense that all the sources of information must work together. He sometimes sampled the initial visual information to get to the word (such as with *paws* and *inside*). On two occasions, he reread and self-corrected errors after he had read beyond the error. Once the error no longer fit the structure of the sentence (*bumps/ bumpy*), and once the error didn't fit the meaning of the sentence (*sōft/soft*). Four errors fit meaning, structure, and visual information and as a result were left uncorrected by Peter: *makes/made* (three times) and *grass/ground*. His accuracy rate was 92% and his self-correction ratio was 1:5. He also falls into the instructional range for this reading, and his comprehension conversation was scored as proficient.

Next Steps for Peter

It will be important for Peter to continue to use all the information sources together as he initially reads texts. The teacher should encourage him to try something at difficulty (*tracks* and *through*), which might involve rereading to regain the momentum of the story (as he did on page 4). The teacher might start with that behavior to reinforce that reading work. As a next step, the teacher might encourage him to check other attempts (*makes/made* and *grass/ground*) further with meaning, structure, or visual information to get at the precise message of the author.

Developing a Self-Extending System

Catherine and Peter are readers who continue to develop the competencies needed at every level, but analysis of their behavior offers evidence of very different processing systems. As shown in the analysis, both are beginning to use sources of information in integrated ways. The goal of reading (and for Catherine and Peter) is to develop a self-extending system. As described in Chapter 15, a self-extending system is an integrated network of understandings that allow the reader to discover more about the process while reading. As you observe your students' processing of text, look for evidence that shows readers are on their way to a self- extending system and are able to apply the strategic actions of self-monitoring, searching for and using multiple information sources, and self-correcting on more difficult texts and for longer and longer stretches of print.

A Look at the Processing Systems
of Two Intermediate Readers

As readers develop, more of the overt processing goes underground. Readers may correct most errors before saying them. Often the reader utters only word beginnings or a part before reading the whole word. You may notice more reading to regroup words in phrases.

Two intermediate readers, Jack and Selma, read *The Glow Below,* a level P text (see Figures 11-11 and 11-12). As you can see, Selma and Jack are reading at the same level with the same accuracy and comprehension. Yet each is working through the same text with a different literacy processing system.

Selma's Reading

Selma is also an active reader at this level, and she works effectively at her problem solving. She uses all three sources of information in an integrated way to read. She samples larger pieces of visual information to problem-solve unknown words: *angler/anglerfish.* Twice she read *dark/darkness* but self-corrected both attempts: once immediately, once as a result of a reread. When she inserted a word and read on, she returned and self-corrected that insertion (*down*). Her five uncorrected errors fit meaning, structure, and visual information and as such she didn't bother to self-correct them: *seemed/seems, the/these, a/an, had/has,* and *glow/glowing.* If you look at her running record, you see longer stretches of accurate reading not interrupted by problem solving of words. That allowed her to gain momentum during her reading and get more from the comprehension conversation afterward. Her accuracy was 97% (instructional), and her self-correction ratio was 1:3. She read in a mostly phrased and fluent way, and her comprehension conversation was determined to be satisfactory for this sample.

Next Steps for Selma

Selma is putting together an effective, efficient processing system, but there are still aspects to attend to. She needs to be directed to look more carefully at the ends of words to get to the precise reading intended by the author. She tends to use much of the visual information effectively, but could benefit from moving through the words more effectively in order to achieve accurate reading. A prompt by the teacher to scan the entire word before reading it may be all that's needed because so much of her reading is accurate. Although she read in a mostly phrased and fluent way, the teacher might want to think specifically about which aspects of fluency could use further prompting for Selma.

We provide a summary of the coding, scoring, and analysis process in Figure 11-13, but over time, you will internalize the process.

Pg.	The Glow Below: Creatures That Light Up the Sea Level P
2	It's Dark Down There! Picture yourself taking a trip to the bottom of the ocean. Down, down you go in your diving machine. The deeper you go, the darker it gets. Sunlight cannot reach the deep ocean floor, so it is darker than night. But when you turn off your ship's lights, you are in for a surprise. Flashes of blue light wink in the dark. Is that a gleaming green bush? A blue cloud seems to appear out of nowhere! Where do these lights come from? The light comes from sea animals that glow in the dark.
4	A Tricky Fish As you look into the dark, you watch a fish that looks like an alien from outer space swim past your ship. It's really a female

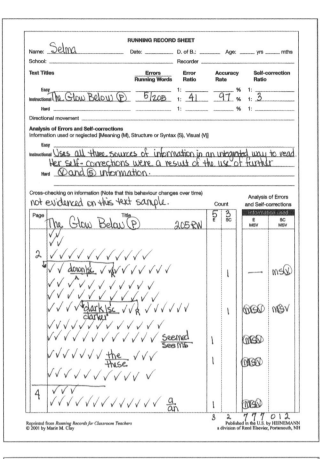

Pg.	The Glow Below Level P
4 (cont.)	anglerfish. She has a glowing stick on her head that looks like a small fishing rod. She uses the stick as a lure, or bait, to attract her prey. Her prey are the animals she is hunting for food. In the darkness, other animals cannot see her body. All they can see is the lure, which looks like a bright, tasty snack. But when a hungry animal gets close to the bait—snap! The anglerfish eats her prey.

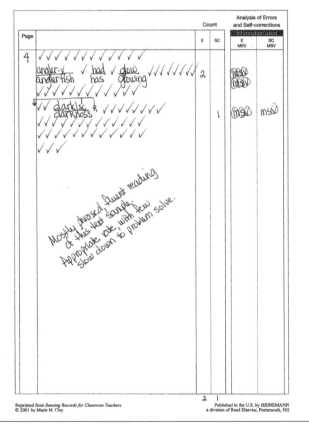

FIGURE 11-11 Selma's Reading of *The Glow Below*

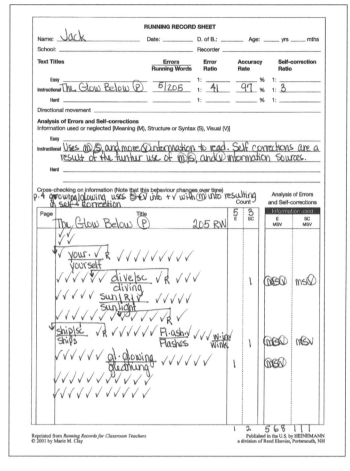

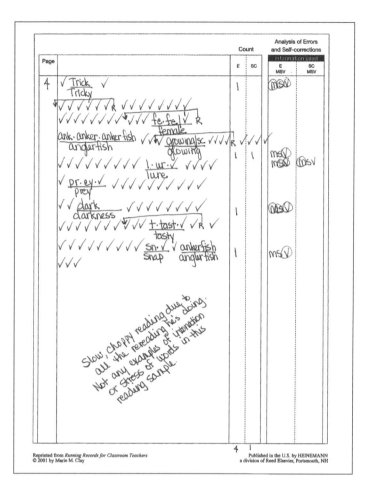

FIGURE 11-12 Jack's Reading of *The Glow Below*

Jack's Reading

Jack is a very active reader, but the work he is doing is ineffective at this level. He rereads much too often to confirm and self-correct his reading and, as such, interrupts the story and its meaning. Sometimes he self-corrects an error and then rereads to confirm it. Other times, he rereads to self-correct. Once he rereads to get beyond the initial visual information to solve the word (*fe.fe.female*). He uses multiple sources of information to read, but not always in an integrated way. For example, on *ankerfish/anglerfish* he uses only visual information in attempting the word. On *growing/glowing* he uses structure and visual information on the initial attempt, but with a further meaning attempt, he self-corrects the error, while *glowing/gleaming*. *Trick/Tricky* and *dark/darkness* use all three sources of information initially without searching for and using further information to self-correct. He samples many unknown words and solves them quickly without rereading. For example: *your/yourself, sun/sunlight, Flash/Flashes, win/wink, pr.ey/pretty, l.ur/lure, tast/tasty* and *sn/snap*. Because of all the work he's doing, there isn't an opportunity to gain any momentum in his reading to move him forward—no long stretches of accurate reading so that the reading is smooth and efficient. His accuracy rate is 97% (instructional), and his self-correction ratio is 1:3; he's correcting 1 in every 3 errors. His comprehension conversation puts this reading into a satisfactory range.

A Summary: Coding, Scoring, and Analyzing Running Records

Coding the Reading	◆ Listen to the student read orally while you code the reading. ◆ Make notes about how the reading sounds. ◆ Make notes about the reader's understanding of the text.
Scoring the Reading (Quantitative Analysis)	◆ Count the total number of words read. ◆ Indicate each error and self-correction in the error and self-correction column. ◆ Count the number of errors and self-corrections. ◆ Determine the error ratio. ◆ Calculate the accuracy rate. ◆ Calculate the self-correction rate.
Analyzing the Reading (Qualitative Analysis)	**Sources of Information Used:** ◆ Write M S V in the column next to each attempt (errors and self-corrections). ◆ Analyze each error and circle M S V if the child likely used it: M–Did the meaning or message influence the response? S–Did the structure of the sentence up to the error influence the response? V–Did visual information from the print influence any part of the error–letters, cluster, word? ◆ Tally the M S V columns. **Self-Correction:** ◆ Analyze each self-correction by circling M S V: ◆ What additional information did the reader add to make the self-correction? ◆ What made the reader go back to fix the error? ◆ Circle M S V. ◆ Tally the self-correction columns. ◆ Consider the overall pattern of use of sources of information. **Strategic Actions:** ◆ Analyze the strategic actions on the left side of the record: ◆ Does the reader initiate problem-solving actions at difficulty or after an error or wait for a told? ◆ Does the reader self-monitor using meaning, structure, or visual information? ◆ Does the reader check one source of information with another? ◆ Does the reader search further when necessary? ◆ Does the reader reread to confirm? ◆ What sources of information does the reader use or neglect? **Fluency:** ◆ Use your notes to score the reader's fluency. ◆ Circle the rating on the rubric. **Comprehension:** ◆ Examine the observable behaviors that indicate comprehension from the oral reading and talk: ◆ Notice the amount of self-correction behavior. ◆ Notice whether the reader's attempts at words make sense. ◆ Notice if the reader rereads to establish or maintain meaning. ◆ Notice if the reader processes with fluency, phrasing, and intonation. ◆ Examine notes on the reader's thinking within, beyond, and about the text as evidenced in the talk after reading.

FIGURE 11-13 A Summary: Coding, Scoring, and Analyzing Running Records

Next Steps for Jack

Although rereading is useful as you're learning how to read and put information sources together, it interrupts the reading of a more proficient reader. Perhaps a focus on phrased, fluent reading would help with Jack's excessive rereading: encouraging him to put his words together in a smooth way so it sounds like talking.

Using Running Records to Document Change over Time

Along with your running records, you may use the Guided Reading section of *The Fountas & Pinnell Literacy Continuum* to help you make notes about the precise behaviors the reader controls, partially controls, and does not yet control at each level of text difficulty. This tool will help you develop a lens for the important behaviors and understandings to notice, teach for, and support at each level.

Over time, you will notice in your informal observations and your standardized running records each reader's unique development. You will notice patterns in their development as readers as they process increasingly challenging texts.

In this book, we have talked about early readers (A-M) and intermediate middle-level readers (N-Z), but these are very broad categories. In the Guided Reading section of *The Literacy Continuum,* you will see (for each level) more precise descriptions of the range of behaviors in each category of the systems of strategic actions.

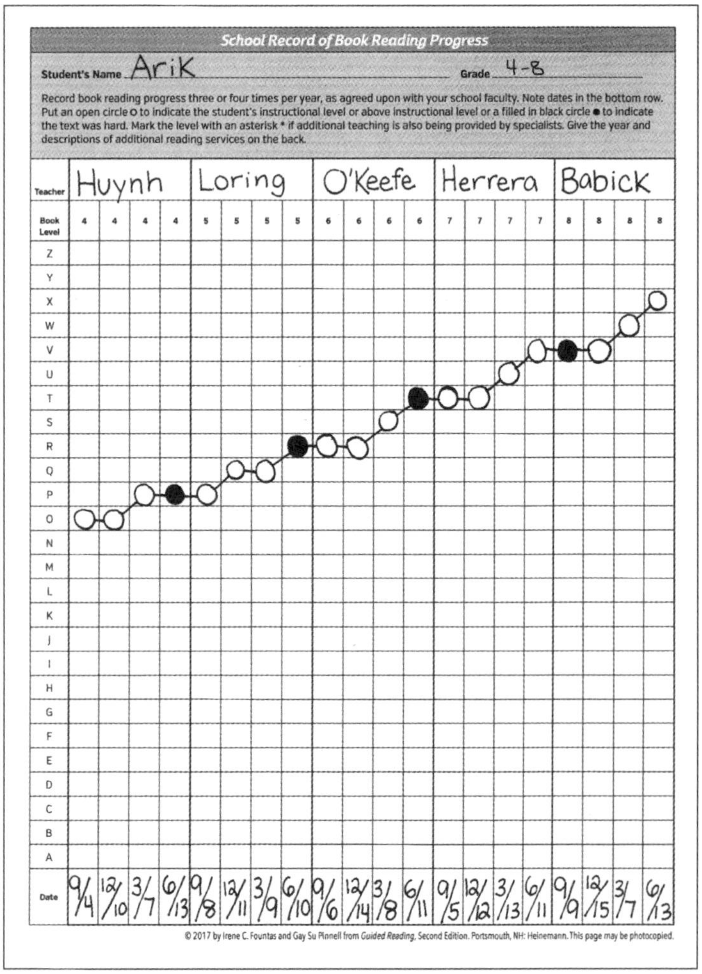

Shifts over Time in Reading Development

Notice Arik's School Record of Reading Progress, which shows the running records taken over time to document his progress in school (see Figure 11-14). The black circles indicate the accuracy level was in the difficult range or the comprehension unsatisfactory. The white circles indicate the reader was processing successfully at an instructional level. This record illustrates how he moved from an early emergent reader to an emergent, transitional, expanding, and advanced reader over five years of schooling. It represents a broad look at change over time in reading development as students learn how to meet increasingly sophisticated demands along the gradient of text.

FIGURE 11-14 Arik's School Record of Reading Progress

A System for Documenting Change over Time

You need a system for taking running records on each student. While you could use printed Recording Forms, we have developed the *Fountas & Pinnell Reading Record App* for iPad (see Figure 11-15) as an electronic alternative. The app is used in conjunction with the Fountas & Pinnell Online Data Management System (ODMS) and is available in the iTunes store. With these tools, you will have a system for capturing and analyzing student reading data to inform future instruction.

The Complexity of Development over Time

Arik's progress as a reader helps us understand development over time, but each reader makes his own journey. Any chart, however useful, is simplistic when matched against the unique pattern of reading behaviors evidenced by individual readers.

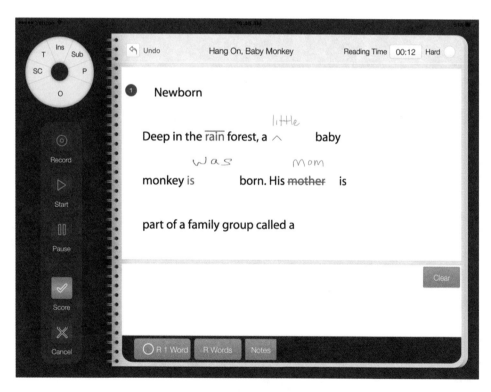

FIGURE 11-15 Fountas & Pinnell Reading Record App

Suggestions for Professional Development

1. Work with a group of colleagues to discuss reading records. Take a video of a student reading at the level of interest for the group. (You may need two readings if your group is diverse.) For each reading, talk with the student informally about the book for 3–4 minutes. You'll need copies of each book.

2. Using the information in this chapter, have the group listen to the reading and conversation after reading. For readers at about levels A through S, have the group use the Guide for Observing and Noting Reading Behaviors, to discuss the reading. Then, invite them to listen again and code the reading and talk about the behaviors they notice.

3. Set another meeting and ask each person to bring a running record for one reader and copies of the book.

4. If you have the *Fountas & Pinnell Benchmark Assessment System 1* or *2*, you might use the reading record tutorial that is available with the system along with copies of the Recording Form.

SECTION **THREE**

Using High-Quality Texts to Support Responsive Teaching

The chapters in Section Three are all about texts. First, we explore the rich collection of high-quality texts that teachers need to use the multitext approach described in Section One. Students need access to a wide range of topics, themes, genres, and forms, as they participate in interactive read-aloud, shared reading, guided reading, book clubs, and independent reading. In addition, they need to experience high-quality leveled texts in guided reading. We describe the text gradient in detail, and we also discuss how you can use it as a teaching tool. We provide specific descriptions of the process of selecting and introducing texts in guided reading lessons, and examples of student and teacher interactions across a wide variety of texts.

CHAPTER 12

Creating a Collection of Texts to Support Literacy Learning

Anyone who calls himself a reader can tell you it starts with great books, heartfelt recommendations, and a community of readers who share this passion.

–Donalyn Miller

In a school that is alive with literacy there is one critical, "must have" element—classrooms filled with good books. Our job as teachers is to assure our students fall in love with books and develop a passion for authors, illustrators, genres, and topics. So the first business of our teaching is to assure our students want to read. All of your expert teaching will not be effective if students have nothing worthwhile to read. So an important early challenge, if you want to implement guided reading within a comprehensive literacy design, is to create a rich text base—a collection of high-quality books in the school and text resources within each classroom. Creating the base will take time, planning, and collaboration among the school team.

A Rich Text Base to Support Literacy

The text base must include books (both print and electronic) to support all dimensions of the developing reading process. You will need books that are in advance of students' abilities to build their competencies through interactive read-aloud and shared reading, leveled books from which you can select to create the ladder of progress they are ascending, and hundreds of single titles from which students can choose to read independently. You cannot expect to assemble all of these books at once—a high-quality collection is built over time.

A Variety of Genres

First, consider the different types of books and genres that are important to include. All literature can be divided into prose and poetry, both of which can be either fiction or nonfiction (see Figure 12-1). Prose and poetry can be further divided into different genres. Fiction texts can be either realism or fantasy. Realism can be divided into realistic fiction or historical fiction; fantasy can be divided into traditional literature (which includes folktales, fairy tales, fables, legends, epics, ballads, and myths) and modern fantasy (which includes animal fantasy, low fantasy, high fantasy, and science fiction). Nonfiction includes informational texts, which can be divided into biographical texts (biography, autobiography, and memoir), narrative nonfiction, expository nonfiction, procedural texts, and persuasive texts. Each of these genres makes specific demands on the reader, so genre is an important text factor to consider. We encourage you to learn about the characteristics of genres so that you can help your students, at the appropriate grade level, attend to the characteristics to develop deep understanding of craft to support comprehension and a shared language to talk with each other about texts.

Fiction Genres

Realism is true to life. Although stories are imagined, settings, characters, and events could exist in real life. Realistic fiction is perhaps closest to students' lives;

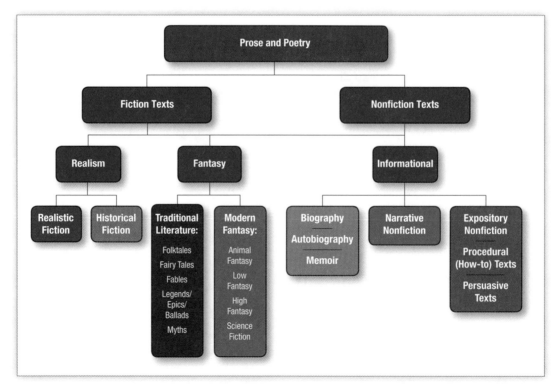

FIGURE 12-1 Fiction and Nonfiction Genres from *Genre Study* (Fountas and Pinnell 2012)

even very simple books can tell a realistic story. Historical fiction adds complexity because the reader must understand the setting of an earlier time that has not been experienced by the reader. Historical fiction often calls for a shift in perspective and considerable background knowledge about a time period or setting.

Fantasy ranges from very simple animal fantasy to highly complex and challenging high fantasy and science fiction. Traditional literature includes simple folktales, including fairy tales and fables. Often, these stories have been passed down over generations. In general, the characters in these stories are "flat" in that they do not change except to learn a lesson or two. These stories were a way to pass along the values of a culture before a large number of people could read; today, traditional stories have been retold or written down but the nature of the tales is the same. Every culture in the world has folktales. Fables are folktales that have an explicitly stated moral lesson at the end; and these, too, were intended to pass along values. Fables often have talking animals. The challenge to the reader is interpreting the larger message of a story even if the characters are far from reality.

Many simple, often humorous stories are animal fantasy (modeled on folktales). These stories feature animal characters that talk and act like people; they may wear clothing; sometimes they learn a "lesson," but character change is not required. High fantasy and science fiction challenge the reader to enter into another world and to understand characters, actions, plots, and the symbolic struggle between good and evil. They often feature alternative worlds, magic, heroes on a quest, and magical objects. Science fiction also includes elements of science and technology, and often space travel.

Nonfiction Genres

Expository nonfiction for beginners is very simple and focuses on everyday events and topics. Usually a nonfiction book has a single topic. For example, a book might show different kinds of baby animals. But categories become more and more complex as you use books across the gradient of difficulty. It is helpful for students to have a mental map of the kinds of categories they can expect. More complex expository texts are like feature articles and sometimes include argument and persuasion. Expository texts often have special features such as headings, subheadings, sidebars, photos with legends, captions, diagrams, maps, and many other features. Readers must learn to gather information from all of these features.

In addition, a nonfiction text may be a true story of any event told in chronological sequence, such as the story of an interesting event or of a process in temporal sequence. This is referred to as narrative nonfiction.

Nonfiction genres also include biographical texts that tell the story of a person's life (or a period of time in their life), and texts that tell true stories of events in history or in contemporary times. These are not exactly like fiction narratives because they don't always have elements like conflict between characters, a climax in the plot, and problem resolution, But they are like narratives in that they are largely told in chronological sequence, although there may be switches in time. Readers need to follow time sequences and detect the significant decision points or emotional reactions within the time period.

Text Structure

All fiction and nonfiction genres use a narrative or non-narrative text structure. A typical fiction narrative consists of an opening, the presentation of a problem, a series of events, a climax in which the problem is solved, followed by "falling action" in which loose ends are tied up. Of course, narrative structure may also be approached in much more complex ways and may vary by culture. Fiction genres are easier to follow if students understand how narrative structure usually works. They have expectations for a book: that the plot will be resolved and the story will end. That is true of all stories whether at level A or level Z on the gradient of text difficulty.

A narrative structure can also be used in nonfiction. A writer may share factual information in a narrative style, told in chronological order. This is characteristic of narrative nonfiction, biography, autobiography, and memoir. Biographical texts often show the decision points in people's lives—the choices they make that lead them to their accomplishments. A memoir usually focuses on a specific, significant period, event, or memory in a writer's life, or it may focus on a place or a time. Narrative nonfiction may recount an inspiring story or a period or event in history, and readers can expect these stories to be told in chronological order.

Non-narrative text structures include expository, persuasive, and procedural. With expository texts, information is typically organized into categories. When you read an informational text, you may notice headings and subheadings. Often, it is not necessary to read an expository text from beginning to end. You can search for the categories of interest and read them in any order. Nevertheless, the writer organizes the text in an intentional, logical way, and the reader should be able to identify and understand the organization and hypothesize the reasons for it.

The structure of factual texts for early readers should be very simple. The text is usually focused on one topic, and examples are familiar. With any factual text, you will want to ask: "What background knowledge will be required for readers to process this text with understanding?"

Text structure can become more complicated when writers embed one structure within another. A narrative may be embedded within an expository text. Factual documents, such as speeches or letters or journals, may be embedded within an historical fiction text.

Nonfiction writers use underlying text structures to communicate information (see Figure 12-2). Often, many of these structural patterns are used in combination within the same nonfiction text. Readers must detect these patterns and use them to derive and understand information. The presence of these underlying structures, especially in combination, can increase the challenge for readers, and they offer excellent opportunities for teaching and learning.

The wide variety of genres that students experience over the course of their years in school is vital to their

Underlying Text Structures in Nonfiction

....

Categories

Description

Chronological Sequence (time order)

Temporal Sequence (the steps or stages in which something takes place)

Compare and Contrast

Cause and Effect

Problem and Solution

Question and Answer

FIGURE 12-2 Underlying Text Structures in Nonfiction

growth as readers. Some genres, for example, historical fiction and science fiction, are challenging in ways that require more experience with texts and more content knowledge to comprehend; but, with these exceptions, students should be exposed to most genres at every grade level through interactive read-aloud. They will build knowledge in a spiraling kind of way as they engage with more and more sophisticated examples. This exposure to a range of genres is important in interactive read-aloud, in book clubs, in the books you use for guided reading, and in the classroom library students use for independent choice. In *Genre Study* (Fountas and Pinnell 2012) we present and discuss ways your students can learn about each genre through an inquiry process that includes interactive read-aloud, minilessons, book clubs, and independent reading.

Texts for Interactive Read-Aloud

We have discussed the important benefits of interactive read-aloud in all of our books (see Figure 12-3). Interactive read-aloud is the foundation of a community that shares literary understandings through thinking and talking together. Students develop a rich common language and shared knowledge of books.

You will need to evaluate texts for interactive read-aloud carefully. The books you ask your school to buy will be texts that you keep and use for many years. The books you acquire from school and public libraries, too, should be the richest, highest quality, and most appropriate to support what you want students to learn. There is a value to selecting and sequencing these books very carefully because read-aloud is much more than just enjoyable space in the day, or a "settle students down" time. There is a strong instructional element to interactive read-aloud that will serve you well as you teach your students to comprehend texts. Here are some important questions to ask about read-aloud texts:

> ▶ *Will this text engage the students' minds and hearts and result in meaningful discussion during and after the reading?* Students need texts that engage their intellect and curiosity and that are relevant to their world. They need to explore multiple perspectives and benefit from the thinking of others. The texts they experience need to bring them pleasure, joy, and deep satisfaction. Books are a connection to all humanity and are the center of every literacy classroom.

> ▶ *Are the texts appropriate to the age of my students?* There are many highly complex texts to choose from. Just because you like a text does not mean it will help

Benefits of Interactive Read-Aloud

Through interactive read-aloud, students can:

- Connect to the lives of others and their world.

- Build and develop ideas together as a community.

- Engage in meaningful conversation.

- Develop deep comprehension about texts without having to decode the words.

- Expand conceptual knowledge, vocabulary, and ability to comprehend texts deeply through listening and talking.

- Acquire complex language structures from listening to and understanding texts.

- Make connections between texts and learn to think across texts to expand comprehension.

- Study the characteristics of a variety of genres in a deep way.

FIGURE 12-3 Benefits of Interactive Read-Aloud

your students (although your own appreciation of a text is important to students). Using mature and abstract texts like *Love You Forever* (Munsch 1986) or *The Giving Tree* (Silverstein 1964) will not necessarily help very young students take on these adult perspectives. Picture books can be simple for primary students and have more complex messages or content for older students. Select books that will delight the age group.

▶ *Am I sequencing a group of related texts so that students can make connections?* Elsewhere (see Fountas and Pinnell, *Genre Study*, 2012 and Fountas and Pinnell, *Teaching for Comprehending and Fluency*, 2006) we have recommended "text sets" or several books that are related by topic, genre, author, illustrator, craft, or element for every grade level to read across the year. Text sets enable students to develop deeper content and literacy knowledge.

School or Public Library

If you are fortunate enough to have a school library and professional librarian, then you have a wonderful resource for your interactive read-aloud planning. You can also visit a variety of local public libraries to get books. The school librarian is an expert at suggesting books for children at different ages, and also knows the school's book collection very well. If you are looking for picture book biographies, for example, set up a time to consult with the librarian and plan for a couple of weeks of interactive read-aloud.

Books for Read-Aloud in the Classroom

Choose your classroom collection of read-aloud books carefully and build a beautiful collection over time. Hardcover books can be expensive, but they last a long time and also show beautiful illustrations at their best. (A big part of interactive read-aloud is helping students develop an aesthetic appreciation for art.) We strongly recommend reading picture books at every grade level through middle school. They can be read in one sitting and there is a great variety of exquisite texts appropriate for every level (see Figure 12-4). A picture book is generally a short story with beautiful art. You may want to borrow a particular book from the public or school library and try it out before buying it. If you find a book that would greatly enhance your teaching and your read-aloud collection, it might make sense to purchase it. Sometimes, schools provide a yearly stipend

FIGURE 12-4 Interactive Read-Aloud in the Classroom

to enrich classroom libraries. These texts have the advantage of staying in the classroom all year, and they become great resources for students as they talk about reading and serve as mentor texts for writing.

Have the books you plan to read in the next week or so available in a tub, basket, or on a display rack near the chair where you read aloud to the students. Be sure to read them all yourself ahead of time and think about:

▶ The big ideas or message in each text

▶ The opportunities for thinking about multiple perspectives

▶ The opportunities for student learning of content, vocabulary, and language

▶ The opportunities to learn about genre as well as text structure

▶ The impact of the illustrations

▶ The relevance of the text to students' lives and their world

▶ The connections students might make between texts

Using language to describe "thinking across texts" requires complex cognitive thinking on the part of students. Use these books as mentor texts for minilessons in writing and reading, and try to keep them in your classroom for a long time, if possible. After reading a book aloud, you can place it on the rack to make it available for students to examine during independent reading time.

Text Sets

A text set is designed for highly intentional teaching through interactive read-aloud. Many teachers have access to small collections of read-aloud books that have features in common and can be grouped into text sets accordingly (see Figure 12-5 and Figure 12-6). A text set enables students to develop deep understandings of a topic, author or illustrator, craft, or genre.

You can build text sets in your classroom library (either permanent or temporary). Sometimes teachers get together and share books to create text sets that travel from classroom to classroom. Often there are baskets with text sets in the school's book room or library.

Grouping Texts by Different Characteristics

Author	Conduct a study of an author by reading four or five works by a single author.
Illustrator	Conduct a study of an illustrator by reading four or five works by a single illustrator.
Topic	Group texts by topics such as family or friends, or by science or social studies content (animals, earth science, space, a particular culture)
Genre	Text sets in like genres are an ideal way to begin the study of genre characteristics, first, by immersing students in four or five clear examples in the genre.
Literary Analysis	Group texts by any aspect of literature, for example, the setting, similar characters, or story problems.
Text Structure	Group nonfiction texts by the organization writers use, for example, categorical structure with headings, or narrative structure.
Themes	Group texts by putting together those with similar messages and themes, for example, overcoming obstacles or appreciating cultural differences.
Award-Winning Books	Organize books that have received critical recognition, such as recipients of the Newberry, Caldecott, or Orbis awards.

FIGURE 12-5 Grouping Texts by Different Characteristics

FIGURE 12-6 A Primary Text Set on Colors and an Intermediate Text Set on Making a Difference

Texts for Book Clubs

You will also need multiple copies (6–8) of trade books for small-group literature discussion. These are books that engage the thinking of your students and that they find relevant. Select titles that include fiction and nonfiction—picture books and some longer chapter books. They should be age and grade appropriate. You can make them accessible to students who can't read them independently (see Chapter 21).

Texts for Shared Reading

Teachers need a rich variety of large-print books, as well as poetry and song charts, to engage readers in shared reading (see Figure 12-7). Big books can be fiction, nonfiction, or collections of poems and songs. Enlarged texts for intermediate readers can be used to examine nonfiction text structures or text features; you can also use large-print books as mentor texts. Often they have interactive features such as cut-outs, flaps, or pop-ups, and are accompanied by small book versions for independent reading or a listening center. You will find your students reading the big book or small book versions over and over.

FIGURE 12-7 Large-Print Shared Reading Books

Classroom Library for Student Choice

Even if there is a library in the school, you will need a high-quality classroom library for student choice. The classroom library includes attractively displayed books (see Chapter 21) in a variety of genres that reflect cultural sensitivity and relevance to the age group. They are organized by categories such as topic, author, illustrator, genre, and award-winning books (see Figure 12-8).

The classroom collection includes many engaging short texts as well as chapter books appropriate to the age of the students. They should not be organized by level for student choice, but at the same time, you'll want to be sure that there are easier and harder texts within each genre or other category. You might include two or three copies of very popular books for intermediate or middle-level students. Some of the books you read aloud may also function as choices in the classroom library, but you may want to keep them separated for convenience, for example, in the "books we've shared" rack or tub.

Early readers may also choose from "browsing boxes," tubs, or baskets of books that you create. These include books they have read before or that are included because they will be easy for the students. They can also look at books they have heard read aloud, espe-

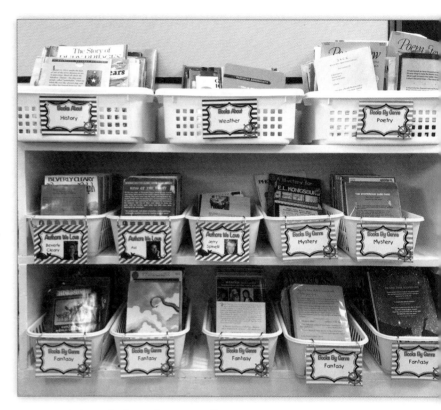

FIGURE 12-8 Books in a Classroom Library

cially favorites they have heard more than once. Small versions of books from shared reading can also be included. Early readers do not mind reading a book over and over, and this reading enables them to develop an early reading foundation as well as to start phrasing their reading. Over the course of grade one, they will be able to choose more and more books from the library that they can read.

Be sure to reflect your students' interests and cultures to the best of your ability as you choose books for the classroom library. Also, keep in mind curriculum areas that you might be studying in science or social studies. Guided reading is not specifically designed to teach subject matter, but it is logical to conclude that:

▶ If students already know something about a topic, then they are more likely to be interested in reading more about it.

▶ The more students read about a topic, the more they know and the more than can bring to further reading.

If you have the technology, you can include electronic versions of books in your classroom library. E-books are limited, though, because you may have only a few tablets and students are often not allowed to take them home. We anticipate advances in technology in the next few years that will make thousands of books available at very low prices. There is no substitute, though, for beautiful picture books to read aloud and for individual copies that are the basis for book club discussions.

Above all, the books in your classroom library are not there for the purpose of "practicing your reading." Students will need to read for a sustained time each and every day, and the purpose is to create lifelong readers who have the power of choice, the ability to make decisions about texts, the freedom to have opinions, the interesting cognitive activity of thinking critically about reading, and the pleasure of reading.

Have the goal of providing hundreds of books in your classroom library. But remember that not all of the books have to be displayed all year. In fact, if you have a huge collection, students may be overwhelmed and browse aimlessly for long periods of time. You may want to keep back some of your books so that you can bring them in as "new" with your brief book talks. The book talks are highly purposeful, one- to two-minute "commercials" about books. Book talks engage students' interest, provide a little background to help them get hooked on a book and help them learn more about the books available in the collection.

Organize books into baskets or tubs with the titles facing out so that students can sort through them. You can put them in labeled tubs, many of which will correspond to the kinds of text sets you are using. Take your cue from popular bookstores and post student recommendations or reviews, or have a box of class favorites.

Leveled Books for Guided Reading

The text gradient (A to Z) provides a basis for organizing the leveled books you use for guided reading instruction.

A School Book Room

With colleagues, you can work together to create a book room for your school that houses a diverse collection of leveled books from levels A through Z that you share with your team. With good planning and an efficient system, it can be a dynamic source of excellent selections for all your guided reading groups (see Figure 12-9).

The book room has a rich variety of fiction and nonfiction texts for guided reading that are shared by all the teachers. (Some schools place big books for shared reading and multiple copies of trade books for literature discussion in the central book room as well.) For estimates and recommendations of numbers, see *Leveled Books for Readers* (Fountas & Pinnell 2002).

The book room should be located in a central place that is convenient for teachers to access. It is wonderful when the room has enough space for teachers to meet in small groups at a table to talk about the books or participate in professional development sessions, but sometimes space is at a premium. You can create a book room that is similar to the "stacks" in a library. In the future, teachers and students will likely be able to access many books electronically, but schools, students, and teachers will need to go through many transformations before that becomes a viable reality. In the meantime, there are advantages to looking over and comparing a large range of books as you begin your instruction in guided reading.

A book room can take several years to develop and doing so involves collaboration. You will need a system for teachers to access or "check out" books and return them to the book room. Once every week or two weeks, you can go to the book room with a basket and "shop" for the books you need for a week or two of

FIGURE 12-9 A School Book Room

guided reading instruction. (Of course, you can always adjust by going back to the book room during the week.) Many schools have a bar code on each book that can be quickly scanned when someone borrows it. If you want a particular book or set of books, you will know who has them and when they will be returned. Some schools have teachers write their name on a card to stick in the box or place a clothespin with their name on it. The book room should be equipped with enough sets of texts at each level so that teachers do not become frustrated.

It takes time and some investment of resources to create and maintain a book room. But, once in place, the system is incredibly economical. The books are a one-time expense, and you can count on them to last for at least five to ten years if cared for properly. Most importantly, the books are a shared resource available to all of the teachers in the school.

For an entire school, you will need books at every level, A-Z (see *The Fountas & Pinnell Literacy Continuum*). Set a goal of fifty titles per level, with six to eight copies of each title, about evenly divided between fiction and nonfiction. The number of titles needed, of course, will depend in part on the size of your school. Also, adjust to the current levels (and envisioned levels) of your students. For example, you may need fewer titles at the upper end at first. But remember, as you work intensively, reading levels will trend upward. The goal is to bring all students to level Z.

An additional benefit of the book room is that it also represents the change over time in reading development, which your students undergo from early elementary to intermediate and middle school. You have a concrete representation of where students are and where they need to go in terms of text difficulty. As you study the books, you enter into informal conversations and share experiences with colleagues as they use them with students. It's very easy to get locked into your own grade level when, in fact, progress should be continuous across grades. It's important for teachers of early readers to have concrete examples of where their students need to go; and it's important for upper-grade teachers to understand where their students have been and the progress they have made. Also, every teacher has students who need more help to achieve grade-level reading, as well as students who are more advanced, and the book room is an ideal resource to meet the needs of this diverse body of readers.

Leveled Book Sets in the Classroom

Sometimes teachers keep their collections of leveled books in their own classrooms (see Figure 12-10), or share them across a grade level. Having a classroom leveled collection makes access and availability easier, but it is not the most economical solution because they are generally not accessible to other teachers. If the leveled book sets are located in the classroom, they should not be available for student selection. They are there so that you can choose books easily for your guided reading lessons. Be sure to put them in a more private place in the classroom that is not accessible to students. If you want to place one of the books in the classroom library, you can always take one copy and put it in the library for a period of time.

FIGURE 12-10 A Leveled Set of Books in the Classroom

Some teachers like to have a small, leveled book collection handy in the classroom that includes only the titles they like very much and have had excellent results using. For an individual collection like this, you would need six to eight copies of each title and a variety of genres and topics. Include a greater number of books with levels that are most used at your grade level, but always think to the future. As you implement a dynamic guided reading program with daily lessons, you may find that you need more books at higher levels.

Sustaining the Collection

As a faculty team, you will always be working on your leveled books in the book room, interactive read-aloud collections, shared reading collections, literature discussion titles, and classroom libraries. Work with the principal and central office in your district to acquire more books over time. Get replacements for timeworn or damaged books (often the most popular titles get worn out the fastest from frequent handling). Local businesses can be a good resource for donating books, and, often, parents will donate books at the end of the year that their children have read and no longer want. Garage sales and bargain bookstores are good places to acquire books over the summer. The process may be ongoing, but the goal is to provide a diverse and high-quality foundation of texts that will carry your students across the year. Every text that your students experience will add to and enrich their lives as readers.

Suggestions for Professional Development

1. If you are using (or plan to use) a multitext approach, it is a good idea to clarify your goals for each type of text you use. Bring together a small collection of texts for teacher analysis. Include:

    ▶ A fiction and nonfiction example of a book to read aloud at the appropriate grade level. (Consider age-appropriate content and student interest.)

    ▶ A fiction and nonfiction example of a text for shared reading at the appropriate grade level. (Consider age-appropriate content and student interest. For beginning readers, also consider the amount of print they will be able to process on a page given the high support of shared reading.)

    ▶ Several fiction and nonfiction examples from the range of levels suggested for the grade level on the text gradient. These would be leveled texts.

    ▶ Several fiction and nonfiction examples that children would be able to choose and read at the grade level. (Include books that reflect a range of difficulty.)

2. Bring together grade-level colleagues and invite them to browse through the texts. (As an alternative, ask each person to bring an example of the four types above.)

3. Working as a group or in pairs, have them identify and list goals (behaviors and understandings) for each type of text. The goals can be specific to the book, but they can also use *The Fountas & Pinnell Literacy Continuum* as a tool.

    ▶ One group or pair can begin with the interactive read-aloud books, listing goals on a large piece of chart paper. The goals should be as specific as possible. Other groups or pairs can start with shared reading, guided reading, and choice reading.

    ▶ When the group has finished one type of text, they pass it (with the chart) to another group. The new group then examines the text and adds any goals they think are important, again using *The Literacy Continuum* where appropriate.

4. When all charts are finished (and everyone has had a chance to add to each), have the group look across the texts and compare the goals and understandings for each context.

    ▶ Identify overlap (common goals).

    ▶ Identify differences.

5. Have an open discussion of a multitext approach and how it can build systems of strategic actions on many levels each day.

    ▶ Address issues like scheduling and materials if needed.

    ▶ Set some goals for the year.

CHAPTER 13

The F & P Text Gradient™
A Tool for Teaching

If children could work on literacy tasks most of the time at a level of success, we would have solved the biggest problem in learning to read and write.

–Don Holdaway

A carefully selected text is a critical element in successful teaching of guided reading. You want your students to process a complex text *with proficiency and ease*. That means that daily reading will be a satisfying and pleasurable experience.

We do want students to be able to process complex texts. But what does "complex text" mean? In our view, text complexity is judged in relation to the individual reader. A text is complex *for the particular reader*. Of course, some texts are inherently more complex than others. In fact, an entire spectrum of text complexity exists. Over a short period of time, a student will read a series of books that offer increasingly significant challenge. With teaching support, he learns from meeting those challenges to the point that he can read these books (and many others like them) independently. What was once a complex text is now a relatively simple text. However, the teacher is always introducing texts that offer more challenge (or we could call these opportunities to learn). So, the student encounters, again, a series of complex texts that get easier with time.

You are engaged in this process any time you learn how to do something. You start with something you *can* do, like making an easy recipe or playing an easy song on a musical instrument. But after a while, the new task becomes too easy and you seek greater challenges and a higher level of expertise. There are gradations of complexity in texts, just as there are in other realms of human activity. But understanding text complexity is in itself a very complex task.

A gradient of text is a powerful tool for you as a teacher. It helps you with the task of selecting texts that will challenge your readers and offer them opportunities to learn. That said, we want to state from the beginning that the gradient is for teacher use only. In this chapter, we describe a gradient as a "ladder of difficulty" and explore ten text characteristics that are used to analyze and "level" texts. We also discuss when and how it is appropriate to use a text gradient (and when it is not) as well as the text gradient in terms of grade-level expectations.

What Is a Text Gradient?

A *leveled set* is a collection of books in which processing demands have been categorized along a continuum from easiest to hardest. This continuum is based on a combination of variables that support and confirm readers' strategic actions and offer the problem-solving opportunities that build the reading process. The "level" of a text has everything to do with an expansion of readers' systems of strategic actions.

It is impossible for a teacher to provide a high-quality guided reading program for students without carefully considering what makes texts difficult or easy for individuals. A gradient of text reflects a defined continuum of characteristics against which you can evaluate texts. It becomes invaluable in the selection process, and also offers guidance in designing lessons. *The Fountas & Pinnell Literacy Continuum* lists detailed text characteristics and goals (behaviors and understandings to notice, teach for, and support) for each level of the gradient, levels A through Z. The twenty-six levels encompass progress from kindergarten through high school. There are ten levels across kindergarten and grade one and three levels each for grades two through six, with one level for middle and high school. Within each level, fiction and nonfiction texts are grouped using a combination of characteristics. The gradient is represented in Figure 13-1.

To create the continuum of text levels, we analyzed the supports and challenges integral to each text (based on a large number of examples), and considered how individual readers need to respond to these supports and challenges. Each text has specific features that support a reader's use of strategic actions and offer new opportunities. This analysis includes the difficulty of the words but goes far beyond that. For example, some early books (levels B to about E) support the use of phrasing by a text layout that keeps phrases together. Each new sentence starts on the left margin. These details can make a big difference for the beginning reader. As you go up the gradient, sentences are longer and more complex, concepts are harder to understand, and the layout is denser. Each category along the continuum presents new or more complex challenges.

A gradient of text is not a precise sequence of texts through which all readers pass. Books are leveled in approximate groups

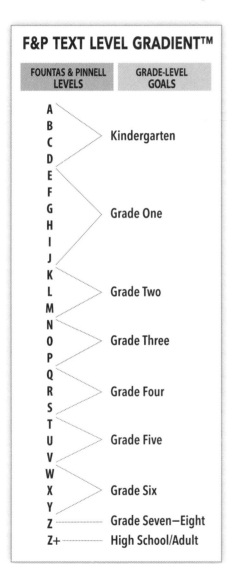

F&P TEXT LEVEL GRADIENT™

FOUNTAS & PINNELL LEVELS	GRADE-LEVEL GOALS
A	
B	
C	Kindergarten
D	
E	
F	
G	Grade One
H	
I	
J	
K	
L	Grade Two
M	
N	
O	Grade Three
P	
Q	
R	Grade Four
S	
T	
U	Grade Five
V	
W	
X	Grade Six
Y	
Z	Grade Seven–Eight
Z+	High School/Adult

FIGURE 13-1 The F&P Text Level Gradient™

from which teachers choose for instruction. The teacher who recognizes the convenience of the gradient yet reminds herself of its limitations will be able to make good choices and test her decisions against students' behaviors while reading and talking about texts. Figure 13-2 sums up what a text gradient *is* and *is not*.

The Uses of a Text Gradient

The gradient provides a basis for analyzing texts and organizing them for instruction. Books for instruction in guided reading are organized by level for teachers' convenience in selecting and using books. The books may be shared in a school book room or in a place in the classroom so that they are not noticed or accessed by students (see Chapter 12). Single copies of selected leveled books can be placed in the classroom library, but they are not leveled or organized by level.

You can compare students' current levels to grade-level expectations in your school or district. That will help you set goals and know which students need intervention. In general, you will want to assure that students who are reading below expectation have guided reading every possible day. In addition, you may need to recommend the student for intervention. The student's reading level represents the range of behaviors and understandings needed to successfully process texts at that level. These very specific behaviors and understandings are listed in *The Literacy Continuum,* and they become goals for instruction. You can select areas of the text for close reading, help students apply strategic actions, and even plan some precise language that will support learners.

The level of difficulty can be a resource for you as you guide student choices for independent reading, but it should not be a limitation or a requirement. Since you are an expert at analyzing and determining the difficulty level of a text, you can predict whether a student will experience frustration in reading it. The level

What Is a Text Gradient?

A text gradient is:	A text gradient is not:
◆ A tool for teachers to use in analyzing texts.	◆ A tool for students to use in choosing books for independent reading.
◆ A tool for selecting books for small-group reading instruction.	◆ A tool for students to use in tracking their own progress.
◆ A tool for recording progress over time in reading.	◆ A label that students attach to themselves as readers.
◆ A reference for teachers in designing lessons and planning teaching moves.	◆ A label for book baskets in a classroom library.
◆ A support for teachers in guiding readers to make good choices for independent reading (when necessary).	◆ An incentive for students to practice reading.
◆ A guide to determining whether readers are meeting grade-level expectations.	◆ A way for students to compare themselves with others.
◆ A signal that a reader may need intensive intervention in reading.	◆ A grade on a report card.
	◆ A label to be communicated to parents.

FIGURE 13-2 What Is a Text Gradient?

does not come into the discussion of the book with the student. Instead, help the student collect some books with elements such as genre, author, or topic that you think will interest the student. Then, teach the student how to explore the book by reading a little and seeing if it engages him.

Cautions in Using the Gradient

Once you've succeeded in finding books to match readers' abilities and helped them progress to more difficult texts, you may make some overgeneralizations that, in the long run, cause great difficulty. Here we raise some cautions to help you avoid these problems.

First, it is destructive to encourage students to measure their own progress by "moving up levels." This does not provide the real motivation that consuming and talking about texts would. Students will fall prey to the superficial (and sometimes pretend) reading they do for pizzas or other rewards. And, the last thing you want is for students to use levels to compare themselves with others or to compete. You are trying to build a community in your classroom where each person is respected, has a sense of agency, and where collaboration is more valuable than competition.

Second, telling students to choose by "level" is not an authentic way to organize for reading. Readers, including adults, do not always read at their highest reading level nor do they choose books by level in a bookstore or library. As much as possible, you want your students to choose books in a way that all readers do—books that interest and engage them. You want your students to have favorite authors, topics, and genres. A classroom library can be organized in many different ways. You can use labeled tubs so that students can easily identify types of books. For example, you might fill a tub with books by the same author, books in a particular genre, or informational books on a topic (see Chapters 21, 22, and 23 for more information on organizing a classroom library). No one chooses very hard books all the time just because they can read the words. Requiring a student to choose only from a particular level will unnaturally limit her reading habits; and this can happen whether a student is reading on, below, or above expectation.

Third, informing parents of the level can make them uneasy because they may see the level as a very precise measure. In fact, students will read and engage with a wide range of texts every day, and texts will vary in the complexity they present. For example, students may reread a big book that was used for shared reading, do research, read science or social studies textbooks and related articles, or read easy books because they love an author or got "hooked" on a series. Even early readers read from the variety of levels they can read. (Remember that if you can read level K, for example, you can usually read all the books from levels A through J.) And, they may try a harder book just because they are fascinated by the topic and already know a lot about it. While we want most of students' reading to be at a level of proficient processing, we would not discourage a highly motivated reader. If a student seems to be consistently choosing hard books just because others are reading them, give him some guidance and help him find similar books that he can read. He can read the book at a later date or you can make it available through an audio version. Since you will probably have audio versions of books available, all students can make use of them, but they are not a substitute for readers' processing a text for themselves.

You would not want parents to be concerned that a student is not reading on a precise level all of the time; that would not be desirable. And, you do not want to have them check with their friends and find that students in another class are reading at a higher level. Too much emphasis on levels can lead to misconceptions on the part of families. When levels become too important, even teachers can become competitive. And, we wish to state very strongly that reading levels of students have no place in teacher evaluation or on a report card. The gradient and set of leveled books are instructional tools for teachers who understand them—nothing more.

Ten Text Characteristics

We analyze text complexity by considering ten characteristics, all of which represent the supports and challenges that face the reader. Looking across all of these factors, you can determine the level of a text along the gradient, remembering that in any one text, several factors are usually combined to raise the challenge level. Text characteristics are summarized in Figure 13-3. Remember that some characteristics and genres enter in very simple form, and are present in more and more complex versions across levels A to Z.

Genre

The lowest levels (levels A and B) include realistic fiction, simple animal fantasy, and simple factual texts. At level C, very simple folktales are included, as well as easy procedural texts. At level E, expository texts on easy topics enter. More complex traditional literature and simple narrative nonfiction are included at level I, and some simple biographies are included at level J. At level L, fantasy and memoir enter. You can find historical fiction and hybrid texts at level N, autobiography at level O, and persuasive texts at level P.

The range of genres increases as you go up the text gradient, and forms and special types change. At about Level P and above, readers have enough reading experience to easily distinguish the genres, each of which has definite characteristics. They have gained this experience not only through reading but also through hearing literature read aloud and discussing it. Interactive read-aloud, in general, is a powerful context for engaging students in the study of genre (see Fountas and Pinnell 2012).

Guided reading is also a place where students can expand their awareness of the characteristics of genres and use that knowledge to comprehend texts more deeply. Even early readers quickly learn the difference between realistic fiction and animal fantasy, and they begin to distinguish between fiction and nonfiction. The range of genres grows broader as the level increases and the challenges to the reader grow as well.

Every genre has unique characteristics and each requires different kinds of processing. To understand historical fiction, for example, you need to realize that everything characters do must be authentic to the times in which they lived. The reader needs to take on the perspectives and problems of characters that live in a particular place and time in the past. Experiencing a variety of genres is very important in the development of reading proficiency, and you will want to include a

Ten Text Characteristics to Consider When Determining Levels

Factor	Definition
Genre	The *genre* is the type of text and refers to a system by which fiction and nonfiction texts are classified. Each genre has characteristic features.
Text Structure	The *structure* is the way the text is organized and presented. It may be *narrative,* as with most fiction texts and some nonfiction texts like biography. Many nonfiction texts use a non-narrative structure, combined with several underlying structural patterns to provide information to readers: *categorization, description, chronological and temporal sequence, comparison/contrast, cause/effect, problem/solution, and question and answer.* The presence of these structures, especially in combination, can increase the challenge for readers.
Content	The *content* refers to the subject matter of the text—the concepts that are important to understand. In fiction, content may be related to the setting or to the kinds of problems characters encounter. In factual texts, content refers to the topic being focused on. For the teacher, content is considered in relation to the prior experience of readers.
Themes and Ideas	The *themes* and *ideas* are the big ideas that are communicated by the text. A text may have multiple themes or a main theme and several supporting themes or ideas. The theme may define a human value and out of it the reader draws the writer's larger message.
Language and Literary Features	Written language is qualitatively different from spoken language. Fiction writers and often nonfiction writers, use dialogue, figurative language, and other literary elements. Fiction and nonfiction writers use description and technical language, albeit for different purposes. In hybrid texts you may find a wide range of literary language. The literary features of texts make them engaging and enjoyable and can also raise complexity.
Sentence Complexity	Meaning is mapped onto the syntax of language. Texts with simpler, more natural sentences are easier to process. Sentences with embedded and conjoined clauses make a text more difficult.
Vocabulary	*Vocabulary* refers to the meaning of words in a spoken language. The more the words are accessible to readers in terms of meaning, the easier a text will be. An individual's *reading and writing vocabularies* are words that they understand and can also read or write. Words have multiple meanings. A word may be used literally or figuratively, and words may also have connotative meanings.
Words	A text contains printed words that must be recognized and solved. The challenge in a text partly depends on the number and difficulty of the words that the reader must solve by recognizing them or decoding them. A text that contains a great many of the same common words makes a text more accessible to readers. In general, the number of multisyllable words in a text is related to difficulty, as is the number of scientific or technical words.
Illustrations	The *illustrations* are the drawings, paintings, or photographs that accompany the text and add meaning and enjoyment. In factual texts, illustrations also include graphic representations that provide a great deal of information readers must integrate with the text. Illustrations are an integral part of a high-quality text. Increasingly, fiction texts include a range of graphics.
Book and Print Features	The *book and print features* are the physical aspects of the text—what readers cope with in terms of length, size, and layout. Book and print features also include tools like the table of contents, glossary, pronunciation guide, index, and sidebars.

FIGURE 13-3 Ten Text Characteristics to Consider When Determining Levels

wide range of genres in your leveled-book collection. Instruction in guided reading usually includes naming the type of text and noticing characteristics that fit the genre.

Text Structure

Text structure is a support (and also a challenge) to comprehension. The *structure* is the way the writer organizes the text. The moment the reader perceives this organization, he can use it as a kind of "road map" to understanding the text. Sometimes we describe the structure as "how the text works." Text structure is closely connected to genre. For example, nonfiction writers may use a narrative structure, which includes biographical texts, stories from history, and narrative nonfiction; or a non-narrative structure, which includes expository, procedural, and persuasive texts. Nonfiction texts may also have underlying text structures, including categorical; chronological sequence (time-ordered), or temporal sequence (something that happens over and over, such as a life cycle); description; compare and contrast; cause and effect; problem and solution; and question and answer.

Fiction texts are usually organized as narratives, which means, "like a story." At the lower levels, narratives are simple—usually involving the introduction of characters and a problem, a series of events, and a plot resolution. As you move up the gradient of text, narratives grow in complexity to include literary devices such as stories within stories, flashbacks and flash forwards, prequels and sequels. The most complex texts may have narratives that require enormous effort from readers to keep track of time, story elements, and characters.

Content

The content of nonfiction texts poses challenges for readers, and one thing is clear: *Reading comprehension cannot be completely separated from background knowledge.* A text is always easier to read if you already know something about the topic or the setting. That is increasingly true as we go up the gradient of texts. As readers read, they accumulate knowledge and vocabulary and are better able to read about more complicated topics. The heavier the content load, the more background experience is required; the more new information (to the readers) presented in a text, the harder it is. Content for early readers would be very simple and related to their typical experiences. But complexity grows from there. Intermediate and middle-level readers are expected to read about topics and ideas far beyond their own experience.

Themes and Ideas

In general, themes for early readers are very simple and obvious—for example, making friends, helping at home, and learning to work with others. Intermediate and middle-level readers are ready to encounter several themes or a main theme with many supporting ideas. The more complex and abstract the text, the harder it is. For example, the text might communicate social responsibility or concern for the environment and the creatures that live there. You want your students, as readers, to fully comprehend the themes and ideas in texts.

Language and Literary Features

Written language has special features such as figurative language, dialogue, description, and technical language. We want students to be able to use academic language to discuss the features of texts. With early readers, this means talking about the title or what characters say. Intermediate and middle-level readers will discuss simile and metaphor, different types of conflict, and descriptive language. The theme usually is a statement of a higher human value or aspiration such as kindness, tolerance, or peace; and out of the theme flows the writer's message, which is always larger than the specific content of the text.

Sentence Complexity

Longer sentences are harder than shorter ones, but not only because of the number of words. Longer sentences can have one or more embedded phrases or clauses:

- The dog went *in the bed.*
- The dog barked *and the people ran.*
- The dog barked *when he saw a car.*
- Mary liked the dog *because he loved her.*
- *When he got home,* he fed the dog.
- *When he got home,* he saw that the dog was hungry, *so he hurried to get some food and put it in the dog's dish;* and the dog ate every morsel.

With language, sentences can be structured in an infinite number of ways. A twenty-word sentence might have numerous embedded prepositional phrases and independent clauses. You can get an idea of the level of challenge by sampling about ten sentences, counting the words, and counting the dependent and independent clauses. Sentence complexity is a classic factor in judging text difficulty. Often sentence complexity has been determined by a mathematical formula. But sentence complexity must be considered as *only one factor* within a complex range of factors that contribute to text difficulty.

Vocabulary

Vocabulary is the classic way of determining text difficulty. After all, knowing the meaning of the words is basic to understanding a text. A person's vocabulary is made up of the words she knows and understands. *Reading vocabulary* refers to the words individuals can recognize in reading. If a person can look at a group of letters and pronounce the word, we usually say he can "read it." But sometimes an individual might read a word without understanding it, and then the reader must take action to derive the meaning, or comprehension can be lost.

If possible, almost all words for early readers should already be in their oral vocabulary and that may be even more of a challenge if you are teaching English language learners. As we move up the gradient, texts are more complex and more words may be new to all learners, especially if they refer to scientific content. Readers need to learn how to derive meaning from the context of the text and how to use tools like a glossary. We also need to remember that there are shades of knowing the meaning of the word. You may know one meaning of a word but not another. To fully "know" a word means to know all meanings in all contexts and also to recognize connotative and figurative use. New words constantly appear in every language and known words take on new meanings.

Vocabulary refers to words and their meanings. It actually refers to an individual's *oral vocabulary,* which is developed through interactions with others, especially adults, and through experience. Reading (or hearing written language read aloud) is an important factor in building oral vocabulary. Children enter school with widely varying oral vocabularies, but through very rich preschool and kindergarten experiences that include interactive read-aloud and shared reading, they add rapidly to the words they know. Having a word in one's oral vocabulary makes it much easier to solve a word and add it to the store of known words in reading. Reading aloud to students of all ages is very important because many words that are frequently used in writing are seldom used in anyone's everyday oral language. Beck, McKeown, and Kulcan (2002) describe three tiers of words:

1. First-tier (Tier 1) words appear frequently in the oral language that early readers have experienced; they are learned without instruction because they are part of daily interaction; for example, *yes, no, come, go, hungry, book.* When children enter school, some experience an expansion of Tier 1 words; for example, *pencil, desk, book basket, notebook.*

2. Second-tier (Tier 2) words are those that appear frequently in the vocabularies of mature language users and in written texts. Some examples are *unfortunate, fascinating, exclaimed, remarked.* You can even find some technical words in Tier 2 that are pervasive across scientific disciplines but not particular to any one, for example, *vacuum, porous, translucent, luminous.*

3. Third-tier (Tier 3) words are specialized and peculiar to scientific domains. They are usually learned through content area study. Even elementary students encounter Tier 3 words in the books they read, especially in nonfiction. Some examples are *ectoplasm, bioluminescence, cerebral cortex.*

It makes sense that the more Tier 2 and Tier 3 words a text includes, the harder it will be. At levels A through J, you will find very few Tier 2 words and almost no Tier 3 words until level M. But these kinds of words occur with increasing frequency as the content load becomes heavier across levels. Guided reading is an excellent context in which you can support students as they add to their vocabularies through encountering complex words in texts. You can support a range of vocabulary development strategies, including the following:

▶ Using context to determine the meaning

▶ Finding synonyms and antonyms

▶ Connecting known words with new words

▶ Using reference tools such as a glossary or dictionary (hard copy or electronic)

▶ Using meaningful parts of words such as roots, bases, and affixes

Vocabulary is a special concern when you're working with English language learners. Here you have an even more complex challenge. Students may meet words in texts they do not know, and they will need to derive the meaning. However, they may know the meaning of the word in their own languages—they just don't know the equivalent in English. So the student not only has to decode the English word but match it to his background knowledge and the language he knows. ELLs need the same competence in vocabulary that native English readers do, but they will need more support as you implement guided reading. Just because a student is reading a word "accurately" doesn't mean deep understanding. ELL students need to expand their understanding through talk. In the text introduction, you can take the opportunity to expand and clarify words that you think students will want to know (or won't know in English); through discussion, you can encourage students to use these new words and provide further clarification if needed. You may also revisit the text to provide opportunities to expand vocabulary.

An area of vocabulary that we should be concerned about is connectives, which are critical not only to understanding the meaning of words but to comprehending language syntax and the relationships among ideas in a text. Connectives are words or phrases that link ideas and clarify meaning in oral and/or written texts. Connectives range from the very simple words that appear in everyday oral language, to highly academic words that are almost always found in writing or in very formal speaking. For example:

- Common (simple) connectives are frequently used in oral language, for example, *and, but, so, because, before, after.*

- Sophisticated connectives are used in written texts but do not appear often in everyday oral language, for example, *although, however, meantime, meanwhile, moreover, otherwise, therefore, though, unless, until, whenever, yet.*

- Academic connectives appear in written texts, often in academic treatises or scientific works, for example, *alternatively, consequently, despite, conversely, eventually, finally, in contrast, initially, likewise, nevertheless, nonetheless, previously, specifically, ultimately, whereas, whereby.*

Many of the sophisticated and academic connectives will be new to students. It's important that they understand how these words function in sentences. They refer to time, to the addition of ideas, to order or sequence, to space, to signal results or an example, to explain purpose, make comparisons, or introduce a summary. Understanding these relationships is basic to comprehension.

Another area of great interest is "academic vocabulary," a term that refers to the Tier 3 words that readers use as they talk in the academic disciplines. It also refers to the terms that readers and students of literature use to refer to literary texts, and this language can be expanded through every context for reading instruction. Even at early levels, children can use terms such as *author* and *title;* as levels expand in difficulty, there is more demand for the use of academic terms. Words like *character, plot,* and *problem* are first used in interactive read-aloud, but they are also intentionally used in guided reading as a natural part of the discussion. Academic language includes academic connectives and words from scientific disciplines.

Words

Students must be able to read the printed words on the page. Readers use a wide range of strategic actions to solve words. In fact, in her study of proficient second-grade readers, Kaye (2006) found over sixty-two different approaches to word solving. The readers used the most efficient actions, which included anticipating language structure and meaning and taking words apart using larger chunks. Word solving on continuous text allows the learner to access a large amount of information both to solve the word and to monitor the accuracy of the reading. But the bottom line is, readers need to be able to read the words accurately.

Reading a word can mean that you: (1) recognize it instantly and automatically; or (2) take it apart to solve it. Readers constantly add to the repertoire of words they recognize automatically; and that is a good thing because no reader could process text with any kind of comprehension if she had to work on every word. Readers need to do their word solving against a backdrop of accurate reading with only a few words to slow down and problem-solve in any one text. If too much work is required, the whole process breaks down and comprehension is severely undermined.

With every level, students encounter more difficult words to solve; the challenge in a text partly depends on the number and complexity of the words that the reader must "decode." For early readers, it is useful to recognize a large number of easy high-frequency words; and texts at levels A through J do generally feature many of the same high-frequency words. But readers cannot depend on simply memorizing words. They need to notice and use the significant features of words, such as these:

- The relationship between the sounds in words and the letters that represent them
- Onsets (the first part of the word, *b-* in *bat*) and rimes (the rest of the word, the part that contains the vowels, *-at* in *bat*)
- Syllables in words (*bat-ter-y*)
- Multiple onsets and rimes (*p-an-h-an-dle*)
- Patterns that appear in words (*bat, battery, fat, sat, cat, catalog*)
- Affixes (prefixes—*display*; suffixes—*graceful*)

Illustrations

Illustrations extend and enhance a written text. Today, with reduction in printing costs and availability of electronic texts, books are more beautifully illustrated than ever. For early readers, the illustrations carry a great deal of information. In fact, the pictures can make a seemingly simple text into a real story just by showing the action. Also, the pictures provide a powerful source of content information. For example, the reader can cross-check the picture (meaning) with the way the word *looks* (visual/phonological information). This strategic action emerges early and requires searching for and using information and self-monitoring.

As fiction texts become more complex and challenging, they include much more print and much less picture support. But illustrations still enhance the meaning of the text. The illustrations extend meaning, make the reading experience enjoyable, and communicate the mood. Design features such as endpapers, decorative margins, borders, and illuminated letters can enhance mood and enjoyment.

Features such as color may have symbolic meaning and be part of comprehension. Skilled readers learn to use the *peritext*. The peritext refers to images and textual elements that are secondary to the main body of the text. The peritext *surrounds* the body of the text and adds meaning and enjoyment.

In nonfiction texts illustrations become increasingly complex and add considerably to the information. A reader needs to interpret graphics such as diagrams, maps, charts, cutaways, photographs, and a variety of graphs providing quantitative information. Often the graphics are critical to the comprehension of a text and can be quite challenging. Graphic texts are made up almost entirely by illustrations, and they may be almost any fiction or nonfiction genre.

Book and Print Features

The physical aspects of a text include features like these:

- Size of print and spaces between words and lines
- Length (number of pages)
- Size (trim size)
- Layout of print
- Punctuation
- Features such as table of contents, glossary, pronunciation guide, indexes, sidebars, insets, headings, and subheadings

All of the features listed above can make a text "friendly" to the reader, or they can increase the challenge. For example, it helps early readers to have clear, easy-to-read print in a simple font, with clear spaces (more than usual) between words and between lines. The number of lines on a page is related to text difficulty for the beginner, and it helps if every new sentence starts on the left margin. As you go up the levels, print becomes much denser; punctuation is complex. Readers are expected to effectively use tools like the glossary and index as well as the headings, sidebars, and insets.

A Continuum of Texts

Following is a general description of some important characteristics of a few selected text levels to give you a sense of how texts become increasingly difficult. We do not have enough space to include them all, but you can find a complete description of all levels in *The Fountas & Pinnell Literacy Continuum*. This will give you a picture of the increasing challenges readers meet as they progress and the characteristics of texts at each level. In *The Literacy Continuum,* you will find a complete analysis for every level, along with instructional goals (behaviors and understandings to notice, teach for, and support). On the Fountas & Pinnell Leveled Books website (*fountasandpinnellleveledbooks.com*), you will find thousands of books at every level that can be sorted in a variety of ways.

Whether a text is easy or hard for a reader depends on more than the characteristics inherent in the text (although as teachers we must know them). Other factors enter into the equation:

▶ The experience and background knowledge a student brings to the reading

▶ The way you introduce the text to the students

▶ Your supportive interactions with readers during and after reading

You are constantly balancing the tension between text level and characteristics and the amount of support you decide to provide. Your knowledge of your students and the way they approach a text is the most valuable tool you have. We have included a sample of selected significant behaviors and understandings with each level presented.

Texts at Levels A and B

Level A and B books are the very easiest for early readers to begin to read. There is a direct correspondence between the print and the pictures; the storylines are very simple; the content is familiar to most six-year-old readers. The language, while not exactly duplicating oral language, includes naturally occurring syntactic structures and is very consistent with oral language. The format is consistent: print appears at the same place on every page, and layout is very easy to follow. Level A has one line of print; level B has two, and sometimes three, lines of print. The print is in a clear regular font and is easy to see. Punctuation usually includes only periods, but occasionally commas, question marks, and quotation marks. Most texts are simple animal fantasy, realistic fiction, or simple factual texts that focus on a single topic.

Examples

Lunch for Monkey (*Fountas & Pinnell Classroom*, in press) is an example of a very simple level A text (see Figure 13-4). It has one line of print on each page, and the story is carried by the pictures. At the end, we see that monkey has made a mess because he tried to put too many things into his lunch bag.

An example of a level B book is *Food for Animals* (*Fountas & Pinnell Classroom*, in press). *Food for Animals* is a simple, two-line informational text with repeating language patterns (see Figure 13-5). The first sentence identifies a kind of food, for example, bug, leaf, and worm. With the pattern, "this is a . . ." The second line tells what animal the food is for. The high-frequency words *this, it, is, for,* and *a* are used on every page. A surprise comes at the end when, after a page identifying seaweed as the food for a fish, the reader sees fish being eaten by a bear.

FIGURE 13-4 Pages 12, 13, and 16 from *Lunch for Monkey*, Level A

This is a leaf.
It is food for a giraffe.

4

5

FIGURE 13-5 Pages 4 and 5 from *Food for Animals*, Level B

Texts at Level C

Books at level C also have simple storylines in fiction; nonfiction texts focus on topics that are familiar to most children. They usually have about two to five lines of print on a page and so the texts have more words. More of the story content is carried by the print, but pictures are still very important in supporting meaning and there is a close match between text and pictures. Print appears on either the left or the right page, but it is still clearly separated from the illustrations. Oral language structures are used and often repeated, and phrasing is supported by print placement. There is a range of punctuation including periods, commas, question marks, and exclamation marks.

Patterns and repetition are used in some books; others support prediction through natural language and meaning. There is more variation in language patterns, requiring readers to attend closely to visual information. Sentences are still short, and the syntax is simple and easy to control. One very important feature, dialogue, is introduced at this level (although some simple dialogue may occasionally appear at level B). The dialogue is always assigned and is usually between two or three characters. Levels C and D typically signal the level at which students enter first grade. If they have experienced a great deal of shared reading (which is a powerful context for teaching early reading behaviors) and some guided reading, then they can begin guided reading at level D with strong instructional support. If not, they need intensive help to move through levels A, B, and C quickly.

Examples

Something for Dinner (*Fountas & Pinnell Classroom*, in press) is an example of a level C text. It is easier at level C to create a storyline, but illustrations are still very important in carrying it (see Figure 13-6).

In this story Dad asks Sam and Pat if they want something for dinner, naming a different vegetable each time and receiving the same answer each time. While there is a repeating language pattern in this text, it is a more complex one. A key concept is that the reader can see in the pictures what Dad is doing but the two children are absorbed in their game and cannot see Dad's cooking. In the end, Dad offers pizza (which has all of the vegetables and the cheese on it), and the kids love it. A reader who is using background knowledge and attending to the pictures may be able to predict the ending.

"Do you want some peppers
for dinner?" asked Dad.

"No, no! I don't like peppers,"
Sam said.

"Do you want some pizza
for dinner?" asked Dad.

FIGURE 13-6 Pages 2–3, 14–15, and 16
from *Something for Dinner*, Level C

Animal Feet (*Fountas & Pinnell Classroom*, in press) is a nonfiction text that focuses on the wonderful variety in nature (see Figure 13-7). Each page spread presents one animal and how it uses its feet. The text offers a great deal of opportunity for beginning readers to talk about how animals are alike and different. Each page of print has three lines of print, and the sentences are simple. High-frequency words include *here, is, a, the, its, to, in, look,* and *at.* The illustrations include clear, simple photographs of animals who are using their feet. The photographs feature only one animal on a page. At the end, we see a penguin holding an egg with its feet.

Texts at Level I

At level I, stories have more complex language and vocabulary and the stories are longer. Nonfiction texts focus on content that is familiar to students, although, depending on the reader's background, some concepts may be new. Dialogue is longer and there are many more lines of print on the page. When there are more lines of print, the font has to become smaller. As in earlier levels, you can expect a plain, clear font with generous spaces between words and lines. Narratives have more episodes and less repetition. Characters do not change much, except for learning the "lesson," which is typical of traditional tales. Nonfiction texts are usually organized around a single topic and incorporate underlying structures such as description, chronological sequence, temporal sequence, and question and answer. Genres include expository and procedural texts, narrative nonfiction, animal fantasy, realistic fiction, and traditional literature. Also, some beginning chapter books with illustrations are included.

Examples

The Ant and the Grasshopper: An Aesop Tale (*Fountas & Pinnell Classroom*, in press) is a retelling of a fable. The dialogue is extensive between two characters, and there are several episodes in the plot. Notice that there are spaces between groups of sentences, indicating a kind of "pre-paragraphing" that you sometimes see at this level (see Figure 13-8).

Bath Time (*Fountas & Pinnell Classroom*, in press), focuses on the idea that there are many ways for animals to keep clean (see Figure 13-9). Readers may be

Here is a penguin.

The penguin uses its feet

to hold on to its egg!

14

15

FIGURE 13-7 Pages 14–15 from *Animal Feet*, Level C

Then fall came.
The leaves turned brown
and fell to the ground.
Grasshopper sang
by a tree.

"The leaves are all gone,
Grasshopper," said Ant.
"What will you eat
in the winter?"

"I'll pick some grass later,"
said Grasshopper.
"The birds and I
are singing now."

FIGURE 13-8 Pages 8–9 from *The Ant and the Grasshopper,* Level I

The zebra uses dust
to take its bath, too.
The zebra rolls
in the dust.

FIGURE 13-9 Pages 8–9 from *Bath Time,* Level I

surprised to learn that some animals use mud and others use dust or their tongues. The text begins with showing a person taking a bath but moves to all the different ways animals keep clean and protect themselves from bugs. It ends with a summary and inset photos of all the baths in the book. There are six to ten lines of print on the pages and many high-frequency words. There are no repeating sentence patterns, and there are many long sentences with prepositional phrases, adjectives, and clauses. There are many descriptive words. The term "take a bath" is applied in a broad, general way to simply mean keeping clean and free of bugs.

Texts at Level J

Typically, level J is a goal for the end of grade one. Students are well underway as readers. Not only do the eyes control directional movement, but also students read silently most of the time. Genres include expository and procedural texts, narrative nonfiction, animal fantasy, realistic fiction, traditional literature, and some simple biographies on familiar subjects. In fiction, characters have attributes but do not change a great deal since the stories are short; however, some development and learning takes place. Sentences are more complex, some over fifteen words long. Sentences may have phrases and clauses, and there are many multisyllable words. Nonfiction texts have some graphic features (photographs with labels, simple maps, diagrams) and features like sidebars.

Examples

Tadpole in a Tree (*Fountas & Pinnell Classroom,* in press) is an informational book about the strawberry poison frog, which has very unusual behaviors (see Figure 13–10). The text uses description and is organized in temporal order from the time the frog lays her eggs, to the time the new frog lays her own eggs. Because it is organized in time order and focuses on one particular frog's experience, it is considered narrative nonfiction. The underlying text structure is temporal sequence, which is summarized in a graphic. This fascinating animal carries her tadpoles up a tree where they swim in the tiny pools that exist in leaves until they turn into frogs. You see here again a plain, clear font with generous spaces between words and lines. The sentences are complex. For example, the first sentence on page 10 has two prepositional phrases. The topic focuses on a frog, which is probably familiar to children as an animal, but this is an exotic frog with unusual characteristics. The text includes labeled photographs and a diagram of the life cycle.

Chester's Sweater (*Fountas & Pinnell Classroom,* in press) is a good example of animal fantasy, and it is also a series book (see Figure 13-11). There is a complex relationship between Chester the pig and his friend Dolly, a sheep. Dolly gives Chester a hand-knitted sweater, which he puts on immediately. Unfortunately, as he rushed to Dolly's house, he catches the sweater on something and it unravels all the way. (This part of the story is told through the pictures.) The dialogue between Dolly and Chester concerns the missing sweater, but clever Dolly figures it out. Chester comes across as a sensitive person who is at the same time a bit bumbling. He doesn't even realize Dolly is the giver of the sweater. She reknits it for him, and he is overjoyed; but then, as the pictures indicate, the same thing is going to happen again.

The small mother frog looks out
for her tadpoles in the tree.
They are safe here.

The mother feeds each tadpole
almost every day.
She lays eggs
in the tiny pools,
but these eggs don't have
baby frogs inside them.
These eggs are food
for the tadpoles.

10

Orange Frogs?
These usually red frogs change
their colors sometimes.
They can change to orange
or even green!

11

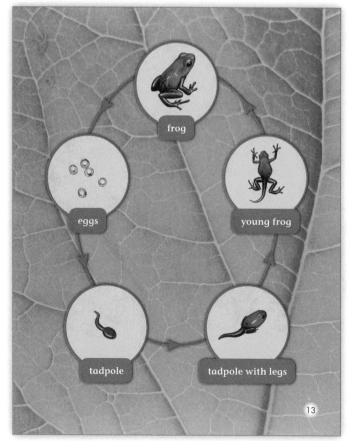

frog

eggs

young frog

tadpole

tadpole with legs

13

FIGURE 13-10 Pages 10, 11, and 13 from *Tadpole in a Tree*, Level J

Chester banged
on Dolly's door.
"Dolly!" he shouted.
"Come and see
my new sweater."

When Dolly opened the door,
Chester twirled around
for her.
Then he said,
"Isn't this the best sweater
in the world?"

"What sweater?" Dolly asked.
"You're not wearing one."

Chester looked down.
Dolly was right.
The sweater was gone.

8

"But where could it be?"
Chester asked.
"I put it on
before I left my house.
I'm *almost* sure
I didn't take it off."

9

FIGURE 13-11 Pages 8, 9, and 16 from *Chester's Sweater*, Level J

"I'm so lucky,"
Chester said.
"I got two sweaters
from Guess Who
in two days.
Dolly will be so surprised!"

And he rushed
from his house
to show his sweater
to his friend.

16

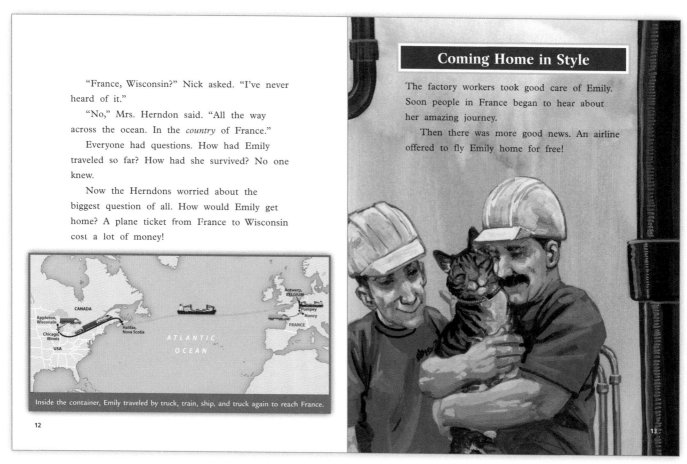

"France, Wisconsin?" Nick asked. "I've never heard of it."

"No," Mrs. Herndon said. "All the way across the ocean. In the *country* of France."

Everyone had questions. How had Emily traveled so far? How had she survived? No one knew.

Now the Herndons worried about the biggest question of all. How would Emily get home? A plane ticket from France to Wisconsin cost a lot of money!

Inside the container, Emily traveled by truck, train, ship, and truck again to reach France.

12

Coming Home in Style

The factory workers took good care of Emily. Soon people in France began to hear about her amazing journey.

Then there was more good news. An airline offered to fly Emily home for free!

13

FIGURE 13-12 Pages 12–13 from *Emily's Amazing Journey*, Level M

Texts at Level M

Texts at level M present a larger range of genres: expository and procedural texts, fantasy, realistic fiction, traditional literature (folktales, fairy tales, fables), biography, memoir, and narrative nonfiction. Also, there are many graphic texts. Some fiction texts are chapter books, and readers are becoming interested in special forms, such as series books. Fiction narratives are straightforward but have more elaborated plots and multiple characters that develop and change over time. The nonfiction texts are generally short, and they may be organized into sections or categories. Nonfiction texts have many features such as table of contents, headings, sidebars, as well as a range of graphics. Writers use underlying structures (description, comparison and contrast, temporal and chronological sequence, question and answer, cause and effect). Sentences include many prepositional phrases, introductory clauses, lists of nouns, verbs, or adjectives. Words require solving by taking apart syllables and/or using base words and affixes. Typically, level M is the expectation for about the end of grade two.

Examples

Emily's Amazing Journey (Fountas & Pinnell Classroom, in press) is narrative nonfiction and tells the story of Emily, a cat who escaped from her home, got trapped in a shipping container, and spent thirty days traveling overseas to France. The map in the book shows the length of her journey (see Figure 13-12).

The girl put Mee-you down and accepted the other kitten. Immediately, Hector stood over his friend, one paw on each side.

"Will you look at that," said Mr. Longleg. "You're really attached to that rascal, aren't you? Well, come on home now, Hector."

Hector stayed put.

"Hector! I said 'Come!'" Mr. Longleg wasn't smiling anymore.

Hector didn't budge. He picked up his kitten friend and stared at Mr. Longleg.

Mr. Longleg scratched his head. "What are you trying to tell me, Hector?" he asked. "Do you want that kitten to come, too?"

Hector barked a muffled bark from his kitten-filled mouth. "Rowf!"

He set the kitten on Mr. Longleg's shoe.

14

15

FIGURE 13-13 Pages 14–15 from *Hector and the Kitten*, Level M

Hector and the Kitten (*Fountas & Pinnell Classroom*, in press) is fantasy, but the setting is the real world. The element that makes it fantasy is the interpretation of the feelings of Hector the dog, who falls in love with a kitten and is devastated when it is adopted (see Figure 13-13). Hector does not talk and in every other way he is a typical dog. There are several episodes in the plot as Hector seeks to solve the problem and the ending is happy.

Texts at Level P

Level P presents a wide range of genres: expository, procedural, and persuasive texts, narrative nonfiction texts, fantasy, realistic fiction, historical fiction, traditional literature (folktales, fairy tales, fables), biography, hybrid texts, and special types of fiction such as mysteries and adventure stories. Leveled texts include both chapter books and shorter texts. There are series books and books with sequels. Fiction narratives have elaborated plots and many episodes; multiple characters develop over time. From level P to level R, the themes are increasingly abstract and mature and include issues related to cultural differences. Some nonfiction texts provide information on multiple topics that are related to a larger concept or idea. Informational texts include underlying structures (description, compare and contrast,

Just as Lone Star stepped forward to make an arrest, hands grabbed him and spun him around. He was face-to-face with a man with a bright red nose. It was a real clown this time.

"You're a lawman, right?" the man said. "Help me! I was about to change into my clown suit. But some low-down rat stole it!"

"I'll help you. Just let go," Lone Star said. He shook himself free. But where was the bull rider?

There he was, running out the barn door. He leaped onto the nearest horse—Trusty. The bull rider was getting away on Lone Star's own horse!

"Hold your horses!" Lone Star yelled.

Folks on the street grabbed the nearest horse.

"Trusty! Hold your horses means STOP!" Lone Star hollered.

Trusty stopped so fast his rider went flying through the air and into a water trough. In a flash, Lone Star grabbed a lasso and hog-tied the sputtering outlaw.

 14

15

FIGURE 13-14 Pages 14–15 from *Lone Star and the Lawman*, Level P

temporal and chronological sequence, problem and solution, cause and effect, categorization, and question and answer). Sentences are complex with multiple phrases and clauses. There are many Tier 2 and some Tier 3 words. Words are complex to solve, including base and root words and words with affixes. Level P is the general expectation for about the end of grade three.

Examples

Lone Star the Lawman (*Fountas & Pinnell Classroom,* in press) is a fantasy that is a kind of spoof on old Westerns. Lone Star and his horse Trusty are chasing clowns who have robbed a bank. The text includes language like "a goner," "pronto," and "low-down rat." The over-the-top plot involves a rodeo and heroic actions by Lone Star (see Figure 13-14).

The Glow Below: Creatures That Light Up the Sea (*Fountas & Pinnell Classroom,* in press) is a nonfiction text that presents bioluminescent sea creatures. The body of the text is divided into sections that present different creatures that live in the dark depths of the ocean. The text has section headings and beautiful photographs with labels. Sidebars provide additional information (see Figure 13-15).

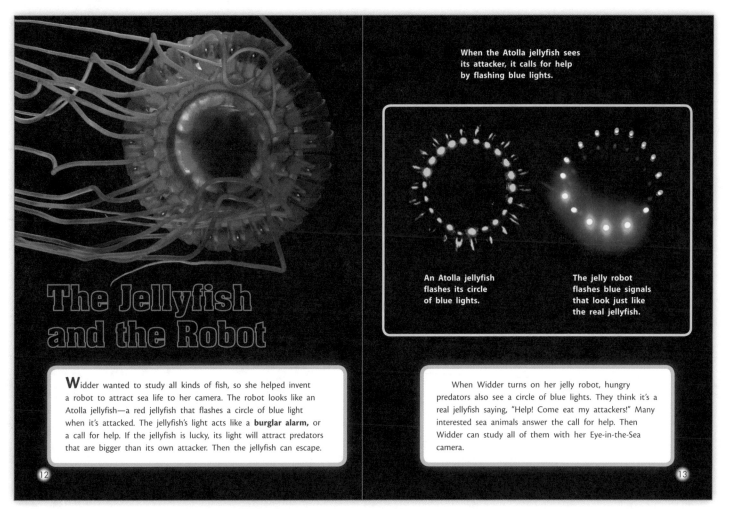

When the Atolla jellyfish sees its attacker, it calls for help by flashing blue lights.

An Atolla jellyfish flashes its circle of blue lights.

The jelly robot flashes blue signals that look just like the real jellyfish.

The Jellyfish and the Robot

Widder wanted to study all kinds of fish, so she helped invent a robot to attract sea life to her camera. The robot looks like an Atolla jellyfish—a red jellyfish that flashes a circle of blue light when it's attacked. The jellyfish's light acts like a **burglar alarm,** or a call for help. If the jellyfish is lucky, its light will attract predators that are bigger than its own attacker. Then the jellyfish can escape.

When Widder turns on her jelly robot, hungry predators also see a circle of blue lights. They think it's a real jellyfish saying, "Help! Come eat my attackers!" Many interested sea animals answer the call for help. Then Widder can study all of them with her Eye-in-the-Sea camera.

12

13

FIGURE 13-15 Pages 12–13 from *The Glow Below*, Level P

Texts at Level S

At levels Q, R, and S, texts continue to increase in complexity, demanding more of readers, particularly in comprehension. Complexity of language and sophistication of language also increase. Level S includes a wide range of genres, including more complex fantasy and science fiction. Special forms, like chapter books with sequels, short stories, and photo essays and news articles are also included, as are graphic texts. Students are reading silently and are required to process texts that have elaborate plots and many multidimensional characters that develop and change over time, and settings that are distant in time and geography. Sentences are long (some over 20 words) and complex, containing many embedded phrases and clauses, and a wide variety of parts of speech including adjectives and adverbs. There are many Tier 2 and Tier 3 words; most are defined in context or in a glossary. In nonfiction, you see extensive use of underlying structures (compare and contrast, description, problem and solution, question and answer, temporal and chronological sequence, categorization, and cause and effect). There are many longer descriptive words as

Learning to Love the Bats

For a time, the future did not look bright for the bats. Then news of the controversy in Austin reached a man named Merlin Tuttle. Tuttle, who lived in Wisconsin, had founded a group called Bat Conservation International (BCI) which was dedicated to saving bats wherever they are threatened.

Tuttle and his group went to Austin to set the record straight about bats. They met with newspaper editors and TV reporters, city officials, residents, and school groups. Over and over, they explained that bats are gentle, beneficial creatures, much more likely to help the city than to harm it. They explained that:

A Mexican free-tailed bat snacks on a corn earworm, a type of moth that damages corn crops.

Bats Control Bugs The bridge bats eat moths, beetles, flying ants, and mosquitoes. A colony of 1.5 million bats can eat 10,000 to 30,000 pounds of insects per night in the summer, benefiting farmers whose crops are eaten by insects.

Bats Spread Seeds Some bats eat fruit, not insects. These bats poop out seeds as they fly around at night, helping to spread the plants.

Bats Pollinate Plants Fruit-eating bats also **pollinate** sugarcane, an important crop in Texas, and other plants. They carry pollen on their fur as they travel from plant to plant.

Bats Are Safe As long as you don't touch a bat, it can't hurt you. Touching a bat that has rabies is very risky, but bats almost never get close enough to people for that to happen. Bats are not aggressive and they won't fly into your hair—that's a myth.

Slowly but surely, Tuttle and the experts from BCI persuaded people to change their minds about the bats. Once people knew the truth—that bats posed no health threat, could be helpful to farmers, and liked to eat pesky insects—they stopped being afraid. Over time, the petitions for their removal began to lose support. After a few years, it was clear: the bats were there to stay.

Merlin Tuttle

10   11

FIGURE 13-16 Pages 10–11 from *Bats in the City*, Level S

well as Tier 2 and Tier 3 words that require using embedded definitions, background knowledge, and reference tools. Texts include many multisyllable words. Level S is the typical expectation for about the end of grade four.

Examples

Bats in the City (*Fountas & Pinnell Classroom*, in press) is a nonfiction text that describes the bats that live under a bridge in Austin, Texas. This expository text describes the life of the bats and why and how they live in Austin in the warmer months (see Figure 13-16).

A feature of the text is the description of the arguments that were posed to change public opinion about the presence of the bats. Another purpose of the writer is to change readers' perspectives on bats by giving them more information. The larger message of the book has to do with recognizing and valuing the connections between the behavior and the function of all living things, and their interdependence.

Introduction

The world is full of frightening things. Snakes. Lightning strikes. Dark, slippery stairways. School dances.

It's pretty scary out there. This book will show you how to avoid the biggest dangers and remain safe. Just carefully follow the directions you read here, and you may actually live to see adulthood.[1]

[1] Footnote: On the other hand, Barbara Dwier, her heirs, the publisher, the book's printer, sales force, and distributers make no promises, legally binding statements, or guarantees. Gosh, you could swallow your own tongue, fall off a cliff, get hit by a bus, trip and fall into a sewer and drown, or die any number of horrible ways today, for all we know.

2

3

FIGURE 13-17 Pages 2–3 from *Run! Duck! Hide! How to Stay Safe,* Level S

Run! Duck! Hide! How to Stay Safe (*Fountas & Pinnell Classroom,* in press) is a humorous fiction text that is a "spoof" on a procedural text (see Figure 13-17). The writer gives directions for how readers can avoid disasters related to bikes, beds, movie theaters, kitchens, and other everyday "dangers." The writer imagines impossible circumstances and ridiculous outcomes. Readers need to understand that the book is meant to be humorous, and part of understanding the humor is the reader's prior knowledge of how procedural texts work. The writer speaks directly to the reader. Sentences are long and complex. There are footnotes (in parody of a nonfiction text). The vocabulary is typical of nonfiction. The illustrations are highly humorous and add considerably to the action.

Texts at Level V

Across levels T, U, and V, readers experience a wider range of genres, as well as more complex narratives. The number of Tier 2 and Tier 3 vocabulary words expands greatly. Level V includes genres such as myths, legends, and high fantasy. There are many graphic texts. Narrative texts include fiction books with chapters related to a single plot and a variety of text structures (flashbacks, flash-forwards, stories-within stories). Texts have a large number of multisyllable words as well as many Tier 2 and Tier 3 words. Themes are mature and abstract. Nonfiction texts have complex graphics and the full range of underlying structural patterns. Forms include speeches. Level V is the typical expectation for about the end of Grade 5.

Examples

Tongue Tied: A Memoir (*Fountas & Pinnell Classroom,* in press) is a memoir of a young girl. The text combines scientific information with a touching personal story. The memoir has larger messages about turning life's challenges into positive experiences and opportunities for personal growth, and the importance of appreciating differences rather than making fun of them (see Figure 13-18).

   Rules (*Fountas & Pinnell Classroom,* in press) is the stark realistic fiction story of a brother and sister who live in a dangerous city area (see Figure 13-19). Their windows are covered with thick blankets. Dion is in charge of his little sister and he chafes at the rules his mother, who is working, adds each week. He calls them

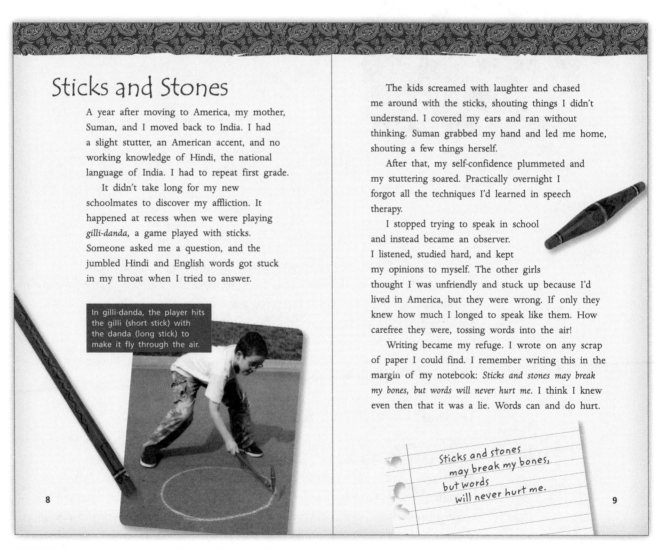

Sticks and Stones

A year after moving to America, my mother, Suman, and I moved back to India. I had a slight stutter, an American accent, and no working knowledge of Hindi, the national language of India. I had to repeat first grade.

   It didn't take long for my new schoolmates to discover my affliction. It happened at recess when we were playing *gilli-danda*, a game played with sticks. Someone asked me a question, and the jumbled Hindi and English words got stuck in my throat when I tried to answer.

In gilli-danda, the player hits the gilli (short stick) with the danda (long stick) to make it fly through the air.

The kids screamed with laughter and chased me around with the sticks, shouting things I didn't understand. I covered my ears and ran without thinking. Suman grabbed my hand and led me home, shouting a few things herself.

   After that, my self-confidence plummeted and my stuttering soared. Practically overnight I forgot all the techniques I'd learned in speech therapy.

   I stopped trying to speak in school and instead became an observer. I listened, studied hard, and kept my opinions to myself. The other girls thought I was unfriendly and stuck up because I'd lived in America, but they were wrong. If only they knew how much I longed to speak like them. How carefree they were, tossing words into the air!

   Writing became my refuge. I wrote on any scrap of paper I could find. I remember writing this in the margin of my notebook: *Sticks and stones may break my bones, but words will never hurt me.* I think I knew even then that it was a lie. Words can and do hurt.

Sticks and stones may break my bones, but words will never hurt me.

8   9

FIGURE 13-18 Pages 8–9 from *Tongue Tied,* Level V

I picked up Sissy from school, as usual.

"Can we get ice cream today, Dion?" she asked, hope all over her face.

"Nope. Gotta go straight home."

Sissy stuck out her lower lip in a pout, but she didn't argue.

My sister was my responsibility after school. I had to take Sissy straight home, no side trips, and no leaving the house when we got home. It seemed like Mom added more rules every week. Those rules really cramped my style. Little kid rules. But if Sissy had to follow them, then I was stuck with them, too.

2

3

FIGURE 13-19 Pages 2–3 from *Rules,* Level V

"little kid rules" and they "cramp his style." Sissy's rules involve staying away from the windows. Dion breaks lots of the rules but never breaks Sissy's rules. Sirens and shots from the street, with shattered glass, makes Dion realize that the rules apply to him too, and he has to be careful to survive. The text has a serious subject matter and complex characters. Dion has to pretend to his younger sister that they are safe, while at the same time protecting her and himself. The challenge lies in understanding the complexity of the problem.

Texts at Levels W, X, Y, and Z

At levels W, X, Y, and Z readers are able to process and understand a wide range of texts, including a full range of genres. Special types of fiction include mystery, satire, parody, horror, and romance. Fiction texts often have unusual narrative structures (flashbacks, flash-forwards, time-lapses). Nonfiction texts combine the full range of underlying structural patterns. In fiction, themes and characters are multidimensional, may be understood on several levels, and are developed in complex ways. Readers are expected to understand and respond to mature themes such as

The next morning, Mary took up her pen and started writing. "It was on a dreary night of November..." the story began.

In her story, an ambitious young man, Victor Frankenstein, believes he's discovered the secret of life. He plans to turn a collection of dead people's body parts into a living human being. Victor means well, but he doesn't think things through. When the stitched-together body comes to life as a huge, hideous monster, Victor runs away, frightened by what he's done.

The abandoned monster is gentle at first. He wanders around trying to make friends, but he inspires only fear. People attack him, and he turns violent. Angry at Victor for creating his miserable life, he kills Victor's brother, best friend, and bride. In the end, Victor tracks the monster to the North Pole, but dies before he can kill him. The monster sails off on an ice raft, also prepared to die.

FIGURE 13-20 Pages 8–9 from *Making a Monster*, Level X

sexuality, abuse, poverty, racism, and war. High fantasy, myths, and legends offer added challenge and require readers to identify classical motifs such as "the quest" and to understand moral issues. Biographies offer a range of stories about individuals and how they have made a difference in human welfare. Readers will encounter challenging genres and literary features such as satire and irony. Texts contain literary language. They contain scientific information with many Tier 2 and Tier 3 words. Many texts require background knowledge of historical events and concepts from science. Levels W, X, Y, and Z are typical of grades 6 through 8 and beyond.

Examples

Making a Monster (*Fountas & Pinnell Classroom,* in press) is the level X nonfiction story of Mary Godwin's creation of the Frankenstein monster (see Figure 13-20). At age 18, Mary wrote the story that became famous for two centuries. Published in 1818, the novel *Frankenstein* has been the subject of many stage plays and movies. It will be interesting to readers that scientists used to steal bodies in order to dissect and study them. This text requires background information and the ability to understand a long period of history. The writer also uses Frankenstein as a simile—for example, "many people worried that the atomic bomb would turn out to be like Frankenstein's monster—uncontrollable and destructive."

Egyptian Mummies: Made to Last (*Fountas & Pinnell Classroom*, in press) reveals important information about Egyptian mummies gathered by digital imaging technology (see Figure 13-21). It is amazing how much scientists can tell about these ancient people. This level Y text reveals startling images of the bodies of mummies. It tells how the art of preserving bodies evolved over time, and it reveals many interesting details about the process and the beliefs of the Egyptians. One section provides a step-by-step description of the procedure for making a mummy—all the way to the sweet smells that embalmers sprinkled between the layers of linen. The text addresses serious subject matter that requires understanding of ancient culture. The text includes a glossary and index.

From Body to Mummy

After the embalmers perfected their method, mummification became very popular in Egypt. Everyone wanted their loved ones to live on after death. With so many customers, the embalmers needed a system to help them handle all the bodies. Here's how some scientists think it worked.

Immediately after death, embalmers took the body to **Ibu** *(ee-boo)*, which means "Place of Washing." There, probably in an open-sided tent near the Nile River, the body was carefully washed in a salty mixture of water and natron.

Next, the body was moved to the "House of Mummification," or **Per-Nefer** *(pair-neff-uhr)*, to be cleaned out and dried. To drain all the fluids, the body was first placed on its back on a slanted table.

The embalmers started their work by removing the brain. They didn't want to damage the head, so they inserted a hooked instrument into one nostril and swirled the hook inside the skull. Then they used a long-handled spoon to scoop out the brain matter. The Egyptians didn't believe the brain was worth anything, so they just threw it away.

Mummification Step by Step

STEP ONE: Ibu
At **Ibu** the body was thoroughly washed. It is likely that this took place near the Nile, but far from any town, so townspeople didn't have to smell the bodies.

STEP TWO: Per-Nefer
At **Per-Nefer** the brain and other organs were removed from the body, and the body was dried in natron so that it would not rot. The body was left to dry for more than a month.

STEP THREE: Wabet
At **Wabet** the body was shaped, rubbed with sweet-smelling oils, and wrapped in cloth.

10

11

FIGURE 13-21 Pages 10–11 from *Egyptian Mummies: Made to Last*, Level Y

Creating a Common Vision for Grade-Level Expectations

Standards and expectations pose a real dilemma for teachers. There is a view that children should be able to develop at their own pace, and that might be the ideal; however, several factors make this goal problematic. First, most children need teaching in the area of literacy learning. Left simply to explore and read, some would probably achieve high levels. But most of us learn best when we interact regularly with others and have the guidance of a more expert person. School is a social situation in which classroom teachers are guiding the learning of twenty to thirty individuals at a time. Much classroom work will involve the entire class; your small-group instruction for reading is a way to provide differentiated instruction. At the same time, responsible teaching means helping students make progress at a rate that will enable them to succeed in school year after year. That means being aware of expected progress and level of reading, which is a daunting task when there is such diversity among every group.

As a teacher, you need to have a vision for your students' progress, and we know that this vision can be accomplished more successfully if teachers work with each other. We are familiar with schools and school districts who set expectations for a year of progress at each grade level; an example of approximate expectations by grade level is shown in Figure 13-22.

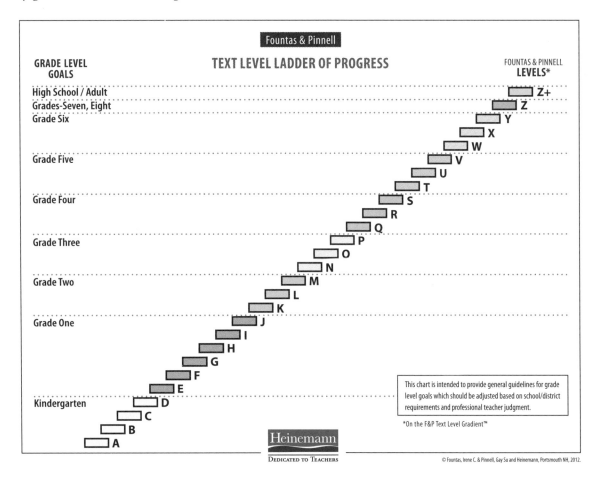

FIGURE 13-22 Text Level Ladder of Progress

We include this figure as a tool for thinking rather than a prescription. Great differences exist across school districts and schools. For example, many districts have half-day rather than full-day kindergarten and that can make a big difference in the early years. (This figure is based on having a literacy-rich, full-day kindergarten.) So, teachers, administrators, and school boards should make their own decisions about expectations for students. Having a clear view of expectations for progress has many benefits:

▶ It gives teachers an opportunity to work together toward common goals.

▶ It helps you identify students who need extra help in the classroom.

▶ It helps your team identify students who need intervention to make faster progress.

▶ It guides the purchasing of leveled books that are needed at each grade.

▶ It makes it possible to look at the overall progress of an age cohort.

A way to think about text levels is shown in Figure 13-23. Across the year, you look carefully at where a student is and work to provide the necessary level of support. This chart is a thinking tool; it does not mean that a student would be expected to read books that are well beyond him. (If the gap is too wide between what he can do and what he is assigned to do, then no instruction will be effective. But with careful choice and effective instruction, you can "up the ante.") Nor does it mean that a student should be required to read at a certain level all of the time.

Since the publication of the first edition of *Guided Reading* over twenty years ago, we have noticed significant changes in early education. The end-of-year expectation for kindergarten is now level D instead of level C; accordingly, entry level for grade 1 is level D and exit level is J, with entry to grade 2 at level J. This does not mean that a child reading at level C at the end of kindergarten is necessarily at risk. It does mean that we want to work toward the goal of independent reading at level C to assure a solid foundation for entry to grade 1.

An examination of data from the Heinemann Data Collection Project and an independent efficacy study of *Leveled Literacy Intervention* conducted by The Center for Research in Educational Policy, University of Memphis revealed that achievement in literacy is trending up. The same trends are supported by decades of data on thousands of children collected by the International Data Evaluation Center of The Ohio State University. From 2003 to 2010, researchers have noticed a steady trend upward. Kindergarten children are entering school with more literacy awareness; they are responding to literacy-rich kindergarten curricula; they are learning fast and clocking up more experience in reading and writing. Earlier and high levels of reading are the result, and that's good news. Expectations are higher and teaching is shifting. We have not changed the continuum but have made minor alterations to grade-level expectations for kindergarten, grade one, and grade two; but you will need to evaluate this shift as it applies to your own setting.

When you set grade-level expectations, you are really establishing long-term goals. *You do not achieve goals simply by setting them*, so you should not look at these expectations as *requirements* for each child to meet. Expectations have everything to do with the implementation of high-level, high-quality *teaching*. There will

Fountas & Pinnell
INSTRUCTIONAL LEVEL EXPECTATIONS FOR READING

	Beginning of Year (Aug.–Sept.)	1st Interval of Year (Nov.–Dec.)	2nd Interval of Year (Feb.–Mar.)	End of Year (May–June)
Grade K		C	D	E
		B	C	D
		A	B	C
				Below C
Grade 1	E	G	I	K
	D	F	H	J
	C	E	G	I
	Below C	Below E	Below G	Below I
Grade 2	K	L	M	N
	J	K	L	M
	I	J	K	L
	Below I	Below J	Below K	Below L
Grade 3	N	O	P	Q
	M	N	O	P
	L	M	N	O
	Below L	Below M	Below N	Below O
Grade 4	Q	R	S	T
	P	Q	R	S
	O	P	Q	R
	Below O	Below P	Below Q	Below R
Grade 5	T	U	V	W
	S	T	U	V
	R	S	T	U
	Below R	Below S	Below T	Below U
Grade 6	W	X	Y	Z
	V	W	X	Y
	U	V	W	X
	Below U	Below V	Below W	Below X
Grades 7–8	Z	Z	Z	Z
	Y	Y	Z	Z
	X	X	Y	Y
	Below X	Below X	Below Y	Below Y

KEY

- Exceeds Expectations
- Meets Expectations
- Approaches Expectations: Needs Short-Term Intervention
- Does Not Meet Expectations: Needs Intensive Intervention

The Instructional Level Expectations for Reading chart is intended to provide general guidelines for grade level goals, which should be adjusted based on school/district requirements and professional teacher judgement.

DEDICATED TO TEACHERS

Fountas & Pinnell LITERACY™

10/26/16

FIGURE 13-23 Instructional Level Expectations for Reading

be readers who need more help, and there will be readers who make faster progress than most. The point of expectations and goals is not to make everyone the same because that would be an impossible task and not even desirable. Our goal is to help every student reach their potential when they are expending their best effort and have expert teaching support. Expectations *can* help you meet readers' needs and support them so that they make optimum progress. The gradient is an invaluable tool in reaching that goal.

Suggestions for Professional Development

Once you have analyzed a variety of texts, you will develop *a way of thinking* that allows you to quickly pick up the text's characteristics just by reading it. You can identify the particular features that offer learning opportunities for your groups; you can select the areas of possible confusion. After this kind of analytic thinking, you will find it easy to plan your book introduction and to identify some potential opportunities for specific teaching. Also, you will have a good idea of what to look for as evidence of student comprehension.

1. Work with a group of colleagues who have established tentative groups of students for teaching in guided reading.

2. Before the meeting, identify the tentative levels of at least two groups for each teacher and assemble a collection of leveled texts at those same levels. (If possible, bring in books that are new to the group so that they will be taking a fresh look rather than relying on one or two teachers' previous experiences.) Have six copies of each title.

3. Have teachers work in groups that have common levels of interest. They select two books and work through the analysis of ten text characteristics quickly, jotting notes on the Text Analysis form (you can download the blank form from Online Resources). Use Figure 13-3 and the descriptions of the ten text characteristics in this chapter as a resource.

4. When finished, the group generates the writer's message for each book. This will be harder than it seems. The message is always a bigger idea than a summary of the plot or the content. It might be a "lesson" in a fiction story, or what the understandings from a nonfiction text might mean for people or the world in general.

5. Then, they write notes about what will be important in introducing the text to one of their groups.

6. At the end, have them lay out the books in order of difficulty and talk about any differences they notice.

7. Each participant can take six copies of a book back to the classroom to introduce to a guided reading group.

8. Set a short follow-up meeting to discuss new insights gleaned from using the texts with groups.

CHAPTER 14

Selecting and Introducing Texts for Guided Reading

A good introduction, leading to a successful first reading by an active reader, sets the stage for a host of teaching ventures around that text.

–Marie Clay

Guided reading has two essential elements related to the texts for an effective lesson. First, the text must provide the right level of support and challenge for the reader's current processing abilities. It must include language and concepts that they either control or can get to (with their present control of strategic actions) while providing a few new things to learn. Second, the text must be introduced in a way that gives readers access to it while leaving some problem solving to do. It is the right amount of problem solving or "reading work" that enables the reader to build the processing system.

Both elements depend on your knowledge of the readers in the group, the reading process, and the demands of the text. Your goal in the text introduction is to orient the readers to the text and anticipate the challenges they will be able to work through and those that will require support. Remove the obstacles requiring support so the readers can work through the text as successfully and as independently as possible.

Before students begin to read a text in the guided reading lesson, (1) select a text that will suit the readers in the group (level, content, language, genre); (2) consider the behaviors and understandings the readers need to take on; and, (3) plan an introduction that will involve the students in the thinking about selected aspects prior to reading it. Some important principles to keep in mind are:

▶ The young child's knowledge of letters, of the way words work, and of the conventions of print (like spacing and directionality) is a factor in the early level books chosen for guided reading and in the way they are mediated.

▶ The students' background knowledge and the language they bring to the process will affect your selections and other decisions. Your precise knowledge of your students helps you provide a customized orientation that makes your teaching powerful.

▶ Varying levels of support are built into the process. You can provide more support for a challenging text and a briefer introduction when the text is easy, fine-tuning the text gradient to provide just the right amount of challenge or reading work for your students.

▶ There will be change over time as different texts are selected and the level of support changes. You may provide more support at the start of a new level, but less support when the students are finding the level easy and you are almost ready to select texts at the next level.

▶ You mediate the text for the readers. By pre-selecting and previewing the book, you can help readers think about how to use their strengths to process or problem-solve the text.

Selecting Books

Start by looking through your set of leveled books. The level helps you narrow your choices. Think about the appropriate level and look at the variety of books available. Consider books that will delight the readers of the age group. Think about the variety of topics, themes, and genres they have experienced. If the students are processing the text well and are finding new learning opportunities on a particular level, the selection is probably about right; however, there are more factors to consider.

▶ Are the concepts in the book familiar to students or can they be made accessible through the introduction?

▶ Is the topic one that will engage the students' intellect or curiosity?

▶ Is the plot interesting? Will it appeal to this group of students?

▶ Is the setting important?

▶ Does the text provide opportunities for this group of students to use what they know?

▶ Are some words in the book known to students?

▶ Are other words accessible through the readers' current ability to use strategic actions such as word analysis and prediction from the language structure or meaning?

▶ Does the text offer a few opportunities to problem-solve, search, and check while reading for meaning?

▶ Do the illustrations or graphics support the reader's search for meaning? Do they extend the meaning of the text?

▶ For emergent and early readers, is the text layout clear? Is the print clear? Are there an appropriate number of lines of text? Is there sufficient space between words?

▶ Is the length of text appropriate for the experience and stamina of the group?

Obviously the book's levels of support and challenge will not be the same even for all students in one guided reading group. They bring different experiences and control of language to the book, so they will search for and use meaning and language structure in different ways. Even if they have been exposed to the same frequently encountered words, they will have paid attention in different ways and each will have an idiosyncratic store of word knowledge and word analysis strengths to bring to any particular text. Nevertheless, with effective teaching and social support, all members of the group can process the new text successfully.

Planning the Introduction to the Text

You will become more efficient in planning text introductions when you have a great deal of experience. You will also get to know your book collection well over time and will be able to anticipate many of the challenges in the texts. You will also be able to add to your knowledge of the text and your knowledge of the particular readers you are teaching. Using a book with many students will help you predict the range of response you can predict. You will find your own way of planning but consider the process shown in Figure 14-1. When you use a sticky note (or two) to

Five Steps to Preparing an Introduction to the Text

❶ Read the text, thinking about how the book works, the messages of the text, and the other text characteristics.

❷ Review the behaviors and understandings in *The Fountas & Pinnell Literacy Continuum*, noting what the readers control and need to learn how to control. Consider learning opportunities in the lesson and how you can attend to a few opportunities in the orientation.

❸ Write a brief opening statement that will immediately engage the readers in thinking about the topic or story.

❹ List page numbers where you mean to take the readers with a brief phrase or note to remind you of what you want to help them notice. (You might also place sticky notes on a few pages.)

❺ Leave the readers with one or two things to think about that will drive them into the text and may initiate the discussion following the reading.

FIGURE 14-1 Five Steps to Preparing an Introduction to the Text

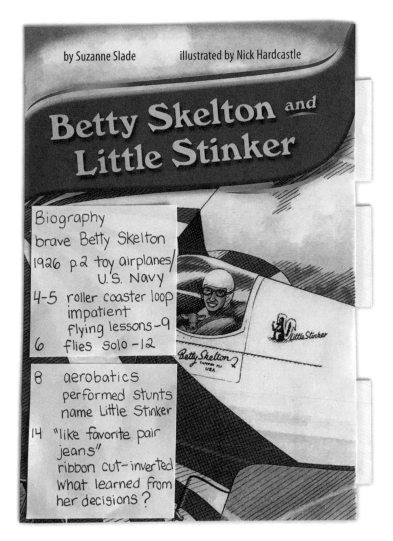

FIGURE 14-2 Using Sticky Notes to Prepare for a Text Introduction

make brief notes, and place it on the cover of the book, you can limit yourself to what is essential and keep yourself from spending time writing long introductions (see Figure 14-2). You can also place a few sticky notes on selected pages where you want to take the students.

Introducing Books

The key to the readers' access to the book is your introduction. "As the child approaches a new text he is entitled to an introduction so that when he reads, the gist of the whole or partly revealed story can provide some guide for a fluent reading," (Clay, *Becoming Literate*, 1991a). A book introduction is defined by Holdaway as, "a brief and lively discussion in which the teacher interests the children in the story and produces an appropriate set for reading it," (1979, 142).

No two book introductions are ever alike. Sometimes teachers are afraid of "giving away" too much when they introduce texts to children, but Clay reminds us to think about it in terms of two people in conversation. For the listener to understand, the speaker must either key in to the listener's prior knowledge or provide some kind of scenario or introduction. Clay says, "This is not a case of telling the children what to expect. It is a process of drawing the children into the activity before passing control to the children and pushing them gently toward problem solving the whole first reading of the story for themselves," (1991b, 265).

Your role is to "prime" the child's processing system to be able to alert him to important aspects of the text that he will need to consider as he moves through it. You are supporting readers in actively anticipating and problem-solving their first reading of a text. Clay's admonition to allow children to read the whole text for themselves is related to building independence in approaching novel texts. The introduction supports and sparks independent problem solving that helps readers build self-extending systems. The balance of support is adjusted for different readers.

Rich introductions will make more challenging texts accessible to a group of students. At other times, the teacher may need to provide only a short, focused introduction or "a few moves to increase accessibility of a new text." When students have developed an independent reading system and they are engaged in taking on many new texts that are well within their control, they introduce texts to themselves, making the "task an unseen, unshared, unhelped activity," (Clay 1991b, 272). The diagram in Figure 14-3 illustrates Clay's description of teacher involvement in book introductions. You shift up or down the gradient of involvement according to the characteristics of the text, your knowledge of the readers in the group, and the relationship between the two.

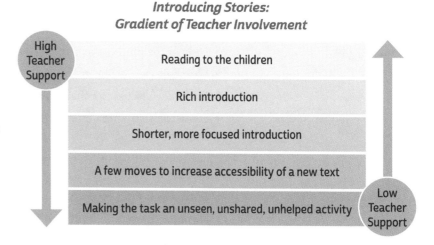

FIGURE 14-3 Introducing Stories—Gradient of Teacher Involvement (Marie Clay)

Be sure to help the readers understand the structure of the story. "Understanding the structure of the whole story provides a kind of scaffold that allows children to focus attention on many new details about print," (Clay, *By Different Paths to Common Outcomes*, 175). The same is true for the organization or structures of a nonfiction text. It helps students to know how the text "works." Your goal is for the reader to read the new text fluently, successfully, and as independently as possible. "The teacher's job is . . . arranging for the problem to be manageable, sustaining the child's problem-solving attempts, emphasizing flexibility," (Johnston 2007, 67).

Drawing from Clay (1991a; 1991b) and Holdaway (1979) we have compiled a list of actions teachers take during book introductions. These characteristics are not a checklist but a repertoire of options. You need to think carefully about a particular group of students so that the introduction can flow much like a conversation among people who are interested in the same thing. The process leaves "room for child input to inform the teacher and for the teacher to make some deliberate teaching moves" (Clay 1991b, 267). Consider how you can provide support for the text meaning, the language structure, and use of the visual information in the print. Consider the conditions under which the reader will be able to process (supporting meaning, language structures, the use of visual and phonological information) the new challenging text successfully. Think about what the reader knows, what he can get to, and obstacles there might be.

In introducing texts, you might:

▶ Build interest in the story or topic.

▶ Invite conversation about a topic, setting, or problem.

▶ Invite students to make predictions, raise questions, and anticipate the text.

▶ Explain important ideas and concepts.

▶ Talk about the meaning of the whole story.

▶ Get individuals wondering about something in the text.

▶ Draw on the learner's personal experiences and background knowledge.

▶ Leave room for the students to bring their ideas and experiences to bear on the story or information.

▶ Help them anticipate the characteristics of the genre.

▶ Discuss the plot or theme of the whole story.

▶ Foreshadow a problem.

▶ Introduce/discuss the characters in the story.

▶ Draw their attention to the organization or structure of the text and help them understand "how the book works."

▶ Say (and sometimes have students repeat) language patterns or vocabulary that are unfamiliar and are critical to the story.

▶ Make them familiar with unusual names.

▶ Use some of the new and challenging vocabulary found in the text.

▶ Draw the readers' attention to a few specific words and punctuation.

▶ Get them to say some unusual words or language structures.

▶ Occasionally address letter-sound relationships or clusters in the pronunciation of unfamiliar words (proper nouns, for example).

▶ Show how to recognize—break apart—two or three new words.

▶ Show how to take apart a multisyllable word.

▶ Explain a few concepts or vocabulary.

▶ Talk about the illustrations or graphics and/or graphic features and help students discover information in them.

▶ Explore any aspects of the text layout that affect the meaning of the story or would be tricky for readers to follow.

▶ Point out unfamiliar text features such as bold type, italics, and ellipses.

▶ Leave room for problem solving.

As Holdaway has said, the introduction serves to "Leave the children with one or two clear questions that will drive them into the text and serve as a continuing impulse to seek meaning when they read," (1979, 143).

The goal is to keep the learning easy. When readers not only hear, but use, the language and content of the text, they will have a greater sense of agency. Be sure not to talk too much or tell too much, which may create noise or clutter in the students' ability to attend. Also, don't give too little support and withhold information the readers need to engage successfully. In Figure 14-4, we describe what the introduction is meant to do, and what it is not meant to do.

Sample Text Introductions

Below are several examples of book introductions with a conversational tone. The texts being introduced are intended for different groups of students reading at a variety of levels with varying strengths.

Introduction to *Family Fun,* Level A

Family Fun (Fountas & Pinnell Classroom, in press) is a simple realistic fiction story set outdoors in what appears to be a park (see Figure 14-5). In this book, a girl talks about the members of her family, saying each is here. The family members are all dressed in athletic clothing and running shoes. Some hints in the illustration indicate that a race is starting. The book ends with the girls saying, "I am here." On the last page, the reader learns that they are involved in a family fun run. A repeating pattern supports beginning readers; high-frequency words are *my, is,* and *here.* Family names are included. In Figure 14-6, you can see a sample introduction for this book.

The Book Introduction Does:	The Book Introduction Does Not:
◆ Create interest in a topic or story.	◆ Laboriously preview every page.
◆ Assess students' background knowledge so that confusions can be cleared up if needed.	◆ Pre-teach vocabulary words.
◆ Help readers understand the text structure as a support for comprehending.	◆ Consist of a "picture walk" in which students look through the text and examine the pictures either individually, or as a group with the teacher.
◆ Familiarize students with tricky language structures.	◆ Remove the challenges from the text by communicating all information in advance.
◆ Draw readers' attention to key information and where they will find it.	◆ Tell readers what to think during and after reading the text.
◆ Draw readers' attention to key vocabulary if needed.	◆ Take longer than it takes to read the text.
◆ Prompt thinking in response to the text.	
◆ Poise the readers to problem-solve their way through the text.	

FIGURE 14-4 What a Book Introduction Is Meant to Do

My brother is here.

10

11

FIGURE 14-5 Pages 10–11 from *Family Fun,* Level A

An Introduction to *Family Fun*, Level A

Speaker	Teacher/Student Interactions	Analysis of Interactions
Mr. H	Today, you are going to read a book with the title, *Family Fun*. Look at the cover and you'll see the girl who is talking in this book. She is holding her little sister's hand. In what kind of place are they?	Draws attention to the setting Introduces the narrator
Raj	A park.	
Mr. H	It looks like a park. Anything else in the picture?	Asks students to search further
Sarah	They're standing on a bench or something.	
Perri	It looks like a walking place or a racetrack and there's a sign.	
Mr. H	That sign says "start" so be thinking about that. Look at page 2. There's her mom in the picture. The girl says, "My mom is here." Now say that with me. *[Children repeat sentence.]* Say *my*. What letter would you expect to see at the beginning of the word *my*?	Points out a clue that foreshadows the ending Asks students to repeat the language structure Draws attention to visual features of a letter
Students	M.	
Mr. H	Find the word *my* and put your finger under it. Let's all say it: *my. [Students say the word while pointing.]*	Draws attention to visual features of a word and how it sounds
Mr. H	Turn to page 6. Think who that might be. And what will she say?	Invites prediction from the picture Invites students to rehearse the language structure
Donald	Her grandma.	
Students	My grandma is here.	
Mr. H	Say the word *is. Is* begins with an "i." Put your finger under it and say it. You will see some other members of her family. On each page, the girl will tell the person in her family that is here. Look at page 14. She is pointing to herself. What is she saying here?	Draws attention to visual features of a high-frequency word Tells readers how the book works (the narrator, the language, and what happens on each page)
Perri	She says, "I am here."	
Mr. H	Yes, she does. Now you are going to go back to the beginning and read this book softly to yourself. Read in a whisper voice and point under each word. On the last page, you will find out why the family is here.	Reminds readers to use voice-print match Prompts anticipation

FIGURE 14-6 An Introduction to *Family Fun*, Level A

Introduction to *The Kite,* Level A

The Kite (*Fountas & Pinnell Classroom,* in press) is an animal fantasy that features the series character, Funny Monkey (see Figure 14-7). Monkey is the narrator of the simple story. On each page, Monkey tells about something he has. There is one line of print on each page and the illustrations carry the story. On pages 14 and 15, we see that Monkey has a kite, and on the last page, the kite carries him skyward as he tries to hold on to it. The sentence structure is very simple with a subject and predicate only. High-frequency words are: *I,* *have,* and *some.* In Figure 14-8, you can see a sample introduction for this book.

FIGURE 14-7 Pages 12–13 from *The Kite,* Level A

An Introduction to *The Kite,* Level A

Speaker	Teacher/Student Interactions	Analysis of Interactions
Mrs. S	You are going to read a book called *The Kite.* There's Funny Monkey on the cover. And do you see the little picture of Funny Monkey down in the corner? That tells you that there is a series of books about the character Funny Monkey. So, you may be reading more books about him. What's Funny Monkey holding in his hands?	Introduces the title and series Draws attention to illustrations and the logo
Kyle	A kite.	
Cynthia	I had a kite that my dad flew.	
Mrs. S	In this book, Monkey tells all the things he has to make a kite. Turn to pages 2 and 3. Monkey says, "I have some paper." Can you say that? Let's read that together. Point under each word as you read. *[Students point and read.]* Do you see the paper in the picture? It's a big piece.	Tells how the book works Prompts for pointing Draws attention to the information in the picture as a way to cross-check

FIGURE 14-8 An Introduction to *The Kite,* Level A

(continues)

Speaker	Teacher/Student Interactions	Analysis of Interactions
Dictson	He's going to make something.	
Mrs. S	Turn the page and take a look at the picture. Now what does he say?	Draws attention to the information in the picture as a way to cross-check
	Yes, he says, "I have some scissors." Say the word *have*. What letter do you expect to see first in *have*?	Prompts searching for a word using visual features
Students	H.	
Mrs. S	Find *have* and put your finger under it. Get a good look. That word will help you on every page.	Prompts children to locate a word and notice the first letter.
Cynthia	He's going to cut the paper.	
Mrs. S	He might cut the paper. On each page he tells something he has. Look at page 9. Now what does he have?	Rehearses the language structure
		Draws attention to the picture and prompts to use meaning
Madeleine	Scissors.	
Kyle	It's glue.	
Dictson	I think he's going to make a kite because I see it on the ground.	
Mrs. S	You are going to read this whole book from the beginning. Remember to point under each word. It has to match. Also, check the pictures to help you know you are right about what he has. Then we will talk about what Monkey makes and what happens to him.	Confirms predictions
		Prompts to match word by word
		Communicates the expectation to talk about reading

FIGURE 14-8 *(continued)*

Introduction to *The Little Hen,* Level B

The Little Hen (Fountas & Pinnell Classroom, in press) is an animal fantasy that represents a very simple version of "The Little Red Hen" (see Figure 14-9). The text has one line of print on each page—a question on one page and an answer on the other. The little hen asks, "Can you help us plant the corn?" The hen is asking a fox, a duck, and a goat; but the speech balloons coming out of each character's mouth say "no." On the next page, the hen says, "Then we will plant the corn." She means that she and her three chicks will plant the corn and that is what the picture shows. The pattern follows with the hen asking the three others to help and each saying "no." We see the fox, duck, and goat, lounging around and watching while the hen and chicks work. Finally, the hen picks the corn, and then the tables turn. This time, the fox, goat, and duck ask, "Can we help you eat the corn?" This time the hen and three chicks answer "no." And the book ends with the little hen and her chicks eating the corn. The book is organized in a question and answer format and some of the text is in speech balloons. The word *we* is in bold on the last page.

Important high-frequency words are *can, you, us, we, will, then*. There is an alternating pattern with the questions and answers. The question always starts with *can* and the answer starts with *then*. In Figure 14-10, you can see a sample introduction for this book.

Can we help you eat the corn?

14

15

FIGURE 14-9 Pages 14–15 from *The Little Hen*, Level B

An Introduction to *The Little Hen*, Level B

Speaker	Teacher/Student Interactions	Analysis of Interactions
Mr. B	You have an animal fantasy book today titled, *The Little Hen* that is retold by Paul Mellon. That means this is a folktale. A folktale is a story that is told over and over by people. Do you know the story of the Little Red Hen?	Names genre and provides a definition Gives the title and author Asks for background information
Michelle	She planted the corn and they didn't help her so she wouldn't let them eat it.	
Mr. B	That's right. The Little Red Hen asked some friends to help her plant the corn and do other things. But they wouldn't help her so they didn't get to eat the corn or the food she made. This is the same story. Look at page 2. You can see the little hen and her three chicks. She is asking the fox, the duck, and the goat a question. She says, "Can you help us plant the corn?" What do you think they say?	Tells the story problem Draws attention to language and speech bubbles
Leland	They say no.	
Forest	No, no, no *[pointing]*.	

FIGURE 14-10 An Introduction to *The Little Red Hen*, Level B

(continues)

Speaker	Teacher/Student Interactions	Analysis of Interactions
Mr. B	They do. Let's all read that, "No. No. No." *[Students point and read the speech balloons.]* Turn to page 4. The little hen always says, "Then we will plant the corn," or whatever else she asked them to do. Say *then*. It starts with "th" just like the word *the*. Put your finger on the word *then*, and have a good look at it.	Rehearses the language structure Draws attention to visual features of high-frequency words Prompts use of visual features of a known word Helps students connect a new word to a known word
Students	*[Reading]* Then we will plant the corn.	
Mr. B	Look at page 6. What do you think the goat and the fox and the duck will say when the hen asks them to water the corn?	Invites prediction
Kate	"No, no, no."	
Mr. B	That's right. Say, *can*. What letter do you expect to see first in *can*? Put your finger under the word *can*, quickly. *[Students locate can.]* So she is going to say, "Then we will water the corn." When she says *we*, who does she mean?	Prompts for sound-to-letter match Prompts searching for visual information to locate a word Clarifies the referent of a pronoun
Kate	Herself and her chicks.	
Mr. B	They are really working hard, aren't they? Look at page 9. What are the duck and the fox and the goat doing?	Draws attention to the meaning in the picture
Michelle	They're not doing anything. They are just sitting around and watching.	
Mr. B	But you know how this story is going to end. Look at page 14. Now who is asking the question?	Prompts use of background knowledge
Forest	The fox and the goat and the duck want to eat the corn.	
Mr. B	They say, "Can we help you eat the corn?" What's the answer?	Rehearses the language structure
Leland	No. No. No. No.	
Mr. B	*Maybe the hen and the chicks will say, "We will eat the corn."* Go back to page 2 and read the whole book. Be thinking about what the hen and the chicks are doing and what the other characters are doing.	Prompts thinking about the conclusion

FIGURE 14-10 *(continued)*

Introduction to *Sticks and Stones for Little Monster,* Level E

Sticks and Stones for Little Monster (*Fountas & Pinnell Classroom,* in press) is a fantasy about an engaging and whimsical character that is part of a series (see Figure 14-11). Little Monster repeatedly piles a series of unlikely things on a table in front of a cave. He keeps putting sticks, stones, worms, weeds, bugs, and mud on top of the table until, finally, he eats them! There is some repetitive language in the book (*got some, put them, on the table, on top of, I need*). The book has four to six lines of print on each page, with one character speaking. Important high-frequency words are *put, got, some, them, them, on, the, of, top*. In Figure 14-12, you can see a sample introduction to this book.

> "I need mud,"
> said Little Monster.
> He put mud on top of
> the stones and the sticks.
> He put mud on the worms,
> the weeds, and the bugs.

12

13

Yum!

16

FIGURE 14-11 Pages 12–13, 16 from *Sticks and Stones for Little Monster*, Level E

An Introduction to *Sticks and Stones for Little Monster*, Level E

Speaker	Teacher/Student Interactions	Analysis of Interactions
Ms. C	Today you are going to read a book about Little Monster. You haven't read a book about Little Monster before. That's Little Monster on the cover. What are you thinking about him? Let's have everyone say what they're thinking.	Says the title and identifies the book as one of a series Encourages talk about the pictures
Cara	He looks funny.	
Pia	This is a pretend book because he couldn't be real.	
Liza	He's got funny feet with big toenails.	
Nadia	And horns.	
John	He might have lived a long time ago.	

FIGURE 14-12 An Introduction to *Sticks and Stones for Little Monster*, Level E

(continues)

Speaker	Teacher/Student Interactions	Analysis of Interactions
Ms. C	This is a book about things that could not happen in real life, so it's, fiction. Put your finger on the logo—the little picture of Little Monster in the lower right-hand corner. This logo, or sign, tells you that this book is in the Little Monster series. The title is *Sticks and Stones for Little Monster*. What does Little Monster seem to be doing here?	Identifies the genre and defines it Helps students identify the series logo Tells title of book and series Helps students identify it Asks for interpretation of the pictures Draws attention to the meaning in the picture
Nadia	He's getting some sticks.	
Pia	There are some stones on the table.	
Ms. C	Stones are rocks. Look at the title page. You can see small pictures of Little Monster and his pet, Spot.	Clarifies meaning of a word Identifies characters in a series
John	Spot is funny. Is he a dog?	
Ms. C	I'm not sure what he is, but he is a pet. Spot is not in this story, but he will be in other stories about Little Monster. Look at page 2. What is happening here?	Recognizes question Asks for interpretation of the pictures
Pia	He's getting the rocks.	
Ms. C	Another word that means the same as *rocks* is *stones*. Little Monster got some stones. And look, he is putting them on the table. Say, *put*. What letter do you expect to see first in *put*? Find the word *put* on this page. [Students locate the word.] Now look at page 5. What's happening?	Uses some of the language Draws students' attention to an important word and the sound of the first letter Prompts to search for visual information Asks for interpretation of the pictures
Nadia	Now he's getting sticks. It's like on the cover.	
Liza	What's he going to do?	
Ms. C	That's a good question. I wonder what he is going to do. On each page of this book, Little Monster gets more things and he puts them on the table. He put the sticks on top of the stones. Find the word *put* on this page.	Recognizes questions Confirms that readers ask questions Tells how the book works Uses some of the language Draws attention to an important word
Students	*[Locate and say* put.*]*	

FIGURE 14-12 *(continued)*

Speaker	Teacher/Student Interactions	Analysis of Interactions
Ms. C	Let's look at some pages and see what other things Little Monster put on the table.	Asks students to think about the content by looking at the pictures
Cara	Some worms, some weeds.	
Liza	It's weird. Now he's getting bugs.	
Ms. C	Now look at page 12. There you can see everything he gets. Little Monster says, "I need mud." And he put the mud on top of everything else he got—the stones, the sticks, the worms, the weeds, and the bugs. He's going to get one more thing—a fork.	Uses some of the language of the story
	Now go back to page 2 and read the whole book. Be thinking about what Little Monster is going to be doing with all of those things. Be sure to use the pictures to help you.	Prompts for predicting throughout the story Prompts for searching the pictures

FIGURE 14-12 *(continued)*

Introduction to *Earl on His Own,* Level L

Earl on His Own (Fountas & Pinnell Classroom, in press) is an animal fantasy in the Earl and Pearl Series (see Figure 14-13). These two badgers talk and act like people. They have their own houses, but in this story, Earl is visiting Pearl. Pearl is a real planner and manager, but today, Earl wants to do something on his own. He decides to explore the town without Pearl. Earl reminds Pearl that she needs to

Earl opened the gate.

"Remember to look both ways when you cross the street," Pearl said.

"I will."

"And don't forget to eat lunch."

"I won't."

"And be careful..."

"Pearl!" Earl shouted. "I am a grown-up badger. I will be fine." He started to walk away.

6

Pearl ran after him. "Wait!" she called. "Take this map with you. You know you always get lost."

"I *never* get lost," Earl snapped. He shoved the map into his pocket. Then he marched down the path that led to town.

7

FIGURE 14-13 Pages 6–7 from *Earl on His Own,* Level L

plant her tulips, but Pearl has doubts about Earl. She reminds Earl to be careful and gives him a map. The rest of the book tells what Earl does in town, and he is unaware that Pearl is following him (shown in the illustrations). He has a good time, but then finds that he is confused about the way to get home. Just then, Pearl takes the map out of Earl's pocket and drops it so that it will come to his attention, and he uses the map to get home to Pearl's house in time for dinner. Earl arrives home not realizing that Pearl has been watching over him all the way. Students need to understand that Pearl is humoring Earl and cares about him. Dialogue is between Earl and Pearl, who says that Earl would never get lost (when, in fact, she knew he would get lost). The story turns on humor that shows the relationship between the sister and brother. Significant information is provided in the illustrations. In Figure 14-14, you can see a sample introduction for this book.

An Introduction to *Earl on His Own*, Level L

Speaker	Teacher/Student Interactions	Analysis of Interactions
Mr. F	Today you are going to read a book about the badgers Earl and Pearl. This is a book in the Earl and Pearl series *[Points to logo]*. What do you know about Earl and Pearl?	Activates prior knowledge
Jasmine	Pearl is Earl's sister, and she's very bossy.	
Wesley	She wants to have everything her own way.	
Mr. F	What do you know about the way Earl and Pearl feel about each other?	Asks for prior knowledge and connection to other texts
Gareth	They like each other.	
Carmine	They're just in the same family. But Earl is one way and Pearl is the other way.	
Mr. F	Say more about that.	Prompts for elaboration
Carmine	Earl doesn't clean up things and he likes them just the way they are and Pearl is always trying to get him to be cleaner.	
Mr. F	They're brother and sister and they're very different. And Pearl is kind of bossy. It's almost like she wants to take care of Earl. The title of this book is *Earl on His Own*. Do you know what it means to be on your own?	States an inference in a tentative way Asks for information about an expression
Gareth	To be by yourself, like if you walk home all by yourself.	
Mr. F	So Earl wants to do something on his own. In this book, he visits Pearl. Look at pages 4 and 5. That is Pearl's house. Earl wants to take a walk and explore Pearl's town. You can see that he has his camera. Pearl needs to plant her tulips, but she is worried about Earl being on his own. Why do you think she's worried?	Briefly outlines the problem Asks for inference
Wesley	He might get lost or something?	

FIGURE 14-14 An Introduction to *Earl on His Own*, Level L

Speaker	Teacher/Student Interactions	Analysis of Interactions
Mr. F	Earl gets lost a lot, and Pearl is worried about all kinds of things. But Earl says, "I am a grown-up badger. I will be fine." What do you think he means by that?	Asks for inference
Jasmine	He's kind of mad because Pearl thinks he can't do anything by himself.	
Carmine	He wants her to stop bugging him because he can do things by himself.	
Mr. F	Look at pages 6 and 7. How do you think Earl is feeling?	Asks for inference
Jasmine	He wants to get away from Pearl. She's so bossy and tells him what to do.	
Carmine	She's getting on his nerves. He looks like he can't stand it.	
Mr. F	The illustrator is really showing you how Earl feels. Look at his face. And, when he walks away on page 7, he's just throwing up his hands. Read page 7 to yourself and then talk about your thinking.	Draws attention to information in the illustrations Asks for interpretation
Gareth	What does *snapped* mean?	
Jasmine	It's kind of like yelling. Because he was mad that Pearl said he always gets lost.	
Wesley	Kind of like you answer back in a snappy way because you're getting annoyed.	
Mr. F	Pearl has given him a map, and you can see it in Earl's pocket. Earl is going to have a nice day in town. He walks all over town. Can you predict what might happen?	Invites prediction based on known information
Gareth	He's going to get lost!	
Mr. F	Is that what you think? [*Students agree.*] Go back to the beginning and read this whole story. Be sure to notice the illustrations because you can get information from them. Then, let's talk about how Pearl feels about Earl.	Prompts for inference Prompts for attention to the illustrations

FIGURE 14-14 *(continued)*

Introduction to *Betty Skelton and Little Stinker,* Level N

Betty Skelton and Little Stinker (*Fountas & Pinnell Classroom,* in press) is a biography of a pioneering woman aviator (see Figure 14-15). Betty Skelton was born in 1926 at a time when women aviators were very rare. The biography begins with Betty's childhood and her early love of flying and tells her story in chronological order to include Betty's solo flight, her aerobatic tricks, and her acquisition of her famous plane, *Little Stinker.* The book gives many interesting details of Betty's life and includes a timeline of significant events. In Figure 14-16, you can see a sample introduction for this book.

The Ribbon Cut

Betty didn't just sit in her plane; she wore it like a favorite pair of jeans. When Betty coughed, *Little Stinker* coughed too! Together they performed many dangerous stunts women weren't supposed to do— inside loops, outside loops, and snap rolls.

Then Betty decided to try something even more dangerous—an inverted ribbon cut. To do this stunt, she would fly *Little Stinker* upside down while her propeller cut a ribbon ten feet (three meters) from the ground. People thought she was crazy. One small mistake could mean disaster. Few men dared try that stunt, and no woman had done it—ever. But Betty wanted to be first.

The first time Betty practiced the stunt, she zoomed *under* the ribbon instead of over it. *Little Stinker* was only a few feet from the ground—and close to crashing—when the engine quit. Betty was able to flip the plane and roll to a stop. After some quick repairs, Betty took off again, but her hands on the wheel were shaking.

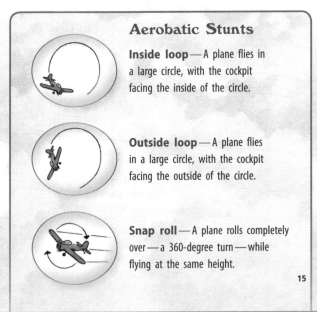

Aerobatic Stunts

Inside loop—A plane flies in a large circle, with the cockpit facing the inside of the circle.

Outside loop—A plane flies in a large circle, with the cockpit facing the outside of the circle.

Snap roll—A plane rolls completely over—a 360-degree turn—while flying at the same height.

14

15

FIGURE 14-15 Pages 14–15 from *Betty Skelton and Little Stinker*, Level N

An Introduction to *Betty Skelton and Little Stinker*, **Level N**

Speaker	Teacher/Student Interactions	Analysis of Interactions
Mrs. R	Today you are going to enjoy reading a biography about an interesting person, Betty Skelton. The title is *Betty Skelton and Little Stinker*. Take a look at the cover and read the back of the book. Then, share your thinking.	Identifies genre, subject, and title Directs attention to information and asks for thinking
Leo	She grew up a long time ago, but she wanted to fly airplanes and she did.	
Jack	Her plane is named *Little Stinker*, and she has her dog with her.	
Shannon	That's a kind of old-looking plane.	

FIGURE 14-16 An Introduction to *Betty Skelton and Little Stinker*, Level N

Speaker	Teacher/Student Interactions	Analysis of Interactions
Mrs. R	It tells on the inside back cover that Betty Skelton was born in 1926. At that time, there were very few women pilots. But Betty flew almost every-thing—planes, helicopters, jets, gliders, and even a blimp. The writer of this book, Suzanne Slade, met Betty once and that inspired her. When some-one is the first, or one of the first, to do something special, they call that person a *pioneer.* Betty was called "a pioneer in aviation." Take a look at page 16 and share your thinking.	Provides background information States a fact
Devon	She's flying upside down. How could she do that?	
Jack	She's a stunt pilot.	
Leo	The timeline shows when she was born and when she started flying.	
Jack	She was only 9 and then she did a solo when she was 12. What does *solo* mean?	
Devon	*Solo* means by yourself.	
Mrs. R	Do you see the word *inverted* under 1949? *Inverted* means upside down. She flew upside down to cut the ribbon. That's amazing and it looks pretty dangerous.	Clarifies the meaning of a word
Maria	She could crash right down into the ground.	
Mrs. R	Look at the picture on page 2 of Betty with *Little Stinker.* As you read, no-tice how the writer has organized and presents the information. Then, let's talk about why you think Betty did such dangerous things and how she felt about flying.	Draws attention to text structure Invites inference
Mrs. R	Look at page 15. There's a graphic that shows you some of the stunts Betty could do. You see the inside loop, the outside loop, and the snap role. This looks pretty difficult!	Draws attention to a graphic
Karey	I don't know how she could do them.	
Jack	It would take a lot of practice.	
Karey	Does she take her little dog with her?	
Mrs. R	She does have a little Chihuahua with her. His name is Little Tinker and you'll read some interesting details about him in this book. As you read, think about the decisions Betty made and notice what makes her a very unusual and special person.	Engages interest Prompts thinking about the significance of the subject

FIGURE 14-16 *(continued)*

Introduction to *Minnie Freeman's Blizzard,* Level O

Minnie Freeman's Blizzard (*Fountas & Pinnell Classroom,* in press) is narrative nonfiction (see Figure 14-17). The writer tells the story of a nineteen-year-old Nebraska teacher, Minnie Freeman, who saves the sixteen students in her one-room schoolhouse during the blizzard of 1888. Background information on the historical time period, the nature of a blizzard, and characteristics of a sod house are provided in sidebars. The dramatic story is told in chronological order, and the text ends with a comparison to current times. In Figure 14-18, you can see a sample introduction for this book.

FIGURE 14-17 Pages 14–15 from *Minnie Freeman's Blizzard*, Level O

An Introduction to *Minnie Freeman's Blizzard*, **Level O**

Speaker	Teacher/Student Interactions	Analysis of Interactions
Mr. H	You are going to read a book today that is a true story about a real person. Look at the front cover of *Minnie Freeman's Blizzard* by Alison Blank. The Illustrations are by Ron Himler. The illustrations are important in this book because this story took place in 1888. What are you thinking from looking at the front cover?	Draws attention to the setting and the illustrations Directs students to the introduction and background information on the back
Ethan	She's dressed in an old-fashioned way, and it looks like the house is in the middle of nowhere.	
James	It's a blizzard.	

FIGURE 14-18 An Introduction to *Minnie Freeman's Blizzard*, Level O

Moira	On the back of the book it says it's a one-room schoolhouse. The roof blows off. So that's really dangerous. They could freeze.	
Mr. H	**Minnie is only nineteen years old, but she's the teacher and she has sixteen students. You've identified the problem. She had to try to save her students. Take a look at pages 2 and 3 and you'll get an idea about the location of Minnie's one-room schoolhouse.**	Provides information Confirms the problem Draws attention to the setting
Jacob	They are in the United States in Nebraska. They have really cold winters there.	
Ethan	The Mira Valley in Nebraska. It's in the middle of nowhere.	
Moira	But it was a long time ago.	
Mr. H	**You can see the students playing at recess time, January 12, 1888. In the sidebar, you'll find out more about what a one-room schoolhouse is like. It was a nice day, but look at page 4.**	Draws attention to the setting and the problem Draws attention to the meaning in the illustrations
Sam	It's snowing out there.	
Mr. H	**A blizzard can start to blow in just a short time. Read the material in italics and then let's talk about Minnie's problem.**	Directs students to information about the problem
Moira	She's afraid they'll be trapped and it will be really hard to stay warm enough.	
Jacob	Maybe they would run out of wood for the fireplace.	
James	She has to try to take care of the really little kids.	
Mr. H	**The wind was so strong that they had to nail the doors and the windows shut. Read the sidebar on page 9 and talk about the information there and what it makes you think.**	Draws attention to elements of the setting and to information revealing the causes of the problem
James	The schoolhouse is just made of grass and dirt. So it might be hard for them to keep warm.	
Ethan	It might even start to turn to mud and dissolve if it rains or snows on it.	
Mr. H	**The roof did blow off. If they stayed there, they would freeze. Remember, the schoolhouse is very far from anywhere else. As you said, Ethan, it's in the middle of nowhere. This is a kind of nonfiction. It's about real people and things that really happened, but it's told like a story. So what is the genre?**	Repeats causes of the problem Clarifies the genre characteristics and asks students to identify the genre
Students	Narrative nonfiction.	
Mr. H	**Yes, it's a true story called narrative nonfiction. Turn back to the beginning and read to find out what happened.**	Confirms genre and directs students to read

FIGURE 14-18 *(continued)*

Introduction to *The Glow Below,* Level P

The Glow Below: Creatures That Light Up the Sea (*Fountas & Pinnell Classroom,* in press) is an informational text focusing on different undersea creatures that glow in the dark (see Figure 14-19). Based on the study of bioluminescence, it also describes the work of marine biologist Edie Widder, and the special "eye-in-the-sea" camera and robot that she uses for her research. This is an expository text, with an introductory section, a section describing each of several species, and three sections describing the work of the biologists. It includes some technical terms (some defined in a glossary), a table of contents, and section headings. It also features amazing underwater photography. In Figure 14-20, you can see a sample introduction for this book.

Lure

A Tricky Fish

As you look into the dark, you watch a fish that looks like an alien from outer space swim past your ship. It's really a female anglerfish. She has a glowing stick on her head that looks like a small fishing rod. She uses the stick as a **lure,** or bait, to attract her **prey**. Her prey are the animals she is hunting for food.

In the darkness, other animals cannot see her body. All they can see is the lure, which looks like a bright, tasty snack. But when a hungry animal gets close to the bait—*snap!* The anglerfish eats her prey.

This female anglerfish waits in the deep, dark water for prey. Her huge mouth is open wide for her next meal.

4

5

FIGURE 14-19 Pages 4–5 from *The Glow Below,* Level P

An Introduction to *The Glow Below*, Level P

Speaker	Teacher/Student Interactions	Analysis of Interactions
Ms. L	You have an informational book today. Take a look at the front cover and read the back of the book. Then share your thinking.	Invites observation and thinking
Madison	It's all about animals that glow in the dark, kind of like fireflies. But these are in the ocean.	
Claire	It says that glowing helps them survive but I don't know how.	
Mallory	For fireflies, it helps them find a mate, so maybe that's it.	
Ms. L	These are very interesting animals. There is some information on the inside back cover about Edie Widder, who is a marine biologist and a specialist in bioluminescence, which is the ability of organisms to produce light. You'll read more about her. Look at pages 2 and 3. You can see her diving machine there. What are you thinking?	Shares background information Defines a technical word Directs attention to the photographs Invites interpretation
Mallory	I'd like to ride in that to the bottom of the ocean.	
Shannon	It's really dark down there.	
Ms. L	These animals are fascinating. Look at pages 4 and 5.	Directs attention to the photographs
Darron	Look at those teeth!	
Bethany	It says the female anglerfish waits with her mouth wide open for her next meal.	
Ms. L	Deep in the ocean it is completely dark, but the stick on her head is a lure. It is bait for other animals. Do you see the word *lure* in bold? What does it mean?	Provides background information Directs attention to the meaning of a word
Darron	It says it's something to attract animals, like fish bait.	
Ms. L	Remember that if you don't know the meaning of a word, you can sometimes find a synonym for it. Here, you see the word *bait*, and you can also look in the glossary. You will read about several of these animals and I know you'll enjoy the photographs. Look at page 10 and read the sidebar.	Articulates to ways to derive the meaning of a word Directs attention to the information in the sidebar
Mallory	That's the camera and a diver.	
Claire	It tells about Edie, the one who is the biologist. She takes the pictures.	
Ms. L	In the last three sections, you'll be reading about Edie and her study of these sea creatures. Read the whole book. Be sure to read the sidebars. Then, you can share your thinking.	Previews the last part of the book Prompts to read sidebars Alerts students that they are expected to share thinking

FIGURE 14-20 An Introduction to *The Glow Below*, Level P

Introduction to *Mission: Earth,* Level T

Mission: Earth (*Fountas & Pinnell Classroom,* in press) is a science fiction text (see Figure 14-21). You get your first clue to the genre immediately from the title and the author line, which says, "Translated from the Draxotian by Michael Sullivan." The story is told as a series of electronic communications from Agent Quark to Commander Z, Draxo Defense Forces. The Commander is considering invading the Earth. The story is told entirely from Agent Quark's perspective, but it is clear to the reader (and supported by the illustrations) that Agent Quark is not where he thinks he is. Quark thinks he is in the Earth's military training program as an "Exchange Student," but he's actually in a middle or high school. Thus, Agent Quark misunderstands and misconstrues everything he sees. When he participates in a basketball game, he misunderstands the rules and high jumps into one of the nets. This whole experience makes Quark believe that members of the Earth's military are very tough. He ends up recommending that the commander discard plans to invade earth. In Figure 14-22, you can see a sample introduction for this book.

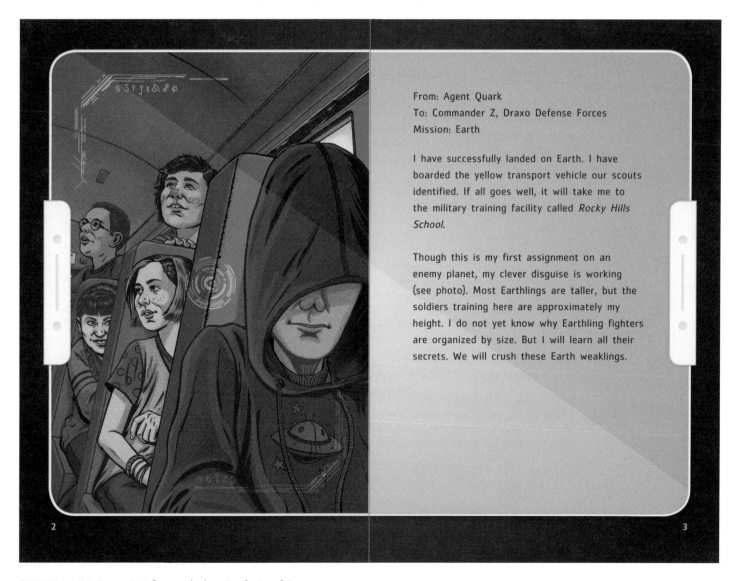

From: Agent Quark
To: Commander Z, Draxo Defense Forces
Mission: Earth

I have successfully landed on Earth. I have boarded the yellow transport vehicle our scouts identified. If all goes well, it will take me to the military training facility called *Rocky Hills School.*

Though this is my first assignment on an enemy planet, my clever disguise is working (see photo). Most Earthlings are taller, but the soldiers training here are approximately my height. I do not yet know why Earthling fighters are organized by size. But I will learn all their secrets. We will crush these Earth weaklings.

FIGURE 14-21 Pages 2–3 from *Mission: Earth,* Level T

An Introduction to *Mission: Earth*, Level T

Speaker	Teacher/Student Interactions	Analysis of Interactions
Mr. A	You are going to read a fiction book today titled *Mission: Earth*. What can you tell about the genre just by reading the front and back covers?	Prompts students to think about genre characteristics and evidence
Ignacio	It's science fiction because it's about outer space.	
Sira	It says it's translated from the Draxotian. There's no such language. They just made that up.	
Aaron	It's kind of funny.	
Mr. A	You're right. It is science fiction and I think you'll find some parts of this book are very funny. Look at pages 2 and 3. Tell what you notice about the illustration and the print.	Confirms student opinion Prompts readers to search for information
Rama	It seems like its e-mail and he's hidden by a hoodie. And his skin is blue!	
Aaron	He looks different from the other kids. They might be on a bus so maybe he's trying to hide. It says, "I have successfully landed on Earth," so he's from another planet.	
Ignacio	A yellow transport might be a school bus.	
Mr. A	Do you see how the whole page layout looks like a tablet of some kind? He's sending pictures and e-mail so you'll want to consider the perspective of each of these layouts. They're on a school bus, but Agent Quark thinks he's at a military training facility on Earth. What kind of confusion could this cause?	Confirms student observations Points out a design characteristic Prompts students to think about perspective Prompts them to think about errors in perspective
Sira	He would be looking at everything like its military.	
Ignacio	What does he want to do?	
Aaron	Maybe he's just checking Earth out.	
Mr. A	Read the last sentence on this page and say what you are thinking.	Asks for literal interpretation
Aaron	He wants to wipe us out!	
Mr. A	He's reporting back to his commander about the invasion of Earth. So as you read this book, notice Agent Quark's thinking. Why is he interpreting everything as he is? We'll talk about that after you finish and we'll also talk about what the writer does to make this book humorous.	Confirms literal interpretation Asks for inference Asks for thinking about the text Communicates expectations

FIGURE 14-22 An Introduction to *Mission: Earth*, Level T

Introduction to *Rules*, Level V

Rules (*Fountas & Pinnell Classroom,* in press) is a realistic fiction text that takes place in an urban neighborhood that is dealing with significant incidences of violence (see Figure 14-23). The main character, teenager Dion, is responsible for taking care of his young sister, Sissy, after school. His mom, who is working, has made "rules" for the two siblings. In Figure 14-24, you can see a sample introduction for this book.

Pop!

I jumped.

"What was that?" Sissy asked, big-eyed.

I secured the bottom lock. "Uh... probably just a car. It must've backfired." I wanted to open the door and look outside in the worst way. Instead I turned the deadbolt tight.

Pop!

I pushed my fingers against the hard metal of the lock. I liked how cold and solid it felt, and I reminded myself I was not scared.

"Sissy! No!"

One second of inattention, that's all it took. Sissy had run to the heavy drapes covering the front window. Well, not really drapes—blankets. Because they were cheaper, Mom said. Thicker, is what I thought.

I grabbed my sister and pulled her back from the window.

6

"Dion, I want to see!" She put her hands on her no-nothing hips and glared at me. "You're not the boss of me."

"There's nothing to see. Besides, you know the rules." I pointed to the wall by the door, where I'd taped rules Mom had dictated. "What are they?"

It was either the diversion or the challenge, but it worked. Sissy had a grumpy look on her face, like an angry little elf, but she turned and recited the list word for word, as if she knew how to read.

"One. Go straight home. Two. Double-lock the door and stay inside. Three. Stay away from the windows."

8

FIGURE 14-23 Pages 6–8 from *Rules*, Level V

An Introduction to *Rules*, Level V

Speaker	Teacher/Student Interactions	Analysis of Interactions
Mr. P	Today you are going to read a book by Patrick Jones. Take a look at the title and the picture on the front of the book. Then read the back and share your thinking.	Draws attention to the title and illustrations Asks readers to search for information about the setting
Janelle	They have rules but maybe they don't follow them.	
Martin	There's a lot of graffiti, and it says the neighborhood is kind of dangerous.	
Charles	He's babysitting for his sister.	
Mr. P	**It's a dangerous neighborhood.** *[Reads the back of the book aloud.]* **On the cover you see Dion and his little sister, Sissy. He's babysitting for her. He picks her up every day from school. She's his responsibility, and his mom has made rules for him to follow when he's taking care of her. For example, he has to take her right home from school. Why do you think that is?**	Communicates information about the characters, setting, and problem
Matthew	If it's a dangerous place, they don't need to be out on the streets or just playing around.	
Charles	But they look like they don't like the rules.	
Julia	My sister and I always have to go straight home after we get off the bus.	
Mr. P	**You will read that this neighborhood is "gang territory." Talk about that.**	Asks for discussion of a significant aspect of the setting
Charles	If it's full of gangs, then it could be dangerous. Even if you're not in a gang, you could end up getting in the middle of something bad.	
Julia	You could get shot.	
Mr. P	**Listen while I read a little of page 8 and look at the picture.** *[Reads the first 14 lines aloud.]* **What's the problem?**	Asks for thinking about the problem
Martin	They've got the windows covered and they have to stay away from them.	
Janelle	A bullet can come in the window, so it's dangerous.	
Mr. P	**How do you think both Dion and Sissy feel about all these rules?**	Asks for inference
Matthew	He doesn't like being tied down to his little sister every day, and she wants to do things like look out the window.	
Charles	They don't like all the rules.	
Mr. P	**You'll learn more about the rules. As you read, think about the problem in this story and how Dion tries to solve it.**	Draws attention to the story problem

FIGURE 14-24 An Introduction to *Rules*, Level V

Assisting Learning

As you look across these introductions, you will notice variations in the way teachers engage students in conversation. While the overarching goals are the same, teachers' selection of goals and language vary as they respond to students who are at different levels. You would not want to standardize a text introduction so much that it becomes a rote performance. Even where we have written lessons to support teachers as they begin to implement guided reading, we use the term "suggested language." We find that as teachers implement lessons, they adjust language in response to students. What is constant is the precision of the language. Skillful teachers try not to make a point over and over, consuming instructional time with their own voices. They are always listening intently to students and responding in a way that confirms in order to take them further. They avoid long, questioning periods looking for the answer they want, and, in general, they avoid extravagant praise. They avoid repeating and/or lecturing on what students have already shown they know. As you grow accustomed to introducing books to students, you will find that you have a kind of repertoire of responses from which you select, keeping the readers in mind.

The selection and introduction to the text work together to help the reader attend to information from different sources while maintaining a strong sense of meaning. Teacher actions related to the text selection and introduction are consistent with the concept of "guided participation," as explained by Rogoff (1990). Rogoff describes how routine activities support children's ability to focus attention on new aspects of a task. Additional features of guided participation include tacit communication, supportive structuring of novices' efforts, and transferring responsibility for handling skills to novices. Teachers support students' learning through tacit as well as explicit communication. In the introductions modeled in this chapter, the teachers demonstrate processes that are important in taking a stance toward a text. The conversational tone, as teacher and students wonder together what will happen, stimulates thinking. In both the selection and introduction, teachers support the novice's efforts. Students can bring their own ideas to the text and use them. Even in rich introductions, teachers begin to transfer responsibility to the readers.

Clay summarizes the critical instructional role that a story introduction can play in helping readers expand their processing systems. "Book introductions enlarge the range of what children can do with whole stories at a first reading. They highlight a particular kind of support for the reader that teaching practice often ignores. With a whole view of the uninterrupted story, children have a feel for the progression of the story through to its climax, so the story itself provides a support within which the detailed processing of information in the text occurs," (Clay *By Different Paths*, 175).

Careful book selection and a thoughtful introduction to a text continue to be important even as readers become increasingly competent. Even as adults, we often benefit from book recommendations and introductions by colleagues. It is a mistake to think of teaching as only what the teacher does when the student is reading the text. The selection and introduction of a text set the scene for successful processing of the text, and support the reader's ability to sustain effective reading behaviors for increasingly longer periods of time. The truest test of a teacher's selection of and introduction to a book is the students' reading of it, which will provide evidence that they understood the text and were able to use it to develop more effective strategic actions.

Suggestions for Professional Development

1. Work with a group of colleagues to collaborate on constructing book introductions.

2. Gather a collection of leveled books at a variety of levels that teachers are likely to use within the next few weeks in guided reading lessons. (As an alternative, have each teacher bring a title that they plan to use with one of their groups.)

3. Have them work with a partner to analyze the text using the Ten Text Characteristics form (available in Online Resources).

4. Then have them work with their partner to prepare a book introduction to the book, even noting some "suggested language." (Of course, they are suggesting the language for themselves, but when they actually work with students in the lesson, they may find changes are needed.)

5. Partners can role play the introduction to get a feel for the interactions while the group observes, and invite further suggestions.

6. Each person leaves the meeting with the goal of implementing the introductions with their students and making a video clip (with a phone or tablet) to bring back and share with colleagues. They can also download the self-reflection form from Online Resources to think about it.

SECTION **FOUR**

Effective Decision Making Within the Guided Reading Lesson

The chapters in this section focus on the very important area of "teaching for strategic actions," to get you started with teaching and prompting that fosters students' agency and independent problem solving as they process a text. Everything you do in the guided reading lesson works toward the goal of students' development of a reading process—one that expands and grows more efficient with use, and one that assures efficient use of information in the text, fluency and phrasing, and a high level of reading comprehension.

We begin with a broad discussion of the systems of strategic actions that readers build in their heads, and then move to examples of teaching in the key areas of monitoring and searching, correcting, solving words, and fluency. The next chapter differs in that it simultaneously offers a summary of understandings about teaching for strategic actions, and a tool for use during your teaching. *The Fountas & Pinnell Literacy Continuum* provides a highly detailed list of behaviors and understandings that a reader needs to use at each level of the text gradient, but in this chapter we identify some specific priorities to get you started. A chart identifies the high-priority areas of strategic actions in oral reading for each level of text in the gradient, and provides examples of language to facilitate the reader's construction of an effective processing system. We have selected key areas of processing observable in oral reading from *The Literacy Continuum*. For each, a specific teacher action is provided. We see this chart as an "in action" tool that will help you teach for the learning students need to accomplish in order to move forward.

Finally, we address teaching for the important dimensions of comprehension across the lesson to assure deep understanding of texts across genres and levels.

CHAPTER 15

Teaching for Systems of Strategic Actions in Guided Reading

I reserve the word "strategy" for in-the-head neural activity initiated by the learner and hidden from the teacher's view.

–Marie Clay

The purpose of guided reading is to help each reader to build an effective, efficient, in-the-head network of strategic actions for processing texts. Every teaching move is directed at helping students become self-initiating, self-regulating readers who are independent, flexible, and confident.

The small group is a social situation in which students can talk with others about a book. They are reading the same book that you have carefully selected because it offers opportunities to learn and it is also one that will engage students and give them plenty to think and talk about. With your skillful teaching the book is within the students' ability to read with proficiency. You have created a setting within which they can work at the edge of their learning, and within which your teaching will be most effective in expanding their reading power.

The goal of every guided reading lesson is to teach readers how to engage in strategic actions that they can apply again the next day and thereafter as they read other texts—they must learn to initiate a set of actions that parallel those of proficient readers. We do not mean that students simply learn one strategy a day, or learn a new word or set of words. They do more than that—they make small but significant, incremental shifts in their processing power as they engage in productive reading behaviors. They learn systems for performing those actions and even at very early levels, they learn in a complex way.

361

A strategic action is not directly observable. Strategies are cognitive operations that take place in the brain. Clay refers to the processing as "fast brainwork." What we can do is look for behavioral evidence and infer that strategic actions are taking place in the head. In *The Literacy Continuum* we have provided detailed descriptions of observable behaviors and understandings that are evidence of strategic actions across the levels of the text gradient. Your goal is to teach in a way that supports the reader in constructing these actions. As Clay says, "Acts of reading are acts of construction, not instruction," (2001, 137). The reader builds and rebuilds the systems as it works on increasingly challenging texts.

Thousands (or an uncountable number) of strategic actions are probably taking place in a reader's head as she processes a text. We have presented these actions in twelve major categories with labels because teachers need words to talk with each other about what they think is going on in the brain (see Figure 15-1).

All of these systems are in use simultaneously as the reader processes print. The reader needs to orchestrate the actions in a smoothly operating process. In the proficient reader, most of the strategic actions are rapidly and unconsciously applied, leaving most of the attention free to become immersed in the story or think about the topic.

Highly competent readers detect the most important information, making the

© 2015 by Irene C. Fountas and Gay Su Pinnell. Portsmouth, NH: Heinemann.

FIGURE 15-1 Systems of Strategic Actions for Reading

most of their efforts. They anticipate what could follow, and as they search for and find new information, they link it to prior knowledge. They employ existing knowledge of genre and how texts are structured and use it as a way to predict and anticipate. They initiate problem-solving actions, demonstrate independence, and engage in self-regulation. They have a sense of agency—they have power over their reading and know they can use it for many different purposes.

We have applied the metaphor of piano playing to show the twelve systems of strategic actions operating in an orchestrated way. When you play the piano, you are not thinking of each note as a single entity; you think of continuous melody. But at the same time, you perform a series of complex actions in a sequence that makes the melody the same whenever you play it. Although beginners may start with learning middle C and even play a scale, it is ridiculous to think of piano playing as exercising each single muscle, one after another. If you focus on one finger at a time, you are likely to stumble along slowly, or, at best, produce a very mechanical version. But, every person might produce a slightly different version based on interpretation. Experience, knowledge, and emotion all feeds into it, just as with reading. It is the thrill of actually producing a simple melody that keeps the beginner going. A beginner may start with a very simple piece, but still make meaningful music. A proficient player might practice a particularly complex part of a piece over and over, but always returns to the larger piece, with the goal of the performance as a whole.

In this chapter we discuss the nature of strategic actions and describe how you can teach for systems of strategic actions across the guided reading lesson. In every part of the lesson, you call for thinking. We have inserted the word "for" after "teach" because everything you do supports the reader in acquiring and expanding strategic actions, which, ultimately, must be constructed by the reader, but not without help. You can demonstrate, prompt for, and reinforce effective actions. But don't make the mistake of thinking you just "sit back" and let the reader do it. Teaching in guided reading is precise and intensive; as a teacher, you are persistent in prompting readers to initiate effective reading behaviors. As they develop, they construct and integrate new ways of thinking because you are gently leading them forward. Almost all children need teaching to achieve the level of reading proficiency required of readers in our future society.

What Is a Strategy?

Clay (2001, 91) describes young children as "assembling working systems" for literacy. These systems are constantly expanding and growing stronger provided the student is reading successfully, and can be built only through processing continuous text. As the reader works on text, reading across words, sentences, and paragraphs, he gathers information from a number of sources. He learns how to find and use the information in print. According to Clay (2001, 98), readers use both visible and invisible information. The visible information includes the letters, the way they are grouped together in words, the spacing, font size, the way the words and punctuation are arranged on the page, and the graphics or illustrations. Everything else is invisible and refers to the information brought to the text by the reader and the author (text experiences, language knowledge, emotions, memories, background knowledge).

> The rules of syntax (the "grammar" or the way words are strung together in regular patterns)

> The phonology or sound system of language (that connects to the letters and letter clusters)

> The meaning or semantic system (the meaning speakers attach to words, phrases, sentences, expressions, and entire sections or texts as well as whole texts)

Every bit of this information is important and essential in reading, which demonstrates that the common polarization of phonics and meaning-based instruction is misguided. We need to teach readers in ways that help them develop strategic actions for efficiently and effectively using *all* the necessary information in a smoothly orchestrated way. This includes teaching for effective word-analysis skills while constructing meaning using language. It is a process of supporting the reader to construct and integrate efficient ways of finding and using the entire range of information in the text.

The beginner reads slowly and may have to access different sources of information in some sequence (according to his attention and current understanding). The proficient reader works on different kinds of information simultaneously, what Clay calls "parallel processing." The strategic actions are a rapid-fire network:

> The learner is gaining a strategic control over how external and internal information is dealt with in the brain. By means of a network of unobservable-in-the-head strategies the reader is able to attend to information from different sources (for example, reading and writing, oral language and visual learning, meaning and phonology). The good reader can work with both internal and external information and make decisions about matches and mismatches in his responses. A dynamic network of interactive strategies allows the reader to change direction at any point in the processing path. (Clay 1991, 328)

Items and Strategies

Another way to look at the way students process texts is to distinguish between items and strategies (Clay 1991). It is essential for the reader to develop a repertoire of many items of information—letters, sounds, letter-sound relationships, words, and parts of words. That's the "raw material" of reading. But strategies or strategic actions are ways of working with this material. At the same time we help the young reader develop a bank of items, such as known letters and their related sounds, he needs to learn to use this information in an efficient way on the run while reading text. The reader can use letter-sound information, for example, to:

> Self-monitor reading by noticing a mismatch between the word he said and the first letter and associated sound.

> Start saying a new word and solve it (in connection with meaning from the pictures and language structure).

> Make connections between a new word and a known word to solve it.

The above description refers to a beginning reader's work on very simple texts in which language structure and meaning are readily available. But by engaging in these actions, the reader learns *how to learn*. He is developing a *system* for learning. A strategy then is a way of operating on print; and through the use of strategies, readers learn more every time they read. As Clay says, "A few items and a powerful strategy might make it very easy to learn a great deal more," (1991, 331).

Readers do need to acquire items of knowledge. They need to learn the letters and their accompanying sounds and they need an ever-increasing repertoire of known words. But working on items only in isolation is perhaps the least efficient way to learn. We once worked at a school where a group of paraprofessionals were charged with using word cards to teach five new words a week to first graders. By Friday, all of the children could read the list perfectly, so on Monday, they were introduced to five more words, with the goal of learning 150+ words by year end. You can guess what happened: by the third week, the children had forgotten most of the words from the first week. Learning five words by drilling each day is easy, and, in fact, children memorizing the list had to use only minimal visual information to distinguish the words from each other. Using them in isolation, they had no other information to self-check their responses.

Readers need to attend to words within meaningful continuous text so that a large amount of information is available to help them self-monitor. In Figure 15-2, you see a diagram by Stouffer (2011, 24), which visually displays the contrast between working with words in isolation and taking words apart while reading. Notice how much more information is available to the reader in learning how to access the words (or visual information) while reading continuous text. The reader

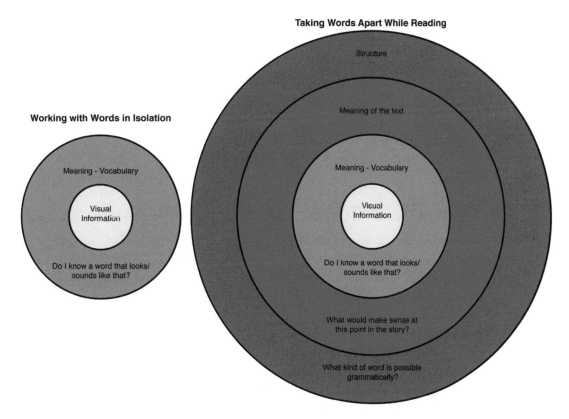

FIGURE 15-2 Sources of Information Available to the Reader When Working with Words in Isolation and Taking Words Apart While Reading Continuous Text

gains the support of the meaning and language structure to learn more about words.

In both isolated word work and reading words in text, the reader can use the visual information—the letters and word parts—and the invisible information—the reader's knowledge of the meaning of the word. The reader can ask herself, "Do I know a word that starts like that?" "Do I know a word that sounds like that?" The reader can use the letters in sequence and connect them with sounds to say the word and can notice larger word parts for efficient solving. The reader can think what the word means to weave more memory around it.

In reading continuous text, the reader can additionally use more information—the meaning of the text and the structure of the language. In addition to the questions above, the reader can ask herself, "What would make sense at this point in the story?" "What kind of word is possible grammatically?" and "What sounds right?" The reader can use this information to learn words and to learn how to monitor and self-correct. Ultimately, a known word can be instantly recognized in isolation as well as within continuous print, but from the beginning the reader must use both.

Reading as Thinking

Reading is thinking, cued by the ideas the writer has expressed in print. Writing and reading are also forms of communication. In its time, written language was an astounding invention. It allowed people to receive messages from distant places or different times. Of course, since the twentieth century, technology has also allowed us to see images and hear the words of people from times past. Nonetheless, written language remains one of the most significant and powerful inventions of all time. And it is even *more* important today with the rapid and constant communication media we now employ.

The reader's in-the-head processing system takes the written signs, and in a smoothly working operation, transforms them into language. The proficient reader doesn't need to voice the sounds and words. Although we cannot directly observe the operations, we can infer that the reader's mind is going directly to the ideas in the writing rather than consciously saying the words, even silently. What we want for all readers is an efficient system that allows them to think about the meaning of texts.

Teaching for Strategies

Just as strategies cannot be directly observed, neither can they simply be "practiced" in a drill-like way. They must be developed through authentic use in pursuit of meaning. Anyone who has taught someone to swim (an orchestrated action far less complex than reading) knows that merely explaining or demonstrating the process will be of little help. The swimmer must get in the water and experience for herself the physical movement of her limbs, the buoyancy of the water (which varies by individual), and the joy of forward movement. The best swimming teachers immerse their students in water play; they have swimmers blow bubbles to get the feel of breathing; they have them float face down and on the back, and experiment with movement. They encourage their students to relax and enjoy the water. We can apply this metaphor to teaching someone to read. Children need to immerse themselves fully in the text, experience it as individuals, and use everything they know to make meaning from it.

When we talk about teaching for strategies, we are not talking about a specific teaching approach for each new strategy, but about a repertoire of responses that help students orchestrate different strategic actions smoothly and simultaneously. In other words, readers do not learn to solve words in grades 1 and 2 and then learn to infer in grade 3, and learn to analyze in grade 4. Every reader uses a developing system of strategies that is like a spiral; it includes the multitude of strategic actions represented in the twelve categories, and the reader applies those strategies every time she reads, throughout her life. The beginning reader's system is not simple, but also not yet fully developed. The beginning reader may need to slow down and consciously apply word solving, monitoring, and searching, but it expands rapidly to the point where readers are applying highly complex operations with lightning speed.

Responsive Teaching

To support the learning described above, your moves must be focused and supportive, designed to bring forward examples that will help readers learn how to read. These skilled teaching moves are informed by your close observation of each readers' behaviors (see Chapter 9, Figure 9-3).

To be powerful, teaching must be responsive to the learner. Of course, you have overall goals guiding your vision of what you want readers to achieve, but your teaching is a bridge that reaches from the learner at this point in time and those high expectations.

Close Observation

As shown in Figure 9-3, you begin with close observation of reading, writing, and language behaviors. If you are using a benchmark assessment system, you will start the year with a great deal of information that will be useful in forming groups, selecting texts, and teaching the first guided reading lessons. But if you are engaging learners in lessons daily and teaching effectively, your readers will change significantly. They may not need a higher level text, but they will gradually exhibit the composite of effective behaviors you have taught them with greater ease and fluency at the level. To detect the shifts in reading behavior that are evidence of effective teaching, engage in ongoing observation. You make these observations "on the run" during every lesson as you listen in to oral reading and observe talk; but, you will also want to take regular running records to give you a systematic source of information. You need a system for taking running records more frequently on the lowest-achieving students (e.g., once a week or every two weeks); less frequently on average readers (e.g., every three or four weeks); and even less frequently on above-grade-level readers (e.g., every 4–6 weeks). Your system also depends on class size and other factors. But you need an efficient system that you can manage, as the information you gain will fuel the direction of your teaching. Without a system of gaining information about each reader, you will be teaching without the children.

A running record will involve a student reading a whole book at lower levels, but at upper levels, between about 150 and 200 words from the whole text is sufficient. It takes only a few minutes. Some teachers have children come in the room, settle down, and read their independent reading books for a little while first thing in the morning. This is a good time to take one record. Sometimes a teacher will take an individual student for a few minutes and then call the guided reading group together, or keep a student after the lesson in order to take a record.

The information you get from observation is invaluable—don't file it away or turn it in and forget it. Instead, look for patterns across time and use it to guide your every action.

Using Behavioral Evidence to Infer in-the-Head Strategic Activities

Just as you administer formal assessment two or three times a year, your ongoing observations provide the data you need to infer in-the-head operations. The reading itself provides powerful evidence of word solving, monitoring, searching, and fluency because you record the reader's stops, starts, and attempts at self-correction—both successful and unsuccessful. You make notes on phrasing and fluency. You can respond to specific behaviors very briefly during reading or go back and teach for processing strategies after reading.

Prioritize Behaviors and Understandings to Notice, Teach for, and Support

You will notice a great many productive reading behaviors as you observe oral reading and listen to the talk about reading.

Before the Reading

Think about the reading behaviors students control and need to control as you plan the introduction to the text. As you orient the students to the text, you can help them learn how to think about challenges, like noticing how to look at a word part, hearing the tricky syntax, and searching for information in illustrations. The introduction to the text is your first teaching opportunity directed at your selected emphases. The task now is to select what will be *most* productive for the readers at this point in time.

During the Reading

For individual prompting while students are reading the text, think about the following questions:

- How does the reader engage with the meaning of the story?
- How is the reader working on problems?

> Where did the reader show an effective behavior that you want his to perpetuate?

> What behavior does the reader nearly know that will help him expand his processing system?

> How does the reader use self-correction?

> How does the reader cope with tricky language structures?

> Is the reading steadily becoming fluent and phrased?

> Where did the reader show confusion that you want to smooth out?

After the Reading

For teaching following the reading, think about what will benefit most of the readers in the group:

> What new, effective behavior did several members of the group demonstrate?

> What effective behavior did one reader demonstrate that others also need to learn?

> What effective behaviors are very important for all readers to learn next?

The Literacy Continuum will be helpful here, because you can continually refer to the particular text level to guide your observation and selection of reading behaviors, to notice, teach for, and support.

Teaching for Change in Strategic Actions

Use *Prompting Guide Part 1 for Oral Reading* as a resource for powerful language that will be helpful to readers. You can use language "on-the-run" for brief encounters during oral reading. You can also use this language for quick teaching after reading. You will find language to *demonstrate,* which you use when the student does not know how to initiate the behavior and needs explicit help. You can find language to *prompt for* the behavior once the student understands it and needs a reminder. You can find language to *reinforce* the behavior once the reader has demonstrated it independently. After the reader is consistently demonstrating the behavior, then you do not need to draw attention to it with specific language; you have other priorities for teaching. Indeed, if you look at *The Literacy Continuum* for each text level, you can see that you will never run out of teaching opportunities! In Chapter 19, we will help you begin to think about how to respond moment to moment to the reading behaviors you observe in oral reading.

Teaching for Strategic Actions Before, During, and After Reading

In the chapters that follow, we will focus on thinking within, beyond, and about the text in specific areas of teaching such as monitoring and searching, visual processing, and fluency. We provide a general introduction and rationales for the kind of action you can take before, during, and after reading to support readers in the development of a processing system (see Figure 15-3).

Teaching for Strategic Actions Across the Guided Reading Lesson

Before the Reading	During the Reading	After the Reading
Introduction • Draw attention to visual features of print, words (letters and word parts), and punctuation. • Familiarize students with complex language structures. • Provide support for thinking about the meaning of words. • Foreshadow the meaning or organization of the whole text. • Provide background information needed for students to make connections and interpret the text.	*Reading the Text* *Teach* • Demonstrate or model for the reader an explicit way to think about problem solving in the text and/or tell the reader explicitly what to do. *Prompt* • Call for the reader to think or act in a particular way that he has learned. • Remind the reader to do what he has been taught how to do to problem-solve. *Reinforce* • Use facilitative language to confirm the reader's independent use of problem-solving actions. • Reinforce only newly emerging behaviors so they will become consistent.	*Discussion* • Probe students' thinking. • Ask for thinking within, beyond, and about the text. • Explore what students noticed about the text. • Ask for evidence to support thinking. *Teach for Processing Strategies* • Draw explicit attention to a part of the text with opportunities to extend thinking beyond and about the text. • Demonstrate, teach for or reinforce problem solving using language structure, meaning, or visual information. • Demonstrate, teach for, or reinforce taking words apart.

FIGURE 15-3 Teaching for Strategic Actions Across the Guided Reading Lesson

Before the Reading

When students enter a challenging text "cold," it may take several pages for them to understand what the book is about, derive the meaning of some unfamiliar words, and understand the organization of the text. By then, interest is considerably diminished and much meaning is lost. The reader needs rich understanding from the beginning of the text so that he can carry it through as a support for integrating the new ideas that are presented as he progresses. Without adequate understanding from the beginning, he won't know how to effectively use multiple sources of information for problem solving. An introduction to the text is essential.

Introducing the Text

Many of us start a new book only to put it down and say, "I just couldn't get into it," or "I found it so confusing," or "I just wasn't interested in the subject matter." Maybe because you are a successful reader (or very determined), you persevere with your reading and find the book, in the end, to be interesting. You learn something fascinating or develop new insights from the reading. Or perhaps you put the book aside; but when others say how good it is, you wonder what they are talking about and sometimes you pick it up again.

Here is another scenario: what if a friend told you something about the book before you began reading—gave you some background information as well as some intriguing clues as to what you might find in the book. The friend might share what she enjoyed about the book or even say, "You need to go beyond the first couple of chapters. It really gets good at this point." This information is brief, but it might help you push forward in the book, past the point at which you may have stopped before.

Remember that early readers and struggling readers are even more vulnerable and tend to lose interest and give up sooner. The introduction is, above all, a time to engage the interest of every reader and help them realize that the book will be worthwhile. In many ways, the whole-class book talk does the same for books that students choose for themselves at the independent level (see Chapter 23); but in guided reading, students are taking on a challenging text and a more supportive introduction is needed.

The introduction allows you to draw students' attention to the text in a way that will support readers' use of multiple sources of information for problem solving. You select features of the text—words, sentences, language structures—that will be useful in monitoring and, when appropriate, self-correcting. Give attention to these features in a way that the students who are reading it immediately afterward can draw on as they move through the text. For example, saying a tricky language pattern in unison helps the student to parse it more easily than reading word by word without support. An example might be:

> "Not giving Mary a present hurt her feelings."

At first glance this might not seem to be so tricky. After all, the words are pretty easy. But to a beginning reader, the word *not* is not usually followed by an *–ing* noun (gerund); and the reader has to understand that the entire phrase, "not giving Mary a present," is the subject of the sentence. Also the reader has to understand that *her* modifies *feelings*. In fact, this is a sentence we would not want in the early books that children read. We would want to challenge the beginning reader with some sentences that are different from oral language, but much of the text should be close to oral language. As readers grow, however, they internalize more and more knowledge of written language syntax from hearing read-alouds and from their own reading; and, they need to encounter a gradually increasingly complexity in syntax.

Attention to a few important words gives the reader agency and familiarity when he is presented with them in the text. Just having heard and seen it recently makes it easier to decode. Knowing the meaning of some of the words eases the ability to understand them as they are processed within sentences and paragraphs. The reader still has to use visual information in connection with meaning, but he has a slight advantage in that he has heard the word within a meaningful context. None of this attention in the introduction is quite enough to place the word into the reader's long-term memory; there is still work to to be done, but he can read the word with the background knowledge of print and meaning.

The introduction also gives readers a "leg up" in terms of the topic and the meaning of the whole text. You provide enough information to help the reader understand the meaning of about two or three key words, the structure of the text (how it "works"), and the topic. Your exposition of this kind of information will depend on your analysis of what the readers already know how to do. But remember that any information you provide in the introduction serves as background information readers can apply while reading, even if they acquired it only a few minutes ago. They get the experience of bringing background information to the comprehension of the text.

Reading the Text

If the text selection and introduction are effective, readers process the text with a *minimum* of support—but that support is selective and powerful. Readers are working through the text, reading for meaning and self-monitoring. Additionally, at about level C, you should expect phrasing and, progressively, you can expect fluent reading (with some slow-downs) even on the first reading. You can listen in and intervene quickly using facilitative language (see *Prompting Guide Part 1*).

You can *teach* for problem-solving actions, which involves showing the student how to, for example:

- Take a word apart.
- Read with phrasing.
- Self-correct noticing the first letter or letters.
- Reread to capture the syntactic pattern.
- Reread to notice the picture and self-correct.
- Use punctuation and reflect it with the voice.

Your selection of actions to demonstrate depends on the level of the text and what the student needs. This, in fact, is the ultimate challenge in teaching—to meet the reader where he is.

You can *prompt* for problem-solving actions, which asks the student to employ a particular action that he knows either because you have taught it or because he has learned it on his own. For example, you can prompt for the student to:

- Notice and use visual information.
- Notice what was wrong.
- Look for a known word part.
- Make it sound like talking.

You can *reinforce* problem-solving actions, confirming the reader's use of them independently. You would use this only when the behavior is newly emerging, and it does not mean simply complimenting or affirming a student's reading, by saying things like, "That's what good readers do." In fact, it is best to avoid this kind of evaluative terminology altogether. It is far more powerful to simply confirm the precise behavior, for example:

- You checked that with your finger all by yourself.
- You noticed the first part and it helped you.
- You knew something was wrong.
- You tried it another way.
- You put your words together and made it sound like talking.

Prompting Guide Part 1 provides many examples of language that have been found to be effective in supporting students' processing during oral reading, but it is important to remember that these interactions are very brief. For every student, most of the time is spent independently processing the text.

Discussion and Teaching for Processing Strategies

There are two opportunities to teach for strategic actions after the reading, and you can move smoothly from one to the other. The *discussion* is a time to ask in an open-ended way, for students to articulate their thinking about the text. Encourage them to talk with each other, to ask for questions, and to clarify points. To guide this discussion, think about the key understandings within, beyond, and about the text that you have identified. You can prompt and ask questions to guide students towards the deeper messages of the text. Ultimately, you want them to derive a message from the text that they can apply to their own lives, and that goes beyond the literal meaning of the text itself.

Based on your observations, select teaching moves that will develop the reader's problem-solving abilities. You have the opportunity to revisit a part of the text to draw attention to information that will prompt any action across the entire range of strategic actions, for example:

- Taking a word apart and checking whether it fits with the meaning or the structure of language.
- Thinking about how the writer reveals the message of the text.
- Noticing how the writer begins a text to engage readers.
- Noticing how characters change and develop.
- Noticing the problem in a story.

Teaching for processing strategies following the discussion takes only a few minutes. It is your opportunity to attend to learning that will be most helpful to the readers based on your observations during today's lesson. Make the most of it with powerful language that tells students directly what to do, prompts them to act, or reinforces actions that build an effective processing system.

Moments Full of Opportunity

You can see that a guided reading lesson is full of opportunity for powerful teaching. Your text analysis and close observation of reading behaviors are the most important resources for your moment-to-moment teaching in guided reading, but the foundation is your tentative and growing understanding of the reading process and the way individuals are learning how to read. These sources of information fuel your teaching and assure each student becomes competent and independent in processing a variety of texts.

Suggestions for Professional Development

1. Work with grade-level colleagues to do some careful observation and analysis of guided reading lessons. You can find examples for observation in several ways:

   ▶ Use *The Continuum of Literacy Learning Teaching Library* (Heinemann 2011) to access videos of guided reading in the range of levels that are of interest to you and your group.

   ▶ Make several videos of guided reading lessons in the same classroom at different levels (you can simply use a smart phone or tablet). Be sure that these lessons are not long because you want to watch at least two, and better three, within about one-and-a-half hours. They should be fifteen to twenty-five minutes in length depending on the level.

   ▶ Select some of the sample teacher/student interactions you have read in this book. Read the text introductions or discussions, first blocking out the third column, which identifies the purpose of the teaching moves (analysis).

   ▶ Have each participant bring a video of at least one part of a guided reading lesson.

2. As a group, work through the parts of each lesson. Ask colleagues to agree that this is not the time to evaluate the lesson or to talk about the "nuts and bolts." Your goal, together, is to identify what the teacher is trying to do—what he is *teaching for.*

   ▶ Don't stop for discussion. You are not trying to "pick the lesson apart." The sole purpose is to identify teaching moves and their goals.

   ▶ Have group members try to capture as many "teaching moves" as they can without discussing them.

   ▶ After viewing, have them work as partners to write the teacher's goal for each move.

   ▶ Bring the group's comments together in a short group discussion (limit to ten minutes).

   ▶ Caution again against evaluation. The purpose of this exercise is to raise self-awareness about the purpose of your teaching decisions.

   ▶ If the teacher is present, have him hold comments until after the group discussion. Sometimes observers see more than the teacher is actually aware of; or, they may have missed some of the teacher's intentions. Then the teacher can respond.

3. It's important in this session to observe and comment on more than one lesson. The idea is not to find lessons to imitate, but to grow in the ability to analyze one's own lessons.

4. Set a follow-up meeting to discuss:

  ▶ Were you more aware of the purpose of your teaching moves in guided reading? How?

  ▶ How was your guided reading teaching different in the last few weeks?

  ▶ View two more lessons in the same way and discuss them.

CHAPTER 16

Teaching for Monitoring, Searching, and Self-Correction Behaviors

All readers need to find and use different kinds of information in print and combine the information they find with what they carry in their heads from their past experiences with language.

–Marie Clay

One of your first goals in teaching for strategic actions is to make your students *active* as readers so that they can learn how to orchestrate in-the-head actions to process text smoothly and efficiently. These readers take *action* as they find and work on information in print to make sure all the sources of information—the meaning, language, and print—fit together. Your students need to understand that when they engage in these in-the-head actions, the result will be successful, meaningful reading, and that even if they make mistakes, they don't give up. This active behavior is even more important than getting the reading "right," because it signals that the learner is constructing a network of strategic actions that will make up the processing system. Of course, they will learn to read accurately, but error behavior can tell you a great deal about whether the reader is self-monitoring and searching actively for all sources of information. Clay (2001) developed the running record as a tool so that teachers would be able to analyze how the reader is building his literacy processing system and can use the information immediately to inform teaching:

> When teachers take records of children reading texts, those teachers record children searching for particular information, finding it, associating it, link-

ing it to prior experience, moving across visual, phonological, language, and semantic information, checking how it is going together, backing up and looking for new hypotheses, self-correcting, reading on, using peripheral vision and syntactic anticipation. (Clay 2001, 114)

Take a look at the text and the running record (Figure 16-1) of Nikki's reading of a level D book, *Maddy's Loose Tooth* (*Fountas & Pinnell Classroom*, in press) shown in Figure 16-2. Nikki's reading process is just beginning to emerge. She is able to read left to right, return to the left, and match voice to print on three lines of text, and has learned about twenty high-frequency words. She knows most of the sounds that are connected to consonants and even a couple of consonant digraphs, but is just beginning to put that knowledge into action on print.

Nikki read *Maddy's Loose Tooth* with 92% accuracy. She corrected one-third of her errors, so that gives you plenty of reading behavior to analyze. At this point, her reading behavior is quite overt, so as a teacher, you will have a great deal of information. Still, treat your thinking as hypotheses rather than certainties. What you are really looking for are patterns of behavior over time. That is how you can truly see the shifts in the reader's processing power.

On page 2, Nikki started the word *tooth* and then read it correctly, so it is not an error. On the second line, she sounded an /m/, perhaps meaning to say *Mike* again, but she stopped quickly and self-corrected, probably using visual information. (It does fit with the syntax, but since *he* is only the first word in the sentence and you analyze only up to the error.) Possibly, she knows the word *he*. Nikki substituted *bits* for *bit* but did not notice a mismatch and read on. Probably she was using visual information because her substitution did not fit meaning or structure.

On page 4, Nikki read the first five words accurately but substituted *tooth* for *too* at the end of the line, an error that did not make sense. Nikki did not self-correct, but she did reread the line, a behavior indicating that she thought something might be wrong. On the third line, she said *didn't* for *did*, which fits the meaning and the structure and represents a close prediction. However, when she came to the word *not*, she read it accurately without correcting the word. Her final reading did not accurately reflect syntax although possibly it was meaningful to her.

On page 8, Nikki started the word *wiggled* with the first part of the word and then read it accurately, but then substituted *little* for *baby*, a meaningful prediction that fits with syntax; but she did not notice the mismatch with the visual information.

On page 10, she read *he* for *she* in the second line. You do not know whether she thought Sam was a boy; if so, she ignored the meaning in the picture and did not notice the mismatch with visual information. She read *pulled* for *pushed*, a substitution that made sense, sounded right with the structure, and also reflected some attention to visual information. When it came to the word *with*, Nikki sounded the /w/ but ended up appealing to the teacher.

On page 12, Nikki again substituted *pulled* for *pushed* but then self-corrected. It may be that she was able to search further for visual information, knew that *pulled* wasn't quite right, and tried another alternative. It may be that she thought about the meaning of what Maddy was doing with her tongue and thought *pushed* was more accurate. It is unlikely that she worked through the word using the visual

Pg.	*Maddy's Loose Tooth* Level D
2	Mike had a loose tooth. He bit into an apple. His tooth came out.
4	Maddy had a loose tooth, too. She bit into an apple. But her tooth did not come out.
6	Ani had a loose tooth. She wiggled and wiggled it. Her tooth came out.

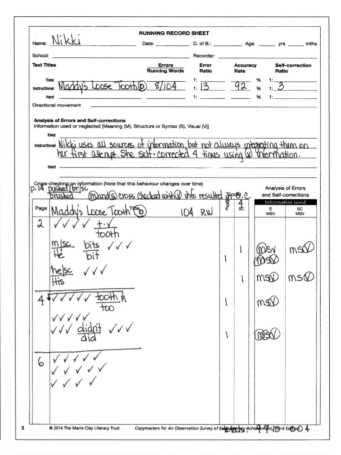

Pg.	*Maddy's Loose Tooth* Level D
8	Maddy wiggled and wiggled her tooth. The tooth did not come out.
10	Sam had a loose tooth. She wiggled and pushed her tooth with her tongue. Her tooth came out.
12	Maddy wiggled and pushed her tooth with her tongue. The tooth did not come out.
14	Maddy brushed her teeth. She brushed and brushed. And her tooth came out!

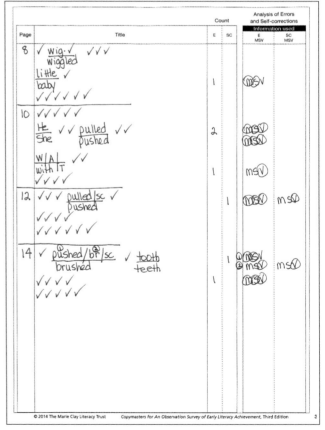

FIGURE 16-1 Nikki's Running Record of *Maddy's Loose Tooth*, Level D

FIGURE 16-2 Pages 8–9 and 14–15 of *Maddy's Loose Tooth*, Level D

information and noticed the /sh/, but it is possible. You will need to watch for more of that kind of behavior.

Page 14 offered another challenge. Nikki read *pushed* (a word she had just figured out) for *brushed*, noticed the *br* and read the word accurately. Perhaps she also glanced at the picture, which clearly showed tooth brushing. We can hypothesize that she noticed visual information because she pronounced the /br/. Having spent energy on *brushed*, she substituted *tooth* for *teeth*, not noticing the mismatch with visual information. Actually, this error could fit with meaning and syntax.

It's important to point out that in spite of all this reading work, Nikki read with a high accuracy rate and good comprehension, indicating that she is processing a text at level D with proficiency. Her record indicates many strengths. All of the accurate reading Nikki is doing indicates that she *can* self-monitor, search for information, and self-correct. Nikki is *active* in her processing. She is using a variety of sources of information, although not consistently. Her behavior provides ample evidence that she can monitor or check using visual information and possibly meaning. Sometimes, she ignores visual mismatches and responds to others, so it will be important to help her be more consistent in monitoring but also in searching for the information she needs.

Nikki's profile informs the direction for teaching. She is already doing much of the work she needs to do at this level. By selecting texts that will provide problem-solving opportunities, and with strong teaching, you can support her in moving forward. Her active reading behaviors contrast with those of many students—even very young ones—who have become passive and simply wait for the teacher to tell them if they don't know a word. Nikki appealed to the teacher only once, when she had no other sources to consult.

In this chapter, we discussed the value of self-monitoring and searching and, ultimately, self-correction. While these behaviors develop fairly early, they have implications for later development as well. Early passive readers turn into later passive readers, who don't think about their reading but simply perform it. As teachers, we know that we must get readers active from the start. In fact, that is a good principle to guide your teaching. It is important to interact with readers in ways that foster their active problem solving at every level (Askew and Fountas 1998).

Teaching for Self-Monitoring

If students are not actively exhibiting evidence of reading that doesn't make sense, sound right, or look right, it's important to teach hard for self-monitoring.

Early Self-Monitoring

Self-monitoring is one of the earliest behaviors to emerge and one of the most powerful. Consider the examples in Figure 16-3.

These readers are exhibiting a very early form of self-monitoring. They are constructing meaning from the pictures but are using very few visual signposts. Nevertheless, they are able to use one-to-one matching to check on themselves. Reader 1 seems to be sensing syllables in words, and she has the idea that you match one syllable to one group of letters. She points very carefully, and it's not until the end of the line that she realizes something is wrong. Reader 2

> **Reading with pointing—Reader 1:**
>
> | | | run | ing | o | ver | the | bridge | "I ran out of words!" |
> | I | am | running | | over | the | | bridge. | |
>
> **Reading with pointing—Reader 2:**
>
> | | | are | going | to | kick | the | ball | [Stops. Looks puzzled.] |
> | The girls | | run | to | | the | ball. | | |

FIGURE 16-3 Examples of Early Self-Monitoring

starts out pointing, but then "invents" a meaningful text based on the picture. At first glance, you might be concerned about both readers, and it's true that they have much to learn. But both realized something was wrong. They stopped. Reader 1 even gave voice to the problem. Simply stopping because something doesn't make sense, doesn't match, doesn't sound right or look right is evidence of monitoring. This is a critical behavior for effective reading. They have *monitored*; what you want these readers to do next is *search*.

These readers show the following strengths:

▶ They understand that the finger pointing and groups of letters (which they are beginning to understand are *words*) need to match. You can't say more or less words than are in the line.

▶ They know how to point under the words in the correct direction, moving left to right.

▶ They understand that what you read has to sound right as a sentence, and they appear to have some sense of the kinds of sentences they are reading in these easy books.

▶ They understand that what you read has to make sense and match the pictures.

▶ Neither produced nonsense, and neither is willing simply to move on without doing something.

Reader 1 has some misconceptions about matching the voice to the print, and Reader 2 is inventing text. Both will profit from gaining some known words and learning more about the visual features of letters, but what you really want the readers to do right away is go back to the beginning of the line and reread, this time matching more carefully—a searching behavior.

Often you will have beginning readers who have somehow learned simply to move on even if there are many mismatches and what they are reading does not make sense. You don't want that. You may need to teach, prompt for, and reinforce self-monitoring as a top priority. It is important that readers learn from the beginning that they need to *actively* self-monitor. Monitoring is key to self-regulation. From there, they can learn how to take action or problem-solve for themselves.

Many readers do not spontaneously self-monitor, especially in the early learning period. Why should they? Some are accustomed to simply looking at the pictures in a book and telling the story, which is helpful for language development; but they may resist pointing to match because it feels constraining. Reading word by word makes it possible for them to notice visual features of words and put to use their growing understanding of the alphabetic system.

Shared reading (see Chapter 3) is an excellent place to demonstrate and have children participate in voice-print matching. When they read small versions of the books and poems they have encountered in shared reading, they have the opportunity to point on a familiar text (they will have seen it done many times before). As a result of shared reading, many children have control of voice-print match when they begin guided reading lessons. In Figure 16-4, you can see some language that is useful in supporting readers to monitor voice-print match and, then, to use it to monitor reading.

Monitoring Voice-Print Match

Teach	Prompt	Reinforce
◆ "If you run out of words, go back and make it match." [Demonstrate] ◆ "You have too many words. You need to go back and make it match. Let me show you." [Demonstrate if needed]	◆ "Did you have enough (or too many) words?" ◆ "Did you run out of words?" ◆ "Read that line (or page) again with your finger and make it match." ◆ "Try that again and make it match."	◆ "You made it match." ◆ "You read it with your finger and made it match." ◆ "You have just enough words."

FIGURE 16-4 Monitoring Voice-Print Match

Notice that the statement, "you can fix that," is very broad and should be used when the student actually knows what to do and how to do it. He only needs a very brief reminder. Another way to do this is to have the reader locate a known word in the sentence or on the page. For example, "Look at the dog." "Show me the ____. Now read it again and make it match." The reader can then use the word as an anchor. Every time he says that word, he knows his finger has to be under the word. If you teach strongly and insist on crisp pointing under the word, the behaviors will be established quickly. Within a relatively short time, the eyes will take over the process.

One of the most productive reading behaviors to watch for is the *partially correct* response. When Nikki read *pulled* for *pushed,* she was almost correct in that her substitution was very similar visually to the accurate word and also made sense in the sentence. In fact, she was so close that on the next page, she self-corrected the substitution, although at this level this error is not a concern because the reader is using three sources of information. To reinforce this kind of self-correction behavior, you could say, "You knew something wasn't quite right." Or, "You knew how to make it right." Again, on page 8, she substituted *little* for *baby,* which made sense. You could prompt, saying, "It could be *little* but look at (point to the *b*). If you make this move, be sure that the reader knows what you are pointing out (the *b*).

Self-Monitoring Across Time

Self-monitoring is important for beginning readers, but it remains a critical factor throughout a reader's life. It's not easy to observe for self-monitoring, but multiple attempts at a word and self-corrections are evidence that monitoring is going on as is accurate reading.

You assume that if the reading is accurate, then monitoring is going on. If a reader talks meaningfully about a text afterward, again, you can assume that self-monitoring was present in the reading. It is possible to read accurately but fail to monitor for full understanding, so comprehension is always important to consider.

As you are reading, you may suddenly realize that you don't remember a character or aren't following the plot. The setting (particularly in historical fiction) might be difficult to understand, or the topic of the book might be highly technical and the book difficult to follow. As an adult, you have choices. You search back in the text, scanning for the information you need to move forward. Or you might continue reading, hoping to pick up the meaning again. If you are unable to pick up the meaning, you might abandon the book entirely. But readers in schools don't always have that choice, and they might continue to struggle with a book, reaching the end without having fully (or even partially) made sense of it.

Readers at all levels need to constantly ask themselves: "Does my reading make sense? Does it sound right?" "Does it look right?" These questions are not conscious; they come into play when something doesn't quite fit. These questions are simple. As readers grow, they ask questions like: "Is the writer giving accurate information? Is this written in an interesting way? Would people really act like this? Is this a satisfying ending?" Again, we are *not* suggesting that readers ask these questions consciously or that teachers should teach them or prompt them to do so. You wouldn't interrupt reading to make the reader ask questions; monitoring is an awareness that hovers at the edge of your thinking but is always in the checking mode. Effective readers monitor their reading.

"At the moment of making an error a child reading for meaning will notice it. To continue, the reader has to take some action. At this moment he's observing his own behavior very closely because he will have to decide which response he should retain and which he should discard." (Clay, 341).

Teaching for Self-Monitoring in Guided Reading

You can support self-monitoring across the guided reading lesson, although, ultimately, the reader performs the action. But, there are many ways to support monitoring with your teaching decisions and your facilitative language.

Before the Reading

You select books that are within the reader's control but with a few challenges that make it important for the reader to monitor, doing so against a backdrop of accurate reading. Then, in the introduction, you make sure that the reader has some "anchors" that will help her notice when something is wrong. You might:

- Have the readers locate one or two new and important words. Having heard these words and seen them before, readers are more likely to notice mismatches.

- Be sure the reader has an idea of the meaning of the whole text to support noticing when something doesn't make sense within this text.

- Rehearse any tricky language patterns that might be new or unusual for the reader.

Give readers the concept of what this text is all about. That will help them understand the whole context so they can anticipate the text.

During the Reading

As you listen to children's oral reading, you may want to take the opportunity to prompt for self-monitoring. You would not want to interrupt the reading unless you see that the reader is neglecting information or is unsatisfied and won't move on, and you don't want to overdo it. In Figure 16-5, you can see some suggested language in response to reading behavior.

After the Reading

The discussion will give you opportunities to gather evidence as to how well students understood the text (and therefore whether they self-monitored). If you think it will benefit all students, you can teach for processing strategies with an emphasis on self-monitoring. For example:

> "Go back to page _____ ."
> "Read the page again and be sure it all makes sense and looks right too." (Students read softly.)
> "You made it look right and make sense."

As students become more proficient, behaviors indicating self-monitoring, searching, and self-correcting will be much less overt; but if you establish self-monitoring early, it will merge with searching and self-correcting behaviors because they will immediately follow.

Suggested Language to Support Self-Monitoring

If the Reader . . .	Say . . .
Stops after an error.	◆ "What is wrong?" ◆ "Why did you stop? What did you notice?"
Makes a substitution and does not stop.	◆ "Watch me check it." [Reread, run your finger left to right under the problem word, and say the word slowly.] "Yes, that looks right" [or "No, that doesn't look right."] ◆ "Find a part that is not quite right." ◆ "Check it. [demonstrate where to check] ◆ "You made a mistake. Can you find it?" ◆ "Did you notice _____?" [point up mismatch] ◆ "What letter would you expect to see first in _____?" ◆ "Does the word you said look like the word on the page?" ◆ "You said _____. Does that make sense? Sound right? Look right?" ◆ "See if you can find what is wrong."
Reads the line/page accurately but looks unsure.	◆ "How did you know you were right?" ◆ "How did you know it was _____?"
Demonstrates self-monitoring by rereading to self-correct.	◆ "You found out what was wrong all by yourself." ◆ "You found the tricky part all by yourself." ◆ "You checked that with your finger all by yourself. You knew something was wrong." ◆ "You knew something wasn't quite right."

FIGURE 16-5 Suggested Language to Support Self-Monitoring

Teaching for Searching and Using Information

Searching is the reader's active, rapid cognitive action to retrieve information that can be from any source:

- The spacing and words in the print
- The meaning in the pictures or graphics
- The meaning in the story or informational book
- The readers' control of language syntax
- What the reader knows (personal experience or background knowledge)
- What the reader knows about texts—the way stories are organized and structured (beginning, middle, end) or other knowledge of craft (literary knowledge)
- What the reader knows about how to use headings, sidebars, and other nonfiction text features to gather information

The reader can search for information previously neglected as well. The reader's goal is to make all sources of information agree.

> . . . at the mismatch the child initiates a search for missing information and *finds* or *attends to* features *previously ignored* . . . By definition the result of a self-correction is agreement between all sources of information in the text. (Clay, 337–339)

Searching involves both confirmation and self-correction. As Clay says, "Different kinds of information may be checked, one against another, to confirm a response," *(Literacy Lessons Design for Individuals,* 112*).* You can teach for active searching across the guided reading lesson, and text selection is very important in providing opportunities for searching.

Searching is important at all levels. The reader is learning to find and use information in print and other text features that are becoming increasingly complex. Readers must continually search all sources to understand a text. Increasingly, background knowledge becomes an important source of information. In the introduction, you may need to provide background information so that readers can apply it immediately while reading and experience success.

Selecting Texts

Select texts that will engage readers' thinking and that are clear examples of the level. Many thousands of books have a level printed on them (we hope on a back cover or in a place that is not prominent). But you still have the responsibility for careful selection. Some texts may be uneven in that they have many simple pages and also some confusing or highly complex pages. Take particular care in selecting books to introduce to English language learners, noting expressions, idioms, difficult syntax, and vocabulary that might be challenging. You can, of course, use the introduction to support the specific needs of the learners, but if the text is too dense, they may lose comprehension. Searching behavior is developed when students are reading continuous print, and at the lower levels, the pictures are very important. Consider the illustrations carefully in your selection. Do they closely reflect the meaning of the text? Are they clear?

Nikki's record of the reading of *Maddy's Loose Tooth* provides a good example of searching after she read *pushed* for *brushed* (see Figure 16-1). *Pushed* was meaningful within the story and sounded right in terms of language syntax. In addition, *pushed* is close visually to the correct word, *brushed,* but Nikki knew something wasn't quite right. She glanced at the picture each time she turned a page, so she could have searched for meaning in the illustrations. At the same time, she paused and looked closely at the word, noticing the *b* or may even the *br.* Notice that she self-corrected at the point of error rather than continuing on and then rereading the line. Your best hypothesis would be that Nikki searched for and used both meaning and visual information to arrive at an accurate reading. But then she carelessly misread *tooth* for *teeth,* seemingly without awareness of error. You may remember, though, that the word *tooth* is used throughout the text while *teeth* appears only once. Nikki's conversation afterward indicates that she did have good understanding of the text. If you think it is important, you could take her back to the page and simply ask her to reread as a teaching point. Our hunch is that she would read it accurately, mainly using meaning. Nikki is probably not yet at a place where she is noticing the middle letters in words. Possibly, a return to *pushed* and *brushed* to affirm her work would be more effective.

In nonfiction texts, graphics offer an additional challenge because readers are required to search for and use information and often the writer provides different or extended information that is not in the body of the text. At some self-selected point, the reader shifts attention from the continuous print in the body to the items of information in sidebars and a variety of graphics such as maps and charts. You will need to teach intermediate readers how to search for and use information from a variety of nonfiction text features (e.g., charts, cutaways, diagrams, maps).

Adam read *Moon Buggies* (*Fountas & Pinnell Classroom,* in press), a level N text (see Figure 16-6). He read the body of the text with high accuracy and then examined the labeled diagram closely. Possibly, he searched his own knowledge of vehicles and batteries to make connections, and his conversation after reading reflected this. He gave only a glance to the sidebar with the picture of a horse-drawn buggy and turned the page without reading it aloud. This decision represents a reader's choice. The information in the sidebar was designed to add interest to the text, but was not essential for comprehension of the entire text, and sometimes, particularly when reading nonfiction, readers do choose to ignore details that do not seem essential (although they sometimes go back to pick up information if they need it further on in the text). It may be that Adam already knew what an old-fashioned buggy was and had little interest.

As a teacher, you can help students know that it is important to read all around the body of the text for additional information. If you think it is important in noticing aspects of the writer's craft, you could quickly prompt Adam to revisit the page and notice the sidebar. After all, the writer is using historical contrast. Or,

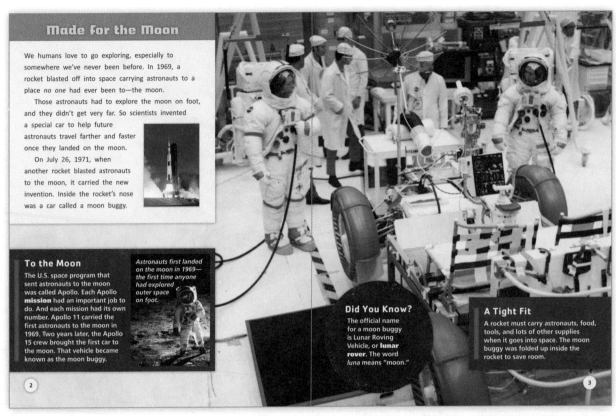

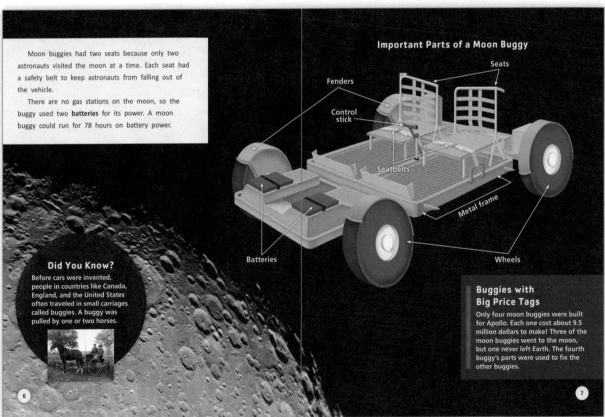

FIGURE 16-6 Pages 2–3 and 6–7 from *Moon Buggies*, Level N

you could take all students to a couple of sidebars as a teaching point, communicating that, often, there is important and/or interesting information in the sidebars. In general, you want students to make a habit of reading all the information on a page. But while searching, the reader will filter the information to gather what is most important.

Introducing the Text

Searching requires engagement, so always begin with an interesting text. You also use the introduction to build interest in a text. At the same time, you can point out useful information that will be important in understanding the text, and that will help to keep the reader persevering throughout the book. For example, in *Moon Buggies,* the sidebars provide additional historical information for the reader. On page 2, the sidebar provides information on the first two Apollo missions; on page 6, you see the historical use of *buggy;* on page 7, you find a sidebar with information about the cost and functionality of moon buggies and other sidebars describe the goals of moon flights and the importance of cars in space. Taken together, the sidebars help the reader understand the magnitude of achievement and the importance of taking cars into space.

These text features contribute significantly to the understanding of the big idea—that a great deal of creativity and scientific understanding can lead to more discoveries about our world. So, you might draw attention to one sidebar and prompt readers to notice the interesting information in them and think about why the writer might have included them. Also, you would help them understand the kind of information provided in the book—the beginnings of moon buggies and the reasons for their invention, several pages of facts about buggies and how these vehicles have been improved, and how they have been used to make important contributions to our knowledge of our earth and moon. That's the way this book works.

In the introduction to *Maddy's Loose Tooth,* you probably wouldn't want to go all the way through the book because you want readers to build expectations about the way Maddy will finally lose her tooth. (Searching their own personal experiences will tell them that, eventually, the tooth will come out.) But you might take one or two examples to show them how the pictures will help and remind them to notice them. Also, you want them to notice that a tooth comes out in some way on almost every page spread, but Maddy keeps trying and trying unsuccessfully.

You want them to make predictions, because the book supports that. In the introduction to the text, you want to:

▶ Build expectations about the plot.

▶ Understand the sequence of events.

▶ Understand the kind of information and how it is organized and presented in the book.

▶ Point out a specific source of information that is critical to understanding.

▶ Give general reminders that will help students search for deeper messages.

Reading the Text

As you sample oral reading, you may want to intervene briefly to teach, prompt for, and reinforce searching behaviors. We emphasize that these encounters are *brief*. They are not for the purpose of testing students' comprehension; rather, use them only if the student:

- Stops and needs help
- Seems confused
- Neglects to self-monitor when important information is needed

Intervening in a student's reading is a big decision because you run the risk of interrupting so much that you actually interfere in the student's ability to search for and use information. Think carefully about the kind of information the student needs or is neglecting:

- Has she lost the meaning or is she neglecting meaning? (Information in the pictures contributes to meaning.)
- Is she neglecting to listen to her reading to be sure it sounds right? (Knowledge of English syntax is a powerful source of information. Here, you may need to give special support to English language learners because their sense of the syntax might be weaker. Or, you may want to teach or show rather than prompt.)
- Is she failing to notice and use visual information? (The letters, words, lines, and punctuation make up the visual information).

In Figure 16-7, you will find some suggested language to use to support active searching for multiple sources of information during the reading.

As students become more active and agile in searching, move quickly to more complex ways of teaching, prompting, and reinforcing problem-solving actions (see Figure 16-8).

Notice that all of the prompts direct the reader toward one or more sources of information. With these prompts, you call for the reader to search for more than one source of information, checking one against the others. You can make the prompts for any combination of sources or for all three. Before long, you'll observe the reader automatically searching actively for multiple sources of information, and you may want to move back to a broad prompt like "try that again," which gives the reader less support and more individual choice. Eventually, the reader must learn to search in such an integrated way that she is using these actions smoothly and rapidly—without conscious attention. The reader makes a conscious effort only when a problem arises, and often that is quick and not observable in behavior.

Teaching for Self-Correction

To self-correct, readers engage in self-monitoring and searching. The whole process comes together in a highly constructive way with the reader engaging in several kinds of integrated brain work. The reader uses all the resources she is capable of and is rewarded by success and meaning, making it a most productive focus for

Suggested Language to Support Searching for and Using Information

	Teach	Prompt	Reinforce
Searching for and Using Meaning	◆ "You can think about the story when you look at the pictures." ◆ "You said _____. That doesn't make sense (or, go with the story)."	◆ "Can the picture help you think about this part of the story?" ◆ "Try that again and think of what would make sense." ◆ "Think about the story." ◆ "Think about what you know about this story."	◆ "That makes sense." ◆ "You were thinking about what would make sense." ◆ "You were thinking about the story." ◆ "You were thinking about what you know."
Searching for and Using Language Structure	◆ "You said _____. That doesn't sound right." ◆ "You said _____. That's not the way the writer would say it in a book." ◆ "Listen to this." (Model two choices.) "Which one sounds better?"	◆ "Would _____ (model correct structure) sound right?" ◆ "Try that again and think what would sound right." ◆ "Try _____" (insert correct structure)	◆ "You made it sound right (after problem-solving)." ◆ "That's how it would sound."
Searching for and Using Visual Information	◆ "You can read it again and start the word." (Model rereading and articulate the first sound.) ◆ "You can get your mouth ready to start the tricky word." (Model.) ◆ "You can say it slowly like when you write it." (Model.) ◆ "You can think of a part you know." (Model.) ◆ "It sounds like that, but it looks different."	◆ "Say the first sound." ◆ "Get your mouth ready for the first sound." ◆ "Do you think it looks like (correct word)?" ◆ "What letter do you see first?" ◆ "Do you know a word like that?" ◆ "Do you know a word that starts (ends) like that?" ◆ "Look at the first part (. . . the middle part . . . the last part)." ◆ "Do you see a part that can help?" ◆ "Think about what you know that might help."	◆ "You thought about the first sound and it helped you." ◆ "You read that again and started the tricky word." ◆ "You thought of another word like that." ◆ "You used a part you know." ◆ "You looked at all the letters." ◆ "You thought about what would look right."

FIGURE 16-7 Suggested Language to Support Searching for and Using Information

Suggested Language to Support Searching for and Using Multiple Sources of Information

Teach	Prompt	Reinforce
◆ "It has to make sense and sound right." ◆ "It has to make sense and look right." ◆ "It has to sound right and look right." ◆ "Listen . . . (say whole sentence). It (combination of any—makes sense, looks right, sounds right)."	◆ "Do you know a word that would make sense and look like _____ (start like, end like)?" ◆ "Think of what would make sense and check with the letters." ◆ "Does that make sense and look right/sound right?" ◆ "Try that again and make it sound right and look right/make sense."	◆ "You made it look right and sound right." ◆ "You made it make sense and look right." ◆ "Does that sound right and look right/make sense?" ◆ "Think of what would make sense, sound right, and look right."

FIGURE 16-8 Suggested Language to Support Searching for and Using Multiple Sources of Information

your teaching. The activity is actually different from an error that occurs and is left without correction. But Clay cautions in italicized print:

> *The argument is not that errors are bad and correcting them is good. That is simplistic. The argument is that errors provide opportunities to become aware of mismatches in redundant information in texts, and when they trigger self-correction processes which involve reading work it is the work done to problem-solve errors which has high tutorial value for the reader.* (Clay 2015, 30)

This problem-solving process has such high value because it actually fuels the construction of the reading process. The reader makes new discriminations, attends to new features, brings the text and the outside world together by making connections, uses several sources of information in concert, and is confirmed by meaningfulness.

Self-correction appears early in the behavior of a reader. "The courage to make mistakes, the 'ear' to recognize that an error had occurred, the patience to search for confirmation—these were the characteristics of children who made good progress in their first year of reading," (Clay 2015, 304). Clay became highly interested in beginning readers when she studied them as part of her doctoral work (reported in Clay 2015). She found a clear difference between high-, medium-, and low-progress beginning readers in the ratio of self-corrections to errors. Clay found that the top fifty percent of children corrected one in every three or four errors while the low group's rates were one in eight and one in twenty! Moreover, the high-progress readers drew information from several different sources.

It is important that self-correction takes place against a background of accurate reading, so it is not a case of "the more self-corrections, the better." You would not want readers to work at nearly every word: the entire process would break down and comprehension would be limited. Note that Nikki read *Maddy's Loose Tooth* at 92 percent accuracy (just as low as you would want accuracy to be), and with a self-correction ratio of 1 to 3—a good ratio. Thus, while Nikki did engage in highly productive reading work, she did not sound like a halting, struggling reader—just one who occasionally paused for successful problem solving. On a second reading of this text, you might predict that she would process it with near perfect accuracy and possibly might have enough attention and energy to work on words like *bit* and *teeth*.

Supporting Self-Correction in Guided Reading

Just about everything you do across the guided reading lesson can support self-correction.

Introducing the Text

The steps you take to support readers through an introduction will make it possible for the reader to read for meaning and monitor her own problem solving. This leads to the extension of the system. When the reader knows how the text works, what to expect in the plot, and some key words, she can bring more to the problem-solving effort. On the other hand, you do not want the introduction to leave the student with no problem solving to do. The reader needs some opportunities for active problem solving to build the processing system.

Reading the Text

As with prompting for other actions, be cautious about interrupting the reading. If a reader shows spontaneous self-correction, a quick confirmation can be a good thing. If the reader is not actively working for self-correction, take the opportunity to teach for and prompt for it. In general, many of the prompts presented for monitoring and searching also move the reader to self-correction. Some language is suggested in Figure 16-9.

Discussion and Teaching for Processing Strategies

Be sure to engage students in conversation so that you have evidence that they have used everything they know how to do to search for and construct meaning. When you find confusions, you can revisit the text to clear them up, especially if you have observed a breakdown in the processing in critical sections.

You can choose to teach for self-correction behaviors. Point out productive self-corrections that you have observed in students' reading. Consider having the student reread a section of the text and use precise language to teach for, prompt, and reinforce problem-solving actions (see Figure 16-9). Of course, with intermediate readers, you would seldom need to teach for self-correction because this action changes quickly and becomes covert.

Change over Time in Self-Correction

When readers self-correct they are either searching further using the same source of information or they are using more than one source to search. As teachers of beginning readers, we know how important self-correction is, but we also know that it

Suggested Language to Support Self-Correction Behaviors

Teach	Prompt	Reinforce
◆ "You can try it again and think what would look right/make sense/sound right" [Model.] ◆ "Watch me check it, [Read the sentence.] Yes, it looks right/sounds right/makes sense."	◆ "You are nearly right. Try that again and think: What would look right/sound right/make sense?" ◆ "You're almost right. Try that again." ◆ "Were you right?" ◆ "You can check to be sure you are right." ◆ "You can fix that." ◆ "Work some more on that."	◆ "You noticed what was wrong." ◆ "You went back and fixed it up." ◆ "You noticed that it didn't make sense/sound right/look right and you worked it out." ◆ "You made it look right, sound right, and make sense." ◆ "You knew something wasn't quite right and you fixed it."

FIGURE 16-9 Suggested Language to Support Self-Correction Behaviors

changes rapidly and then seems to disappear. Early readers may reread an entire line (and sometimes an entire page) before self-correcting, but as abilities expand, self-correction will shift closer to the point of error (to the beginning of the sentence, to the beginning of the phrase, to the word) and will even occur after sounding the first letter or *before* any overt action is taken. Clay (2015, 339) has summarized these shifts in self-correction behaviors:

▶ From overt to covert

▶ From slow to fast

▶ From after the error to after the first sound of the error response

▶ From long stretches of text involved in the self-correction to only local information

In Clay's (1968) readers, overt self-correction virtually disappeared within about a year, and that is our experience as well. You would not want to see a great many self-corrections in experienced, expert reading. Much overt processing would mean that the reader is working too hard to give attention to the more complex ideas in the text. The text would be broken up. Even a high accuracy rate is undesirable if the reader has to work too hard on processing. Sometimes more experienced readers have even learned to "over correct." When reading aloud, highly proficient readers tend to overtly self-correct *only* when there is a purpose to it—for example, if the error would cause listeners to misperceive. You can notice that behavior in television newscasters, who are reading aloud. When reading silently, the reader probably does self-correct but it is part of one smooth set of actions.

Teachers of intermediate or middle-level readers have less opportunity to observe evidence of cognitive actions, and you want that to be the case. But you can look at other evidence—for example, smoothness and fluency, pausing, and conversation after reading—to be sure that the reader has taken maximum meaning from the text, and you can help them revisit it for close reading. You can make hypotheses about the reader's silent processing by examining regular samples of oral reading.

We have discussed the high tutorial value of readers engaging in the active monitoring, searching, and correcting behaviors that build an effective, efficient processing system as they read continuous text. Your teaching decisions—introduction, wait time, use of facilitative language, teaching points, discussion—will be important factors in the development of these self-initiating, self-regulating behaviors.

Suggestions for Professional Development

1. Plan a session with colleagues to hone your ability to detect evidence of monitoring, searching, and self-correcting. (Obviously, it will be easiest to detect self-correction; but you want to be able to notice all behavior related to this important area.) The key to this kind of observation is the analysis of behavior leading to the coding of M, S, and V on the running record.

2. Collect several running records of readers at the levels that interest you and your group. The reading should be coded but without the completed M S V analysis. If you have video to accompany the record, it will allow you and your colleagues to be more observant.

   ▶ If you have the *Benchmark Assessment System 1* or *2,* you will find individual readers on the Tutorial video. Play the video without commentary and take the reading record using the form.

   ▶ Each teacher can also bring a video and record of one reader.

   ▶ You can take a video of several readers at your school and code the reading (you can use a smart phone or tablet).

3. The purpose of this meeting is not to code the reading but to focus *only* on monitoring, searching, and self-correcting. Listen to at least three readings with this focus.

   ▶ Watch the reading and follow the coding on the form but leave the M S V analysis.

   ▶ Then you can work with a partner to identify:

      ▶ What evidence is there that the reader is monitoring? (Remember that accurate reading always indicates some monitoring.) What is the reader using to monitor in this instance? Consult this chapter for a discussion of monitoring.

      ▶ What evidence is there that the reader is searching? What kind of information is the reader searching for? Consult this chapter for a discussion of searching.

      ▶ What evidence is there of self-correction? What kind of information is the reader using *in addition* to the information that led to the error? Or what sent the reader back to work or search for more information?

   ▶ Partners can complete the M S V analysis and compare it with others in the group.

4. Have a general discussion of the importance of monitoring, searching, and self-correcting. Emphasize the importance of monitoring and searching behavior even if the reading is not, ultimately, accurate.

CHAPTER 17

Teaching for Visual Processing over Time

Solving Words

The teacher's job is . . . arranging for the problem to be manageable, sustaining the child's problem-solving attempts, emphasizing flexibility.

–Peter Johnston

As you think about what children need to learn to process print efficiently, consider Clay's (1991a) words, "reading for meaning with divided attention." Clay's (1991a, reprinted in 2015) theory of reading continuous text suggests that readers must *simultaneously* notice and use visual and phonological information while thinking about the ideas communicated through the language. They must divide their attention so that it is possible not only to decode the words but also to comprehend the text. Most of the time, the reader's attention is on the meaning, and words are recognized effortlessly. But when a reader notices mismatches or other challenges arise, attention will shift directly to the word in order to apply problem-solving actions. The reader might:

▶ Recognize the word as known with a quick look and recall.

▶ Recognize and use known word parts.

▶ Search for and use meaning in illustrations or graphics.

▶ Predict possibilities based on meaning or syntax and check with the visual information.

▶ Use the redundant information in print to increase resources.

▶ Partially sound the letters of the word and fit this partial information with meaning and language structure.

▶ Analyze the word letter by letter, sometimes using individual letters, sometimes letter clusters, and sometimes parts.

▶ Derive the word by analogy to a word or words he already knows (use *my* and *tree* to solve *try;* use *nation* to read *revolution*).

Remember that proficient readers, even early ones, use the most efficient approach possible to solve words, and have many different ways to solve them (Kaye 2008). The readers Kaye observed took words apart in multisyllable segments (*elec-electricity*), syllables (*voy-age*), root words and endings (*strength-ened*), halves of compound words (*earth, worm*), or onset and rime (*th-eory*). Readers are helped by the redundancy in language. For example, in the sentence, "I saw several cows grazing in the field," plurality is communicated by both the word *several* and the *s* ending. The better the reader can predict, the smoother the word solving will be because the reader needs to give only enough attention to the visual information to check the prediction. The opportunity to read continuous text offers the reader support in using a number of sources of information to solve words. The reader needs many encounters with letters and words in a variety of contexts: in shared reading, guided reading, independent reading, writing, and word study lessons.

The Role of Phonics

The relationship between the phonological aspects of language (the sounds) and the graphic signs (the letters and combinations of letters) is an important source of information for readers. The reader needs to notice the visual form and its features, hear the sound in the spoken word and link to its visual form while reading text. According to Clay (1991a), a competent reader "uses not just the sounds of letters but phonological information from several levels of language. He can provide phonological identities for letters, digraphs, clusters, syllables, prefixes and suffixes, root words, phrases, and non-language strings. He will select a larger rather than a smaller unit for efficiency and may check one source of information against another," (290).

In the discussion about how to help children learn letter/sound relationships, it is useful to distinguish among several important terms (see Figure 17-1). We often use a "shorthand" speech describing young children's use of "phonics" to read, but in fact, they are using graphophonemic relationships. Phonics is an approach to teaching students how to read words, not a linguistic term. It's a fine difference but we think it is worth mentioning in order to keep attention on what readers are actually doing.

Phonological (or phoneme) awareness instruction, often called "training," is designed to help young children acquire the ability to hear and distinguish the sounds in words. It might include becoming aware of words that rhyme or words that begin or end alike. It might mean separating a word into phonemes orally or putting together a string of phonemes that are said in a segmented way with space between them. In this kind of instruction, we are not talking about the use of letters, only the sound. Very little phonemic awareness training is needed. A review of research found that about twenty total hours was optimal and suggested that more could be confusing (National Institute of Child Health and Human Development 2000).

While you will find that a few playful oral exercises focusing directly on phonemes may be helpful, we suggest that you immerse children in rhymes and songs and the use of sounds and letters within meaningful print. In general, the study of letters and sounds together gives energy and power to the process of learning.

English Language Learners

We inject a note of caution in the instruction of phonemic awareness and letter/sound relationships (or graphophonological understanding) when working with English language learners. All languages have different phonological systems and they may differ slightly (or a great deal) from English. The student may have excellent phonological awareness in his own language but it will differ from English. Meaningless "training" for long periods of time on English phonology may be confusing or boring. Every experience a student has in English needs to be packed with as much meaning as possible. In that case, work with students to focus on the letters and accept dialects that vary. Help them to notice how the word *looks*. If students are young enough, they may quickly acquire almost standard English phonology; or, they may always have slight variations that do not get in the way of decoding and comprehending text. If they are older, they can still process and understand the text.

Terms Related to the Teaching of Letter/Sound Relationships

Phonological System	The sound system of a language.
Phonology	Phonology refers to the study of the way the sounds are organized in languages. It is a branch of linguistics.
Phoneme	A phoneme is a unit of sound that makes it possible to distinguish one word from another. A single sound can distinguish a word; words like *him* and *hit* are called minimal pairs. There may be a little variation, for example the /r/ in *run* and *drill* are not precisely the same but are so close that they are classified as allophones (slight variations of) the same phoneme.
Phonological Awareness	An individual's awareness of the phonological structure of words (e.g., individual phonemes, onsets, rimes, syllables).
Phonemic Awareness	An individual's ability to hear, identify and manipulate the individual phonemes in a word (a subset of phonological awareness).
Letter (Grapheme)	A letter is a written character (called a grapheme) in an alphabetic system of writing. An alphabetic system is a language based on the principle that a letter or group of letters represent the sounds of the spoken language. The letters used to represent English are also used for several other languages.
Phonics	A method for teaching reading that involves developing learners' ability to hear and manipulate sounds and to learn the correspondence between sounds and spelling patterns.

FIGURE 17-1 Terms Related to the Teaching of Letter/Sound Relationships

Vocabulary Learning

Every language has a *lexicon,* a body of words that speakers use to communicate with each other. An individual's vocabulary represents the body of words he knows, and this refers to oral vocabulary. Vocabulary is spoken of in different ways, for example:

- *Speaking vocabulary* means the words an individual can use in conversation.
- *Listening vocabulary* means the words an individual can understand while listening (probably will be larger than the speaking vocabulary).
- *Reading vocabulary* means the words an individual can recognize with understanding (for early readers, usually much smaller than the oral vocabulary).
- *Writing vocabulary* means the words an individual can use in writing (and spell in a way approaching conventionality; may be smaller than the reading vocabulary).

All of these vocabularies constantly inform each other. You might hear a word many times in a meaningful context and begin to use it in oral language. You might learn to read a word and connect it to oral vocabulary, or you might read a completely new word and add it to your reading vocabulary. The more words you recognize in reading, the easier it will be to use them in writing. You might learn to recognize a word and understand its meaning, but seldom use it in oral language (for example, *luminescence*). But it would be available to you if you become engaged in a relevant topic.

Vocabulary is integral to reading and is certainly an important part of word solving. If readers do not understand the meaning of the words they read, the process becomes meaningless decoding. No reader should ever have to struggle along, producing what to him is nonsense. Students need to understand a wide range of words. An important part of comprehending is quick, fluent access to word meanings.

What does it mean to "know" a word? Experts (see Beck et al. 1987; Dale 1965) have identified a continuum ranging from being completely unfamiliar with a word to having a rich network of meaning attached to it. Often, you might encounter a word, for example *semaphoring.* "John is semaphoring from the yard and that means the steaks are done." The word might have a vague familiarity, but seeing it in isolation, you might be stumped. Probably you would move right on because the context of the sentence would give you enough meaning to understand that the word is a gerund and John must be gesturing. However, if the word intrigues you, you might take a closer look and connect it with *semantic;* both words have the root *sema* which comes from a Greek word meaning *sign* or *token.* A *semaphore,* you'd discover, is a system for signaling (such as two flags or lights). You see people *semaphoring* every time you take off and land in an airplane. Further, you might even know that the root *–phore* is from Greek and means *to carry;* connect with *metaphor* and *euphoria.* To carry a signal. How easy is that?

Partial recognition, supported by context, often lets us read on without losing meaning. Today, we read many texts in electronic form and the meaning of most unknown words is immediately available at a touch. (This tool breaks down considerably when you encounter dialect or archaic language.) If you encounter a partially recognized word several times, you build a network of meaning around it. In this way avid readers add constantly to their vocabularies. They know thousands of words that they might not use in oral language (or even in their own writing), but they can handle them competently when they meet them in a text.

Words are known along a continuum from unknown, to partially known, to known (at least one definition), to richly known. Beck has suggested that when readers truly know a word, they are able to use it in a decontextualized way, extending it to other situations and perhaps even using it metaphorically. Knowing a word means, in many cases, understanding multiple meanings and being able to choose from those definitions the one the writer means within the context of use. To add to the complexity, words often have connotations that go beyond literal meaning. A writer can use a word in an ironic or sarcastic way to mean the opposite of what is stated. These meanings can also vary by cultural setting; a word's meaning may be profane in one culture and perfectly acceptable in another. Finally, word meaning changes over time. Scientific words like *teflon* sneak into everyday use; the word *nice* used to mean *clean*. Virtually every word has a social history that continually attaches meaning to it and many words change with use.

Nuances of language as well as idioms can be very difficult when you are trying to learn another language, and this is something to remember when working with English language learners. They need to encounter and use a word again and again within meaningful contexts. Over time, they can build a system for learning new words. The learning is, in itself, complex. Students need to learn how to:

▶ Use the meanings they know while reading text.

▶ Recognize words quickly and automatically while reading for meaning.

▶ Figure out partially known words by using contextual information and making connections to known words.

▶ Call up related concepts when they encounter a partially known word or a word for which they know only one definition.

▶ Recognize when they need to consult an authority (dictionary, glossary) and when other strategies can be used effectively.

▶ Recognize whether a word's meaning is important to the comprehension of a text and when it peripheral.

▶ Notice the structure of a whole text as a source of information.

▶ Monitor their own level of comprehension.

▶ Realize that connotation can be an important part of understanding a piece of writing.

▶ Use the words they read in their own talk and writing.

It is seldom productive to have students copy and memorize definitions of long lists of words; nor do we see any value to the "word of the day" for the whole school (usually an esoteric and seldom used word that has no meaning in students' lives). Nevertheless, students probably need to add about 3,000 words per year to their vocabularies (Anderson and Nagy 1992). There is a case for the inclusion of both direct teaching of vocabulary and indirect teaching through interactive read-aloud and through wide reading. Some guiding principles for effective vocabulary instruction are:

▶ New words should be connected with familiar words and concepts.

▶ Students should experience new words in repeated, meaningful encounters.

▶ Students need the opportunity to use new words in oral discourse and in writing.

▶ Students need the opportunity to experience new words in texts that they can read so that they have rich contextual information.

▶ Students need to learn how to look closely at words and use meaningful word parts (base words, prefixes, and suffixes).

▶ Word history can be very helpful (Latin and Greek roots as well as other languages).

Learning to Solve Words Across Instructional Contexts

A reader's familiarity with the graphophonological system is developed in several settings in addition to guided reading lessons.

Writing

Shared writing offers a powerful demonstration of how meaningful written language is constructed. Shared writing is a demonstration that slows down the process of relating sounds and words to letters and word parts so that it becomes more visible and easy to understand. The teacher may take the opportunity to involve students in the spelling of a word or may point out useful word parts.

During interactive writing, early writers construct words in conjunction with other students and their teacher. They say words slowly, becoming aware of the sequence of sounds, and then link these sounds to the letters they know. As they reread the group messages they produce, their knowledge expands rapidly.

You can use children's own names to draw attention to letters, teaching not only the letter names but the features of letters and how to recognize one from another. The goal is learning to use information from letters that are embedded in continuous print. Words that are written, located, and read many times become strategic "anchors" for students as they begin to recognize them in continuous print and use them to monitor their reading. A known word can also be used to decode unknown words.

Writing provides many opportunities for learning about words. As students engage in their own independent writing, they have the opportunity to apply everything they know about letters and sounds and how print works. Early readers can attend to using spaces to define words or to saying words slowly to hear the sounds and represent them with letters. In younger children, you will find "temporary" spellings based on their current understandings of the graphophonological system (for example, *CHRN* for *train*). They are representing what they hear. You do not need to correct every one of these temporary representations, just appreciate them, but very soon you want students to think not only about what they hear, but also about what they expect to see. You want them to make the word "look right," and this is where reading helps. With voluminous reading, learners meet words hundreds (or even thousands) of times, and develop a visual memory of how a word looks. (When trying to spell a difficult word you might say, "I'll write it down," in order to see if it "looks right.")

Interactive Read-Aloud, Book Clubs, Independent Reading

Interactive read-aloud, and the talking opportunities it brings, is an ideal place for helping students acquire new vocabulary that they might not experience in ordinary oral language. The discussion in interactive read-aloud is *text based*. The text you have read aloud is a rich resource of language. By talking about texts, during and immediately after the reading, students have the opportunity to notice and try out new language. Also, you can draw attention to interesting words as you read and bring them up afterward, all within a conversation about the writer's meaning or style.

Book clubs, too, offer a setting that demands text-based talk. Here, students do most of the talking about issues that have meaning for them. They offer examples or evidence from the text and are using academic vocabulary. Some of the facilitative language you use (see *Prompting Guide Part 2 for Comprehension*) can help students get back into the language of the book, for example:

▶ "When she said _____, what do you think she meant?"

▶ "When the writer said _____, what did that mean?"

▶ "Let's do a slow reread of that paragraph (page) to notice more."

The more students read, the more likely they are to increase their vocabularies, and this is true even if they are reading books on a level that they can process independently. Students will use text-based talk during the share period as they talk with a partner or a group of four. Encourage them to include interesting words in their responses in their reader's notebooks.

Essential Areas of Phonics and Word Learning

The principles students need to understand are organized into nine areas of learning, all related to the levels of texts that students are reading over the years (see Figure 17-2). The first three apply to grades PreK through Grade 1, but all of the others are important PreK through Grade 8.

Structure for Phonics and Word Study Lessons

You can schedule your phonics or word study minilesson any time during the school day (see Chapters 22 and 23). Many teachers like to schedule it early in the day as part of a whole-class meeting and ask students to participate in application

Nine Important Areas of Learning for Phonics and Word Study

Early Literacy Concepts (PreK to Grade 1)	Even before they can read, children begin to develop some awareness of how written language works, and they continue to develop concepts about processing print as they read their first books.
Phonological Awareness (PreK to Grade 1)	A key understanding in becoming literate is the ability to hear the individual sounds in words, and rhymes, as well as word parts.
Letter Knowledge (PreK to Grade 1)	Letter knowledge refers to what students need to know about the graphic characters in the English alphabet—how the letters look, how to distinguish one from another, how to detect them within continuous print, how to use them in words, and the names we use to talk about them.
Letter-Sound Relationships	Students continue to learn about the relationships between letters and sounds in English throughout the elementary school years. In addition to the sounds connected to individual letters, they learn the way alternative sounds may be attached to a letter and they learn to look for letter combinations (blends and digraphs) and to see them as units.
Spelling Patterns	Efficient word solvers look for and find patterns in the ways words are constructed. Knowing spelling patterns helps students notice and use larger parts of words, thus making word solving faster and easier. Students begin with simple phonograms (*sat, mat, cat*) but progress to learning much more complex patterns (*-ign, -ight*) and to the recognition of patterns in multisyllable words.
High-Frequency Words	Knowing how to read and write a core of high-frequency words is a valuable resource for students as they build their reading and writing processing systems. We can also call these "high-utility words" because they appear often in print and can sometimes be used to help in solving other words.
Word Meaning and Vocabulary	Students need to know the meaning of the words in the texts they read, and they need a continually expanding vocabulary to use in writing. Expanding vocabulary means developing categories of words: labels, concept words, synonyms, antonyms, homonyms, and so on. It also refers to words that appear in print but are not usually used in speech, to technical words, and to academic vocabulary.
Word Structure	Looking at the structure of words will help students learn how words are related to one another and how they can be changed by adding letters, letter clusters, and larger word parts. Students work with base words and affixes (prefixes and suffixes); they can also learn about word roots (Greek or Latin origins). Principles related to word structure include understanding the meaning and structure of compound words, contractions, plurals, and possessives.
Word-Solving Actions	Word solving is related to all of the categories of learning in this chart, but this category specifically focuses on the effective moves readers and writers make when they use their knowledge of the language system while reading and writing continuous text.

FIGURE 17-2 Nine Important Areas of Learning for Phonics and Word Study

activities while they teach guided reading groups. Others like to confine phonics and word study to one thirty-minute period. However you work word study into your day, you can follow a general structure:

> **Phonics Minilesson:** Teach a short, explicit, inquiry-based lesson on one principle related to any of the nine areas of study. Place examples on a chart and have students generalize the principle through inquiry whenever possible.
>
> **Application:** Students engage in some kind of 'hands-on" application. They can work with a partner or individually. (In this period of time, they can also use activities related to learning how to study words, for example, look, say, cover, write, check, as outline in *Word Matters* (Pinnell and Fountas 1998).
>
> **Group Share:** Students gather for a whole-class meeting and they share their discoveries during the application activity.

We would expect students to have whole-class lessons on phonics or word analysis that is based on what will benefit most of the students in terms of the behaviors and understandings in *The Literacy Continuum*. Using an inquiry approach, students learn important principles that are reinforced in the word work segment of the guided reading lesson as appropriate.

Students need opportunities to work on meaningful print in many ways during the school day. Attending to words allows the reader/writer to notice the details. It is very helpful to readers to work with magnetic letters to develop automatically and flexibility for picking up print information as they read. The students need to learn how to construct words and take them apart. This does not mean you should teach all the words before readers encounter them in a text. The goal is to expose them to how words work.

A Variety of Opportunities to Apply Learning

There are many further opportunities for students to apply phonics and word study learning, independently, as partners, or in small or large groups. Some of the following are specific to early readers. Suggestions may be used with the whole group, small group, or with partners for teaching and practice. Some will be useful in the letter/word work segment of the guided reading lesson.

Alphabet Linking Chart

Many teachers use a chart of letter forms and simple pictures that provide a clear letter-sound link to key words (see Figure 17-3 and Online Resources). Start using this chart with the entire group, building the knowledge together with kindergartners and first graders who have limited letter knowledge and are just beginning to learn how to look at print. You can also use the chart with small groups and, eventually, each student will have his own small version. The chart can be used in many different ways, including:

- ▶ Read every other box.
- ▶ Read only the letters.
- ▶ Read only the words.

> Read only the vowels.

> Read only the consonants.

> Read the pictures.

> Read the letters in your name.

> Sing the chart.

> Cover some letters with sticky notes and ask for predictions, then remove the stickers.

Consonant Cluster Linking Chart

As students progress, use a Consonant Cluster Linking Chart that gives students another link to the connections between letters and words (see Figure 17-4 and Online Resources). You can use this chart in the same ways, but you are now helping your students learn how to use letter clusters or larger word beginnings.

FIGURE 17-3 Alphabet Linking Chart

FIGURE 17-4 Consonant Cluster Linking Chart

Alphabet Books

Collect a wide range of simple alphabet books for children to read to themselves or with a partner. This activity will provide much practice in using letter names, recognizing letter forms, and developing many new letter-sound associations.

Children can match magnetic letters to the book or the pictures. They will enjoy making alphabet books, and the alphabet provides an organizing frame. At first, you may want to use interactive writing to model making a group alphabet book. These books can reflect a theme like animals or food. Children's names can be included in the class alphabet book. Or children can make a book with just the letters in their names. Older students can come up with clever and sophisticated alphabet books that have interesting content and new vocabulary words.

Individual Letter Mini Books

One way for young children to get acquainted with letters and begin to connect them with words that reflect letter-sound relationships is to "read" individual letter books (see Figure 17-5 and Online Resources). The books match the Alphabet Linking Chart and readers can read each word and practice to expand their knowledge of letter-sound relationships. You might have children read selected letter mini books in the letter/word work segment of the guided reading lesson. The books have the advantage of drawing children's attention to the distinctive features of letters and can help in developing fast, efficient letter knowledge.

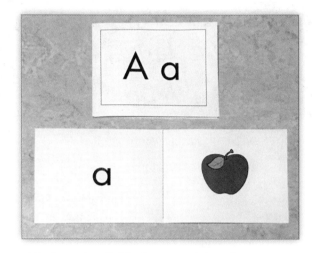

FIGURE 17-5 Individual Letter Mini Book

Matching and Sorting Letters

Children's first efforts at matching and sorting may be with letters of different shapes or colors, but they can soon learn to sort letters, match letters, find letters with features in common such as tails, circles, short sticks, tall sticks, tunnels, dots, capitals, and so on (see Figure 17-6). Their time spent sorting letters in a myriad of ways is essential to learning how to look at print in the early levels. They need to develop fast, flexible recognition of letters. Begin with just a few letters rather than all twenty-six, and concentrate on the lowercase letters and get the children to develop speed in matching or sorting.

Sorting Words

Word sorting can be a very simple activity (such as sorting words by first letter or letter cluster) for primary students, but it can evolve into being able to notice highly complex characteristics of words (see Figure 17-7) for intermediate/middle-level students.

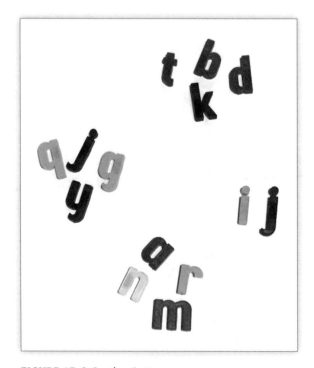

FIGURE 17-6 Sorting Letters

Students can work with a partner and they can add an example of each category to their reader's notebooks. Here are some categories:

▶ Put together rhyming words.

▶ Match words with the same initial or final letter or letters.

▶ Sort words by initial of final letter clusters (*spring/sprout, last/fast*).

▶ Sort words by phonogram.

▶ Sort words by number of syllables.

▶ Sort words by spelling patterns.

▶ Put together words with the same inflectional endings, prefixes, or suffixes.

▶ Put together words that reflect particular spelling rules.

▶ Sort words by type of plural.

▶ Sort words by base words or word roots.

▶ Sort words by vowel sound.

FIGURE 17-7 Sorting Words

The above sorts are usually "closed sorts," in which students work to put words in a designated category. The sort can also be "open," where students sort a selection of words and then identify the principle that makes them the same. They can create and label categories. One student can sort words and another can guess the reasons behind the categories. There are endless variations to sorting (see *Word Matters* 1998). Once you have the word cards made for a sort, you can use them over and over again.

Making Words

Making words can also be simple or more sophisticated. Students can work with magnetic letters, tile letters, foam letters, or letter cards (see Figure 17-8). More advanced students can write words. Here are some possibilities. Give students a set of letters. Make or write words:

▶ With the same first letter.

▶ With the same final letter.

▶ With the same amount of letters.

▶ With particular letter sequences.

▶ With letter clusters at the beginning or end.

▶ With the same phonogram (*hat, cat, bat*)

▶ With an *e* (or other vowel) or a silent *e*.

▶ With silent letters.

▶ With the same base word.

▶ With the same root.

▶ With the same affix (prefix or suffix).

▶ That go from present to past tense.

▶ That go from singular to plural.

FIGURE 17-8 Making Words with Magnetic Letters

in	as	do	net	an
pin	has	dog	nest	and
pen	ham	dig	next	sand
open	hat	digging		candy
opens	hit			
opening	hits			
Reopening	hitting			

FIGURE 17-9 Word Ladders

Word Ladders

Working from a word they know, students can add and remove letters to construct a "ladder" (see Figure 17-9).

Teaching for Word Solving in Guided Reading Lessons

Guided reading provides the most intensive and effective opportunity to teach powerful word-solving actions that are essential for processing texts at a particular level. It is most helpful because you are providing the teaching or prompting at the point that the reader needs it in processing a text. When the reader processes continuous text, she has support in using a number of sources of information in order to solve words. You'll find ample evidence of word solving as you observe readers process continuous text. In intermediate readers, there will be much less evidence of overt processing, but you can still get information from error behavior. A key piece of information also comes from the running records you take on a regular basis (see Chapter 11).

Here is an example of evidence that an early reader is solving words while reading *Food for Animals (Fountas & Pinnell Classroom,* in press), a level B nonfiction text (see Figure 17-10).

On page 2, Andy substituted *frog* for *bug.* As he read on further, he sensed something wasn't right (possibly because he realized a frog isn't food for a frog), and he reread to the beginning of the sentence. When he got to the error, he articulated the first sound of the word and self-corrected his error. This is an emerging behavior and certainly cause for celebration—he used the meaning (picture) and the visual information (print on page) to check his reading.

Andy substituted *a* for *an* on page 6, but at this level you wouldn't spend time here as it's very common for early beginning readers to make syntactical errors. The examples on page 8 are also interesting. Andy is again able to start a word and to say it accurately, possibly using the meaning in the picture. But when he comes to the word *rabbit,* the word *bunny* would also be accurate and the picture would only take him so far. He had to look again and notice the visual information to make the choice of *rabbit.*

Pg.	*Food for Animals* Level B
2	This is a bug. It is food for a frog.
4	This is a leaf. It is food for a giraffe.
6	This is an egg. It is food for a snake.
8	This is grass. It is food for a rabbit.

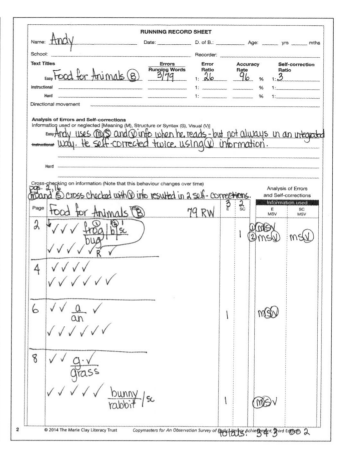

FIGURE 17-10 Record of Andy's Reading of *Food for Animals*, Level B

Below is an excerpt from a student reading *Dragon Quest* (*Fountas & Pinnell Classroom,* in press), a level Q book (see Figure 17-11). Cliff shows that he is capable of taking words apart. He noticed the first syllable of *forbidden* and went on to say the word. He made two attempts at *perilous*, finally saying the word. This behavior indicates the ability to use syllables and parts of words.

Clay (1991a) has identified a range of actions that readers use to solve words while reading continuous text. Readers can use them in any combination. These actions are overt in the behavior of beginning readers as they read orally, but as readers learn, they do not need to engage in this overt problem solving. They find that overt correction is inefficient and that they can perform operations more rapidly in their heads. Even when they read aloud, the teacher seldom hears overt processing like this, and you do not want to. Some of them are:

▶ Using the meaning of the whole text, the paragraph, the sentence and/or understanding of oral language to anticipate the word and confirming it with visual and phonological information.

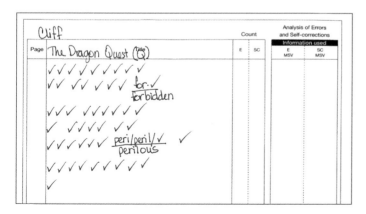

FIGURE 17-11 Record of Cliff's Reading of *Dragon Quest*, Level Q

- Repeating the line up to the problem word and making the sound of the first letter. This allows readers to remember the preceding meaning and language structure so that they can make an attempt on a word that looks right but also sounds right and makes sense.

- Noticing letter, sounds, and parts of words and then linking them to known oral vocabulary words. This is commonly called "decoding" or "cracking the code." The reader should make sure the word sounds right and makes sense before moving on.

- Noticing a part of the new word that is like a known word. Noticing meaningful chunks speeds up the word-solving process, and it can be an efficient strategy for intermediate/middle-readers as well.

- Solving words by cumulative letter-by-letter analysis. This allows readers to sample as much of the word as needed while thinking what would make sense. Often, the reader does not need to sound out all of the word but solves it with just the first two or three sounds. It is necessary, of course to notice word endings, but the redundancy of language is often helpful there.

As readers grow in proficiency, they tend to take longer words apart by parts or syllables, but they employ many of the same actions mentioned above to each. By now, the process is rapid and automatic, but even proficient readers sometimes find that they need to slow down, take a word apart, and look at it in detail, especially if it is highly technical.

Introducing the Text

You do not select a text only for the particular word-decoding challenges it offers. Other factors are important—interesting content, accessibility of language, level of vocabulary—but you will want to consider the difficulty of the words in the text and the opportunities for students to engage in problem solving. For early readers, you may want to use a word in conversation and help students connect the pictures with the words to support their use of meaning. For example, in *Food for Animals* (Figure 17-12), you might want to take students to several pages of the book and say the names of animals. Having just heard the words in connection with the pictures will help them solve the words when they come to them.

This is a leaf.
It is food for a giraffe.

4

5

FIGURE 17-12 Pages 4–5 from *Food for Animals*

You may also want to draw attention to a high-frequency word that is key to the language structure and meaning of the text. The word *this* is an example. Have them locate it on several pages. You may want to have students locate a key word like *food* by predicting the first letter and finding the word.

> Teacher: Do you see the leaf in the picture? The leaf is food for a giraffe. What letter would you expect to see at the beginning of the word *food*?
>
> Students: F.
>
> Teacher: Find *food* in the second line. Run your finger under it. *Food* is an important word. This book is all about food for animals.

For intermediate/middle readers, you will also want to draw attention to key words—both the meaning and the word structure. For example, in introducing *Dragon Quest* (*Fountas & Pinnell Classroom*, in press), you might draw attention to *pampered* on page 12 (see Figure 17-13). While the word is not difficult to decode, students might not have seen it before in written text, and it is important to the meaning. Fathom, the prince who goes out to fight the dragon says, "To prove myself. To show everyone I am brave, not just a pampered prince."

> Teacher: Turn to page 12, the third paragraph, and read it. Find the word *pampered*. Say it.
>
> Students: Pampered.
>
> Teacher: This word is important to understanding the character of Fathom. What do you think this word might mean?
>
> Elena: He doesn't want to just be safe and like a little kid. He wants to be brave.
>
> Teacher: So *pamper* means to take care of and make safe and comfortable.
>
> Teacher: All through this book, Fathom wants *not* to be a pampered prince but to be brave. So, you'll see whether he does it.

The writer of this book uses metaphors, so you might make other choices. For example, the dragon Huffalot says, "Why are you here, trying to skewer me with that toothpick you call a sword?" This sentence shows how tiny and insignificant Fathom is compared to the dragon. But you might decide students can comprehend this on their own. Every introduction involves a great deal of decision making, and word solving is only one of the areas to which you can give attention. We strongly advise against pre-teaching every word you think might give students challenge. For one thing, that would take all of the time for the introduction and would additionally deprive students of the challenge of solving words.

Reading the Text

As students read the text, you have the opportunity to observe oral reading, and that will give you a great deal of information even from the reading of a couple of pages of text. Many teachers use notation to code just a little oral reading on their observation sheets. Early readers will be reading audibly in a whisper and will soon progress to reading silently, but you can tap a student's hand to signal that he should raise his voice to a point that you can hear. (You might want to move around the round or horseshoe table on a small stool in order to sit behind the stu-

FIGURE 17-13 Pages 12–13 from *Dragon Quest*

dent. Then, all that is required is that the student turn slightly to read into your ear.) In this way, you can discover a great deal about what students know about word solving as they process text.

Occasionally, while listening to oral reading, you will want to use facilitative language to teach for, prompt, or reinforce word solving. The application of this kind of language will depend on the reader's specific behavior, so be selective. Remember, you can't prompt for actions the reader does not yet control. You'll find many examples of facilitative language in *Prompting Guide Part 1*. Some examples of prompts for early word solving are in Figure 17-14.

Clay has described various levels of teacher support you can use while students are processing text (Clay 2005). The level of support will depend on the reader's ability to search for and use visual information, or take words apart on the run and the particular word in the text that needs solving. Review the levels of support and think about how you may use the language up and down the scale with your students (see Figure 17-15).

Suggested Language to Teach for, Prompt for, and Reinforce Early Word Solving

Teach	Prompt	Reinforce
◆ "Listen to how I start it." ◆ "Look at the beginning." ◆ "You can get your mouth ready to start it." ◆ "You can read that again and try something else. [Model.]"	◆ "Say the first part." ◆ "Get your mouth ready to start the word." ◆ "Say the first sound." ◆ "Say more."	◆ "You got your mouth ready to start the word." ◆ "You said the first sound and it helped you."

FIGURE 17-14 Facilitative Language to Teach for, Prompt for, and Reinforce Early Word Solving

Levels of Support for Taking Words Apart While Reading

More Student Independence	Teacher/Reader	Teaching	Facilitative Language
↑	◆ Reader solves the word.	Confirm the reader's effective action.	◆ *You worked that out.*
	◆ Prompts the reader to use any known word part (beginning–initial letter or cluster, root, prefix), middle, end (inflection, rime, suffix).	Direct the reader to the tricky word or word part.	◆ *Do you know a word that starts (or ends) with those letters?* ◆ *What do you know that might help?*
	◆ Reader divides word with pointer finger or uses a card strip.	Direct the reader to the tricky word or word part.	◆ *Look for a part you know.* ◆ *What do you see that might help?*
	◆ Say the part and reader finds it.	Say the word part and have the reader find it (e.g., *sh*). Have the reader find it.	◆ *Does that part help you?*
	◆ Show a word part with a pointer finger or card strip.	Direct the reader's attention to a known word part.	◆ *Look at this part.* ◆ *You know this part.* ◆ *Do you know a word like that?*
↓ More Teacher Support	◆ Use magnet letters or a whiteboard to construct part of the word or to break a word apart.	Show the reader how to break the word apart.	◆ *Break it like this.* ◆ *Here is a word you know.* ◆ *If you change this part, you can make _____.*

FIGURE 17-15 Levels of Support for Taking Words Apart While Reading

Some of these examples are more for early readers than for students who are further along, but some intermediate students may still need this kind of prompting. As students are reading silently and rapidly, you will seldom want to intervene, although you may still sample oral reading to check on your perceptions.

Discussion

In the discussion, you invite students to talk about their thinking. You now have the opportunity to facilitate conversation and also notice how they are using the vocabulary of the text. As you listen carefully you will find evidence, for example:

"Snakes eat leafs and birds eat worms. It's all food."

"Fathom didn't want to be pampered like a baby. He wanted everybody to respect him because he faced the dragon. And he did that even though the dragon wasn't dangerous. He was really smart."

Teaching for Processing Strategies

Be selective about your teaching decisions after students read the text. Your students need to deeply comprehend the text and also be efficient with word analysis. Showing students something about word solving is an important option if there is a pattern in the processing that shows a need. You might select a productive example of student behavior that you think will help all students. For example,

> Teacher: Turn to page 8. Andy noticed the picture that that helped him understand what this page is about. He started to say *bunny*, but then he noticed. . . ?
>
> Students: *R* for *rabbit*.
>
> Teacher: The first letter of the word helped him say the word.

Early readers can benefit from quick location of a word in the text. For example:

> Teacher: Turn to page 10 and put your finger under the word *for*.
>
> (Students locate the word *for*.)
>
> Teacher: Now find *for* on page 2 . . . quickly. Find *for* on page 14.

You can also support students in looking closely at print. Notice that on the last page of *Food for Animals* there is a slight pattern variation (see Figure 17-16).

> Teacher: Turn to page 14 and find the word *this*. Get a good look at it.
>
> Now find *this* on page 16.
>
> Now put your finger under the word *and* on that page.
>
> It starts with uppercase *A*.

FIGURE 17-16 Page 16 of *Food for Animals*

For intermediate/middle readers, also, you might want to focus some teaching on word solving. An opportunity might arise in a text like *Dragon Quest*. For example, you might want students to understand the ironic meaning of a word (see Figure 17-17).

> Teacher: Go to page 10 and read the first three paragraphs. Then, talk with a partner about the meaning of the word *admirable*.
>
> (Students talk and report to the group.)
>
> Students: It means that he admires the king. He's saying he's a good king.
>
> Teacher: You did see the base word *admire* and the *–able* ending makes it an adjective, that means 'something to be admired.' Normally, that's something good. But listen while I read that paragraph and the next one to you and think about what the dragon is really thinking.
>
> (The teacher reads the paragraphs with expression.)
>
> Students: He doesn't really mean that he likes the king. He thinks the king is silly. He's getting Fathom to think about if the dragon really burns fields and villages.
>
> Teacher: Huffalot doesn't really admire the king. He is using the word in a sarcastic or ironic way. He means just the opposite. Sometimes writers use words in an ironic way for emphasis or humor.

Remember that teaching points can focus on any of the behaviors and understandings listed in *The Literacy Continuum* based on your observation of how the readers are processing the visual information.

Word Work

In word work at the end of the guided reading lesson, take the opportunity to zero in on any facet of letter or word learning. You are teaching the readers to look at the distinctive features of letters or to take words apart in continuous text. The teaching is enhanced by helping students attend to features in isolation. Word work is preplanned based on patterns of your students' needs as evidenced in your observations of text reading. Word work can focus on letters, letter-sound relationships, word patterns, word structure, or high-frequency words. The goal is for your students to learn to break the same words apart in many different ways quickly and flexibly. When readers look at letters or words in isolation, noticing their similarities and differences, they build systems for attending to the distinctive features of letters or segments of words that proficient readers use. They learn to become flexible and increase speed in picking up print features.

Think about what they need not only to learn but to use quickly with ease and flexibility. In guided reading, you have the opportunity to work with students in a small group to address their particular word analysis needs. Word work is very short—two to three minutes—but it can be powerful in helping readers develop flexibility in using word parts.

FIGURE 17-17 Pages 10–11 of *Dragon Quest*

Word work is *active;* students are engaged rather than simply watching and listening. They need to get their hands on manipulative materials. Some supportive materials are:

- Magnetic letters
- Teacher whiteboard and erasable marker or small chalkboard
- Small student whiteboards and erasable markers
- Word cards for high-frequency words
- Word cards for sorting
- Base words and prefixes or suffixes on cards
- Sound or letter box cards for students to write on

Some basic types of activities for letter or word work are:

▶ Give early readers a pile or cup of multicolored magnet letters to sort in specific ways.

▶ Give students sets of magnetic letters on a small metal tray (cookie sheet, stove burner covers, or other surface about 8 x 10 inches). Presort the letters rather than waiting for students to choose them from a full set. You can also have the sets of letters ready to use in small plastic bags or a cup. Have students make words quickly, take them apart, and make them again and break them apart. They can also add or substitute letters to make new words.

▶ Give students sound or letter box whiteboards on which they write—the box frames are permanent and students write inside with an erasable marker. At first, dictate a few words with three clear sounds. When the children gain good control of saying words slowly and hearing three sounds in sequence, use words with four sounds. Then, as the children show strong sound awareness, move to using letter boxes with four or five letters so they can learn how to think not only about the sounds they hear, but now think about how words look. The children have now shifted from phonemic awareness (sound awareness) to letter awareness (spelling). (See Figure 17-18.)

▶ Have students use individual small whiteboards (or chalkboards) to make and change words to demonstrate principles. Each student can have a small eraser or old sock on one hand.

▶ Use magnetic letters on a vertical board. Magnetic letters are particularly helpful when demonstrating how to take words apart or change words to make new ones. Have students manipulate the letters or words on their individual boards. Sometimes they can work as partners.

▶ Give students small plastic bags with word cards representing high-frequency words that they need to know. Early readers will benefit from having their own bags or envelopes of words that they know. They can work with these words in various ways and, finally, take home words that are well known.

For each text level in the Guided Reading section of *The Literacy Continuum,* you will find a section labeled, "Planning for Word Work After Guided Reading." These sections are consistent with the phonics and word study continuum, but they are specifically designed to involve students actively in working flexibly with the kind of concepts that they need to read this level with proficiency. Some examples are shown in Figure 17-19.

You will find these suggestions to be "generic" in that you can apply them over and over with different examples.

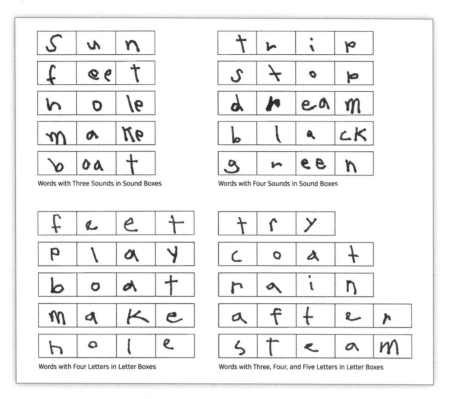

FIGURE 17-18 Sound and Letter Box Cards

Examples of Suggested Word Work

Level B	Match or sort letters by a variety of features quickly (uppercase or lowercase; tall or short; with and without sticks, circles, tails, dots, tunnels).
Level E	Using phonogram patterns, make new words by changing first and last letters (*pin/pit/hit*).
Level K	Take apart words with consonant blends and digraphs at the ends of words (*help*, *path*)
Level N	Work flexibly with base words, making new words by changing letters and adding prefixes and suffixes (*tip/tie/untie*; *grow/row/growing*).
Level Q	Work flexibly with base words, making new words by changing letters (*found/sound*) and adding and removing prefixes (*dis-like*, *un-sound*) and suffixes (*sound-ly*, *found-er*, *sound-less*).
Level S	Read frequently appearing syllable patterns in multi-syllable words (*-er*, *-ice*, *-tion*)
Level V	Read and derive meaning of words that are related to each other because they have the same base or root word (*monarch, monarchy, oligarchy, patriarch, matriarch*).

FIGURE 17-19 Examples of Suggested Word Work

A Meaningful Context for Word Solving

We have discussed how students acquire understandings about letters, sounds, and how words work across a long continuum of learning. The goal during the school years is to develop powerful systems for learning words. Students will need to continue learning about words throughout their years of schooling and as they enter the work force. But almost all of that learning will need to be accomplished independently through reading, so the patterns established in these early years of school are important.

We have described elements of word study that can take place in another block of time. But guided reading is a powerful context for focusing students' attention on aspects of words, as well as giving them many opportunities to use their word-study understandings in action while reading for meaning.

Suggestions for Professional Development

1. Meet in grade-level groups to work together on the letter/word work at the end of a guided reading lesson. Have each teacher bring some supplies:

   ▶ A set of magnetic letters

   ▶ A small whiteboard and markers

   ▶ Some cards that can be used to make word cards

2. Use *The Fountas and Pinnell Literacy Continuum,* Guided Reading section.

3. Identify levels of interest to teachers in the group.

4. Divide into pairs or small groups and assign a level or two to each group. Then, dig into the "Suggestions for Word Work" at the end of the "Within the Text" goals for the level and operationalize them.

   ▶ Each pair or group can identify at least four ways of working with letters or words at the end of a guided reading lesson.

   ▶ Using the materials they have, they role play in a way that will help them demonstrate it to the group. (The particular letters or words they use do not have to come from a particular book. They can draw on their understanding of what is typical knowledge of the children they teach. The idea is to provide powerful examples.)

   ▶ Groups should remember that this "word work" must be concrete, fast, and efficient. They will have one, two, or three minutes for each, and the materials need to be easy to reach and give to students.

5. Have pairs or groups take the whole group to the goal in *The Literacy Continuum* and then demonstrate the activity. These activities represent routines that students learn to use very quickly. This short activity can be related to the phonics/word study/spelling lesson they have had in the classroom, but it may be a little easier or a little more advanced depending on the level.

6. At the end of the session, consider the following questions:

   ▶ How can an activity such as sorting be used again and again with different letters or words?

   ▶ How can the routine be taught to students so that they are very efficient?

   ▶ Does each activity involve some kind of student action (rather than just teacher demonstration)?

7. Have an open discussion of the benefits to students of fast, active word work.

CHAPTER 18

Teaching for Phrased, Fluent Reading in Guided Reading Lessons

Fluency in reading leads to greater reading volume and greater reading volume leads to gains in fluency—fluency and reading volume are cause and consequence of one another.

–Timothy V. Rasinski

Slow, halting reading with many stops to do word solving is sometimes typical of struggling readers; but sometimes even proficient readers do not demonstrate aspects of fluency such as phrasing, appropriate word stress, and intonation to reflect meaning. We all know readers who can read fast with high accuracy, and yet have serious gaps in comprehension. Demonstrating reading proficiency also means reading with fluency, so it makes sense to teach for fluency in guided reading. The teaching is based on assessment. There is no substitute for listening to a segment of oral reading, and there is no other way to determine the degree to which readers can reflect the meaning of written language with their voices.

Consider that in social and work situations, reading fluency is often scrutinized and is sometimes the only indicator of a reader's skills. Many adults hesitate to read aloud because they feel awkward and unsure of themselves, for example, when asked to read in church or to read a speech. It takes practice to become a good oral reader, and even teachers, who must read aloud frequently, read and think about the expression and pace *before* they read to an audience. For the proficient reader, oral reading is performance.

We recommend strong teaching for oral fluent reading as part of the literacy curriculum for the following reasons:

▶ Throughout a student's school career, he will be judged by the quality of his oral reading.

▶ Oral reading fluency is an important social skill.

▶ It is an essential part of reading assessment.

▶ It is an outcome of smooth, efficient processing.

▶ Fluency contributes to a readers' ability to expand the processing system.

▶ Students must read at an appropriate pace to be able to complete work in school and in the workplace.

▶ Oral reading fluency is connected to fluent processing, which underlies all proficient silent reading.

▶ Oral reading should reveal the deeper meanings that the writer has mapped out in language; it is intimately connected to comprehension.

In this chapter, we discuss four contributors to fluent reading. Then, we examine the nature of fluency by presenting multiple dimensions and we discuss ways to teach for fluency in guided reading lessons.

Contributors to Reading Fluency

In general, reading fluency is based on how the reader solves the words in the text, on the reader's background knowledge of language and the world, and on the reader's experience with written language. While there are a multitude of contributors, we have identified four that we will discuss here (see Figure 18-1).

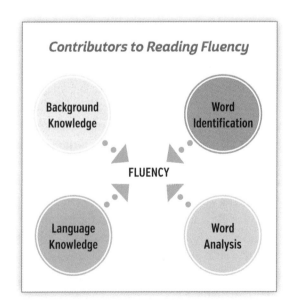

FIGURE 18-1 Contributors to Reading Fluency

Background Knowledge

The more the reader knows about the content of the text the easier it is to read with fluency. Readers know the meaning of the words (even if they are new to reading). They have heard stories read aloud and understand a basic narrative structure so that they can anticipate problem resolutions and endings. They can anticipate what a character is likely to do. Anticipation fuels fluent reading as it acts as a "feed-forward mechanism." The range of background knowledge that contributes to fluency includes: (1) content knowledge; (2) knowledge of texts; and (3) genre knowledge.

Content

If the reader has some familiarity with the topic of a nonfiction book, then more vocabulary words or phrases will be familiar. When they know the meaning of the words or have heard the words, even though they have never read them, word solving will be quicker and reading can be smoother as a result. Readers' background knowledge helps them predict the kinds of information they are reading and how ideas are related to each other. It's more than the meaning of discipline-specific words; writers in different disciplines have ways of using language to talk about the discipline or topic. These ways may involve style, grammar, punctuation, and literary conventions particular to works like feature articles, editorials, or reports. At higher levels, we call this "academic language," and it takes skill to read it with fluency.

Content knowledge also plays a role in reading fiction with fluency. For example, knowing the time period or the setting is helpful to readers. Having some understanding of technology helps in understanding science fiction. Even for young children, content knowledge of everyday procedures will help in following a description of a temporal sequence. The content of the text may be supported by their own personal experiences (like making a pizza or planting a garden). Yet, these are often the kinds of texts that we as adults find ourselves reading aloud.

Texts

Experience in processing texts builds students' content knowledge, but it also helps students internalize the structure or organization of texts. In many texts, information is presented in chronological order; in others, the writer uses categories. If students have a great deal of experience with hearing texts read aloud, they learn how to anticipate the way the text "works." Their knowledge of the organizational patterns helps to fast-forward reading. In addition, nonfiction writers often use underlying structural patterns like compare and contrast, problem and solution, cause and effect, and chronological or temporal sequence. Familiarity with text structure gives readers a kind of "road map" for rapidly understanding the information and producing reading with appropriate word stress and intonation.

Genre

In our book *Genre Study: Teaching with Fiction and Nonfiction Books, Grades K-8+* (2012), we describe an inquiry process for immersing students in a genre in order to internalize its characteristics. Text structure and genre are intimately connected because text structure is one characteristic of a genre; but each genre also has other important characteristics. Understanding of genre characteristics helps readers know when the setting is important to the problem in the story, as well as how to identify the problem and predict the solution. Different genres sometimes have characteristic language; for example, historical fiction and traditional tales often include archaic language. Science fiction and fantasy may have author-created words that label procedures and events that do not exist in the real world. The writing style of the exposition of characters, setting, and plot signal a fiction genre to the reader, who forms expectations around the way the text works.

Nonfiction genres have special features that propel the reader through the text. As in fiction, the writer's lead and the revealing of the topic signals a nonfiction genre. The information in headings and subheadings, for example, helps the reader quickly identify the category of information that will follow. They can raise questions in their minds and look for answers. Nonfiction writers use a wide range of graphics, from which readers take information, which often helps them to better understand the text.

Language Knowledge

Students' language knowledge includes vocabulary, syntax, and the way language is used to express meaning. For the young reader, knowledge of syntax is probably the most powerful system for supporting fluency. They have an intuitive sense for how the reading should sound like talking. Readers use their knowledge of how oral language is structured to anticipate word order. You are probably thinking that will be a tricky area for ELLs, and you are right. But these speakers do have a sense that language should "sound right," because they follow syntactic rules to communicate in their home language. They may need more rehearsal to get a sense of English syntax, and shared reading can be helpful.

The better students understand the grammatical structure of English, the easier it will be for them to read with fluency. Young children begin with the syntax they have learned in their homes and communities. It's important to point out that all languages as well as dialects and types of English have "rules" by which words are put together to make meaning (see Chapter 17). So, the child learns that language is rule-governed, and he should use this knowledge to monitor whether reading "sounds right" and "makes sense."

Students' knowledge of language structure grows exponentially when they hear books read aloud and when they talk with others about books. Ahead of their individual reading, they expand their knowledge of the syntax of written language, which is different in many ways from oral language. As they read for themselves and listen to their own reading, they further expand the syntax they control.

Word Identification and Word Analysis

Every proficient reader has a huge body of words that he recognizes instantly and without effort, and readers constantly add to that repertoire. Rapid action from the brain that recognizes letter and word patterns fast is an aspect of effective processing. But language structure also plays a key role. If the reading is phrased, there is a chance the reader will also be attending to the meaning. Developing readers need to process a text that has potential for new learning, but they need to do this problem solving against a backdrop of accurate reading. Fast processing of letter information and known words makes the meaning and language structure available to students as they work to solve unknown words.

Beginning readers may produce the kind of staccato reading characteristic of children who are gaining control of word-by-word matching, but as they become more experienced, reading words that were once new become effortless and automatic, leaving attention to learning. "Slow" word-by-word reading should not last long because the reader, guided by meaning, will begin to use all of his word knowledge and to phrase and stress words to make the reading sound very much like oral language.

Clay (2005) has cautioned teachers not to allow slow reading: "It is the nature of the brain to move with urgency from early slow processing to fast processing on things the brain can recognize. That leaves space and time for slower processing on the things you do not know. At no time in the Reading Recovery® lesson series should the child be a slow reader of the things he knows." (Clay 2005, 151.)

Keep in mind that Clay is referring here to Reading Recovery, an intervention program for young children who are having difficulty learning to read and write. They are expected to read fluently! We believe that the same is true for students who are making satisfactory progress and at all grade levels. In general, rate and fluency should increase as children go up the grades. One reason for this is that the increase in known words is enormous. But after the first few levels on the text level gradient on which readers are learning to match the voice with print, the reading should *sound fluent at every level.*

We still find intermediate students reading with very high accuracy but sounding slow and plodding (sometimes even pointing at words with a pencil long after the eyes can control the process). In other words, slow and not-fluent reading may actually become a habit. When students can recognize words with high accuracy but are still not reading fluently, you need to work intensively for more fluent reading. And, that work is not simple. It requires teaching moves on several fronts at once, and word solving is necessary (although not sufficient) to assure fluent reading. Readers need a body of known words they can recognize with automaticity, and that body of known words needs to grow every year.

Word analysis usually requires a "slow down" to problem-solve. The reader links the oral sounds of language to the symbols that represent them in simple and highly complex ways. Readers look at letters, letter clusters, and larger parts of words to monitor their reading and to make attempts. Beginners may need to look across the word, processing the letters and connecting them to sounds, but very quickly, children learn to use known words and patterns to solve new words. For example, if you know *the,* it is easier to read *then.* If you know *it,* you can solve *is.* If you know *the* and *at,* it's easier to solve *that.* Intermediate readers can deal with complex multi-syllable words in much the same way—if you know *misery,* it's easier to solve *miserable* or *miserably.*

There is some belief that readers always solve words by noting individual letters and connecting them to sounds, and that is a myth. Proficient readers do understand individual letters (and letter clusters) and how they connect to sounds *but they always do the most efficient action*—the one that will take less time and effort and they check it with what would make sense and sound right. Kaye (2006) completed a large study of proficient second graders' reading behaviors across a school year. She examined more than 2,500 readings and found that the proficient readers visibly demonstrated more than sixty ways (both one-step and multi-step actions) to solve words, and presumably more of their actions could not be observed because they took place in the head. She found that these proficient readers:

- Had the ability to "sound out" words letter by letter but never articulated words phoneme by phoneme while reading (they used more efficient strategies).
- Took more efficient or "economical" approaches, such as using larger word parts.
- Were extremely active in problem solving.
- Never appealed to the teacher without first initiating an attempt.

You need to teach your students a range of word-analysis strategies that they can employ in flexible ways to support fluent processing; that is, if one approach doesn't work, they try another. You'll find a detailed description of these strategic actions in the word solving and searching for and using visual information sections of each level, A–Z, in the Guided Reading section of *The Literacy Continuum.*

What Is Reading Fluency?

Fluency is not a word that applies only to reading (although as teachers we become accustomed to thinking that). Think about anything that you do with fluency. Maybe you can play the piano, ice skate, knit, exercise, or text furiously. Chefs move through the actions of cooking with a minimum of motions, high efficiency, and graceful movements, some while talking nonstop to a television audience. Fluency means:

- Having high expertise in the motor movements of a task.
- Being able to perform a large number of actions so automatically that they require no attention.
- Having an eye to the ultimate goal, realizing (not always consciously) how every action leads to it.
- Being able to orchestrate *simultaneously* a number of complex actions in search of the goal.
- Monitoring in a way that gives you feedback about how it is going so that you can correct action.
- Varying rate according to purpose and interpretation of a text.
- Feeling a constant sense of satisfaction at the fluent performing.

Reading fluency is a product—an outcome of a reader's integration or orchestration of strategic actions. It's much more than automatic word recognition, although that is one contributor. But it is also a process. Reading fluency itself fuels the reading system because it enables the reader to make maximum use of all the information he has—oral language structure and meaning, knowledge of the visual features or words, and understanding of the story or informational book that is being processed. Because the reading is moving along at a pace that resembles language (rather than slow, isolated word calling), the reader can constantly check whether the language processed is making sense.

We want to make it clear that fluency is not synonymous with speed in reading. Too much emphasis has been placed on speed to the detriment of comprehension. Fluency is multidimensional and it varies with the type of reading that the student is processing. Sometimes readers "gobble up" the story, racing ahead. Sometimes they pause and search back for evidence. Sometimes they stop to reflect on what is read and to reread for deeper comprehension. Sometimes they skim and scan, looking for specific information. Fluency is a highly complex process and cannot be measured by a simple "words per minute" assessment or even a "correct words per minute." (In this case, any smart reader would simply skip all words that require work and the reading can become incoherent!)

We are mindful of Newkirk's advice in *The Art of Slow Reading* (2012). The fluent reader is demonstrating comprehension, taking cues from the text, and taking pleasure in finding the right tempo for the text. That is why goals for reading rate must be so wide. The norms for reading speed have gone up, but these increases have not been matched by improvement in comprehension. The way reading fluency has been measured has influenced practice, and in some places, it has had a devastating effect on reading itself. Have you seen students who read rapidly, robotically, skipping words without working for accuracy and meaning? Now think about practicing that kind of reading every day, all day.

Newkirk hastens to explain that by slow reading he does not mean the laborious, word-to-word struggle to read something that is clearly too hard. Instead, he means the thoughtful consideration of the text. There is no ideal speed; the speed, for Newkirk, has to do with the relationship the reader has with what he reads. Newkirk describes his own entry to a book:

> I enter a book carefully, trying to get a feel for this writer/narrator/teller that I will spend time with. I hear the language, feel the movement of sentences, pay attention to punctuation, sense pauses, feel the writer's energy (or lack of it), and construct the voice and temperament of the writer. Even as I read 'silently,' I am still in a world of sound. My connection to writers, my pleasure in reading, even my capacity for comprehension depends on this sound, on the voiced quality of print. (1–2)

He goes on to say that he doesn't hear this voice all the time—not when skimming the Internet or reading interminable lengthy letters from administrators. But the reading that truly matters asks him to be continuously present:

> I am thrown off my reading game when I am forced to go too fast. I can feel the connection slipping away. I lose this vital sense of language and rhythm. I am forced to skip, scan and sample when I feel myself on the clock . . . and one of my favorite and most pleasurable activities becomes suddenly unpleasant. (2)

You don't want to treat teaching for fluency as teaching for speed, although a reasonable rate is one dimension to develop. When readers attend to and make their reading reflect the multiple dimensions of fluency, then, rate tends to follow. Stouffer (2011) explains that it makes sense to help readers listen to themselves as they read so that they can become more aware of the links between language and meaning. If reading is too fast or robotic, the listener can't make sense of it. The oral reading provides additional information, especially for the beginning reader:

> As the child reads, his eyes are searching through the arbitrary symbols of print and generating a spoken response. As sounds or words are generated, the child can listen to the sound of his own voice to weigh up what he has just said against his general knowledge, the plot of the story (meaning), spoken language (structure), and the text symbols he is seeing (visual information). (Stouffer 2011, 17)

In this way, listening to his own voice helps the reader engage in the self-monitoring that is essential for building a reading process. Others have argued (for example, see a review by Reutzel, Jones, Fawson and Smith 2008), that oral reading provides developing readers with useful feedback. Oral reading or interpretation prompts intermediate readers to think deeply about the writer's meaning so that they can reflect it with the voice. Oral reading of plays and readers' theater scripts give students an authentic reason to read aloud. It is a team effort that promotes the sense of community. Intermediate students can also enjoy reading famous speeches, concentrating on the delivery of the speaker's message.

Promoting oral reading does not mean engaging students in the kind of tedious "round robin" exercise in which students take turns reading aloud in a small group (and certainly not in a whole-class setting). This process can be highly distressing to students who do not read with high accuracy or fluency and can be very boring to others. While they are not reading, students tend to stop listening. Thinking about the text may be limited. What we will examine here is how you can work with your students in guided reading to help them improve in all aspects of the complex process we call fluent reading.

Dimensions of Fluency

We have described fluency as having five characteristics, or dimensions, with a sixth being the smooth integration or orchestration of all these dimensions (see Figure 18-2). You can focus students' attention on any one of these dimensions or on the integration of all.

The quality of reading that we often call "expression" in reading is a characteristic of language called *prosody*. This word is derived from an Ancient Greek word that means "song sung to music; tone or accent of a syllable." The variables that make up the prosody of a language are not the individual phonemes attached to vowels and consonants. They are attached to syllables and larger units of speech. It is prosody that allows a speaker to express emotion, use sarcasm, argue with emphasis, convey a sense of calm. Prosody also may convey meaning to a listener that is not obvious just by looking at the words chosen. Consider this exchange:

> "Well, you took your time getting here." (Meaning: you were slow, you're late, and I'm mad about it.)

Dimensions of Fluency

Dimension	Description	Value in Reading Processing
Pausing	Readers use punctuation to guide the voice (short breath at a comma, longer pause at ending punctuation, anticipatory pause at a colon). Pausing and phrasing are highly related.	Recognizing the role of punctuation helps readers process the syntax of the written language and to understand the relationship among words, clauses, and sentences.
Phrasing	Readers put words together in meaningful groups as they read, and these are marked with short breaths or pauses. Phrasing makes oral reading sound like language.	These brief pauses show that groups of words belong together in a way that communicates the syntactic patterns of the language and meaningful units (for example, prepositional phrases).
Stress	Readers place emphasis on particular words in a sentence to reflect meaning and structure, just as in oral language.	Emphasizing selected words in a sentence communicates specific meaning, which can differ if other words are selected.
Intonation	Readers vary the tone of the voice (rising or falling, pitch, and volume) to show the meaning of the text.	The pitch or tone of voice signals purpose (for example, asking a question), as well as strength and emotions. Intonation communicates that readers are inferring meaning beyond the bare words.
Rate	Readers move through the text at an appropriate rate. They may read rapidly to gather information or show action in a fiction text. They may slow down for emphasis or to take a thoughtful and reflective tone. But, overall, they avoid extremely long pauses, stops, and starts.	Moving with good momentum through the text means that the readers are solving words efficiently (recognizing most without conscious effort). A satisfactory rate frees attention so that readers can process the language and meaning.
Integration	Readers consistently orchestrate their reading, using pausing, phrasing, stress, intonation, and rate in a smoothly integrated way.	Integration of all dimensions of fluency makes oral reading sound like meaningful language. It requires readers not only read the words but interpret the meaning of the text.

FIGURE 18-2 Dimensions of Fluency

"You don't have to take that tone with me!" (Meaning: I think you're scolding me.)

"All I said was that you took your time." (Meaning: What do you mean? I was just making a statement.)

We all know that seemingly mild statements can be said in a way that causes offense, and this can happen whether intended or not. It's all in the prosody and the listener's interpretation. Many comedians use prosody in a highly skilled way. With excellent timing, they can make a "jab" that hits home and surprises the audience. Of course, prosody in oral language is accompanied by nonverbal behavior—

gestures, facial expressions, body stance; and comedians make good use of those, but the voice is crucial.

Language consists of strings of meaningful word units spoken one after another in grammatical patterns. (This does not necessarily mean "proper" grammar as in English class but any patterns that are meaningful to the speakers of a language or a dialect of a language.) Listeners must follow a speaker and "parse the sentence so far to make sure that he or she is receiving a 'possible' message," (Clay 2001, 101). Parsing involves understanding the correct relationships between spoken words, and it involves analyzing a string of symbols (the sounds in words, the words, the phrases, sentences, etc.). We all do it constantly every day—the behavior is unconscious and automatic. But we occasionally become aware of the process if we mishear something, if the speaker uses grammatical patterns that are new to us or that vary from the standard language we have learned, or if a speaker uses a new expression.

Written language has meaningful words arranged in grammatical patterns and with helpful punctuation included. Like the listener, the reader parses the string of symbols—this time letters and words—to identify meaningful language patterns. The beginning reader is helped by the fact that many easy books have simple and natural language patterns, so he can use everything he learned about parsing as he acquired oral language. But all readers must also analyze sentences that differ from oral language and have increasingly complex grammatical patterns to parse. Unlike the listener, the reader must either listen to himself reading the language aloud, or "hear" the language in the head in order to parse the grammar. Attributes of prosody include:

▶ Awareness of the sound system, which informs intonation. The reader uses pitch, stress, tempo, rhythm, and pausing to reflect meaning.

▶ Awareness of the meaning system, including the grammar onto which meanings are mapped, the way words are stressed or accented, conversational interaction called discourse, and emotion.

So language—both oral and written—is ultimately a social device that represents meaning through words, but also through a number of other complex communication devices. Oral reading reflects all of these through the voice. In dramatic plays and films, though actors are reciting memorized written language, they are able to incorporate nonverbal behavior to fully communicate meaning.

Pausing

For purposes of reliable assessment, we have defined pausing as the time a reader stops briefly when cued by punctuation. However, pausing and phrasing are actually interrelated because readers use brief pauses to define phrase units even if no punctuation indicates it. Pausing, then, refers to the way a reader recognizes punctuation with a distinct pause, for example:

▶ Full stop at a period with the voice falling.

▶ Full stop at an exclamation point with the voice placing emphasis on the last word.

- ◗ Brief breath at a comma.

- ◗ Pause at a semicolon with voice at the same pitch.

- ◗ Pause at a semicolon with the voice at the same pitch, communicating anticipation.

- ◗ Pause at a dash (next word may be emphasized or stressed).

- ◗ Full stop at a question mark with a rising tone in the voice.

- ◗ Pause at open and closing parenthesis, phrasing the material in the middle.

- ◗ Longer pause at ellipses with the voice staying at the same pitch or rising slightly.

- ◗ Brief pause to set off a quotation at the beginning and ending marks, and reading the material in the quotes as if talking.

- ◗ Bullets indicate the reader should present a list, with pause between the end of a bullet and the beginning of another one.

There are some exceptions to the above guidelines, for example, periods are also used to abbreviate words (U.S., Feb.) and in this case the reader doesn't stop but treats the abbreviation as a word.

Except for beginning readers who are just beginning to notice these marks, these pauses and changes in voice pitch do not happen at the point in time that the reader sees the punctuation mark. The reader usually anticipates the punctuation by recognizing syntactic patterns and using the meaning of words. For example, when you say, "Where is the car?" you know at the beginning of the sentence that your voice will rise. Even early readers learn that words like *when* signal that the voice will rise.

You want readers to reflect the punctuation rather than reading right over the marks in a monotone or using inappropriate intonation and pausing. Beginning readers who are learning to match one spoken word with one written word may pause after *every* word, but you do not want this behavior to continue very long. It is important that students process continuous print as *language* so that they can sense appropriate responses to punctuation; this process becomes automatic very quickly.

Phrasing

As mentioned, the reader uses brief pauses to show phrase units. Even beginning readers who are pointing can do some phrasing by putting two words together, for example "the park" or "said Mom." Phrases reflect groups of words and these are indicated by knowledge of language patterns and meaning in addition to punctuation. In the paragraph below from *Bear and the Little Snakes* (*Fountas & Pinnell Classroom,* in press), we have inserted slashes to indicate where a reader paused to show phrases.

Mrs. Snake / was at the door/. Her three little snakes / were with her.
"I'm going /to the store,"/ she said. / "Will you take care of / my three little snakes?"/
Bear did not want to take care of /the little snakes,/ but they crawled inside. / Mrs. Snake smiled, /and then she left./

Many well-designed books for beginners are laid out in a way that helps children to group words into phrased units. There are only a few lines of print on each page (see Figure 18-3). In the example below, notice how the line breaks indicate places to pause. We are not saying that you would teach children to use line breaks, because that kind of layout will not apply as they move into higher levels of text. But you can demonstrate reading with excellent phrasing and ask them to "put these words together as you read."

> Page 4:
> "Will you take care of
> my three little snakes?"
> Page 5:
> Bear did not want to take care of
> the little snakes . . ."

Clay cautions us that, "expert readers know that there is nothing precise about phrasing. This is where being tentative and flexible pays off. How many words and which words are grouped together cannot be predicted. Two different groupings might give you two different messages; but they might also give you the same message." (Clay 2005, 151) So, much phrasing is left to the individual reader's interpretation. The important thing is for readers to realize that phrasing is needed.

Stress

In connection with pausing and phrasing, proficient readers use word stress, and this factor too is related to the reader's interpretation of the text. Consider the difference in meaning that you communicate by stressing different words in the same sentence (see Figure 18-4).

FIGURE 18-3 Pages 4–5 from *Bear and the Little Snakes*

It's amazing how a simple question like this one can come across as negative, depending on which word is stressed. That may be the reason so many texts or emails are interpreted as offensive—there's no prosody in those messages! The differences are subtle but real. By stressing different words the speaker indicates variations in the underlying connotations. Fluent readers reflect their interpretation of those connotations through stress.

Intonation

Each of the dimensions mentioned above have something to do with intonation (for example, the tones at end punctuation). The readers use different tones and pitches to show the meaning of the text. You may listen to books using audio recordings, and this experience is pleasurable because the actors reading the texts are highly practiced in using intonation to reflect meaning. They vary the pace and pitch of the voice to show suspense, reflection, and deep emotion. Of course, early and even higher-level readers are not professionally trained actors, and you would not expect this kind of performance; but you do want them to take pleasure in the reading and use tone of voice to show interpretation of the meaning of the text.

Word Stress Within a Sentence

Word Stress Within Sentence	Meaning	Interpretation
Why did you call me today?	I want to know the reason you called today.	Straightforward, neutral question (unless said with angry intonation).
Why *did* you call me today?	I suddenly realized that I don't know the reason you called today.	Just wanting to know why the person called (or it could be said with suspicion).
Why did *you* call me today?	I'm surprised that you were the one to call me today.	May imply that the caller acted inappropriately or that another person is not meeting expectations.
Why did you *call* me today?	You should have contacted me another way (text, email, or personal visit).	Implies inappropriate action.
Why did you call *me* today?	I'm not the person you should have called today (you should have called someone else).	Implies detachment.
Why did you call me *today*?	You should have called me at another time (earlier or later). Or, you knew today would be a very busy time.	Implies exasperation.

FIGURE 18-4 Word Stress Within a Sentence

Rate

As a positive aspect of reading, you could say that rate is highly overrated. Many people, including some educators and researchers, seem to equate reading speed with reading quality, and the two are not necessarily synonymous. If you read at a very fast rate but retain little of the meaning (or only a very superficial idea), then what have you accomplished? In general, as readers grow more proficient in solving words and processing written language, of course, they progress at a faster rate. Speed or rate of reading can't be ignored either as it may be evidence of excessively slow processing of text. Slow, labored reading may be a symptom of inefficient word analysis or lack of awareness of how reading should sound. The proficient ten-year-old reader can read more lines of text than a proficient seven-year-old reader in the same length of time. And, silent reading is faster than oral reading simply because of the time needed to audibly pronounce the words. Clay concluded, "What is certain is that when a person is reading continuous text, reading speed and reading fluency are linked to increasing improvements of reading test scores in older readers." (Clay 2005, 151)

It is true that faster rates of reading have been correlated to higher comprehension (Allington 2001), but we don't know whether there is a causal link. It may be that better comprehension contributes to fluency. It is also true that moving along at a satisfactory rate contributes to the reader's ability to process the text as language. After that early period when children take on word-by-word matching, you can expect the reading rate increases each year throughout elementary school. But you should not make a "faster is better" simplistic assumption, nor should you allow your students to believe such assumptions. You want thoughtfulness in reading; but while that is true, you also need to include in your teaching goals the support of students' achieving momentum as they read. Increased phrasing, pausing, word stress, and intonation usually lead to a faster rate.

Integration

The real test of fluency is how the reader uses all of the dimensions in an integrated way. All sources of information must be orchestrated to process text quickly, efficiently, and smoothly. When an individual reads aloud, the voice communicates to listeners the meaning of the story or nonfiction book. It is effortless. Expression includes pausing, phrasing, stress, and intonation working together in a way that gives listeners pleasure in accessing the meaning of the text—following the story or encountering and thinking about interesting ideas. You do it every day in interactive read-aloud. You will not be expecting early readers to demonstrate the skills of a highly proficient teacher, but they should be working toward the same goal of reading not only with accuracy, but also in a way that communicates meaning to listeners by interpreting the text with their voice.

What About Silent Reading?

The reason you assess reading fluency by listening to oral reading is that it is virtually impossible to assess it through silent reading. You could set the reader a task of reading a selection silently and telling you when he finishes, but you would still have no idea of *how* he processed the text. He could have skimmed or skipped sections. You have to assume that in many ways, fluent oral reading reflects the ability of the reader to move through the text. You might assume that readers:

▶ Recognize phrases and punctuation.

▶ "Hear" word stress and intonation in their heads.

▶ Move their eyes along the print in a fluid motion (although there will be backtracks).

The most important ability students develop is silent reading—that is the way they do most of their reading in school and in life. But it is not true that they should never read aloud. There is a place for authentic oral reading in the literacy design and for the development of proficiency in that area.

Teaching for Fluency in Guided Reading

We assume that guided reading is implemented within an instructional design that includes:

▶ Interactive read-aloud, in which students have ample opportunity to hear demonstrations of fluent reading, to process the meaning and syntax of texts, and to talk about texts.

▶ Shared reading, in which students have the opportunity to join in with the support of the group, experiencing fluent reading, and to practice the performance of oral reading. Repeated readings of a familiar text supports the reader's orchestration of all dimensions of fluency.

▶ Independent reading, in which students engage in reading massive amounts of continuous text at an independent level.

▶ Phonics/word study minilessons and application, in which students learn a range of efficient word analysis strategies so they can pick up print information quickly with the eye.

▶ Writing, in which students grow in familiarity with words and the distinguishing features of letters and words.

You have many opportunities to teach for fluency across the guided reading lesson.

Selecting the Text

Choose books that will allow your students to recognize most words automatically but have a few challenges so that they can problem-solve against a background of accurate reading. The more the reader brings to the text, the smoother the processing. As you select texts, notice language structures that will likely be easy, and those that will be difficult for your students. Consider how the print and layout will support fluent, phrased reading. Take into account those students who are English language learners. Seemingly easy English sentences may pose difficulty. English language learners will likely have difficulty reading what they cannot say, so you might have them listen and then repeat the language. Make a plan for supporting readers for fluent reading and this may include attention to particular visual features of words that are difficult. If children hear a new word, especially one that might not be in their English vocabularies, then it will be more accessible to them when they process a text.

> Rooster was so angry
> turned dark red. But he knew more than
> one way to get a worm. Rooster decided
> to trick Crow.
>
> "Oh mighty Crow!" he crooned.
> "That was a fast flight. Your strong
> wings flap like the wings of an eagle."
> The proud crow thought, "That
> rooster has spoken the truth for once."
> So he flapped his wings and showed
> them off to the whole meadow.
>
> **9**

FIGURE 18-5 Marking the Text With a Card

> Rooster was so angry his comb
> turned dark red. But he knew more than
> one way to get a worm. Rooster decided
> to trick Crow.
>
> he crooned.
> "That was a fast flight. Your strong
> wings flap like the wings of an eagle."
> The proud crow thought, "That
> rooster has spoken the truth for once."
> So he flapped his wings and showed
> them off to the whole meadow.
>
> **9**

FIGURE 18-6 Sliding Card Left to Right

Introducing the Text

The introduction to the text provides support for using meaning, language structure, and visual or graphophonic information—all of which are important in supporting reading fluency. In the introduction, you can:

❭ Draw attention to the features of a complex or known word.

❭ Support students in practicing a difficult language structure. You might have them repeat the structure aloud.

❭ Help students understand the genre or how the text is organized.

Almost everything you do in the orientation to connect students to the meaning of the text, its organization and language structures, will support fluency, along with comprehension.

Reading the Text

While students are reading the text (softly to themselves or silently) you can take the opportunity to sample some oral reading, and, for very brief intervals, you may want to teach for and prompt for dimensions of fluency.

For young children (and even some older readers who are habitually lacking fluency) a high priority is to begin to read in phrases, which will automatically increase rate while asking the reader to think about the meaning and to connect the written language to their own oral language. While you are drawing attention to the phrasing, though, you want to maintain a sense of the whole sentence or the short paragraph. Clay (2005) has suggested some very explicit teaching aimed at a fluency problem: "mark the text with a card or your thumb, exposing two or three words at a time, ask the child to 'read it all'" (see Figure 18-5).

Another of Clay's suggestions is to slide a card over the text, left to right, so that the child's eyes can work ahead of the voice (see Figure 18-6). These techniques are effective when you are sure the child can read the words, and they can also be used during the rereading of a text.

Based on the student's reading, make a decision about whether you want to teach, prompt, or reinforce behavior. Some sample prompts for each dimension of fluency are illustrated in Figure 18-7. You can find an extensive list of prompts to use in teaching for fluent reading in *Prompting Guide Part 1*. Your goal is to internalize the language so you can respond precisely to the reading behaviors you observe.

These kinds of interactions should be very brief so as not to interrupt the students' construction of meaning while reading the text. Intermediate/middle students

Suggested Language for Teaching for, Prompting, and Reinforcing Fluency

Dimension	Teach	Prompt	Reinforce
Pausing	◆ Listen to me read this. Can you hear me take a little breath at the comma (period, dash). ◆ Listen to me read this. Can you hear my voice go down at the period (question mark)?	◆ Take a little (or short) pause when you see the comma (or dash). ◆ Stop at the period. ◆ Make your voice go down when you see the period. ◆ Set off the parentheses by stopping before them and after them. ◆ Read the punctuation.	◆ You stopped at the period. ◆ You made your voice go up when you saw the question mark. ◆ You made your voice go down when you saw the period.
Phrasing	◆ Read it like this (model phrase units). ◆ Read this much all together (cover part of the print, exposing phrase unit).	◆ Read these words together (indicate). ◆ These words make sense together. Read them together. ◆ Put your words together so it sounds like the way you talk.	◆ You put your words together. You make it sound like talking. ◆ You made your words almost touch each other that time.
Stress	◆ Listen to how this sounds. (Model appropriate word stress.) ◆ When you see this print (boldface, capital letters), make these words sound important.	◆ Try that again and make that word sound important. ◆ Try that again and say the dark word (or word in all capital letters) louder.	◆ You made that word sound important. ◆ You made the dark word (or the word in all capital letters) louder that time.
Intonation	◆ Listen to me read this. Can you hear how excited my voice sounds? ◆ Listen to me read this. Can you hear how I sound like the characters who are talking?	◆ Make your voice show excitement when you see the exclamation point. ◆ Make your voice sound like the character is talking when you see the speech marks (talking marks, quotation marks). ◆ Read the punctuation. ◆ Are you listening to yourself? ◆ Make it sound like a story you listen to.	◆ You sounded excited when you read that part. ◆ You read the punctuation. ◆ You made it sound like the character(s) were talking. ◆ You made that story (part) interesting.
Rate	◆ Listen to how I read this quickly.	◆ Read these words quickly (model if needed).	◆ You read it faster that time.
Integration	◆ Listen to how I read this. Can you read it the same way? ◆ Make your reading sound smooth like this. (Model.)	◆ Read it all smoothly. ◆ Read it like the author is telling the story. ◆ How do you think your reading sounds?	◆ You made your reading sound interesting that time. ◆ You are reading it like you are telling a story. ◆ You sounded smooth that time.

FIGURE 18-7 Suggested Language for Teaching for, Prompting, and Reinforcing Fluency

who have learned fluency throughout their years of school will probably need little prompting, but you may want to work for greater fluency in the teaching after the reading if it is not achieved.

Discussing the Text and Making Teaching Points

First, invite students to talk about the text. Everything you do to help students articulate their thinking will expand comprehension of the text and contribute to fluency. Moving smoothly out of the discussion, you make one or two teaching points that will support the reader's use of strategic actions. You may choose to focus on fluency.

A Range of Instructional Procedures to Support Phrased, Fluent Reading

One of the simplest approaches with early readers is engaging students in rereading familiar texts. The following are a variety of other approaches you might use in your teaching to get shifts in processing.

Echo Reading

Select a short segment of the text to revisit. A sentence or two, or a short paragraph, is enough. You can emphasize any aspect of fluency, or just work for integration. You may want to consider:

- An exciting, emotional, or funny part of a story
- A short stretch of dialogue
- A summary of information in a nonfiction text
- An interview with a real person in a nonfiction text
- A statement of the lesson or larger message of a fiction or nonfiction text
- Any piece of the text that offers a chance to use punctuation

Say to the students, "Listen while I read this." Then, read the segment to the students. You can have them read it in unison right after you, or say, "What did you notice about how I read that?" You can ask them to talk about:

- What your voice did at punctuation
- What words you read all at once (phrased)
- Which words you stressed and why
- How your voice made it sound like talking
- How your voice showed the meaning

You can repeat the process, working for greater fluency, and/or have students practice with a partner.

Phrased Reading

Give students a typed copy of a paragraph drawn from the text or work with an enlarged version. Read the text to the students with appropriate pausing. Then, read it again and either mark the phrases with slashes on the enlarged copy or have students mark them on their individual copies. Have them work in pairs to practice phrasing.

Assisted Reading

Read a selected sentence or paragraph with fluency. Then, have the students read the same text in unison. When you see that the students are reading with fluency, you can let your voice drop off while they continue to read.

"Let's read it again together. I may drop my voice but you keep going." After students know this routine, they can work with a partner, taking turns assisting each other.

Rate Mover

Select a paragraph from the text and read it to the students two or three times. The first reading should be a bit slow, but not exaggerated; the second reading can be faster; and the third reading can be at ideal speed (although not too fast). Talk with the students about what an appropriate reading rate will be, always realizing that it may vary by the type of text. They should not strive to read so fast that others cannot understand them and they do not reflect the meaning.

Students can then read the paragraph to a partner several times, each time getting a little more fluent. Students can become very good at listening to each other and in the process they become more aware of their own reading.

You can incorporate the routine previously described (moving a small card across the text) if you have time to work with individual students. This practice is probably more suitable for younger students who are not reading dense text.

Self-Monitoring Rate

You may occasionally want students to time their reading, although this practice should be employed with caution. Students actually enjoy timing their reading or each other's reading. The danger is that they may become so enthusiastic that they read too fast at the expense of accuracy and meaning. They can always work as partners to find the "best" rate instead of just the fastest.

Paired Reading

In paired reading (Topping 1989), you pair more and less fluent readers. The partners read together and help each other with some problem solving. They reread, taking turns listening to each other and working for fluency (not speed). Multiple readings contribute to fluent, phrased reading.

Notice and Use Sentence Structure

An understanding of the sentence structure (grammar of a language) is important in helping readers know how to pause and vary the voice when reading the language. The writer has mapped meaning onto the structure of sentences and the reader knows how to reflect the underlying meaning with the voice. You can combine any of the routines listed above to help students use the parts of a sentence to guide fluency, for example:

▶ A prepositional phrase is often read together with emphasis on the noun (e.g., in the house).

▶ Phrases that assign dialogue are often grouped together (e.g., said the girl).

▶ An introductory dependent or independent clause is read all at once, usually with one word stressed, and with a pause at the end of the clause. The second clause (or third) is then read like a sentence (e.g., When I go to New York, I'll see the parade).

▶ An interrogatory statement (question) will end on a rising tone.

▶ Strong action verbs (". . . bounded into the room.") are often stressed.

▶ Adverbs ("He stomped furiously around the room.") often receive primary or secondary stress.

▶ A connective ("Meanwhile, . . ." "Nevertheless, . . .") may be offset with a comma and are usually stressed with a slight rising or even tone to show that something important is to follow.

▶ Understanding that subject, verb, and object must "agree" ("Children should wear their hats.") helps to automatically generate the probable words, pronounce them, and give them appropriate intonation.

▶ Strings of modifiers (". . . a round and delicious, juicy, red apple . . .") is read with slight pauses and often with equal emphasis on the words. Adjectives connected by "and" do not require a pause.

Punctuation usually works hand in hand with structure, so marks like commas and quotation marks are helpful. But it is the structure of the sentence itself—not the punctuation alone—that cues the reader.

Students can work with a partner to practice the sentences or a short paragraph. They need to be aware of punctuation but also to access the underlying structure. Students can present their oral reading interpretations to their peers for feedback, and they can talk about the choices they made and why.

Readers' Theater

One of the most enjoyable ways to work on fluency is readers' theater (see Chapters 3 and 4 for a more detailed description). You can use a short version of readers' theater to teach for fluency in guided reading.

Select a part of a text or the whole text and read it as a readers' theater script. Some guided reading books actually have a short play at the end. If not, you can simply have students read a stretch of dialogue in parts, omitting the words that assign dialogue ("said Mom"). If you have time, you can also create a short readers' theater script (see Figure 18–8).

Notice that you do not need to incorporate every part of the story into the script. This example has dialogue, which, of course, carries the play. After they learn the routines for readers' theater, students can work in small groups to read them. There is no need for them to stand in a line or have elaborate props or costumes. This activity does not need to become a performance, nor do students need to memorize the lines. It should be short and enjoyable. You'll find that students can read scripts like the one shown in one or two minutes.

Readers' Theater Script for *Dinner with a Python* (Level I)

Parts: Bradley, Mom, Narrator 1, Narrator 2

Bradley: May I bring a friend to dinner?

Mom: Does your friend have good manners?

Bradley: Yes.

Narrator 1: Bradley brought a python to dinner. The python flicked his tongue at the pizza.

Mom: He's sticking out his tongue. He has bad manners.

Bradley: He has good manners for a python. Pythons smell with their tongues.

Narrator 2: The python wrapped around the pizza.

Mom: He's touching the food. He has very bad manners.

Bradley: He has good manners for a python. Pythons squeeze their food before they eat it.

Narrator 1: The python swallowed the whole pizza.

Mom: He didn't chew his food! He has very bad manners.

Bradley: But he has good manners for a python. Pythons swallow their food in one bite.

Narrator 1: The python fell asleep on the floor.

Bradley: Pythons need to rest after they eat.

Mom: Terrible, horrible manners!

Narrator 2: The python finally went home.

Bradley: May I bring a new friend to dinner?

Mom: You may bring a friend with good manners.

Bradley: My new friend has good manners . . . for a lizard.

FIGURE 18-8 Readers' Theater Script for *Dinner with a Python*

Assessing Fluency

We have designed a four-point holistic rubric that you may want to use to keep a record of your students' growth as fluent readers (see Figure 18–9). Listen carefully to how the reading sounds. You can use the rubric any time you sample oral reading from a student and particularly when you take a running record (see Chapter 11).

As you use the rubric, consider each dimension of fluency as well as the student's overall integration of them. At each level of text (after about level C), teach for a score of 3. If your assessment reveals student needs, you can be specific in your teaching.

After listening to a reader process a text (or after taking a running record) select the number that most closely resembles the description of 0, 1, 2 or 3. Your goal in teaching during the guided reading lesson is always to teach toward a 3.

A Fluency Rubric

0	Reads primarily word by word with occasional but infrequent or inappropriate phrasing; no smooth or expressive interpretation, irregular pausing, and no attention to author's meaning or punctuation; no stress or inappropriate stress, and slow rate.
1	Reads primarily in two-word phrases with some three- and four-word groups and some word-by-word reading; almost no smooth, expressive interpretation or pausing guided by author's meaning and punctuation; almost no stress or inappropriate stress, with slow rate most of the time.
2	Reads primarily in three- or four-word phrase groups; some smooth, expressive interpretation and pausing guided by author's meaning and punctuation; mostly appropriate stress and rate with some slowdowns.
3	Reads primarily in larger, meaningful phrases or word groups; mostly smooth, expressive interpretation and pausing guided by author's meaning and punctuation; appropriate stress and rate with only a few slowdowns.

FIGURE 18-9 A Fluency Rubric

Teaching for Fluency

There are many factors involved in the building of a processing system. All dimensions of fluent reading contribute to the building of a smooth, efficient process and fluent reading is a characteristic of effective processing. You need to monitor how reading sounds, and teach hard for phrased, fluent reading whenever you do not observe it.

"Fluent reading will arise from teacher attention to the role of oral language, and thinking and meaning, and increasing experience with the visual information in print, and practice in orchestrating complex processing on just-difficult-enough texts. It is a matter of successful experience over a period of time moving up a gradient of difficulty of text which can support fluent and successful reading." (Clay 1993, 53)

Effective reading at every level of text (with the exception of levels A and B, with C as a transition) is essential to reading for meaning using the language and print. Your readers need to develop a concept of fluency and your teaching needs to show persistence and insistence on reading with phrasing that reflects the language and interprets the author's meaning with the voice.

Suggestions for Professional Development

1. Invite colleagues for a discussion of the six dimensions of fluency.

2. Begin by listening to a fluent, expressive reader. You can provide this demonstration yourself, or play an audio of a young reader. Be sure that the reader is not just "fast." The reading should reflect all dimensions of fluency. Have the group generate a list of the characteristics they noticed. They should be as descriptive as possible.

3. Then, play several more audio or video recordings of readers at any level. There should be a good variety. (If you have the *Benchmark Assessment System 1* or *2*, you will find recordings of individual readers there.) After listening to each reader, ask:

   ‣ What characteristics of fluency do you notice in this reading?

   ‣ What is the reader neglecting?

   ‣ Where should teaching be focused?

   ‣ How much teaching is needed?

   ‣ What prompts or teaching would be helpful?

4. Set up a follow-up meeting to discuss the readers in your school. Have each teacher come to the meeting with a video or audio recording of two students. The recordings should be only about three minutes and the student should be reading an instructional level text.

   ‣ Have the group consider each reader in turn and use the four-point rubric.

   ‣ The teacher can explain some of the ways she has been teaching for fluency with this reader in mind.

   ‣ The group can briefly engage in problem solving to identify areas of teaching needed and prompts that would be appropriate.

CHAPTER 19

The Role of Facilitative Talk in Supporting Change over Time in Processing Systems

> *Give thoughtful attention to the level of help the child needs and decide when you are prompting for processing or when you should be supplying information that the learner does not have (teaching).*
>
> –Marie Clay

Throughout this section we have emphasized the importance of careful observation and precise responses to individual learners. Your clear, specific language facilitates the reader's construction of a neural network or system for working on written language, a network that becomes smart enough to extend itself (Clay 2005). We have referred to the language that you might use to teach for, prompt, or reinforce strategic activities as "facilitative" talk and have given many examples in this book. Some of the prompts call the reader's attention to behaviors that assist in problem solving while reading a text orally—searching for and using information, monitoring and correcting, solving words, and maintaining fluency. We will explore examples of these in this chapter. We will discuss prompts to support comprehending in the discussion following reading, or when revisiting the text, in Chapter 20.

Prompts are very short, clear, direct statements or questions that give the reader the maximum information in the fewest words and are used sparingly. They are used when readers encounter difficulty, after an error to support the reader's problem solving, or after successful problem solving to reinforce effective processing. Too much talk clutters the teaching, so think about how to use the fewest words to accomplish your goal and use those words carefully.

Each prompt is a call to action. It evokes something the reader can do. You need to teach for the strategic action before you can call for the reader to engage it. When you see the reader is engaging in the behaviors independently, you move beyond prompting to reinforce it. For example, the prompt may invite the reader to think about the meaning or structure, to check something, to point the reader to what he knows, to encourage the reader to solve something, or to attend to fluency. Your prompting calls the reader's attention to behaviors that you have previously taught. The behaviors assist him in problem solving. The ultimate goal is for the reader to initiate the action without the need for the external prompt. This cycle is followed for hundreds of actions that readers take—teach, prompt, reinforce. Of course, all of this learning proceeds at an amazingly rapid pace. Students will demonstrate some behaviors spontaneously and no teaching or reinforcing is needed; some will be learned the first time a behavior is demonstrated. Sometimes no prompting will be necessary but you will still want to reinforce the effective action quickly. You don't want to waste time teaching for, prompting for, or reinforcing a behavior that is already established; that's a principle of learning and teaching. All of this depends on your moment-to-moment decision making as you interact with students during reading. You select language in response to the reading behaviors you observe.

In the *Prompting Guides,* we have provided numerous examples to assist in your teaching for all the systems of strategic actions. They are there for your *selection* (based on your knowledge of the reader and on the behavior you see at the moment). The prompts are not specific to any book; rather they are generative and can apply to any text the student is reading. If you use the facilitative language frequently, you will internalize it and use the language naturally to respond to the behaviors you observe. Your students will also benefit from the common language used by each of their teachers.

We have organized a small sampling of the range of important behaviors and understandings to notice, teach for, and support while students are reading orally or for selecting as emphases for teaching after the discussion. We hope these selected examples will give you a sense of how your teaching will shift over time as readers gain increasing control of the "fast brainwork" needed to process increasingly challenging texts. You will notice that the overt behaviors of oral reading become controlled and go underground as readers become more proficient and the demands on comprehension become greater. But you may want to sample oral reading and assess behaviors, and have brief interactions with students.

In each of the charts provided in this chapter, we identify the reading behaviors that can be observed while students read orally and describe how to teach for it, using a sample of the precise language that might be used to demonstrate, prompt, or reinforce the reader's actions. We have organized the sample behaviors and prompts as presented for a range of levels. Some behaviors, you will find, are the same across many levels. They are high-priority behaviors and readers must engage the actions again and again over increasingly complex texts. Some behaviors may require an important shift be established, and then sink to an automatic level. Remember, though, when new learning occurs or a reader encounters new challenges in a text, he may temporarily need to think consciously about a previously established behavior.

The charts included here represent a starting point—some high-priority areas that are essential for supporting oral reading. But reading is highly complex and cannot be described in a list like this one. Refer to *The Literacy Continuum* for the complex range of behaviors and understandings readers need to control at each level in these four areas as well as the behaviors in the other eight systems of strategic actions. Prompts to support comprehending (thinking within, beyond, and about the text) would not generally be used while the children are processing the text because they would interrupt the reading. They are more suited for supporting readers in the discussion or revisiting the text following reading or might have implications for the introduction of the text.

We refer you to the many works of Clay (Clay 2001; 2005) whose meticulous analyses of reading behavior and teacher responses have changed the face of teaching. Her complex theory and her description of the role of teacher language in supporting the reader's construction of a processing system for literacy is grounded in observable behaviors. Clay's work provides compelling evidence that skilled teaching makes a difference for learners in very visible ways.

You may be new to this process. When you first begin to use precise language, you may feel a bit awkward. You may find yourself using great facilitative language in the wrong place or at the wrong time. You may need to refer to your notes or the guide often. With teacher colleagues, we began working in this way about thirty years ago; and we observed and interviewed expert teachers over time to learn their perspectives and describe their learning (see Lyons, Pinnell and DeFord 1993). Teachers found that during the first year they had to refer to notes and probably applied some language in a way that wasn't the most powerful; however, they began to internalize it so that soon the dialogue was "just part of the way I teach." They developed a smoothly working link between observation and the language they used. We could call this precision teaching because it is so specifically responsive to the reader and is characterized by such economy of words.

As you use this language in response to precise observations of reading behavior, you will realize more power in your teaching. Watch the behavior or your students as they take your specific direction and then initiate it on their own. That is your cue to take it further.

See the complete range of behaviors and understandings to teach for, notice, and support at each level in *The Fountas & Pinnell Literacy Continuum* and the wide variety of prompts needed for teaching in *Prompting Guide Part 1 for Oral Reading* and *Prompting Guide Part 2 for Comprehension.*

Levels A–D

Readers at the early levels are learning how to handle books and to look at the distinctive features of print, read from left to right, and return to the left again. Early writing plays a strong role in supporting early reading behaviors. The child draws on his knowledge of language, of the world, and of how books work to build a strong early-reading process. Across these levels readers are learning how to match one spoken word with one printed word and by about level C, they no longer need to use a finger as a support (except occasionally at difficulty), because their eyes have taken over the process. Through reading these natural language texts, they are learning some letter/sound relationships and building a core of high-frequency words that they use as anchors in print. These readers search for and use information from pictures, sentence meaning, and language structure to self-monitor and correct errors as well as confirm reading. At level C, they begin to read in phrases, with intonation, and vary their voices to read periods, questions, and speech marks.

Levels A–D

Reading Behavior	Teach	Prompt	Reinforce
Searching for and Using Information			
Read left to right [A].	Demonstrate reading one line of text from left to right, pointing under each word. ◆ *Watch me read. I start here and move my eyes and my pointer finger this way.*	◆ *Start here and move your eyes. Use your pointer finger.*	◆ *You read it with your eyes and your finger helped you.*
Slow down speech to assist in voice-print match [A–B].	Show how to read with a tiny breath between words, not too slow to disrupt syntax. ◆ *Watch me read this with my pointer finger under each word.*	◆ *Put your pointer finger under each word.*	◆ *You put your pointer finger under each word.*
Read with voice-print match on one line of text [A]. Read with voice-print match on more than one line of text [B].	Show how to point precisely under each word as you demonstrate reading one (or more) lines of text. ◆ *Look at how I point and read. I make it match.*	◆ *Point under each word.* ◆ *Read it with your finger.* ◆ *Did it match?* ◆ *Were you right?*	◆ *You pointed under each word.* ◆ *You read it with your finger.* ◆ *You made it match.*

FIGURE 19-1 Facilitative Talk: Levels A–D

Levels A–D

Reading Behavior	Teach	Prompt	Reinforce
Read left to right and start again on the left on more than one line of text [B].	Demonstrate reading two lines of text–reading to the end of the line and returning to the left. ◆ *Watch me read with my pointer finger under each word. I read this way and then all the way back to start again.*	◆ *Read it this way and then go all the way back and start again.*	◆ *You read it and then went all the way back.*
Begin to read without finger pointing [C].	Demonstrate reading a page with your eyes. Tell the student to read with his eyes. Insist that the student not point under words as he reads. ◆ *Watch me read with my eyes.*	◆ *Read it with your eyes.*	◆ *You read it with your eyes.*
Use information from pictures to support meaning.	Refer to the picture and tell what would make sense. ◆ *See how the picture shows _____*	◆ *Look at the picture.* ◆ *Check the picture and think what would make sense.*	◆ *You checked the picture and thought about what would make sense.*
Use meaning to predict what would make sense.	Demonstrate reading a sentence, stopping very briefly, and reading the word. Then say, "That makes sense." ◆ *When you come to a tricky word, think what would make sense.*	◆ *Try _____ . Does that make sense?* ◆ *Think what would make sense.*	◆ *You made it make sense.*
Use a new language pattern [A–B].	Read the sentence while the student listens. ◆ *Listen to me read this.*	◆ *Now you read it with me.*	◆ *You read it.*
Use oral language syntax to predict what would sound right.	Demonstrate reading a sentence, stopping very briefly, and reading the word. Then say, "That sounds right." ◆ *When you come to a tricky word, think what would sound right.*	◆ *Try _____ . Does that sound right?*	◆ *You made it sound right.*

FIGURE 19-1 (continued)

Levels A–D

Reading Behavior	Teach	Prompt	Reinforce
Reread to search for information from language or meaning.	Show how to reread the sentence and think about what would make sense or sound right. • *You can read that again and think what would make sense (or sound right).*	• *Try that again and think what would make sense (or sound right).* • *Try that again.*	• *You made it make sense.* • *You made it sound right.* • *You tried that again.*
Locate known and new words.	Show a word on a page and have children find it and put a finger under it. • *This is _____. Can you find it?*	• *Find _____ and put your finger under it.*	• *You found _____.*
Use visual information (known words).	Tell a high-frequency word. Show it with magnetic letters or write it on a whiteboard. • *This is _____ .*	• *Find _____ . Get a good look.*	• *You know that word.*
Use visual information (first letter) to predict a word.	Demonstrate how to read the sentence and start the tricky word. • *You can get your mouth ready to start the tricky word.*	• *Get your mouth ready for the first sound.*	• *You got your mouth ready for the first sound and it helped you.*
Use visual information to predict, check, or confirm reading.	Cover up the unknown word with your pointer finger.	• *Say ____. What letter would you expect to see at the beginning of (or at the end of) ____?* • *Does it look like ____?*	• *You found ___.*

Monitoring and Self-Correcting

Reading Behavior	Teach	Prompt	Reinforce
Check one's reading by using word by word matching, noticing known words in text, and noticing mismatches in meaning or language.	Tell the student when she notices something isn't right, she should try again. • *When you read, if you notice something isn't right, try again.*	• *Were you right?* • *Was that okay?* • *Does that match?* • *Does that make sense?* • *Does that sound right?* • *Does that look right?*	• *You checked on yourself.* • *You made it match.* • *You made it make sense.* • *You made it sound right.* • *You made it look right.*
Cross-check one source of information with another.	Tell the student when he reads it has to make sense and look right (or sound right). • *When you read, it has to make sense and look right (or sound right).*	• *That makes sense, but does it sound right?* • *That makes sense, but does it look right?* • *That looks right, but does it make sense?*	• *That makes sense and sounds right, too.* • *That makes sense and looks right, too.* • *That looks right and makes sense, too.*

FIGURE 19-1 *(continued)*

Levels A–D

Reading Behavior	Teach	Prompt	Reinforce
Reread a sentence to confirm or self-correct.	Show how to reread the sentence and check to be sure it makes sense or sounds right or looks right. ◆ *You can read that again and check to see if it makes sense (or sounds right or looks right).*	◆ *Try that again and check to see it makes sense (or sounds right or looks right).*	◆ *You made it make sense.* ◆ *You made it sound right.* ◆ *You made it look right.*
Self-monitoring using language and visual information.	Have the child predict the word based on language structure. Cover the tricky word and ask for something known about the word. ◆ *Listen to how I read it (say the word). Think about how it starts (or ends).*	◆ *Cover the word.* ◆ *Think what would sound right.* ◆ *Run your finger under it.* ◆ *What letter do you expect to see first? After the s? At the end?*	◆ *You checked it.* ◆ *That sounds right and looks right.*
Solving Words			
Say a word and predict its first letter before locating it.	Show how to say a word and think about the first sound and letter. ◆ *Listen to me say _____. I expect to see _____ at the beginning.*	◆ *Say _____ . What letter do you expect to see first?* ◆ *Find _____ , move your finger under it, and check it.*	◆ *You found _____ .*
Build a core of high-frequency words.	Choose books with natural language that includes many high-frequency words. Have children locate a word or two occasionally after reading. ◆ *This is _____.* ◆ *Find _____.* Say an easy high-frequency word and show how to find it. (e.g., *I, the, at, look*) ◆ *I put my finger under _____.*	◆ *You found _____ . That's a word you know.* ◆ *Say _____ . Put your finger under it.*	◆ *You knew that word.* ◆ *You found _____ .*

FIGURE 19-1 *(continued)*

Levels A–D

Reading Behavior	Teach	Prompt	Reinforce
Maintaining Fluency			
Use intonation to show the end of a sentence or a question.	Demonstrate reading a sentence with a period (and show how your voice goes down) and reading a question (with voice tone going up). ◆ *Listen to how I read this.*	◆ *Make your voice go down at the period.* ◆ *Make your voice go up at the question.*	◆ *You made your voice go down at the period.* ◆ *You made your voice go up at the question.*
Read dialogue with intonation (C–D).	Demonstrate reading dialogue with intonation. ◆ *Listen to how my reading sounds like talking.*	◆ *Make it sound like talking.*	◆ *You made it sound like talking.*
Use oral language knowledge to read with phrasing (C–D).	Demonstrate reading a sentence with phrasing and have students repeat. ◆ *Listen to how I put my words together.*	◆ *Put your words together.*	◆ *You put your words together.*

FIGURE 19-1 *(continued)*

Levels E–J

Readers at levels E–J have firmly established the behaviors of early emergent readers. They have built up their knowledge of high-frequency words and are developing flexibility in solving words using first letters and word parts. They are integrating several sources of information in their attempts and using multiple sources of information to monitor and self-correct consistently. Self-corrections are made closer to the point of error instead of constantly rereading the sentences. They control longer sentences, reading some language that has moved from natural to more literary. Readers show evidence of the orchestration of processing, phrasing, appropriate word stress, intonation, and rate. They notice and use a range of punctuation and read dialogue. Across the span of levels, the readers are relying more on the print to construct meaning. Overt processing is moving to covert and some of the readers are beginning to process more texts silently with confidence and a faster rate.

Levels E–J

Reading Behavior	Teach	Prompt	Reinforce
Searching for and Using information			
Reread to search for information from language or meaning.	Show how to reread the sentence to problem solve. ◆ *You can read that again and think what would make sense (and sound right or look right).*	◆ *Try that again and think what would make sense (or sound right).* ◆ *Try that again.*	◆ *You made it make sense.* ◆ *You made it sound right.* ◆ *You tried that again.*
Reread to problem-solve using the first letter (early).	Show how to read the sentence again and use the first part of the word (letter, cluster). ◆ *You can read that again and start the word.*	◆ *Try that again.* ◆ *Try that again and start the tricky word.*	◆ *You tried that again.* ◆ *You worked on that.*
Use visual information to predict, check, or confirm reading (early).	Cover up the unknown word with your finger.	◆ *Say _____. What letter would you expect to see at the beginning of (or at the end of) ____?* ◆ *Does it look like _____?*	◆ *You found _____.*
Solve new words independently.	Tell the student that if he comes to a tricky part, he needs to work it out.	◆ *Look for something that can help you.* ◆ *Do you know a word like that?* ◆ *What can you try?* ◆ *How can you help yourself?*	◆ *You worked that out for yourself.*
Search for and use multiple sources of information.	Tell the student it has to make sense, sound right, and look right. ◆ *You can try that again and think what would make sense, sound right, and look right.*	◆ *It needs to make sense and look right.* ◆ *Try that again.*	◆ *You made it make sense, sound right, and look right.*
Monitoring and Self-Correcting			
Reread to confirm.	Show the student how to reread the sentence. ◆ *You can read that again and check to see if you are right.* ◆ *You can read it again.*	◆ *Read that again to check if you are right.* ◆ *Try that again.*	◆ *You read that again and checked to see if you were right.* ◆ *You read that again.*

FIGURE 19-2 Facilitative Talk: Levels E–J

Levels E–J

Reading Behavior	Teach	Prompt	Reinforce
Monitor structure.	Tell the student it has to sound right. [Demonstrate.] • When you read, it has to make sense and sound right too.	• Can we say it that way?	• You made it sound right.
Monitor visual information.	Tell the student it has to look right. [Demonstrate.] • When you read, it has to make sense and look right.	• Does that look right?	• You made it look right.
Cross-check one source of information with another [E].	Tell the student that what she reads needs to make sense and look right [or sound right]. [Demonstrate.] • When you read, it has to make sense [and sound right, or look right].	• It could be ____ but look at ____. • That makes sense, but does it sound right? • That makes sense, but does it look right? • That looks right, but does it make sense?	• That makes sense and sounds right, too. • That makes sense and looks right, too. • That looks right and makes sense, too.
Self-correct close to point of error.	Tell the student what he reads has to make sense, sound right, and look right. • If you notice something isn't right, try again and fix the tricky part.	• You can fix that quickly.	• You fixed that quickly.
Self-correct using multiple sources of information.	Tell the student that what she reads needs to make sense and look right [or sound right]. [Demonstrate.] • When you read, it has to make sense and look right [or sound right].	• Were you right? • Try that again. • Something was not quite right.	• You tried it again. • You fixed it all by yourself.

Solving Words

Reading Behavior	Teach	Prompt	Reinforce
Say a word and predict its first letter before locating it.	Show how to say a word and think about the first sound and letter. • Listen to me say ____. I expect to see _____ at the beginning.	• Say _____. What letter do you expect to see first? • Find _____. Put your finger under it and get a good look.	• You found _____.

FIGURE 19-2 *(continued)*

Levels E–J

Reading Behavior	Teach	Prompt	Reinforce
Build a core of high-frequency words.	Choose books with natural language that include many high-frequency words. Occasionally have children locate a word or two after reading. ◆ *This is _____.* ◆ *Find _____.*	◆ *You found _____ . That's a word you know.*	◆ *You knew that word.*
Use known words and word parts to problem-solve new words.	Show the student how to notice a word part. ◆ *Use your pointer finger to mask part of the word and show a known word part.* ◆ *Look at this part.*	◆ *Look for something you know* (may use pointer finger early). ◆ *Do you know a word that starts and ends with those letters?* ◆ *What do you know that might help?* ◆ *Look carefully and think what you know that can help.*	◆ *You used a part you knew.*
Take words apart while reading for meaning.	Tell the student the reading needs to make sense and look right too. ◆ *That makes sense, but look at this part.*	◆ *Find the tricky part.* ◆ *Where can you break that word?*	◆ *You broke that word apart.* ◆ *Now it makes sense and looks right too.*

Maintaining Fluency

Reading Behavior	Teach	Prompt	Reinforce
Read with phrasing.	Tell the student he needs to listen to his reading and make it sound good. ◆ *Listen to how I put my words together so it sounds like talking.*	◆ *Put your words together so it sounds like talking.*	◆ *You made it sound like talking.*
Read with appropriate stress and intonation.	Tell the student she needs to make her reading sound interesting. ◆ *Listen to how I make my reading sound interesting.*	◆ *Listen to yourself.* ◆ *Make your reading sound interesting.*	◆ *You made your reading sound interesting.*
Demonstrate fluent reading.	Tell the student her reading needs to sound smooth. [Demonstrate]. ◆ *Listen to how I make my reading sounds smooth.*	◆ *Make your reading sound smooth.*	◆ *You made your reading sound smooth.*

FIGURE 19-2 *(continued)*

Levels K–M

Readers show increasing stamina to process longer texts, orchestrating the use of multiple sources of information. They process texts with some literary language and have flexible ways of taking words apart. They are reading texts of a greater variety of genres with multiple short episodes or a greater range of information structuring. With consistent self-monitoring, self-correction has become mostly covert. They demonstrate smooth, phrased, fluent reading and the ability to read assigned and unassigned dialogue with intonation and understanding.

Levels K–M

Reading Behavior	Teach	Prompt	Reinforce
Searching for and Using information			
Search for and use multiple sources of information.	Tell the student that it has to make sense, sound right, and look right. It has to all fit. ◆ *When you read, it has to make sense, sound right, and look right.*	◆ *Try that again.* ◆ *That made sense and sounded right, but did it look right?*	◆ *You made it all fit.* ◆ *It makes sense, sounds right, and looks right, too.*
Monitoring and Self-Correcting			
Self-monitor consistently.	Tell the student that it has to make sense, sound right, and look right. ◆ *You need to check to be sure it makes sense and look right (or sound right).*	◆ *Try that again.* ◆ *What did you notice?*	◆ *You tried again and you fixed it.*
Self-correct using multiple sources of information.	Tell the student that it needs to make sense and look right (or sound right). ◆ *When you read, it has to make sense and look right (or sound right).*	◆ *Were you right?* ◆ *Try that again.* ◆ *Something was not quite right.* ◆ *You made a mistake on that page. Can you find it?*	◆ *You tried it again.* ◆ *You fixed it all by yourself.*
Self-correct close to point of error.	Tell the student what he reads has to make sense, sound right, and look right. ◆ *When you notice something doesn't fit, think what would make sense, sound right, and look right.*	◆ *You can fix that quickly.*	◆ *You fixed that quickly.*

FIGURE 19-3 Facilitative Talk: Levels K–M

Levels K–M

Reading Behavior	Teach	Prompt	Reinforce
Solving Words			
Use known words and word parts to problem-solve new words.	Tell the student to use his pointer finger to mask part of the word and show a known word part. ♦ *Look at this part. It says ___.*	♦ *Look for a part you know* (may use pointer finger early).	♦ *You used a part you knew.*
Take apart new words.	Tell the student to use her pointer finger or a piece of sentence strip to show how to look at parts. ♦ *You can look at the parts like this* [show].	♦ *Look for a part that can help.* ♦ *What do you see that can help?* ♦ *Where can you break it?*	♦ *You looked at the parts.*
Solve new words independently.	Tell the student that if he comes to a tricky part, he needs to work it out. ♦ *You can work it out.*	♦ *How can you help yourself?* ♦ *What can you try?*	♦ *You worked that out for yourself.*
Maintaining Fluency			
Monitor fluent, phrased reading.	Tell the student that he needs to listen to how his reading sounds. ♦ *Listen to how I make my reading sound interesting.*	♦ *Make your reading sound interesting.* ♦ *Listen to how your reading sounds.* ♦ *Did it sound interesting?*	♦ *You listened to how your reading sounds.* ♦ *Your reading sounds interesting.*
Use a variety of punctuation to read for meaning.	Demonstrate using your voice at periods, question marks, and speech marks. Tell the student she needs to read the punctuation. ♦ *Listen to me read this.* ♦ *Change your voice when you see the marks on the page.*	♦ *Make your voice read the punctuation.*	♦ *You read the punctuation.*
Read with all dimensions of fluency.	Tell the student that he needs to make his reading sound smooth like talking. ♦ *Listen to how I make my reading sound like talking.*	♦ *Listen to yourself.* ♦ *Did it sound smooth?* ♦ *Put your words together and make it sound like talking.*	♦ *You made it sound smooth.* ♦ *You made it sound like talking.*
Read with phrasing at a good rate.	Slide the strip of card left to right across the line of text. ♦ *Watch me move my eyes.*	♦ *Read this smoothly with your eyes.*	♦ *You read that smoothly.*

FIGURE 19-3 *(continued)*

Levels N–S

Readers have made a shift to smooth, fluent processing of a wide range of genres, reading silently with momentum. While focusing on meaning in fiction and information texts that are increasingly dependent on more background, vocabulary knowledge and literary knowledge, they read mostly silently and in oral reading show minimal overt processing. They show a wide variety of flexible word-solving strategies and can access much new vocabulary defined in the text, by using morphemes or other reference tools such as a glossary. They process sentences that are complex, containing prepositional phrases, introductory clauses, and lists of nouns, verbs, or adjectives. They read silently; oral reading shows the orchestration of all dimensions of fluency.

Levels N–S

Reading Behavior	Teach	Prompt	Reinforce
Searching for and Using Information			
Search for and use multiple sources of information.	Tell the student it has to make sense, sound right, and look right. It has to all fit. ♦ *When you read, it has to make sense, sound right, and look right.*	♦ *Try that again.*	♦ *You made it all fit.* ♦ *It makes sense, sounds right, and looks right, too.*
Search for and use information from dialogue presented in a variety of ways.	Tell the student when she reads dialogue, she needs to notice and use the punctuation. ♦ *When you read, notice how the punctuation tells you how to read it. Listen to me read this.*	♦ *Read the punctuation.*	♦ *You read the punctuation.*
Search for and use information from a wide variety of illustrations and graphics.	Show the student how to read all the information on a page. ♦ *See how this ____ gives you more information about ____.* ♦ *You can read the ____ before or after you read the page.*	♦ *Read all the information on the page.*	♦ *You noticed and read all the information.*

FIGURE 19-4 Facilitative Talk: Levels N–S

Levels N–S

Reading Behavior	Teach	Prompt	Reinforce
Monitoring and Self-Correcting			
Self-correct covertly prior to or after an error.	Tell the student that as he reads, he needs to think and make sure everything fits. ♦ *Listen to how I think and check to be sure it all fits.*	♦ *Check on yourself as you read.*	♦ *You checked on yourself.*
Self-monitor reading using multiple sources of information.	Tell the student to check to be sure the reading makes sense, sounds right, and looks right. ♦ *You need to check to see if it makes sense, sounds right, and looks right.*	♦ *Check it.*	♦ *You checked it and fixed it.*
Demonstrate flexibility using different strategies to solve words.	Tell the student that he can use what he knows to solve words. Show a word and different ways to take it apart. ♦ *Here's a tricky word. Look at the part ___.*	♦ *Do you see something that can help you?*	♦ *You found something can help.*
Monitor consistently across long stretches of text.	Tell the student he needs to check on himself when he reads. ♦ *You need to check on yourself to be sure it makes sense, sounds right, and looks right.*	♦ *You made a mistake on that page.* ♦ *Can you find it?* ♦ *Something was not right.*	♦ *You checked on yourself.*
Self-correct at point of error.	Tell the student what she reads has to make sense, sound right, and look right. ♦ *When you notice something doesn't fit, think about what would make sense, sound right, and look right.*	♦ *You can fix that quickly.*	♦ *You fixed that quickly.*

FIGURE 19-4 *(continued)*

Levels N–S

Reading Behavior	Teach	Prompt	Reinforce
Solving Words			
Take apart new words.	Tell the student to use her pointer finger or a piece of sentence strip to look at parts. ♦ *You can look at the parts like this* [show].	♦ *Look for a part that can help.* ♦ *What do you see that can help?* ♦ *Where can you break it?*	♦ *You looked at the parts.*
Solve multisyllable words by taking them apart using syllables.	Show the student how to notice and use word parts [show with pointer finger or card]. ♦ *You can look at this part.*	♦ *Do you see a part you know?*	♦ *You noticed a part and it helped you.*
Notice parts of words and connect them to words to solve them.	Show the student a part in a word she knows. ♦ *You know this word.* ♦ *You can look for a part that can help.*	♦ *Do you know a word like that?* ♦ *Do you know something that starts with those letters?* ♦ *Do you know something that ends with those letters?*	♦ *You noticed a part and it helped you.*
Use flexible ways to solve new words–noticing parts, suffixes, and prefixes.	Show the student how to notice parts. ♦ *You can look for parts you know.*	♦ *Do you know a word like that?* ♦ *Do you know a word that starts [ends] like that?*	♦ *You noticed the parts.*
Maintaining Fluency			
Notice a variety of punctuation and reflect with the voice.	Tell the student he needs to read the punctuation. ♦ *Change your voice when you see the marks on the page.*	♦ *Make your voice read the punctuation.*	♦ *You read the punctuation.*
Read with all dimensions of fluency.	Tell the student she needs to make her reading sound smooth and like talking. ♦ *Listen to how my reading sounds.*	♦ *Listen to yourself.* ♦ *Did it sound smooth?* ♦ *Put your words together and make it sound like talking.*	♦ *Your reading sounded smooth.* ♦ *You made it sound like talking.*
Read with phrasing and intonation.	Slide the strip of card left to right across the line of text. ♦ *Watch me move my eyes.*	♦ *Read this smoothly with your eyes.*	♦ *You read that smoothly.*

FIGURE 19-4 (continued)

Levels T–Z

Readers at these levels have the confidence and ability to read complex fiction and specific technical information texts with multiple perspectives and long, complex language structures, some including diverse dialects or archaic language. They search for and use information in an integrated way, taking apart new words smoothly and efficiently with a range of flexible word-solving strategies. Most reading is silent and all aspects of fluency are well-orchestrated in oral reading.

Levels T–Z

Reading Behavior	Teach	Prompt	Reinforce
Searching for and Using information			
Sustain searching over long and highly complex sentences that include multiple phrases, clauses and lists, and the full range of punctuation marks.	Tell the student that her voice needs to show what the writer means. ◆ *Listen to how I read it the way the writer means.*	◆ *Read it like the writer means it.*	◆ *You made it sound the way the writer means it.*
Search for and use multiple sources of information.	Tell the student it has to make sense, sound right, and look right. It has to all fit. ◆ *When you read, it has to make sense, sound right, and look right.*	◆ *Try that again.*	◆ *You made it all fit.* ◆ *It makes sense, sounds right, and looks right, too.*
Search for and use information from a wide variety of illustrations and graphics.	Show the student how to read all the information on a page. ◆ *See how this ____ gives you more information about ____.* ◆ *You can read the ____ before or after you read the page.*	◆ *Read all the information on the page*	◆ *You noticed and read all the information.*
Monitoring and Self-Correcting			
Continue to monitor accuracy, self-correcting, and searching at difficulty.	Tell the student she needs to check to be sure everything makes sense and looks right. ◆ *When you read, you need to check to be sure it makes sense and looks right.*	◆ *Were you right?* ◆ *Check it.* ◆ *Something was not quite right.*	◆ *You checked on yourself.*
Monitor understanding of text.	Tell the student he needs to stop and reread if it doesn't make sense. ◆ *When something doesn't make sense, you need to stop and think. You might need to reread to fix it.*	◆ *What is wrong?* ◆ *Why did you stop?* ◆ *What doesn't make sense?* ◆ *Try that again.*	◆ *You went back to be sure it made sense.*

FIGURE 19-5 Facilitative Talk: Levels T–Z

Levels T–Z

Reading Behavior	Teach	Prompt	Reinforce
Self-correct covertly prior to or after an error.	Tell the student that as he reads, he needs to think and check to be sure everything fits. ♦ Listen to how I think and check to be sure it all fits.	♦ Check on yourself as you read.	♦ You checked on yourself.
Solving Words			
Access a large reading vocabulary and without conscious effort, keeping attention on the meaning and language of the text.	Tell the student when she reads, she needs to read smoothly, solving new words as she reads. ♦ Listen to how I solve words quickly and smoothly as I read.	♦ Solve words quickly and smoothly.	♦ You solved words quickly and smoothly.
Solve words repeatedly while processing continuous text and with minimum overt self-correction.	Tell the student when he reads, he needs to read smoothly, solving new words as he reads. ♦ Listen to how I read smoothly.	♦ Read it all smoothly.	♦ You read that smoothly.
Take multisyllable words apart flexibly, efficiently, and quickly.	Tell the student when she reads, she needs to solve new words quickly using anything she knows. ♦ Listen to how I read and quickly solve the tricky word.	♦ What can you try? ♦ Do you see something that can help? ♦ Look for something that can help you.	♦ You solved that quickly.
Maintaining Fluency			
Read orally in a way that demonstrates all dimensions of fluency.	Tell the student she needs to make her reading sound smooth like talking. ♦ Listen to how I make my reading sound smooth.	♦ Listen to yourself. ♦ Did it sound smooth? ♦ Put your words together and make it sound like talking.	♦ You made it sound smooth. ♦ You made it sound like talking.
Read smoothly, interpreting the writer's message.	Tell the student when he reads, his voice needs to show what the writer means. ♦ Listen to how my voice shows what the writer means.	♦ Listen to yourself. ♦ Read smoothly and have your voice show what the writer means.	♦ You read smoothly. ♦ You showed what the writer means.
Read orally (and silently) at a good rate.	Tell the student that she needs to read smoothly. Demonstrate reading smoothly at a good rate–not too fast and not too slow. ♦ Listen to me read smoothly–not too fast and not too slow.	♦ Read that smoothly. ♦ Keep your reading going–not too fast and not too slow.	♦ Your reading was not too fast and not too slow.

FIGURE 19-5 *(continued)*

Progress over Time

In this chapter we have given several examples of how to teach for some of the important behaviors and understandings while a student is reading orally and has an opportunity to engage in "reading work." As you know, much more is going on in the brain than is observable to you as a teacher. At the same time the reader is learning to process text and you are prompting him to engage in productive and efficient behaviors, he is simultaneously thinking about the meaning of the text. Each of the language examples is a general suggestion for getting the student to notice and use problem-solving behaviors while processing text, but the brief language interaction does not interfere with comprehension. It supports comprehension. You will tailor each response to the precise behavior you observe. Each interaction is directed toward supporting the readers' construction of the "fast brainwork" needed to engage in the actions independently. You want the learning to take place as fast as possible, realizing that this will be different for every learner and will take adjustment on your part.

As the reader becomes more proficient, in some ways it becomes more difficult to teach because reading behaviors "go underground." They are less overt and at the same time more complex. You will not be able to notice errors because the reader will covertly correct them *before* or *after* making them. In fact, mature readers have even been known to change words or syntax after an error made earlier in the text so that the reading sounds right and the error will not be noticed by listeners. The mature reader is processing the *whole text,* including the graphophonemic information, the syntax, the meaning, and the deeper messages at the same time.

Use of precise language in your interactions will have a lasting effect. From the beginnings of reading to highly sophisticated levels, the reader will access this precise language as he encounters a difficulty in reading, after an error, or when experiencing a mismatch or a lack of comprehension. He will listen to himself read orally and attend to the same strategic actions in silent reading. None of this will be conscious, after time. It will be part of the reader's internalized system of understandings that allow for unconsciously applied actions and understandings. All of this is applied automatically and without effort, and that is partly why researchers have had so many problems taking apart what readers do. It's a little like riding a bike—only a thousand times more complex. When you ride a bike, you don't think about what your feet or eyes or hands are doing, but you keep your eyes on the road and every part of your body is coordinated towards moving along that road. At some point in the process of learning how to ride a bike, you had to learn all of these coordinated actions. Every biker might learn in a slightly different way and they might reach different levels of competency, but all will develop what is essentially the same set of competencies.

As a responsive teacher, you will enable each reader to build an effective processing system. As you select texts with increasing challenges, each reader will "assemble working systems" and become self-regulating readers who take "different paths to common outcomes," (Clay 1998).

Suggestions for Professional Development

Responding to the reader with precise language is perhaps the most challenging element of effective teaching. It takes the longest to develop, but it is what makes the difference in teaching *all* the children with success. Researchers have often been puzzled when they look at the results of large studies that compare two or three methodologies. Instruction can "look" much the same in fifty different classrooms, but the results may be excellent in 40% of them, satisfactory in 40% of them, and miserable in 20% of them. In other words, everything works or nothing works.

The inevitable conclusion is that it is the teacher that makes the difference, and few studies look below the surface to the intimate, individual interactions that permeate the instruction. There's good reason for that. An in-depth look at teaching takes thousands of hours of time and analysis. It costs a great deal to uncover even minute examples. But you can, through self-reflection, uncover your own effective moves in your classroom. Colleagues can help. Begin with a self-awareness exercise. This session will probably be more effective at a grade-level meeting or in grade level groups, but try to think of the *range* of students in your classroom. If you find that difficult, think of just one.

1. Bring together a group of colleagues and have each person bring assessment data or notes (as detailed as possible) on the individuals from one reading group.

2. Have a discussion of some of the ideas in this chapter.

   ▶ What does responsive teaching really mean when you consider individual interactions with readers? (Responsive teaching is a larger term that can be applied to everything you do in the classroom, but it means something very specific when it comes to your interactions with individual readers.)

   ▶ Talk about some of the examples of language in this chapter. What characterizes them?

   ▶ Have you used of these responses effectively? Which ones and why were they effective?

   ▶ How is this kind of language different from telling? From correcting? From praise? (Remember that in *assessment,* the most neutral response is to tell the word; but this is *teaching.*) You create opportunities for the learner to problem-solve when you prompt.

3. Have teachers work with a partner to examine the samples of reading behavior on the Responsive Teaching form in Figure 19-6 (found also in Online Resources). Use this chapter or *Prompting Guide Part 1,* as a resource. (You may want to use your own running records for more examples or select from the examples here.) Caution that sometimes, the best response might be to say nothing!

   ▶ For each observable behavior, discuss what might be the cause. Keep the readers in your group in mind.

   ▶ Then, for each behavior, write some language that you could use in response.

   ▶ Finally, identify whether your language means "teach," "prompt," or "reinforce."

4. Have a summary discussion.

5. Have each person note some language that might be productive and use it over the next two weeks when working with students. (They may want to try this first with individuals and then when interacting with individuals during small-group instruction.)

Responsive Teaching During Oral Reading		
Reading Behavior The reader:	**Potential Response**	**Teach, Prompt, or Reinforce**
Stops and cannot go further.		
Stops and appeals for help.		
Reads *truck* for *van* and goes on.		
Rereads the sentence twice, making the same error.		
Rereads and self-corrects.		
Reads *said* for *saw* and stops.		
Makes three attempts at the word *something: this, said, some,* and stops.		
Rereads the same sentence twice, both times correctly.		
Reads *the* for *this* three times on two pages.		
Reads *can, cook, cooking* for *camping.*		
Reads "*he is the go*" for "*here is the toy.*"		
Reads "*Same animals take a bath with their tongues*" for "*Some animals use their tongues to take a bath.*"		
Reads "*b, o, boat, b, but*" for *books.*		
Is reading very slowly and monotonously.		
Reads with inappropriate stress—stressing every word or the wrong words.		
Reads *but* for *boat* and self-corrects right after the error.		
Stops at a hard word and scans the picture.		
Ignores the punctuation.		
Stops at a new word, scans the picture, makes the first sound of the word, and reads it correctly.		
Reads words in quotation marks with phrasing and intonation.		
Reads the material in a graphic and then rereads some of the body of the text.		
Stops, looks puzzled, and backs up to reread a paragraph.		
Stops and says, "I don't understand this."		
Stops at a four-syllable word.		
Reads *please* for *unpleasant* and goes on.		
Reads *unpleased* for *unpleasant* and goes on.		
Reads *street* for *straight* and stops.		

FIGURE 19-6 Responsive Teaching During Oral Reading

CHAPTER 20

Teaching for Comprehending

Helping Students Think Within, Beyond, and About the Text

---

*I regard meaning as the "given" in all reading—
the source of anticipation, the guide to being on
track, and the outcome and reward of the effort.*

–Marie Clay

As readers build a processing system, they learn items of information such as letters and words, but the reader's construction of meaning using language and print is central in the process. All of the systems (see Chapter 15) work simultaneously in the comprehending of texts—comprehending is an active, meaning-making process, not simply an isolated outcome or product after reading.

It used to be common practice to think of reading as a sequence of steps that the reader engages in: you see the letters and decode the words in order, and comprehension comes out as a result. In this scenario, comprehension is a product of decoding—first translating into words, then understanding the words, and then understanding the text. Almost every voice in the research on literacy learning—even among scientists who disagree vociferously with each other—would agree that this is a gross oversimplification of a complex process. But it was common for this message to be communicated to practitioners through some of the published materials they were expected to use. Here are some practices we have observed (and even used!) in our many years of experience in education:

▶ Teaching all the words (sometimes all week) before allowing children to read the text.

▶ Introducing a text *only* by pre-teaching the new words.

▶ Teaching phonogram patterns and then giving students texts that are written with single patterns or only a few phonogram patterns (Nan can fan Dan).

▶ Correcting students immediately when they make a mistake.

▶ Telling the word immediately when a student pauses rather than leaving room for problem solving.

▶ Having students do "round robin" reading so that each student reads only a little bit of text.

▶ Reading every text "cold" rather than revisiting familiar texts.

▶ Providing no support before reading a text "cold" to see what the students can do (this is testing).

▶ Consistently asking students to "sound it out" (as a sole strategy) when they meet a word that is unknown.

▶ Asking a series of questions after reading to test comprehension; most concerned with literal comprehension.

This last practice is very common today. In some published materials, teachers are given a series of questions to ask *after* the reading of a whole text or a section of text. Asking students questions after reading is a form of testing, not teaching. You are not able to influence the process because the reading is completed. To influence how readers construct meaning as they work through a text, your teaching moves before and during the reading will support the most important new learning.

In guided reading, our underlying belief about reading as a complex process means the practice must be different:

▶ You provide engaging, complex texts.

▶ You *foreground* comprehension with the introduction to the text, with students actively participating.

▶ You teach for comprehending within the reading of continuous text.

▶ You observe carefully and sometimes support students' meaning-making while reading.

▶ You invite students to engage in conversation after reading.

▶ You engage them in revisiting the text to ignite deeper thinking.

Reading is thinking, in response to the messages in print. Comprehending is a dynamic, ongoing process. Readers comprehend before, during, after, and sometimes long after, reading. Talking fuels thinking. When you talk with others about a book you have read, you often gain new insights, even if you read the book some time ago. You gain a richer understanding than you could get on your own. As you read more, your thinking about the original text may change yet again. Nonfiction texts such as articles or even reports of current events may remind you of fiction books you have read in the past (and vice versa). Every text you have read stays in your memory (although not in your consciousness), and some texts emerge as important touchstones that change or evolve your thinking over time.

In this chapter, we discuss some procedures for expanding students' ability to comprehend texts. We provide examples for teaching students about:

- Summarizing (thinking within the text);
- Predicting, making connections, synthesizing, and inferring (thinking beyond the text);
- Analyzing and critiquing (thinking about the text).

What Does Teaching for Comprehending Mean?

Though we will refer to each system of strategic actions one at a time to show how you can gently guide students' attention; it is important to remember that these actions are *never applied one at a time* by the reader. Consider how all of these actions occur:

- A student who is automatically **solving words** and **monitoring** his comprehension might realize it and pause to reread or **search** for more information. He might also **search** his background knowledge, **make connections,** and, by comparing present knowledge to new learning, **synthesize** new ideas.
- A student who is **monitoring** his understanding of key words might **solve** one by taking it apart by syllables, **connect** to known words, gain insight into or **infer** the motives of a character, and **predict** what the character will do to resolve the problem he has **analyzed.**

A sequence of actions is implied in these scenarios only because we have to present written language in some order. How else would we do it? But, in fact, these actions happen rapidly and many take place simultaneously as fast brainwork. And no matter how detailed we make these descriptions, they are still far from describing the complexity of what is going on. The rapid nature of these cognitive actions makes it very difficult for an individual to know exactly what the brain is doing.

Much is currently made of *metacognition* as the answer to reading problems, in particular, comprehension problems (Palincsar and Brown 1984). Metacognition means the awareness a person has of her own thinking processes. It is literally *thinking about thinking*. Metacognitive knowledge refers to knowing what you know and what you don't know and also knowing how you approach different kinds of learning (Flavel 1976, 1987). If metacognition is broadly defined, then the following understandings could be considered to have some element of metacognition:

> "I know that it helps me to say the first sound of a word and think what would make sense."
>
> "The side heading gives you an idea what you will find in this part of the book."

> "If I don't know what the words mean, I look for a synonym or I read the paragraph to find information about the word."
>
> "I am more interested when I read nonfiction than when I read fiction."
>
> "I like to read stories that tell about someone overcoming obstacles."

Study skills involve metacognition. For example, students can be taught to develop a plan for studying a topic. Students can learn to find evidence for an argument or to detect it when a writer is using compare and contrast. Metacognitive regulation involves adjusting one's own metacognitive strategies to become more efficient or effective. The idea is that individuals can have a repertoire of strategies for analyzing and accomplishing a number of tasks, including comprehension, and many people believe such strategies can be taught and then transferred to new tasks (Halpern 1996; Pressley, Borkowski and Schneider 1987).

Most of the research on metacognitive strategies has been focused on older students (middle and high school) and many experiments are brief. We don't have evidence of long-term value. In our view, students do learn about their own learning simply by engaging in it, and, over time, they can benefit from reflecting on their reading and making some adjustments to understand a text at a deeper level, to read with greater fluency, or to get better at deriving the meaning of words. It is true that self-regulated use of comprehension strategies is evident in skilled adult readers (Pressley and Afflerback 1995). Reciprocal teaching, in particular, has been shown to have positive effects on strategies like summarization and self-questioning (Palincsar and Brown 1984; Pressley 2000). Reciprocal teaching focuses on multiple strategies and follows a rather rigid sequence of activity, but within the framework, there can be some flexible discussion of texts.

We don't, however, see it as productive to have students memorize the *names* of strategies, and that is especially true for beginning readers. Children can learn big words, but whether that actually helps them engage deeply with texts is questionable. In our experience, some students begin to think like this: "Ok, I have my connection to report." Or, "I made an inference so I'm finished." For these reasons, we don't see "strategy groups" as an effective use of teacher and student small-group time. Often, students engage in the empty application of one strategy, and that's not the way effective reading works. Rather than digging deeper into a text that they all share, students in strategy groups often focus on naming instead of engaging in the thinking. As a result, the conversation *must be* at the metacognitive level with each student talking about what the brain is doing. We don't think the way to learn strategies is simply to talk about them at that level—instead, students must be engaged in talking about the range of meaning they are taking from specific texts. There are some academic terms that are useful for talking about texts, but they need to be appropriate for the age and grade level.

In this chapter, we focus on creating a situation within which students *can* engage in the complex application of a network of strategic actions. First, they enjoy reading the fiction or nonfiction text and respond to it as readers. They share their thinking through talk. Then, as a teaching point, you might choose to have students go back into the text for a closer look, and here is where you can support more complex comprehending. We (and many others) have been talking and writing about the close analysis of texts for a long time (Fountas and Pinnell 2006). Close reading involves examining a section of text for the specific purposes of thinking analytically and reflecting on the meaning. Promoting such analysis means keeping students' discussion "grounded" in the text while thinking and talking about the meaning. By directing their attention to a particular part or feature of the text, you can promote analytical and critical thinking.

At the same time, remember that the comprehension of a text is a transaction between the reader and the text (Rosenblatt 1978, 1983). The text conveys meaning as expressed by the writer, but the reader connects that meaning to her own understandings in some unique ways. The stance you take toward a text—the purpose for reading—influences how you focus attention. For example, Rosenblatt says that an *efferent* stance means that the reader is primarily seeking information, whereas an *aesthetic* stance means the reader is seeking enjoyment or appreciating something about the writer's craft—the language, the feelings of characters and how they are revealed, or how the book arouses an emotional response.

This is not the same as the difference between reading fiction and nonfiction—any text can be read with an efferent or aesthetic stance or some combination of the two. It is always important to listen to the expression of students' own interpretations. Ultimately, they construct their own meaning, but this doesn't mean that your teaching begins and ends with whatever a student wants to talk about. Instead, work with your students to expand their understandings and guide them to develop socially shared meanings through communication with others. Inquiry arises from and contributes to the socially shared meanings that exist within the group, and these are built over time (Bakhtin 1981). As both individual meaning and shared meanings are experienced, new learning happens.

Teaching for Comprehending Across the Guided Reading Lesson

The components of the guided reading lesson work together to promote student comprehension before, during, and after reading. All roads lead to comprehending the writer's message and going beyond it to connect to the other texts and experiences that make up an individual's thinking. We give general examples in this chapter of facilitative language that will support the kind of discussion that promotes comprehension, but you can also consult *Prompting Guide Part 2 for Comprehension, Genre Prompting Guide for Fiction,* and *Genre Prompting Guide for Nonfiction* for additional prompts to facilitate discussion.

Selecting Texts

To begin with, select texts that offer rich opportunities for thinking. When selecting a text, it's not as simple as saying, "it should be complex," because complexity is a relative term. The text also has to be within reach for the reader. It is very hard to think in complex ways and to reflect thinking in talking if the text is so hard that the reader stumbles over every other word, or even a significant percentage of words. The idea is for readers to constantly move forward in the texts they can process proficiently. Remember that in a multitext approach you are also teaching for comprehending in interactive read-aloud with age-appropriate texts.

Teaching for comprehending is one reason that we recommend the selection of short texts for guided reading. Longer texts are appropriate for choice reading and book clubs. Short texts can be highly complex and offer a great deal for readers to think and talk about. When you use short texts, students can experience a great variety of texts in a short time—as many as three to five a week! This experience broadens their knowledge of the variety of texts in many genres and gives them many different opportunities to think about characters, story problems and resolutions, ways of organizing information, and all the other aspects of texts they need to consider. What readers learn how to do on a short text they can take to their reading of a longer text in independent reading or book club discussions. You can occasionally use a chapter book in guided reading, but again, you might want to select books like *A Long Walk to Water* (Park 2010) that can be read within about a week. In any case, if you occasionally use a chapter book to build stamina, plan to have students read the book in about one to two weeks.

Introducing the Text

It is in the introduction to the text that you engage the readers in a conversation and carefully set the scene for comprehending. You wouldn't want to tell students what to think but you can point out helpful information and raise questions in their minds. As you introduce the text, you might choose to get readers starting to think about any important aspect of the text. For example, you can ask them to consider the genre and check their expectations or untangle the meaning of a few new and important words that are key to understanding the text. When introducing a fiction text, you might draw attention to the setting, the problem, the characters, or some basic conflict. For a nonfiction text, you might point out one or two examples of important information or ask students to consider comparison or arguments. Right before students begin reading, you can choose to remind them to notice something about the text. This kind of advance information gives comprehending a "boost."

Summarize. As you read a text, you start to summarize by noticing the important information in the text—big ideas and evidence in a nonfiction text, and plot, characters, and problem resolution in a fiction text. As you move through the text, you are constantly making judgments about the important information. (Sometimes, you even go back to check something that you have forgotten or neglected.) At the end of the reading, you are able to construct and articulate a logically organized summary that includes all (or almost all) of the important information and your interpretation of the message or messages. Summarizing is different from retelling, in which even minor or unimportant details and information are shared. If a student knows he will be expected to retell, he will be likely to share every detail, and that can undermine the reader's grasping of the most important ideas or information. On the other hand, a reader who expects to summarize will look for the important information and ideas, and articulation will be briefer and more succinct and organized than a retelling.

If you intend to help students learn how to summarize, it may be helpful to remind students of what to keep in mind before they begin reading, for example:

> "As you read today, notice the important information and the writer's message(s) so that we can talk about them together."

"As you read today, notice the important things that happen in the story and the writer's message(s) so that we can create a summary."

For some intermediate/middle students, you may think this approach is too leading, and they may know very well how to automatically summarize a piece of writing by selecting the most important information, but that is not necessarily so. In our experience, summarizing is pretty high level and needs to be taught. For beginners who are reading very simple texts, the summary might include almost all of the events or information, or it may be quite short, but still, they need to consider what is important to tell in talking about a story or nonfiction text.

Predict. It is easy to get students thinking about predicting during the text introduction. You can reveal just enough information about the setting, characters, or problem to start this thinking. Let's look at an example of a teacher introducing a level V book, *Elephant Rescue* (*Fountas & Pinnell Classroom*, in press) (see Figures 20-1 and 20-2).

As they move through a fiction or nonfiction text, readers constantly make predictions and either confirm or discard them. It works in

FIGURE 20-1 Front and Back Cover of *Elephant Rescue*, Level V

An Introduction to *Elephant Rescue*, Level V

Mr. G	Today you are going to read *Elephant Rescue* by Jill Rubalcaba. This book is fiction. The author wrote it because she was inspired by the work of Dr. Caitlin O'Connell who observed elephant families for twenty years. Take a look at the front cover and read the back cover.
Max	It looks like they're watching the elephants from some sort of tower.
Ali	She doesn't like helping her mom watch elephants, but I would.
Mr. G	You can see by what the back cover says that Jan is not happy with her summer vacation. They are doing what Dr. O'Connell does—observing elephants in Africa. The front cover shows them observing the elephants. Do you think Jan will get more involved with the elephants?
Ali	Maybe she tries to help them somehow because the title of the book is *Elephant Rescue*.
Max	That might be dangerous to do because an injured elephant could hurt you.
Josh	But if she starts helping them then she might change her mind about summer.
Mr. G	Maybe that could happen. As you read, you'll get to see whether your predictions are right.

FIGURE 20-2 An Introduction to *Elephant Rescue*, Level V

a slightly different way in nonfiction and fiction. In fiction texts, readers use what they are finding out about the characters and the story problem to make predictions about:

- What is likely to happen next.
- How the characters will solve the problem.
- What a character will do next.
- How the story will end.

If the setting is relevant to the plot, readers use their understanding of it to make predictions about:

- Whether the characters will have to deal with challenges related to the setting (and why you think so).
- Whether the title and the illustrations offer clues that help you predict what the story will be about.

Nonfiction texts typically do not have a plot, although some biographical texts and narrative nonfiction texts are told in chronological order, like a story. For a narrative nonfiction text like *Minnie Freeman's Blizzard* (see Figure 14-17), the readers might predict in a way similar to fiction:

- What will Minnie do to keep the children safe?
- What will happen at the end of the story?

Predictions in expository nonfiction have to do with the kind of information the readers will find in the text or the arguments or ideas the writer might present. Predictions might be about:

- The way the writer has organized the text, or what a particular section will be about, based on the headings.
- The side of the argument the writer might take, based on the writer's style.
- What the reader might learn about a specific topic or idea.

Based on how much information you have drawn students' attention to in the introduction to the text, you can work some prompts or reminders into the introduction, or at the end. The introduction is an opportunity for readers to begin to actively make predictions.

Make Connections. The more connections students can make to their lives, to the world, and to other texts, the richer the comprehension will be. The guided reading lesson is a setting that allows you to support students in making connections and, in the process, communicate to them the value of making connections. You can:

- Ask them what they already know about the topic of a nonfiction book.
- Remind them if they have read (or heard read) another book by the author or illustrator.
- Remind them of another book in a series.
- Ask what they will expect of a text based on what they know about the genre or topic or author.

▶ Ask them if they are like any of the characters and in what ways.

▶ Ask what questions they have about a topic.

▶ Ask if they think this book will be like another book with a similar setting.

▶ Give them some information about the setting so that they can apply background knowledge immediately while reading.

▶ Help them think about the times in which the narrative or biography takes place.

▶ Remind them to think about what they know while reading.

▶ Remind them to think about the importance of the topic in light of what you know about the world (or world problems).

▶ Ask what an illustration or another graphic reminds them of.

The specific way you raise readers' awareness of connections depends on the nature of the text and, of course, what readers already know. For example, if students are reading *Elephant Rescue,* you would want them to think of what they already know about animal sanctuaries and elephant families in particular. You might want them to have some awareness of the threats to elephants or the danger in trying to help a mother elephant that is trying to protect her calf. In contrast, if students are reading *Bad Day in Doomsville* (*Fountas & Pinnell Classroom,* in press), it would be important for them to have some understanding of the genre of Western movies so that they can appreciate the humor (see Figure 20-3). Even very easy books require readers to connect to prior knowledge.

Frankie wasn't big and she wasn't strong. But she was smart and determined. She'd just have to save Doomsville all by herself.

Just then the Magees galloped by, swinging their lassos over their heads, the ropes swirling and hissing like snakes.

Frankie stepped out onto Main Street. "Just what do you want?" she shouted at them.

"Lots and lots of everything!" was the reply.

Then, before Frankie could say, "horned toads and polliwogs," one of the Magees swooped her up and plunked her on his horse.

FIGURE 20-3 *Bad Day in Doomsville, Pages 8 and 9*

Bear's Flowers (*Fountas & Pinnell Classroom,* in press) a fiction text, features Bear and Rabbit (see Figure 20-4). Bear plants a garden, Rabbit eats the flowers, and, as a result, Bear is very angry. But Rabbit is so grateful that Bear ends up planting a garden for him. Readers would call on what they know about gardens and rabbits, any disappointing experiences they may have had, and how friends should treat each other. In addition, Bear is a character in a series of books, and he is always kind. Children who have read other books in the series will feel they are meeting an old friend and might be able to predict what he will do based on the character traits they learned from previous books in the series.

Synthesize. Readers encounter new information and ideas as they read, and this is true in both fiction and nonfiction texts. They make connections to what they already know and to current thinking, and often, reading a new book can change a reader's attitudes, make him think in new ways, or expand conceptual knowledge. As they read fiction, they vicariously experience human problems and learn from characters. Through nonfiction, they greatly expand understanding. In both fiction and nonfiction, readers find messages that teach them about life and about their world.

In the introduction, you can foreshadow and prompt for synthesizing by asking students to think about the writer's message (what the writer is really trying to say). In a high-quality text, the message or "big idea" is always greater than the "facts." The big idea or message goes beyond the particular book; it is not a summary. It refers to the "so what" or relevance of the text to the reader. What message

Rabbit hugged Bear.
"Thank you, Bear!" he said.
"Those flowers tasted so good!"

Bear did not know what to say.
But soon he had an idea.

10

11

FIGURE 20-4 *Bear's Flowers,* Pages 10–11

does the story or nonfiction text give to the person who reads the text? You can ask them to reflect on what they already know about a topic and notice new or surprising information. You can, if appropriate, remind students that after reading (perhaps about a controversial topic), everyone in the group can share whether and how their thinking has changed.

Infer. As with other categories of strategic actions, you can "set the scene" for inferring in the introduction to the text. You can't do the inferring *for* students, nor would you want to interfere with thinking by having them mark the page or make a note every time they "make an inference," as some advise teachers to do. You do want students to be on the alert to what the writer is really saying. Inferring and synthesizing are both involved because you have to think about what the writer is *implying* rather than telling and also to compare the ideas with your own knowledge and thinking.

In the introduction you can prompt or question to raise students' awareness, for example:

> ▶ As you read, think about how the author shows his point of view.

> ▶ As you read, remember that sometimes the writer says something and means more, so think about what she is really saying.

> ▶ As you read, think about how the writer feels about the topic.

> ▶ As you read, think about how the character feels (or about why a character behaves like that).

> ▶ As you read, notice the conflict in the story.

> ▶ As you read, notice how the setting affects the characters and what they do.

> ▶ Remember to think about what the writer wants readers to learn.

Analyze. As a category, *analyze* includes a wide range of actions that readers take to notice aspects of the writers craft. The reader is analyzing the writer's use of literary craft in fiction, for example, exposition of setting, characters, plot, character development, literary language, plot resolution, use of symbolism, and others. In nonfiction, the writer notices the writer's use of techniques for organizing and revealing information, including the "lead," selection of information to support argument, and the use of underlying structural patterns such as compare and contrast, problem and solution, temporal and chronological sequence, and others. High-quality leveled texts of both fiction and nonfiction can have literary quality.

In the introduction to a text, you can draw readers' attention to information in a way that will prompt them to think analytically about it. *Lion and Tiger (Fountas & Pinnell Classroom,* in press) is a level K text (see Figure 20-5). Following is an excerpt from an introduction to the text (Figure 20-6). In this introduction, the teacher prompts students to notice character development and how the writer shows it.

For nonfiction texts, you might help students notice when the writer is using underlying text structures that are so characteristic of nonfiction genres.

The sky began to darken.
Tiger said, "Lion, I think we are lost."
Lion said, "I think you are right. For once."

"We must stay here for the night," said Tiger. "Then tomorrow we can find our way home."
Lion said, "I think you are right. For the second time in one day."

FIGURE 20-5 Pages 8–9 from *Lion and Tiger*

An Introduction to *Lion and Tiger*, Level K

Ms. P	We've talked about how Lion and Tiger were always saying almost the same thing.
Richard	They both thought they were the greatest, and they didn't like each other.
Marguerite	They always bragged that they were the best.
Ms. P	They went for a walk every day and argued. Each one would talk about what made them the best. Take a look at pages 8 and 9. What do you think is happening?
Inez	It's getting dark.
Cathy	They are lost.
Ms. P	It could be! So, as you read, notice whether Lion and Tiger change their feelings; and if they do, notice how the writer shows it.

FIGURE 20-6 An Introduction to *Lion and Tiger*, Level K

Critique. The introduction can also prepare the readers to think critically about the text, in this case, *Ants for Lunch* (*Fountas & Pinnell Classroom*, in press). (see Figures 20-7 and 20-8). Critiquing involves a very important set of cognitive actions. All readers need to ask questions like these:

- Is this text accurate and unbiased?
- Is it written in an interesting way?
- Are the writer's arguments valid? Does the writer offer counterarguments or neglect important facts?

▶ What is the writer's point of view?

▶ Does the text show a particular group of people in a bad light (perpetuates any racist or gender stereotypes)?

▶ Is the writer clear in stating his points?

▶ Is the organization appropriate for the topic?

As with other strategic actions, you can remind readers to read critically and share their opinions with the group after reading.

FIGURE 20-7 Pages 2–3 from *Ants for Lunch*, Level O

An Introduction to *Ants for Lunch*, **Level O**

Mr. H	Based on the front and back cover, you know that this nonfiction book is about the anteater. The way a writer starts a nonfiction book—the lead—gives you an idea what the whole book will be about. Sometimes the writer uses comparison. Read the first paragraph and then talk with a partner about what this writer is comparing. Read silently and then turn and talk.
Mr. H	What did you find out?
Alan	It's about the anteater's body. The snout is like a vacuum cleaner hose.
Mr. H	You noticed that the writer is comparing the anteater's snout to a vacuum cleaner hose to help readers understand what that part of its body is like. As you read, notice other ways the writer uses comparisons in this book.

FIGURE 20-8 An Introduction to *Ants for Lunch*, Level O

As a note of caution, if you prompt readers in the ways mentioned above, you want to do it very lightly and stay grounded in *this* text. Readers need to engage with the text and apply the systems of strategic actions—not just think in an abstract way. It is important when introducing the text, not to overload the reader. Too many reminders will make the reading a tedious task rather than a meaningful, enjoyable experience, and might also interfere with comprehension.

Reading the Text

Students who are reading levels A through about level H or I, generally are reading aloud softly. You can listen in and interact when a reader has some difficulty, seems confused, or asks for help. While readers at higher levels are reading the text, you might sample oral reading and may interact briefly with them.

As needed, you might support the reader's attention to the meaning of the text with a variety of brief prompts that support the reader's use of meaningful information. For example:

- Try that again and think what would make sense.
- That looks right, but does it make sense?
- It has to make sense. Try that again.

You might also support the reader's phrased, fluent reading with prompts that focus attention on interpreting the meaning of the text. There is a strong correlation between fluent reading and comprehension (see Chapter 18):

- Put your words together so it sounds like talking.
- Make it sound like the character is talking.

With students who are reading silently, be cautious about interfering with the reading, although you may need to sample oral reading to check on the effectiveness of your text selection and introduction. Or, you may observe that the reader is puzzled or "stuck," and sometimes readers ask for help. In that case, you can prompt for any action that the reader can take to solve a problem.

It is easy to fall into the trap of questioning the student or asking for action in a way that amounts to a test of the student's understanding. It's best to avoid having a "comprehension conversation" with a single student during reading, because even a good conversation can go on for several minutes and interrupt the reader's processing of the text. The student may lose his train of thought and will find it difficult to get back into the book. Instead, at point of difficulty, you can choose to prompt briefly for students to problem solve and move on.

Discussing the Text

The beginning of the discussion should be an open invitation to students to share their thinking with each other about the text, for example:

- "What are you thinking about this story?"
- "What do you think about _____ (the topic of this book)?"
- "What did this book make you think about?"

Students need the opportunity to provide their personal responses to the meaning of the text and to respond to each other. This is a time for the students to wonder, with each other, ask for clarification, link to and build on each other's thinking, and support their thinking with personal experience or evidence from the text. You will probably find that they spontaneously talk about how their predictions were confirmed (or not), what new understandings they have gained, the insights they have developed about characters, what they have noticed about the problem and the resolution, and how they found the text engaging (or not). You can guide this discussion and help students respond to each other with language like this:

▶ "Who can add something to what _____ said?"

▶ "What do you think about what _____ said?"

▶ "Do you agree (or disagree) with _____ and why?"

In addition, to extend the discussion, you can ask:

▶ "Were your predictions right about _____?"

▶ "How was the problem resolved?" (Or, "How did they solve the problem?")

▶ "Do you think the ending was good? (Or, "Was the ending satisfying?")

▶ "Did you notice how (character) changed?" "How and why?" (Or, "What lesson did (character) learn?"

▶ "What do you think was the author's message?"

▶ "Have you changed any of your thinking after reading this book?" Or, "Did you learn anything new? What?"

In *Prompting Guide Part 2, Genre Prompting Guide for Fiction,* and *Genre Prompting Guide for Nonfiction Poetry, and Test Taking,* you can see many more examples of facilitative talk that supports readers in thinking in new ways or reflecting on a text. Remember you can also use this kind of language when students *revisit* the text after the discussion. This facilitative language lets students do the thinking and talking but helps them become more specific in what they notice, and the prompts can direct attention to new thinking. You may even use these examples of talk more in revisiting the text than during reading.

The more you can keep such questions rooted in text they are reading, the better. Don't ask these questions in an abstract way (for example, "What inferring did you do?"). Readers need to go back into the text as much as possible. The discussion is all about expressing their thinking, but the readers need to give evidence from the text. You can use language like:

▶ "Take us to the part that supports your thinking."

▶ "Can you tell us the page to look at for an example?"

▶ "What makes you think that?"

The discussion in guided reading is not long, but it should give you some important information about the meaning that the students have taken from the text.

Teaching Points

Following the discussion, and based on your observations, take students back into the text to teach for any strategic actions, for example, to take a word apart, think about the meaning of a new vocabulary word, read more fluently, to examine a tricky sentence structure, or to think about the message of a text.

You can also choose to have students revisit the text to attend to any of the categories in thinking within, beyond, or about the text, or to use in close reading, which can be a way to expand comprehension and help them think analytically about the text. You can use the *Prompting Guides* for facilitative language that will help students go deeper into the text, and it is more effective in close reading because students have already had the opportunity to process the entire text and have a background of meaning and familiarity. When they reread a short portion of the text, they are able to have new insights.

Summarize. A summary is a short report that includes the important information in as few words as possible. Sometimes a text can be summarized in one sentence; but it may be as long as a paragraph. Constructing a summary is not a simple task; many students are tempted to include every detail, important or not, as if they are trying to prove that they read the selection. Usually, students have to be taught how to summarize and they need many examples. Fortunately, writers sometimes end a text with a summary—mostly in nonfiction. The summary may not be strictly an academic one because the writer takes literary license to engage readers and also may want to drive home the message; however, such summaries can serve as examples for students. As a teaching point, you may want to revisit the summary to closely examine it. The writer provided a summary in this example from *Ants for Lunch* (Figure 20-9). Notice how the teacher teaches for summarizing in the following example (see Figure 20-10).

In Figure 20-11, you can see another example of teaching for summarizing at level N. The teacher helps the students talk

Built for Survival

The anteater is an odd-looking creature, but it looks this way for a reason. Its physical features help it survive. From its snout to its tail, the anteater's body helps it get the food it needs to stay alive and healthy.

The next time you see a strange-looking animal, ask yourself how it survives in the wild. You may find that the animal no longer looks so strange to you.

FIGURE 20-9 Page 15 from *Ants for Lunch*, Level O

about the important information and compose a summary using shared writing (see Figure 20-12).

Summarizing is an excellent skill but it takes years to develop. Being able to concisely summarize is an important skill that they will use all of their lives.

Predict. The human brain is constantly making predictions—predicting potential danger is what keeps us safe. Readers make predictions throughout the reading process—from the time they pick up a book, until the end. After the reading, during the discussion and in the teaching point, you can have students discuss whether their predictions were confirmed or disconfirmed and take them to pages where this happened. You can find suggested language for discussion in *Prompting Guide Part 2 for Comprehension, Prompting Guide for Fiction,* and *Prompting Guide for Nonfiction, Poetry, and Test Taking.*

Students don't always have to verbalize or report on their predictions, so be selective. Often they can turn and talk with a partner about any surprises they found

Teaching for Summarizing Using *Ants for Lunch,* Level O

Ms. R	Go to page 15. Reread the page and then talk with a partner about the information on this last page. Then, let's list what the writer is doing.
Students	*(Read and then talk).*
Ms. R	What did you and your partner find?
Ira	She says the anteater's body looks funny but it helps it survive.
Kyeara	His body helps him get food.
Diana	She talks about his snout and his tail.
Ms. R	You've captured the meaning in the first paragraph. Anything else?
Susan	She says you should look at other animals that look strange and think how their bodies help them stay alive.
Ms. R	So the writer makes a statement of what this whole book is about and then alerts readers to think about all animals' bodies and how they help them survive. That is a short way of telling the most important information in the book. It's called a summary. A summary can be just a couple of sentences. There are several ways to write a summary, but a summary always shows the important information and the writer's message, and a summary is always short. Is there any other way the author could have written this summary?
Mary	She could have just told us that parts of animals' bodies help them survive.
Ms. R	She could. It seems to me that she wrote it as a question to get readers thinking about the message instead of just telling. When you are writing a summary for a test, you could just tell the message as you understand it.
Kelly	She could have included an example.
Diana	The snout and the tail are examples.
Ms. R	All the writer had to do was mention the examples because the reader has just read about them, but if you are writing a summary for a test, you could tell why the example is good. Remember that you can look for a summary at the end of a nonfiction book like this one. Summaries are short. They tell the important information in the book and the message. Sometimes they include one or two examples. A summary generally follows a sequence if that is the way the text is organized.

FIGURE 20-10 Teaching for Summarizing Using *Ants for Lunch,* Level O

Teaching for Summarizing Using *The Motata Tree*, Level N

Ms. R	Sometimes after you read a book, you need to tell about it in just a few sentences. Let's do that for *The Motata Tree*. What happened in this book?
Students	*[Spend a few minutes talking about the events in the book based on an African folktale].*
Ms. R	You know a lot about what happened. Let's organize our summary. First, let's tell who is in the story and what the problem is.
Greg	Giraffe and Elephant wanted to eat fruit that was in the tree but they couldn't reach it.
Harry	And Turtle was there. They went to see the Great Lion.
Ms. R	*[Writes: Giraffe and Elephant and Turtle wanted to eat fruit but they could not reach it.]* Who went first?
Bertie	Giraffe did and the Great Lion said he had to say the name of the tree, but Giraffe forgot it. Then Elephant went and he just thought of a lot of other things and forgot it. Then Turtle went and he said the name over and over—like Motata. And he remembered it because he made up a song.
Ms. R	*[Works together with students and produces a summary.]* Sometimes a fiction story in which several things happen will be a little longer. Our summary has all the important things that happened. If we needed to, could we make it shorter?
Greg	We could just say that all three animals went to see the Great Lion but Turtle was the only one who remembered the name of the tree because he made it into a song.
Ms. R	We could and that would shorten it quite a bit. Sometimes you can do a longer summary and sometimes you can make it very short.

FIGURE 20-11 Teaching for Summarizing Using *The Motata Tree*

Summary of The Motata Tree

Giraffe and Elephant and Turtle were very hungry and wanted to eat fruit. Giraffe and Elephant went to the Great Lion and he told them the name of the tree so they could get the fruit, but they forgot it. Turtle went and remembered it, so they learned a lesson about remembering things.

FIGURE 20-12 Summary of *The Motata Tree*

in a book—a general direction that prompts for confirming or disconfirming predictions, reporting new learning, or something they found interesting or engaging.

Make Connections. Students make connections with everything they know—their own personal experiences, their content knowledge of the world (background knowledge or academic disciplines as they develop such knowledge, and their experience and understanding of other texts.) Even if you did not specifically prompt students to make connections to their own understanding of a topic and notice new information, you would expect this to happen every time they read a nonfiction text. As students read fiction texts, they can also articulate personal, world, or textual connections across a range of characteristics of literature. After reading, you can prompt them to articulate some of the connections they have made. As students develop ease in linking what they read to their own experiences or knowledge, you can make prompts more general.

Synthesize. In a sense, all human beings synthesize all of the time because they learn from experiences. They are constantly adding to their knowledge and changing their understandings. In fact, that's what makes life interesting. Readers are engaged in texts when they find something new and surprising or encounter ideas that intrigue them. Our ideal is for students to learn something new or think in a new way with every book they read. That's a pretty high goal, but if we reach for it, we increase the likelihood of success. We want students to value reading because of the way it stretches them. During the discussion or in your teaching for points after reading, you can ask students to articulate changes in their thinking with specific language.

Infer. Students are always making inferences as they read, but you can help them probe deeper into the meaning with interaction. Ask students to revisit a part of the text and think about what it tells them about what character is like or what it shows about a character's feelings. For example, Earl and Pearl are brother and sister in a series, and Pearl is always taking care of Earl (see Figure 20-13). After reading *Earl on His Own,* level K, you might say: "Beginning on page 6, look through several pages of the book and just notice the illustrations. Then, talk with a partner about what these illustrations tell you about Pearl as a sister and how she feels about Earl." Students will be able to infer that Pearl really cares about Earl and wants to take care of him. But she also wants him to feel independent. All of this is shown in the illustrations.

Another example is *A School Made Out of Trash* (*Fountas & Pinnell Classroom,* in press). In this level M narrative nonfiction text, young students in Guatemala create a school building out of trash (see Figure 20-14).

After reading *A School Made Out of Trash,* you might say: "Go to page 6 and reread it. As you read, think about why these young students worked so hard on filling the empty soda bottles with plastic bags to make something like bricks." Students will be able to infer that the students really wanted a school building big enough for them even though their town couldn't afford to finish the building. They also wanted to solve the problem of too much trash in the garbage dump. They were happy to work hard to solve both problems.

You don't need to use words like "infer" until students have had a great deal of experience articulating what a writer really means, how a character feels, or why a character behaves as he does. You can explain that often writers mean more than

Just then, Earl felt something fall out of his pocket.

"What's that?" he wondered and turned to look.

"Why, it's Pearl's map!" he shouted. "Hooray!"

14

Earl looked carefully at the map.

"Now I see which way to go," he said. "I'll be at Pearl's house in time for dinner!"

Earl hurried down the road, whistling all the way.

15

FIGURE 20-13 Pages 14–15 from *Earl on His Own*, Level K

Making Bricks from Trash

When they had collected a huge pile of soda bottles and plastic bags, the kids were ready to begin. Children from kindergarten to sixth grade helped to fill the empty soda bottles with plastic bags. They stuffed bottles before school, during lunch, and after school. Some bottles now contained *hundreds* of bags. When the bottles were full, they were as hard as bricks. Stuffing bottles was very hard work. Yet no one quit, because the students all wanted a new school. Some students even got **blisters** on their hands, but they still kept working. Together the children filled *six thousand bottles*.

Children filling bottles with used grocery bags, chip bags, and other plastic trash.

stick

plastic bottle

plastic bags

6

7

FIGURE 20-14 Pages 6–7 from *A School Made Out of Trash*, Level M

they say. When students are able to articulate these kinds of understandings, then it may be useful to communicate the vocabulary of inferring, what is implied but not stated, especially if students are working on "showing, not telling" in their own writing. Sometimes people describe inferring as "reading between the lines." This is one of the most important elements of comprehension so we want to develop it, but not as a meaningless (or superficially understood) label.

Analyze. Thinking analytically about a text raises the reader's awareness of the craft of writing. Even for sophisticated adult readers, it's hard to analyze a text on the first reading—usually a reader is just immersing himself in the story. But even adults go back and engage in close reading to think analytically about a text. After the reading, you can take the readers back into the text to analyze it. For example, the nonfiction text, *Coley's Journey* (*Fountas & Pinnell Classroom,* in press), Level Q, features an osprey that makes a yearly journey from South America to New York City and back again. Coley is assisting scientists by wearing a tiny GPS system. You might say: "Go back to pages 10 and 11. Reread the page and take a look at the map. As you read, think about how the writer is showing how amazing Coley's journey is. Then, talk to a partner about it." Students can notice that the journey is very long and covers a lot of distance because the writer has used a diary format to tell about the 15-day, 7-hour trip, and also shows the route on a map. The illustration (with a caption) shows an osprey waiting out a storm, one of the dangers of the trip (see Figure 20-15).

Stormy Weather

March 12
Coley is finally back in the USA. He spends the night in a tree in a neighborhood near Orlando, Florida. The next day he heads north again. The weather is good for flying.

March 18
Bad luck! A huge winter storm hits the East Coast of the USA. The state of Virginia is blasted by heavy rain and strong winds. Coley must stop in Virginia to wait out the storm. He finds a safe shelter near a river.

March 19
When the weather clears, Coley begins his journey again. He still has more than 200 miles (322 kilometers) to go. For a person driving a car, it would take three or four hours. How long will it take Coley?

Like Coley, this osprey has found a safe place to wait out a storm.

Coley's Route

10

11

FIGURE 20-15 Pages 10–11 from *Coley's Journey,* Level Q

Another example is *How to Find a Prince* (*Fountas & Pinnell Classroom,* in press), level N. In this book, Princess Poppy tries to find a prince (see Figure 20-16). You might say: "Reread pages 10 and 11. As you read, think about what the writer is doing to make this book funny and to show what Poppy is like as a person." Students can notice that the writer is presenting a "how-to" book for finding a prince that makes connections to traditional tales like Rapunzel. Students may notice that the princess in this story doesn't just wait for a prince to come to her—she becomes bored waiting in her tower and becomes an excellent wall climber. This is a princess who does things for herself. Readers can conclude that the writer has created a spoof (or "take off") on the traditional depiction of a princess.

You can spend much of your time teaching for processing strategies in the area of analytical thinking because readers grow in this ability over the years. Students can revisit the text to discuss how a writer:

▶ Reveals characters

▶ Exposes the problem of the plot

▶ Chooses a genre to show the main idea

▶ Makes the topic/story interesting

▶ Shows the solution to problems

▶ Uses the "lead" to get readers interested

▶ Uses language to describe, compare, and connect ideas

You will never run out of teaching points that will help students analyze a text.

Critique. Students need to learn to think critically as they read, and this is increasingly important as they encounter more sophisticated texts. Beginning readers

Princess Poppy read Chapter 3.

> For a foolproof way to find a prince, climb a tower and grow your hair. Hang it out the window. A prince is sure to climb your hair and rescue you.

"That sounds unlikely," said Princess Poppy. Still, she was a princess, through and through, and she would do what a princess should do.

She found a tower, climbed to the top, and poured a whole bottle of hair-grow oil on her head. Soon her hair grew so long it hung out the window.

10

Princess Poppy got bored waiting for a prince to arrive. She passed the time climbing the tower wall. She became an excellent climber.

11

FIGURE 20-16 Pages 10–11 from *How to Find a Prince,* Level N

may simply discuss whether the story or nonfiction book was good or interesting and what made it so. You can bring this up in the discussion or decide to have them show a place in the book that is especially funny or interesting and talk about why they think that.

As they grow in sophistication, you can use close reading to help students re-visit the text in a way the helps them evaluate the quality. They can revisit the text with questions in mind. For example, the nonfiction text, *Animals and Their Dreams (Fountas & Pinnell Classroom,* in press), the writer argues that many different kinds of animals dream (see Figure 20-17a and 20-17b).

FIGURE 20-17a Pages 6–7 from *Animals and Their Dreams*

FIGURE 20-17b Pages 8–9 from *Animals and Their Dreams*

As a teaching point, you might say: "What is the writer of this book arguing? (Students can respond that the writer is arguing that many animals dream). "Reread pages 6 and 7 of *Animals and Their Dreams*. As you read, think about whether the writer is supporting his argument. Then talk with a partner." Students can discuss the scientific experiment involving rats that the writer included. The writer used words like "seemed" to show that scientists were developing theories.

You might choose a different point in this text for a slightly different angle on critical thinking about the argument. "This book presents an argument with some evidence and some theories that scientists have. Reread pages 8 and 9, and then talk with a partner about what is likely to be factual and what is not yet proven to be true." Students can notice that while there is good evidence that mammals dream, the ideas of what they dream about don't really have proof. The writer uses words like "might" and "it's possible."

In critiquing a text, a reader should consider:

▶ The writer's qualifications

▶ References to scientific information

▶ Documentation

▶ The objectivity of the writer

▶ How the text fits the characteristics of the genre

▶ How interesting the text is

▶ The quality of the writing

▶ The quality of the illustrations

Thinking critically is perhaps the most complex thinking readers are expected to do. It is amazing how easily many readers accept the truth of something just because it is in written language—even if it comes from the Internet in a form that is not reviewed or vetted. We consider critical reading to be a significant responsibility of educators as we work to develop informed citizens.

Being Selective

As you have read this chapter, you have probably noticed that you have hundreds (if not thousands) of choices for making teaching decisions on what to teach for after reading.

Although it may be difficult to think about, your teaching can actually interfere with comprehension. You may, with the best of intentions, fall into the trap of this kind of interference (see Figure 20-18).

Keep in mind that analytical and critical thinking are difficult for young children—they need to talk about the text in language they understand, and you must attune your language to the current language of students. A general rule is that you need evidence that students can engage in the kind of thinking you want before asking for it in academic language (using words like *infer* and *perspective*). In *The Literacy Continuum* you will find suggested academic language that might be appropriate for each level, A to Z. This is not a "rule," but it may help in adjusting your language to the readers. Teacher language determines the quality of language and thinking of the students. When teachers are doing most of the talking, students tend to do less thinking. The one who talks is the one who learns.

You can involve them in close reading to focus their attention on any of a huge number of understandings related to reading comprehension. It is tempting to explore every possible teaching opportunity in a text, and we have seen guided reading lessons that last an hour (thus neglecting other students and wearing out those with whom you are working); or revisiting a single text for several days (thus taking too much time and risking boring the students). It is not possible to teach everything in a text—the lesson would become tedious and students would stop listening. You need to select one (at the most two) clear teaching opportunities, which forces you to be selective. Think about what your students are most in need of learning and then connect those goals with the opportunities in the text. The *Literacy Continuum* will be helpful. Think about what the students can learn and how they can apply their learning to other texts. As the students are reading short texts, every day will bring a new opportunity and over the course of the school year, these will be numerous.

Writing About Reading

You might engage students in writing about reading after they have read and discussed the text and you have made your teaching point. If you choose this option, students can complete the writing at the table while you have individual conferences or even teach another group. Or they can complete the writing individually at their desks or tables. But we want to emphasize that writing about reading is *optional*. You don't want to communicate to students that they must write about every text they read. That kind of practice could lead to a dread of reading!

But occasionally, for specific purposes, you may want students to articulate in writing their understanding of the text they have read in a guided reading lesson. This activity should be productive and include follow up—the purpose of writing about reading is not simply to keep students busy. There are several kinds of writing about reading that you might select, including:

> ▸ *Shared writing* in which you are the scribe but students give input. For beginning readers, you can use interactive writing in which students contribute some of the writing of letters and/or words. For students who are farther along, you want to avoid having students wait for one student to write. Just write it quickly yourself. In this kind of writing, students

Ways That the Teacher May Interfere with Reading Comprehension

1. Do most of the talking.

2. Have students practice a strategy or skill.

3. Interrupt the oral or silent reading to have students talk about their thinking and label it.

4. Interrupt the oral or silent reading to test students' comprehension.

5. Ask students to prove they read a text.

6. Tell students what to think.

7. Go back to every part of the text and question students to test their understanding.

8. Use big words that students don't understand.

9. Ask students to use big words that they don't really understand.

10. Have a metacognitive conversation that talks about thinking in an abstract way instead of genuine responses to a specific text.

FIGURE 20-18 Ways That the Teacher May Interfere with Reading Comprehension

are freed from the mechanical activity of writing so that they can give full attention to the construction of the message.

▶ *Dictated writing* in which you read the short piece of writing to students and they write it in their reader's notebooks. In this way, you can demonstrate many ways of writing about reading. Students will be able to refer back to models that they have recorded in their own handwriting in their notebooks.

▶ *Independent writing* in which students construct and record their own responses to reading as guided by the teacher's prompts.

The ultimate goal is for students to be able to engage in independent writing about reading, but they may need the demonstrations provided by shared, interactive, and dictated writing. When exploring an area of thinking (to be expressed in writing about reading), consider demonstrating shared or dictated writing first and then asking for independent writing. A general sequence is:

1. Select an area of response (any of the systems of strategic actions) that you have previously demonstrated through shared and/or dictated writing.

2. Direct the students to write in a way that is connected with the discussion or your teaching for processing strategies.

3. Give students enough time to write a *short* response.

4. Bring students back together to share their writing (either the same day or the next day in the small group).

5. Engage students in extended discussion emerging from their writing.

Some of the criteria for writing about reading in guided reading are:

▶ The writing should be short and take only a little time (a quick write rather than a long "report").

▶ It should be directly related to some aspect of the text.

▶ It should emerge from the discussion or teaching following the discussion.

▶ Students should use the text as a resource.

▶ The writing should be something that students share with each other and serves as a springboard for further discussion.

▶ The writing should not be a "test" that asks students to prove they read the text, but it should reveal their thinking.

If you are using a reader's notebook, then have students record their writing about reading from guided reading there. In this way, they'll keep a record of their thinking. Across the year, engage the students in different ways of writing about reading to provide opportunities for them to think within, beyond, and about a text.

Summarizing

Over time, students need to be able to summarize, not retell. With your demonstration in shared writing, students will be able to summarize independently in their reader's notebooks. Students were asked to summarize *Coley's Journey* in independent writing (see Figure 20-19). Notice how the student was able to put the important information in a few sentences.

Predicting

Students can do a quick write about how their predictions were confirmed or disconfirmed in two columns in their reader's notebooks. You could ask students to write about how the title helped them predict what the students would do in *A School Made Out of Trash*, and what it didn't help them predict (see Figure 20-20).

Making Connections

After talking about their personal connections to *A Peeper Sings* (*Fountas & Pinnell Classroom*, in press), shown in Figure 20-21, students wrote about their own

In the beginning Coley (osprey) got a backpack GPS on his back so when he goes back to his nest in New York City people can know where he is.
In the middle, Coley sets off to New York City. He went several places. In the end he made it to New York City and got a mate and had two chicks.

FIGURE 20-19 Student Summary of *Coley's Journey*

My Predictions: School Made Out of Trash

Before	After
From the title I think the students will fill big boxes with trash and pack them up.	But they stuffed plastic bottles with plastic bags and made hard plastic bricks.

FIGURE 20-20 Student Predictions for *A School Made of Trash*

Spring

The frogs are called peepers.
Their song means
that spring is here.

The snow melts,
and the air gets warmer.

peeper

4

5

FIGURE 20-21 Pages 4–5 from *A Peeper Sings*

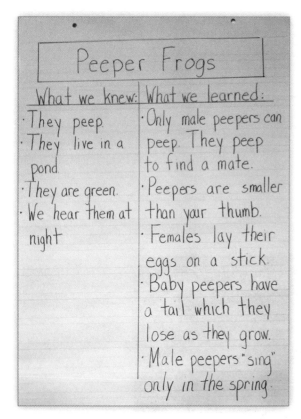

FIGURE 20-22 Student Connections to *A Peeper Sings*

FIGURE 20-23 Shared Writing Chart for *A Peeper Sings*

Nolan

How I'm like Earl or had an expierence like him is when My Mom & I went to Wal★Mart and she let me walk around on My own.

FIGURE 20-24 Short Write for *Earl On His Own*

experiences in listening to night sounds in their reader's notebooks (see Figure 20-22).

Synthesizing

This teacher used this same text and shared writing to make a chart with two columns and the headings, "What We Knew" and "What We Learned" about peeper frogs (see Figure 20-23).

Inferring

A short write is a few sentences that students write in less than five minutes. It does not have to be a crafted paragraph. It's an expressive reaction. After discussion about a character, students did a "short write" to express their thoughts about a character's attributes, feelings, or emotions in their readers' notebooks. One student explained how he had an experience like Earl. (see Figure 20-24).

Analyzing

After discussion of *Lion and Tiger,* using shared writing, the teacher invited the students' thinking to construct a list of how the writer showed that Lion and Tiger really cared about each other (see Figure 20-25).

FIGURE 20-25 Shared Writing List of Evidence for *Lion and Tiger*

Critiquing

After reading and discussing *Animals and their Dreams*, the students made a two-column list of evidence that supported the idea that animals dream in the first column and statements that are not proven by scientific research in the second column (see Figure 20-26).

Using Writing About Reading Effectively

Writing can support comprehending because it allows readers to slow down, reflect, and carefully consider what they think about their reading. Keep it in the arena of thinking rather than performing. If students believe that they are writing just to prove they have read something, then the writing will become a routine task. The more you can help them understand writing about reading as thinking, the more effective it will be. In general:

Scientific Evidence	Possible Explanations (but not proven)
• Rats go throught REM sleep like when they are running through a maze	• animals dream
	• dogs dream about bones
	• mice dream about mazes
• Cuttlefish dream/ (Rem sleep)	• dogs dream about flying

FIGURE 20-26 Two-Column List for *Animals and Their Dreams*

- ▶ Demonstrate through shared or interactive writing—students work together on the construction and the teacher is the scribe.
- ▶ Use dictated writing to demonstrate a writing form (e.g., a list, two-column writing, a summary).
- ▶ Keep writing focused on sharing thinking about reading.
- ▶ Keep it short and use it as a springboard for thinking.
- ▶ Use organization tools like graphic organizers but not "worksheets" to fill out.
- ▶ Have students work together as partners to talk about and/or create writing.

You may want to consult the Writing About Reading section of *The Literacy Continuum* to get an idea of the many possibilities for engaging students in writing about reading.

A Light Touch

We have discussed a variety of ways to teach for comprehending in guided reading. Comprehending is the overarching goal of guided reading, and there are many routes that lead to it. Readers ultimately arrive at a deep understanding of a text in highly individual ways. As a teacher, you can support, prompt, and scaffold their learning. But they need to engage actively with texts, think about what they mean, talk about their understandings, and connect them with their own lives. As teachers we want to support this engagement, scaffold students in extending their understanding, and avoid interfering. This is indeed a challenge and one that requires reflection and practice. But thoughtful planning, precise language, and selective teaching can be enormously powerful in helping students enjoy their reading and build a rich understanding of each text they read.

Suggestions for Professional Development

To teach for deep comprehension, you need a clear vision of what it "looks like and sounds like." You want to be able to infer from students' comments whether they are thinking within, beyond, and about the text; and, almost always, this will be accomplished while teaching lessons with very little time to reflect. If you are in tune with the comprehension demands of each text you use in guided reading, you can plan for the kind of thinking that will be essential. With this vision in mind, you can make a quick assessment of students' comments. At the same time, you can prompt for (and demonstrate when necessary) the behavior that shows evidence of understanding.

Hold a meeting to focus on the thinking that texts demand. You can work with grade-level colleagues, but it might be a good idea to work across grades so that teachers can gain a vision of how the demands grow across the levels.

1. Assemble a collection of books appropriate for guided reading at various levels. Have teachers work with a partner to look at one book at a level of interest. They specify key understandings that the reader needs to construct for:

   ▶ Thinking within the text

   ▶ Thinking beyond the text

   ▶ Thinking about the text

2. Have partners place their thinking on a chart in three rows—one each for within, beyond, and about the text.

3. Encourage teachers to be rigorous and to think of what they—as proficient readers—understand about the text. (In other words, you wouldn't expect a lower level of understanding for ELLs, for struggling readers, or for younger readers. A text is a text in what it demands of the readers).

4. When they have finished, line up the charts from lowest text level to the highest text level. You should be able to more or less "line up" the within, beyond, and about columns.

5. The group can then talk through the books one at a time with the people who did the analyses leading.

6. Then, have a whole-group discussion of the changes over time in the demands of comprehension that we can expect from students.

7. Discuss how you will apply these understandings to your own work in guided reading, for example, in the introduction, discussion, teaching for points, and in writing about reading.

SECTION **FIVE**

Thinking, Talking, Reading, and Writing in a Classroom Community

In this section, we move to the larger context of the classroom. Guided reading is most successful if you consider not only the intellectual but also the emotional lives of your students. Select and use books that help them think more deeply about important ideas and issues, about themselves and the world they live in, about their roles as global citizens, and about developing empathy for others. Foster a sense of community within the classroom where students spend so much of their lives.

We discuss how teachers and students can work together to build a community of readers and writers across the grades. We also specifically address classroom management, describing alternatives for students in the early years as well as transitions that you might make across time. Finally, we describe a comprehensive design for literacy education. All students, and especially struggling readers, need consistent and clear messages across instructional contexts. Our belief is that the curriculum must have a coherent design and a coherent underlying literacy theory rather than simply being a mix of "this and that," without an eye to how different parts work together to form a cohesive whole.

CHAPTER 21

Building a Community of Readers Across the Grades

If we want to know what is going on in our students' minds, we have to arrange conditions in which they will want to speak their minds—to risk revealing themselves and their thinking.

–Peter Johnston

Your classroom is a place where students learn how to read, write, and expand all of their language skills, but it is much more. It is a laboratory where they learn how to be confident, self-determined, kind, and democratic members of a community. It is common for those who don't understand the culture of a classroom or a school to blame students for actions that are not productive or that disrupt learning, saying, "parents should teach children how to behave." But those of us who spend hundreds of hours in classrooms realize that almost no homes truly prepare children for the challenges they will meet as they enter school and become part of a large group of learners. Even the previous year's classroom doesn't fully prepare students for the challenges of the current year.

Additionally, many students are constantly under stress. Their lives are in constant flux, their classrooms change, their teachers change, and they need to meet new expectations. Many move geographically several times during their time in school and some have arrived in a new country. When a student walks into your classroom, at the beginning of a school year, he is expected to live and work with some twenty to thirty other human beings, in a space that is a little larger than the average living room, for the better part of a year.

Just think about the social and emotional learning that students must do during their years of school. We list all of the behaviors that are expected of children from entry through middle school (see Figure 21-1). Look carefully at the list.

Behavioral and Emotional Expectations of School

Social Interaction	◆ Listen to others in small- and large-group settings
	◆ Work well as part of a group
	◆ Communicate clearly with others
	◆ Adjust communication to help others understand a point
	◆ Share details about one's own life
	◆ Give others personal space
	◆ Demonstrate conversational skill (taking turns, getting a turn in a polite way)
	◆ Interact with others in a positive way
	◆ Know how to ask for help
Empathy	◆ Recognize and appreciate individual differences in others
	◆ Understand and feel sympathy for the feelings of others
	◆ Consider the opinions of others in a small or large group
	◆ Ask others how they feel or what they think
	◆ Take action to help others
	◆ Work to see the perspectives of others
Sense of Community	◆ Work cooperatively with others to take care of materials in the classroom
	◆ Share materials with others
	◆ Ask for help when needed
	◆ Help others when needed
	◆ Make decisions cooperatively with others
	◆ Support the group's needs
Emotional Well-Being	◆ Be aware of one's own feelings
	◆ Grow in the ability to understand one's reasons for actions
	◆ Use language to express both positive and negative feelings constructively
	◆ Wait with patience
	◆ Use constructive talk instead of physical action to express anger or frustration
	◆ Like other people and make friends
	◆ Get excited about ideas
	◆ Consistently look for connections between ideas
	◆ Look forward to school
	◆ Feel confident and successful daily
	◆ Believe in oneself (self-efficacy)
	◆ Have a sense of agency
	◆ Feel accepted and valued in the classroom
Self-Regulation	◆ Make one's own decisions about learning (materials, texts, and tasks)
	◆ Move into a task quickly
	◆ Sustain independent work on a task to completion
	◆ Stay focused
	◆ Know when a task is complete
	◆ Self-evaluate and reflect on work
	◆ Maintain awareness of self in relation to physical space
	◆ Know when one needs help
	◆ Expend one's best effort

FIGURE 21-1 Behavioral and Emotional Expectations of School

Not all of these can be learned in the home. What you see amounts to a curriculum! This grid represents a portrait of the traits we would like to see in a successful student.

The good news is that you provide numerous opportunities for students to learn these behaviors and understandings throughout the school day. If they are to grow as thoughtful users of literacy, students need to build social and emotional abilities. It is worthwhile to consciously teach social and emotional health along with literacy. As teachers we want to communicate daily in a way that honors readers and writers as people and helps them develop a sense of agency—people who believe that they can act with effectiveness.

Social and Emotional Health

In this chapter, we focus on the social and emotional growth that we want students to make as a result of schooling. From the time they enter school, at about age five, and over the next twelve or thirteen years, students spend just about as much time in classrooms as they do at home. They will learn and grow into productive, responsible, and empathetic citizens based on their experiences in school. In this chapter, we discuss how you can foster students' emotional health as well as help them grow intellectually. Some factors to consider are:

- How the classroom climate contributes to learning and a sense of community
- The physical space and what it communicates to students
- How you can create predictability to help students feel secure
- The environment in which students work individually and with each other
- How you can foster empathy and kindness among the members of the community
- The extent to which students can exercise control over their learning
- How active learning and inquiry contribute to emotional and intellectual growth
- The goal of self-regulation

These interrelated factors are important in creating a community of learners and in building a sense of self-efficacy in your students. In recent years, the emotional and affective sides of learning have been pushed to last place while competition and test scores are given top priority. Students even compete to see who can "read" the most books, but we question the depth and meaningfulness of this kind of reading experience. We believe that supporting the emotional health of students is critical to success in learning.

Burkins and Yaris (2014) suggest that we need to think not only of alignment with standards but with the goals of lifelong learning. In their view, aligning with our "inner teacher," (5) involves thinking about how the consequences of our actions may affect what children become. We agree. To us, this means becoming conscious of the positive and also, however unintended, possible negative effects of the decisions we make. Reading and writing instruction are often solitary activities even though the whole class is involved. Schools can be places where competition is more common than collaboration, and students are tested as much as they are taught. No area is more stressful than literacy. Burkins and Yaris suggest asking ourselves questions like: "How will habituating what they are practicing in this lesson make students more 'well' as readers?" (8). Reading "wellness" is characterized by energy, purpose, and joy; and most children depend on school to achieve it. You can accomplish this by sincerely asking students what they think about books and encouraging them to share their thinking with others.

Buckley (2015) describes social and emotional development as learning "languages," much like learning oral and written language, so that students can communicate their thoughts and emotions. She recommends:

▶ Teaching students how to tell oral stories to share their lives and their feelings. Connect life in the classroom to students' own life events.

▶ Bringing emotions to the surface and talking about them *before* incidents happen.

▶ Setting clear expectations and obvious consequences (distinguished from punishment).

▶ Giving students choices and some control over their learning.

▶ Modeling and demonstrating positive ways of handling conflict and emotions.

▶ Talking about the role of kindness in the classroom.

▶ Helping students understand that often there is more than one point of view on a subject.

▶ Observing behavior closely and making hypotheses about students' possible needs.

▶ Recognizing the importance of self-regulation (often called executive functioning), which affects student performance in every area.

▶ Helping students make the connection between persistence and success.

Building a community of readers and writers in your classroom is a way of teaching them what it means to be human. Reading and writing are not isolated, competitive skills that must be constantly tested. Written language was invented as a way of recording truth and communicating it. In this chapter we discuss physical space, choice, predictability, peacefulness, empathy and kindness, and self-regulation as factors in building the classroom community. In the following two chapters we describe classroom management, which is also strongly related to the building of community.

A Climate of Acceptance

Both verbally and nonverbally, you can communicate to students that you are interested in what they want to say. Accept one word or phrase or incomplete or incorrect sentences. The main point the student wants to make is more important than the grammar or syntax. Work to understand the meaning and check with students to be sure you got it right. Remember that students who are learning English can always understand more than they can produce. Don't correct a student's speech in front of their peers; set the model and encourage all students to listen to each other and interact.

As much as possible, select books for interactive read-aloud, shared reading, and guided reading that reflect the variety in your classroom and in the world. Every culture has a set of beliefs and values that are often carried in traditional literature. It is easy to unthinkingly give students the same diet of books that you have for years; look at the collection carefully to see the extent to which it is biased toward white, European culture.

Creating an Inclusive Environment

A diverse class is an asset; your resources are rich and varied. Students bring their own cultures and language histories into the classroom, and that is increasingly so in almost all of our schools. You can make the most of these resources if the classroom communicates an environment of acceptance and inclusion. When we value students' background and culture, the point comes across loud and clear; unfortunately, the opposite is also true. Most teachers are (or will be in a few years) in schools with highly varied populations as the number of immigrants swells and families where English is not the first language spoken in the home, grow. Even students who speak the same language may come from very different cultures and family educational backgrounds. Faced with these new challenges, many teachers may feel inadequate or fearful that they cannot meet student needs. Seeking professional development is always a good idea, but start with the basic climate of your classroom. (See Chapter 7 for a discussion on working with English language learners.)

Working Actively to Create Inclusion

It is not enough to create acceptance; you also have to work actively to include students. Take the attitude that all students in the class have much to learn from each other; they have the responsibility and opportunity to help their peers learn.

Walk into your empty classroom. Does it extend a welcome to every student? Are their names prominent? They should see themselves and their work on the walls. Work hard to pronounce their names correctly. Ask also for their name in their native language. They will enjoy helping you, and in the process, you are communicating not only that they are important, but also that you value their languages even if you cannot speak them. For example, if you are reading aloud or talking about a new word, ask students how the word would be said in another language (like Spanish or Urdu). You can easily put common phrases like "please and thank you" or "good morning" on the wall in every language represented in your classroom. All students will enjoy using a bit of another language.

Physical Space

The classroom is simultaneously a laboratory, a library, an office, and a living room for your students. The design of the classroom supports the building of community. Preparing the classroom means taking into account both individual and group needs. You can look around your classroom and envision the work students will do and what will take place there. If a visitor walks into your classroom, he should be able to see immediately what is valued there. In Figures 21-2 and 21-3, you see some photographs of classrooms that illustrate this.

Although the materials and organization of space will vary from grade to grade, all of these classrooms have the following characteristics:

▶ *Welcoming and Inviting.* When you walk into the classroom, you want to feel that you are coming into a welcoming place. Bright colors are helpful. Many teachers have incorporated some beanbag chairs, bright cushions, a rocking chair or other chair, lamps, and small side tables. The intention is not to fill the room with furniture. After all, this is also a workspace where people are engaged in productive enterprise. But you do want to create a pleasant, comfortable place for students who will spend six or seven hours a day, 180+ days a year, working to meet high expectations and constantly reflecting on their own productivity.

▶ *Organized and Tidy.* Clutter increases stress. Hunting for materials increases stress and dependence on the teacher. The more organized the classroom, the more independent your students will become, *the less of your time they will require*, and the more time you will have for teaching. Materials (even for older students) should be clearly organized and labeled. The work that takes place in each area should be visible at a glance. We show sample "layouts" of a primary classroom and an upper elementary classroom (see Figures 21-4 and 21-5). Notice how different activities and the materials they require are clearly marked. By walking through each of these classrooms, you can easily tell what goes on here. No one needs to go around the room to collect the materials they need. Everything is accessible.

▶ *Rich with Materials.* By materials we mean books, writing tools, art materials, manipulatives, references, computers, tablets, and other technological resources. This can be a difficult criterion to meet because it depends on the resources of the school district. But, at least where books are concerned, you can increase the richness with a number of money-saving moves—visiting garage sales, checking out books from libraries, asking parents and friends to donate, writing for grants, appealing to the business and social community. In our book, *Leveled Books for Readers,* we include guidelines for collecting books in many ways, including letters and sample grant proposals.

▶ *Includes Group Meeting Space.* If you want to form a community, students must have a place to meet together and talk every day. You use this space for many occasions—group meeting, minilessons, interactive read-aloud, shared reading and writing, interactive writing, sharing after independent reading and writing workshop, discussion of problems. For young children, a colorful rug with space enough to accommodate the class sitting on the floor without students having to touch each other works well. They can sit together in rows or make a circle. Older students can also sit on the floor in a circle or they can move chairs away from their tables to make a circle in the same area. If the class is very large and students are older, you may have to use two circles (some sitting on the floor and some behind in chairs). In intermediate grades or middle school, students sometimes sit at individual tables or desks, especially if the class is large, but this is less effective than a circle. You can link desks to make group tables or make a horseshoe out of the furniture so students can see each other.

FIGURE 21-2 Photos of Primary Classrooms

FIGURE 21-3 Photos of Intermediate Classrooms

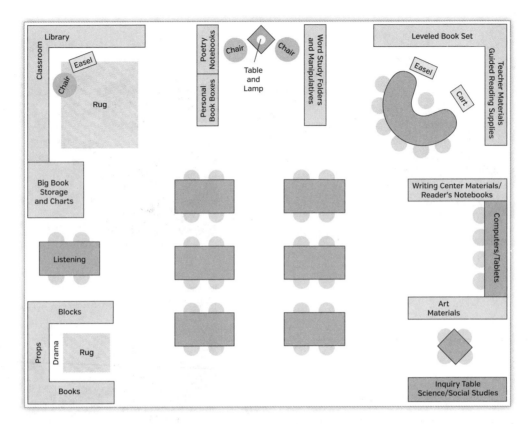

FIGURE 21-4 Layout of a Primary Classroom

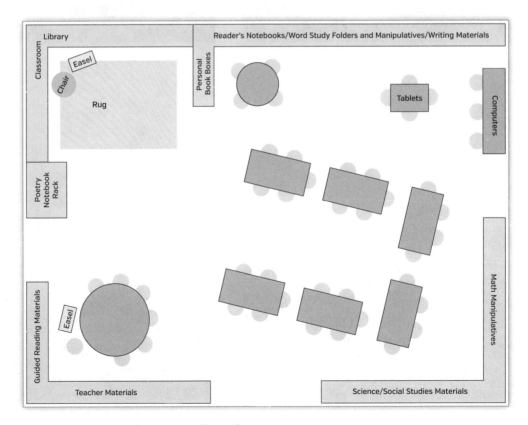

FIGURE 21-5 Layout of an Intermediate Classroom

▶ *Includes Personal Space.* For many years, we have assumed that each student should have an individual desk. But that assumption goes back to the days when desks were bolted to the floor. Now, many teachers use tables or "airplane" desks that can be combined in flexible ways, or push desks together to make tables. This allows for more flexibility to engage in group project work and discussion. But students also need a personal space. If they do not have a desk, they can have a cubby or personal book box (a magazine-type holder) where they keep personal documents like a reader's notebook, a writer's notebook, independent reading books, a take-home portfolio, and textbooks. (Of course, they have locker or cloakroom space for coats and backpacks.) The bottom line is that every student has personal storage needs.

▶ *Shows What is Valued.* A classroom must be alive with student work. From kindergarten to grade six, almost all of the displays in the classroom show student work and student thinking. You do not need posters with motivational slogans. You can start the year with relatively blank walls because your students are going to fill them with a variety of products that show student input and student work, including: minilesson charts made with student contributions, interactive and shared writing constructed with student contributions, student writing and drawing, and artifacts showing student work in inquiry projects (math, science, social studies). The greatest motivation you can give your students is to display their work (see Figures 21-6 and 21-7). Change displays as the year progresses. And, at year's end, let students take them home. You'll be starting again with a new group.

FIGURE 21-6 Photo of a Wall Display in a Primary Classroom

There is no question that the physical space of the classroom is important. The moment the students walk into your classroom they need to feel that it is:

▶ A happy and welcoming place

▶ A place where people take care of the materials they use

▶ A place that has a space for me

▶ A place where I'll be expected to cooperate with other people

▶ A place where I help others and can get the help I need

Within a few days, a student will feel that the walls of his classroom "reflect" him and his fellow classmates, because the walls will show individual and cooperative work with others—perhaps even language that the student has contributed. (We

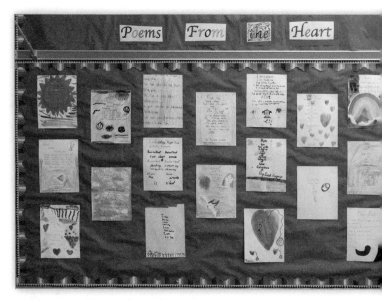

FIGURE 21-7 Photo of a Wall Display in an Intermediate Classroom

have found that even months after the creation of a piece of interactive writing, young students can remember the language and writing that they contributed.) And, certainly students can remember their own contributions to group-created charts or their own drawing and writing. The bottom line is that students must ultimately feel that the classroom is theirs.

Predictability

Create in your classroom a predictable structure within which students can work independently and with each other, and achieve self-regulation. A workable, consistent schedule and classroom routines contribute to predictability. Students get into the rhythm of the day and have expectations for themselves and others when there is consistency, clarity, and predictability.

Routines

From school entry to the end of elementary school, the key to teaching students to make good choices is to establish and teach routines for each activity in the classroom. A routine is a set of actions or steps that you repeat for accomplishing something. Don't have too many routines and don't make them too complex because even intermediate or middle-level students can find it difficult to remember a long list. During the first week of school, demonstrate and teach a few routines to get started, and then use them over and over. In Chapter 22, we talk more about teaching the routines and transitions in the primary grades, and we provide a sample morning schedule. In Chapter 23 we talk about some options for independent work with intermediate students, and we provide a detailed plan for getting a readers' workshop started in thirty days.

Intermediate and middle students also need routines, and you will need to teach these routines to them. In fact, the first thirty days of independent reading (see Chapter 23) involves teaching the routines that make a reading workshop possible. Each routine is taught through a minilesson that explains the rationale for the routine and demonstrates it. For example, you begin the year by teaching minilessons on how to select books and read them silently. You also teach how readers choose books and how they talk about their reading. It will take several different minilessons to teach some routines, for example, teaching students how to use a reader's notebook. These minilessons take some time but they establish routines that students will use all year. See Chapter 23 for more information on establishing routines with intermediate and middle students.

Schedule

Having a predictable daily schedule also supports stability. When students know what they are going to do each day, they feel secure and you spend less time explaining and directing. Of course, there will be adjustments as you work with the students to make the schedule right for what you want to accomplish together. There will be days when there are interruptions, but as much as possible, keep them to a minimum. You can see a sample schedule for a primary class and one for an intermediate class (see Figures 21-8 and 21-9). These are samples only of how a

A Sample Grade One Schedule

Time	Action	Description
8:15	Arrival	Students come into the room and put their items in a cubbyhole (reserved with their names).
	Independent Reading	Students take their individual book boxes (or a book they are reading) or choose from browsing boxes and go to their desks or places at a table (with their names reserving seats). They read until everyone is seated. The teacher circulates and greets children, reminding them to start reading.
	Assessment	The teacher may take a running record with one or two students while the others read independently.
8:30	Community Meeting	Students gather in the meeting area for an introduction to the day. This is a time for students to talk with each other. If there are any problems to solve, they can address them together.
8:35	Shared Reading	The teacher engages students in the shared reading of some enlarged poems, chants, songs, or a big book.
8:45	Interactive Read-Aloud	The teacher reads aloud a fiction or nonfiction text from a text set, with students sharing their thinking at selected points.
	Interactive Writing Option	The teacher talks with the children and constructs a piece of writing that may relate to the read aloud or shared reading book by "sharing the pen."
9:10	Reading Minilesson	The teacher provides a minilesson using recent read aloud books as mentor texts. At the beginning of the year, these lessons are mostly procedural (e.g., how to choose books).
9:15	Independent Literacy Work	Independent work tasks for the day are explained if needed. They may include literacy tasks signaled by a workboard (e.g. independent reading from browsing boxes, poetry notebook, word work, listening, pocket chart, writing center).
	Guided Reading	The teacher works with about three guided reading groups. Later the teacher may also convene book clubs.
	Group Share	Students meet as a class to share books; talk may be related to the minilesson principle.
10:45	Snack	
10:50	Writing Minilesson	The teacher provides a minilesson on any aspect of the writing process, craft or conventions. At the beginning of the year, the lessons are mostly procedural (e.g., how to get started, getting materials).
	Independent Writing and Conferring	Students write independently while the teacher moves around to confer with individuals. The students may be working on any aspect of their writing pieces. The teacher may bring together a guided writing group with similar needs.
	Group Share	The students meet as a class to share their progress; talk may be related to the minilesson principle.

FIGURE 21-8 A Sample Grade One Schedule

(continues)

A Sample Grade One Schedule

Time	Action	Description
11:50	Lunch/Recess	
12:35	Mathematics	Students engage in inquiry-based mathematics. The teacher provides a lesson, students apply the learning independently or with a partner, and the class convenes for summary and evaluation.
1:35	Projects: Group Meeting	Teacher and students plan to share their progress on science/social studies projects. Teacher may introduce new content, resources, or materials.
	Project Work	
	Group Share	Students may work with a partner or in small groups on science and/or social studies projects that involve inquiry, art, technology, and collaboration.
		Students provide an update on projects. They can then assess their productivity and identify any problems that arose.
2:15	Interactive Writing	The teacher and students talk and construct an interactive (or shared) writing piece that may be connected to math, social studies, or science learning. They reread it several times.
2:35	Phonics/Word-Study Minilesson	The teacher teaches an inquiry-based minilesson on a phonics principle that children will apply individually, or as partners at independent work time.
	Group Meeting	Students reflect on and evaluate the day.
3:00	Dismissal	Students gather materials and go home.

FIGURE 21-8 *(continued)*

A Sample Grade Five Schedule

Time	Action	Description
8:30	Arrival	Students enter, sign in, indicate the status of their homework, and place their homework in an appropriate tray.
	Independent Reading	Students have something to do as soon as they settle in to their seats (for example, read a choice book or finish a piece in their reader's or writer's notebook).
	Assessment	The teacher may take a reading record with one or two students.
8:40	Community Meeting	Students gather in the meeting area for an introduction to the day. This is a time for students to talk with each other. If there are any problems to solve, they can address them together.
	Interactive Read-Aloud and/or Shared Reading	The teacher reads aloud or revisits a fiction or nonfiction book that has been carefully selected and may be part of a text set. The text may be part of a genre study inquiry and may serve as a mentor text for reading minilessons. Sometimes the text is a poem or the teacher engages students in shared reading.

FIGURE 21-9 A Sample Grade Five Schedule

A Sample Grade Five Schedule

Time	Action	Description
9:00	Reading Minilesson	The teacher gives a couple of quick "book talks" to acquaint students with possible book choices. Then, the teacher provides a minilesson on an aspect of the reading process (e.g., genre, compare and contrast, writer's use of language). At the beginning of the year, minilessons may focus on procedures (e.g., choosing books).
9:10	Independent Reading and Writing About Reading	Students read books of their choice and/or write about reading in their reader's notebooks. The teacher may confer with a few individuals.
	Guided Reading/Book Clubs	The teacher provides guided reading lessons to small, homogeneous groups, and/or meets with small heterogeneous groups in book clubs.
	Group Share	Students meet as a class to share their thinking about their reading and to revisit the minilesson principle. They also reflect on their accomplishments.
10:15	Break	
10:30	Word-Study Minilesson	The teacher provides a minilesson on some aspect of word study (e.g., word structure, spelling patterns, or vocabulary.)
	Application	Students apply the word-study principle independently or they may work with a partner.
	Group Share	Students meet as a class to share what they may have discovered about word structure or word meaning.
11:00	Mathematics	The teacher teaches an inquiry-based lesson and students apply the learning independently or with a partner. The group convenes for sharing and evaluation.
12:00	Lunch/Recess	
12:45	Writing Minilesson	The teacher provides a quick "writers' talk" (a brief talk about a published writer's process). Then, the teacher provides a minilesson on any aspect of the writing process, craft, or conventions.
	Independent Writing and Conferring	Students write independently while the teacher moves around to confer with individuals. Sometimes students do a quick write or write in their writer's notebooks. The students may be working on pieces at any phase of the writing process. The teacher may bring together a guided writing group of writers with similar needs or interests.
	Group Share	Students meet as a class to share their progress; talk may be related to the minilesson principle.
1:45	Science/Social Studies Meeting	Students meet to share their progress on science/social studies projects. The teacher may engage the group with new thinking, new materials, or resources.
	Project Work	Students may work individually, with a partner, or in small groups on science and/or social studies projects that involve collaborative work and inquiry.
	Group Meeting	Students provide an update on projects. They assess the productivity of the day and identify any problems that arose. The teacher reminds them of homework assignments.
3:00	Dismissal	Students gather materials and go home.

FIGURE 21-9 *(continued)*

day might be planned out. Of course you will need to weave in time for specialist teaching such as art, music, or physical education. It's a good idea to place the necessary blocks of time on cards and move them around until you have a workable schedule within the constraints of your situation. Once you have a good schedule, as much as possible, *follow it every day.*

Both of the elementary schedules offer predictable movement between whole-class, small-group, and independent work. The amount of time for reading (which includes integrated science and social studies content) at the primary level is about two hours with an additional hour for writing. At the intermediate level, ideally the amount of time for reading (including read-aloud and integrated science and social studies content) is about ninety minutes with another hour for writing (although many teachers have only sixty to seventy-five minutes and adjust times). The schedule at the middle school will feel very different in a departmentalized context. In the ideal, students in middle school will have fifty-five to sixty minutes for reading and fifty-five to sixty minutes for writing. Even more important, there is planned time for students to meet and talk with each other. Through this process, you can bring them together as a community. Use language like:

> "Our books."
> "Our classroom."
> "Our class meeting."
> "We have a problem to solve."
> "How did we help each other do our best work today?"

Knowing that the schedule will provide plenty of opportunity for them to get the attention of the teacher and of other students, to have a turn, and to engage in their favorite activities goes a long way in helping them to wait patiently and stay focused. They have the confidence of knowing what will happen and that the day will unfold as expected. There will be surprises, but they will add to the day rather than detract.

A Peaceful Environment

The classroom is a busy, lively, and sometimes noisy place. It is almost never a completely silent place and, in the case of test taking, can sometimes be too silent. While students should know that it's okay to get excited about a project or laugh when something is funny, you generally want your classroom to have a peaceful and serene ambiance.

Students should move about the space quietly, set books down gently, handle materials carefully, and help each other. All of these behaviors must be taught as part of your curriculum. If students are squabbling over space or materials, then that's a problem to be solved as a group. Maybe better organization is needed or the schedule needs to be revised. Students will not always agree, but teach them how to disagree with language like:

> "I disagree with what you said because . . ."
> "I agree with _____ but not with _____ because . . ."

"Can you say more about that because I understand it differently?"

"I understand what you are saying, but what about _____?"

"I'm thinking differently about that. Can I explain what I think?"

"Can you help me understand why you think that?"

You'll find that book club meetings are a great context for studying literature, but also for learning the language of polite and respectful social discourse. You will find that this kind of language carries over to class meetings.

The classroom should be a place where people speak to each other with respect and listen courteously. The general tone of voice should be soft, and the first step in making that happen is to speak in a quiet tone of voice yourself. You need to speak loudly enough to be heard, but it's true that the louder you talk, the louder your students will talk; and noise has a tendency to escalate.

You need to teach voice volume as carefully as you teach everything else, because it matters. Volume can contribute to or detract from the peacefulness of the classroom. Some teachers have been very successful using a voice volume chart. You can see one version of such a chart (Figure 21-10). It is helpful to create the actual chart in a discussion with your students so they can understand the rationales.

All you need to do is say "zero voice" or "three voice" to signal volume. Have students practice demonstrating the different levels. Self-monitoring the level of their voices is another way students learn to handle themselves in a variety of settings.

Empathy and Kindness

One of the hardest things for students to learn is that other people have different perspectives and that they need to understand them. Becoming aware of the feelings of others is especially difficult for young children because, developmentally, they are centered on themselves. School is their opportunity to learn that others have feelings to consider, that kindness is valued, and that they can feel more

Voice Volume Chart

	0	1	2	3	4
During	Reading Time Writing Time Drawing Hallways	Literacy Centers Reading and Writing Conferences	Snack Time Partner Work Group Work	Book Clubs Whole-Class Meeting Read-Aloud	Outside Recess
Your Voice Should Be	Silent	Soft Whisper	Quiet Voice	Strong Speaker	Outside Voice

FIGURE 21-10 Voice Volume Chart

confident and powerful if they help others. Buckley (2015) describes a "friendship workshop" in which you actively teach young children to recognize differences and work with others. She teaches children that it's not wrong to feel angry, but that they need to express their anger in words, and practice those words, for example: "I feel (angry/happy) because . . ." "I'm sorry that I . . ." and, "Are you okay?"

In Buckley's workshop, children learn to respect personal space, for example, by walking around the room without touching anything or anyone. The real test of these lessons, of course, is the students' behavior on a daily basis. Participating in a community year after year will build these social skills.

Some intermediate/middle students have not learned how to feel (or at least express) empathy for or kindness toward other students. You cannot undo the events of their lives or what they have learned or not learned, but you can help them start down the road to becoming positive members of the community. A feeling of collaborative ownership and responsibility in the classroom and school will go a long way toward creating empathetic members of that community. Model and even "act out" the behaviors you want students to use in an automatic way. We caution against moralistic, "preachy" lessons that have no connection to real life. Involving students in the cooperative solving of real classroom problems provides an opportunity to demonstrate empathy and kindness daily.

Choice

Having control over one's learning nourishes the sense of agency. Buckley (2015) describes how even very young children can learn to make choices, and they are more eager, have more stamina, and are more likely to demonstrate on-task behavior when they see themselves as having a role in their own learning. Young children can make choices such as which books to look at from the classroom library. They can select from a few simple activities that they know well, like drawing, "writing," art, small blocks, or projects. As they begin to read independently, they can choose from a "browsing box" that contains books they either have read before or that the teacher knows they can read (see Figure 21-11). The teacher simply tells a guided reading group that they will find many good choices in the blue or green or purple basket. Of course, you cannot present young children with dozens of choices and expect them to manage themselves; it takes a long time to develop self-regulation in a room filled with people and materials. Some children are accustomed to flitting quickly from toy to toy or activity to activity at home, and many have not learned to share space or materials. The secret is an instructional process that begins when children enter school and continues every year, building responsibility along with choice.

As students grow older, it makes logical sense that they can exercise more choice; however, sometimes the opposite happens. The requirements of the curriculum become more demanding every year until students have almost no choices. We have to consider the realities of standards, but we need to strive for balance between "getting through" the required curriculum and helping students develop an independent reading life. There is a lot of evidence, for example, that adolescents

FIGURE 21-11 Browsing Boxes

read very little but no evidence that a required list of literature for every year of school builds successful independent reading (Kittle 2012).

In many places, under the guise of "equal access to texts," educators go to the extreme of having every child in the district reading the same book on the same page despite an appalling lack of evidence that this approach works. Nothing could be more unequal. Some children will find the book interesting; others will be bored. Some will find it easy and read quickly; some will find it hard and take three times the amount of time. As an experiment, just try assembling twenty—or even ten— adults, and giving them a challenging text (for example, a research article) one page at a time, using a timer. We guarantee that some in the group will pretend to read; others will start fiddling with their phones. According to Allington (2001), "I know of no evidence that suggests that any curriculum plan that had all children working in the same books all day, all week, all year, ever produced high achievement in all children, or even in most children." (118) Kittle (2012, 47) calls assigned reading, "the narrow door into reading." To teach "book love," she recommends getting kids reading something that engages them. That's a wide-open door.

Of course, not all the books students read will be those of their choice. After all, there need to be some requirements so that you are meeting your responsibility as mentor and guide. Students need to broaden their experiences. But there should be plenty of room for students to make their own selections. You can require a certain number of books in each genre, for example, with plenty of books in a choice genre. If you are required to read a biography, it helps to be able to choose which one. Besides choosing their own books for book clubs and for independent reading, intermediate students may make choices like:

- When and what to write in their reader's and writer's notebooks (within the week)
- Topics for science and social studies projects
- PowerPoint® and other tools for media/text presentations

They can also participate in group decisions concerning the time schedule, order of activities, and special events.

Inquiry

Exciting learning is driven by intellectual curiosity, not memorization. The more students can become engaged in the process of true inquiry, the more they will learn and the more they will learn how to learn. Inquiry happens when students work together to pursue understanding; for example, they:

▶ Search for patterns and examples

▶ Consider evidence and draw tentative conclusions

▶ Test their ideas and affirm or reject them

▶ Look for "clues" to solve a dilemma

Inquiry means investigation. In our book *Genre Study* (Fountas and Pinnell 2012) we propose an inquiry process for learning and internalizing the characteristics of written genres. You begin by immersing students in many good examples of texts in a genre, and, over time, make it possible for them to construct their own definitions and characteristics. The whole process is much more interesting than being given a definition, for example, of "biography," and then learning a list of characteristics.

Inquiry makes learning come alive and it puts students into a context of natural collaboration, within which they are learning to be citizens of the classroom. With the resources available today, students can select topics and engage in inquiry projects to do with mathematics, history, social studies, science and the environment, or political forces. Within necessary constraints for safety, the whole world is open to them. There is no need to limit their study to dry textbooks when they can view authentic documents and events at the tap of a key. But you will also want them to engage in inquiry through "hands-on" work with materials and objects.

Accountability

When we talk about accountability, we mean being accountable to the community. The greatest accountability is to your peers in a social situation—students need to feel they have an obligation not only to their teacher but also to their fellow students, and that they are contributing to the learning of everyone in the class.

In a collaborative culture it is important for every member to contribute to each other's learning. At the same time students must be aware of their own learning and self-evaluate. As a partner in your students' learning, you can help them reflect on what they learned and on the evidence of their growing competencies.

As a teacher, you need to provide an evaluation of the students' achievement. We hope this evaluation takes into account multiple indicators of progress.

Learning and Helping Others Learn

Instead of comparing himself to others, each student needs to do his own best learning every day, and each should see himself as supporting the learning of others. The attitude should be: "We are all responsible for all the learning that happens here." If a student is distracting others or leaves materials in disarray, then he is not helping others learn. Students should take credit for all the learning that takes place every day. That's one sure way to grow in self-efficacy.

We had a recent conversation with a young teacher who was concerned because she had so little time to teach reading. The reason given was: "With these children, I have to spend a lot of time every day teaching the social/emotional curriculum, so that they will know how to be respectful of each other." This is quite puzzling, because surely mutual respect is built through sharing the work (reading, writing, talking, drawing, inquiry) of the classroom. Her curriculum consisted of a series of didactic, moralizing "lessons" and books urging students to be kind and respectful. We can't comment on whether this approach actually worked, but we continue to believe that respect is learned best by collaboration in the process of pursuing worthwhile work. Students need to learn to politely ask for help and to freely give help. "Please" and "thanks" continue to be good words, but they don't exist in a vacuum. They are part of the everyday expected behavior.

It's a mistake to assume that children have to learn respectful behavior at home or they will never exhibit it. We actually have known quite a few children who are fine at home but feel threatened and lose control in a classroom. And plenty of children from pretty boisterous families fit well into the norms of an orderly classroom with routines. Actually, a good rule of thumb is that you learn how to behave in a place *in that place*. And, usually, someone has to teach you.

School is also where your students can learn the power of collaboration with others. The more they take ownership for the classroom and assist each other, the more enjoyable school will be for everyone; and learning will increase exponentially. Just as important, your students will build a sense of self-efficacy that will serve them well beyond the school walls. Self-efficacy will enable them to persist even when things are hard for them, to solve problems, and to see a positive future. What we have talked about in this chapter is not just about literacy skills; it's about life skills. The good news is that with attention to the classroom climate and ways of working together, we can achieve both goals.

Self-Regulation

Self-regulation is both an outcome of everything we have mentioned so far and a source of exactly the kind of learning we want students to achieve. A goal of education is helping students achieve a sense of agency, which is quite different from motivation. A student with a sense of agency believes that he can achieve his goals; this emotion is internal rather than being "motivated" by the teacher.

Many students lack a sense of agency. This feeling has broad consequences in life, but in the case of literacy, it is disastrous. A student may believe she is not good at reading and/or writing and has no power to become better. She may have a perception that she lacks power, and even her best efforts will change nothing (Dweck 2006). Every experience reinforces this feeling. And, surprisingly, many students who can read with some competence feel the same way and avoid reading except when required (and we know that it is very easy to "fake" the reading of a book). Agency does not grow from empty praise; it grows from a true sense of accomplishment. Agency is built from within through day after day of positive experiences. A "growth mindset" is one that underscores the importance of the students' understanding that with effort they can achieve more and they control their potential. When teachers have a "growth mindset," they show high expectations for every student.

Agency is a critical element in self-regulation. If you have power over your own learning and a chance to change, then you are able to manage your progress toward the goal. The earliest readers can read very short books and they read so many, so they can feel a sense of accomplishment as they stack them up or even count them. As they grow more proficient in writing and reading, they can begin to keep a record of their reading and their thinking about books. Readers in the intermediate/middle grades keep records of their reading and the genres so they can see their progress over time (see Figure 21-12).

The student who constructed this notebook is able to look back on an entire year of reading in which she read fifty-five books in a variety of genres and wrote weekly letters or other forms of response to her teacher. It is a body of work.

Start working for self-regulation the moment students enter school. The structure of the classroom space, the schedule, and the routines help. Students need to learn to manage themselves within the requirements and the space that also includes twenty to thirty other people. If they view the other students who they share space with as their friends and partners, then it is easier for them to see their own place within the classroom community.

Self-regulation is required in the general behavior in the classroom and in the management of independent work, but it is also a major factor in reading achievement. An early reader who is self-regulated is not content with attempts at words that do not make sense, sound right, or match the visual information on the page. And you should see in older readers a lack of satisfaction when they sense that they do not understand the text. You want readers who are not satisfied with accurate reading alone; instead, they need to feel that they have the ability to reach for deep understanding. We can talk about reading achievement, but it will not be possible to achieve unless we can foster students who know that they have the ability to affect their own learning. And that means for *all* our students, not just most of them.

Reading List

Select a book to read. Enter the title and author on your reading list. When you have completed it, write the genre and the date. If you have abandoned it, write an A and the date you abandoned it in the date column. Write an E if the book was easy for you to read, a JR if it was just right for you, and a D if it was difficult for you to read and understand. Place an asterisk (*) next to the code in the genre column if your book is a graphic text.

#	Title	Author	Genre Code	Date Completed	E, JR, D
1	Henry and mudge and the Careful Cousin	Cynthia Rylant	RF	Sept. 10,2015	E
2	Henry and mudge and the happy Cat	Cynthia Rylant	RF	Sept. 14,2015	E
3	The Case of the Climbing Cat	Cynthia Rylant	RF	Sept. 15,2015	E
4	Cam Jansen and the mystery of the television dog	David Adler	RF	Sept. 18,2015	JR
5	Horrible Henry at Halloween	Suzy Kline	RF	Sept. 23,2015	JR
6	Cam Jansen and the ghostly mystery	David Adler	RF	Sept. 28,2015	JR
7	Wild Wild Wolves	Joyce Milton	I	Sept. 29,2015	E
8	Life in the Tundra	Christine Caputo	I	Sept. 30,2015	JR
9	Molly's Pilgrim	Barbora Cohen	HF	Oct. 07,2015	JR
10	Jigsaw Jones	James Preller	RF	Oct. 08,2015	JR
11	A to z mystery The Canary Caper	ron ray	RF	Oct. 13,2015	JR
12	A to z mystery The Falcon's Feathers	ron ray	RF	Oct. 16,2015	JR
13	The Courage of Sarah Noble	Alice Dalgliesh	HF	Oct. 23,2015	D

© 2011 by I. C. Fountas & G. S. Pinnell from *Reader's Notebook*. Portsmouth, NH: Heinemann.

#	Title	Author	Genre Code	Date Completed	E, JR, D
14	The littles and the grate Halloween Scare	John Peterson	F	Oct. 26,2015	JR
15	The Halloween house	Erica Silverman	F	oct. 29,2015	JR
16	The Witch Who lives down the hall	Donna Guthrie	F	Oct. 30,2015	JR
17	In the Haunted House	Eve Bunting	F	oct. 31,2015	E
18	The Chalk Box Kid	Clyde Bulla	RF	nov. 1,2015	JR
19	The Paint brush Kid	Clyde Bulla	RF	nov. 16,2015	JR
20	Diary of a Wimpy Kid	Jeff Kinney	RF	nov. 25,2015	JR
21	Ice wreck	Lucille Donner	I	nov. 27,2015	JR
22	The Christmas Cup	Nancy Patterson	RF	Dec. 08,2015	D
23	Kate Shelley and the midnight Express	Charles Wetterer	HF	Dec. 11,2015	JR
24	Foss Earth Materials	Delta Education	I	Dec. 14,2015	JR
25	Balto	Natalie Standiford	B	Dec. 15,2015	JR
26	Diary of a Wimpy Kid old School	Jeff Kinney	RF	Dec. 22,2015	JR
27	Rain School	James Ramford	I	Jan 05,2016	JR
28	The Chocolate touch	Patrick Colling	F	Jan 06,2016	JR
29	Fary Realm	Emily Rodda	F	Jan 10,2016	JR
30	The Littles and the Lost Children	John Peterson	F	Jan 13,2016	JR
31	The Littles	John Peterson	F	Jan 15,2016	JR

© 2011 by I. C. Fountas & G. S. Pinnell from *Reader's Notebook*. Portsmouth, NH: Heinemann.

#	Title	Author	Genre Code	Date Completed	E, JR, D
32	The librarian of Basra	Jeanette Winter	B	Jan 18,2016	JR
33	Lon Po Po	Ed Young	TL	Jan 19,2016	D
34	Nasreen's secret School	Jeanette Winter	B	Jan 20,2016	D
35	My Librarian is a Camel	Margriet Rurrs	I	Jan 20,2016	D
36	Helen Keller Girl of Courage	Francene Sabin	B	Jan 28,2016	JR
37	Amelia Earhart	John Parlin	B	Feb 02,2016	JR
38	Rosa Parks	Keith Brandt	B	Feb 10,2016	JR
39	Thomas Edison	Louis Sabin	B	Feb 24,2016	JR
40	A Picture Book of Harriet tubman	David Adler	B	Feb 26,2016	JR
41	If You Traveled on the Underground Railroad	Ellen Levine	I	March 01,2016	JR
42	A Picture Book of Amelia Earhart	Jeff Fisher	B	March 04,2016	JR
43	The story of Ruby Bridges	Robert Coles	B	March 08,2016	JR
44	I survived Hurricane Katrina 2005	Lauren Tarshis	RF	March 12,2016	JR
45	Magic tree house Ghosts	Mary Pope Osborn	RF	March 17,2016	E
46	Birdie's Lighthouse	Deborah Hopkinson	M	March 21,2016	E
47	only opal a young girl The Diary of	Barbara Cooney	M	March 23,2016	E
48	Keep the lights Burning Abbie	Connie Roop	B	march 29,2016	E
49	The Three little Wolves	Eugene Trivizas	TL	april 05,2016	E

© 2011 by I. C. Fountas & G. S. Pinnell from *Reader's Notebook*. Portsmouth, NH: Heinemann.

#	Title	Author	Genre Code	Date Completed	E, JR, D
50	The Three Little Javelinas	Susan Lowell	TL	April 11,2016	JR
51	Strega Nona	Tomie de Paola	TL	April 13,2016	JR
52	Cinderella	Barbora Karlin	TL	April 14,2016	E
53	The Talking Eggs	Robert P. SanSouci	TL	April 15,2016	JR
54	Aesops Fables The Wolf and the Crane	Jerry Pinkney Retold	TL	April 15,2016	D
55	Face to Face with Wolves	Jim and Judy Brandenburg	I	April 28,2016	D

© 2011 by I. C. Fountas & G. S. Pinnell from *Reader's Notebook*. Portsmouth, NH: Heinemann.

FIGURE 21-12 A Completed Reading List from a Readers' Notebook

Suggestions for Professional Development

1. Meet with a small group of colleagues to self-assess your school and classrooms as a community. You might involve the leadership team and/or grade-level colleagues. Or, you might just work with a colleague.

2. Try to see your school from the students' perspective as you walk through the school, your classrooms, and the library. Ask:

   ▶ Is there evidence that students' homes and neighborhoods are valued?

   ▶ Does the school reflect the cultural and linguistic diversity in the school?

   ▶ Is there evidence that student work is valued?

   ▶ Do you see order, cleanliness, bright color, and a welcoming environment?

   ▶ Is there evidence of good management?

   ▶ Are there signals to students that let them know what to do and create predictability (guides, directions)?

3. Chances are you will find many positive aspects; but look hard for areas of improvement. Work as a group to identify some short term and long term goals. There may be one or two goals that you can accomplish right away.

4. Now do the same for your own classroom, for example, ask:

   ▶ Are there clearly designated meeting areas?

   ▶ Is the meeting area attractive, comfortable, and functional?

   ▶ Does each student have an organized way of keeping personal items and supplies?

   ▶ Is there evidence that the classroom reflects students' homes, languages, and culture?

   ▶ Is there evidence that student work is valued?

   ▶ Is the room orderly: Are supplies well organized and labeled? Are work areas designated?

   ▶ Is there evidence that students have been engaged in collaboration? In inquiry?

   ▶ Are the students' names posted and used in a variety of places (e.g., cubbies, name charts, and folders)?

5. Again, define some short-term and long-term goals. You may want to implement some of the ideas in this chapter, but your colleagues can give you many more.

    ▸ Create a short-term plan for at least one idea that you can implement right away.

    ▸ Start to think about next term or next year and make a plan for creating a community environment from the beginning.

6. As you work toward developing your classroom environment, it will help to invite a friend into the room to walk about and then just tell you his first impressions.

CHAPTER 22

Managing Independent Learning in the Early Grades

Children learn and develop best when they are part of a community of learners—a community in which all participants consider and contribute to one another's well being and learning.

–Carol Copple and Sue Bredekamp

When we talk with teachers about guided reading, this question always comes up: "While I'm working with a small group, what are the rest of the children doing?" That question can be complicated when it comes to younger children who are just getting used to the constraints of being members of a group of twenty or thirty—all expected to learn and to be busy all of the time.

When implementing guided reading, your first challenges will be:

1. Designing an organized environment that supports students' literacy learning and becoming independent and responsible.

2. Managing the classroom so that you can work in a focused, uninterrupted way with small groups of students.

As you address these challenges, there are some criteria that really matter:

▶ Independent tasks must be authentic and *worthwhile*. Each must have learning value, especially in the area of literacy, rather than simply keeping students busy. Children need to spend their time thinking, talking, reading, writing, and listening.

- Independent tasks must be simple enough that even younger students can learn to perform a series of them successfully with very little help from you. They need to be able to see the purpose and value of the tasks.

- Students must be able to access materials and put them away neatly so that others can use them. They need to learn the responsibility of caring for materials and sharing them with others.

- Independent tasks must be relatively quiet but can be social in nature. Children learn and enjoy the process when they can work alongside each other or with a partner. They learn how to modulate their voices appropriately for the context.

- Independent tasks must be active and constructive. Children do not respond well to boring, repetitive drills on something they already know. The task should engage their interest, curiosity, and intellect. They need to have generative value.

In this chapter we share some ways that teachers of young children can organize the environment for use and teach students how to work independently within it. We call the process "managed independent learning," and it can be particularly effective in helping children develop the self-management skills that they will increasingly need as they go through school and life.

An Organized Learning Environment, Rich with Opportunity

Set up your classroom before students enter, but in the first week, as your students need to become acquainted with every area in the classroom and to take ownership of the room—a place they will be working in all year. In fact, familiarity with all of the spaces in the classroom will make them feel secure and at home. In Chapter 21, we described the role of the classroom space in helping students become a community and included sample diagrams of a classroom layout for primary and intermediate students. Here we go into more detail about the spaces and materials that you will find there.

Class Meeting Area

You need a large group meeting area that can include the entire class and areas for small-group and independent work (see Figure 22-1). Young children usually sit on the floor for the class meeting, but the meeting area must be large enough that children can sit on their bottoms without touching each other. It is very helpful to have a large, colorful rug; or you can use carpet samples (small squares) that can alternately be stacked

FIGURE 22-1 Classroom Meeting Area

and picked up by children to sit on. Some teachers prefer to make the meeting area central, with areas like the classroom library opening off of it.

Others prefer to use a corner of the classroom. The teacher sits in a chair or on a slightly raised seat (a stool, small trunk, student chair, etc.) and faces the classroom door. Students sit on the floor facing the teacher so that people passing in the hallway or entering the classroom are less distracting to them. Still others use the classroom library as the center of the room with bookracks or tubs on shelves surrounding the area, which is large enough for students to sit. This plan allows student desks or tables to be spread out around it. The class meeting can take place in the center. Your decisions depend on the size and characteristics of your classroom as well as your furniture options.

In the meeting area it is ideal to have two easels, one for group writing on charts and one for enlarged texts for shared reading. You will want to have an organized supply area near your chair with all materials you might need. (It causes too much disruption to constantly walk away from the group in search of materials.) Materials needed for group meetings are listed in Figure 22-2.

Some teachers also have enough small whiteboards and erasable markers for each child in the class to use. (Sometimes they have small erasers, or an old sock will work.) These materials can be helpful, but may also be expensive and time-consuming to pass out and use.

Independent Work Areas

Later in this chapter, we suggest two alternatives for independent work—a simple list option where students perform three or four independent tasks at their tables and a more active (but complex) option where students move to centers in the classroom. In either case, you need categorized areas to store materials in a way that students can access them independently and put them back in good order. It is not wise to spend your teaching time (and it can amount to quite a lot during a day) passing out materials to every child. Nor do you want them rummaging through individual desks to find materials. Inevitably, a number of children will discover that they can't find paper, pencils, markers, or crayons, or they discover that their pencils need sharpening. At all costs, avoid the line and the disruptive noise at the pencil sharpener by keeping cans of sharpened pencils available. You can allow one or two students to do the sharpening for you at the end of the morning or afternoon.

If students are working at the independent work centers (for example, writing),

---

Materials in the Class Meeting Area

- Big books or enlarged print charts
- Long pointer
- Children's literature you plan to read aloud this week
- Chart paper for writing
- Pocket chart for sentence strips
- Markers
- White correction tape (or mailing labels)
- Markers in a dark color (black, blue)
- Markers for emphasis (red, yellow highlighter)
- Magnetic letters organized on a cookie sheet or other magnetic surface
- Sticky notes
- Sentence strips for writing
- Small whiteboard for writing letters/ words
- Highlighter tape in various sizes and colors
- Masking card
- Name chart of children in the classroom (PreK, Kindergarten, Grade One, Grade Two)
- The Alphabet Linking Chart and Consonant Cluster Linking Chart (as appropriate for level)

FIGURE 22-2 Materials in the Class Meeting Area

they will need sufficient space to work and for their own materials. If students are working in a center, the work area should have enough space, materials, and chairs for the number of children who will typically be there. Crowding makes it frustrating for children to work together productively. Whatever way the work areas are organized, it is important to have ample display space. You can put student work on the walls as well as very simple directions for using the center. Many of these pieces of writing will be produced through shared and interactive writing—including directions—which means that children have ownership of them.

Bookshelves, tables, and other furniture can be used to create work areas where materials can be stored and groups of children can work alongside each other. You can group some traditional desks together to form a table surface if needed. It is not a good idea to create tall barriers in the classroom. Everything should be about student height so that as you scan the room, you can look across the room and see every part of it at a glance and know what everyone is doing. Tall shelves should be placed against the wall. Divisions need only to be suggested. For example, a cardboard back on a desk can signal a space to work. You can even use a cardboard triangle in the middle of a group of four desks to designate a temporary center. Dividers can do double duty by displaying instructions, examples of children's work, or reference materials like the Alphabet Linking Chart, and lists of Words We Know.

Personal Storage Space

Each student needs personal storage space for materials such as a basket, bin, or cubbyhole, and each child needs a "home seat." It may be at a round table (or desks pushed together). Having assigned seats allows you to say, "Find your seat," and have children quickly sit. You can teach them to do this in a game-like way. They march around the room to music or say a rhyme or song and when it stops, they find their seats (with their name printed and taped to it) as quickly as possible without running. Having a chair with a name on it gives a child a place to go when arriving first thing in the morning. But the supplies do not need to be housed in traditional school desks, which typically are dark caverns that make it very difficult to find anything. Some teachers hang a cloth bag over the back of each chair. The bag has compartments into which materials can be organized. Students may have a book to take home (from guided reading), some personal pencils and markers. In some schools, even young students have business-like portfolios in which materials to take home are organized. In most classrooms, there are bins or baskets that have the student's reader's notebooks, writing folders, sketchbooks, and word study folders.

Guided Reading Area

You will need a designated area for small-group reading instruction. You can say something like, "I'd like the group that read *Tongues* yesterday to come to the table." Those students then know what to do. Situate the guided reading table in a quiet corner of the room, and sit so that you can scan the room to identify any students who need more help staying on task independently. Students in the group are generally turned away from the activity of the classroom. A round or horseshoe table is ideal, as all students can face you and see your chart and you can lean over to observe each reader.

Keep a complete set of supplies at the table or on a small table or shelf nearby. Some teachers use a plastic caddy or tub; others use a wheeled cart with a few shelves that they place next to the table. You'll need:

▶ Leveled books for the week for each group

▶ Your records of students' reading, reading graphs, and plans for the week (written or technological)

▶ Paper and writing materials for students

▶ Thin markers and pencils

▶ A whiteboard or chalkboard to which magnetic letters will stick

▶ Two sets of lower-case magnetic letters organized into a tackle box for student use (see Figure 22-3)

▶ One set of magnet letters organized alphabetically on a cookie sheet for quick access in demonstrating (see Figure 22-3)

FIGURE 22-3 Magnetic Letters

▶ An easel with chart paper large enough for students in the group to see (Sometimes the whiteboard is part of the easel)

▶ Small whiteboards, dry-erase markers, and erasers for students to use

▶ Small cookie sheets, stovetop burner covers, or other surfaces for students to use for work with magnetic letters

▶ Plastic baggies to house magnetic letters or word cards

▶ Sentence strips (small)

▶ Cards to write words on (either tag board or magnetic strips)

▶ Individual sound and letter box cards for students to write words with three, four, or five sounds or letters in word work (see Chapter 17, Figure 17-18)

Students may store their reader's notebooks in a common place close to the reading table or they may have them in their personal spaces and bring them to the table as needed. A reader's notebook is not needed for every lesson.

A Print-Rich Classroom

Early readers are still learning how to look at print and how it works. They need an environment filled with meaningful print, including much that is at eye level for them. A favorite activity for young children is to "read the walls" in a designated part of the room using pointers (see Figure 22-4). Children who are proficient at reading print will seldom read the walls but may still use it as a resource for spelling words.

Below, you can see a list of the kinds of print you will find in a classroom for children in the first three years of school.

▶ Charts of poems and songs (on a rack as you collect more of them)

▶ Labels and directions for using materials at the poetry center, listening center, pocket chart, and so on.

FIGURE 22-4 Student Reading the Walls of the Classroom

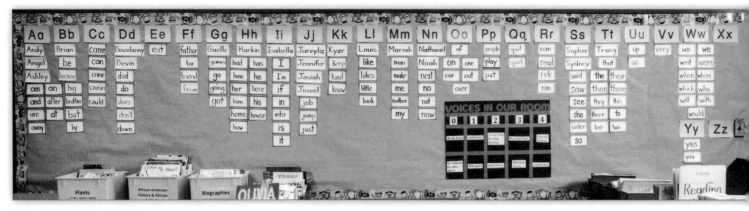

FIGURE 22-5 Word Wall

▶ Informational books located in investigation centers (science/social studies/math)

▶ A class schedule for the day, listed in strips in a pocket chart (e.g., community meeting, read-aloud, interactive writing, readers' workshop, and so on.)

▶ Stories, messages, lists, letters, records of science experiments, and other written materials produced through shared and interactive writing

▶ A word wall, organized alphabetically, of frequently used words and other content words that children can use as a resource for writing (teacher and children create this wall together through the year) (See Figure 22-5)

▶ A class name chart (first names for children beginning to read and both names for students farther along) (See Figure 22-6)

▶ A list of books we've shared (books that have been read aloud to the students); small copies of book covers may be next to each title (See Figure 22-7)

▶ Word charts showing different patterns (phonograms, compound words, high-frequency words) which children have studied through phonics lessons

▶ Published versions of children's independent writing for others to read

▶ A classroom library with varied labels on baskets

▶ Alphabet charts and similar reference materials

▶ A rack of personal poetry books

▶ Pocket charts with sentence strip stories and poems

▶ Whiteboards (or a section of the large chalk or whiteboard) to which magnetic letters and magnetic word cards will stick

▶ A message board for the daily message. This can be read as children come into the classroom.

▶ Writing center with labeled materials and supplies

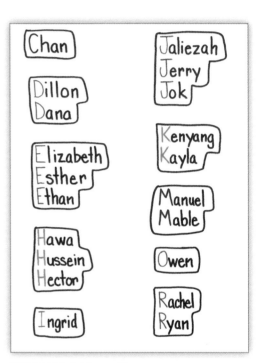

FIGURE 22-6 Name Chart

FIGURE 22-7 List of Books We've Shared

- A sign-in sheet for children to use, or a board with photos and names of children

- Mailboxes for each student so that the teacher and members of the class can deliver "memo" notes or other important messages

- A photo board (which can later become an album) that shows children in the class and pictures of their families, pets, or favorite toys and sometimes a sentence about each

- Labeled materials and supplies—label with sample of tub contents glued to the outside of the tub

The classroom reflects a lot of work! But you create this environment with the children. When they enter at the beginning of the year, you can have some poems to read and many things labeled. Some things can be labeled with the students in order for them to understand what they are for and to build ownership. You can create the name chart on the first day of school. It welcomes children and gives them a wonderful resource for linking sounds and letters. A good beginning of the year activity for preschool and kindergarten is a manila envelope with the child's name carefully printed on it. Inside, are the letters of the child's name on separate squares (see Figure 22-8). Children can put together the name puzzle, left to right, and match it or check it with the model. As children become more proficient with print, you may add last names. Finally, the child can take it home

The print that children are expected to read on charts should:

- Be written in dark ink (black, blue, or other)

- Be legible and use simple standard print

- Use standard spelling

FIGURE 22-8 Name Puzzle

▶ Have clear spaces between words and between lines.

▶ Be at eye level or reachable with a short pointer.

Classroom Library

The classroom library is a rich resource for all of the activities taking place in your classroom and you do not want to hide it with books shelved tightly together. The more it resembles an inviting bookstore or library, the better. It will help to have a carpeted area and cushions. In Chapter 2, we described a multitext approach, and the classroom library is the heart of it (see Figure 22-9). Display high-quality, colorful, and engaging books of varying sizes and genres face front across the tops of bookcases. Plate stands are useful for this purpose. On the shelves and other surfaces place tubs or baskets of books with covers facing out. Clearly label the tub or basket with the topic, author, series, genre, and illustrator. In each basket are books of a range of difficulty. Some teachers of young children put a colored dot on the label and a dot of the same color on the back of each book. If they run out of colors, they put the same kind of sticker or shape on the books that go together (star, cat, stripe, circle, and so on.) Children match them and this, in itself, is an exercise in visual discrimination. The sticker and label assists the students in looking for books and also enable them to return them to the appropriate place. (You can always change a book's category by changing the dot.) Teach students by demonstration and practice how to select a book and replace it right side up, face out, in the tub from which they took it. Don't assume that they will already know this or can figure it out. You might also have an empty basket in which they can put a book if they don't remember where it goes.

The classroom library will have both hardcover and paperback books. In Figure 22-10, you see some possible categories, but there will be many others. The

FIGURE 22-9 A Primary Classroom Library

Books in the Classroom Library	Description
Books We Have Shared	After you read a book aloud, place it in this tub. Students will often revisit it even though it is usually too difficult for them to read. Also, you will be able to find it to use as a mentor text.
Books About Animals	If you have many nonfiction books about animals, you can create separate tubs for each, or pull out one kind of animal that students find especially interesting.
Animal Fantasy	For young children, you can label this in any meaningful way that the children will understand. Place books here that feature animal characters that act like people.
Folktales	Folktales are very popular in the early grades, and children learn a great deal about genre from studying them. If you have several versions of the same tale, create a separate tub (for example, "The Three Bears").
Author's or Illustrator's Name	Kindergarten is not too soon for children to acquire a favorite author (for example, Kevin Henkes, Mo Willems, Denise Fleming, or Donald Crews). If you have several books by an author or illustrator, make a special tub for her. A great idea is to stick a little picture of the author or illustrator on each book. Children need to see writers and illustrators as people.
Poetry Books	Choose books with simple poems and read many of them aloud to the students. If you have many poetry books, you can make special tubs like "Poems About Animals."
Series Books	You can put together books that have the same main characters, such as Henry and Mudge, Poppleton, and Elephant and Piggy. Children fall in love with a book and want to continue to read books in the series.
Books on Topics (nonfiction)	If you have picture books related to what children are currently studying (community, rocks), you can collect them in one tub and label it with the topic. Include a variety of science and social studies topics that will fascinate children.
Books on Themes (both fiction and nonfiction)	You can put together books on concepts you want students to understand (friendship, sharing, being yourself, working together, appreciating differences).
Colors or Shapes	Many picture books feature colors or shapes.
Math	You may have counting books or other books that feature mathematical concepts.

FIGURE 22-10 Books in the Classroom Library

categories are almost limitless and depend on the nature of your collection, the interests of your children, and what you are emphasizing in your curriculum. The one category you should not have is the "level" of the book. Readers do not choose books by level, and all of them tend to read a range of levels. Very young children will enjoy revisiting and talking about many of the picture books in the library, but they will also want to find books they can read independently. But placing books in leveled tubs will not be helpful. Instead, create "browsing boxes" of books students have read before or new texts that you know will be accessible. Students learn that they can read the books in the yellow, blue, or green browsing box, but each has a variety after the first week or so of instruction. The boxes are revised frequently, with new titles added and others "retired." Begin the year with books you predict many of the children can read right away.

It will be important to add books to the classroom library each year. There are many ways that you can acquire free or very inexpensive books. An extensive library may be overwhelming to children at first, and you may want to begin with a limited number of books while you teach them how to use the library. You can introduce a few new books or a basket at a time, introducing them through "book talks" that call attention to the books and prompt students to select them at independent reading time.

Centers

A center is a physical space organized for specific learning purposes. The center has appropriate materials to enable children to explore and work independently (as individuals or with partners or, rarely, in small groups). If you choose to have students work at their tables or desks, you will still need an organized area for materials. As with all materials in the room, place only one type of material at a time in a container; for example, avoid mixing crayons, pencils, and scissors together in the same box or it will take students a long time to locate what they need. Label the can, box, or tub clearly. Also label the place on the shelf or table where the materials should be kept when not in use; this will keep your shelves orderly. For young children, cut a colored piece of contact paper in the exact shape of the container and place it on the shelf so that they can match the can, box, or tub with it and replace it precisely.

You will have some permanent centers that stay in use all year except for changing content (see Figure 22-11). You may also have some temporary centers with a particular focus, for example, a project that is underway. A center should not be a one-time activity. Some criteria for using centers are listed below:

1. A center should involve students in active exploration rather than being a close-ended "exercise."

2. A center should not involve a large amount of teacher preparation for a short-term activity.

3. The purpose of a center is to learn, not to simply keep children busy. The center should offer learning opportunities for a variety of levels.

4. The activity in a center should grow out of your ongoing teaching. For example, the phonics minilesson principle is applied in the Letter/Word Study (ABC) center.

5. All materials needed should be clearly organized and labeled on the box container and the shelf.

6. Keep *only* the centers you will use actively. You don't want to dedicate space to something that is used only a few times a year. Establish and post clear routines for participating in centers (for example, there may be a limit per day).

Year-Long Permanent Centers

Year-Long Centers	Materials
Independent Reading	The classroom library, with many organized baskets, becomes a year-long opportunity for independent reading. Organize books by topic, author, illustrator, genre, and series. Include colored browsing baskets geared to each guided reading group.
Writing Center	Pencils, paper, markers, stapler, scissors, glue, pre-made blank books for book making, cover-up tape, sticky notes, crayons, and date stamp. Teach students how to use equipment like the stapler and how to make books. Student writing folders can also be stored here.
Math Center	Counters in various forms (animals, cars, blocks, disks), Legos™, popsicle sticks, pattern blocks, Unifix™ cubes, big buttons, shape puzzles.
Word Work (ABCs)	Blank word cards, wall of high-frequency words, magnetic letters, games, words to sort, phonogram pattern charts. Students can apply here what they learned in the daily phonics lesson.
Listening Center	Player (iPod™, iPhone™, tablet). Teach students to play it softly. Post a clear set of directions with picture clues. Multiple copies of books organized in boxes or plastic bags.
Poetry Center (can be adjacent to the writing center so that supplies can be shared)	Personal poetry books for each student, copies of poems they have read in shared reading, glue, crayons, markers, and decorative stickers. The poetry center may include large-print poems, poetry cards mounted on stiff paper, small books of poems, a class book of poems, and individual copies of large-print poems, jigsaw poems for children to put together and read, and individual copies of poems to read, glue, and illustrate. It can be near the pocket chart (so children can assemble sentence strips and reread poems).
Art Center	Colored paper, paint, scissors, pencils, pens, crayons, markers, materials like feathers and felt, glue, glue sticks, and recycle materials.
Science/Investigation Center	The topic or focus may change. Include objects for children to handle, explore, sort, and describe. Include beautiful picture books related to the topic. This center invites hands-on inquiry.
Pocket Chart	The pocket chart hangs from a rack or is fastened firmly to the wall. You can have sentence strips and individual words in a basket by the chart. Children can reconstruct favorite stories, poems, and songs on the chart and then read them—perhaps to a partner while using a pointer. They can insert their own names or other words in familiar sentences of poems: "I like chocolate, yummy, yummy. I like chocolate in my tummy."

FIGURE 22-11 Year-Long Permanent Centers

7. Teach how to use centers one at a time, opening just a few during the first two weeks.

8. Keep all the materials children need *in* the center. You'll need many duplicates of materials such as pencils, paper, markers, sticky notes, scissors, and glue. You don't want boxes of materials traveling around the room, and you don't want students wasting time looking for them.

All of the centers described above are relatively quiet. Some teachers plan for two different center times—a quiet center time and another time later in the day for noisier learning such as art, drama, sand table, or blocks. If you have the room and equipment, it is wonderful to have centers that involve more physical activity and talk (a sand or water table, blocks for building, music). You might have a drama center with dress-up clothing and puppets, or a house or store where children can engage in dramatic play. These offer extremely valuable learning opportunities for young children. If you can, schedule a time for children to be involved in such activities, giving them a choice. But it is probably best not to have such centers in use while you are teaching your guided reading groups.

Storage

You will also need places for students to store work in progress as well as finished work that will be used to assess their progress. Some suggestions are:

▶ Writing folders for each child with resources fastened in the center brackets and work in progress in pockets. Store folders in a labeled tub or file in the writing center. Children should be able to easily find their names, clearly printed at the top. We suggest using four different colors for folders as children can find theirs easily, or four different children can distribute them at writing time.

▶ A plastic crate with hanging files for finished writing work and/or portfolios (or scan and keep electronically).

▶ A rack for storing personal poetry books so that the decorated covers can be displayed. (Students thoughtfully decorate the covers after they have collected and illustrated a few poems.)

▶ Students may have sketchbooks, handwriting books, or other small items. You can use covered cereal boxes, cut in half, as files, and they can be placed in the middle of tables.

▶ A personal box of books to read for each child. You can also use cereal boxes for these. Ask parents to send them in!

▶ A basket for reader's notebooks. You might place four different color stickers on the upper-right corner and have students place them in four baskets. They can access them more quickly and you can review a pile with a particular color each day.

Student Tools for Literacy Learning

As we have described, the children have a variety of tools for organizing and collecting their thinking. Notebooks such as a sketchbook for drawing and writing, a poetry notebook, a writing folder, and a reader's notebook help children see

FIGURE 22-12 Cover of *Readers' Notebook: Primary*

FIGURE 22-13 Reading Time Activities

progress across a school year. They also become important tools for teacher assessment and use in parent conferences.

The *Reader's Notebook: Primary* (K–2) (Fountas and Pinnell 2014) is an important tool to support independence and response to books (see Figure 22-12). It includes a variety of sections for the child to tell about himself, a section for the child to list and respond to books he reads or listens to, a section for the child to list words he knows, and several letter and word resources. We will discuss the notebook as one of the options during literacy time (see Chapter 23 for information regarding *Reader's Notebook* (2–4), and *Reader's Notebook: Advanced* (4–8)). A reader's notebook becomes a record of reading and response to books that becomes one of the child's treasured artifacts of early literacy learning.

Managing the Classroom

Once you have created a well-organized environment, you have made significant progress toward managing the classroom so that students can work independently while you meet with small groups in guided reading. Granted the principle that all independent activities must be meaningful, productive, and usually related to literacy, we offer two options, drawn from teachers with wide experience in implementing guided reading. You may want to use a combination of approaches or start with one and move to the other.

A Simple System: Four Activities a Day

Some teachers are uncomfortable with movement or feel too inexperienced to manage centers. They prefer to have children work at their desks or tables. Still, they want students to be working actively at tasks that promote literacy learning. A simple system involves children in the same four or five activities every day. They can choose to do them in any order or you can suggest an order (see Figure 22-13).

Read a Book

This is independent reading. The children need to learn how to select books and enjoy reading them silently. Read a book means choice reading or rereading little books that have been read before. As you begin the year, you will need to have all students doing the same thing at the same time to learn the routine. Start with short periods where students "practice" doing each activity and then self-evaluate "how they did." Each day, lengthen the period for each. Then, start to vary. If you have a system that includes shared reading of large-print books with corresponding small books of the same title, you can quickly build a collection of books that everyone can read. As you introduce the classroom library, that can also be an option. You can assign students to:

- Read the books in their individual book boxes or baggies. The students have read these books before or you have provided them because you know they can read them independently. As students grow more proficient, have them remove old books and put new ones in.

- Read the books in the browsing boxes. They may need to be assigned to a particular colored or labeled box (with books at a variety of levels once they progress past level C). Have students go to the browsing box, select four or five books, read them, and return them.

- Read or look at books in the classroom library (including large print books).

After they are familiar with the routines and areas of the classroom, you can suggest that they choose from the three options above for reading time. You can vary the "read a book" task by assigning book buddies and having children take turns reading to each other.

Listen to a Book

With the technology now available, it is easy to acquire a collection of audio books to go with your read-aloud collection or you can simply record your reading of a book using a smart phone or tablet. You can even record the group reading a big book. Students can then use an iPod, tablet, or other device to listen. Place the device in the middle of a table and teach the children how to use it. Unless each child has reliable ear buds or headphones, listening to a book is best accomplished in the classroom library or a listening area that is located at some distance from the guided reading table. Show the students how to set the volume loud enough for three or four to hear as they look at the book, but not so loud that it disturbs others. As children are learning to listen, you can preset the story and have the book available. As they become more sophisticated with the technology (and some will arrive at school with thorough knowledge), they can choose from the library of audio books or you can continue to assign particular books.

Word Work (ABCs)

The Word Work center will take a little more work because you will want to connect it to your phonics lesson (see *Phonics Lessons, Grades K, 1, and 2* for examples). The activities range from very simple work with the alphabet (such as the name puzzle or sorting letters) to more complex work with letter or word sorts. You can have a task that changes every few days or weekly. Here are some examples:

- Put together your name puzzle and have a friend check it letter by letter. The name puzzle is the child's first name cut up into individual letters in an envelope with her name on the front. As they learn more, add the last name (see Figure 22-8).

- Make your name in magnetic letters and check it with the name puzzle.

- Write your name and something about yourself (or draw a picture of yourself).

The activities listed above could take a couple of days for all children to do. Words can be sorted in many ways, for example, beginning letters, ending letters, and patterns like phonograms. The word-work tasks would need to be preplanned and taught to the children during the phonics lesson. Materials can be stored in plastic tubs with tops. Unless you want to make a set for every child, children would need to share materials and might work with a partner.

If you wish to add a fifth task, you might add other tasks such as: read a book to a partner; write about a book you read; or read your poem book. The more children read and write and enjoy it, the better. Just be sure to keep the tasks worthwhile and simple.

Work on Writing

Teach students how to get materials from the writing center and return them when finished. You can have a stapler for students to make a book or have a variety of pre-made books. It is helpful to have a variety of types of paper, including pages that have a box at the top for a picture and either blank space to write or some lines. Children can also use blank paper. Show them how to fold the paper in half so that the picture goes on one part of the page and writing on the other. Often, young children like to draw the picture first and then write some labels, some kind of description, or something about their lives (see Figure 22-14). Even children who can write very little will work with concentration on a picture and come up with wonderful attempts at writing. Over time, as they listen to stories read aloud and begin to read little books for themselves, their books will grow in length and structure.

FIGURE 22-14 Sample of Child's Writing

Teach children how to plan and write books. You can provide demonstrations and supportive instruction during writers' workshop. Begin by having the child tell a story orally and lay out several pages. She might want to do the picture first. Then staple the pages together to make a book. You can have a variety of blank books in different sizes with different-colored covers already assembled in the writing center so that children can choose from them to make a book during independent work time. During this time, children can work on a variety of forms of writing—cards, thank-you notes, letters, stories, alphabet books, how-to books, or all-about books. They can work on pieces they started in writers' workshop. You can provide them with directions for what writing to work on by explaining at the community meeting and posting directions at the writing center. After children have learned the procedures, the two tasks above will require little preparation time on your part.

Maintaining the Materials

In this system you need to keep the browsing boxes and library fresh and orderly, always adding a few new books, and the writing center will need to be supplied.

Over time, teach students to check for tidiness, sharpen pencils, pick up paper, and put books back in order at the end of the day or work period. Many teachers have a chart of responsibilities with names assigned. It only takes a few moments and gives students a chance to take care of *their* classroom.

Using Centers and a Work Board

Another more active option is to have children rotate and work independently at centers, which allows them to stretch and move more often. Also, work can be very productive because the children in proximity are working on the same kind of activity and they can help each other or work as partners. (You can always use a combination of work at tables and work at centers if you have enough space in the classroom.) We have also seen teachers work successfully with a few centers using the children's own desks or tables by putting up a foldable center divider with labels and instructions on it. If you are using the center option, a work board will be very helpful (see Figure 22-15). A work board is a large diagram that includes:

▶ *Names of all children in groups.* These are not ability groups or even guided reading groups but heterogeneous groups of children who have the same schedule of tasks for the day. When a child's name is called for reading table, he stops what he is doing as a task and goes to reading, then returns to the task. Don't worry if every student does not completely finish the morning tasks. There is another day! (Do worry if the child consistently doesn't finish.) These groups can stay intact for a period of time, perhaps a month before you vary the composition of the groups.

▶ *Names and pictures (icons) of routine tasks for independent work time.* These tasks usually involve literacy, though some teachers have reasons to include a greater range of activities, for example, investigations or math.

▶ *Flexible ways of rotating tasks and children's names on the board to provide variety and assure all children experience a range of literacy events across the week.* You move the groups each day so that their schedule varies.

Locate the work board on a wall where all students can see it easily so that they may refer to it as needed. As with everything else, learning to use the work board will require demonstration and practice. Each icon signals a series of actions and that's complex learning for the young child. You may want to begin with just one activity and gradually increase the independent work time. You can design your work board to meet your needs. A large

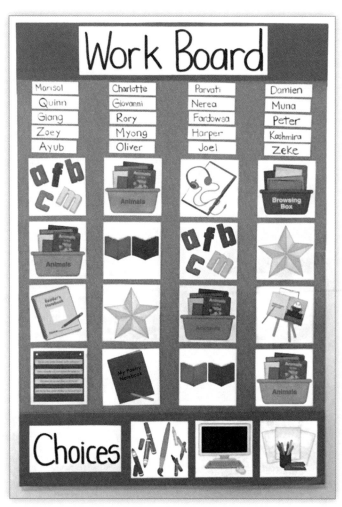

FIGURE 22-15 Classroom Work Board

number of icons can be downloaded from Online Resources (resources.fountasand-pinnell.com). The icons measure about 4 x 4 inches in size, but you could reduce or enlarge them. Print them in color on cardstock and, if possible, laminate them.

We have created a list of the icons with brief descriptions of each (see Figure 22-16 and Online Resources), but feel free to make them fit your specific goals. On the Online Resources we provide a blank square to create your icon as well. We will also continue to make small refinements and/or additions, so check Online Resources periodically for updates.

Getting Started

When you first begin to implement the work board, children will probably need your guidance, so take a few days to supervise and support them as they work independently and gradually increase in the number of tasks. You will need to teach and model how to use each center you introduce. Then provide guided practice time. Also be sure to discuss how to solve any probable "what-ifs" that may arise in the future. You may use a signal to tell them it is time to move to another activity temporarily while you are teaching routines. They put things away, look at the work board to check their schedules, and move to the next area. Emphasize getting right to the task at each center. After they are familiar with the routines, they can move at an individual pace. Have them self-evaluate at the end of the period. Be sure they consider their personal effort and their consideration for the learning of others.

Time

Your young students are just beginning to learn to manage time, which is a very valuable life skill. If they have four tasks, they should spend about ten or fifteen minutes in each. Remember that many students will be in a guided reading group for about fifteen to twenty minutes during the period. When you call a group, they simply stop what they are doing, move to the table, and go back to the same activity when the group is finished.

Changes

You do want to make changes in independent work to keep it fresh and interesting. Remember that your students are always reading new books and writing new stories so that will add to the engagement. When it is time to make a change, we recommend that you introduce no more than one new activity each day and you introduce the change by teaching it as a lesson.

Task Completion

As with anything else, children will approach their work in centers differently. Some will tend to rush through the tasks, finishing before others and not doing a thorough job. Others will dawdle and fail to complete anything. These are problems to solve. At the class meeting at the end of the period, encourage students to self-evaluate. Did I finish my schedule? Did I do a good job? Did I hurry too much? Did I consider others? Sharing some of their discoveries or things they enjoyed at

A Variety of Icons

Icon	Description
	Independent Reading: The children read a book from the classroom library (or browsing baskets) independently, or read a big book using a chopstick pointer.
	Big Book Reading: The children use a pointer or chopstick to read a big book.
	Read Around the Room: With a pointer, the children read all the print on the walls, charts, and lists around the room.
	Browsing Boxes: The children select books from the browsing boxes. The teacher places some books a group of children have already read in guided reading, as well as several new books they might enjoy, in colored boxes.
	Buddy Reading: The children take turns reading a book (or a big book) to a partner.
	Literature Circle: The children, with their books in hand, talk about a book and its illustrations with each other.
	Pocket Chart: The children place sentence strips from a familiar poem or story in correct order in the chart and take turns reading it. They may also innovate some texts by changing some of the words.
	Poetry Notebook: The children reread a small poem they read in shared reading, glue it in their notebook, illustrate it, read it to themselves, and read it to a partner.
	Reader's Notebook: The children work on various sections of their reader's notebook as assigned by the teacher.
	Listening Center: The children, with books in hand, listen to an audio recording of a book and follow along with the reading.
	Writing Center: The children use a variety of paper and writing utensils to make books or cards, write letters, or create any other form of writing.
	Word Work: The children work with a variety of letters and words. The activity is generally an application of the phonics/minilesson principle that was taught.
	Computer: The children engage with various programs on the computer.
	Tablets: The children use a variety of apps and tools on a tablet.
	Drama: The children put on simple puppet plays, readers' theater, or use the play corner to role play a variety of contexts, such as restaurants, doctor's office, or store.
	Art: The children use a variety of art materials to paint, draw, or create projects related to books.
	Math: The children use a variety of manipulatives to learn and practice math concepts.
	Games: The children play a variety of card or board games to reinforce what they are learning about letters or words.
	Science: The children investigate a variety of topics using the tools and artifacts of a scientist.
	Building: The children use a variety of materials (e.g., blocks, Legos) and props to build.
	Sand/Water Table: The children play with sand or water in a special table using a variety of utensils.
	Choice: Children choose from a variety of activities in the classroom. The teacher may give limited choices or choice may be open-ended.

FIGURE 22-16 A Variety of Icons in Reduced Size

the end of the time period goes a long way toward accountability and children are motivated to have "something to say." Avoid tedious, hard-to-manage record-keeping systems. Children might spend more time "signing" or checking than they do on the activity and your time is better spent on other things. If you are worried about a particular student, check in on her often. If students do not finish the last activity, put it on the schedule for the next day in a different order.

Choice

The star icon signals choice, which is usually limited to two or three options, although by the end of the year, children may be able to handle more. There may be many more possibilities just as long as you and your students can work within the guidelines you have taught. Notice that on this work board, there are three activities students can choose after they finish the schedule. You can also place a star in one of the work board spaces to indicate free choice.

Icons

As mentioned above, the icons serve as a signal for the activities. Each is a recognizable picture without distracting detail. You will teach (demonstrate) a routine for each icon so that the icon brings the steps to students' minds.

Here are some examples:

- ▶ The Writing Center icon reminds students to choose materials, write, put materials away, and file their finished or unfinished work in their writing folders. If you decide to provide a writing prompt for the week, you can have children draw and write in response to any kind of reading in which children have been engaged. Or they can write about their own topics. You may want to post a list of the kinds of writing they can choose and add to the list as they learn to do different kinds of writing. Students should have experienced each of these kinds of writing first through shared or interactive writing and then through "trying it out" and self-evaluating before you add it to the list.

- ▶ The Independent Reading icon reminds students to choose (the number of books you think is feasible), read each one, front to back, and return the books to the tub or box.

- ▶ The Big Book icon means that students will take a pointer and read the big book that is placed on an easel or other big books or enlarged charts in the book area. They might work with a partner.

- ▶ The Pocket Chart icon reminds students to go to the pocket chart and take out a plastic bag with a set of sentences, a story, or a poem. They put the strips in order in the pocket chart and then read it with a pointer, often working with a partner.

Create a simple routine with not too many steps for each icon. Then teach and practice the routine. Children will feel confident. They know what is expected and that leads to a sense of security. Everyone needs to feel like an expert at least once a day.

Teaching the Routines and Transitions

At the beginning of the year, put children in "the big picture" by taking a tour of the room. Introduce children to their "home" seat at a table and to the different areas of the classroom. Play a game that involves coming to the meeting area, sitting on the rug, and going quickly and quietly back to the home seat. You will not use all the centers (even the major ones) right away. Begin with large-group experiences and introduce materials and work areas one at a time. Your goal is self-initiated movement so children develop and practice self-regulation as they transition from one center to the next. You may find it helpful to use these steps:

1. Talk about and demonstrate the routine yourself.

2. Have one or two children demonstrate and affirm their efforts. (Everyone claps!) If necessary, repeat this process with more students.

3. If everyone can use a center simultaneously (for example, the classroom library) have all students at once demonstrate the routine. For example, browsing boxes might mean reading three books; listening center may mean listen to one book and write or draw about it in your reader's notebook; poetry notebook might mean read the poem, glue it in your poetry notebook, illustrate it, and read it to a partner. Post directions for the students at each location for their reference. Watch and describe what they are doing to affirm their efforts. If the center is small, have each small group start working there and observe them closely affirming their efforts the first time. Teach them how to transition to the next center.

4. Introduce the basic centers first—the ones you will be using almost every day.

5. Observe children in the center until you are comfortable that they are consistently using the area independently and are being respectful of others and of the materials. (This may take only a short time.) If some children are inexperienced or find self-regulation challenging, reteach. Children will soon learn to help each other achieve self-regulation.

6. Build in extra support for students who find it difficult to work independently (for example, a check-in between groups).

7. Then work on helping students learn how to clean up and organize the materials at the center before transitioning or moving on to the next center. Demonstrate explicitly or have a few students demonstrate for the class what is needed for each type of center.

8. Encourage children to self-evaluate and problem-solve at the end of the independent work period.

Remember that as you use shared and guided reading, you will build up texts students can read. Through interactive writing, you also create a great deal of writing that children can read and use as resources. Since work groups are mixed, some children will be more advanced in reading and writing than others. The extent to which group members assist each other can be part of their self-evaluation.

Every time you introduce a new task, or if you decide to change the task in a center, help children make the transition. Again, demonstrate and have children act out the change. *Don't assume that telling is enough*. After a time, children learn how to make such transitions and they will take on new tasks more quickly and with independence so you can work with guided reading groups without interruption.

Managing Guided Reading Within a Two-Hour Block of Time

Although guided reading may take place any time during the day, most teachers implement it in the morning because they are more likely to have a large block of uninterrupted time for all the language arts including read-aloud, phonics, and other contexts (about 2.5 to 3 hours). A daily schedule was presented in Chapter 21. On the following page is another sample schedule for a language and literacy block (see Figure 22-17).

If you have less than two-and-a-half or three hours, you will need to make adjustments. You may find that you can teach only three reading groups per day. In that case, rotate children so that each group gets three or four lessons a week. You will want your least experienced readers (who may be ones who have trouble benefitting from independent work) to have guided reading five days each week. You may need to reduce the time for other elements or do some alternate days. It is most important, however, to have guided reading, writers' workshop, and interactive read-aloud every day.

The schedule must fit the particular needs of children and the constraints of your school day. There are no bathroom breaks or recess periods on this schedule, so you'll want to work those in (some teachers make snack a center). Use sticky notes and move things around until you have a workable weekly schedule. Be flexible, but avoid daily fluctuations if possible. The closer you can stick to a predictable weekly schedule, the better—children like to know what to expect.

Norms

You may be wondering why, in a chapter on classroom management, we discuss norms, rules, or agreements about how people will work together, so near the end. You do need understandings among all members of the community, that will work. Any time twenty-five or so people work together for hours every day in one room, they need agreements about how members of the group will work together so the time and space works well for everyone. We see rules as "ways of working together" or "descriptions of how the community is organized and operates." Rules are just agreed upon behaviors and they grow out of the educational process. Gather your students and have a talk about how they feel they can best learn and share what you need to offer your best teaching. Create a set of norms together for your classroom using either shared or interactive writing, as you discuss rationales. You can also agree to revisit the norms as needed. As students learn the procedures for routines, they are also learning and internalizing important descriptors for the kinds of behaviors that are required so that everyone can enjoy their work and learn. This goes back to the idea that everyone in the class is responsible for her own learning as well as the learning of others.

A Sample Morning Schedule for Teaching Reading and Writing

Time	Activity	Description
8:00	Independent Reading	Students come into the room and go to the classroom library where they choose a book. They can sit on the rug. The teacher can take attendance, lunch count, and so on, during this time.
8:05	Community Meeting	Students get a preview of the day's work. You can teach any new routines needed.
8:10	Interactive Read-Aloud (or Shared Reading and/or Interactive Writing)	This reading may be related to any topic, including the book(s) just read in a text set.
8:30	Reading Minilesson	Engage students in thinking about one simple understanding related to reading or to ways of working together using the recent interactive read-aloud texts as mentor texts. You have several clear examples to ground the minilesson (e.g. story problem and solution, important characters, kind of book, information learned).
8:40	Reading Time (Guided Reading and Independent Work Time)	Invite students to look at the work board. After they know the icons, they will need very little time to understand their schedules for the day. For the youngest children who are reading very short texts, a guided reading lesson will take only about 10 minutes. Take the groups as soon as the children settle in to independent work so that you may be able to teach three or four groups. You can take a walk around the room (a couple of minutes) between each group to check on individuals.
9:45	Class Meeting	Debrief the morning by having students share something interesting they learned or did.
10:00	Snack	
10:15	Writers' Workshop	Teach a minilesson and then support individual students as they work on their own pieces of writing or convene a guided writing group. End the period with sharing.
11:15	Phonics/Word Study Lesson	Phonics lessons are brief and based on inquiry and an understanding about how words work. The application activity can be demonstrated and students can work on it in the ABC center during independent work time the next day or several days later.
11:30	Lunch	

FIGURE 22-17 A Sample Morning Schedule for Teaching Reading and Writing

> ## Our Class
>
> We will take good care of our classroom.
> We will do our best learning.
> We will help others learn.
> We will be kind to others.
> We will respect others.
> We will talk about problems and solve them together.
>
> Latasha Ariel Harmony Iris
> Zachary Lucien Ayla
> Emma Josh Jayden Dion Sophia Tuani
> Brianna Kayla Ben Coby Tyson

FIGURE 22-18 Norms for a Primary Classroom

You will want a simple list of these descriptive guidelines to which you can refer if needed. Post them on the wall where students can easily see them. Some general guidelines for norms are:

▶ Encourage students to participate in constructing the list.

▶ Don't make a long list—keep it short.

▶ State the agreements in positive terms.

▶ Norms should describe specific behaviors as much as possible.

▶ Revisit the list during self-assessment.

▶ Add items if problems arise and another is needed.

Here is an example of norms from a primary classroom that the teacher and students created using shared writing (see Figure 22-18). Notice that the students signed their names after the teacher recorded their thinking.

Getting Started: The First Eight Weeks

We suggest a plan for the first eight weeks of school (see Figure 22-19) to establish the community and expectations. The "getting started" period sets the tone for the year. You can pull back and "start over" if you have to, but it's best to get things right from the start. The first few weeks, students are most willing to behave in the new ways you (and the community) expect.

The Importance of Management

In this chapter, we may seem to be overstressing the role of management and the necessity of teaching routines in a very explicit way. Children come to us from many different home environments and it isn't our role to criticize any of them; but what works for a family in the home is almost always different from what works in a classroom with twenty to thirty people all the same age and only one adult. *None of the children will come into your room already knowing how to behave there.* We agree that "the most lavishly appointed classroom may turn into a shambles if routines for using it have not been established." (New Zealand Department of Education 1985, 143).

It is critical for the teacher of young children to establish an organized, predictable, safe environment within which they can learn to be independent. Responsibility for organization cannot be abdicated to young children who have no experience in group learning. In the beginning, you will need to demonstrate and direct. But this very direction will create independence because it frees both you and the

The First Eight Weeks:
Kindergarten and Grade One

	Suggestions for Working with Children	Materials Needed
Weeks 1–2	◆ Use mostly whole-group or individual table activities (reading aloud, shared reading, writing, poetry notebook). ◆ Involve students in simple shared or interactive writing appropriate to their experience. ◆ Give children a product that they can take home and read (for example, simple poems you have read together). ◆ Take a tour of the room to name the centers (and have students do it). Introduce main centers (or supplies centers) for writing/drawing, and reading (library). ◆ Establish morning meeting. ◆ Practice moving between meeting space and home table. ◆ Teach children routines for using the classroom library for independent reading and the writing center. Have them self-evaluate. ◆ Have children work with their names (puzzles, magnetic letters, etc.). ◆ Make a name chart with the children. ◆ Have them find their names (using a model). ◆ Begin making and using class charts like Alphabet Linking Charts. ◆ When children are involved in table activities, do some assessment conferences.	◆ Labels on everything. ◆ Preselected read-aloud books. ◆ Chart and other materials ready for interactive writing. ◆ Teacher made charts like the Alphabet Linking Chart or Consonant Cluster Linking Chart (you'll make another with students). ◆ Have the meeting area ready and names on desks or tables for students' "home" seats or tables. ◆ Have baskets or cubbyholes ready for students' personal materials. They can hunt for their baskets by matching their names. ◆ Have a name puzzle prepared for each student (first name and last for grade one). Advanced students can compare their names to others. ◆ Have one name chart already made, but make another with the students. ◆ Have students' names up in every part of the room and try to use names in as many places as possible (helper chart, name chart, stories about them (to which you can add pictures), name cards in the pocket chart). ◆ Have a variety of pre-made books and other kinds of paper at the Writing Center. ◆ Already set up for assessment with all materials ready.
Weeks 3–4	◆ Open one new area at a time; for example the pocket chart or listening center. Demonstrate and practice. ◆ Work with students toward rotations to two or three centers and you interact while encouraging them. ◆ Continue to read aloud and use shared reading and interactive writing to establish the learning community and build up common reading materials and models for writing. ◆ Teach students to use browsing boxes. ◆ Begin phonics lessons with simple applications that students do simultaneously at tables. Teach them to work with a partner. ◆ Continue assessment conferences any time students are working independently.	◆ Materials for all centers you are using and for the meeting area. ◆ Preselected read-aloud books. ◆ Materials for phonics lessons and application activity (choose one that all students can do simultaneously). ◆ Browsing boxes for students. ◆ Organized assessment materials.

FIGURE 22-19 The First Eight Weeks: Kindergarten and Grade One

(continues)

The First Eight Weeks:
Kindergarten and Grade One

	Suggestions for Working with Children	Materials Needed
Weeks 5–6	◆ Establish the routine of working in small groups in centers (or at tables) for a period of time–working toward 50 or 60 minutes. ◆ Emphasize independence during the morning meeting and in a self-evaluation meeting at the end. ◆ Have phonics application activities at tables. Students can work as partners. ◆ Complete individual assessments and form tentative groups to begin in week 6. ◆ Hold at least four very short (10 minutes) guided reading groups a day in week 6. Since you are teaching the routine, you can use any book students can read quickly, even ones they have previously read in shared reading. ◆ Explain the table to students and what they will be doing there. The idea is to establish the routine of the reading table. Explain why you need no interruptions. With short lessons, you can take a quick walk around the room after each group. ◆ Establish writing folders for each student and teach them how to use them. ◆ Introduce the reader's notebook (grade 1; may start kindergarten later). ◆ Begin personal poetry books with one poem that they illustrate. Don't have them decorate the front cover right away; they need to think about the poetry and the importance of their cover art. ◆ Teach children how to store their writing folders, reader's notebooks, and their personal poetry books.	◆ Materials for phonics lesson and application. ◆ Books for shared reading, including poetry book. ◆ Materials for guided reading groups. ◆ All materials for community meeting and interactive writing. ◆ Individual personal poetry books for students. Small copies of a poem for students. ◆ Writing folder for each student. ◆ Reader's notebooks for each student. ◆ Storage place for writing folders and personal poetry books.
Weeks 7–8	◆ Continue the full schedule of activities. ◆ Go over the schedule as refined with students so that they understand the way the week will go. ◆ Continue guided reading groups, increasing time but still keeping them short. Regroup as needed. ◆ Continue to monitor independent work and help students self-assess and problem-solve as needed. Revise center work as needed. ◆ Fully implement writers' workshop.	◆ Keep the classroom supplied with all needed materials for everything on the schedule. ◆ Continue to bring out new books for the classroom library and refresh browsing boxes.

FIGURE 22-19 *(continued)*

children from constant distractions related to management. It establishes a trusting relationship between you and the children because school becomes a place where you know what is expected of you and you are able to participate successfully. It helps children to become organized to learn and it helps you to be organized to teach. Self-management promotes self-regulation, one of the most important skills an individual can learn. Self-regulation has been defined as "the ability to contain and manage one's own behavior without relying on others for impulse control. It is an internalized mechanism that develops through instruction and support, much the way math or literacy must be learned, and is a central agility to success in school and life." (Copple and Bredekamp 2009, 269).

Children are capable of social learning and they can learn to regulate their own behavior. They need the demonstrations and support that will foster that learning. The use of the work board is not only a means of building meaningful learning, but is also a tool for developing critical social competencies that children will need throughout their lives. Moving through centers in a self-regulated way provides children with opportunities to problem-solve for themselves. Teachers will need to be proactive in teaching students some problem-solving strategies before problems arise. A sense of independence, choice, and autonomy are fostered when children take control of their movement from center to center. Through independent work and self-management, they can develop the sense of agency they need to learn in a group across many school years.

Suggestions for Professional Development

This chapter can be used as a resource for looking at classrooms and refining management plans. Hold a grade-level meeting to create your own plan for the first eight weeks of school. Having the plan will give you time to reflect and refine it over the vacation period, and to gather and organize supplies before the term starts.

1. As a group, look at the plan for the first eight weeks. Discuss each item and then select those you think are most appropriate for your classrooms/school. Add other items that you think will be helpful.

2. Then, as individuals or grade-level colleagues, draw up a general plan for the first eight weeks of school that is doable in your own circumstances.

3. Make a list of the materials and supplies you will need, including materials such as plastic buckets for organizing books, cans for holding pencils and other writing tools, trays for paper, and so on. Have a creative discussion of how to acquire these materials at little or no cost.

4. Finally, make an "action plan" of tasks that you need to do to make the start of school dynamic and successful. Each person may want to work on her own; or, you may find it useful to pool resources and assign a few tasks to each person.

Hold a meeting on the first day that you are in the school to go over the plan and share what you have gathered and thought about over the vacation time. Hold another meeting at the end of the first two weeks to compare progress and solve problems.

Alternatively, you may meet during the school year and plan to make small improvements to your existing classroom plan. Use the following questions to consider the classroom environment:

▶ Are there well-defined areas for large, small, and independent work?

▶ Is the classroom library inviting and well-organized?

▶ Are books easy to find and return?

▶ Are books integrated into the work centers?

▶ Are there numerous displays of written language at eye-level (print for "reading around the room")?

▶ Are pocket charts used in several locations?

▶ Are all materials clearly labeled? Are there simple written directions where appropriate?

▶ Are there resources such as poems, charts, big books, and other print materials readily available for children to read?

▶ Are all materials organized for easy access and return?

▶ Is furniture, and are dividers arranged so that you can have a full view of the classroom?

▶ Is there a comfortable and well-supplied area for independent reading? Independent writing?

▶ Are noisy and quiet areas separated?

▶ Are there neat, usable places to store, remove, and replace student work?

▶ Is there a well-organized place for your materials?

CHAPTER 23

Managing Literacy in the Intermediate/Middle Grades

It is said that we make time for what we value,
and if we value reading, we must make time for it.

–Donalyn Miller

Self-management is even more critical for older students; and, like younger students, they need to be taught how to learn within the classroom community. The goal of self-management is more encompassing even than the goal of becoming highly literate. You want your students to grow as responsible, empathetic human beings who can collaborate with others and feel they have something to contribute to the community. You want them to have self-awareness, self-discipline, agency, and self-motivation. For *most* of the year, they spend *most* of their waking hours at school. Those hours inevitably help to shape the people they become.

The development of self-management happens in a place where students feel safe and where they feel they belong to a group or community. "Belonging to a group means being needed as well as to need, and believing that you have something vital to contribute," (Charney 2002, 22). Charney (2002) points out that being useful and helpful to others is an inherent human need. But, it doesn't automatically flourish. Children have to have a chance to engage in meaningful work that they can feel is a genuine contribution. "Creating community means giving children the power to care," (Charney 2002, 22).

Management isn't just a matter of keeping your students busy and quiet. Students who do not feel that the work they are doing is meaningful, who do not connect with others or feel they are making a contribution, will not be engaged enough to profit from "activities" (or independent work). Teachers are always searching for a guaranteed-to-be-good "activity" that will occupy the rest of the class while they work with small reading groups. Cambourne and his colleagues (2001) took an in-depth look at teaching-learning activities (the name given to students' independent work during the guided reading time) in nine classrooms. All of the classrooms in the study were located in lower socioeconomic school districts, and focused on students in grades one through five. Researchers were able to compile an enormous database over a period of nine years, including hundreds of hours of video and audio records and thousands of pages of transcripts and notes. These data were subjected to rigorous analysis. The researchers expected their findings to reveal that some activities were more successful than others, but they also found that a teaching-learning activity could be very successful in one classroom and unsuccessful in another, even though both teachers used the same procedures. In fact, they found a profound relationship between the success of teaching-learning activities and the culture of the classroom where the activities were taking place.

The researchers looked below the surface to find *how* the teaching-learning activities were implemented, and they identified a number of characteristics that describe what makes for an effective teaching-learning activity. Three characteristics are especially applicable to our work in guided reading.

> ▌ *"Effective teaching-learning activities were explicitly linked to other parts of the class,"* (Cambourne 2001, 128). This means that the teacher intentionally planned strong connections between other lessons or parts of the school day, and students were conscious of the connections. So when students read, write about reading, and talk with others in sharing time or book club, they can relate what they have noticed to their minilessons (not only today but past lessons), to the mentor texts they have heard read aloud, to the inquiry they experienced in genre study or content area a study, and to what they are learning in guided reading with expected responses.

> ▌ *"Effective teaching-learning activities were ones in which students had to engage in social interaction and cognitive collaboration,"* (Cambourne 2001, 132). Students do need to engage in reflection, which can be a solitary activity, but they also need to share their thinking and learning with other students. Learning is social and meaningful and engages students' intellect.

> ▌ *"Effective teaching-learning activities were structured so that learners were able to offer a range of acceptable responses,"* (Cambourne 2001, 133). When students engage in reading, writing, and talking about books, their first goal is to express their thinking rather than to answer a set of prepared questions.

In this chapter we describe ways to manage a sixty- to ninety-minute literacy period for students in grades two through the upper-elementary grades. We encourage middle-level teachers to work toward fifty-five or sixty-minute periods to offer a readers' workshop structure to their students. (If you are teaching second grade, decide how well students can manage to work independently. You may need to begin the year with a task structure as described in Chapter 22, and end with the systems proposed here. Or, you may want to shorten the literacy block or break it up with a read-aloud session or other activity.) We'll suggest a simple option using independent reading and writing about reading, and then we'll describe a slightly more complex structure that frames independent reading and writing about reading in a readers' workshop structure.

We start with the assumption that students in grade two and above are able to sustain attention to reading and writing for longer periods of time than their younger counterparts. As you get to know your students, you may want to start with a fairly short period of time and gradually lengthen it. One principle to follow is that you want to observe the length of time that students can sustain independent activity and that will tell you how long you have to work with small groups.

Option #1: Independent Reading with a Reader's Notebook

Your goal is to engage your students in interesting, satisfying independent work that represents authentic reading and responses in writing. In a two-stage process, teach your students to:

1. Choose books for independent reading and read them silently at their desks or tables.

2. Use a reader's notebook to record their thoughts about reading.

Each step will take several days to establish. Teach each of these steps in a short whole-class lesson, which we call a minilesson to emphasize that it is short and explicit (usually about five to eight minutes). After each minilesson, students read independently a book of choice with an awareness of the principle in the lesson. Walk around the room conferring with individuals to support them in engaging with texts that they can enjoy.

Establish Independent Choice Reading

The words "independent" and "choice" are important. You cannot expect students to engage in independent reading for any sustained period of time if:

- ▸ The books are not ones they want to read.
- ▸ The books are too hard for them to read.

The following steps will be helpful.

Step 1: Create a Well-Organized, Attractive Classroom Library

Create a classroom library that includes a variety of genres—about half fiction and half nonfiction. Include poetry collections and magazines. The classroom library is the essential component of the management system. The fiction and nonfiction books available for student choice should reflect a wide range of interests and levels of difficulty. The books should *not* be labeled by level but instead should be grouped by topic (nonfiction), author, genre, type, series, or other categorizations such as animals, friendship, survival, or sports. Have books sorted into labeled tubs (and label the shelf where the tub belongs) and place them with covers facing out

FIGURE 23-1 Book Tubs in a Classroom Library

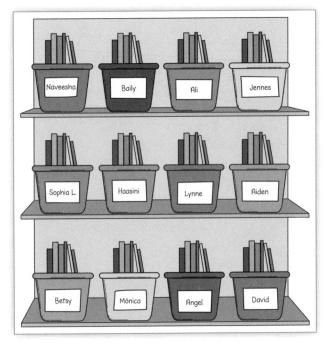

FIGURE 23-2 Student Boxes

so students can flip through the titles (see Figure 23-1). You might have one basket where students can put a book when they can't remember the basket they took it from. Students usually know where they get the book and can learn to return them to the same place, but you want to do everything you can to keep the library in order. Wasting time searching for books increases stress or wondering where to return them takes time and increases stress, too.

Start with a good number of books in baskets, but not so many that students will be overwhelmed. (Take into account the reading levels you have learned through assessing the students at the beginning of the year so that you are sure there are books that every student can read.) Add books to the library all year and "retire" some books that are no longer of interest. Our publication, *Leveled Books K-8: Matching Texts to Readers for Effective Teaching,* 2006, has many suggestions for acquiring and organizing a rich classroom library.

Step 2: Identify a Personal Place for Student Materials for Independent Reading

Create a place for each student to keep his book of choice and a reader's notebook, as well as other materials such as a writer's notebook, poetry notebook, or word study folder. This personal space could be a desk, a cubby, or a magazine box. Indicate students' places with their names. The magazine boxes labeled with students' names can go on one shelf or set of shelves (see Figure 23-2). Teach them to put materials in the same order in the box. We have spent enough time waiting for students to find materials within a stuffed traditional desk to know that an orderly shelf of labeled boxes or tubs works much better.

Step 3: Introduce the Classroom Library

Introduce the classroom library to the students during a whole-class minilesson that is designed to create excitement about the library. ("Boys and girls, we have wonderful books in our library, and you are going to choose and read so many of them this year!") Explain the baskets and the ways books are organized. Demonstrate how to choose books and how to put them back if not chosen or when students are finished reading them, and how to place them in one's personal magazine box at the end of reading time if needed to continue reading.

Give some book talks featuring books that you think might be of interest to students. Be sure to include books at a variety of levels. A book talk is a way to spark students' interest in particular texts. As you add new books to the library all year, you give these short talks, which act as brief (one- to two-minute) "commercials" for specific books. The most effective book talks, of course, feature books that you have read and loved; but you can also give book talks on those you have not read. You can comment on the author, a particular aspect of the plot, interesting characters, and other unique aspects of text. For example:

- Talk about the title and the author.
- Show the cover and some of the illustrations (if applicable).
- Read aloud the lead or a particularly interesting part of the book (without giving away the outcome).
- Connect the book to students' lives in some way.
- Tell a little about the plot or characters.
- Tell why the book interests you and/or might interest your students.
- Talk about what is special about the writing.

Get students to explore the baskets in an orderly way and to choose a book to start reading. Many students will be able to choose a book they are interested in, though you may need to offer guidance to a few. Give assistance to those who need it. But at the end of the period, every student should have chosen a book and read a little bit of it. As students choose and read books, constantly circulate so that you are conferring briefly with each student to ensure they are feeling good about their choices.

Step 4: Teach Students to Make Good Choices

For any reader—but especially for students who have some difficulty in reading—choosing books is complex. As adult readers, we have a wide range of choice; and all of us read "lighter" and "heavier" material according to our moods and inclinations. Your students will also need to consider whether a book is too hard or easy for them. This decision is not that easy. As they begin a book, they need to ask themselves:

- Can I read this book without stopping or are there places I have to work a lot on the words and language?
- Are there too many hard words or can I figure most of them out?
- Am I understanding the book?
- Is this book interesting enough to continue?
- Am I fascinated by the topic, the characters, or the plot?

Teach students to explore a book and make a decision whether this is a good book to read now or whether it should be saved for a time in future. You can extend this teaching to your individual conferences with students. You might also put together a temporary basket of just-right books as an interim step for a student who is having a consistently hard time choosing books.

Step 5: Continue to Introduce New Books to Students and Develop the Habit of Reading Silently for a Period of Time

Students should be seated comfortably at desks or tables when they read. Some teachers have comfortable chairs, a side table and lamp, and a rug in the library area and students can take turns using those, but we discourage students lying on the floor. It's too easy to trip over them or for them to start to roll. Students should have their own space without being crowded by others.

Establish the Use of a Reader's Notebook

The reader's notebook is an exciting way to increase the depth of reader response. It is practical and easy to use and it builds a student's awareness of reading's many dimensions. A reader's notebook is a vehicle for students to record and save their own written responses to their reading. We find that a letter to the teacher is a good format to use because students can move from an oral conversation to a written conversation. You are a real audience for your students and you can respond. The letter represents their own thinking—a thoughtful, critical reflection on a text that grows in sophistication as the reader processes increasingly challenging texts.

Writing about reading is not a "test" but it does provide excellent evidence of a student's progress in reading. In the beginning, expect students to write one thoughtful letter to the teacher each week to describe their thinking about any book they have heard read aloud or that they have read in guided reading. But they should give special attention to the books they choose to read independently. They can use a reader's notebook any time you want them to respond to texts; and as they become accustomed to using it, you can vary the forms of writing about reading they use, for example:

- Letters to the teacher (which you answer). See *Guiding Readers and Writers* (Fountas and Pinnell 2000) for specific descriptors and examples.
- Two-column writing (e.g., a quote and response).
- Sketching or drawing about reading.
- Analyses of texts (for example problem/solution).

A reader's notebook can be a simple spiral bound (or any kind of binding) blank book. We have created three versions of a *Reader's Notebook* (Fountas and Pinnell 2011) specifically for each set of grade levels (K-1, 2–4, 4–8), shown in Figure 23-3, but if you don't have access, you can create your own using the same type of information. The following are sections of the notebook for grades 2–4:

- Guidelines for readers' workshop
- Genre requirements for the year
- List of genres and descriptions of each
- Reading list (number, title, author, genre, date completed, and student assessment as easy, just-right, or difficult)
- Tips for choosing books
- How to give a book talk

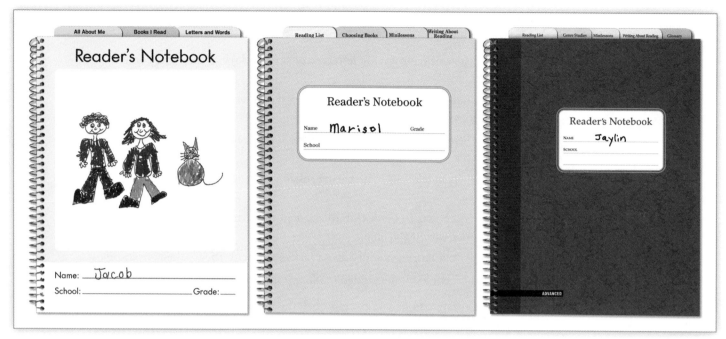

FIGURE 23-3 Different Versions of the Fountas and Pinnell *Reader's Noteboook* (K–1, 2–4, 4–8)

▶ Books to read (title, author, place to check when completed)

▶ Record of minilessons (includes how fiction and nonfiction are organized)

▶ Writing about reading (includes forms for writing about reading and guidelines for checking your writing)

You will also find reproducible versions of many of these pages in the back of our book, *Guiding Readers and Writers*. You can reproduce these pages and glue them in a blank notebook, saying to students: "I have made a reader's notebook that you will use all year to collect your thinking about your reading."

We have also developed an *Advanced Reader's Notebook* for upper elementary and middle school (see Chapter 22 for more about *Reader's Notebook* for primary). A major focus of the notebook is engaging in the inquiry process related to genre characteristics and keeping a record of minilessons (*Genre Study*, 2011).

These notebooks are valuable tools that take the place of worksheets or workbooks and other materials that require more teacher time and have little value for students. If a student records his thinking year after year in these notebooks, an incredibly rich record of progress is created. Students keep their reader's notebooks in their personal book boxes, along with a book of choice for independent reading time. The reader's notebook assignment is completed during class time rather than as homework (although students do have the option of taking it home if they need more time). Entries should be proofread carefully by the student and should represent the best writing the student can do. (You do not "red pencil" or correct the writing, although you can note for yourself areas of spelling or grammar that indicate where many students need instruction at a later time).

Reader's notebooks are constantly used during classroom literacy activities.

During independent reading, students should always have their notebooks with them. For example, students can:

- Write parts of their weekly letters over several days as thoughts come to mind.
- Write in their notebooks during book talks to record titles of books they want to read.
- Bring their notebooks to the minilesson if the teacher asks them to take notes or to do a "quick write" or sketch.
- Bring their notebooks to a sharing session so they can use them as a resource.
- Bring notebooks to book club to share notes or responses that they want to talk about with the group.
- Discuss their entries in individual conferences with the teacher.
- Bring notebooks to the guided reading lesson to work in if needed.

The following steps can be used to establish the use of a reader's notebook in your classroom.

Step 1: Introduce the Reader's Notebook

Write a letter to the students that you duplicate and place in each reader's notebook. Give each student a notebook and read aloud the letter you have placed in it. Take them to the Reading List section and demonstrate how to record the information. Explain that today, they will write the title, author, and genre of the book they are reading on the first line. Explain that when they finish the book, they will write the date in the last space.

That same day, ask each student to write a letter to you in the notebook about a common text, one that students have talked about previously as a class, such as a book that you have read aloud to the group. Have a short discussion about what they might write in a letter to you about the book. Students can also (additionally) write about the book they have chosen to read independently. Circulate around the room, offering assistance as students need it. You can quickly read some responses and ask questions to give suggestions to help students extend their responses (see Figure 23-4).

It is a good idea to begin using the notebook on a Friday, because you will want to answer every letter the first time they turn in their notebooks. When students enter the classroom on Monday, they will find your response in their notebooks; we have found that this practice makes a strong impression on students. You show them that you take their thinking (and this task) very seriously. If it is faster for you to use word processing for your letters, you can print them and glue them in the students' notebooks. It is important that your letters be placed in the notebooks so that they are in one place and students can look back on the thinking and the dialogue as they reflect. Scattered emails will not do that job, but you can print and glue them in. Also, there are applications for electronic journals that might work if your students have sole control of a tablet. There will be many times when you want all students to have their notebooks at the same time. But many

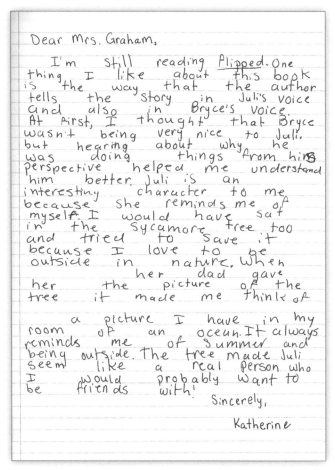

Dear Mrs. Graham,

I'm still reading <u>Flipped</u>. One thing I like about this book is the way that the author tells the story in Juli's voice and also in Bryce's voice. At first, I thought that Bryce wasn't being very nice to Juli, but hearing about why he was doing things from his perspective helped me understand him better. Juli is an interesting character to me because she reminds me of myself. I would have sat in the sycamore tree too and tried to save it because I love to be outside in nature. When her dad gave her the picture of the tree it made me think of a picture I have in my room of an ocean. It always reminds me of summer and being outside. The tree made Juli seem like a real person who I would probably want to be friends with!

Sincerely,

Katherine

Dear Katherine,

I'm glad that you're enjoying <u>Flipped</u>, and that you noticed the unusual way the author tells the story. Showing both of the characters' perspectives helps you understand them, and it also let's you see why they sometimes misunderstood each other.

Did you think about the title of the book and how it relates to the two different characters and how the author uses both of the characters' voices? What other meanings do you think the title might have?

The author of Flipped, Wendelin Van Draanen, also wrote the Sammy Keyes mystery series, which you might enjoy. The main character in that series, Sammy, is an independent and resourceful girl, just like Juli in Flipped. Do you think the narrator's voice is important in a book?

From,
Mrs. Graham

FIGURE 23-4 Letters Between a Student and Teacher from a *Reader's Notebook*

teachers quickly write responses in longhand, limiting themselves to five minutes per student and a few students each day. In your letter:

- Demonstrate the use of good form and sentence structure.

- Emphasize that you want students to write about their thinking—not just a summary of the book.

- Ask questions that require students to explain their thinking or give evidence. You'll expect them to answer these questions in the next letter.

- Make suggestions of books you think the student would like.

Step 2: Explain the Letter-Writing Process and Accountability

Prompt students to read your letter and to share their thinking about it. Invite them to share some of the things they talked about in their letters. Students can learn from others' suggestions. You may want to write these suggestions on a chart.

We have found that it works very well to have students write one thoughtful letter to you a week to begin using their notebooks. They develop voice because they are writing to a real audience. To make this system manageable for you, divide students into four groups, with each group having the letter due on a different day: the Monday, Tuesday, Wednesday, and Thursday kids. This allows you to answer the students in each group each day so that you will not have the entire load of responses at the same time or on the weekend. Each day, remind the students who have letters due the following day.

Step 3: Demonstrate the Elements of an Effective Letter

If students are new to the process of using a reader's notebook, it will take some time to learn to use it to maximum advantage. Consider writing a letter to share your thinking about a book you read to the class or about a book you read yourself. In your letter, demonstrate appropriate form and also share your thinking. The letter can be an enlarged chart that everyone can see, and you can invite students to underline in red the statements that express your thinking, and in green the evidence you provide. Invite students to talk about what makes the letter a good example. Later, you will provide minilessons on other writing forms.

Step 4: Teach Minilessons on Using the Different Parts of the Reader's Notebook

Over several weeks, visit each part of the notebook to show students how to use the tools effectively. For example, visit the genre requirements page and show students how to tally the books they have read in each required genre. For younger students who are just beginning to use a notebook, you might distinguish only between fiction and nonfiction, but eventually, you will want to assure the reading of a range of genres (with a great deal of free choice) and that will change over the grades. You can have minilessons on proofreading, listing books students want to read or topics and genres of interest. For each minilesson:

- Show an enlarged version of the page or reproduce it on a chart.
- Fill in examples so that students have a good model of how to use the page.
- Invite student observations about how they find the page useful as well as their questions.
- Leave the chart posted for several days so that students can refer to it.

Moving Toward Independence

After you have established independent reading and the use of the notebook, you will be poised to convene small groups of students for guided reading. The independent reading and reader's notebook, while highly beneficial in themselves, also act as your management system.

During independent reading, you will want to ask students to maintain a "zero voice" time (see Chapter 21, Figure 21-10). While you will want to make time for students to talk about their books with others, it is not helpful to have many different conversations going on while you are teaching guided reading groups. And, there are many opportunities for students to be distracted if others are talking and moving around the room. Independent reading should be a very quiet time. The only voices heard would be your individual conferences with students, which are conducted in whispers or the low voices of your students and you in the small group.

As you would for younger students, place your guided reading table in a corner and position yourself so that you can keep an eye on the students who are reading independently. In this way, you can identify any problems that arise and can make a note to confer quickly—at the end of one group—with students who seem to be at loose ends.

It is never wise to shout across the room at a student who is off task. This disturbs and interrupts other students and risks making even more of them lose concentration. Simply walk over and whisper to the student. When students have fully internalized the operating procedures of the classroom, they will often be self-aware of their inappropriate behavior at the catch of your eye! You want your students to see reading time as a serene, quiet, and serious work period. Many students welcome this quiet time of the day when they can read books of their choice. At the end of the time, you can involve the students in evaluating how everyone supported their ability to focus on their reading and writing.

Option #2: A Readers' Workshop Structure

The structure of the readers' workshop puts a strong instructional frame around independent reading and also provides regular opportunities for students to share their thinking with each other. The structure is shown in Figure 23-5.

If you have already established independent reading and the reader's notebook, it takes just a few steps more to implement the full structure of a readers' workshop. In general, the workshop moves from a whole-class meeting to individual reading and small-group work, and back to a whole-class meeting. Your use of time will depend on the amount of time you have for the entire class period. Ideally you have seventy-five to ninety minutes, though many teachers have only sixty minutes. You will need to adjust accordingly.

Book Talks and Minilessons

Use the very short books talks, as discussed previously, to engage students' interest in books. They can write down titles in their notebooks for later reference. Often, you will find students taking the books right out of your hands following a book talk! Remember to give book talks on a variety of genres and for easier and harder books, without mentioning levels.

Minilessons are short, concise, very purposeful lessons. The term *minilessons* is used by many educational researchers to emphasize that these are short (five- to

Structure of Readers' Workshop

Book Talks and Minilessons		5—10 minutes
Students: • Independent Reading • Writing in a Reader's Notebook	Teacher: • Guided Reading Groups (about 20–25 minutes each) • Book Clubs (about 20 minutes each) • Individual Conferences (3–5 minutes each)	50-60 minutes
Group Share		5 minutes

FIGURE 23-5 Structure of Readers' Workshop

ten-minute), powerful, focused lessons with practical application (rather than lengthy lectures). A minilesson has an opening statement and engages students in inquiry, usually using mentor texts, that leads to a principle. You use several texts that the students have already heard in read aloud as examples from which the students generalize the understanding. Lessons build on each other, and often you will make a visual representation in the form of a chart that can be referred to again. (For greater detail, see *Guiding Readers and Writers* (2000), *Teaching for Comprehending and Fluency* (2006), and *Genre Study* (2012). We describe *umbrella minilessons* as broader categories within which there are several related minilessons. For example, "character" or "biography" may be umbrellas for several lessons within the category. This enables you to help your students develop deep knowledge of concepts instead of jumping from one lesson to another.

Minilessons can be further categorized as:

1. *Management Minilessons*. These lessons cover the routines of reading workshop, how readers choose books, and how and why they might abandon a book. Most of your minilessons at the beginning of the year will focus on management so you can get the workshop going smoothly. But you will continue to use management minilessons to help students work in more complex ways and to take care of any problems that might arise.

2. *Literary Analysis Minilessons*. You can use literary analysis minilessons to build students' awareness of the characteristics of various genres and of the elements of fiction and nonfiction texts. Literary analysis minilessons are an important component of genre study. You are always implicitly teaching about literary analysis in interactive read-aloud sessions; consider carrying these mentor texts over to minilessons to make them explicit. Discuss examples of literary elements and techniques and have students then apply their understanding to their books of choice.

3. *Strategies and Skills Minilessons*. Most teaching that has to do with processing a text effectively is best done in guided reading lessons with an appropriate-level book for the students. There are a few general lessons that may serve as reminders and may be helpful to the group such as noticing parts in words and reading punctuation.

4. *Writing About Reading Minilessons*. Writing about reading supports comprehension and offers an opportunity for students to reflect on their understanding of a text by drawing about it or writing about it. Writing about Reading Minilessons introduce the idea of keeping a reader's notebook, and provide examples of ways that students can respond to both fiction and nonfiction texts.

Establish routines for the minilesson. Students should have a specific place to sit—sitting on a carpet or on their chairs works well. Be sure that everyone can see your chart and hear you (see Figure 23-6), and can see and hear each other. If your class is too large for one circle, you could have a smaller circle on the carpet and others behind them in chairs. But be sure that students are not packed too closely together, where they might distract each other. The main goal is for them to have a comfortable place to listen, view, and talk.

FIGURE 23-6 A Minilesson in a Fourth-Grade Classroom

Independent Reading, Individual Conferences, and Small-Group Work

After the minilesson, students engage in silent, independent reading of the books they choose. The process is identical to that described above except for the following:

▶ Usually they will take something from the minilesson to intensify their attention during reading. For example, you might teach a brief minilesson using mentor texts (from interactive read-aloud) on the main characters in a book and how the author reveals them. As they read, students notice the characters in their own books. Of course, this example applies only to fiction, but you can teach a variety of minilessons to include concepts and principles that apply to nonfiction or to both fiction and nonfiction. Rosemary worked with her students to state the writer's message in several of the books she had read aloud to them (see Figure 23-7). Students were accustomed to talking about the writer's purpose and the writer's main message (or messages), so Rosemary could quickly write a statement of message next to the title and author on a chart. Then say, "Today when you are reading your book, think about what the writer is

Think about the author's message to help you understand the story.		
Title	Author	Message(s)
When Jessie Came Across the Sea	Amy Hest	When you face your fears, you learn to believe in yourself. With hope and optimism, you can achieve your goals.
Uncle Jed's Barbershop	Margaree King Mitchell	With hard work and determination, you can overcome great obstacles and realize your dreams. Love can sustain you through difficult times.
Crow Call	Lois Lowry	Time and love can heal many wounds. It's important to enjoy the time you have with people you love.

FIGURE 23-7 Minilesson Chart: Identifying Messages in a Story

really trying to say—the message of the book, and we'll share your thinking at the end of our time." Students thus were more purposeful in reading—not to get "the right answer" but to have some thoughts to share with their peers.

▌ You might ask students to include their thinking about the minilesson principle in their weekly letters, leaving the chart as a reminder. It will help students to write their letters when they have these suggestions. In the example described above, Rosemary reminded students to write a paragraph describing the writer's message for their independent reading books.

While students are reading independently, you can choose to engage students in one or more of three instructional approaches.

Individual Conferences. You can have individual conferences with students. These conferences are brief (three to five minutes) and they serve the following purposes:

▌ Reviewing what the student is reading and asking for his response.

▌ Reviewing the students' reading list and making suggestions.

▌ Sampling some oral reading to check on accuracy and fluency.

▌ Taking a systematic reading record as ongoing assessment data.

▌ Helping the student understand something about the book he is reading.

▌ Teaching for specific strategic actions, for example, fluency or word analysis following the sampling of oral reading.

▌ Finding out more about the students' preferences and interests, including genres.

▌ Focusing on the minilesson principle as applied to this student's reading, which often results in the student having something specific to share at the end of the period.

▌ Helping the student choose a book or write in their reader's notebook.

When you first begin the readers' workshop, you will spend all or most of your time engaging students in individual conferences to get to know them. Be sure they are making good book choices and help them become self-managed.

Guided Reading Groups. You can bring together small groups of students for guided reading lessons while students are reading silently or writing in their notebooks. Most teachers find that they can hold about two to three guided reading groups per day and two or three individual conferences. Sometimes, while students are in the guided reading group (and if you do not feel the need to listen to every student read orally), you can leave the table for two or three individual conferences, coming back for the discussion, teaching points, and word work.

If you have four reading groups, then, you might need to rotate them so that each group has at least three or four lessons per week with greater frequency for the lowest achieving readers if possible (see Figure 23-8). C and D have seven guided readings groups in a two-week period, and Groups A and B have eight. You can equalize this by taking four groups for two days in the two-week period. Or, you might decide that some students need less support and some need more. You could vary this schedule by having the groups who need the most help meet five

Guided Reading Group Schedule: Option 1

	Monday	Tuesday	Wednesday	Thursday	Friday
Week 1	Group A Group B Group C	Group D Group A Group B	Group C Group D Group A	Group B Group C Group D	Group A Group B Group C
Week 2	Group D Group A Group B	Group C Group D Group A	Group B Group C Group D	Group A Group B Group C	Group D Group A Group B

FIGURE 23-8 Guided Reading Group Schedule, Option 1

Guided Reading Group Schedule: Option 2

Monday	Tuesday	Wednesday	Thursday	Friday
Group A	Group A	Group C	Group B	Group A
Group B	Group D	Group D	Group C	Group B
Group C	Group B	Group A	Group A	Group D

FIGURE 23-9 Guided Reading Group Schedule, Option 2

days a week and other groups meet three or four days (see Figure 23-9). It is important to be systematic in planning for a two- or three-week period so that you can prepare for groups and do not unintentionally neglect any group of students.

Book clubs. You can find a great deal of information on book clubs (literature discussion groups) in our books *Teaching for Comprehending and Fluency, Guiding Readers and Writers,* and *Genre Study.* You can also view book clubs on *The Continuum of Literacy Learning Teaching Library* video collection.

Book clubs are a highly enjoyable and productive way to help students deepen their thinking about books by bringing their thinking together with that of their peers (see Figure 23-10). You give students a choice of three or four books, which you have carefully selected to be excellent subjects for discussion. Students select their books of choice, and that book becomes the book they read during independent reading time and/or at home. Schedule book

FIGURE 23-10 Students and Teacher Participating in Book Club

clubs in a way that leaves students time to complete the reading of the book. Another approach is to have students meet after reading a section of a book (several chapters), discuss that part of the book, and then meet again after reading more. As with other books they hear and read independently, they can write about their book club texts in their reader's notebook.

The critical characteristic of book clubs is that students learn more about conversing with each other about a book that they have read in common. Groups are *not* organized by level; instead, students make their choices according to their own interests. If the book is too hard for some of them to read independently, you may make it available as an audio book. (For students' first book clubs, you might start with books you have read aloud to them if you have multiple paperback copies.)

Book clubs are an excellent instructional approach but they do not take the place of guided reading in which you can make strong instructional moves to lift the individual student's control of strategic actions. But once guided reading lessons are going well and the management system is working, you may want to schedule book clubs for all students about once or twice a month. Make your decisions according to the needs of your class.

Your presence in the book club is just as important as your presence in guided reading. Book club is not a situation where you can simply leave students together and tell them to "talk about the book." They may not know *how* (this is the usual case), and only your guidance can keep them grounded in the text and push them to deeper understanding. Students may make points about the book but may not be listening or responding to each other, or be able to back up their points with evidence from the book. Much of the time, they will be talking to and responding to each other, so your role may not look as important as it does in guided reading; however, your intervention and guidance at the right moment can make all the difference.

Sharing Time

At the end of each readers' workshop period, bring students together for a brief sharing period (about five minutes). Usually, you go back to the minilesson principle, asking students for their comments on the texts they are reading. For example, you might ask students to quickly state the writer's message in the books they are currently reading. They hold the book up, state the title and author, and make a brief statement of the writer's message. At other times, you might have students "buzz" with a partner, in triads, or in a group of four to share thinking about some aspect of a text. Students enjoy being "the authority" on the books they are reading. Often, the session sparks interest in books that their peers are reading. The sharing session also gives you an opportunity to assess the effectiveness of your minilesson.

Transitioning with Younger Children

In grade two or even grade three, you may have students who are just beginning to sustain attention to texts and have little experience managing themselves independently. You may want to structure the independent work period so that it includes three independent tasks:

- ❱ Reading books of their choice.
- ❱ Writing in a reader's notebook.
- ❱ Completing one carefully designed word study/phonics activity with a partner.

The word-study activity can be an outcome of the phonics/word-study minilesson that you teach at another part of the day. These activities can be individual or involve partners or a group of four using quiet voices. Students can learn to complete three tasks during the alloted time.

When students are called to the guided reading group during independent work time, they set aside their materials and go to the group. Then, they return to whatever they were doing. This kind of transition may not be needed very long as students begin to build stamina for reading for increasing amounts of time.

Getting Started with a Readers' Workshop

It is obvious that a good start has big payoff in classroom management, students' time independently reading, and on talking and writing about reading. In our book, *Guiding Readers and Writers* we described in detail the first twenty to thirty days of independent reading, and we have received feedback from teachers that the chapter is helpful. In Figure 23-11, we summarize briefly an example of steps for getting a readers' workshop started. There may be many variations but you can get a sense of how the readers are learning some foundational principles.

Of course, the sequence would need to be adjusted to fit the competencies of your students. You may need to digress to repeat a minilesson on managing the readers' workshop. It will help students if each minilesson has a visual artifact—a chart you can display so that they can refer to it as they carry out their reading. Students need to learn that they can monitor their own preferences and progress over time so that they understand how they are changing.

Readers' workshop must be viewed by students not as a tedious assignment that they are doing for someone else but as a normal, everyday activity that they are engaging in for themselves. They have choice, and that means they have power and self-efficacy. At the same time, they are part of a community in which readers share their thinking on a regular basis and are responsible for listening to and responding to each other. The readers' workshop brings together both individual interests and the shared experiences of a literate community. Students read at a sharper edge when they know they will be sharing their thoughts with peers in their classroom. They are personally motivated because they have choice. In addition to providing an excellent management system, the workshop engages students in massive amounts of daily reading and in writing about reading.

We have written in depth about the teacher's role in helping students learn how to use a variety of forms to write about their reading (*Teaching for Comprehending and Fluency* 2006, *Genre Study* 2012, *Guiding Readers and Writers* 2001). When students write about their reading they share their thinking and deepen their understandings about texts. They develop academic vocabulary and a sense of agency. Refer to *The Literacy Continuum* (Writing About Reading section) for goals specific to your grade level.

Getting a Readers' Workshop Started in Thirty Days

GOAL(S)	KEY PRINCIPLES FOR STUDENTS TO LEARN
DAY 1 — Introduce the organization of the classroom library. Help students learn how to select and return books. Explain voice levels.	▶ There are specific ways to select and return books in the classroom so that all students can find and use them easily. ▶ Choose a book that will be interesting and enjoyable to you. ▶ Read silently and do not talk with others so you and your peers can do your best thinking while reading.
DAY 2 — Help students understand how to choose books.	▶ Choose books in many different ways (e.g., topic, author, genre). ▶ Think carefully about your book choices.
DAY 3 — Show students how to make good book choices.	▶ Books can be easy, just-right, or difficult for you. ▶ Choose just-right books most of the time.
DAY 4 — Ask students to think about their reading.	▶ Reading is thinking. Think about what you understand and about how you feel about what you understand.
DAY 5 — Help students talk with others about their thinking.	▶ You can talk with a partner or a small group to share your thinking about your reading. ▶ You can understand more about a book by talking with others about your reading.
DAY 6 — Help students understand that they can abandon a book if they have a reason.	▶ Abandon a book for a specific reason after giving it a good try (not interesting, too hard, want very much to read another book right now).
DAY 7 — Show students that they can choose books from a variety of fiction and nonfiction genres.	▶ There are fiction and nonfiction books, and you need to know the difference between them. ▶ Within fiction and nonfiction, there are different genres.
DAY 8 — Help students understand that there are different genres of fiction books.	▶ Within fiction texts, there are different genres. Over time, you need to distinguish between them (realistic fiction, fantasy, historical fiction, science fiction).
DAY 9 — Help students understand that there are different genres of nonfiction books.	▶ A biography is the story of a person's life and it is usually told in chronological order. ▶ Some nonfiction books may be told in chronological order and they are narrative nonfiction. ▶ Nonfiction books may be organized to present information in categories. These books have an expository structure.

FIGURE 23-11 Getting a Readers' Workshop Started in Thirty Days

| DAY 10 | Introduce the reader's notebook to the students. | ▶ Record thinking about reading in a letter in the reader's notebook. |

| DAY 11 | Ask students to write a letter to you in the readers' notebook. (Provide a model letter that you have written about your reading.) | ▶ Share thinking about reading by writing a letter in a reader's notebook.
▶ You can use the your teacher's example to write your first letter. |

| DAY 12 | Invite students to talk about their letters and your response. | ▶ Letters should express your thinking about books.
▶ Your teacher will respond to your letters. |

| DAY 13 | Teach students to keep a record of their reading in a reader's notebook. | ▶ You can keep a list of books you've read so that you can evaluate the quantity and quality of your reading. |

| DAY 14 | Teach students the guidelines for readers' workshop. | ▶ In the classroom, there are specific guidelines about how we can work together and help each other learn. |

| DAY 15 | Teach students to write one thoughtful letter (or other writing form) a week on the assigned day: Monday, Tuesday, Wednesday, Thursday | ▶ In the classroom, you need to share your thinking about your reading in a letter once a week.
▶ Your teacher will respond to you. |

| DAY 16 | Teach students to proofread their letters before putting them in the basket. | ▶ The letters you write in your notebook need to show your best work.
▶ Proofread the letter using guidelines. |

| DAY 17 | Help students understand that there are a variety of topics they can write about in letters. | ▶ There are many different kinds of thinking that you can write about in your reader's notebook (what the book is about, how the book makes you feel, why you think the author wrote the book, whether you would recommend the book to another reader, what you predict will happen, what you found interesting.) |

| DAY 18 | Teach students how to remember their thinking to prepare for writing in the reader's notebook. | ▶ Quick notes (stick-on or in the notebook) help you remember your thinking so you can use it to write letters or when you confer with your teacher. |

| DAY 19 | Teach students to create a list of their reading interests. | ▶ You can keep a list of your reading interests that will help you choose another book quickly.
▶ You can list authors you like, topics you are interested in, or genres you like.
▶ You can write titles of books that others have told you about. |

FIGURE 23-11 *(continued)*

DAY 20	Teach students how to make book recommendations for others.	▶ Choose books by listening to the recommendations of others. ▶ You can recommend books to others (tell something about the book that is interesting).
DAY 21	Help students notice when they lose understanding of a text. They need to search for information.	▶ Notice when the text doesn't make sense to you. ▶ Look for information to help you understand the writer's message.
DAY 22	Teach students strategies for solving unknown words (decoding).	▶ Use a variety of strategies to solve a new word. Take it apart by syllables or connect it to a word you already know.
DAY 23	Teach students strategies for deriving the meaning of new vocabulary words.	▶ Use the context of the sentence or paragraph to learn the meaning of new words in a book. ▶ Take words apart by syllables or connect with words you know to learn the meaning of a new word.
DAY 24	Help students understand how the punctuation helps them understand a text.	▶ Use punctuation to help you understand the writer's message.
DAY 25	Teach students how to improve their letters in the reader's notebook.	▶ You can look at examples of letters to analyze how other readers describe their thinking.
DAY 26	Help students infer the writer's message from the texts they are reading.	▶ As you read, think about why the writer wrote the book and what he is really trying to say. ▶ You can talk about your interpretation of the writer's message. Different people might have different interpretations.
DAY 27	Teach students to make notes in the reader's notebook to help in sharing time.	▶ Make brief notes on sticky notes or in your notebook. Be prepared to share with others what you have noticed about your reading.
DAY 28	Help students expand the ways they can write about their reading in the reader's notebook.	▶ Write about the story problem and resolution or about character change in fiction. ▶ Write about the problem and solution or cause and effect in nonfiction. ▶ Write in a variety of forms, (e.g., two-column writing, short write, web, etc.).
DAY 29	Help students understand the characteristics of genres.	▶ When you read, you need to think about the genre of the book and how it helps you read and understand it.
DAY 30	Teach students to describe the characteristics of genres.	▶ You can list characteristics of a genre after you have read some examples. ▶ You can categorize books according to the genre based on characteristics.

FIGURE 23-11 *(continued)*

Suggestions for Professional Development

This chapter can be used as a resource for looking at classrooms and refining management plans. Let's focus on the first thirty days of readers' workshop. Teachers can implement these first thirty days any time that they start to implement readers' workshop, but they should have all of the materials in place (classroom library, readers' notebooks, and read-aloud books). As an alternative, hold the meeting toward the end of school, focusing on the beginning of the new school year. Having the plan will give teachers time to reflect and refine it over the vacation period, and to gather and organize supplies before the term starts.

1. As a group, look at the plan for the first thirty days. Talk about changes you would make and revise the plan to meet your needs. (You may want to extend it to a forty or fifty-day plan).

2. Then, as individuals or as a group, draw up a general plan for the first thirty days of readers' workshop that is doable in your own circumstances.

3. Make a list of the materials and supplies you will need, including materials such as books for choosing in the classroom library, reader's notebook, and so on. Have a creative discussion of how to acquire these materials at little or no cost.

4. Finally, make an "action plan" of tasks that you need to do to make the start of school dynamic and successful. Each person may want to work on her own; or, you may find it useful to pool resources and assign a few tasks to each person.

Hold a meeting on the first day that teachers are in the school to go over the plan and share what you have gathered and thought about over the vacation time. Hold another meeting at the end of the month of implementation to compare progress and solve problems.

CHAPTER 24

A Design for Language and Literacy Instruction

The secret of change is to focus all of your energy, not on fighting the old, but on building the new.

—Socrates

As you have read the chapters in this book, we hope some core values and beliefs about language and literacy learning come through again and again. The classroom is a place where students, as a diverse community, are thinking, talking, reading, and writing about their world. In a sense, the classroom is a sheltered environment within a noisy world where everything interferes with high-level intellectual discourse and time for reading and writing. But in these short years students have a chance to live a literate life that expands their empathy, curiosity, and competencies. Literacy is their *job*. If they are not provided time for literacy in school, then when can they become immersed in the wonderful world of books and the doors they open to understanding themselves and their world? When students spend their time thinking, reading, writing, and talking every day, they get a message about what is valued in your classroom and they begin to develop their own values.

You may have a vision for what you would *like* your classroom to be but find the concept so overwhelming that it is hard to know where to start. There are real constraints, and money is not even the most important of them. Too many times, school and district personnel have spent large proportions of the budget on sets of materials that *promised* instant success and delivered little. We recall an enormously expensive set of audio materials and textbooks designed to help elementary students develop "economic understandings" that did little more than teaching the words *consumers* and *producers* (both of which were immediately forgotten). It will be a shock for you to learn that the program started with first graders. It didn't take long for these materials to begin gathering dust on the shelves taking up a lot of room. And, unfortunately, that is what happens with many expensive educational materials.

It would be nice to have unlimited funds, but you wouldn't want to buy even good materials with "one click" because many costly mistakes would be made. You want to collect materials, *mostly* good books, carefully, perhaps acquiring them in a modular way, and be sure that you are ready to put forth the effort and acquire the expertise to use them effectively.

The major constraint is the enormous amount of decision making that must go into the landscaping of literacy education in every classroom. The process begins with imagining it and having a vision for what literacy classrooms can be like. It's challenging, but that doesn't mean you shouldn't start. Even the first steps can be exciting. The development of your own expertise is of prime importance in the process. Think of the process of change as a journey that will take several years, if not more. In fact, teaching is a profession that requires continuous learning. The more you learn, the more you understand about what there is to learn; and the reward comes as you see your highly engaged students and their growing competencies.

Effective teaching is *responsive* to the learners. It means that you are able to notice the strengths of individuals and build on their competencies. Instead of expecting them to be where you are, you have to bring the teaching to where they are. To us this means teaching in a way that recognizes individual strengths and needs. It means respecting linguistic and cultural diversity. Responsive teachers have real conversations with students; they value their thinking and opinions; they encourage talk. Lessons are carefully planned and systematic; but there is always room for moment-to-moment adjustment given student response. Classroom routines are established so that teachers and students are free to engage in the conversations that are needed to extend thinking.

Responsive teaching also means creating in the classroom a microcosm of democracy. Students are responsible, sensitive members of a community; they learn to work together, help each other and solve problems together. Teachers are concerned not only about *what* students learn but also about *how* they learn. A spirit of inquiry and intellectual curiosity permeates the classroom. And the educators in the school offer a model of collaboration and continual learning.

Throughout these chapters we have emphasized the importance of your expertise in several essential areas:

- Systematic observation and assessment of reading and writing behaviors.
- Understanding the systems of strategic actions within the reading process—behaviors and understandings to notice, teach for, and support.
- The characteristics of texts—how texts support readers and provide opportunities to learn.
- Making effective teaching decisions within the guided reading lesson.
- Documenting student learning over time.
- Teaching students to be self-regulated learners.
- Planning and organizing for efficient, effective teaching.
- Responding to the precise learning needs of individuals.

Once you have started to imagine what you want your classroom to be, begin to develop the common set of understandings and values that make up a vision. This is easier to accomplish if you and your colleagues work as a team toward a common vision so that, from grade to grade, your students will have consistent, coherent opportunities as literate people from grade to grade.

Guided reading is not the entire literacy program; rather, it is a vital and necessary part of it. In this chapter, we discuss a design for literacy—one that can be built over time. We have titled this chapter "A Design for Language and Literacy Instruction" (rather than just for literacy) to indicate that language is an integral part of the teaching. All of your students are constantly learning language as they extend their literacy, so, you are also a language teacher.

From Vision to Design

Turning a vision into action requires the process of design. Design is a plan for a system that works in a coherent way. Every component fits with others in a streamlined whole and works for the accomplishment of a worthy goal. In our case, that goal is the growth of individuals who not only use literacy in a highly proficient way but use literacy to create a high quality of life. That means having a sense of agency and finding enjoyment and *pleasure*.

A good design has aesthetic, functional, economic, and sociopolitical elements. It may seem lofty to think of the classroom as if it is a giant software company; yet, we can see some parallels.

▶ *Aesthetic.* You want the classroom to be a beautiful, hospitable, and comfortable place that welcomes all students. You could spend an entire year just creating the environment for learning! Luckily, once the basic classroom structure is established, your students can and will help because they have ownership.

▶ *Functional.* The classroom is well organized and accessible to the members of the community. You may have to try several different arrangements before you find exactly what works best, but your students will contribute.

▶ *Economic.* The most must be made of every dollar, so that students have the books and other materials they need and deserve. Once a precious item is acquired, everyone pitches in to take care of it. You don't need to have conflicting materials (such as twenty-four copies of one hardback book that only a few students at a time will be reading) and you don't need storage for materials you never use. Be efficient and economical. Remember, you don't really need a lot of "stuff." Real books, notebooks, folders, paper, chart paper, materials for working with words, writing and drawing tools, and technological tools for communication and research—that's about it.

▶ *Sociopolitical.* The more your classroom is like a community and the less like a factory, the happier you and your students will be and the higher the achievement. The classroom must be culturally responsive and inclusive of every student that learns there.

So if you have read this book, regard it not as an end point but just the beginning of learning more.

The Vision of a Learning Community

There are two ways to go about teaching: (1) close your door and, within limits, teach the way you know and like; (2) become part of a learning community that actively pursues a common vision. The first choice avoids criticism and the time needed for collaboration, but it limits your growth and opportunities for your students to benefit from the community. Teaching is an increasingly public activity so that it is neither wise nor desirable to take the "behind the door" position. Besides, it just isn't much fun. On your greatest days, you want to share the thrilling evidence of learning you see; on your low days, you need empathetic and useful advice from colleagues.

We favor embracing the open door and becoming part of a learning community of colleagues—all of whom share common goals, take risks, and find the rewards of continuous professional growth. This takes time and problem solving but if achieved, it will have big payoff for students. Here we talk not only of your teacher colleagues at your grade level but of *everyone* in the school—from the maintenance staff, to the office and administration, to teachers at every grade level, to specialist educators who serve particular populations. Work together with other adults to achieve the kind of consistency and coherence that students need, including a predictable environment and a clear sense of what is expected of them across the grades and across subject matter. In this way, every time they engage in problem-solving actions, they will learn more. Messages will not be mixed; confusions will be avoided. Almost all of us have experienced the varying definition of "good" from one setting to another. When students receive consistent signals, *school makes sense to them.* They learn what it means to collaborate, solve problems, articulate rationales, and share ownership of outcomes.

We know that teachers are individuals, and of course, you develop your own individual styles. But in pursuit of coherence, hold some things in common across the school for the benefit of student learning. Some examples are listed below.

Common Values and Beliefs

Work with colleagues in your school to establish a set of core values that will form the backbone for every decision you make. Many values are implied across the chapters in this book, for example:

- Students learn to read by reading continuous text.
- Students need time to think and talk about reading.
- Students need time to think and talk about writing.
- Students need time to engage in authentic reading and writing, behaving as literate people.

As you work toward a set of core values, you can generate a long list, but you don't want too many. A set of values is not the same as a comprehensive curriculum. It's a known set of statements that gives you a touchstone against which to measure your decisions.

Common Understandings About Learning

When teachers with a common vision work together over time, and have the lift of excellent professional learning, they develop a common knowledge about the nature of learning. When you and your colleagues share a view of the constructive learner and the zone of proximal development (see Chapter 8), then everyone is watching for the same kind of evidence. Colleagues work at the cutting edge of student learning, support independence and student agency, and understand the critical role of teaching in leading learning forward. Teachers need a common theory of the reading and writing process to ground teaching. In this book we have discussed reading and writing as complex processes. Give yourself time to develop your theory as you engage in practice.

Common Curriculum Goals

We constructed *The Fountas & Pinnell Literacy Continuum* to be used as a tool for planning and assessing language and literacy. We described the behaviors and understandings that are observable in proficient readers and writers at each grade level and at each text level on the gradient for guided reading. This is a curriculum of proficiency. The evidence is in what students do as readers and writers and in what they say. You will find that it exceeds local, state, and national standards and provides great specificity to guide assessment and teaching. A common curriculum means coherence across the grades and supports a common language for talking about teaching and learning.

Common Ways of Assessing Learning

There can be no coherence if everyone evaluates learning in a different way. Common assessments drive coherent instruction. From grade to grade, students need the secure sense that their progress is appreciated by the adults who teach them. Teachers, too, need ways of talking about progress so that they have the satisfaction of seeing "our students" move toward high levels of literacy.

Common Language

Language weaves a community together, and it is developed through communication and problem solving. A common language has two advantages: (1) it enables teachers to talk with each other in a meaningful way; and, (2) it communicates most clearly to students. The same or similar language coming from a variety of sources constantly prompts and reinforces problem solving and deeper thinking. The *Prompting Guides* are designed as a resource for facilitative language that, once learned, becomes part of the fabric of teaching.

Common Instructional Procedures

What if students learn the routines for independent reading (see Chapters 2 and 22) in grade one, and they continue to engage with the same although with increasingly challenging content, instructional procedures throughout the next five or six years? Would it be easier to implement the literacy design? Even if half the students move away, the other half will be there to demonstrate and teach the instructional routines. Books change and grow astronomically in complexity; the interactions change; and the readers change. Sustained concentration time increases (to the limits of time available). But the basic instructional routines remain the same.

We do recommend a shared set of instructional practices that teachers are helping each other to implement. They can share materials, ideas, successes, and problems. Moving toward a coherent set of instructional procedures is, again, a journey. You might not be able to implement everything the first year. But when critical numbers of teachers implement these practices in a school, always improving over time, energy builds. Students enter new classrooms and experience some welcome familiarity. You and your colleagues find it easier and smoother to implement them. While you always refresh your book collections and think of new ideas, you have some very dependable pieces on which to build.

Some Differences

All of the above commonalities are *not the same as having all students on the same page in the same materials in the same sequence.* While values, language, and instructional practice are held in common, teachers choose materials. Instruction is differentiated. Groups are formed for many reasons and in many ways. You cannot achieve coherence simply by adopting a massive core system and forcing it into place. There are too many negative consequences. Thousands of times, districts have made big purchases with the promise of raising achievement and they have been disappointed.

Moving Toward High Expertise

At first, just as with anything new, you may find that some of the assessment and teaching actions we have described feel awkward and that you are implementing them in a clumsy way. It may take more time. It is true that the acquisition of new learning sometimes causes a "shake up" of existing knowledge, so everything is disturbed. As the new learning takes hold, though, you reconcile what you know already with the new understandings, and smoothly operating procedures grow as a result. Remember, we all have more learning to do every year of teaching. As McKay (2012) says, "You Don't Have to Be a Bad Teacher to Get Better." We have recommended professional development as a necessary support for all teachers at all levels, and it can take different forms:

Engage in self-study. Today, many resources are available in addition to excellent professional books. Our website, for example, offers video samples of lessons and other materials. You can join "chats" and follow blogs, always keeping in mind that you may encounter an overload of opposing views and a confusing array of "tips." Talk with a colleague to sort out what is truly helpful and coherent with your understandings of literacy learning. Don't try to do everything. Your classroom and your school need to be simple and clear—not "Christmas trees" on which you just hang everything you find.

Find more expert others. You can take the opportunity to observe more experienced teachers in your school or district. If you are lucky there will be a great mentor right in your school, and keep in mind that within a few years, you will be assuming that role. If you are already in a mentoring position, be sure that your protégée gets a chance to see many examples of teaching and to discuss them with you. The strongest learning comes from viewing many examples of the same kinds of lessons and generalizing across them. Otherwise, learning becomes imitation rather than thinking.

Self-assess. Take the time to reflect on your teaching. Select one instructional setting a week and analyze: How did it go? How did students respond? What shifts in learning are you confident that took place? Don't get mired in the details or expect to do everything perfectly, but notice whether you and your students are beginning to handle routines smoothly and automatically, leaving more time for rich talk and thinking. Call in a colleague to observe, and talk through your self-assessment with her. For the purpose of guided reading, we include A Guide for Self-Assessment in Guided Reading at the end of this chapter and in Online Resources (resources.fountasandpinnell.com). It is comprehensive, but you can select one or only a few areas at a time. We also include a simpler and more abbreviated self-reflection form (Self-Assessment: Getting Started with Guided Reading) at the end of this chapter and in Online Resources. In our other professional books and on our website, you will find many such tools to support your continuous learning. Perhaps the most valuable aspect of self-reflection and professional development is the talk and problem solving that takes place between colleagues as a result.

Engage in coaching. Many schools are moving in the direction of having a teacher leader or a trained literacy coach to support teachers, and this has been shown to have a highly positive effect (see Biancarosa, Bryk, and Dexter 2010). There should be some cautions: A literacy coach is not an "inspector" to be sure teachers are "doing it right." Nor, is the literacy coach the person to simply tell teachers what to do. A literacy coach is a partner and a leader in the process of inquiring into practice. If you have a literacy coach in your school, take advantage of the opportunity to get an experienced observer to work with you. You may *be* a literacy coach; in this case, we offer *The Literacy Continuum* as a resource for collaborative inquiry. You "corner the conversation" by keeping the focus on student learning and you engage in continuous inquiry as you think together about teaching and learning. Sometimes, teachers gain a great deal from "peer coaching." Colleagues work together with neither having huge reservoirs of expertise, but they use resources like this book and *The Literacy Continuum,* as they work to make sense of their observations and build their expertise in a direction of coherence.

Participate in school-based and off-site professional development. Meetings are the staple of professional development for teachers. This kind of training is least effective when someone just gets a speaker, and the group comes together expecting to be entertained. A series of speakers with no relationship to each other can lead to fragmented learning at best. Sometimes, a person with high expertise can be brought into a school for a period of time both to coach and to conduct sessions on a particular topic. The best kind of professional development is not a "one off," but consists of an ongoing series that supports growth in expertise over time.

Seek the best professional learning opportunities you can find. Don't be discouraged if you are occasionally disappointed, but do find something to think about and learn from every experience you have. Luckily, opportunities to learn are much more available now even for teachers in wide-apart, rural communities. You can find virtual learning communities. We created the Fountas & Pinnell Literacy™ community (www.fountasandpinnell.com) to offer an Internet "home" for teachers, literacy leaders, and district administrators who have similar values and beliefs and are engaged in the kinds of practices we discuss here. It is a way to connect and converse with others and to select resources that elevate your expertise. Make www.fountasandpinnell.com your daily literacy retreat to reflect, recharge, research, and redefine your literacy instruction. We invite you to join the conversation and become a member today.

A Comprehensive Design

A comprehensive design offers opportunities for language and literacy learning with an underlying coherent theory of the reading and writing process. Instructional routines are built on understandings about learning and how students develop as readers, writers, and language users.

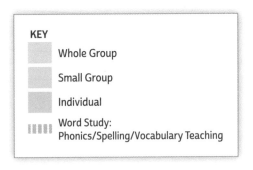

FIGURE 24-1 Key for Different Settings in a Coherent Literacy Design

Each setting is described in different parts of this book and in our other professional books. We will define them briefly here as a kind of summary. Notice the key that applies to the different settings. (See Figure 24-1)

In Figure 24-2, you see a layout of a basic coherent literacy design. This broad approach can be adapted to meet local needs. And, you will want to select where you start and collaboratively decide where you go next. There are some variations for primary and intermediate students of course, and time periods will vary (see sample schedules in Chapter 21). The middle school plan with departmentalization may incorporate a limited number of the elements. But, in general a group of teachers across the grades can share the design for instruction and students benefit from the predictability and consistency they experience.

Whole-Group Teaching

Whole-group instructional contexts are signaled by the color green. It is highly efficient in terms of your instructional time to do some things with the entire class at once. It is also helpful in building community to have several times a day when the whole group meets together to share learning. They are:

- *Interactive Read-Aloud.* You select a text (usually a group of texts that are connected in some way) and read-aloud to the class. Students are invited to discuss the text. Interactive read aloud includes specialized studies that focus on genre, authors, illustrators, or the craft of writing.

- *Shared/Interactive Writing.* You invite students to collaboratively compose a message, story, or informational text and then act as their scribe. In interactive writing you "share the pen." Students take ownership for the

A Design for Responsive Literacy Teaching

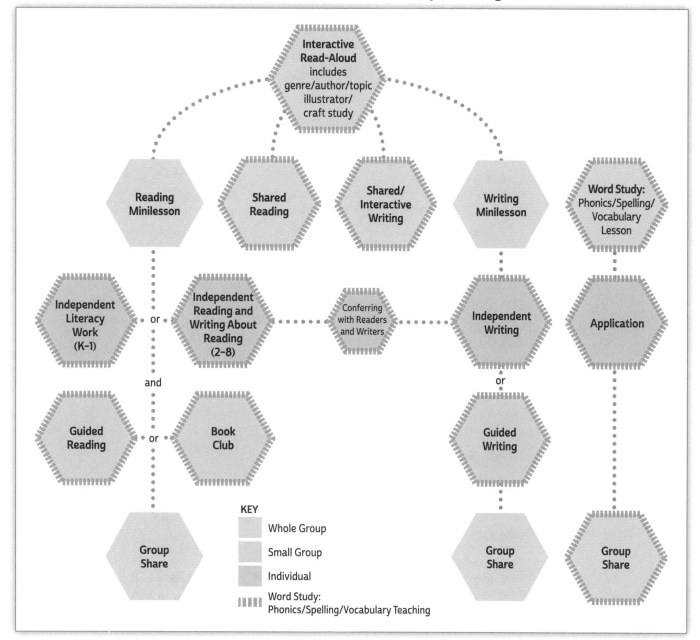

© 2017 by Irene C. Fountas and Gay Su Pinnell from *Guided Reading*, Second Edition. Portsmouth, NH: Heinemann.

FIGURE 24-2 A Design for Responsive Literacy Teaching

piece of writing and it can be used to extend reading. In the course of constructing, or writing, the text, there are opportunities to teach *phonics, spelling, and vocabulary.*

▶ *Shared Reading.* Students read together from a common text (either enlarged or individually held copies). Texts are read several times and in the process there is the opportunity to teach *phonics, spelling, and vocabulary.* (See Chapters 3 and 4.)

▶ *Reading Minilessons.* You present a pre-planned, short explicit minilesson on any aspect of reading (using the mentor text from read aloud) and students immediately apply the principle as they read independently.

▶ *Writing Minilessons.* You present a pre-planned, short explicit minilesson on any aspect of writing—craft, conventions, or process. Students immediately apply the minilesson principle to their own independent writing.

▶ *Word Study Minilessons (phonics, spelling, and vocabulary).* You present a pre-planned, brief minilesson to help students learn an important principle about how words work and what they mean. Phonics lessons are sequential, inquiry based, and highly systematic (see Phonics Section, *The Literacy Continuum* and *Phonics Lessons: K, 1, 2, and Word Study 3).* An application activity enables active involvement and opportunity to discover more.

▶ *Group Share.* After independent and small group work in word study, reading, and writing, you bring the whole class together again so that students can share their learning. You will have several "group shares" a day. They take about five minutes and relate back to the principles students have learned and applied.

Small-Group Teaching

Small-group teaching is signaled by the color blue. We see three kinds of small group teaching for literacy, with one (guided reading) engaging students who are similar in level of development in reading a common text, one heterogeneous group (book club) and one needs-based group (guided writing).

▶ *Guided Reading.* Through careful assessment and observation, you bring together a group of students who are similar enough in the development of a reading process that they can be taught together. You select a text that has learning opportunities for each member, introduce it, and support the students in reading it. Guided reading is characterized by discussion, and it offers an opportunity for very specific teaching. At the end of the lesson, you engage in some specific teaching of *phonics or vocabulary.*

▶ *Book Clubs.* Thinking about the interests of your group and the instructional goals you have, you select a set of texts that will spark good discussion. Students choose one of the texts and you form book clubs. During independent reading time, students prepare for the discussion. Book clubs are convened in a way similar to guided reading groups but students do not need to be at a similar level. The emphasis is on discussion; students learn to talk with each other about books and deepen their thinking. There is opportunity to expand *vocabulary* and awareness of the literary characteristics of texts.

▶ *Guided Writing.* During writer's workshop, you may bring together a small group of students who for a temporary period need to work on the same aspect of writing—conventions, craft, or process. (You make this determination through conferences and by examining their writing.) It makes sense to teach them efficiently in a group. When the new learning is accomplished, the group is disbanded.

Individual Teaching

Individual teaching is signaled by the color purple. It's hard to find time for individual teaching, but it adds greatly not only to your knowledge of students' progress but to the impact you make on them. We identify four times you can have individual instruction for literacy:

▶ *Word Study Application.* After the minilessons, students engage in a "hands on" activity that allows them to apply the principle. They work with a partner or a small group; they may work at tables or the word study center. You can take the opportunity to circulate, checking the progress of individuals and interacting briefly. Over several days, you will have done some individual teaching with each student and have a good idea of their understanding.

▶ *Independent Literacy Work (K–1).* While you are working with small groups of students, younger readers engage in a range of routines that you have carefully taught. These include independent reading, writing, and work with words. It may also involve poetry or other literacy-related tasks. Between groups, you may decide to have brief conferences with individuals so that you hear some of their reading and have a chance to discuss reading with them.

▶ *Independent Reading and Writing About Reading* (2–8). After the minilessons, students have a period of time that they use for independent reading of books that they choose. Also, they write about their reading in a reader's notebook. During this time, you can take the opportunity to hold individual reading conferences that include looking at the reader's notebook with the student, talking about the books and genres he has read, discussing the book he is currently reading or is going to read next. You may sample some oral reading and take the time to do some individual teaching. These conferences are brief, but you learn a great deal about the student and can help him make good choices.

▶ *Independent Writing.* After the writing minilessons, students work individually on their own pieces of writing. They may be at any place in the process of planting seeds in a writer's notebook, drafting, revising, editing, or final draft. You can hold individual writing conferences to go over the writing with the student and do some individual teaching.

Varied Opportunities

Talk permeates each of the contexts listed here; and the talk is different within each. There are different opportunities for learning across this design but all contribute to the goal of creating active, thoughtful readers and writers.

The Goals of Responsive Teaching

We see no reason not to dream for our students. Our goal is to give them the opportunity for a literate life—not just to achieve a minimum test score. This means learning how to behave in the ways that are characteristic of real readers and writers; that is, the way literate citizens of the world think, talk, and act. Within the social world of the classrooms, students learn what it means to be a citizen of a democratic society. Through books and electronic media they learn outside the classroom walls. They learn how to collaborate, how to learn, how to solve problems. They become individuals who:

- Read a lot, read voluntarily, read in many genres, and read with enthusiasm
- Write a lot, write voluntarily, use writing as a tool for thinking and a basis for talking, write about their reading
- Use reading and writing for real purposes
- Read in many genres; write in many genres
- Base decisions on the purpose for reading or writing
- Collect books and refer to favorites again, drawing on a rich repertoire as a resource for writing and for comprehending other texts
- Know authors, illustrators, genres, forms, and styles of writing
- Recommend books, authors, series, and genres to others
- Reflect on their reading and writing accomplishments and set goals
- Talk about their reading and writing with others
- Think critically about texts they read
- Discuss texts with feeling and intensity
- Write passionately about their own thinking and beliefs
- Access powerful language in the writing of others
- Construct arguments in talk and writing with logic and evidence
- Value the thinking of other readers and writers
- See themselves as contributing to the learning of others
- See themselves as readers and writers

We hope we can describe ourselves as highly literate people who demonstrate daily the characteristics listed above and who open doors for our students to do the same.

Suggestions for Professional Development

A Group Meeting to Begin the Vision

1. Convene a group of colleagues to answer the question: "If students are living a literate life in our school, what will we see if we walk through every classroom during literacy time?" Set some "ground rules," for example,

    ▶ Make every statement descriptive (something you can see or hear)?

    ▶ Don't tear down or criticize anyone's idea (or say "we already tried that" or "that can't happen here").

    ▶ Build on the ideas of others.

    ▶ Pause to wait and continue until all ideas have been exhausted.

2. Write responses on a large piece of chart paper. (If there are more than ten people at the meeting, consider dividing into small groups and having each group produce its own list and share them. Then, consolidate the items, removing duplications.)

3. Lead a discussion of the statements. Do these statements reflect what we really value here—our core values?

4. Ask the group to consider the list, give everyone four stick-on dots in four colors. Each person can place a dot on his/her top priorities as follows: Priority 1 = red; 2 = blue; 3 = yellow; 4 = green (or any order you wish) An individual can place one, or even all dots on an item.

5. Discuss the list. Remove items (or place them on a "wait" list) that receive no priorities. You now have a prioritized list of what everyone sees as important and the beginnings of a vision. Have a recorder type the list, with the "red" items first.

6. Hold another meeting to start planning steps toward the design.

Personal Reflection

1. Use your phone to make an audio or video recording of a guided reading lesson that you teach. (It's more interesting if you have a colleagues do the recording and reflect with you. You and a partner could take turns.)

2. Select one of the Self-Assessment forms in Figures 24-3 and 24-4 at the end of this chapter or in Online Resources (resources.fountasandpinnell.com) to reflect on your lesson.

3. Identify areas where you'd like to make some changes.

4. Write down a goal and three steps to take (or changes to make). You can't change everything at once.

5. Teach the same group for about two weeks, implementing between one and three changes.

6. Record the group again and use the form. Identify areas of progress and further need to refine your teaching of guided reading.

Self-Assessment: Getting Started with Guided Reading

Materials and Management	❑ Do I have a set of leveled books organized for selection (or access to a school book room)? ❑ Do I have the materials I need (chart or easel, magnetic letters, whiteboards, markers, sticky notes, white correction tape) accessible for efficient use at the table where I am teaching? ❑ Do I have an appropriate teaching table in a location that will enable students to view instruction and allow me to view the entire class?
Assessment and Record Keeping	❑ Do I have beginning-of-the year evidence of students' text reading at an appropriate instructional level so that I can form tentative groups? ❑ Do I have record-keeping forms organized for note taking during teaching? ❑ Do I have a plan for taking running records (or reading records) regularly with individual readers? ❑ Do I make notes during and after teaching that will help me plan for my next lesson?
Text Selection and Preparation	❑ Do I select appropriate texts for the group (content, language structures)? ❑ Do I **read the text** and contemplate the obstacles students may encounter so I can prepare a brief introduction and prepare them for valuable problem-solving? ❑ Do I consider the special considerations needed to support English Language Learners? ❑ Do I select important aspects of the text to discuss prior to reading? ❑ Do I note a few selected places to take students to during the introduction?

Teaching

Introduction to the Text	❑ Do I introduce the text to readers in a conversational way, so the students share their thinking and anticipate the text? ❑ Are the students engaged and interactive in the orientation? ❑ In the orientation, do I support the students' use of meaning, language, and visual information for their independent processing of the text?
Reading the Text	❑ Do I provide brief, helpful support to students as needed? ❑ Do I make notes of significant reading behaviors observed during reading?
Discussing and Revisiting the Text	❑ Do I engage the students in a meaningful discussion of the book? ❑ Do I promote the sharing of thinking by students instead of questioning only?
Teaching Decisions After Reading	❑ Do I make teaching decisions that help the readers process this book proficiently, but also apply what they learned how to do as readers to the proficient processing of other books?
Word Work	❑ Do I preplan one to three minutes of word work that actively engages students with letters and words? ❑ Do I have materials for active student work? ❑ Are word study materials organized for maximum efficiency?
Pace	❑ Am I able to teach lessons with all components within the time I have? ❑ Do I move efficiently from one part of the lesson to another?
Engagement	❑ Are students engaged and active throughout the lesson?

FIGURE 24-3 Self-Assessment: Getting Started with Guided Reading

Self-Assessment for Guided Reading

Teacher _____ **Date** _____

Grade Level   K   1   2   3   4   5   6   7   8

Directions: Use this rubric to make an assessment of your progress in teaching guided reading and to set goals. Mark the characteristic within each category that most clearly describes your teaching of guided reading at this time. There are two parts: (1) Getting Started, and (2) Reflection on Teaching.

GETTING STARTED

1. Classroom Management: My goal is to engage students in meaningful and productive independent literacy work while I am working with small groups and conferring with individuals during the reading time.

❏ I have not yet established a management system for implementing guided reading. ❏ I have identified some possible ideas for independent work. ❏ I am considering the implementation of independent reading with a reader's notebook for independent work but have not taught students how to use one. ❏ I want to begin teaching guided reading groups but students have not learned how to work productively in an independent way.	❏ I have decided on the management system that I want to have and have made a workable schedule, which I have implemented in my classroom. ❏ I am still teaching students the routines for independent work and/or the routines for independent reading with a reader's notebook. ❏ My students can work independently for short periods of time but they still need my help.	❏ My system for independent reading is well established and I am conferring with individuals. ❏ Students can sustain independent work using established routines and/or independent reading and the reader's notebook. ❏ I am beginning to work with small groups in guided reading.	❏ My classroom is well managed during the entire reading time. ❏ Students are engaged in silent independent reading and/or writing in a reader's notebook. They work in a completely independent way. ❏ I meet with guided reading groups on a regular schedule and have time to confer with individuals.

2. Materials: My goal is to have all necessary materials organized and accessible for the implementation of efficient guided reading lessons.

❏ My books and other materials are at a beginning point in terms of acquisition and organization. ❏ I am just learning about how to keep records of reading behavior and how to use reader's notebooks. ❏ I am beginning to collect the materials I need for the management system.	❏ I have or have access to a leveled collection of books, but it is minimal and not adequate for the needs of my class. ❏ I have some materials but they are not yet organized for student use. ❏ I know about record keeping and reader's notebooks but am not yet using them.	❏ I have or have access to a leveled collection of books and I am using it. ❏ I have easels, white boards, papers, markers, and other materials ready for use. ❏ My students have reader's notebooks (and/or I have word study and other materials organized for independent work.). ❏ I am beginning to keep records. I am beginning to teach the routines in the lesson.	❏ I have or have access to a leveled, well-organized, and trusted collection of books that are ready for use. ❏ I have an organized area for guided reading with easels, white boards, paper, markers and other materials. ❏ My students know how to use reader's notebooks (and/or independent work materials). I have a well-organized and useful record keeping system.

FIGURE 24-4 Self-Assessment for Guided Reading

Self-Assessment for Guided Reading *(continued)*

GETTING STARTED *(continued)*

3. Initial Assessment: My goal is to have sound assessment data on each student in my class that will enable me to form initial groups for reading and to make efficient and effective teaching decisions.

❏ I do not have an initial assessment system yet. ❏ I need to make decisions about assessment. ❏ I am looking for a way to fit it into my schedule.	❏ I have an initial assessment system and am beginning to learn to use it. ❏ I am learning how to code and score running records or reading records, and have tried it a few times. ❏ I have a tentative plan to complete assessment of all students.	❏ I have initial assessment data on all students and am in the process of interpreting it in preparation for grouping and teaching. ❏ I am beginning to use the *Literacy Continuum* (or other curriculum tool) to plan for and assess teaching.	❏ I have assessment data on all the students in my class and have established tentative groups for guided reading instruction. ❏ I am using the *Literacy Continuum* (or other curriculum documents) to determine specific teaching goals for each group and for each student.

4. Grouping: My goal is to form small groups of students who are similar in their development of a reading process and can read the same instructional level text so that I can teach them effectively. I can identify particular strengths and needs to determine emphases for teaching.

❏ Small group teaching is new to me. I usually teach the whole class or confer with individuals, but I have occasionally met with small groups. ❏ I am making decisions about the kind of assessment I will use and about how I will work it into my schedule.	❏ I have identified an assessment system, learned to use it, and almost completed the initial assessment of all students in my class. ❏ I am in the process of using data to group students for guided reading instruction. ❏ I am using the *Literacy Continuum* (or other curriculum document) to set instructional goals for groups and individuals.	❏ I have established level-based groups and used assessment data to establish specific goals for groups and individuals using the *Literacy Continuum* (or other curriculum document). ❏ I am keeping regular records of reading behavior. I meet with at least one group each day.	❏ I teach guided reading groups daily and also convene book clubs periodically. ❏ I take running records (or reading records) on a regular basis and keep observational notes, which helps me use the *Literacy Continuum* (or other curriculum document) to continually revise goals. ❏ My groups are formed and reformed on the basis of systematic observation. ❏ Every student in my class has the opportunity for small group instruction.

5. Lesson Management: My goal is to provide a fast-paced, lively, engaging lessons with components working together effectively.

❏ I have not yet implemented any of the components of guided reading.	❏ I have begun to implement the components of guided reading, but I am still working on smoothness and including all elements. ❏ I am working on using time effectively and being efficient with materials. Lessons are uneven. ❏ I don't get very many lessons taught in a week.	❏ I am implementing guided reading groups daily but am still working on efficiency and including all elements. ❏ Sometimes lessons are either too short or too long. ❏ I find some components easier to implement than others. ❏ My students are not engaging in the routines in an expert way.	❏ My lessons are well timed and smoothly managed. They include all elements in the lesson structure. ❏ I work efficiently with books and other materials. ❏ Students are responsive, participate actively, and understand the routines. ❏ I am using time in a way that assures all of my students have 3-4 guided reading lessons each week.

FIGURE 24-4 *(continued)*

Self-Assessment for Guided Reading *(continued)*			

REFLECTION ON TEACHING

1. Text Selection and Analysis: My goal is to select texts that are appropriate in terms of level for my groups, analyze their demands, and offer opportunities to extend their processing strategies across the guided reading lesson.

❑ I am just beginning to select texts from my collection. ❑ I am not sure how to analyze the texts to make decisions about selection and introductions.	❑ I am selecting texts with attention to level and am beginning to analyze them using the text characteristics. ❑ My analysis does not help me very much with my introductions.	❑ I can select texts that meet the needs of my groups and I can get them started with an introduction. ❑ I am still learning how to use my analysis of text characteristics to help students extend their thinking across the lesson.	❑ I can select texts that are appropriate for my students and offer opportunities for them to learn. ❑ I can analyze the texts to uncover learning opportunities and adjust the introduction, prompting, discussion, and teaching decisions to meet the needs of the students in each group.

2. Text Variation: My goal is to provide students with experiences across a wide range of fiction and nonfiction texts in guided reading so they can apply their understandings to independent reading.

❑ I am just beginning to learn about genres and how they vary in structure and other characteristics. ❑ My book collection does not provide enough variety to meet my students' needs. I tend to choose books by level only.	❑ I can identify genres and know about their structure and characteristics. ❑ I am just beginning to analyze what my students know and to plan for more variety in my guided reading selections.	❑ I have acquired or have access to a varied book collection, and I understand and use my knowledge of characteristics of genre in planning for guided reading. ❑ My students are provided with a variety of fiction and non-fiction texts on a regular basis.	❑ The book collection is rich and varied. I have an in-depth knowledge of the characteristics of different genres. ❑ I plan students' guided reading lessons carefully so that they are introduced to new genres in guided reading and incorporate them in independent reading.

3. Introduction to the Text: My goal is to introduce texts in a way that provides access for students to the meaning, language, and print of fiction and non-fiction texts.

❑ I provide an introduction but I seem to be using the techniques suggested in former reading systems I have used. ❑ I tend to use approaches like pre-teaching words and I neglect aspects of the text that are important. ❑ I either say too much or too little. ❑ I am not feeling successful in engaging students. ❑ I am just learning how to introduce texts in a way that prepares students to use effective processing strategies and comprehend within, beyond, and about the text.	❑ I regularly introduce texts by previewing the meaning and directing children's attention to some features of the text. ❑ Sometimes, my introductions are too supportive and sometimes they do not seem to provide enough support. ❑ I am beginning to plan text introductions based on my observations of students' reading behaviors rather than implementing the older routines I previously used.	❑ I introduce texts in a way that provides students with the support they need to read and comprehend texts at a level that is more challenging. ❑ My introductions are well-planned and based on students' reading behaviors. ❑ My students are engaged and responsive during introductions and they want to read the books. ❑ I leave opportunities for them to problem-solve and learn.	❑ My text introductions are carefully planned, smooth, and well paced. They provide students with access to meaning, language, print, and text features but leave important problem solving for them to do. ❑ My introductions are based on my assessment of the students' processing strategies and make it possible for students to learn more from their own reading.

FIGURE 24-4 *(continued)*

Self-Assessment for Guided Reading *(continued)*

REFLECTION ON TEACHING *(continued)*

4. Text Reading: My goal is to observe students' reading behaviors and to support students at error or at point of difficulty or by teaching, prompting, and reinforcing effective reading behaviors as they process text.

❑ I am unsure as to whether or not to intervene while students are reading the text. ❑ I tend to stop the student for long teaching interactions (meaning that the student does not finish the book).	❑ I observe oral reading and sometimes interact with students, but I tend to give students clues for guessing or I tell the words. ❑ I am unsure how to intervene in a way that supports the reader's construction of effective processing behaviors.	❑ I am learning precise language for supporting effective processing behaviors and my observations are helping me know a good time to interact with students. ❑ I am still working on the preciseness of my language and the length of my interactions.	❑ I observe oral reading and when appropriate, I interact with individuals to teach, prompt for, or reinforce effective reading behaviors that are based on what individual readers need to know how to do for themselves. ❑ My interactions are brief, to the point, and do not interrupt the reading.

5. Discussion after the Reading: My goal is to engage students in a rich discussion that supports their ability to think within, beyond, and about the text.

❑ My students either talk little about the story or engage in talk completely separate from the story. ❑ I spend time questioning and have not prompted much conversation.	❑ My students do talk about the story, but not in a way that furthers their understanding. ❑ Talk is distracting and random at times. ❑ I am learning how to guide the discussion, allowing for maximum text-based talk and thinking that is more than literal.	❑ I engage students in talk about the text, and most of the talk is text-based, but I continue to do much questioning. ❑ Some of the time, I can guide the discussion so that students have opportunity to talk and build on each other's comments. ❑ Student comments provide some evidence of thinking within, beyond, and about the text.	❑ I engage students in a rich discussion. ❑ There is evidence of a great deal of text-based talk initiated by the students. They often build on each other's comments. ❑ They have maximum opportunity to share their thinking and the discussion helps them extend their understanding within, beyond, and about the text.

6. Teaching Decisions after the Reading: My goal is to make precise, clear teaching points that help students engage in effective processing of texts and extend their understandings.

❑ I am currently engaging in very few teaching interactions after the discussion in lessons. ❑ Those I do try are not based on my observations of students and do not seem to have an impact on the effectiveness of the students' processing.	❑ I tend to make teaching points after the discussion in each lesson, but my teaching does not seem to help students engage in effective processing of texts. ❑ I am unsure how to make these teaching points in a way that helps readers learn how to problem-solve for themselves.	❑ I am learning to use *The Literacy Continuum* (or other curriculum document) in connection with my assessment and observation to make some effective teaching decisions. ❑ Some of them seem understood by students but I am not sure they are helping them become more independent as readers or understand the text more deeply.	❑ Using *The Literacy Continuum* (or other curriculum document) in connection with my assessment and observation of students, I am able to make expert teaching decisions that help students initiate effective actions. ❑ I have evidence that students are responding with more effective reading behaviors.

FIGURE 24-4 *(continued)*

Self-Assessment for Guided Reading *(continued)*

REFLECTION ON TEACHING *(continued)*

7. Word Work: My goal is to show students something explicit and strategic about how words work so that they are fluent and flexible in taking words apart while reading.

❑ I sometimes show students something about how words work but the activities I choose are either too easy or too hard (and time consuming). ❑ Usually, I demonstrate rather than engaging students actively.	❑ I engage students in working with words for a short time but not in an active way. ❑ Word work sometimes takes too long. ❑ I am unsure how to plan for word work.	❑ I am learning how to select word work using *The Literacy Continuum* (or other curriculum document) in connection with the word solving behaviors of my students. ❑ I observe as students process text and my observations inform my teaching. ❑ I can engage them efficiently with "hands on" activities some of the time.	❑ I am able to plan word work using *The Literacy Continuum* (or other curriculum document) in connection with my assessment and observation of word solving behaviors. ❑ Students are highly engaged in "hands on" activities and there is evidence that they are applying understandings to their independent word solving as they process texts.

8. Teaching for Processing Strategies Across the Lesson: My goal is to teach effectively in every part of the guided reading lesson in order to expand my students' ability to use background knowledge, self-monitor and correct, solve words, access and use information, maintain phrased, fluent reading, think beyond a text, connect the text to self, world and other texts, and think analytically and critically about the text.

❑ I am just beginning to understanding processing strategies and to observe students' reading behaviors for evidence. ❑ I am unsure how to teach for strategic actions.	❑ I am able to observe students' reading behaviors for evidence of processing strategies. ❑ I see behaviors that I want to encourage and I can think of what students need to learn how to do, but I am unsure of how to teach.	❑ I observe students' reading behaviors continuously and am able to find examples that are evidence of strategic actions. ❑ I have a good idea of what they need to learn how to do and also some teaching decisions that will support strategic actions, but I am inconsistent across the lesson. ❑ Some components go better than others.	❑ My decisions and interactions are well timed and powerful in illustrating processing strategies for students. ❑ My decisions allow students to use what they know to process a text. I am aware of and teach for a wide range of processing strategies and I see evidence of self-initiated, self-regulated strategic actions. ❑ I am consistently working toward my goals across the lesson.

9. Student Talk Across the Lesson: My goal is to engage children in talking about the meaning of the story and noticing the information in the text.

❑ There is little student talk across my guided reading lessons except for some talk that is not text-based.	❑ Students talk about the texts but not in a way that furthers their understanding. ❑ I am unsure how to elicit productive talk. ❑ Students tend to become distracted when they talk. ❑ Only a few students tend to talk.	❑ I can engage some students in talk that is mostly text-based. ❑ Some students dominate the talk. Some talk furthers their understanding of the meaning. ❑ I would like to sharpen discussion to support effective thinking about the text.	❑ There is evidence that students are engaging in highly productive, text-based talk that furthers their understanding of the meaning and assists them in using effective processing strategies. ❑ All students work at a high level of participation.

FIGURE 24-4 *(continued)*

Self-Assessment for Guided Reading *(continued)*

REFLECTION ON TEACHING *(continued)*

10. Engagement Across the Lesson: My goal is to engage students' attention throughout the lesson.

❏ I am frequently interrupted during lessons because my management system isn't working. ❏ Student attention is inconsistent across the lesson. ❏ Students are engaged only a little of the time.	❏ I can work with a group with few interruptions, but student engagement is still low. ❏ I have difficulty keeping students on task and focusing on the text across the lesson.	❏ I can work with groups with almost no interruptions. ❏ Students in the groups are attentive but the focus is uneven across the group. ❏ I am working towards a higher level of engagement in all lesson elements.	❏ Students' attention and interest is evident almost all of the time across the guided reading lesson. ❏ Students' talk and response to each other indicates that they are thoughtful, highly engaged, and interested in the comments of others.

11. Pace of the Lesson: My goal is to lead a fast-paced lesson with students who read fluently and are excited about the new book. A related goal is to use all components of guided reading within a 10 to 30 minute period.

❏ My lessons seem to "bog me down." ❏ I either have difficulty finishing all of the components of guided reading or the lessons take much too long.	❏ I am able to use all or most of the components of guided reading but the lesson is slow-paced and I often run out of time, making it impossible to teach several groups in a day.	❏ I can include all elements of the lesson (introduction, text reading, discussion, teaching points, and word work), but I would like it to be more fast-paced and to engage the students.	❏ My guided reading lesson is fast-paced and includes all the elements (introduction, text reading, discussion, teaching points, and word work). ❏ Students read fluently and I stay within time constraints to support my overall classroom management program.

12. Continuous Assessment: My goal is to have an efficient system for periodically stepping out of teaching to collect data on each reader and to use the information to inform the emphases of teaching and show the effects of my instruction on student learning.

❏ I am currently observing readers and taking some notes, but I have not been able to take running records (or reading records) with students. ❏ I try to use my notes to inform teaching.	❏ I am making observational notes and taking running records with a few students but I am not consistent. ❏ I am beginning to understand how to analyze the information to inform teaching.	❏ I am making efficient observational notes and have begun to create a system for taking regular running records (or reading records). ❏ I have begun using the information to identify emphases consistently.	❏ I have an efficient workable system for taking running records (or reading records) at selected intervals, more frequently with lower achieving students. ❏ I analyze the information and consistently use it with the *Literacy Continuum* to plan for and guide teaching decisions.

Comments:

FIGURE 24-4 *(continued)*

References

Children's Literature

Adams, J. in press a. *Bear and the Little Snakes*. Portsmouth, NH: Heinemann.

———. in press b. *Dinner with a Python*. Portsmouth, NH: Heinemann.

———. in press c. *The Mysterious Fossa*. Portsmouth, NH: Heinemann.

Barnes, I. J. in press. *A Trip to the City*. Portsmouth, NH: Heinemann.

Bensen, R. in press. *Sticks and Stones for Little Monster*. Portsmouth, NH: Heinemann.

Best, C. in press. *Earl on His Own*. Portsmouth, NH: Heinemann.

Blank, A. in press. *Minnie Freeman's Blizzard*. Portsmouth, NH: Heinemann.

Bodach, V. in press. *Tongue-Tied*. Portsmouth, NH: Heinemann.

Carle, E. and B. Martin Jr. 1996. *Brown Bear, Brown Bear, What Do You See?* New York: Henry Holt and Co.

Cary, A. in press. *Emily's Amazing Journey*. Portsmouth, NH: Heinemann.

Charles, D. in press. *Something for Dinner*. Portsmouth, NH: Heinemann.

Creech, S. 2001. *Love That Dog*. New York: HarperCollins.

Dion, M. in press. *Hector and the Kitten*. Portsmouth, NH: Heinemann.

Edwin, D. in press. *Baxter's Red Ball*. Portsmouth, NH: Heinemann.

Friend, C. in press. *Animal Feet*. Portsmouth, NH: Heinemann.

———. in press. *Stripes*. Portsmouth, NH: Heinemann.

Hall, M. C. in press. *All Kinds of Eggs*. Portsmouth, NH: Heinemann.

Hall, P. in press. *Food for Animals*. Portsmouth, NH: Heinemann.

Hermansson, C. in press. *The Rooster and the Crow: An Aesop Fable*. Portsmouth, NH: Heinemann.

Hesse, K. 1997. *Out of the Dust*. New York, NY: Scholastic Press.

Hill, E. 1980. *Where's Spot? The Original Lift-the-Flap Book*. New York: The Penguin Group.

Iasevoli, B. in press. *Saving Cranes*. Portsmouth, NH: Heinemann.

in press. *Rain, Sun, Wind, Snow: Poems About the Seasons*. Portsmouth, NH: Heinemann.

Jones, P. in press. *Rules*. Portsmouth, NH: Heinemann.

Landecker, H. in press. *Once Upon a Time Machine*. Portsmouth, NH: Heinemann.

Latham, D. 2008. *More Than a Pet*. Portsmouth, NH: Heinemann.

Latimer, J. in press. *Tadpole in a Tree*. Portsmouth, NH: Heinemann.

Latta, S. L. in press. *The Glow Below: Creatures That Light Up the Sea*. Portsmouth, NH: Heinemann.

McCloskey, S. 2008. *Edwin's Haircut*. Portsmouth, NH: Heinemann.

McKerley, J. in press. *Lone Star the Lawman*. Portsmouth, NH: Heinemann.

Mellon, P. in press. *The Little Hen*. Portsmouth, NH: Heinemann.

Moore, A. in press. *On the Go*. Portsmouth NH: Heinemann.

Morais, C. in press. *Animal Tracks*. Portsmouth, NH: Heinemann.

Munsch, R. 1986. *Love You Forever*. Buffalo, NY: Firefly Books, Inc.

Nichols, C. in press. *Chester's Sweater*. Portsmouth, NH: Heinemann.

Park, L. S. 2010. *A Long Walk to Water*. New York: Clarion Books.

Paulsen, G. 1987. *Hatchet*. Seattle, WA: Bradbury Press.

Peterson, C. in press. *Bird Feet*. Portsmouth, NH: Heinemann.

Phillips, A. W. in press. *Lunch for Monkey*. Portsmouth, NH: Heinemann.

———. 2017. *The Kite*. Portsmouth, NH: Heinemann.

Pickerill, M. in press. *Bats in the City*. Portsmouth, NH: Heinemann.

Rosen, M. 1989. *We're Going on a Bear Hunt*. New York: Margaret K. McElderry Books.

Santos, R. in press. *The Ant and the Grasshopper: An Aesop Tale*. Portsmouth, NH: Heinemann.

Schwartz, J. in press. *From Beans to Chocolate*. Portsmouth, NH: Heinemann.

Sigman, M. in press. *Splash, Plop, Leap!* Portsmouth, NH: Heinemann.

Silverstein, S. 1964. *The Giving Tree*. New York: Harper & Row.

Simon, Jane. in press. *Morning on the Farm*. Portsmouth, NH: Heinemann.

Slade, S. in press. *Betty Skelton and Little Stinker*. Portsmouth, NH: Heinemann.

Stratton, P. in press. *Family Fun*. Portsmouth, NH: Heinemann.

Stribling, Anne. in press. *The Wheels on the Bike*. Portsmouth, NH: Heinemann.

Sullivan, M. in press. *Dragon Quest*. Portsmouth, NH: Heinemann.

———. in press. *Mission: Earth*. Portsmouth, NH: Heinemann.

The Wheels on the Bus. 2003. Minneapolis, MN: Picture Window Books.

Van Allen, L. in press. *Making a Sandwich*. Portsmouth, NH: Heinemann.

Vassos, P. in press. *Yard Sale*. Portsmouth, NH: Heinemann.

Professional References

Allington, R. L. 2001. *What Really Matters for Struggling Readers*. New York City, NY: Addison Wesley Longman.

Anderson, R. C., and W. E. Nagy. 1992. "The Vocabulary Conundrum." *American Educator*. 16(4):14–18, 44–47.

Askew, B. J., and I. C. Fountas. 1998. "Building an Early Reading Process: Active from the Start!" *The Reading Teacher*. 52:126–34.

August, D., and T. Shanahan. 2006. "Developing Literacy in Second-Language Learners: Report of the National Literacy Panel on Language-Minority Children and Youth." Lawrence Erlbaum Associates. Mahwah, NJ: Center for Applied Linguistics.

Bakhtin, M. M. 1981. *The Dialogic Imagination*. Austin, TX: University of Austin Press.

Beck, I., M. McKeown, and L. Kucan. 2002. *Choosing Words to Teach: Three Tier Model of Vocabulary Words*. New York: The Guilford Press.

Beck, I., M. G. McKeown, and R. C. Omanson. 1987. "The Effects and Uses of Diverse Vocabulary Instructional Techniques." Hillsdale, NJ: Erlbaum.

Biancarosa, G., A. S. Bryk, and E. R. Dexter. 2010. "Assessing the Value-Added Effects of Literacy Collaborative Professional Development on Student Learning." *The Elementary School Journal.* 111(1): 7–34.

Britton, J. 1970. *Language and Learning.* Coral Gables, FL: University of Miami Press.

Brown, S. 2004. *Shared Reading.* Wellington, NZ: Learning Media Limited.

Buckley, M. A. 2015. *Sharing the Blue Crayon.* Portland, ME: Stenhouse.

Burkins, J. M., and K. Yaris. 2014. *Reading Wellness.* Portland, ME: Stenhouse.

Cambourne, B, L. D. Labbo, and M. Carpenter. 2001. "What Do I Do with the Rest of the Class?: The Nature of Teaching Learning Activities." *Language Arts.* 79(2):124–35.

Cambourne, B. 1988. *The Whole Story: Natural Learning and the Acquisition of Literacy.* Auckland, NZ: Ashton Scholastic.

Cappelini, M. 2005. *Balancing Reading and Language Learning.* Portland, ME: Stenhouse.

Cazden, C. 2001. *Classroom Discourse: The Language of Teaching and Learning.* Portsmouth, NH: Heinemann.

Charney, R. S. 2002. *Teaching Children to Care: Classroom Management for Ethical and Academic Growth, K–8.* 2d ed. Greenfield, MA: Northeast Foundation for Children.

———. 1991. *Teaching Children to Care: Management in the Responsive Classroom.* Greenfield, MA: Northeast Foundation for Children.

Clay, M. M. 2015. 1991a. *Becoming Literate: The Construction of Inner Control.* Auckland, NZ: Global Education Systems.

———. 2005a. *Literacy Lessons Designed for Individuals, Part One—Why? When? And How?* Auckland, NZ: Heinemann Education.

———. 2005b. *Literacy Lessons Designed For Individuals, Part Two: Teaching Procedures.* Auckland, NZ: Heinemann Education.

———. 2001. *Change Over Time in Children's Literacy Development.* Portsmouth, NH: Heinemann.

———. 2000. *Running Records for Classroom Teachers.* Portsmouth, NH: Heinemann.

———. 1998. *By Different Paths to Common Outcomes.* Portland, ME: Stenhouse.

———. 1993. *An Observation Survey of Early Literacy Achievement.* Portsmouth, NH: Heinemann.

———. 1991. "Introducing a New Storybook to Young Readers." *The Reading Teacher* 45(4):264–73.

———. 1979. *Reading: The Patterning of Complex Behavior.* Portsmouth, NH: Heinemann.

Copple, C., and S. Bredekamp. 2009. *Developmentally Appropriate Practice in Early Childhood Programs Serving Children From Birth Through Age 8.* 3d ed. National Association for the Education of Young Children. http://www.naeyc.org/files/naeyc/file/positions/PSDAP.pdf.

Cormack, P. 1992. "School-Related Barriers to Success in Reading and Writing." *The Australian Journal of Language and Literacy* 15(3):175–86.

Dale, E. 1965. "Vocabulary Measurement: Techniques and Major Findings." *Elementary English*. 42(8):895–901, 948.

DeHaven, L. 2014. "What Are Some Ways to Effectively Record Anecdotes During Guided Reading?" [blog]. *University Center for Reading Recovery and Literacy Collaborative*. May 7. https://lesleyuniversitycrrlc.wordpress.com/2014/05/07/what-are-some ways-to-effectively-record-anecdotes-during-guided-reading/.

Department of Education. 1985. *Reading in Junior Classes*. Wellington, NZ: Department of Education.

Dinan, S. 2014. "An Eye-Popping 20% of U.S. Residents Abandon English at Home." *The Washington Times* (October 6).

Downend, C. n.d. "Ensuring Quality Instruction for All in the Literacy Collaborative Classroom." *Literacy Collaborative*. http://literacycollaborative.org/blog/ensuring quality-instruction-for-all-in-the-literacy-collaborative-classroom/#more-104.

———. "Using Data Walls as a Tool for Monitoring Student Achievement." Presentation, Lesley University, March 26, 2012.

Drucker, M. J. 2003. "What Reading Teachers Should Know About ESL Learners." *The Reading Teacher*. 57(1):22–29.

DuFour, R. 2004. "What Is a 'Professional Learning Community?" *Educational Leadership*. 61:6–11.

Dweck, C. S. 2006. *Mindset: The New Psychology of Success*. New York: Random House.

Elkonin, D. B. 1973. "Comparative Reading: Cross-National Studies of Behavior and Processes in Reading and Writing." *J. Downing (Ed.), U.S.S.R.*

Flavell, J. H. 1987. "Speculations About the Nature and Development of Metacognition." In F. E. Weinert & R. H. Kluwe (Eds.), *Metacognition, Motivation, and Understanding*. Hillside, NJ: Lawrence Erlbaum Associates. 21–29.

———. 1976. "Metacognitive Aspects of Problem Solving." In L. B. Resnick (Ed.) *The Nature of Intelligence*. Hillsdale, NJ: Lawrence Erlbaum Associates. 231–236.

"Fountasandpinnell.com." n.d. fountasandpinnell.com.

Fountas, I. C., and G. S. Pinnell. 2017. *Fountas & Pinnell Classroom*. Portsmouth, NH: Heinemann.

———. 2012a. *Genre Prompting Guide for Fiction, Grades K–8+*. Portsmouth, NH: Heinemann.

———. 2012b. *Genre Prompting Guide for Nonfiction, Poetry, and Test Taking, Grades K–8+*. Portsmouth, NH: Heinemann.

———. 2012. *Genre Study: Teaching with Fiction and Nonfiction Books, Grades K–8+*. Portsmouth, NH: Heinemann.

———. 2012, 2009. *Prompting Guide, Part 1, for Oral Reading and Early Writing*. Portsmouth, NH: Heinemann.

———. 2012, 2009. *Prompting Guide, Part 2, for Comprehension: Thinking, Talking, and Writing*. Portsmouth, NH: Heinemann.

———. 2011, 2008. *Fountas & Pinnell Benchmark Assessment Systems 1 & 2*. 2nd ed. Portsmouth, NH: Heinemann.

———. 2009. *Leveled Literacy Intervention*. Portsmouth, NH: Heinemann.

———. 2006. *Leveled Books K–8: Matching Texts to Readers for Effective Teaching.* Portsmouth, NH: Heinemann.

———. 2006. *Teaching for Comprehending and Fluency.* Portsmouth, NH: Heinemann.

———. 2001. *Guiding Readers and Writers: Teaching Comprehension, Genre, and Content Literacy.* Portsmouth, NH: Heinemann.

———. 1996. *Guided Reading: Good First Teaching for All Children.* Portsmouth, NH: Heinemann.

———. n.d. "Leveled Books." *Fountasandpinnell.com.* http://www.heinemann.com/fountasandpinnell/.

Halpern, D. F. 1996. *Thought and Knowledge: An Introduction to Critical Thinking.* Mahwah, New Jersey: Lawrence Erlbaum Associates.

"Heinemann." n.d. *Heinemann.* http://www.heinemann.com/.

Hill, J. D., and K. M. Flynn. 2006. *Classroom Instruction That Works with English Language Learners.* Boston: Houghton Mifflin Harcourt.

Holdaway, D. 1979. *The Foundations of Literacy.* Sydney, Australia: Ashton Scholastic.

International Data Evaluation Center. 2015. "2014–2015 Reading Recovery National Summary Report for the United States." International Data Evaluation Center, Columbus OH: The Ohio State University.

Johnston, P. 2007. "Revolutionary Contributions." *Journal of Reading Recovery.* 7(1):67–68.

———. 2005. "Literacy Assessment and the Future." *The Reading Teacher.* 58(7):684–86.

Kaye, E. 2006. "Second Graders' Reading Behaviors: A Study of Variety, Complexity, and Change." *Literacy Teaching and Learning.* 10(2):51–75.

Kittle, P. 2012. *Book Love.* Portsmouth, NH: Heinemann.

Lyons, C., Pinnell, G. S., and DeFord, D. 1993. *Partners in Learning.* New York: Teacher's College Press.

Lysaker, J., and E. Hopper. 2015. "A Kindergartner's Emergent Strategy Use During Wordless Picture Book Reading." *The Reading Teacher.* 68(8):649–57.

McKay, C. 2012. *You Don't Have to Be a Bad Teacher to Get Better: A Leaders Guide to Improving Teacher Quality.* Newbury Park, CA: Corwin.

National Institute of Child Health and Human Development (NICHD). 2000. "Teaching Children to Read: An Evidence-Based Assessment of the Scientific Research Literature on Reading and Its Implications for Reading Instruction: Reports of the Subgroups." NIH Publication No. 00–4754. Washington, D.C.: U.S. Government Printing Office. http://www.nichd.nih.gov/publications/nrp/report.htm.

Newkirk, T. 2012. *The Art of Slow Reading.* Portsmouth, NH: Heinemann.

n.d. *What Works Clearinghouse.* http://www.w-w-c.org/.

Palincsar and Brown. 1984 "Reciprocal Teaching of Comprehension-Fostering and Comprehension-Monitoring Activities." In *Cognition and Instruction.* Mahwah NJ: Lawrence Erlbaum Associates, Inc.

Parkes, B. 2000. *Read It Again!* Portland ME: Stenhouse.

Pearson, P. D., and M. Gallagher. 1983. "The Instruction of Reading Comprehension." *Contemporary Educational Psychology.* 8:317–44.

Pinnell, G. S., and I. C. Fountas. 2011. *The Continuum of Literacy Learning, Grades PreK–8: A Guide to Teaching.* 2nd ed. Portsmouth, NH: Heinemann.

———. 2003a. *Phonics Lessons: Letters, Words, and How They Work (Grade 2).* Portsmouth, NH: Heinemann.

———. 2003b. *Phonics Lessons: Letters, Words, and How They Work (Grade K).* Portsmouth, NH: Heinemann.

———. 2003c. *Phonics Lessons: Letters, Words, and How They Work (Grade 1).* Portsmouth, NH: Heinemann.

———. 2002. *Leveled Books for Readers, Grades 3–6.* Portsmouth, NH: Heinemann.

———. 1998. *Word Matters: Teaching Phonics and Spelling in the Reading/Writing Classroom.* Portsmouth, NH: Heinemann.

Pressley, M. 2000. "Comprehension Instruction in Elementary School: A Quarter-Century of Research Progress." In B.M. Taylor, M. G. Graves, and P. Van Den Broek (Eds.). *Reading for Meaning: Fostering Comprehension in the Middle Grades.* New York: Teachers College Press and Newark, DE: International Reading Association. 70–94.

Pressley, M., and P. Afflerbach. 1995. *Verbal Protocols of Reading: The Nature of Constructively Responsive Reading.* New York: Routledge.

Pressley, M., J. G. Borkowski, , and W. Schneider. 1987. Cognitive Strategies: Good Strategy Users Coordinate Metacognition and Knowledge. In R. Vasta, and G. Whitehurst , *Annals of Child Development.* Greenwich, CT: JAI Press. 4:80–129.

Ransford-Kaldon, C., E. S. Flynt, C. Ross, L. Franceschini, T. Zoblotsky, Y. Huang, and B. Gallagher. 2009–2010. "Implementation of Effective Intervention: An Empirical Study to Evaluate the Efficacy of Fountas & Pinnell's Leveled Literacy Intervention System (LLI)." The Center for Research in Educational Policy: The University of Memphis.

Ray, K. W., and M. Glover. 2008. *Already Ready: Nurturing Writers in Preschool and Kindergarten.* Portsmouth, NH: Heinemann.

Reutzel, D. R., C. D. Jones, P. C. Fawson, and J. A. Smith. 2008. "Scaffolded Silent Reading: A Complement to Guided Repeated Oral Reading." *The Reading Teacher.* 62(3):194–207.

Rodriguez-Eagle, C., and A. Torres-Elias. 2009. "Refining the Craft of Teaching English Language Learners." *Journal of Reading Recovery* (Fall). 53–61.

Rogoff, B. 1990. *Apprenticeship in Thinking: Cognitive Development in Social Context.* New York: Oxford University Press.

Rosenblatt, L. M. 1978. *The Reader, the Text, the Poem: The Transactional Theory of the Literary Work.* Carbondale, IL: Southern Illinois University Press.

———. 1938. *Literature as Exploration.* New York: Noble and Noble Publishers.

Rumelhart, D. E. 1985. "Toward an Interactive Model of Reading." In *Theoretical Models and Processes of Reading.* 3d ed. Newark, DE: International Reading Association.

Saavedra, D. R.M. 2016. "Empathy Is the Gateway." *Educational Leadership,* February. 66–69.

Smith, F. 1998. *The Book of Learning and Forgetting.* New York City: Teachers College Press.

Smith, J. W., and W. B. Elley. 1995. *Learning to Read in New Zealand.* New York: Richard C. Owen.

Soltero, S. W. 2011. *Schoolwide Approaches to Educating ELLs: Creating Linguistically and Culturally Responsive K–12 Schools.* Portsmouth, NH: Heinemann.

Stanovich, K. E. 1986. "Matthew Effects in Reading: Some Consequences of Individual Differences in the Acquisition of Literacy." *Reading Research Quarterly.* 21(4): 360–407.

Stouffer, J. 2011. "Listening to Yourself Reading: Exploring the Influence of Auditory Input in Literacy Processing." *Journal of Reading Recovery.* 15–28.

Topping, K. 1989. "Peer Tutoring and Paired Reading: Combining Two Powerful Techniques." *The Reading Teacher.* 42(7):488–94.

Vygotsky, L. S. 1978. *Mind in Society: The Development of Higher Psychological Processes.* Cambridge, MA: Harvard University Press.

Ward, E. 2009–2010. "Leveled Literacy Intervention: Research and Data Collection Project." Portsmouth, NH: Heinemann.

Weir, R. H. 1970, 1962. *Language in the Crib.* 2nd ed. The Hague: Mouton.

"WIDA Classroom Consortium." n.d. www.wida.us.

Index

Credits

Figure 15-2 from "Listening to Yourself Reading: Exploring the Influence of Auditory Input in Literacy Processing," by J. Stouffer, 2011, *The Journal of Reading Recovery,* 11(1), p. 24. Copyright 2011 by Reading Recovery Council of North America. Reprinted with permission.

Photograph Credit Lines

p. 89 (May) © NatPar Collection/Alamy Stock Photo, (June) © Tom Lynn/Getty Images, (July) © Tom Lynn/Getty Images, (August) © Danita Delimont/Alamy, (September) © Robbie George/Getty Images, (river background) © June J/Shutterstock, (caring parents background) © Danita Delimont/Alamy, (crane puppet inset) © Gertan/Shutterstock, (crane puppet background) © Tom Lynn/Getty Images; p. 90 (3 chocolate truffles) © Aprilphoto/Shutterstock, (chocolate drip) © Elic/Shutterstock, (chocolate bar) © LightShed Photography Studio, (chocolate shop) © Deyan Georgiev/Alamy, (molds) © Gary Moss Photography/Getty Images, (nibs) © Diana Taliun/Shutterstock, (beans) © simon de glanville/Alamy Stock Photo, (pod) © Dr. Morley Read/Shutterstock, (tree) © 167/Taylor S. Kennedy/Corbis, (cocoa pods) © Leungchopan/Shutterstock, (large chocolate truffle) © Mia V /Shutterstock, (Cocoa worker, Tamana, Trinidad) © John Harper/Getty Images; p. 95 (snake) © Matt Jeppson/Shutterstock, (caterpillar) © jordache/Shutterstock, (eel) © TAGSTOCK1/Shutterstock; p. 97 (bottom background) © Dudarev Mikhail/Shutterstock, (top inset) © Luke Dollar, (middle inset) © Luke Dollar, (bottom inset) © Luke Dollar; p. 109 © Robinson, James/Animals Animals; p. 109 © amana images inc./Alamy; p. 138 (background image) © marco silvestri/Alamy, (inset No Durians) © Greg Benz/Shutterstock; p. 139 (bats roosting) © Brian Keeley, Bat Conservation International; p. 171 (background) © Picture Alliance/Photoshot, (inset) © Sohns/imageBROKER/AGE footstock; p. 175 © Dave Bradley Photography, Inc.; p. 180 © Scott Linstead/Science Source; p. 223 (boys and dogs on beach) © image100/Alamy, (service dog and owner) © Alan & Sandy Carey/Science Source, (therapy dogs) © David Grossman/The Image Works; p. 305 © MyImages—Micha/ Shutterstock; p. 308 © amana images inc./Alamy; p. 309 © James Hager/Getty Images; p. 311 © Justin Yeager–Department of Ecology and Evolutionary Biology, Tulane University, (leaf background) © GraphicStock; p. 316 © Dr. Edith Widder, ORCA; p. 317 (background) © Merlin D. Tuttle, Bat Conservation International, (foreground bat) © Merlin D. Tuttle, Bat Conservation International; p. 319 (paisley border) © GraphicStock, (boy playing gilli-danda) courtesy of Vijaya Bodach, (danda) © Robert Reynolds, (paper from notebook) © GraphicStock, (gili) © Robert Reynolds; p. 340 © Dr. Edith Widder, ORCA; p. 378 courtesy of NASA, © Procy/Shutterstock, (inset starry background) © seecreateimages/Shutterstock, (horse and buggy) © Kirn Vintage Stock/Getty Images; p. 401 © MyImages—Micha/ Shutterstock; p. 405 © Galyna Andrushko/Shutterstock; p. 471 © Francois Gohier/Science Source, (upper border) © GraphicStock; p. 474 © Roberto Tetsuo Okamura/Shutterstock, (upper border) © GraphicStock; p. 478 © Hug It Forward, (top border) © Laura Kutner, (bottom border) © Design Instruct; p. 479 © Superstock; p. 481 (mouse) © Rubberball/ Mike Kemp/Getty Images, (dog) © Kuznetsov Alexey/Shutterstock, (bone) © canbedone/ Shutterstock